In recent years some evangelical scholars have claimed that the Gospel writers were allowed by contemporary literary conventions to present events one way even when the historical reality was different. This involves a number of distinct claims about writing conventions, each of which requires individual investigation. McGrew has done her homework and systematically considers the evidence for each convention, ultimately finding them all wanting. At the same time she amasses evidence that the gospels should be read in a way lay readers are likely to read them anyway. I am grateful for her knowledgeable contributions to Gospel studies.

Peter J. Williams, Principal, Tyndale House, Cambridge

As Thomas Kuhn pointed out long ago, it is often someone from a different discipline who has the epistemic distance and objectivity to evaluate a widely accepted paradigm/methodology in another discipline, because practitioners in the latter tend to look at things the way they were trained and, thus, cannot see things accurately. Kuhn's remarks are right on target when it comes to philosopher Lydia McGrew's critique of widespread methodological practices in New Testament studies. While *The Mirror or the Mask* is very easy to read, it is also a massive piece of first-rate, rigorous scholarship that leaves no stone unturned. Replete with very careful distinctions, *The Mirror or the Mask* offers a precise analysis of the contemporary practice of employing "fictionalization" to exegete various Gospel texts. McGrew's careful analysis finds such a practice wanting and dangerous and replaces this practice with an approach that treats the Gospels as honest historical reports based on eyewitness testimony. This book is a must read for all who are interested in the historical accuracy of our portraits of Jesus. I highly recommend it.

J.P. Moreland, Distinguished Professor of Philosophy,
Talbot School of Theology

Readers can learn a lot about good historical method, ancient and modern, from McGrew's extremely thorough and meticulous analysis. However, three clarifications are essential: (1) This book is not about literary devices in general but about fictionalizing devices. (2) The approaches most criticized are not common among inerrantist Gospel scholars. (3) The evangelical scholars criticized, both inerrantist and non-inerrantist, have overall been significant defenders of Gospel reliability and of the Christian faith more generally.

Craig L. Blomberg, Distinguished Professor of
New Testament, Denver Seminary

Lydia McGrew's critique of the literary reductionism employed by many New Testament scholars, including some influential evangelicals, is the definitive refutation of this sad methodology, which dehistoricises the text, destroys any possible apologetic for its truth-value, and leaves the Christian in a position where he or she ends up with faith in the literary style of early church writers rather than faith in a historical Jesus. But *only the Christ of history* is the Way, the Truth and the Life. Faith in the literary creativity of human writers, whether believers or not, has never saved anyone. McGrew's book is therefore a needed corrective to an approach that destroys both mind and soul.

John Warwick Montgomery, Ph.D., D.Théol., LL.D.
Professor Emeritus of Law and Humanities, University of Bedfordshire, England/UK Director, International Academy of Apologetics, Strasbourg, France (www.apologeticsacademy.eu)

Speaking as a specialist in Biblical studies, I find Dr McGrew's work here to be a cold breeze right in the face: it is both *bracing* and *refreshing*. It is *bracing* because of the scrupulous attention to detail in the primary sources and the relentless logic of the analysis. But it is *refreshing*, not only for its clarity of presentation but also for the sense that good scholarship actually brings us a greater confidence that the Gospels really do tell us things that Jesus did and said and that he entrusted his apostles to remember. I commend this work to my fellow specialists and to all who enjoy clear thinking.

C. John ("Jack") Collins, Professor of Old Testament, Covenant Theological Seminary

Diamonds are valued by reference to four criteria; carat (weight); clarity; color; and cut. Lydia McGrew has provided us with a literary gem that rates highly on all four tests. Her new book, *The Mirror or the Mask,* is, firstly, a timely and weighty defense of the historical reliability of the New Testament's foundational writings. Secondly, it exhibits a clarity of thought and argumentation that is all too rare in theological debate today. Thirdly, it is no mere academic treatise but glows with the "color" and warmth of a love for God's revealed truth. And fourthly, the "cut" or presentation of its case is exemplary in its logical development. The book needs to be read and taken to heart by all who profess the biblical Christian faith, whether in the pulpit or the pew.

Edgar Andrews, Professor Emeritus, University of London

Whatever conclusions one reaches at the end of this careful book on the nature of ancient history and Biblical texts, Dr. McGrew has written a clear, masterful argument for the perspective that the Gospels contain history and that ancient historians or writers did not add "fiction" to their narratives. As such, her book challenges the arguments of Professor Licona and others. As someone who studies and reads ancient philosophy, I can say that McGrew has done all of us, not just New Testament scholars, an important service. McGrew's work covers important details about the methods of writers around the time of the New Testament, and the range of her scholarship is immense. Her impressive set of arguments will need careful examination by those like Professor Licona who have relied on different assumptions about literature in the ancient world.

John Mark N. Reynolds, President, The Saint Constantine School

Nothing has been more contentious in Evangelical New Testament scholarship over the last decade than the claim that the Gospels are examples of Greco-Roman biography, a genre that allowed its writer to alter or rearrange facts and speeches while still giving a generally reliable impression of its subject. Supporters believe that this recognition allows them to affirm biblical inerrancy while avoiding artificial harmonization, and opponents argue that it renders the very concept of inerrancy meaningless. Analytic epistemologist Lydia McGrew subjects the claims to exhaustive and incisive examination to conclude that readers should be dubious when scholars say, "This does not mean that the Gospels are unreliable, because these things were permitted at the time." That is a non sequitur, because "permissible" misrepresentations of facts are still misrepresentations. Are the Gospels presenting straightforward history or merely accounts "based on" the real events? McGrew concludes that it matters greatly which type of document the Gospels are and that the case that they share the characteristics of Greco-Roman biographies has not been convincingly made. Significant, timely, and well argued, this book is a must read for anyone concerned with the historical grounds of our faith in the Jesus the Gospels present.

Donald Williams, R. A. Forrest Scholar at Toccoa Falls College
Past president of the International Society of Christian Apologetics

Unlike most books in New Testament studies, *The Mirror or The Mask* is not obfuscated by unnecessary and ambiguous jargon, its assumptions are examined and defended, and the author provides many arguments and evidences that remain rigorous yet accessible to non-experts for its claims. For these reasons, I have no doubt that McGrew's critics will chastise her for not following the normal pattern of New Testament scholars, but the rest of us can celebrate the clarity and cogency of a text that actually helps its readers understand and defend the historical claims of the New Testament. In this book McGrew completely routs the literary device theory and establishes a beachhead for the reportage model. Anyone interested in thinking about why there are differences between the Gospels must read this book.

John M. DePoe, Ph.D., Academic Dean of the Schools of
Logic and Rhetoric, Kingdom Preparatory Academy

For a number of years, I accepted and repeated claims that other scholars were making about the genre and nature of the Gospels, assuming that they must mean by those claims more or less the same things that I did and that they must have solid grounds for making them. But I have gradually come to realize that both of these assumptions were unwarranted. The Gospels are biographies—well, fine, in some minimal sense; but it is another thing altogether to say that they were influenced by Greco-Roman conventions and that we should expect a certain amount of fictionalization in them for this very reason. The Gospels contain paraphrases—yes, of course; but the notion of paraphrase cannot be stretched to indefinite lengths. I thought that evangelical scholars, at least, were making modest statements and stood on firm historical ground when they used these expressions. I was wrong. This meticulously researched book contains the arguments that changed my mind.

Tim McGrew, Professor of Philosophy
Western Michigan University

Dr. Lydia McGrew is an iconoclast who is single-handedly reshaping the terrain of New Testament research. Her ability to think outside of the conventional guild of contemporary scholarship gives her a unique perspective on the New Testament. With her previous book, *Hidden in Plain View,* Dr. McGrew provided ample, and powerful, evidence for viewing the Gospels as what they purport to be—reliable historical reportage concerning the life and times of Jesus of Nazareth. In her new book, *The Mirror or the Mask,* Dr. McGrew extends this thesis further and champions source harmonization as a sound principle in ancient historiography. Simple harmonization theories, argues Dr. McGrew, should always be preferred over more complex and extravagant theories. As such, Dr. McGrew challenges the habit among many well-known Gospel scholars of explaining away Gospel differences by invocation of implausible literary device theories. Thus, this book calls into question an approach to the Gospels that has been adopted uncritically by all too many contemporary Christian leaders and apologists. In fact, argues Dr. McGrew, such an approach undermines the epistemic basis of belief in the resurrection, rather than contributing to it. The book has something to offend everybody and is not for one whose sensibilities are easily offended. Dr. McGrew's new book is a very valuable contribution to Gospel scholarship, and lay apologists and scholars alike would do well to consider carefully what she says.

Jonathan McLatchie, Christian Apologist

In *The Mirror or the Mask,* Lydia McGrew argues that the Gospels were intended by their authors to report what happened without altering or inventing facts about what Jesus said and did. In defending this position, she engages polemically against the views of such evangelical Gospel scholars as Michael Licona, Craig Keener, and Craig Evans, whom she contends often employ literary interpretations of Gospel differences that undermine their historical reliability. The extent to which differences among the Gospels can and should be harmonized and to what extent literary explanations should be employed is a difficult and complex issue. McGrew's vigorous defense of a thoroughgoing harmonization approach in this book will not be the last word, but as a provocative counterpoint to the dominant viewpoint it provides an opportunity for evangelical scholars to develop and present their positions with greater rigor and clarity.

Robert M. Bowman Jr., President
Faith Thinkers Inc.

Tightly reasoned and passionately written, *The Mirror or the Mask* dissects the shoddy argumentation of New Testament scholars who have appealed to literary devices to explain apparent contradictions and discrepancies in the Gospels. These moves, ostensibly intended to rescue Scripture from its critics, in fact bury the Gospel narratives in confusion while sacrificing the historical claims of the witnesses to Jesus' life and ministry. Lydia McGrew's analytical acumen and passion for truth stand out on every page. Highly recommended.

Paul Nelson, Senior Fellow, Discovery Institute

The Mirror or the Mask is consistently interesting and remarkably readable, especially in view of the massive detail McGrew puts forward in it. And she puts that detail to work, forming a case that's both reasoned and persuasive. Her argument is sure to catch attention where it matters most: among pastors, teachers, writers and others who lead in discipling Christians everywhere. Her work cannot be ignored—not without ignoring the very people whom scholarship should serve. For this is no mere scholarly sideshow. The outcome will determine how reliably we can know what Jesus actually said, and what he actually did.

Tom Gilson, Senior Editor, *The Stream*
Author of *A Christian Mind: Thoughts on Life and Truth in Jesus Christ*

THE MIRROR OR THE MASK

Liberating the Gospels from Literary Devices

The Mirror or the Mask

Liberating the Gospels From Literary Devices

Lydia McGrew

DeWard
for your journey

To Tim

who introduced me to good friends in old books

and

To J. P. Moreland and J. W. Montgomery

whose early, public support of this project
has been a key encouragement.

Contents

Part Four—The Mirror or the Mask in Gospel Examples

Preface

The Mirror or the Mask and its projected companion volume on John, *The Eye of the Beholder*, have grown out of my study of the claim that the Gospels contain compositional devices in which the authors deliberately alter facts for literary or theological reasons. This study began in its earlier stages with a careful analysis of Michael Licona's 2017 book *Why Are There Differences in the Gospels? What We Can Learn from Ancient Biography* and branched out to include the work of other scholars who make similar claims.

From the outset, I have had several questions in mind: 1) If true, how much would this claim affect our understanding of the reliability of the Gospels? 2) Does independent, non-biblical evidence support the claim that these compositional devices were indeed known and widely accepted in secular literature that is relevant to our understanding of the Gospels? 3) Does the evidence from the Gospels support the claim that the Gospel authors themselves used such compositional devices? The first two parts of *The Mirror or the Mask* are broadly structured by questions 1 and 2. Part Three presents and provides evidence for an alternative model—a commonsense model of the Gospels as honest historical reportage, based on eyewitness testimony, in which Jesus and the disciples are treated as real persons rather than as literary characters to be moved about by the author. Part Four analyzes a large number of Gospel examples that the theorists believe plausibly or probably exemplify fact-altering changes.

If the answer to the first question above is that this view would affect our understanding a great deal, this conclusion should motivate readers *not* to set aside these issues as unimportant, especially not if they are inclined to accept the literary device views. That is to say, if the literary device view *would* make a substantial, negative difference to our understanding of the reliability of the Gospels, it should not be accepted lightly. The arguments for it should be subjected to careful scrutiny before one accepts it. I wish to be absolutely clear: I am *not* saying that we should reject a view out of fear of its consequences for our understanding of the Gospels. I am saying that, because of its epistemic consequences, we should not think it a trivial matter nor accept the theory without rigorous examination. Nor is it enough to say that some scholars regarded as experts endorse it, nor even that many scholars endorse some aspects of it. Truth is not decided by majority vote, and especially not by majority vote of those who happen to be alive at a given time. If the robust reliability of the Gospels is important (as I'm sure many readers agree that it is), then any view that would undermine that robust reliability is a serious matter.

I want to assure laymen as well as scholars who have not specialized in these particular topics that they are indeed capable of evaluating the evidence on these issues for themselves. I mention this point because unfortunately credentialism has sometimes been used to dismiss the views I argue for here. This book itself illustrates that one does not need some specific credential in order to assess the relevant evidence, as it lays out and evaluates the arguments point by point. I have placed some of the supporting material concerning ancient compositional textbooks, Plutarch, and composite Gospel discourses in appendices in order to improve the flow and readability of the book. Readers are warmly invited to delve into any of this material for themselves. For that very reason I have provided links to freely available English translations of Greco-Roman literature. One of my major points in this debate is that we should not blindly follow designated experts. I have no desire to set myself up merely as a competing expert, asking the reader to follow me blindly.

It may be asked why I focus so much on evangelical scholars rather than, for example, on a skeptical, liberal scholar such as Bart Ehrman. The decision to do so is quite deliberate. The reason that literary device views are becoming more widely accepted by conservative Christian apologists, pastors, seminarians, and laymen is precisely *because* some New Testament scholars deemed to be conservative and evangelical advocate them. The natural assumption is that, if these scholars accept these views, the evidence must be truly compelling, since these scholars could not possibly have any liberal bias driving them in this direction. But I shall argue that such an assumption leads in the wrong direction. Whatever the sociological causes may be, these scholars *have* accepted these views on shaky grounds, against evidence to the contrary, and hence have made unnecessary, damaging concessions.

By focusing on the work of evangelical New Testament scholars, I also provide in the very course of doing so a more robust response to a liberal scholar such as Bart Ehrman. If evangelicals like Michael Licona and Craig Evans (who both debate Ehrman) have conceded too much ground, Ehrman's more extreme skepticism is even more unjustified. We can and should take a stronger, more forward position in responding to the likes of Ehrman in the future. This stronger position will outlast the specific scholarly movements that gave rise to this book. If these specific literary device views cease to be popular in some later time period, the robust defense of the reportage model of the Gospels found here will be applicable to whatever comes to take their place.

A word is in order concerning persons and ideas. In the words of the late, great Justice Antonin Scalia, I attack ideas; I don't attack people. One of my goals in this book is to discuss and refute ideas that I consider to be wrong-headed, and importantly so. I also intend to remind readers of a venerable and better alternative. In no way does any of this amount to a personal attack on the scholars whose ideas I criticize. Scholarly interaction will always and should always involve the vigorous exchange of ideas and arguments on different sides of an issue. It is in this way that we ensure that scholarship, and Christian scholarship in particular, does not stagnate, becoming a game of "inside baseball" without internal critique or disagreement. I pray, personally, for those whose ideas I critique in this volume, and I wish them God's richest blessings. I believe that one of the blessings God sends is the opportunity to engage with those who disagree, so that we may test our ideas against the best arguments that can be made against them. I call upon those whose ideas I discuss in these books to join me in the sincere, difficult, vigorous, and clear-eyed search for truth about such vital matters.

The prominence of Michael Licona as a foil in these pages is chiefly the result of this fact: Dr. Licona has worked hard to lay out the literary device view clearly, together with a lengthy and explicit case for it. His body of work, being both so comprehensive and so relatively recent, and being aimed at an audience including lay and scholarly readers and Christian apologists (which is also my audience), has thus provided both an entry point for these ideas into the evangelical world and a salient point of departure for critiquing them.

Because I am interacting with the work of living scholars who often explain and elaborate upon their views in venues other than their formal scholarly work, I have freely drawn upon sources such as debates, podcasts, and interviews, as well (of course) as their formal writing. All references to audio or video recordings are publicly available on-line and cited in such a way that the reader can check them for himself.

The Mirror or the Mask: Liberating the Gospels from Literary Devices is intended to be the first volume in a set of two. The next volume, tentatively titled *The Eye of the Beholder*, will focus on the Gospel of John, defending the historicity of the Gospel that has received the most sweeping application of dehistoricizing theories.

I published a significant part of my initial writing on these subjects at the blog *What's Wrong With the World*, and those scholarly posts have been deemed quite controversial. I have carried out the work on those posts and on this book, both in public and in private, against a certain amount of opposition. Sometimes that opposition has taken the form of marked, explicit refusal to engage, together with statements that I am unqualified to write on these matters. Sometimes it has been vocal and even at times personal. I could not have pushed through to the point of publication without the help and encouragement of others. For assistance both in my preliminary work and in the writing of this book, I have many people—too many to name—to thank.

I owe incalculable gratitude first to my husband, Timothy McGrew, who has been strongly supportive of my work all along. Tim first taught me to think clearly of the Gospels as historical reports and provided me with enormous quantities of evidence for that model. He has taught me to love older writers who faced similar objections and wrong-headed theories and answered them long ago. He has taught me that we read to know that we are not alone and that the democracy of the dead and the communion of saints have a better right to a voice in our councils than the temporary consensus of those who happen to be on earth at the same time as ourselves.

I also thank my eldest daughter, Bethel, who has been unwaveringly encouraging and always willing to listen and exchange thoughts about both the scholarly and the interpersonal issues involved. I thank my editor at *What's Wrong With the World*, Paul Cella, for his support and for not resenting the near-takeover of our group blog by my New Testament preoccupations. Thanks to my good friend Mia Langford, who has constantly urged me to keep going and trust in the Lord. Mia also helped me to find the main title for this book.

Enormous thanks are due to Nathan Ward of DeWard Publishing, without whose encouragement this book would almost certainly not exist. It was because Nathan was interested in publishing this material in book form that I persevered.

Thanks to Jonathan McLatchie who, at real personal cost, invited me to present webinars on these controversial topics at Apologetics Academy.

My debt to J. P. Moreland for his staunch encouragement and support is enormous. My only regret is that I waited as long as I did to seek his support, when it was always available. Thanks as well to John W. Montgomery, who invited me to write a full-length review essay of Licona's *Why Are There Differences in the Gospels?* for the *Global Journal of Classic Theology*.

I thank Tom Gilson, who publicly argued that those I have critiqued should engage with my ideas, and Rob Bowman, who said publicly that these issues should be decided not on the basis of credentials but rather of arguments. My thanks to all who agreed to write "blurbs" for this book, thus acknowledging the value of taking the work into consideration, whether or not they agree with everything I have written here.

Finally, my sincere thanks to all those (you and God know who you are) who have written to me to tell me how much my work on the New Testament means to you and to urge me to continue. It has meant more than you can possibly know.

My deepest and highest gratitude goes to the One who empowers us for ministry and who has assured us, in our search for truth, that He is the way, the truth, and the life and that we shall find Him if we seek for Him with all our hearts. This work is presented, despite whatever flaws remain, to the greater glory of God.

Lydia McGrew
Kalamazoo, MI
April, 2019

PART ONE

Masking History

I

What if the Gospels Were Only
Based on True Events?

1. Why does all of this matter?

Why do Christians need to know the words and deeds of the real, historical Jesus? Why is it important to present Jesus as he really was to non-Christians? Are details important in the Gospels, or is it enough if the Gospels just give "the big picture" while altering or inventing details?

Christians have always believed that they are supposed to know Jesus, to love him, and to imitate him. "To know Christ and to make him known" has been a goal of the Christian life ever since the Apostle Paul declared that his greatest desire was "that I may know Him and the power of His resurrection and the fellowship of His sufferings" (Phil. 3.10) and ever since he told the same audience, "Let this mind be in you, which was also in Christ Jesus" (Phil. 2.5, KJV).[1] How can we imitate one whom we do not know? But if we are to know Jesus, we must know him as he was historically—that compelling, difficult, cryptic, explosive, real person who walked on a particular part of the globe at a particular point in time.

Jesus calls us to invite others to follow him and to be willing to risk everything for him. "When God calls a man," said Dietrich Bonhoeffer, "he bids him come and die." Jesus himself said (or at least the Gospels *say* that he said) that we are to "make disciples of all the nations" (Matt. 28.19). Of whom are they to be disciples, and how are they to know what he said and taught, if the sayings attributed to him must, as in the previous sentence, be tacitly asterisked, because they might or might not be historical? And why should we be willing to give our lives for one whose life and teachings we can know only at some high level of generality?

---

[1] Unless otherwise indicated, Bible quotations are from the NASB.

Indeed, how well can we even be sure that he rose from the dead if the accounts that allegedly came from witnesses to that event are cast into doubt?[2]

The scholars I am answering in this book are arguing, quite clearly, that the Gospel authors considered themselves licensed to change the facts in their stories. Sometimes they argue that the evangelists invisibly and deliberately altered details because they were trying to tell only some more minimal "core" accurately. Sometimes they hypothesize that the evangelists may well have invented or radically altered what we would normally call entire incidents. According to this view, the evangelists are writing literary and theological treatises in which they consider it legitimate to invent sayings, details, and even some incidents, change days and times deliberately, suppress events and details to give a slanted impression, and make many other factual changes within the "story world" of their documents. They may be trying to make a better story, to follow the compositional conventions of their time, or to make a theological point. It is quite clear that an author of this kind will give us much less information about Jesus than an author who tries to tell what happened in a more straightforward fashion.

How much accurate information do the Gospels give us? This question is intimately connected with the question of what evidence Christians should expect to find for the reliability of Scripture. My previous book, *Hidden in Plain View: Undesigned Coincidences in the Gospels and Acts*, revived an argument for the eyewitness nature and high reliability of the Gospels, based upon details and side incidents within larger incidents. But Christians cannot have it both ways. If the argument in *Hidden in Plain View* has force, it supports the conclusion that the Gospel

---

[2] See Chapter XVI, where I discuss and respond to doubts cast upon the resurrection accounts. In a paper on the resurrection of Jesus, Timothy McGrew and I argue, using the details of the Gospel accounts, that the evidence strongly supports the resurrection. It is central to our argument that the accounts, including details such as eating with Jesus, his being tangible, etc., represent what was claimed by those who were in a position to know. See Timothy and Lydia McGrew, "The Argument from Miracles: A Cumulative Case for the Resurrection of Jesus of Nazareth," in W. L. Craig and J. P. Moreland, eds., *The Blackwell Companion to Natural Theology* (Oxford: Wiley-Blackwell, 2009), pp. 593–662. See also Lydia McGrew, "Minimal Facts vs. Maximal Data Approaches to the Resurrection," April 12, 2018, webinar for Apologetics Academy, https://www.youtube.com/watch?v=RUt3r3dXBr4. In contrast, in *The Resurrection of Jesus: A New Historiographical Approach* (Downer's Grover: IVP Academic, 2010), p. 372, Michael Licona questions whether historical investigation warrants accepting the detailed resurrection appearances as recorded in the Gospels. He affirms that there was at least one occasion on which a group of disciples had an experience that convinced them that Jesus was risen but adds, "Did other experiences reported by the Gospels occur as well, such as the appearances to the women, Thomas, the Emmaus disciples, and the multiple group appearances reported by the tradition in I Corinthians 15:3–7 and John? Where did these experiences occur? Historians may be going beyond what the data warrants in assigning a verdict with much confidence to these questions."

authors told their stories honestly, not massaging the truth. If Christians accept and use that argument as confirmation, they cannot, at the same time, consistently accept this alternative view of the evangelists and what they were trying to do. In Chapter XI, we will see how what I call the fictionalizing literary device approach blinds scholars to evidence for the historicity of the Gospels.

These issues are also relevant to the doctrine and practice of Christianity, which we often base upon the historical teachings of Jesus. I encourage pastors, apologists, and laymen to ask themselves how often they cite the *specific* teachings and actions of Jesus recorded in the Gospels when making a theological point. Do you ever cite the fact that Jesus cried out in thirst on the cross when discussing his humanity? Then you should be interested in the question of whether that record is historically accurate. Do you ever discuss the gentleness of Jesus with Mary Magdalene in the scene at the tomb and the glorious turn when she cries out, "Rabboni"? Then you have an interest in finding out whether or not that dialogue was created as part of a "relocation" of the appearance to Mary. Do you argue, perhaps when talking with Jehovah's Witnesses, from Jesus' statement, "I and the Father are one" that Jesus claimed to be God? Would you like to have the option of doing so? Then it is in your interest to know whether the saying is recognizably historical. Do you ever use Jesus' words, "I am the true vine" to motivate yourself and fellow Christians to abide in him, as he enjoins his disciples to do? Then you might like to know whether this was merely the extrapolated meditation of the Johannine community rather than something Jesus really said. Do you think that Jesus really healed the blind before John the Baptist's disciples arrived and that his words, "Go and report to John what you hear and see; the blind receive sight" as recorded in Matt. 11.4–5 refer to real previous events? Then you might be a bit concerned if you concluded that Matthew invented an earlier healing of the blind (Matt. 9.27–29) for Jesus to refer to in Chapter 11.

Scholars—not just secular scholars or scholars thought of as liberal but even some evangelical scholars—have questioned every one of these sayings or scenes. Moreover, there is nothing whatsoever in these theories that confines them only to the passages the scholars have chosen to question so far. To the contrary, if the theories are true, the idea that such changes were part and parcel of the genre, together with their invisibility, would make it likely that there are many more, unbeknownst to us.

The view I am addressing in this book significantly alters our concept of the historicity of the Gospels. It is therefore important to know whether or not it is true.

2. Movies and question marks

What does all of this remind one of? At some time in our lives, most of us have read a book or watched a movie that was "based on true events." This might be as creative as an historical novel about the Civil War, in which only the broadest events are factual, while the unique characters of the novel are entirely invented. It might be a somewhat more historical dramatization of real events in the lives of real people, where much of the dialogue is invented, characters are inserted into scenes who were not present, people's motives are manipulated according to the decisions of the director, and various events and details are altered as a matter of artistic license. Or it might be a somewhat more accurate biographical or autobiographical work containing *some* dramatization in which we have only some doubts about a few of the scenes or events.

In all of these cases, multiple factors are involved in the reader's or viewer's decision to put question marks over the historicity of the work and to rate particular scenes or events as factual or fictional. Any clear indication of a fictional or partly fictional genre is helpful. If the work is designated "a novel" on the front cover, that tells us a lot right to begin with, even if Queen Victoria (an historical character) appears in its pages. Occasionally the author himself will tell us in a preliminary note what kinds of alterations he has made. Sometimes we may think that the dialogue sounds stilted and will guess on that basis that the dialogue was partly or wholly created by the author. Occasionally an author will put a semi-humorous "tag" in the text by which an alert reader can see that the event is partly invented.[3] Sometimes those who were personally acquainted with the events or the author will explain later that the author made up or altered some events.[4]

The ethical evaluation of such alterations will vary, depending upon whether we think that the author or director gave the impression that his work was entirely factual, whether there was a note such as "based on true events" at the beginning,

---

[3] Such a humorous tag probably occurs in the partially fictional memoirs of Yorkshire veterinarian Alf Wight, writing under the pen name James Herriot, when he tells a story of an eccentric dog owner. According to the story, Mrs. Pumphrey tells the vet that her Pekingese, Tricki Woo, has written to the editor of a dog magazine asking the editor to find him a pen pal. She says that for purposes of correspondence Tricki has decided to take the name Mr. Utterbunkum. The phrase "utter bunkum" means "complete nonsense." The besotted Mrs. Pumphrey, as described in the story, would have been very unlikely to have her pet take on this name. It seems to be Herriot's wink to the reader that this story is invented—that it is "utter bunkum." James Herriot, *All Creatures Great and Small* (New York: St. Martin's Press, 1972), p. 85.

[4] Concerning Alf Wight, such revelations occur in the affectionate biography by his son, James Wight, *The Real James Herriot: A Memoir of My Father* (New York: Random House, 1999).

and so forth. We may be annoyed by changes that the author made for propagandistic purposes—to put a slant on the events to serve some contemporary agenda. But in all cases, the *ethical* evaluation that the author or producer of the work was or was not deceptive or manipulative is a different matter from the *epistemic* effects of factual alteration. Whenever we think that the author or producer considered himself licensed to alter facts, whatever the reasons (even if wholly ethical), we will take events in the work with the proverbial grain of salt unless we can confirm them from some more down-to-earth historical source. And the less we can confirm independently, the more difficult it will be to separate fact from fiction and the harder it will be to gain, from that work, information about what really happened and what the historical characters were like. We may consider it morally allowable for the producers of the work to take artistic license while, at the same time, recognizing that the artistic license renders the work a poor historical source for the events in question.

The theories I will be responding to in this book place such an epistemic question mark, and a fairly large one, over the Gospels. Michael Licona, who will be a frequent foil in these pages, makes explicit the analogy between ancient literature, including the Gospels, and a movie based on true events:

> The historical accuracy of ancient literature may be viewed in a manner similar to what we observe in movie theaters today. Some movies claim at the beginning to be "based on true events" while others claim to be "inspired by true events."[5]

Often the proponents of these theories will argue that they do not make the Gospels unreliable *because* the fact-changing compositional devices they describe were allowed at the time of their writing or because the audiences would not have *minded* if they had known that facts were changed.[6] But this argument confuses ethical evaluation with epistemic evaluation. *Even if it were true* (and I will argue that it is *not* true) that the Gospel authors considered themselves licensed by the

---

[5] Michael Licona, *Why Are There Differences in the Gospels? What We Can Learn from Ancient Biography* (Oxford: Oxford University Press, 2017), p. 6.

[6] See Craig A. Evans, Foreword to Licona, *Why Are There Differences*, p. ix and Licona, *Why Are There Differences*, p. 17. William Lane Craig says, concerning one of the few literary devices he has endorsed, "What I've said is that I don't think by the standards of that day for John to move the cleansing of the temple to early in Jesus' ministry rather than during Passion Week is an error. This by the standards of that day would be permitted by ancient standards of historiography and therefore this is not incompatible with the reliability of the Gospels." "An Objection to the Minimal Facts Argument," May 6, 2018, https://www.reasonablefaith.org/media/reasonable-faith-podcast/an-objection-to-the-minimal-facts-argument/. But this is a *non sequitur*.

standards of the time to change facts knowingly in their works, this would not ameliorate the epistemic effects. If they really were taking artistic license as suggested by the literary device theorists, and if they placed no tag in their works by which one could tell the true from the false, then their works become epistemically questionable sources for the life and teaching of Jesus, regardless of whether or not the "standards of the time" allowed such factual changes.

The same is true in our own time. Let's consider a concrete case from the late 20th century. The 1981 movie *Chariots of Fire* dramatizes some historical events of the 1924 Olympics from the perspective of two runners, Eric Liddell and Harold Abrahams, who competed and won medals that year. The film also portrays their friends who compete in the same Olympic Games, some of them historical persons. As it turns out, the movie made quite a number of substantial factual changes. For example, the historical Harold Abrahams did marry a woman named Sybil, but the movie identifies her as Sybil Gordon, an opera singer (a real historical character, but not Abrahams's wife) and portrays them as meeting while Abrahams is preparing for the Olympics. Abrahams's wife in historical fact was Sybil Evers, a different singer in the same company whom he did not meet until some years after the events portrayed in the movie.[7] The movie portrays Eric Liddell's sister Jennie as disapproving of his running, expressing concern that it is coming between him and his commitment to God and to missions. The real Jennie Liddell was only a child in China at the time, and Eric's family supported his running.[8] Perhaps most striking of all, the lovable Lord Lindsay of the movie is a largely fictional creation, based only loosely upon David Cecil, known as Lord Burghley.[9]

It is entirely true to say that the "standards of the time" (i.e., 1981) allowed the artistic license taken in the movie. It was only based upon the events of the early 1920s, and everyone knew this. It did not present itself as anything else. It would

---

[7] Jeffrey Richards, "Chariots of Fire," *History Today*, August 8, 2012, https://www.historyto-day.com/reviews/chariots-fire; "Sybil Evers (1930–31)," *The Gilbert and Sullivan Archive*, January 28, 2002, https://www.gsarchive.net/whowaswho/E/EversSybil.htm. "Sybil Gordon (1926–1930, 1931)," *The Gilbert and Sullivan Archive*, July 11, 2002, https://www.gsarchive.net/whowaswho/G/GordonSybil.htm.

[8] Maev Kennedy, "Eric Liddell exhibition for champion who wouldn't run on Sundays," *The Guardian*, July 8, 2012, https://www.theguardian.com/sport/2012/jul/08/liddell-chariots-daughter; Gina Davidson, "My Daddy: The Flying Scotsman," *The Scotsman*, June 19, 2012, https://www.scots-man.com/news/my-daddy-the-flying-scotsman-1-2362795.

[9] Nick Mason, "Yesterday's Anti-Heroes: Champion Toff Misrepresented in the Movies," *The Guardian*, Sept. 28, 2000, https://www.theguardian.com/sydney/story/0,,374383,00.html.

have been naïve to think that everything presented in it was factual. Those who go to such movies expect, or should expect, some degree of artistic license, and if it is important to you to know whether Lord Lindsay really gave up his place to Eric Liddell in 1924, so that Liddell could avoid running on Sunday but still compete in the Olympics, you should realize that you have to consult an historical source more reliable than *Chariots of Fire*. In other words, the changes in *Chariots of Fire* are classic cases of morally permissible, fact-altering literary devices, and the producers of the movie are not morally culpable or deceptive for making the movie in the way that they did.

But by the same token, it follows that *Chariots of Fire* is not an historical source, except in the very loosest of senses. It follows, more to the point, that it is not a *reliable* historical source. It follows that we have to *check up on* its representations from *other*, factual sources in order to find out if they are true. In other words, the epistemic issue remains even if we don't think of the moviemakers as deceptive.

What if *Chariots of Fire* were our only historical source for those years? Or what if all that we had as sources for Liddell's and Abrahams's Olympic story were *Chariots of Fire* and a handful of other movies that were also only "based on true events" and contained a variety of similar factual alterations? It would then become much harder to "mine" or "glean" historical fact concerning those events from such sources. The problem would be exacerbated if we also had reason to believe that some of the movies were actually based upon each other rather than more directly based upon historical knowledge. And once we started to decide (somehow) that portions of the movies were changed or invented, the questions would start rolling in: If Lord Lindsay didn't exist, did Aubrey Montague, Harold Abrahams's friend in *Chariots of Fire*, exist? Did Eric Liddell have a problem in the Olympics because he refused to run on Sunday or because of some other religious scruple concerning the Olympic regulations? Did he win a gold medal or a bronze? Our picture of the events would be much more foggy than it is now. The reason it is not foggy now is because we can look things up elsewhere, using better sources than partially fictionalized movies to make our historical decisions.

With this understanding in mind, readers should be dubious when they hear a scholar say, "This does not mean that the Gospels are unreliable, because these things were permitted at the time." That is a *non sequitur*. If invisible, unexpected alterations *were* widely and uncontroversially allowed at the time, and if the authors did consider themselves licensed to use them (both of which I shall argue are untrue), this conclusion would render the Gospels unreliable as historical sources. One is always rightly cautious about historical conclusions drawn from biopics or dramatizations merely "based on true events." This is why it is important to find out if the Gospels really are that type of document.

3. Fictionalizing literary devices

Let us, then, consider the concept of a fictionalizing literary device, which will come up often in the course of this book. The term "fictionalizing" is not a flourish of rhetoric,[10] still less an insult directed at the scholars who attribute such devices to the evangelists. Michael Licona himself uses the analogy of a movie based on true events in his description of ancient literature. Yet if we were discussing such a movie, we would unhesitatingly say that it is partially fictional.

To avoid any misunderstanding, the following three criteria show what I mean by saying that an alteration of fact is fictionalization. The term is used throughout this book as a technical term, explicitly defined.

1) What is presented in a seemingly realistic fashion in the work is actually contrary to fact. The real facts have been altered.

For example, an event presented as occurring in a certain year actually occurred in a different year. A discussion presented in the work did not recognizably occur in the historical context in which it is presented. An event presented realistically in the work was invented. And so forth.

2) The alteration of fact was made by the author deliberately.

The author did not (if the act is a fictionalization) make a mere mistake while trying to tell the truth. He did not misremember. He did not make a reasonable inference about what happened that turned out to be false. He did not present a good paraphrase of a person's speech, based upon memory or sources he had reason to believe are accurate (a point I shall return to later). He did not merely write quickly or carelessly in a way that accidentally gave a misimpression. He knew that what he presented *did not happen* or else he knew that he had *no good reason at all* to think that it did happen, yet he wrote as he did with the deliberate intention of presenting the event "as if" it happened that way in the narrative.

---

[10] Licona has objected to the term "fictionalizing" by saying "that's just going too far with the rhetoric." "Bonus Episode 15: Mike Licona Answers More Questions on the Gospels," *The Freethinking Podcast*, May 2, 2018, minute 4:35, http://freethinkingministries.com/bonus-ep-15-mike-licona-answers-more-questions-on-the-gospels/.

3) The alteration of fact is invisible to the audience within that work itself.

There is no "tag" in the text, no "wink" within the movie, to show that this is not true. There is no equivalent of "once upon a time" or "there once was a man" within the artistic work that signals, "What follows did not really happen." One may *guess* that the facts might have been altered by using independent historical considerations, a vague sense of implausibility, comparison with other works, accidental roughness of style, etc., or other critical methods. One may directly check a more serious historical source and conclude that the change has been made. But *within the work itself*, the presentation appears seamless and historical.

In Chapter IX, section 1, I will discuss a fourth condition that literary device theorists themselves are insistent upon—namely, that the type of device in question was widely accepted at the time. This is consistent with condition #3. "Accepted at the time" does *not* mean that it was recognizable within the work. It merely means that the audience would allegedly not have been bothered if they later learned that this alteration of fact had been made, even though, when reading the work, they had no way of telling. This fourth condition is meant to distinguish the use of a literary device from *ordinary* deception or disregard for truth. For right now, I present conditions 1–3 to define what I mean by "fictionalization." In this way, when we have in hand quotations from the theorists, we will be able to see that they are, indeed, advocating literary devices that fictionalize.

4. Fictionalization and the mask on the Gospels

The trouble, of course, in the case of the Gospels is that they are our closest extant primary source documents for the life and teaching of Jesus. Most of the specifics we want to know, from whether Jesus taught that he was God to whether or not he took little children in his arms to whether he predicted his own death and resurrection, are unknowable aside from the Gospels. If the Gospel authors felt free to craft their stories using fictionalizing literary devices, we do not have other, more solid sources with a better claim to historicity that are going to tell us a clear "yes" or "no" if we have to check the Gospel incidents and sayings on a case-by-case basis. The epistemic effect if the Gospel authors did consider themselves free to use such devices would be a serious one.

It is important to stress that, on the literary device theory, *even the original audience* would have found such devices invisible within the work itself, though it is *occasionally* suggested that the original audience would have considered one

Gospel more historically authoritative than another. Just as an audience member in the late 20th century could not tell just from watching *Chariots of Fire* that Lord Lindsay was non-historical but Aubrey Montague was historical, the original readers of Matthew, Mark, Luke, and John would not (on the literary device theory) have had some special, ancient way of telling, by reading a given document, which parts of it were factually true and which were not.

Since the Gospel authors knew that their works would be used as a means for their audience to know about the life of Jesus (see, for example, Luke 1.1–4), and since Jesus was extremely important both to the Gospel authors and to their audience, we should wonder even more whether they would make it difficult for their audience to know the facts from reading their books. Simply saying that such devices were accepted at the time does not answer this point. Partially fictionalized movies were accepted in 1981, but if someone wanted to write a biography or produce a film from which people could be confident that they were gaining accurate information about the specifics of Liddell's 1924 Olympic run, he would not produce a movie like *Chariots of Fire*. He would produce a researched documentary or factual biography instead. I will return in Chapter X, section 2, to the point that the Gospel authors wanted their readers to be able to know the factual truth from their works.

If the literary device theorists are right, it matters. We will have to rethink radically, not just a little bit, the reliability of the Gospels. By way of illustration, I list below twenty places where literary device theorists of the Gospels throw factual historicity into doubt. In some cases, the author does not *definitely conclude* that a particular theory is true—e.g., that an evangelist invented an incident. He may merely raise this as a very serious possibility, or conclude that we do not know what happened. In every case, the historicity of the events related is seriously called into question by treating the possibility of fictionalization as a very live contender. And in many of these cases (as we shall see as we go along) the authors definitely argue that fictionalization has occurred.

I want to note here that the word "perhaps" does not produce an historical free pass. Suppose that an historian, writing about the death of John F. Kennedy, were to say, "Perhaps he was killed by aliens" and were then to consider this possibility solemnly for a paragraph or two, concluding eventually in heavy tones that it appears *more* probable that Kennedy was shot by Lee Harvey Oswald than that he was killed by aliens. The fact that he used the term "perhaps" before seriously contemplating the alien hypothesis would not, and should not, prevent astonishment that he would take it so seriously. I bring up this extreme example merely to point out that a scholar's serious consideration of a hypothesis *is itself an evaluation of plausibility*. Scholars take time to discuss in that manner those hypotheses they consider to be "on the table," not hypotheses they consider simply silly. If a scholar thinks a hypothesis is completely absurd and is considering it only because it has garnered unfortunate support from misguided people, he will make that clear. But these theories are being raised by literary device theorists as (in their opinion) real contenders, plausible explanations of the text. If a New Testament scholar says that "perhaps" John invented the entire doubting Thomas sequence, though "perhaps" instead Luke deliberately conflated two different appearances of Jesus, he is treating both of these as quite plausible and casting doubt on the historicity of the events related in both Gospels. This is the case even if he eventually narrowly concludes that the seemingly less radical option (that Luke deliberately conflated two appearances) is the correct explanation.

Here, then, is a sample list, taken from several different theorists, showing the range of the historical questions evangelical scholars are raising about the Gospels:

1) Did Luke move a saying of Jesus about causing little ones to stumble to a different context, try to erase all traces of his chronological change, but leave some clues behind accidentally?[11]

2) Did John move Jesus' cleansing of the Temple by three years, deliberately making it look like he cleansed the Temple early in his ministry, when in fact he did it shortly before his crucifixion?[12]

3) Did Matthew invent the involvement of the mother of James and John in asking that her sons sit on Jesus' left and right hands, when in fact she was not involved at all?[13]

4) Did Matthew invent dialogue between Jesus and the Pharisees when Jesus was going to heal a man with the withered hand, when in fact the Pharisees kept silent?[14]

---

[11] Licona, *Why Are There Differences*, p. 244 n. 46; Michael Licona, "Why Are There Differences in the Gospels," April 19, 2014, minute 47:35, https://youtu.be/xtemSTrkogE?t=2855.

[12] Licona, *Why Are There Differences*, p. 195. Craig Keener, *The Gospel of John: A Commentary* (Grand Rapids, MI: Baker Academic, 2003), pp. 518–519.

[13] Craig A. Evans, *Matthew* (New Cambridge Bible Commentary) (Cambridge: Cambridge University Press, 2012), p. 353.

[14] Licona, *Why Are There Differences*, p. 128.

5) Did Mark or did John deliberately move the day on which a woman anointed Jesus' feet shortly before his death?[15]

6) Did Mark deliberately suppress the conversion of the thief on the cross in order to make Jesus appear to have been rejected by all?[16]

7) Did Mark put into Jesus' mouth a prohibition against a woman's divorcing her husband, not uttered by Jesus, as an extrapolation for a Gentile audience?[17]

8) Did Luke deliberately put all of the events after Jesus' resurrection *on Easter Day* in his Gospel, though he knew that they really took forty days instead?[18]

9) Did Luke move the location of Jesus' first appearance to his male disciples to Jerusalem, when he knew that it really occurred in Galilee, in order to make it possible for all of the appearances to occur on Easter Day?[19]

10) Did John invent the story of Thomas's doubts and Jesus' invitation to Thomas to touch his scars in order to rebuke those who doubted Jesus' resurrection, or (instead) did Luke deliberately conflate two different appearances to the disciples at which different numbers of disciples were present?[20]

11) Did John invent the incident in which Jesus breathes on his disciples after his resurrection in order to allude to Pentecost, since he was not narrating the real Pentecost?[21]

12) Did Jesus say, "I am thirsty" from the cross, or did John invent those words as a theological alteration of the tradition that Jesus said, "My God, why have you forsaken me?"[22]

---

[15] Ibid., p. 150.

[16] Ibid., p. 165.

[17] Daniel B. Wallace, "An Apologia for a Broad Use of *Ipsissima Vox*," unpublished paper presented at the meeting of the Evangelical Theological Society, Danvers, MA, November 18, 1999, p. 12.

[18] Licona, *Why Are There Differences*, pp. 177, 180. Licona, *The Resurrection of Jesus*, p. 596, n. 449.

[19] Licona, *Why Are There Differences*, pp. 177–180. Bart Ehrman vs. Michael Licona, "Are the Gospels Historically Reliable," Kennesaw State University, February 21, 2018, minute 1:46:20, https://youtu.be/qP7RrCfDkO4?t=1h46m20s.

[20] Licona, *Why Are There Differences*, p. 177.

[21] Ibid., p. 181; Keener, *John*, pp. 1196–2000.

[22] Licona, *Why Are There Differences*, p. 166; Daniel B. Wallace, "*Ipsissima Vox* and the Seven Words From the Cross," unpublished paper presented to the Society for Biblical Literature Southwest Re-

13) Did Jesus actually say, "It is finished," or did John invent that saying as a "redaction of the tradition" that Jesus said, "Father, into your hands I commit my spirit"?[23]

14) Did John invent the scene between Jesus and Mary Magdalene in the garden after Jesus' resurrection in order to "relocate" the first meeting between Jesus and Mary Magdalene? Or instead did Matthew deliberately try to make it look like Jesus appeared to Mary Magdalene with the other women when he knew that she actually met Jesus alone, as recounted in John?[24]

15) Did John deliberately change the day of the crucifixion to make a theological point?[25]

16) Did Matthew make up an extra demoniac and/or an extra blind man in an incident where they were not present in order to compensate for not telling different healing stories?[26]

17) Did Matthew invent a "doublet" incident in which Jesus healed two blind men early in his ministry in order to create a healing to which Jesus could allude in response to John the Baptist's disciples?[27]

18) Did the disciples dispute about who would be the greatest on the night of the Last Supper, or did Luke invent the connection between this incident (which he took from a different time recorded in Mark) and the Last Supper and redact Jesus' words to make it seem to fit with the context of the Last Supper?[28]

19) Are Jesus' "I am" sayings with predicates such as "I am the true vine" and "I am the bread of life" the dramatic creations of the Johannine community based upon their theological reflections on Jesus' other teaching?[29]

---

gional meeting, March 5, 2000, pp. 4–9.

[23] Licona, *Why Are There Differences*, p. 166; Daniel B. Wallace, "*Ipsissima Vox* and the Seven Words From the Cross," pp. 10–11.

[24] Licona, *Why Are There Differences*, pp. 175–176.

[25] Ibid., p. 163; Keener, *John*, pp. 1100–1103, 1129–31.

[26] Licona, *Why Are There Differences*, pp. 131, 135.

[27] Ibid., p. 135.

[28] Ibid., p. 141.

[29] Craig A. Evans vs. Bart Ehrman, "Does the New Testament Present a Historically Reliable Portrait of the Historical Jesus?" Saint Mary's University, January 19, 2012, minute 1:36:59, https://youtu.be/ueRIdrlZsvs?t=1h36m59s.

20) Are Jesus' relatively explicit claims to deity in John, such as "I and the Father are one" in John 10.30, inventions by the author that make clearer the implicit claims to deity in entirely different incidents recorded in Matthew, Mark, and Luke?[30]

This is the mask upon the historical Jesus. This sample of alterations suggested by the literary device theorists shows how their ideas cast a redactive fog over Jesus' life and teachings. And that is why this study is important. If the Gospels are the kind of artistic works that manipulate Jesus, his disciples, and other characters in these ways, we need to know that, and a major recalibration of our ability to get historical information from the Gospels will be in order. If these theories are true, we are confronted with a mask, which shows us the face of the historical Jesus only as the artistic author chooses to make the mask sufficiently like the face beneath.

Previously most Christians have thought that the Gospels are more like a mirror, which shows the face of the Master by the natural process of historical reporting. Such a serious recalibration would be a great loss. It will, therefore, prevent a great loss if we find upon examination that these theories are false.

---

[30] Michael Licona, "Are We Reading an Adapted Form of Jesus' Teachings in John's Gospel?" *Risen Jesus*, Sept. 29, 2017, https://www.risenjesus.com/reading-adapted-form-jesus-teachings-johns-gospel; "Bonus Episode 15," *The Freethinking Podcast*, minute 9:20 and following.

Summary
What if the Gospels Were Only Based on True Events?

- Christians have an interest in knowing Jesus' actions and teachings clearly. The Gospels are our main primary sources for the life and teachings of Jesus. If the Gospel authors felt free to change facts about Jesus, this will make a significant difference to how much we can know him.

- Even small details are important to confirming the Gospels' reliability.

- If the Gospels were like movies that are only based on true events, this would make it hard to know what really happened. The fact that it is culturally acceptable to make such movies in our own time does not turn them into reliable historical sources. If it were acceptable at the time of the Gospels to write a document that was only based on true events, this would mean that it was acceptable to write a document that was *not* a significantly reliable historical primary source. If the Gospels were such documents, they would not be reliable historical documents.

- I define a fictionalizing literary device as a deliberate alteration of fact that would have been invisible in the document itself. The narrative in that document would appear realistic. The term "fictionalization" is a carefully defined, clear designation of what literary device theorists themselves claim occurred in the Gospels, though they do not use this term.

- The literary device theorists I will discuss in this book question the historicity of a wide array of Jesus' words and actions and of the events in the Gospels, including things that would not normally be regarded as trivial details.

II

A Handful of Crucial Distinctions

1. Doing without chronology vs. changing chronology

It may be asked whether I am representing the theorists correctly. Are they really saying that the Gospel authors made invisible changes of fact? Could they perhaps be saying *merely* that the authors sometimes narrated *without specifying* chronology? Isn't it true that ancient authors sometimes didn't worry too much about chronological precision? Isn't there a thing called "telescoping" in which authors compress events, and isn't that legitimate?

In Chapter III, and throughout this book, I will be quoting New Testament scholars in their own words telling us what they are alleging the Gospel authors did. Here I want to make some crucial distinctions that must be kept in mind when discussing these issues. By keeping our concepts clear, we can avoid confusion as we interpret what scholars are saying and consider the claim that the Gospel authors used compositional devices in their narratives.

It will be useful to have a couple of coined words to help us deal with chronology (time ordering). I will be using the term "achronological" for narration that does not have a chronology stated or implied, as intended by the author. I will use "dyschronological" for narration that *does* imply or state a chronology that the author believes is *different from* what happened in the real world.

Consider an example. Suppose that John is talking to his wife Jane over dinner about his day.

Jane: So, how was your day?

John: Oh, it was okay. I got a lot of work done. Had a great conversation with my boss about the new project. But I didn't really like the new menu at the cafeteria.

Now, let's suppose that the conversation with John's boss was at the beginning of the day. Here he mentions the conversation after saying that he "got a lot of work done." Does that mean that John is *changing* the order of the events, since he had the conversation *before* getting any work done? Not at all. His "I got a lot of work done" is a summary of the day's work. It neither says nor is meant to imply that he got a lot of work done *before* the conversation with his boss. Often, when a person narrates several things that all happened at around the same time, we need not assume that the order of narration was the order in which the events occurred. The same was true in the ancient world, though they perhaps did somewhat more achronological narration than we do.

Contrast that with this dialogue:

Jane: So, how was your day?

John: It was okay. First thing, I sat down and did a lot of work, so that made me feel like I had accomplished something no matter what happened the rest of the day. After that, the boss came in and wanted to have a talk, and that went really well. But I didn't like the new menu at the cafeteria.

Now suppose that the conversation with the boss happened before John's profitable day got going and that he remembers that quite well. In that case, he is narrating dyschronologically.

Bear these two dialogues in mind when we consider the literary device called "displacement." If an author is deliberately trying to make it look, within his narrative, like Event A took place before Event B, though he knows that B took place first, he is narrating dyschronologically. If, on the other hand, he is just narrating a "heap" of events without specifying an order and without intending to make it look like they happened in the order narrated, he is narrating achronologically, like John in the first dialogue.

One of the only New Testament scholars I have been able to find who distinguishes achronological narration from dyschronological narration and expressly blocks the inference of the latter from the former is Allan Chapple, in an article about the Temple cleansing. Chapple argues for two cleansings and expressly rejects the claim that John's moving the cleansing is unproblematic because ancient people did not always narrate chronologically:

The second step in our argument involves challenging the widely held view that John had theological reasons for moving this event to the beginning of Jesus' ministry. Scholars generally see no problem here, on the grounds that the Gospel writers often arrange material thematically rather than chronologically. That this occurs in the Gospels is obvious enough—but is there any parallel for such a major departure from the actual order of events? It is one thing to recognize, for example, that Matthew has grouped together a series of miracle stories without any regard for their precise chronological setting (Matt 8:1–9:34). This is only a matter, first, of not recording specific dates and times for the events being reported, and second, of selecting representative incidents from the early stages of Jesus' ministry. All we get is a rough idea of when they happened—but a rough idea is all that we need. But to bring forward to the beginning of Jesus' ministry an event that occurred only at the end—and, what is more, an event that played a significant part in bringing his ministry to an end—is not at all the same kind of thing. *This does not give us just a rough idea of what happened; it gives us the wrong idea.*[1]

It is rather disturbing that so many scholars elide the crucial distinction between giving a rough idea and giving the wrong idea. Chapple's clarity on this point, and his recognition that dyschronological narration is unlikely, are as commendable as they are rare.

We can see something similar with a concept sometimes called "compression" or "telescoping." Consider the following hypothetical narrative about a battle:

> The final attack on the city opened with a volley of fire arrows. But as time went on, the besiegers grew low on ammunition. Then relief arrived in the form of General Tremayne with one thousand cavalry. They scattered the besiegers before them like the wind and halted before the city gate, from which a sortie had just emerged. The city was saved!

Let us supposed that, in the real world, the fire arrows were fired over the walls on the morning of one day and General Tremayne arrived to lift the siege about thirty-six hours later. Even if the author of the history book knew this, this passage could nonetheless be an example of achronological compression—merely relating briefly and without giving a lot of detail. The author might well not be trying to give the impression that General Tremayne and his cavalry arrived to save the city on the *same day* as the initial volley of fire arrows. He could simply be bypassing that question with the phrase "as time went on" and the word "then," being inexplicit about precisely *how much* time went by before General Tremayne arrived.

Contrast that version with this one:

---

[1] Allan Chapple, "Jesus' Intervention in the Temple: Once or Twice?" *JETS* 58:3 (2015), p. 551. Contrast Chapple's clarity here with Craig Keener's severely confused use of Augustine and the concept of achronological narration when he argues that John moved the Temple cleansing. See the discussion in Chapter X, section 1. Emphasis added.

The final attack on the city opened early in the morning with a volley of fire arrows. Things looked grim for the defenders. As the morning wore on, however, the besiegers grew low on ammunition. Just after noon, a shout of joy went up from the watchers on the wall. Over the plain they could see relief arriving—General Tremayne, with one thousand cavalry. Scattering the besiegers before them like the wind, they galloped up to the gate, where they were joined by a sortie of the defenders within. The city was saved!

Here the implication that all of the events occurred on a single day is unmistakable and must be deliberate. If the author *knows* that General Tremayne *did not* arrive until thirty-six hours after the opening volley of fire arrows, he is knowingly changing the facts to make it appear in this version that the entire series of events happened within a shorter time than it really did. This would be dyschronological compression, not the uncontroversial compression that is merely a result of inexplicitness or haste in narration, as in the previous paragraph.

So we have different concepts of both "displacement" and "compression" or "telescoping." These must be kept distinct when deciding whether or not an author is engaging in a fictionalizing literary device.

2. Paraphrase vs. "paraphrase"

What about paraphrase? Here I want to emphasize that the special use of this term made by some New Testament critics is not like *any* ordinary use of the word at all and is bound to confuse. To understand this confusing usage, let's begin with a made-up example. Suppose that my friend Bill says to me, in his exact words,

> I'm really bummed about what the city council is doing with the roads around here. It's all unnecessary. Man, they decided to turn South Street into only one lane each way and put a giant turning lane in the middle. It was fine the way it was! We didn't need a turning lane. We needed two lanes of traffic going each way. We're near the highway, and we get a lot of traffic on that road. At 8:30 a.m. when I'm going to work that place is going to look like Chicago.

Suppose that I am talking to someone else about Bill, and I say the following:

> Bill is really ticked off about what the city council is doing to South Street. He told me, "During rush hour when people are going to work that street is going to be like Chicago."

This is normal paraphrase. I don't recall Bill's exact words. I remember that he was talking about a time of day that is rush hour (though as it happens he didn't use that phrase). I remember that he referred to going to work, though his exact words mentioned himself going to work. And so forth. This is what would legitimately be called "giving the gist" of what Bill said. The content and even some wording are quite close, well within the normal, expected range of what is known as "paraphrase." I am doing my best to tell my listener what Bill said, and I'm doing a good job.

But suppose, instead, that Bill said the above and also on a *different occasion* said to me, "I really don't trust the city council" but went into *no further detail* about what he suspects. Suppose that on both of these occasions we were alone. Now suppose that I put together Bill's general expression of distrust in the city council (which might indicate that he suspects corruption, though he did not say so) and his expression of dissatisfaction with the road project and constructed a short "discourse," with a setting, like this:

> Bill was talking to a group of people the other day right outside my house about the city council. He's really ticked off. He said to us, "The city council is carrying out projects all over this city that are unnecessary. They are taking away our driving space on South Street, and they have started a completely pointless project of digging up the sewer lines on Front Street that were just replaced last year. Are they getting kickbacks from the contractors? Is someone on the council the cousin of the guy who got the contract for the road work? We need more transparency about this process."

Now, obviously, if Bill did not recognizably say those things standing outside my house and if that content is largely my *extrapolation* from his comments about rush hour, South Street, and not trusting the council, this short "discourse" is heavily invented. This is *not* paraphrase. It contains insinuations about the council's corruption that Bill never recognizably uttered. It contains a complaint about a project (the sewer project) that Bill never brought up. And the setting of the comments is quite different from the setting of any of his relevant comments in real life.

Unfortunately, some literary device theorists use the term "paraphrase" for alterations up to and including this kind of invention. Sometimes a technical-sounding pair of terms will be used. The phrase *ipsissima verba*, meaning "exact words" will be used for just what it sounds like—someone's exact words, just as he said them. The phrase *ipsissima vox*, meaning "the very voice," will be used by scholars for *some sort* of paraphrase or alteration of the words. There is nothing wrong with this concept of "the very voice" in some uses. But *ipsissima vox* can be used in either a narrow or a broad sense. The narrow sense could refer to the fact that, for example, Jesus may have spoken in Aramaic, whereas our New Testament was originally written in Greek. In those cases the words of Jesus in the New Testament *must* be at least to that extent different from the words Jesus originally uttered. *Ipsissima vox* could also refer merely to normal, recognizable paraphrase. For example, if God the Father said, "You are my beloved Son" as recorded at Jesus' baptism in Mark 1.11 and someone to whom Matthew spoke recalled and recounted this as, "This is my beloved Son," which was recorded in Matt. 3.17, the second would be ordinary paraphrase or an *ipsissima vox* rendering of the words uttered by the voice from heaven. Nor would it have been changed deliberately for some special theological reason.[2] This is merely telling a story in slightly different words.

In contrast, when some scholars use "paraphrase" or *ipsissima vox* in a much broader sense, they mean something quite different, though what they mean is not always made clear to the audience. Such so-called "paraphrase" can be so extreme that the use of the phrase "the very voice" is highly questionable. For example, some scholars have suggested that Jesus did not recognizably claim to be God in such a relatively clear manner as we find in sayings in John, such as "I and the Father are one." On this theory, these sayings in John are John's theological extrapolation, placed into Jesus' mouth, from the implicit claims to deity indicated in *completely different incidents* recounted in other Gospels.[3] For example, in Mark 2.1–12, Jesus claims to be able to forgive sins, and in Mark 2.28 he claims to be Lord of the Sabbath. These incidents take place in completely different geographical and interpersonal settings from the claims to deity in John, though they also seem to imply that Jesus is God. Like my invented "discourse" for Bill with its accusation of corruption against the city council, the dialogues and sayings surrounding Jesus' claims to deity in John are completely different incidents from the "implicit" claims to deity on which they are allegedly based. If John made up the

---

[2] On this difference, Michael Licona postulates an extremely deliberate change on Matthew's part rather than casual paraphrase such as happens in witness testimonial variation. He says that, if asked about the different wording, Matthew would have said, "I changed it so that the voice addresses my readers, so that they personally hear God saying that Jesus is his Son and he's pleased with him." This is quite an unnecessarily complicated hypothesis. "Bonus Episode 14: Mike Licona Answers Your Questions on the Gospels," *The Freethinking Podcast*, minute 26:30, http://freethinkingministries.com/bonus-ep-14-mike-licona-answers-your-questions-on-the-gospels/.

[3] Michael Licona, "Are We Reading an Adapted Form of Jesus' Teachings in John's Gospel?" *Risen Jesus*, Sept. 29, 2017, https://www.risenjesus.com/reading-adapted-form-jesus-teachings-johns-gospel.

sayings and settings of John 8.58 or John 10.30 because he believed that Jesus really did imply that he was God, based on *other events*, the phrase *ipsissima vox* (the very voice) should not be used at all to describe such fictional extrapolation. To use "paraphrase," "loose paraphrase," or *ipsissima vox* for such extrapolative inventions of scenes and sayings is bound to create confusion.[4] Creating scenes in which to set invented discourses and sayings based on what one believes to be the theology of the alleged speaker is not "loose paraphrase."[5]

It is entirely possible to believe that moderate, recognizable paraphrase is plausible within the Gospels while thinking it quite implausible that the authors invented in this way and while absolutely refusing to use the confusing term "paraphrase" for such invention. Laymen need to know that a scholar who says he simply "believes in paraphrase" in the Gospels may mean something quite different from what the listener would spontaneously understand by that phrase.

It is important here not to be confused by what philosophers call a sorites paradox. A sorites is a heap, and the paradox concerns the following fact: If we gradually add a single grain of sand to other grains of sand, there is not a sharp line where we say that we have a heap of sand rather than a few grains. Or consider a beard. When does a man merely have five-o-clock shadow and when does he have a beard? Yet the fact that there is not a sharp line in these cases does not prevent us from recognizing clear instances of heaps and beards. This point is relevant to the issue of paraphrase. At what point does a restatement of a person's words cease to be a paraphrase and become one's own free interpretation or outright invention? There may not be a sharp line differentiating moderate from loose paraphrase and loose paraphrase from extrapolative invention, but there are paradigmatic cases of each. Scholars who use the term "paraphrase" for what would undeniably be invented sayings and speeches should not be given a free pass in doing so merely because we can envisage borderline cases.

Moreover, there is an important distinction between deliberately changing what someone said, while presenting it as his words, because you think that you

---

[4] Daniel B. Wallace suggests that Jesus' words of comfort about going to prepare a place for his people in John 14.1–4 might be a broad *ipsissima vox* rendering of the Olivet Discourse in the Synoptic Gospels (Matthew 24–25, Mark 13, and Luke 21). The Olivet Discourse describes the horrors of the destruction of Jerusalem and the end times and bears not the remotest resemblance to Jesus' words about the many dwelling places in his Father's house in John 14.1–4. Daniel B. Wallace, "*Ipsissima Vox* and the Seven Words From the Cross," unpublished paper presented to the Society for Biblical Literature Southwest Regional meeting, March 5, 2000, p. 12.

[5] Licona attempts to say that these changes in John should be considered "loose paraphrase." "Bonus Episode 14," *The Freethinking Podcast*, minute 23:30 and following.

can say it better, and paraphrasing because you have no choice given a gap of time or space. Consciously "upgrading" Jesus' words (or someone else's words) for theological or literary reasons is a different sort of activity from moderate paraphrase undertaken because exact replication is not possible.

3. Transferral

Another term that we need to disambiguate is "transferral." Even in our own time, we have a usage in which an action can be attributed to Person A when in fact Person A hired or commissioned Person B to do it for him. If we use "transferral" in this sense, there may be some ambiguity without the intention to report contrary to fact. For example, if I say, "George asked me to lend him fifty dollars," it may be that George sent our mutual friend Jack to say, "George wants to know if you can lend him fifty dollars." While the hearer might understandably get the idea that George came to me personally and asked for the fifty dollars, this would be a mere accident, arising from an abbreviated way of telling the story. It need not be the case that I suppressed Jack's involvement in order to "have" George come to me in person in my "story world." Therefore, this need not be a fictionalizing type of transferral.

An instance likely to cause even less confusion would be my saying, "George is building a house not far from here" when George himself is not a builder or handyman, in a culture where professional builders usually construct houses. The hearers are likely to understand immediately that George is probably not wielding a hammer at the building site. Non-fictionalizing transferral occurs when one makes (at most) a potentially ambiguous statement that Person A did something in a situation where Person B acted as an agent or intermediary.

If, however, the conversation took place in the context of the frontier, the utterance, "George is building a house not far from here" would probably mean that George really is wielding a hammer, and it would be understood in that way.

Suppose that I said, "George came to me and asked for fifty dollars. He looked pretty tense about it." This would make it sound like George came to me personally and asked for the money, since I described his appearance. Or suppose that I said, "George is building a house not far from here. I went out to the site to talk to him, and he was up on some scaffolding with a hammer, so I had to wait." This would certainly give the strong impression that George was personally involved in building the house. If in these cases someone else were carrying out the action and George was not present at all, my statements would be fictionalizing. "Transferral" in which one says that Person A did something, in a way that will be understood to mean that Person A carried it out personally, when one knows that Person B really did it instead, is fictionalizing transferral.

4. Meaningful reliability

One more very important word that needs to be defined is "reliable" and its cognates ("unreliable," "reliability," etc.). Once we have a working definition, we need to distinguish reliability in these normative and usual senses from a specialized and confused sense of "reliability" that has crept into the usage of some evangelical New Testament scholars in recent years.

Probability theorist and philosopher John Earman has defined what he calls a "minimal reliability condition" for testimony. Expressed non-technically, this minimal reliability condition is that the testimony is *more likely* if what it attests is true than if what it attests is false.[6] What this amounts to in informal terms is that that testimony, *all by itself*, gives us some reason to think that what it attests is true. It may be a weaker or a stronger reason, depending on how much more likely the testimony is given the truth of its contents than given the falsehood. There are special conditions under which we might colloquially say that a witness is unreliable (e.g., he often tells lies) but he could be reliable in this minimal sense. For example, a known liar who testifies against his own interests in some given case may meet the minimal reliability condition when he gives that testimony. His testimony, since it appears to go against his own interests, can give us some reason to believe that what he says is true. We can also have empirical data indicating that a witness is unreliable about one sort of thing but reliable about a different sort of thing. For example, a witness who has poor vision but excellent hearing would be unreliable for visual recognition of a criminal but might be very reliable at voice recognition.

Quite commonly, when we do not have specialized information, we will take a witness or document to be reliable only if we believe that what he or it says is usually true. This corresponds to a higher notion of reliability than Earman's minimal reliability criterion—namely, that the attestation of a witness or document gives us *quite a good* reason to believe what it asserts. We might say in that case that the source is highly reliable.

Whether we consider a document just barely (minimally) reliable or highly reliable, or somewhere in between, what remains constant is this: The document

---

[6] John Earman, *Hume's Abject Failure: The Argument Against Miracles* (New York: Oxford University Press, 2000), p. 55.

or witness does not have to be separately confirmed in order for its attestation to count in favor of what it attests. What is common to all of these cases, even the unusual ones, is that "reliability" must be understood in terms of what we know *before checking out* the fact attested to. "Reliable" never means merely, "This person happened to get this fact right, as we figured out by checking in some separate way." Happening to get something right, as determined in some independent way, and being reliable are not the same thing at all. Why not? Because even a stopped clock is right twice a day. We may, of course, re-evaluate the reliability of a source *after* finding it repeatedly correct by independent checking. But in that case, given enough confirmation, its further testimony to new statements can come to meet the minimal reliability condition, or an even higher standard, even if it did not before. It will then give us, all by itself, some reason to believe what it says in the future. As long as we regard a document's or person's testimony as individually valueless and must always check it out separately, we are treating it as unreliable.

Notice the way that this understanding dovetails with the discussion of movies. One does find some historical facts even in an historical novel or in a movie based on true events. But they are not usually very historically reliable sources in themselves. Rather, one figures out after the fact which aspects of them are factually correct based upon double-checking with more genuinely historical documents. Or one may make guesses. But if one merely guesses, one must hold one's conclusions to be tentative.

One may eventually conclude after much research that a given historical novelist tends to be (for example) accurate in recounting the external facts but fictionally invents the characters' feelings, personalities, and motivations. This would be like concluding that a witness has good hearing but poor vision. In that case, one would divide the portrayals in the novels into the types of things about which the novelist is reliable and the types of things about which he is unreliable. One would not simply declare him to be reliable because he has *some* correct information.

What has happened in recent years in the evangelical apologetics community is that a new and quite odd definition of "Gospel reliability" has come on the scene. On this concept, a Gospel is considered reliable if it *contains true historical material* and/or if it is possible to *get some historical information out of it*.

Craig A. Evans has articulated this concept in the course of his opening statement in a debate on the question "Does the New Testament present a reliable portrait of the historical Jesus?" Evans answered this question "yes" on the grounds that it is possible to "find substantial historical material in the Gospels."[7] Evans characterized the nature of this historical material by offering a list of seven generic propositions conceded by liberal New Testament scholar E. P. Sanders. (Evans himself emphasizes Sanders's non-conservative scholarly inclinations.) These included such facts as that Jesus was baptized by John the Baptist and was crucified by Roman authorities. To this list Evans added a few more, such as that the public viewed Jesus as a prophet and that he spoke often of the kingdom of God. In other words, what Evans means in the debate when he says that the Gospels present a "reliable historical portrait of Jesus" is that there is *some* broadly-conceived historical material *in them* that we can find by applying various techniques, criteria, and conjectures, as Sanders does.

This does not, however, mean that any one of the Gospels is reliable in the sense that its attestation, by itself, gives us reason to believe that what it says occurred. In other words, it does not mean that any of the Gospels is even minimally reliable as defined above. And as we shall see in the next section, Evans does not consider the Gospel of John to be as historical as Matthew, Mark, and Luke. This is a very confusing and attenuated concept of Gospel reliability, and it is not surprising that Evans's skeptical opponent, Bart Ehrman, states that it constitutes a "sleight of hand" concerning the meaning of "reliable" or "accurate."[8]

William Lane Craig, who accepts a couple of fictionalizing literary devices in the Gospels, has said, "I'll concede for the sake of argument virtually all the errors and inconsistencies in the Old and New Testaments that [the unbeliever] wants to bring up, while insisting that the documents are fundamentally reliable when it comes to the central facts undergirding the claims and fate of Jesus of Nazareth."[9] By "reliable when it comes to the central facts" he seems to mean that these really

---

[7] Craig A. Evans vs. Bart Ehrman, "Does the New Testament Present a Historically Reliable Portrait of the Historical Jesus?," Acadia University, January 20, 2012, minute 13:02, https://youtu.be/UvCVnlHoFow?t=13m1s.

[8] Craig A. Evans vs. Bart Ehrman, "Does the New Testament Present a Historically Reliable Portrait of the Historical Jesus?" Saint Mary's University, January 19, 2012, minute 2:16:27, https://youtu.be/ueRIdrlZsvs?t=1h12m47s.

[9] William Lane Craig, "Scriptural Inerrancy and the Apologetic Task," *Reasonable Faith*, December 27, 2015, https://www.reasonablefaith.org/question-answer/P110/scriptural-inerrancy-and-the-apologetic-task/. For further discussion of this topic see Lydia McGrew, "When Minimal is Minimizing," *What's Wrong With the World*, March 1, 2018, http://whatswrongwiththeworld.net/2018/03/when_minimal_is_minimizing.html. For a response from Dr. Craig, see "An Objection to the Minimal Facts Argument," May 8, 2018, https://www.reasonablefaith.org/media/reasonable-faith-podcast/an-objection-to-the-minimal-facts-argument/. For my further response, see "On minimalism, the Resurrection, and More: Response to Dr. Craig's Podcast," *What's Wrong With the World*, May 7, 2018, http://whatswrongwiththeworld.net/2018/05/response_to_dr_craigs_podcast.html.

are facts—in other words, that the Gospels do get those facts right. He also seems to mean that we have some way of figuring out that the Gospels get those specific facts right, even after he has "conceded for the sake of the argument virtually all the errors and inconsistencies" that the unbeliever wants to bring up. While Craig's list of facts, including Jesus' resurrection, is much more robust than Evans's list taken from E. P. Sanders, the confusion about reliability remains. For a source to be reliable is not merely for it to be right "when it comes to" some list that we have checked up on by some other, elaborate means, even though the source is chock-full of errors and inconsistencies. The list of alleged errors and inconsistencies that a skeptic will "find" in the Gospels is, of course, quite long. A document's being correct about some things is not at all the same thing as its being reliable.

Interestingly, Craig expressed a similar idea rather differently more than a decade earlier, without the confusing use of the term "reliable." In the preface to the third edition of *Reasonable Faith*, Craig said this, concerning his decision to eliminate a chapter from the new edition of that work:

> The inclusion of this chapter [on the reliability of the Gospels]…perpetuated the misimpression, all too common among evangelicals, that a historical case for Jesus' radical self-understanding and resurrection depends upon showing that the Gospels are generally reliable historical documents. The overriding lesson of two centuries of biblical criticism is that such an assumption is false. Even documents which are generally unreliable may contain valuable historical nuggets, and it will be the historian's task to mine these documents in order to discover them.[10]

I *strongly* disagree with Craig's statement that the defense of the basics of Christianity is independent of an argument for the general reliability of the Gospels.[11] But it is interesting to notice that here Craig was using "reliability" and "unreliability" somewhat more clearly. In this quotation from the 3rd edition of *Reasonable Faith*, the idea is that *even if the Gospels were unreliable* we could "mine" them for a few important truths. In the other quotation, however, Craig seems to imply that the Gospels *count as reliable* if we can mine them for such truths.

One of the most striking instances of a confusing, redefined use of "reliable" arises when Michael Licona is discussing the possibility that Jesus did not and indeed would not historically claim to be God "in such a clear manner as we find John reporting" in John 8.58 and John 10.30. Licona insists,

[10] William Lane Craig, *Reasonable Faith*, 3rd edition (Wheaton, IL: Crossway Books, 2008), p. 11.

[11] Lydia McGrew, "Minimal Facts vs. Maximal Data Approaches to the Resurrection," *Apologetics Academy*, April 12, 2018, https://www.youtube.com/watch?v=RUt3r3dXBr4.

By no means does this mean John is historically unreliable. It means that John is often communicating Jesus' teachings in a manner closer to a modern paraphrase than a literal translation. Stated differently, John will often recast Jesus saying something explicitly the Synoptics have Him saying implicitly.[12]

This claim about reliability is quite astonishing, and here the confusing use of "paraphrase," already discussed, and the confusing use of "reliable" come together. As already pointed out, such a change is not anything like "modern paraphrase." An author who would craft entire scenes, as John must have done in order to "recast Jesus saying explicitly" that he is God, based on completely different scenes in the Synoptics where he implies that he is God, is an author who is *unreliable* in his accounts of Jesus' teaching and his interactions with the people. These sayings occur in the context of dialogue which itself would have to be invented in order to give them a setting, as would other clues about where the incident allegedly occurred. E.g., John 10.22–23 says that it was winter, at the Feast of Dedication, and that Jesus was walking in Solomon's Porch in Jerusalem when he had the discussion leading up to the statement, "I and the Father are one." Jesus is nearly stoned after both of these claims to deity in John. Were the attempted stonings also invented, or did they happen apropos of some entirely different, unknown exchanges with the crowd? Licona's statement that "by no means does this mean that John is historically unreliable" is flatly untrue if one uses "reliable" in any meaningful sense. He must be radically redefining it. Why should we consider an author reliable who invents this sort of crucial material?

Elsewhere, Licona makes an explicit statement about John's Gospel that certainly calls its reliability into question:

> John often chose to sacrifice accuracy on the ground level of precise reporting, preferring to provide his readers with an accurate, higher-level view of the person and mission of Jesus.[13]

This claim is virtually impossible to square with reliability even in the minimal sense that the presence of a statement in the document gives us some reason

---

[12] Michael Licona, "Are We Reading an Adapted Form of Jesus' Teachings in John's Gospel?" In this post Licona does not commit himself to the claim in question, but he does defend it, giving only arguments that he thinks support it.

[13] Licona, *Why Are There Differences*, p. 115. The word "precise" in this sentence should not distract attention from the inventions in question. See the list and references at the end of the previous chapter. When Licona says that John "sacrifice[s] accuracy" at the "ground level," he is not talking about something like using round numbers.

to believe that it is factually true. If John *often* chose to sacrifice accuracy at the ground level of literal reporting, then how is he historically reliable? "Reliable" must be redefined in order to give meaning to any assertion that the Gospel is historically reliable while simultaneously holding that the author often chose to sacrifice literal accuracy in the service of higher theological truth. Those who ask about Gospel reliability are asking whether the documents are stating historical fact, not whether they are giving an accurate "higher-level view" that requires sacrificing ordinary historical truth. And if the idea is that John may be reliable (as an historical novelist might be) about matters of, say, geography but not about Jesus' teaching and interaction with the crowds, then he is *unreliable* about the latter.

"Reliable," then, can and should be understood to mean that we have some reason to accept what a document or witness says (individually) as true. But theorists sometimes use it in a redefined sense that means only that the document *contains* some historical facts or that some historical facts can be *gleaned from* it. These are quite different meanings.

With these distinctions in hand, let's see more of what the theorists themselves have to say.

Summary
A Handful of Crucial Distinctions

- New Testament scholars sometimes use words in ways that are ambiguous and that make their claims appear less controversial than they really are.

- It is important to distinguish fictionalizing from non-fictionalizing uses of various terms and phrases like "not narrating in chronological order," "paraphrase," and "transferral." Theorists will not always clarify what they mean by these terms, so readers need to be alert and ask questions.

- Some evangelical scholars are using the term "reliability" in a way that is confusing and attributing reliability to the Gospels while making concessions that undermine meaningful reliability.

III

A Bushel of Quotations

1. Definitions and fictionalization

In *Why Are There Differences in the Gospels?*, Michael Licona defines several of the compositional devices he is discussing in explicit terms that show that they do fall under the heading of fictionalization as I carefully defined it in Chapter I, section 3, though Licona himself objects to the term "fictionalization."[1] Part Four of this book will give quotations concerning particular passages in the Gospels.

Consider Licona's own definition of "compression":

Compression: When an author knowingly portrays events over a shorter period of time than the actual time it took for those events to occur, the author has compressed the story.[2]

The word "knowingly" is especially notable. "Compression" as Licona is using it does not merely mean telling an incident briefly or hastily, leaving out details, or being inexplicit about how much time passed, as in the first battle narrative in the previous chapter. Rather, the author who uses this type of compression *deliberately* writes *as if* the incident took place over a shorter period of time than was actually the case. Licona attributes this type of fictionalization to Luke in Luke 24 by saying that "Luke compresses all of the appearances [of Jesus after his resurrection] and the ascension to have occurred on the same day as Jesus' resurrection," despite the fact that Luke knew that they really took place over the much longer period of forty days.[3]

---

[1] "Bonus Episode 15: Mike Licona Answers More Questions on the Gospels," *The Freethinking Podcast*, May 2, 2018, minute 4:35, http://freethinkingministries.com/bonus-ep-15-mike-licona-an-swers-more-questions-on-the-gospels/.

[2] Licona, *Why Are There Differences in the Gospels: What We Can Learn from Ancient Biography* (Oxford: Oxford University Press, 2017), p. 20.

[3] Ibid., pp. 177, 180. Licona likens compression as an ancient compositional device to the "guy

Licona also gives a fictionalizing definition of "displacement":

Displacement: When an author knowingly uproots an event from its original context and transplants it in another, the author has displaced the event.[4]

Again, the author in this case is supposed to have uprooted the event *knowingly* from its original context and to have placed it deliberately into a different temporal context. The idea that the event happened at a different time is not a mere accidental impression the reader might get. Here, too, Licona's usage bears out the understanding of this as a fictionalizing literary device. He states that Matthew and Mark have the healing of a leper (Mark 1.40–45, Matt. 8.1–4) at different points in time and that they are both using "explicit chronologies." He guesses that Matthew was the one responsible for "altering the chronology."[5] There would be no point in speaking of altering the chronology if the impression of chronological change were an accident. Licona is explicit when he says that either John or Mark changed the day when Jesus' feet were anointed in Passion Week:

Either Mark or John appear to have changed the day, using synthetic chronological placement in order to *bind the anointing explicitly to a different context than where it actually occurred*....The event is presented as historical, but *the stated chronology is artificial.*[6]

Licona's definition of transferral also appears fictionalizing:

Transferal: When an author knowingly attributes words or deeds to a person that actually belonged to another person, the author has transferred the words or deeds.[7]

This is saying that the words or deeds are definitely attributed to someone who did not carry them out, which would be fictionalization. In contrast, if I say that

version" of a story in contrast to the female version. Women, he says, like all the details, whereas men prefer to leave out details that may not be relevant. "Licona Responds to Ehrman on New Testament Reliability," https://thebestschools.org/special/ehrman-licona-dialogue-reliability-new-testament/licona-detailed-response/. But if anyone, male or female, deliberately *put* a series of events onto a single day, attempting to give the impression in the narrative that they all occurred on a single day, while knowing that they took place over forty days, that would be a highly misleading narrative. The difference between such a narrative and a factual historical version would be something far more than an unimportant difference between a briefer "guy version" and a longer "girl version."

[4] Licona, *Why Are There Differences*, p. 20.

[5] Ibid., p. 192.

[6] Ibid., p. 191. Emphasis added.

[7] Ibid., p. 20.

George asked me for fifty dollars, and if (as it happens) he did so by way of sending a mutual friend with the message, I am not attributing to George words or deeds that actually belong to another person, since George *really did* ask me for fifty dollars by way of an intermediary. The expression is merely potentially ambiguous. (See the discussion in the previous chapter.)

Here Licona's usage creates confusion in practice, since he just occasionally applies the word to an activity that would not be fictionalizing. At one point in Plutarch's *Lives*, Caesar makes a request to Pompey; in another place Plutarch says Clodius made the request. Licona says that perhaps Clodius conveyed Caesar's wishes to Pompey and calls this "transferal via substitution."[8] This would be the non-fictionalizing type of transferral, since Plutarch's statement about Caesar is inexplicit enough that it could refer non-fictionally to a request made by means of sending a message through an intermediary. Licona confusingly includes a non-fictionalizing hypothetical example concerning the Gospels as well. He says that if someone reported that Pilate crucified Jesus, no one would think that Pilate personally nailed Jesus to the cross.[9]

But in another instance, he says that Plutarch may have transferred some insults (calling Caesar a robber) in the Roman senate from one opponent of Caesar to another.[10] But in this case there would have been no such intermediary relationship, and Licona does not claim that there was. The claim is not that one senator was conveying the insults on behalf of another senator. In that case, the idea is simply that Plutarch decided to "make" a different senator utter the insults, rather than reporting the person who actually uttered them. This would be a fictionalizing type of transferral. Similarly, Licona says that Plutarch has engaged in transferral when, in one place, Plutarch emphasizes expressly that Pompey appeared *in person* in court to give a speech, whereas in another version Plutarch says that Pompey did not appear in person but rather sent an emissary with his message. This would obviously be a fictionalizing type of transferral if it were deliberate, since Plutarch emphasizes explicitly that Pompey came in person.[11]

---

[8] Ibid., p. 49.

[9] Ibid., p. 107. Licona may here be influenced by John 19.1, which says that Pilate took Jesus and scourged him—of course, not that Pilate carried out the action personally.

[10] Ibid., pp. 64–65.

[11] Ibid., p. 60. I am inclined to think that Plutarch either forgot what he had written earlier and/or obtained additional information in between his two accounts. An apparent contradiction does not equal a literary device, as I shall argue at length in later sections. If it did, there would be no ordinary discrepancies between historical accounts.

In his scriptural examples, Licona suggests that perhaps John placed into John the Baptist's mouth the statement that he was the voice of one crying in the wilderness, when he did not actually utter this statement. Licona calls this transferral, though it would be a fictionalizing sort.[12] He also suggests that Matthew transferred a question about who would be the greatest in the kingdom by having the disciples ask that question (Matt. 18.1, compare Mark 9.33ff). What is allegedly "transferred" is the initiation of the discussion, since in Mark Jesus asks them what they were discussing on the road.[13] If this occurred—that is, if Matthew "made" the disciples ask Jesus a question that they did not really ask—this would be a fictionalizing type of transferral, since (of course) in no sense would the disciples be acting on behalf of Jesus.

Licona's definition of "conflation" is also that of deliberate alteration of fact, especially in its connection with displacement and transferral:

> Conflation: When an author combines elements from two or more events or people and narrates them as one, the author has conflated them. Accordingly, some displacement and/or transferal will always occur in the conflation of stories.[14]

In conflation, then, an author knowingly and deliberately combines two or more different events when he knows that they were separate. He deliberately writes as if only one event took place.

Licona also includes in his list a broadly defined "compositional device" that involves simply making things up:

> Expansion of Narrative Details:…If minor details were unknown, they could be invented to improve the narrative while maintaining historical verisimilitude. In many instances, the added details reflect plausible circumstances. This has been called "creative reconstruction" and "free composition."[15]

In an illuminating footnote to this definition, Licona adds,

> I have here conflated two compositional devices described by [classical scholar Christopher] Pelling…"the *expansion* of inadequate material, normally by the fabrication of circumstantial detail" and "the *fabrication of a context*."[16]

---

[12] Licona, *Why Are There Differences*, p. 121.

[13] Ibid., p. 140.

[14] Ibid., p. 20.

[15] Ibid.

[16] Ibid., p. 228, n. 34. Italics in original.

Licona does not balk at the term "fabrication" when used by classicist Pelling to describe one of the compositional devices.

It is important to bear in mind that in none of these definitions is Licona alleging that the original audience would have recognized some "tag" in a passage that would show the readers when the author did not intend to narrate historically. As explained in the definition of "fictionalization" in Chapter I, section 3, these devices are invisible within the document. While Licona asserts that readers would not have been *disturbed* if they learned that an author deliberately bent the facts,[17] he makes it quite clear throughout that readers would not in general have been *able to tell* whether such a device was being used in that location. On the contrary, he repeatedly indicates that they might well have been led to an *incorrect* literal belief by such a device. For example, concerning Plutarch he expressly says that "Plutarch gives the reader the impression that ..." events took place in one order in one of his *Lives* while giving readers a contradictory impression elsewhere.[18] When arguing that John changed the relationship between the Last Supper and the beginning of Passover for theological reasons, he says, "John *appears deliberate in his attempts to lead his readers to think* the Last Supper was not a Passover meal" even though, per the Synoptics, it was in fact a Passover meal.[19] The phrase "appears deliberate in his attempts to lead his readers to think" makes it unequivocally clear that this alteration was not recognizable in the passage, even for the original audience. In addition, phrases such as "narrated as though" or "describes as though" appear throughout the book.[20] Licona also repeatedly says that it is "impossible to know," "impossible to tell," or "impossible to discern" whether a given author has used "literary artistry," changed a day, or put words into a figure's mouth. He does not imply at all that the original audience would have been able to tell.[21] The point of the use of "artistry" is that the author is deliberately writing "as if" things were a certain way, though this is contrary to fact.

Both Licona's explicit definitions of the devices and his applications indicate that the use of these devices was (on his theory) both a deliberate change of facts and also normally invisible in the document. Moreover, the connection between these alleged devices and the alleged genre of the Gospels would give us reason

---

[17] Ibid., p. 17.

[18] Ibid., p. 50.

[19] Ibid., pp. 156, 163. Emphasis added.

[20] Ibid., pp. 39, 46, 55, 157, 177.

[21] Ibid., pp. 116, 117, 121, 129, 165.

to expect them to be quite widespread, if Licona's theories were correct. In a written interview, Licona states that these devices are "part and parcel" of the genre of the Gospels:

> The majority of New Testament scholars agree that, at minimum, the Gospels share much in common with the genre of Greco-Roman biography. Therefore, it should be of no surprise to observe the Gospel authors using the compositional devices that were part-and-parcel of that genre. In fact, we should be surprised if we did *not* observe it.[22]

In the same written interview, he even states that one should seek such compositional devices *before* attempting to harmonize the texts, apparently because of the high antecedent expectation that the authors are using them:

> Where I differ [from most evangelicals] is, I place a priority on genre over harmonization. So, *before seeking to harmonize Gospel texts*, one should read the Gospels in view of their biographical genre, which includes their authors' use of the various compositional devices commonly used when writing history and biography.[23]

Here, again, it is worth quoting Licona's words concerning the Gospel of John:

> John often chose to sacrifice accuracy on the ground level of precise reporting, preferring to provide his readers with an accurate, higher-level view of the person and mission of Jesus.[24]

These statements help to explain why Licona (as we shall see in Part Four of this book) so often concludes that an author changed the facts even when an entirely reasonable harmonization is available and in some cases when there is *no apparent contradiction at all* requiring harmonization. Such strong statements about the expectation of fact-changing literary devices must also be borne in mind when we consider how important these matters are.

Here I should briefly discuss one supposed "literary device" discussed by Licona that is neither literary, nor a device, nor particularly ancient, nor fictionalizing. Nor is it original to Licona. This is "spotlighting." Licona defines "spotlighting" in this way:

[22] Jonathan Peterson and Michael Licona, "Why Are There Differences in the Gospels? An Interview With Michael R. Licona," *Bible Gateway Blog*, June 27, 2017, https://www.biblegateway.com/blog/2017/06/why-are-there-differences-in-the-gospels-an-interview-with-michael-r-licona/. Emphasis in original.

[23] Ibid. Emphasis added.

[24] Licona, *Why Are There Differences*, p. 115.

Spotlighting: When an author focuses attention on a person so that the person's involvement in a scene is clearly described, whereas mention of others who were likewise involved is neglected, the author has shined his literary spotlight on that person.[25]

In other words, "spotlighting" is just talking about one person in a scene and not mentioning others, which in itself implies no intention to make it look like others were not present in one's version of the story. Such a so-called device occurs, for example, in the Gospels' accounts of the blind men healed near Jericho. Matt. 20.29ff mentions two blind men whereas Mark 10.46ff mentions only one, named Bartimaeus. Licona considers the possibility that Mark was "shining his literary spotlight" on one of these,[26] while both were present, but this is hardly a new idea for which the study of Plutarch or other ancient literature is particularly helpful. The 19th-century preacher Alexander McLaren long ago noted, apropos of this passage in Mark, that "[t]he greater includes the less; silence is not contradiction" and also that Bartimaeus might have been known to Mark's readers.[27] Charles Ellicott, a 19th-century bishop and Bible commentator, makes a similar point concerning the two demoniacs in Matthew 8.28,[28] as does the traditional harmonizer and inerrantist Gleason Archer.[29] The idea that an author is "spotlighting," though not under that specific name, has long been a widely accepted type of harmonization. Labeling normal reporting behavior of the author as "spotlighting," a Greco-Roman "compositional device," does not add to our understanding of the Gospels, but it does serve to give the impression that there are far more legitimate, unique compositional devices in the Gospels taken from Greco-Roman literature than there are. "Spotlighting" does not in any way support the existence of the fictionalizing devices Licona discusses. It should therefore be kept completely separate from Licona's arguments for the fact-changing literary devices he claims to have found in Plutarch and other ancient authors and in the Gospels.

---

[25] Ibid., p. 20.

[26] Ibid., p. 135. Licona also considers various fictionalizing theories about the two blind men, treating them as if they are equally probable. One of these, already mentioned, is the theory that Matthew may have invented a "doublet" of two blind men healed in Matt. 9.

[27] Alexander McLaren, *Expositions of Holy Scripture* (New York: Hodder & Stoughton, 1900), *in loc.*

[28] Charles Ellicott, *Commentary for English Readers* (New York: E.P. Dutton & Co., 1878), *in loc.*

[29] Gleason Archer, *Encyclopedia of Bible Difficulties* (Grand Rapids, MI: Zondervan Publishing, 1982), *in loc.*

2. Dehistoricizing the Gospels

Quotations from other scholars indicate that the alterations they suggest are fictionalizing as I have defined the term. Craig A. Evans has been particularly clear in comments he has made concerning the Gospel of John in contrast to Matthew, Mark, and Luke (the Synoptics). Evans has indicated that he considers the Gospel of John to be only partially historical. Speaking to skeptical New Testament scholar Bart Ehrman, he says this:

> I suspect we don't have too much difference on John. My view is the Gospel of John is a horse of another color altogether. It's a different genre....So, I don't disagree with you too much on that point. I think John is studded with historical details. Maybe you called them nuggets. That's not a bad way of describing John. But I think the Synoptics are more than just some nuggets.[30]

When Ehrman re-expresses this by saying that Evans does not consider John historically accurate, Evans objects:

> And by the way, Bart, I object to saying it's not historically accurate. Well, if something that isn't...exactly historical, how is it not historically accurate? It'd be like saying "You mean the parable, the parable was a fiction Jesus told? It's not historically accurate?"[31]

In other words, Evans takes the very category of "historical accuracy" to be inapplicable to John, except for some "nuggets" of historicity. It is on this basis that he objects to saying that he does not consider John historically accurate: He rejects that category as irrelevant to John in the first place.

His comments about what are called the "I am sayings with predicates" (such as "I am the bread of life") are particularly unequivocal:

> On a historical level let us suppose we could go back into time with a camera team and audio and video record the historical Jesus and we followed him about throughout his ministry. I would be very surprised if we caught him uttering, "I am this" and "I am that" and one of these big long speeches that we find in John. This aspect of the Gospel of John I would not put in the category of historical. It's a genre question.
>
> The real question then would be, do these from a theological point of view reflect an accurate theological understanding of Jesus' person, his accomplishment, what he's achieved, what he brings to his believers? Is he the light of the world?

---

[30] Craig A. Evans vs. Bart Ehrman, "Does the New Testament Present a Historically Reliable Portrait of the Historical Jesus?" Saint Mary's University, January 19, 2012, minute 1:34:45, https://youtu.be/ueRIdrlZsvs?t=1h34m45s.

[31] Ibid., minute 1:36:59, https://youtu.be/ueRIdrlZsvs?t=1h36m59s.

Is he…the way, the truth, the life? Is he the bread of life? See? And that's what Christians can affirm…. So you could say, theologically, these affirmations of who Jesus is in fact do derive from Jesus. Not because he walked around and said them. But because of what he did, what he said…and because of his resurrection. And so this community that comes together in the aftermath of Easter says, "You know what? This Jesus who said these various things, whose teaching we cling to and interpret and present and adapt and so on, he is for us the way, the truth, the life, the true vine. He is the bread of life," and so on. And so that gets presented in a very creative, dramatic, and metaphorical way, in what we now call the Gospel of John.[32]

In the next volume, *The Eye of the Beholder*, I will be discussing at more length these comments about John. I bring them up here to show that Evans's view is one of fictionalizing changes. Although the passages in John that Evans questions are presented as if Jesus really said the things in them, Evans believes that they were invented as theological extrapolations by the later Christian community.

Evans also believes that the Synoptic authors sometimes fictionalized, though less radically than did John or the "Johannine community." He says regarding all of the evangelists that they had "the freedom and, I would argue, the obligation to reshape Jesus' teaching" and holds that this freedom explains differences in the Synoptic Gospels as well as between the Synoptics and John.[33] Evans does not confine his speculations to Jesus' teaching, as can be seen from his brief treatment of the passage in Matt. 20.20ff where the mother of James and John asks Jesus to allow them to sit on his left and right hands in his kingdom:

> Because the request arouses the indignation of the other disciples (v. 24), we should not be surprised that the scene is mitigated by Matthew, who in various ways seeks to put the disciples in a better light. According to vv. 20–21, it is the *mother* of James and John who makes the request. But it is clear that Matthew knows Mark's version, for he has Jesus reply: "You [pl.] do not know what you [pl.] are asking" (cf. Mark 10:38).[34]

---

[32] Ibid., minute 2:02:45, https://youtu.be/ueRIdrlZsvs?t=2h2m45s.

[33] Craig A. Evans vs. Lydia McGrew, "Is John's Gospel Historically Accurate?" *Unbelievable*, May 18, 2018, minute 36, http://unbelievable.podbean.com/e/is-john%E2%80%99s-gospel-historically-accurate-lydia-mcgrew-craig-evans-debate/; see also the debate transcript, https://www.premierchristianradio.com/Shows/Saturday/Unbelievable/Unbelievable-blog/Lydia-McGrew-vs.-Craig-Evans-on-the-Historical-Reliability-of-John-s-Gospel-Full-Transcript; Craig A. Evans vs. Bart Ehrman, "Does the New Testament Present a Historically Reliable Portrait of the Historical Jesus?" Evans's opening statement, Acadia University, January 20, 2012, minute 19:50, https://youtu.be/UvCVnlHoFow?t=13m1s.

[34] Craig A. Evans, *Matthew* (New Cambridge Bible Commentary) (Cambridge: Cambridge University Press, 2012), p. 353.

If one reads quickly, these sentences might go by without realizing what Evans is saying: He is saying that the mother was not really involved and that Matthew *invented her out of whole cloth* (at least in this scene) in order to "mitigate" the ambitiousness of James and John, making it appear that, perhaps, this pushy question was partly her idea. This is not apparent in the scene at all, where Matthew realistically narrates that the mother comes to Jesus, kneels before him, and makes a request. Evans's analysis depends upon the invisibility of the fictionalizing change. For Matthew could hardly "put the disciples in a better light" if his story did not make it appear that the mother *was* involved. If the audience knew for a fact that her involvement was a literary creation, they would think just as they previously had thought (based upon Mark's account) about James and John's ambitiousness. If Matthew's narrative did not portray her realistically, her sons would not appear in a better light. This is an especially clear instance of the invisible and hence confusing nature of fictionalizing literary devices, yet Evans does not hesitate to attribute this action and motive to the author of the Gospel of Matthew.[35]

Craig Keener has also made statements that indicate that he advocates the theory of fictionalizing alteration—again, with particular emphasis upon the Gospel of John:

> A close examination of the Fourth Gospel reveals that John has rearranged many details, apparently in the service of his symbolic message. This is especially clear in the Passion Narrative, where direct conflicts with the presumably widely known passion tradition ... fulfill symbolic narrative functions.[36]

> John takes significant liberties with the way he reports his events, especially in several symbolic adaptations in the passion narrative, whereas Luke follows, where we can test him ..., the procedures of a good Hellenistic historian.[37]

In *The Eye of the Beholder* I will discuss and rebut these claims concerning John. I quote them here to display another evangelical scholar asserting the presence of fictionalizing adaptations in the Gospels. Note that Keener states that the Syn-

---

[35] Evans also implies that Matthew has invented John the Baptist's protest that he has need to be baptized by Jesus and Jesus' answer in Matt. 3.14ff, in order to "mitigate" the concern that Jesus' baptism by John implies that John is greater than Jesus. "Because it is assumed that he who baptizes is greater than he who is baptized, Matthew cannot simply repeat Mark's brief version of the story.... Matthew's version of the story mitigates these difficult questions." Ibid., p. 76.

[36] Craig Keener, *The Gospel of John: A Commentary* (Grand Rapids, MI: Baker Academic, 2003), pp. 42–43.

[37] Craig Keener, *Acts: An Exegetical Commentary* (Grand Rapids, MI: Baker Academic 2012), vol. 1, p. 793.

optic passion tradition was "presumably widely known." His implication, made clearer in his treatment of John's allegedly moving the Temple cleansing,[38] is that the original audience would have treated what they had already read or heard from the Synoptic Gospels as historical and would have treated John's different narratives (where Keener thinks there are "direct conflicts") as symbolic. This is a highly conjectural and dubious hypothesis about the original audience, and Keener does not base it upon an unrealistic appearance in John itself. Why would the audience have agreed with Keener in the first place that there are "direct conflicts" in the cases he has in mind? That point itself is certainly open to question.[39] If the original audience did agree that there were "direct conflicts," how would they know that John was not attempting to *correct* the earlier version? Why should they have thought of the symbolic meanings that Keener thinks of? Why would they not simply have been confused about what happened? In short, Keener is trying to save John from the charge of being deceptive by presuming that the original audience thought like a 21st-century New Testament critic and came to the same conclusions that critic has come to concerning a) whether the accounts are harmonizable, b) which account is historically true, and c) what theological point the author was trying to make by fictionalizing. This would be a very thin basis upon which to excuse John, in his realistic narrative, from the charge of misleading his audience if we were to agree with Keener that he changed the facts. I note here that St. Augustine, a good deal closer to the time of John's Gospel and highly trained in ancient rhetoric, took it as *evident* that there were two Temple cleansings, not that John changed the chronology of the Temple cleansing.[40]

Keener's reference to the Synoptic tradition as "presumably widely known" is relevant here because it fits with my definition of fictionalization as involving changes that were invisible *within the fictionalized document itself*. Keener's only suggested method for the original audience to detect John's "significant liberties" would have been to treat a Synoptic tradition (that is, what we find in the other Gospels) as more historically accurate than John, to conclude that John was in conflict with it, and to use the other Gospels as a check upon John.[41] Within John

---

[38] Keener, *John*, pp. 518–519.

[39] Keener's specific claims of "direct conflict" will be discussed more in *The Eye of the Beholder*. A version of my discussion exists already in "Does John 'Narrate Theologically'? On the Perils of Theological Theory in History," *What's Wrong With the World*, June 14, 2018, http://whatswrongwiththe-world.net/2018/06/does_john_narrate_theologicall.html.

[40] St. Augustine, *The Harmony of the Gospels*, II.67.129.

[41] This implication, implied in passing by Keener, that the original audience might have had a hier-

itself, on Keener's theory, the change is invisible; John sometimes deliberately narrates realistically but contrary to fact within his "story world."[42] The phrase "story world," referring to John's coherent narrative world which might or might not correspond to historical reality, occurs countless times in Keener's commentary on John's Gospel.[43]

The examples given in Chapter I, section 4, concerning Jesus' words on the cross in John come from Daniel B. Wallace and were brought to light more recently because Michael Licona adopts and cites those theories about "I thirst" and "It is finished"—namely, that they did not occur historically but rather were John's

---

archy of historicity for the Gospels and would have thus been able to use the Synoptics to "decode" the ahistorical segments of John is not the most common idea of literary device theorists. On the contrary, as noted above, Licona says that John "appears deliberate in his attempts to lead his readers to think the Last Supper was not a Passover meal." Moreover, Keener has no evidence whatsoever that the early church held that John or any other Gospel was systematically less historical than other Gospels, nor that the early Christians presumed John to be "narrating theologically" (i.e. non-historically) when it contains material that needs to be harmonized with other Gospels or that is not contained in other Gospels. Certainly the mere fact that the "Synoptic tradition" was already "widely known" by the time John wrote would not have been enough for the original audience to conclude any such thing. As I will discuss in a later chapter, John is extremely historical in his narration of the Temple cleansing. If he changed the chronology of that event, he did so in a way that appeared so firmly historically tied down that it would be difficult to clear him of the charge of deliberate deception. This is, of course, another reason to believe that he did not do anything of the sort.

[42] In a work that I am not discussing much in this book, because its influence has waned in recent years, Robert Gundry made a similar suggestion concerning Matthew. Gundry sometimes implied that Matthew's Jewish readers, though probably not his Gentile readers, would have somehow just *known* that Mark and an "expanded Q" tradition were historical but that Matthew was using a "spirit of free adaptation and embellishment" to make up non-historical material and weave it into his narrative. Robert H. Gundry, *Matthew: A Commentary on His Literary and Theological Art* (Grand Rapids, MI: Eerdmans, 1982), 634ff. Gundry, "A Response to Matthew and Midrash," *JETS* 26 (1983), pp. 50, 54–55. Because Gundry made this suggestion, Craig Blomberg accepted that Gundry's position was consistent with inerrancy, though Blomberg did not find Gundry's theory persuasive. Craig L. Blomberg, "A Constructive Traditional Response to New Testament Criticism" in James K. Hoffmeier and Dennis R. Magary, eds., *Do Historical Matters Matter to Faith* (Wheaton, IL: Crossway Books, 2012), pp. 348–349. Blomberg may not have realized, however, that Gundry himself was *not* basing his claim of non-deceptiveness on what the audience would have known and was not even consistent in his claims about what the audience would have known. While Gundry would sometimes seem to imply that the Jewish members of the original audience could have detected places where Matthew was fictionalizing by comparing Matthew with the Mark-Q tradition and preferring the latter historically, he apparently realized the extreme implausibility of this thesis and simultaneously dismissed the whole question as anachronistic. He held that the original audience, being ancient people, and specifically Jewish ancient people, would not have *cared* whether or not they could figure out where Matthew was embellishing (*Matthew*, pp. 634–635). Like more recent literary device theorists, Gundry excused Matthew from deception in his far-reaching embellishment *not* on the grounds that the original audience could have told fact from fiction but on the grounds that they did not care whether they could tell the difference because they did not have our allegedly modern hang-ups.

[43] Keener, *John*, pp. 86, 108, 433, 467, 504, 519, and more.

symbolic adaptations of entirely different sayings.[44] Neither Wallace nor Licona alleges that there was a "tag in the text" by which one could tell that John did this. John's narration of these sayings certainly appears to be historical, including the fact that in John a bystander gets a drink for Jesus after he cries out, "I am thirsty" (John 19.29).[45]

Wallace foreshadowed what he was going to do with John in a paper presented just a year before in which he said,

> Thus, if a broader view of *ipsissima vox* is needed for the synoptic gospels, how much more is it needed for John (an issue I hope to address in a later paper)?[46]

He bases this "so much the more" argument upon the alleged fact that, while Luke is the most "historically sensitive" evangelist, John lies on the other side of a continuum and is the most "theologically sensitive," implying that theological sensitivity and literal historical accuracy are in opposition.[47] Obviously, the "later paper" alluded to here is the paper on the words from the cross, presented the following year.

Here I want to highlight what Wallace says about some alleged changes in Matthew and Mark, both to show that the broad view of the Gospel authors' alleged license applies to the Synoptics as well as to John and to point to some methodological statements. Wallace's unpublished 1999 paper, delivered to a meeting of the Evangelical Theological Society, is entitled "An Apologia for a Broad Use of *Ipsissima Vox*," and in it he argues at length that evangelicals have been too rigid in their ideas of the ways in which the Gospel authors considered themselves licensed to change Jesus' words deliberately.

Wallace suggests, for example, that both Matthew and Mark have deliberately added to Jesus' words about divorce. Concerning Mark, he says that "it seems

---

[44] Licona, *Why Are There Differences*, p. 166; Daniel B. Wallace, "*Ipsissima Vox* and the Seven Words From the Cross," unpublished paper presented to the Society for Biblical Literature Southwest Regional meeting, March 5, 2000, pp. 4–11.

[45] Wallace goes so far as to say that the fact that the bystanders get wine for Jesus when he cries out means that the response to Jesus' cry represents a misunderstanding (Ibid., p. 9). This makes no sense whatsoever, since John portrays Jesus as literally crying out that he is thirsty and the bystanders as getting wine. John's narrative is completely coherent at this point; the offer of wine appears to indicate that the bystanders heard Jesus say that he was thirsty. What would it mean *in John* for the bystanders to misunderstand Jesus' cry of thirst, since the narrative portrays him as literally crying out in thirst? Wallace's theory is hyper-literary to the point of being incoherent.

[46] Daniel B. Wallace, "An Apologia for a Broad Use of *Ipsissima Vox*," unpublished paper presented at the meeting of the Evangelical Theological Society, Danvers, MA, November 18, 1999, p. 7.

[47] Ibid., p. 5.

difficult to claim that 'And if she divorces her husband and marries another, she commits adultery' really belongs to Jesus' original utterance." His idea is that Mark has deliberately added words and put them in Jesus' mouth for the sake of his own audience:

> However, since Mark was writing to Gentiles in Rome (where women had been permitted to divorce their husbands for over one hundred years), he is apparently extrapolating a legitimate principle from Jesus' utterance.[48]

Wallace's only arguments for this claim are the fact that the clause is unique to Mark and that it would have allegedly been irrelevant to Jesus' original audience. He then quotes approvingly the theory of NT scholar Robert Stein that Matthew also put words in Jesus' mouth concerning divorce—namely, the clause "except for fornication" in Matt. 19.9:

> If we assume that the "exception clause" is a Matthean comment, of what value is this? The value lies in the fact that it reveals how Matthew understood Jesus' teaching on divorce, i.e., that it was an example of overstatement for effect ....Matthew provides us with an implication and submeaning of the statement, which he believed Jesus would accept and which is equally authoritative.[49]

Again, the only argument (and even this is implicit) is that Jesus' statement *without* the exception clause may be hyperbolic and that the clause does not occur in other Gospels. Wallace's conclusion from this and other examples is that "within the synoptic gospels, interpretive additions to the words of Jesus seem to occur."[50]

These deliberate interpretive additions are not, in Wallace's view, tagged as glosses by the author. Rather, Wallace is arguing that the authors put them into Jesus' mouth invisibly. In fact, he expressly argues against the idea that these comments about divorce were parenthetical remarks by the author, and his argument implies that the change would *not* have been noted as non-original by the audience:

> One expedient on the divorce passages for those who feel uncomfortable about Mark's and Matthew's apparent additions is simply to place the extra material in

---

[48] Ibid., p. 12. The claim that Jesus would not have mentioned a woman's divorcing her husband to his original audience is historically uninformed. It is not implausible that he would have addressed this possibility because of a situation that would have been in the minds of his audience: Herodias' divorcing Philip in order to marry Herod Antipas. See Josephus *Antiquities* XVIII.5.18. This case even comes up in Mark's own Gospel (Mark 6.17ff) as the occasion of the death of John the Baptist.

[49] Robert Stein, *The Synoptic Problem: An Introduction* (Grand Rapids: Baker Books), p. 153, as quoted in Daniel B. Wallace, "An Apologia for a Broad Use of *Ipsissima Vox*," p. 12.

[50] Ibid., p. 10.

parentheses (so as to flag editorial comments by the evangelist). But this really does not do justice to how the original audience would have read such texts. To expect them to make side by side comparisons with the other synoptic gospels—especially when not all had yet been written…—and to discern on that basis what Jesus said and did not say seems to be quite unlikely.[51]

I agree with Wallace that it is *quite unlikely* that audiences would have concluded by comparison with another Gospel that a clause appearing right in the middle of Jesus' words was an authorial gloss; in any event, if Mark were the first Gospel published, there would have been no earlier document to which to compare Jesus' words about divorce in Mark. It is good for Wallace himself to admit this point, as it makes it even clearer that Wallace deems these changes to be both *deliberate* and *invisible* within the apparently historical document itself. Hence, they fall under fictionalizing alteration as I have defined it in Chapter I, section 3.

My goal in this chapter has been to begin to show readers, from the scholars' own words, that I am correctly representing their views when I refer to the alterations they hypothesize as fictionalizing (as I have defined that term) and when I argue that, being invisible and apparently realistic, the use of such devices would make it especially difficult to know what occurred historically.

---

[51] Ibid., p. 12

Summary
A Bushel of Quotations

- The definitions of "compression," "displacement," "transferral," "conflation," and "expansion of narrative details" given in Michael Licona's book *Why Are There Differences in the Gospels?*, together with Licona's usage, make it clear that they meet the careful definition of "fictionalizing literary devices" that I gave in the previous chapter.

- The theorists I am most discussing in this book expect such alterations to be fairly widespread in the documents.

- The non-fictionalizing move that Licona dubs "spotlighting" has been known to traditional harmonizers for a long time and is not a special insight gained from Greco-Roman literature.

- Other evangelical scholars have made surprising statements about changes of historical fact in the Gospels. There is often a special emphasis in such statements on the Gospel of John, though they are not confined to John.

IV

Whither Inerrancy?

1. Inerrancy: The elephant in the room

I thought hard about whether or not to include this chapter in this book. In the end I decided that the questions it addresses are inevitable. They *will* occur to readers, and it is better to discuss them openly than to evade them. If inerrancy is the proverbial elephant in the room in these discussions, it is better not to ignore it.

The major points that I hope readers will take from this chapter are these:

1) The refutation of literary device theories in this book is not only compatible with but, in an important sense, supportive of, inerrancy in its older sense. Which is to say, the sense of that term when not severely qualified by literary device theories.[1] Like *Hidden in Plain View*, the argument in this book that the Gospels are artless reports can function as part of an *inductive* case for inerrancy: If the Gospels are *this* reliable and are *this* type of report, perhaps they have no errors at all.

---

[1] An example of this older sense of "inerrancy," not redefined by literary device views, is the Chicago Statement on Biblical Inerrancy as further explained by the Chicago Statement on Biblical Hermeneutics. Article XVIII of the former says, "WE DENY the legitimacy of any treatment of the text or quest for sources lying behind it that leads to relativizing, dehistoricizing, or discounting its teaching, or rejecting its claims to authorship." See http://www.bible-researcher.com/chicago1.html. Articles XIII and XIV of the Chicago Statement on Biblical Hermeneutics were expressly added in 1983 to emphasize that genre classifications cannot (on this definition of inerrancy) be used to assert that passages not otherwise "tagged" (like parables), appearing in putatively historical works, are non-factual. Article XIII states, "WE DENY that generic categories which negate historicity may rightly be imposed on biblical narratives which present themselves as factual." Article XIV says, "WE DENY that any event, discourse or saying reported in Scripture was invented by the biblical writers or by the traditions they incorporated." See http://www.bible-researcher.com/chicago2.html. These clauses were included in order to rule out, as incompatible with inerrancy, the very type of move being made by the literary device theorists I am discussing in this book.

2)   The objections to literary device theories in this book are not "about inerrancy." The arguments here cannot be dismissed (as some might try to dismiss them) by saying that they are part of a narrow, internecine, evangelical squabble about the meaning of a term that some Christians don't care about. Nor are the objections I raise here motivated by an *a priori* commitment to inerrancy. The objections to literary device views are evidential and historical. I am arguing that such views seriously undermine the historical reliability of the Gospels and that they are based on poor historical arguments—methodology that is not a good way to find out the historical facts. These theses are worth consideration even by Christians who do not consider themselves inerrantists. For that matter, the argument of this book is relevant to non-Christians as well, since the historical reliability of the Gospels indirectly supports the truth of Christianity, which non-Christians would do well to consider.

3)   Inerrantists should not embrace literary device views. Such views constitute a Pyrrhic victory for "inerrancy." One continues to use the bare term, redefined, while gutting it of the meaning that gave it historical value and at the expense of making the Gospels—hitherto regarded as paradigmatically historical books within the biblical canon—significantly historically unreliable. The concept of a document that is "inerrant" but historically unreliable, like a movie only based on true events, is a bitter oxymoron. It is no gain to eschew *accidental* errors, made in good faith while attempting to get the facts right, while embracing *deliberate*, invisible alterations of fact. Even a neutral observer of the debate can see that this is true.

2. Supporting inerrancy without assuming it

The first point is fairly easy to see. If the Gospel authors are honest reporters trying to tell what they knew (either from their own witness memories or from information they have gathered from others), and if they were "in the know" about what occurred, then this makes it less likely that their documents will contain errors and more likely that they will contain factually accurate information. Less likely and more likely, that is, *all else being equal*. But if the authors considered themselves licensed to change and invent historical material deliberately, then all else is not equal. That theory introduces another possible source of factually inaccurate information. By arguing *against* that view of artistic license and continuing to uphold the picture of the authors as honest reporters in the ordinary sense of the term, my argument supports the absence of errors in the documents with at least the possibility that this absence of error might be complete—i.e., that they are inerrant.

The second point—that this critique does not arise from an *a priori* theological commitment to inerrancy—requires more explanation. In this entire part of the book (Part One: Masking History) I am openly and unabashedly attempting to motivate readers to investigate this issue by pointing out that the literary device views undermine Gospel reliability. How does this not amount to being driven by *a priori* theological considerations? One way that it does not amount to that is that one may be motivated by an interest in reliability without being motivated by the doctrine of inerrancy. A document or witness (even a secular document) can be *highly* reliable while still making a few good-faith errors. Someone may therefore be concerned about these views because of concerns about reliability rather than concerns about inerrancy. That is to say, a non-inerrantist could consider this an urgent matter.

But also, and more importantly, we must distinguish the *motive* for investigation from the *grounds* of our conclusions. The literary device theorists should have to make their case. They should not be given a pass by way of an assumption that none of this matters very much anyway. It does matter, deeply. But that is not the same thing as saying that they are wrong *because*, if they were right, the Gospels would be historically unreliable. Before these theories about the Gospels are granted credence, they deserve careful scrutiny on the part of orthodox Christians if for no other reason than that, if true, they would be seriously detrimental to the cause of the Gospel. But I do not argue that the harmful nature of these ideas is a reason for rejecting them *a priori*. They should be rejected, rather, because they cannot withstand careful scrutiny once it is brought to bear. They should be rejected because the evidence does not support them.

The methodological problems with these approaches can be seen by non-inerrantists and inerrantists alike. For that matter, they can even be seen by non-Christians. When these methods are used in secular history, they are damaging to our understanding of secular history, substituting over-complex theories for more justified, simpler theories, as my discussions of examples from Plutarch and other authors in Part Two will show. Hence, one should reject literary device views and even conclude that the Gospels manifest the characteristics of artless testimony because that is the way the evidence points, not because one wants to "save" inerrancy.

3. The inerrancy-friendly non-inerrantist

Having said all of this, I realize that readers may still be wondering, "But are you an inerrantist yourself?" On a number of public occasions, I have stated openly that I do not label myself an inerrantist, and I will state here openly as well that I do not take that label to myself, for two main reasons: Most of the time, the term "inerrancy" refers to an *a priori* approach in which one assumes for theological reasons related to the doctrine of inspiration that the biblical documents are inerrant (in their original manuscripts). That certainly does not describe me. I think we have to see whether or not there are errors by investigation. But also, there are places, even in the Gospels, where it does not seem to me implausible that some minor error of fact might have been made by the authors. Some of these will come up as this book proceeds.[2]

In the examples in Part Four of this book, I will occasionally (not often) raise the possibility of a minor error as *one possible explanation* of the data. In any such cases, I encourage inerrantist readers to consider other options, which might mean simply concluding that they do not know right now what the accurate harmonization is in that instance. I would not, I admit, raise those possibilities if I thought they were highly implausible. As stated in an earlier chapter, scholars don't bring up hypotheses for serious consideration if they consider them to be no more than logically possible. I do not follow the scholarly trope of saying "perhaps" and then trying to dodge criticism for bringing up a theory. Occasionally the possibility of a witness error seems more plausible to me than the harmonizations I'm aware of.

---

[2] The reader will understandably be curious about examples. One example concerns the day of the week on which Jesus' feet were anointed shortly before his crucifixion. Setting aside the foot anointing recorded in Luke 7 as a separate occasion (as I believe it was), there remain the records given in John 12 and Matthew 26/Mark 14. The last two are quite obviously the same incident, and I think it highly likely that John 12 records the same incident as Matthew and Mark. John indicates fairly clearly that the anointing occurred on the evening before the Triumphal Entry (hence, Saturday), whereas Matthew and Mark appear to give the time as the Wednesday, two days before the crucifixion. If that is the case, one or the other is apparently a minor error. See discussion in Chapter XIV, section 6. Another example concerns whether or not Luke refers to "the eleven" in Luke 24.33 under the mistaken impression that eleven disciples were literally present, or whether he is using the phrase "the eleven" as a group name. See Chapter XVI, section 4. I am roughly balanced between these two options and present both in Chapter XVI, but I lean very slightly toward the option that Luke simply did not know that Thomas was absent on that occasion and that he means "the eleven" literally. If that is correct, this would seem to count as an error in Luke 24.33. Another example concerns the centurion and whether or not he came personally to Jesus. As discussed in Chapter XIV, section 3, I am not fully satisfied with the traditional harmonization on that point. Of course I also consider the fictionalization change alleged there to be an overly complex interpretation of the passage. It is simpler to assume that, if Matthew portrays the centurion as *personally* coming to Jesus, he believed that this was what happened.

But at the same time, by no means does any reader have to accept that option, and *by no means* do my objections to literary device views rest upon an assumption that the Gospels *do* contain errors.

In the case of Plutarch and other secular authors, all scholars should be *completely* open to the possibility of ordinary human error. No one, presumably, is committed to the inerrancy of Plutarch or Tacitus, either in an old-fashioned or in a redefined sense. It is extremely misguided to assume at the outset that an author like Plutarch virtually never made an ordinary error and to look first for some more complex explanation of an apparent discrepancy. The discussion of the flowchart I have developed in Part Two will explain this point at greater length. It is very important to consider the possibility of error for secular authors in those sections of the book, because Michael Licona uses those authors to infer what one might call a baseline for the existence and frequency of compositional devices in ancient literature. If Plutarch's making a simple error or obtaining more information is a good explanation in those secular examples, this conclusion greatly weakens the case for thinking that fictionalizing literary devices were used by secular authors and accepted by audiences at the time. So we cannot set aside the possibility of ordinary error *in general* or we will end up treating non-biblical literature in an artificial and over-literary manner.

Moreover, since Licona himself has emphasized the requirement for him, as a neutral historian examining the Bible, to be open to *all* options and *not* to be bound by theological considerations such as inerrancy,[3] he cannot refuse to consider the possibility of an error even in a biblical document. From a purely neutral historical point of view, a normal human error is often going to be a simpler conclusion than an elaborate literary device, and this is true in the Gospels as in other documents. These considerations help to explain why I occasionally raise the possibility of a minor error in the Gospels along with possible harmonizations.

One of the major messages of this book is that harmonization in general is good historical practice. Harmonization is not an esoteric or religious exercise. Christians studying the Bible should not allow themselves to be bullied by the

---

[3] Licona says, "[I]f I as a Christian historian want to conduct an investigation in the Gospels with integrity, I cannot bring a theological conviction that the Bible is God's infallible Word to that investigation. Historians who practice with integrity must come to an investigation being as open as possible to what it may yield, even if what it yields suggests something that I presently believe should be modified or abandoned. Otherwise, one ends up being guided more by his or her presuppositions rather than the historical data. That's practicing theology or philosophy, not history." Michael Licona, "Are We Reading an Adapted Form of Jesus' Teachings in John's Gospel?" *Risen Jesus*, Sept. 29, 2017, https://www.risenjesus.com/reading-adapted-form-jesus-teachings-johns-gospel.

implication that they are engaging in harmonization only because of their theological commitments and hence are fudging the data for non-scholarly reasons. To the contrary, reliable historical sources can be expected to be harmonizable, and they normally are harmonizable when all the facts are known. Attempting to see how they fit together is an extremely fruitful method to pursue, sometimes even giving rise to connections such as the undesigned coincidences discussed in *Hidden in Plain View*. This is why I pursue ordinary harmonization between historical sources and why I often conclude that a harmonization is correct.

Ironically, there are many who do adopt the label of "inerrantist" who think that, for example, two Temple cleansings by Jesus strain our credulity. William Lane Craig is rather emphatic about insisting that there was only one cleansing, which John chronologically moved. He even makes a kind of story out of his own progression away from (what he considers) strained harmonization:

> I once believed, as a younger Christian, that Jesus cleansed the temple twice. The way I harmonized this apparent inconsistency was to say that early in his ministry there was a cleansing of the temple, and then later on in his ministry, in the final week of his life, he did it again. But we don't have to have recourse to any such artificial harmonization ... [4]

In contrast, though not considering myself an inerrantist, I think it almost certain that Jesus did cleanse the Temple twice. This seems to me by far the most likely historical conclusion, and I will come back to it several more times in this book.[5] Jesus' Temple cleansing was a form of protest, and just as in our own day people often engage in similar protests at the same location (abortion clinic protests, to take just one example), and these protests take a similar form on different occasions and even encounter similar outrage and opposition, so it was with Jesus: He protested the Temple practices surrounding buying and selling once early in his ministry. The sellers and money changers returned to their previous activities when the disturbance was over. Jesus then made a similar protest against these practices shortly before his crucifixion, about three years after the first occasion. Arguments that the Jewish leaders "would not" have allowed Jesus to do this twice or "would

---

[4] William Lane Craig, "Biblical Inerrancy," *Reasonable Faith*, December 24, 2014, https://www.reasonablefaith.org/podcasts/defenders-podcast-series-3/s3-doctrine-of-revelation/doctrine-of-revelation-part-7/.

[5] See Chapter X, section 1, on the confusion between achronological and dyschronological narration as applied to this incident, Chapter XI, section 6, on external confirmation, and Chapter XIV, section 2, on other arguments against two cleansings.

not" have allowed him to live and continue in ministry for so long after the first Temple cleansing manifest the worst tendencies of armchair historical speculation.[6] Both John's Gospel and Mark's Gospel give entirely plausible historical pictures of Jesus as getting away with the activities they describe at the times they describe, and even in Mark itself Jesus re-enters the Temple precincts boldly the very next day after cleansing the Temple. We cannot decide what *has* happened in history by deciding what we think would have been allowed to happen. Most concrete history can be described in a fashion that makes it sound improbable.

I have discussed this example of the Temple cleansing a bit here to illustrate that, if I am a non-inerrantist, I am an unusual one, and to illustrate that my methodological approach is one that old-fashioned inerrantists can readily embrace even though we disagree on some particular passages.

4. The pointlessness of redefined "inerrancy"

Point three—what inerrantists themselves have to gain or lose from the literary device views and whether literary device "inerrancy" counts as inerrancy—is probably the most sensitive topic addressed in this chapter. This is partly a matter of recent history into which I do not intend to delve at length. Very briefly, after Michael Licona published *The Resurrection of Jesus: A New Historiographical Approach* in 2010, there was debate over the question of whether some of the positions he took in that book were compatible with inerrancy. These included his questioning the historicity of the raising of the saints at Jesus' crucifixion and the literal nature of the angels at Jesus' tomb and his statements about the possible inclusion of legend in Greco-Roman *bioi*, the genre to which he thinks the Gospels belong, and hence by extension in the Gospels.[7,8] Conservative scholars Norman Geisler,

---

[6] See, e.g., Craig Keener, *The Gospel of John: A Commentary* (Grand Rapids, MI: Baker Academic, 2003), pp. 518–519.

[7] Michael Licona, *The Resurrection of Jesus: A New Historiographical Approach* (Downer's Grover: IVP Academic, 2010), pp. 185–186, 548–549.

[8] I have decided not to write at length in this book about the passage concerning the raising of the saints in Matt. 27. Licona claimed at the time that, if it was not historical, Matthew's readers would have understood that it was an instance of non-historical apocalyptic language. Thus, according to the theory, the literary device in question would *not* have been invisible in the text itself. While Licona himself seems not to understand the importance of this point, it does distinguish the claim concerning the raising of the saints from the literary device claims that I am answering through much of this book. Licona's argument for the claim about what Matthew or his readers would have understood was, however, quite weak. I have examined that case in more detail elsewhere, showing that neither the Greco-Roman nor the Jewish examples Licona considers establish the existence of an apocalyptic convention in this passage. There is some evidence that, when a Roman historian reported portents, he either believed the report himself or at least expected his audience to do so. Lydia McGrew, "On

F. David Farnell, and some others noted Licona's statements and argued that his position was not compatible with inerrancy.[9] The ensuing controversy left a great deal of nervousness and weariness in the evangelical community at large. Some felt that Licona had been the victim of a personal witch-hunt based upon an overly narrow definition of inerrancy; some decided that they were uninterested in the controversy over what inerrancy really means, thinking of this as a parochial dispute in which the larger Christian community has no interest. Above all, many were concerned not to be associated even indirectly with anything that might be viewed as a personal attack against a fellow Christian. That past history and the social muddle resulting from it hang over this book of mine, despite the fact that I was not involved in those exchanges. Because of this background, and because I am trying to dispel the idea that I am motivated by any *a priori* commitment to inerrancy, I have sometimes been reluctant to discuss the question of what counts as inerrancy. But in a book-length treatment of the subject of literary device views, including Licona's, it must be addressed.

To be forthright, my own position is that, if I were an inerrantist, I would consider it pointless and meaningless to affirm inerrancy while also affirming the presence of fictionalizing literary devices in the Gospels. I will go further. It is *more* detrimental to Gospel reliability, which ought to be one of the points of inerrancy, to affirm literary devices than to affirm good-faith errors on the same points. To see why this is the case, consider the following scenario: You are in court listening to a witness testify. Perhaps he is giving an alibi for the accused, or perhaps he is a witness for the prosecution who claims to have witnessed the crime. Suppose that the witness says that a certain event in his testimony happened on a Saturday. The opposing lawyer brings other witnesses who say that it happened on a Wednesday. He then confronts the first witness with the discrepancy. Now imagine two different possibilities. On the one hand, suppose that the witness says, "Wow, I'm sorry, you're right. It was a Wednesday. We did some similar things on the Saturday, and

---

That (In)famous 'Saints Rising' Passage in Matthew 27," *What's Wrong With the World*, Feb. 5, 2019, http://whatswrongwiththeworld.net/2019/02/on_that_infamous_saints_rising.html. See also an excellent analysis of the church fathers and ancient pseudopigraphical works by Christopher Haun. Haun shows the uniformity with which the raising of the saints was taken as historical, which is strong evidence that Matthew's readers would not have understood it to be intended non-historically. "Did Roman Christians Detect the Influence of Ancient Historiography in Matthew 27:45–54," *Defending Inerrancy*, April 30, 2014, http://defendinginerrancy.com/historical-testing-for-the-genre-theories/.

[9] See, for example, Norman L. Geisler, *Preserving Orthodoxy: Maintaining Continuity with the Historic Christian Faith on Scripture* (Matthews, NC: Bastion Books, 2017), Chapter 6, and the collection of posts here, http://normangeisler.com/category/inerrancy-v-errancy/licona/.

that was how I got confused. My apologies." On the other hand, suppose that the witness says, "Yes, I knew all along that it happened on a Wednesday. I changed that in my earlier testimony to make a better story. It was a literary device." Which of these two statements would undermine your confidence in that witness more? It is absolutely obvious that the second scenario would be far worse for the witness's future credibility.

Why would it be worse? We all know that a witness with good intentions might make accidental errors anyway. That is already a possibility. This strange motive to change apparent facts to make (somehow) a better story adds *another* possible source of non-factual material in the witness's testimony. Moreover, if the witness is not even *trying* to tell the story straight, then doubt spreads much faster to other things he says than it would if he were both knowledgeable and truthful. We have some idea of how often knowledgeable witnesses make good-faith errors when they are trying to tell the truth. But a witness who deliberately bends the truth in the service of making a better story is far more difficult to calibrate for. After all, it's very difficult to tell what *he* will think makes a better story. Perhaps his motives or his idea that some change improves the story are surprising or opaque to us. If we add to the mix the claim that the witness sometimes had secret symbolic or metaphoric motives, known only to himself, his fact-altering changes are unpredictable.

This, by the way, is often the case in the literary device theories, as we shall see in later sections and in the next book concerning John's Gospel. The psychological claims about why the author would have thought the changed version would be "better" are far-fetched and made up after the fact. One would be hard-pressed to guess ahead of time that an author would consider it either literarily or theologically better to make *that* change. In one case, Licona says that Luke may have made a given alteration just to "change things up slightly."[10] He generalizes that, "The evangelists' use of these devices most often appear to have no objective other than to follow the literary conventions of their day," as if this were an end in itself.[11] When he is not satisfied with available non-fictionalizing explanations but does not believe he can identify a specific compositional device, he says broadly that the authors may have "crafted [details], or even creatively reconstructed them as part of their literary artistry in writing a quality narrative."[12]

---

[10] Licona, *Why Are There Differences in the Gospels? What We Can Learn from Ancient Biography* (Oxford: Oxford University Press, 2017), p. 167.

[11] Ibid., p. 183.

[12] Ibid., p. 184.

In some cases, highly convoluted theological motives (such as avoiding "My God, why have you forsaken me?" and expressing metaphoric spiritual thirst)[13] are attributed to the author. In empirical terms, it is virtually impossible to control for the motives leading to such changes.

This is why an inerrantist has every interest in questioning literary device theories. Here we should ask a question: What is inerrancy *for*? It would be self-evidently pointless if an affirmation of inerrancy were merely a set of marks on a page, electronic pixels, or sounds in the air. Presumably the concept is supposed to mean something and, more importantly, safeguard something from an epistemic point of view. Is not at least one of the points of inerrancy supposed to be that, when the books in question appear to be historical in nature, we can believe what they say in a *fairly* straightforward way? To be sure, biblical scholars engage in endless wrangling over the degree and nature of the historicity of certain parts of the Bible, most notably the first chapters of Genesis. But if the Gospels, purporting to tell the life of Jesus as the foundation of the historical religion of Christianity and written within living memory of Jesus' death, are not straightforwardly historical in genre, what parts of the New Testament are?[14] What the theorists I am answering want to do is to carve out a special category in which the Gospels are *somewhat* historical, *partly* historical, not *entirely* ahistorical, but also partly fictionally altered. I submit that such a view of the Gospels' nature is epistemically and conceptually incompatible with any "inerrancy" worth the name.

Occasionally a literary device theorist will make an unhelpful analogy to anthropomorphic language such as the references to God in poetic language as sleeping.[15] The intention is, presumably, to point out that literary and poetic conventions need to be taken into account in deciding what is literally true in the Bible. But such references are irrelevant. No mature, minimally knowledgeable reader of the Bible is confused by Old Testament references to God's sleep or God's ear. To imply that someone who objects to the dehistoricizing of the Gospels is akin to someone who is insensitive to obviously poetic language in the Psalms is merely insulting and should not commend the view in question to inerrantists or to anyone else.

---

[13] Ibid., p. 166; Daniel B. Wallace, "*Ipsissima Vox* and the Seven Words From the Cross," unpublished paper presented to the Society for Biblical Literature Southwest Regional meeting, March 5, 2000, pp. 4–9.

[14] The theorists believe that there are historical truths in the Gospels. But the Gospels as a whole supposedly belong to a genre that mingles fact and embellishment.

[15] "Bonus Episode 15: Mike Licona Answers More Questions on the Gospels," *The Freethinking Podcast*, May 2, 2018, minute 8:20 and following, http://freethinkingministries.com/bonus-ep-15-mike-licona-answers-more-questions-on-the-gospels/.

I am not saying that inerrantists should be closed-minded. If the evidence pointed sufficiently strongly toward literary device theories, it would be necessary, at least for those who put a premium on following the evidence, to accept them. But in that case, there is no reason to call the resulting position "inerrancy." If one has been forced to admit that the Gospels are like movies or books merely based on true events, one should say openly and without dodging that one can no longer hold them to be inerrant. After all, no one would ever say that *Chariots of Fire* is without historical error, even if every single deviation from history were deliberate. Merely saying that the screen-writer *meant* to change facts doesn't make the factual implication—e.g., that Lord Lindsay raced Harold Abrahams around the courtyard at Cambridge—historically true. The scene is realistically portrayed. It certainly is not cast as a parable or non-historical portion of the movie's story-line. Taken at face value it has certain propositional content. That propositional content is, as it happens, false. As discussed in Chapter I, section 2, that does not all by itself make the movie-makers *deceptive*. But it would be ludicrous to call the movie inerrant.

A fascinating quotation by Craig Blomberg makes a similar point concerning error. Blomberg is addressing the work of biblical scholar Kenton Sparks and, in particular, Sparks's contention that John deliberately changed the day of Jesus' crucifixion for theological reasons. A similar thesis about the day of crucifixion, and many of the same arguments for it, are put forward by Michael Licona and Craig Keener,[16] though they are both more conservative scholars than Sparks. Here Blomberg is addressing the question of whether Sparks's position is compatible with inerrancy:

> [W]hen Sparks insists that John has gone out of his way to tell us that Jesus was crucified during a certain twenty-four-hour period of time in order to exploit the symbolism that alone attached to that period of time, when in fact Jesus was crucified during a different twenty-four-hour period of time, and that the language used by John in its historical and literal contexts unambiguously referred to those day-long periods of time, I do not see how John can be spared the charge of both error and duplicity.[17]

It is possible that Blomberg would say something different about duplicity if Sparks had claimed that John's readers expected him to change facts invisibly at

---

[16] Licona, *Why Are There Differences*, p. 163; Keener, *John*, pp. 1100–3, 1129–31.

[17] Craig Blomberg, "A Constructive Traditional Response to New Testament Criticism" in James K. Hoffmeier and Dennis R. Magary, eds., *Do Historical Matters Matter to Faith* (Wheaton, IL: Crossway Books, 2012), p. 360.

unpredictable intervals. Sparks does not seem to have availed himself of that option. But Blomberg's point about error stands regardless.

Any inerrantist considering literary device theories should ask himself some questions concerning an alleged change of fact in the Gospels. Take, for concreteness, the claim that Jesus first appeared to his male disciples in Galilee after his resurrection but that Luke changed this and had him appear to them in Jerusalem first in order to fit all of the post-resurrection events onto one day in his Gospel. In that case, the appearance to the disciples, placed firmly by Luke's narrative in Jerusalem (Luke 24.33ff), did not really take place in Jerusalem. On this theory, the proposition that Jesus appeared on Easter Day to a group of his male disciples in Jerusalem is false. Other things would have to be false as well. For example, in Luke the two disciples who saw Jesus on the road to Emmaus have just come back to report and are with the other disciples on that occasion when Jesus first comes among them. That must be false if Jesus first appeared in Galilee. In Luke, Jesus appears unexpectedly, whereas if he first appeared in Galilee to his disciples who went there deliberately expecting to meet him, this is not true. This is an important point from an evidential point of view, since some skeptics would try to use the expectation to raise the probability of a hallucination or other religious experience "of" the resurrected Jesus on the part of the disciples.

To be absolutely clear, I do not think that any of this is the case. As I will argue in Part Four, I think that Luke is completely correct that this appearance took place in Jerusalem; there is no conflict with Matthew 28, which narrates only a later appearance in Galilee. But one literary device theory is that Luke geographically moved this appearance to Jerusalem because he was chronologically compressing all of the events onto Easter Day.[18]

Now ask yourself as an inerrantist *what you have gained* if you decide that Luke changed things and so included false propositional content in his Gospel. How does the deliberateness of the change help your inerrancy? Do the falsehoods cease to be false if included deliberately? Do they even cease to be false if (you decide) readers expected realistic, invisible falsehoods to crop up from time to time in such works? Remember: To say that this was allowed by the standards of the time *does not mean* that the original audience could tell *from that document* that a fictional element was included *at that point*. Of course the idea is supposed to be that Luke corrected this misimpression in Acts 1, saying there that Jesus appeared

---

[18] Licona, *Why Are There Differences*, pp. 177–180; Bart Ehrman vs. Michael Licona, "Are the Gospels Historically Reliable," Kennesaw State University, February 21, 2018, minute 1:46:20, https://youtu.be/qP7RrCfDkO4?t=1h46m20s.

over a period of forty days to his disciples. But why should we select Acts 1 as the historical report on this point and take Luke 24 to be factually altered? After all, for Jesus to appear repeatedly over forty days obviously has apologetic value. And the number "forty" might be deemed theologically symbolic. If Luke was the sort of author to alter facts, perhaps he reported without factual warrant in Acts 1, while really thinking that Jesus appeared to his disciples only over a much shorter period of time. How was Theophilus (Luke's recipient) to know which account to prefer, historically, if they really are contradictory?

I submit that the view of Luke as the sort of author who did that sort of thing is a great loss to you, as an inerrantist and as a Christian. I note, too, that such theories have ramifying effects, for John also places Jesus' first appearance to his disciples in Jerusalem, as well as another appearance about a week later; it is in this sequence that the doubts of Thomas arise and are satisfied (John 20.19–29). One might think that the first appearance in Jerusalem should count as multiply attested by Luke and John, especially given their varying details about the incident, but evidently that is not the direction the literary device theorist leans. If Luke's placement of the first appearance in Jerusalem is non-factual, then the first appearance in Jerusalem is not multiply attested with factual intent.

One also finds it difficult to imagine how the doubting Thomas sequence can be fitted *at all* into a theory according to which the risen Jesus did not appear to his disciples in Jerusalem as John and Luke recount. Did Thomas travel to Galilee, still doubting? Why would he travel to Galilee to see Jesus if he dismissed the women's testimony? And what about the fact that Matthew 28.16 says that "the eleven" went to Galilee and saw Jesus there together? If one rejects (as Licona does) the use of "the eleven" to refer to a smaller group, and if one takes this account to describe the first meeting with Jesus, then the doubting Thomas sequence is ruled out.[19] So the claim that the first appearance really happened in Galilee and that Luke non-factually altered its location casts doubt upon other important aspects of the resurrection narratives. Ironically, these other parts of the Gospels actually fit very well with an historical interpretation of Luke 24.

And you, as an inerrantist, have gained nothing if you accept such a theory, for the documents (on that view) actually do contain errors, but the theory simply tells you not to *call* them errors, since they were allegedly "allowed at the time" and were allegedly inserted deliberately. Such word magic is, ultimately, of no value for the goals that inerrancy was supposed to serve. Hence, a commitment to inerrancy

---

[19] See Chapter XVI, sections 4 and 6.

cannot *support* literary device theories. An inerrantist should never think that he has to be ready, *qua* inerrantist, to accept fictionalizing literary devices as a fallback, lest he otherwise be in danger of accepting a good-faith error. The usual fallback of old-fashioned inerrantists when dissatisfied with all known harmonizations has been to say that we simply don't know for now how to resolve a difficulty. Unlike fictionalizing literary devices, that position is fully compatible with inerrancy.

I therefore suggest that inerrantists should join me in investigating whether, in fact, the Gospels are like stories only based on true events. Is the history portrayed in the Gospels really a mask—a realistic façade, which might or might not faithfully represent the truth beneath? In the next part of this book I will investigate the claim that such a view is independently supported by the norms and compositional devices of Greco-Roman literature of the time.

Summary
Whither Inerrancy?

- The refutation of literary device theories in this book is not only compatible with but even supportive of inerrancy in its older sense.

- The argument of this book does not assume inerrancy. I do not identify myself as an inerrantist and am open to the possibility of minor, good-faith errors in the Gospels. The argument of this book is relevant to non-inerrantists who are interested in Gospel reliability.

- Inerrancy does not support literary device views. Someone who is an inerrantist has a great deal to lose in terms of the factual truthfulness of the Gospels if he accepts fictionalizing literary devices.

- Inerrancy redefined to accommodate fictionalizing literary devices is pointless.

PART TWO

Unmasking
Ancient History

V

Are the Gospels Greco-Roman Biographies?

1. The Gospels as βίοι: Limiting both unreliability and reliability

It would be difficult to exaggerate the acceptance that the claim, "The Gospels are Greco-Roman biographies" or even "The Gospels are something very much like Greco-Roman biographies" enjoys in the current evangelical scholarly milieu. The popularity of this claim, based most of all upon the book *What Are the Gospels?* by classicist Richard Burridge, has only grown since that book's first publication in 1994 and its release in a second edition in 2004.[1] The idea was not unique to Burridge or new with his work, but Burridge's book gave the claim an apparently rigorous basis in genre criticism and word statistics, and it is now considered quite radical to question it.

So well-established is Burridge's genre identification considered to be that a large anthology entitled *Biographies and Jesus: What Does it Mean for the Gospels to be Biographies?*[2], published in 2016, took the identification as a given and set out to decide what effect this unquestioned premise should have upon our understanding of the Gospels. The authors surveyed a variety of Greco-Roman literature, trying to decide how factually reliable those works were and then making closing suggestions at the end of every essay about how the results might apply to the Gospels. The anthology, edited by eminent New Testament scholar Craig Keener, consisted chiefly of essays by Keener's doctoral students at Asbury seminary, along with contributions by Keener and a short essay by Michael Licona previewing his (then)

---

[1] Richard Burridge, *What Are the Gospels? A Comparison With Greco-Roman Biography* (Grand Rapids, Eerdmans, 2004).

[2] Craig S. Keener and Edward T. Wright, eds., *Biographies and Jesus: What Does it Mean for the Gospels to be Biographies?* (Lexington, KY: Emeth Press, 2016).

forthcoming book *Why Are There Differences in the Gospels?* There is much that is of interest in the anthology, and I will be discussing one of its essays in a later chapter and one in Appendix 2; my point here is simply that the anthology does not claim to provide *new* evidence for the thesis that the Gospels fall into this identified genre. That assumption is the foundation of the entire enterprise; the goal of the book is to see how much more we can learn about the Gospels by studying extra-biblical literature that also falls into or resembles that category.

Even before Burridge's book was published, the thesis that the Gospels are Greco-Roman biographies (βίοι) was a known possibility and was taken to support their historical reliability by rebutting the claim that they are myth or some other strongly fictional genre.[3] Since Burridge's work argues for a connection between the Gospels and a genre that is in some sense historical, evangelicals have hailed it as a counterweight to hyper-skeptical New Testament criticism.

What has become evident, however, is that matters are by no means that simple. Once again, the work of Michael Licona is particularly clear and instructive in explaining the complex nature of the thesis that the Gospels "are" or "have much in common with" Greco-Roman βίοι. As Licona uses the genre identification, it establishes what one might call both a "floor" and a "ceiling" for the historicity of the Gospels. The idea is that the Gospels, at least the Synoptics, are *no less* historical than some lower limit. We can think of this lower limit as the "floor" of their historicity. (Licona, like Craig Evans, tends to treat John as *more* mysterious and *less* historical than the Synoptics.[4] Hence, the expected "floor" for John's historicity in Licona's work appears to be even lower than the "floor" of historicity in the Synoptics.) So the Gospels are *at least* historical to some significant degree, on this view. But on the other hand, for all of the Gospels, Licona treats their resemblance to Greco-Roman βίοι as meaning that their historicity also has a "ceiling." That is to say, their being Greco-Roman βίοι means, according to Licona, that we should consider it antecedently quite plausible that they contain invisible, non-historical portions.

Authorial intent often eludes us, and the motives behind the reports are often difficult to determine. This is a challenge when we consider the four earliest ex-

---

[3] See, for example, the allusion to this theory by Douglas Moo (when the theory was less widely held) in his debate with Robert Gundry in the pages of *JETS*. Douglas J. Moo, "Once Again, 'Matthew and Midrash': A Rejoinder to Robert Gundry," *JETS* 26 (1983), p. 68. Gundry claimed that Matthew was "midrash" and hence (as he conceived of this category) contained a great deal of fabrication. Moo suggested that Matthew might be Greco-Roman biography instead and hence historical.

[4] Michael Licona, *Why Are There Differences in the Gospels? What We Can Learn From Ancient Biography* (Oxford: Oxford University Press, 2017), pp. 114–116.

tant biographies of Jesus, known as the canonical Gospels. There is somewhat of a consensus…that the Gospels belong to the genre of Greco-Roman biography *(bios)*….Because *bios* was a flexible genre, it is often difficult to determine where history ends and legend begins.[5]

In other words, if the Gospels belong to the genre of Greco-Roman biography, that *in and of itself* means that we will find it difficult to determine whether their reports have an historical intention and where history ends and legend begins.

Licona concludes directly from the genre that the individual authors would have considered themselves at liberty to invent speeches and change other material, and he tries to use this concession to answer objections from Bart Ehrman based upon alleged Gospel contradictions:

> This objection is not nearly as strong as Ehrman supposes. Responsible method requires that historians take genre into consideration. I have noted above that there is now somewhat of a consensus…that the Gospels belong to the genre of Greco-Roman biography (*bioi*) and that this genre offered biographers a great deal of flexibility to rearrange material [and] invent speeches to communicate the teachings…of the subject.[6]

Licona reasons that we should positively expect the Gospels to contain *at least* a certain amount of fictionalization, as I have defined it in the previous section. In one of his strongest statements, already quoted in Chapter III, Licona actually says that we should be surprised if we did *not* find the Gospel authors using compositional devices such as displacement, transferral, and so forth. I have discussed Licona's definitions of these devices above and will be giving many examples as this book proceeds. Licona calls these devices "part-and-parcel of that genre" and draws a strong, direct inference about the *prior probability* that such devices will be found in the Gospels.

> The majority of New Testament scholars agree that, at minimum, the Gospels share much in common with the genre of Greco-Roman biography. Therefore, it should be of no surprise to observe the Gospel authors using the compositional devices that were part-and-parcel of that genre. In fact, we should be surprised if we did *not* observe it.[7]

---

[5] Michael Licona, *The Resurrection of Jesus: A New Historiographical Approach* (Downer's Grover: IVP Academic, 2010), p. 34.

[6] Ibid., p. 593.

[7] Jonathan Peterson and Michael Licona, "Why Are There Differences in the Gospels? An Interview With Michael R. Licona," *Bible Gateway Blog*, June 27, 2017, https://www.biblegateway.com/

This is a remarkably bold claim, especially given the qualification that the Gospels may only "share much in common with" the genre.

2. Two questions about the Gospels as Greco-Roman βίοι

Broadly speaking, we can consider the relevance of Greco-Roman βίοι to the Gospels by examining two questions:

1) Do the Gospels belong to or resemble the genre of Greco-Roman βίος in the informative sense that the authors were probably influenced by the conventions of this genre and chose to write their Gospels according to the conventions of this genre?

2) Do Greco-Roman standards of history generally and the practices of Greco-Roman βίος in particular support the claim that some degree of fictionalization was part and parcel of this genre and that we should therefore expect that any document in this genre would use fictionalizing literary devices?

The present chapter will examine the first of these questions. All of the other chapters in Part Two will be relevant to the second. It will come as no surprise to readers that my answer to both questions is "no." But given the amount of material in existence asserting the contrary, it will be necessary to argue these points at length. To address question 2, I will have to answer not only generalizations about "ancient standards of truth" but also specific alleged examples from Greco-Roman biographies where, scholars claim, these literary devices occur. I will also have to discuss the Greek exercise books used for teaching writing to boys, since literary device theorists allege that these books support the claim that fictionalizing alteration was deeply imbedded in Greco-Roman historical practice.

There is much detail involved in these arguments, and they are bound to be of less interest to some readers than to others. Yet one of my goals in this book is to encourage readers not to take the word of an expert unquestioningly. This applies to me as well. I do not want anyone to choose me as his "designated expert" and to take my word for what is or is not found in (e.g.) Plutarch's *Lives*. At the same time I do not want to bog down readers in too much detail. As a partial solution to this dilemma, I have included some additional supporting examples both from Greco-Roman works (where a fictionalizing literary device is alleged) and some

---

blog/2017/06/why-are-there-differences-in-the-gospels-an-interview-with-michael-r-licona/. Emphasis in original. Licona repeats this strong claim in slightly different wording in *Why Are There Differences in the Gospels?* p. 5.

additional points about the Greek exercise books in appendices. Beyond this, I will say something more radical: If you find yourself bogging down, feel free to skip ahead and read Part Three and Part Four. You can come back to this part of the book later as your time and interest permit.

The discussion of alleged ancient literary parallels to the Gospels is unavoidable, since it forms a large part of the literary device theorists' argument for a high prior probability that the Gospels contain such devices. It is on the basis of the supposed affinities between the Gospels and Greco-Roman βίοι and the supposed practices of Greco-Roman writers that Licona has made such a strong methodological statement, already quoted in Chapter III:

> Where I differ [from most evangelicals] is, I place a priority on genre over harmonization. So, *before seeking to harmonize Gospel texts*, one should read the Gospels in view of their biographical genre, which includes their authors' use of the various compositional devices commonly used when writing history and biography.[8]

This background claim about genre is supposed to provide a baseline for our expectations in the Gospels. Licona uses it to justify a hermeneutical approach in which he rejects available harmonizations or even treats mere difference without apparent discrepancy as grounds for considering very seriously that a Gospel author has deliberately altered fact. It is therefore valuable to see that the background information does not support such an approach at all.

If we were to defer to Licona's research, assuming without further investigation that he must be right about what the Gospels are and about what Plutarch and other writers do, we would set out with a much higher expectation of finding fictionalizing literary devices in the Gospels than if we were to examine only the passages in the Gospels themselves and the differences among them.

If, on the other hand, we are convinced that we should answer "no" to the two questions asked above, the case for the evangelists' use of fictionalizing literary devices is much weaker. If we have little reason to think that three out of four of the Gospel authors would have been conversant at all in any specific conventions of Greco-Roman βίος, the question becomes largely moot. And if we go so far as to conclude (as I shall argue) that there is no case for the objective existence of the defined devices (such as displacement, transferral, etc.) *even in Greco-Roman literature itself*, we have no reason to think that they exist in the Gospels, either. At

---

[8] Jonathan Peterson and Michael Licona, "Why Are There Differences in the Gospels? An Interview With Michael R. Licona." Emphasis added.

that point the question about what to think of the Gospels' supposed discrepancies returns to a much older debate concerning the plausibility of individual harmonizations and what we should think if we are not satisfied with any of the available harmonizations. Moreover, when there is not even an apparent discrepancy but merely a difference between Gospels and when a theorist alleges a fictionalization, that move will be seen for the unforced error that it is.[9]

3. Are the Gospels βίοι in an informative sense?

With all of that in place, let us turn to this question:

> Do the Gospels belong to or resemble the genre of Greco-Roman βίος in the informative sense that the authors were probably influenced by the conventions of this genre and chose to write their Gospels according to the conventions of this genre?

One might think that it is unnecessary for the authors actually to be influenced by this genre. Wouldn't it be enough if they simply *resembled* the genre? But remember, the very question at issue is whether they resemble the genre in certain important respects, such as the fidelity to literal, historical truth and the use of particular conventions. On the one hand, evangelicals are hoping that placing the Gospels in the genre of βίος means that they are at least substantially historical. But if the authors were not aware of the genre nor influenced by it, how can we draw that positive conclusion? It is hard to see how the genre can give us a "floor" of historicity—the Gospels are no less historical than *this*—if they do not lie within the genre in the sense that there is a genuine causal connection between the existence of the genre in the culture and the intentions of the authors. Such

---

[9] As discussed in Part Four, there are places where Licona does not even allege a *specific* compositional device in the Gospels that he claims to have found in Plutarch or other ancient biographies, yet he writes as though his study supports a Gospel alteration of fact in these places as well. (See, for example, *Why Are There Differences*, pp. 184–185.) In one of these instances, the claim that either Matthew or John has "relocated" Jesus' resurrection appearance to Mary Magdalene, Licona even draws a moral for the reader—"This shows the extent to which at least one of the evangelists or the sources from which he drew felt free to craft the story" (p. 176). This despite the fact that, by his own admission (p. 184), such a "relocation" would not correspond to a clear Greco-Roman literary device. Licona's willingness to allege fictionalization without specific literary devices is interesting. His approach to finding passages to which to apply fictionalization theory appears to be that he questions passages whose historicity scholars *otherwise* challenge rather than consistently finding objective, independent evidence from Greco-Roman literature and recognizing clear similarities in the Gospels. See also the suggestions that John invented the incident in which Jesus breathed on the disciples, pp. 180–181, and that Matthew has invented Jesus' early healing of two blind men as a "doublet," pp. 131, 135. Neither of these corresponds to any alleged specific literary device.

a causal connection is needed to provide us with stable expectations based on the authors' decision to write in this genre.

On the other side, the controversial claim on Licona's part is that, since the Gospels resemble the genre in respects such as length, focus on a single character, the number of verbs that have the main character as their subject, containing a mixture of stories and sayings, relatively little psychological analysis,[10] and the like, we should also expect the evangelists to use fact-altering compositional devices that were (he claims) "part and parcel" of the genre of βίος. For this purpose, mere broad resemblance that has come about by accident is obviously not sufficient. The authors must be aware of the conventions of the genre if they are to use them, especially since the conventions in question—the literary devices—are both esoteric and impossible to fall into by accident. Remember that one of the criteria of a fictionalizing device is that the author does it deliberately, as the literary device theorists themselves state. If fictionalizing conventions existed, they wouldn't be obvious. The evangelists would need a fairly high level of understanding in order to use them. And they certainly would not know about the conventions if they had no acquaintance at all with works in that genre. Licona even says, "The evangelists' use of these devices most often appear to have no objective other than to follow the literary conventions of their day."[11] The evangelists could not have deliberately tried to "follow the literary conventions of their day" if they were not influenced by the relevant works.

The literary device theorist, then, must meet a burden of proof to establish the claim that the Gospels resemble Greco-Roman βίοι in an informative sense for our expectations of their truthfulness or their use of literary conventions. With this in mind, one finds it rather surprising that Richard Burridge spends so little effort arguing for actual influence. To begin with, his criteria for what constitutes a βίος are scarcely so specific or unusual that, if a document satisfies them, the conclusion is almost inescapable that it has been influenced by other documents of the same sort.

Several examples of the bland nature of the criteria suffice to make the point. Length is one feature of βίοι—they usually fell into the medium length of between 10,000 and 25,000 words, with 25,000 words being about the amount that a scroll would hold.[12] This last point is significant, since it provides an obvious rationale for a work to fall into that length range without any need for influence

---

[10] Ibid., p. 3. These criteria are taken from Burridge's work.

[11] Ibid., p. 183.

[12] Ibid., p. 4.

by a genre.[13] Moreover, being of such a medium length seems entirely natural for the story of a person's life composed in an age when everything had to be written by hand on scrolls. Or consider the claim that a skewed proportion of the verbs in the document have the subject of the story as their subject, while many others occur in sayings or speeches by the subject. Surely this is quite natural in a work that is focused on the life of a single, important individual. Again, no influence by other works is necessary. Then there is the fact that the character is illuminated by his words and deeds rather than by psychological analysis. But surely we can acknowledge that a strong focus in a biography upon psychological analysis is a convention of a later time without concluding that the Gospels were influenced by other works that show a similar absence of modern preoccupations. If some higher critics were so anachronistic as to fault the biographical intentions of the Gospel authors on the basis of their lack of psychoanalytic reflection,[14] it hardly follows that the proper corrective is to think that the Gospel authors were literary people who had encountered and been influenced by Greco-Roman biographies. These features, then, would be well explained by the desire of an author to write an historical work of a medium length, focused on a particular person, in an age not deeply interested in psychoanalysis.

Burridge points out that some older critics thought that the Gospels could not be biographical and historical in intention because they spent so much time upon the passion and death of Jesus. Burridge counters that a heavy focus upon the death of the hero is common in Greco-Roman biography.[15] But the objection he is answering just further illustrates the obtuseness of higher critics. The answer shows that historical intention is compatible with a focus on the death of the main character. According to Christians, Jesus redeemed the entire world from sin by his death. This theological belief provides plenty of reason for the evangelists to spend a lot of time on the story of Jesus' passion and death without any need for literary influences. Other ancient authors may have had their own reasons for spending a disproportionate amount of time on their heroes' deaths, but they need not have influenced the Gospel authors.

Here I must pause and make a terminological point: To say that the Gospels are biographies in the extremely broad sense that they are, as the church father Justin

---

[13] A point made by Robert Stein in his review of *Why Are There Differences in the Gospels? What We Can Learn from Ancient Biography, Journal of the Evangelical Theological Society,* 61 (March, 2018), p. 183.

[14] Richard Burridge, *What Are the Gospels?,* pp. 117, 199.

[15] Ibid., pp. 192–193.

Martyr said, memoirs of the apostles,[16] and that they tell with historical accuracy the life of Jesus, is *not at all* the same thing as saying that they are Greco-Roman βίοι. The latter is a far more specific, literary claim, and we must not be confused into a false dichotomy according to which the Gospels are either specifically Greco-Roman βίοι or else they are not *prima facie* historical documents that tell the life of Christ.

Astonishingly, Burridge himself admits openly that a document may "be" a βίος in the sense that it bears a "family resemblance" to other works in that genre without the author's having knowledge of the genre. That is to say, he envisages that a document may fall into the genre by accident. He appears to consider this hypothesis fairly plausible for the Gospel of Mark:

> [Mark] may have been consciously writing about Jesus in a way which was similar to βίοι of philosophers, or he may have done it unconsciously, falling into a βίος pattern *simply because it is the natural genre for any text concentrating on the deeds and words of a single person.*[17]

> Mark's biographical genre may be a natural, if unconscious, consequence of his decision to present his Christian message with such a concentration on the life, deeds and words of Jesus of Nazareth.[18]

New Testament scholar Robert Stein makes similar points about the generic nature of the criteria for Licona and Burridge to declare something a Greco-Roman βίος. Stein, who is not by any measure an extreme conservative (see the discussion of Stein's theory about the divorce clause in Matthew in Chapter XIII, section 6), considers that Licona and others have overestimated the strength of the case:

> Licona points out that a normal scroll held about 25,000 words. This suggests that it may not have been so much the genre of biography that was the determiner of length but rather the size of the scroll! …Did the Gospel writers need to know Greco-Roman rhetoric to remember that they should focus on Jesus in telling the story of Jesus Christ (Mark 1:1)? Can one write a biography of Jesus and not follow this rule?[19]

Stein praises Licona for not acquiescing too readily (as Stein views it) in accepting harmonizations,[20] but the bulk of his review is focused on questioning the ancient

---

[16] Justin Martyr, *The First Apology*, 66–67; *Dialogue With Trypho*, 100–107.

[17] Burridge, *What Are the Gospels?*, p. 241. Emphasis added.

[18] Ibid., p. 246.

[19] Robert Stein, review of *Why Are There Differences in the Gospels? What We Can Learn from Ancient Biography*, p. 183.

[20] Ibid., pp. 183–184.

parallels that Licona claims for the Gospels. The question of influence is central to the use of Greco-Roman βίοι in the literary device theorists' program, and challenges like mine and Stein's cannot be set aside merely by the statement that the Gospels "share much in common with" that genre. Accidental resemblance will not do.

Burridge's work is also noteworthy for the extent to which he overlooks evidence for the traditional authorship of the Gospels. This is relevant to his thesis because traditional authorship would mean that at least three out of four Gospels—Matthew, Mark, and John—were written by Jews who were likely not educated in a Hellenistic fashion. Then too there is the probability that Peter, a Galilean Jew, was a major oral source for Mark's Gospel (the latter point noted by Stein). The evidence that Matthew, Mark, and John were written by their traditionally ascribed authors tends to disconfirm the thesis that they were influenced by Greco-Roman literature. How likely is it that Matthew the tax collector, John Mark, Peter, or even John the son of Zebedee would have read or heard the earlier writers of biography discussed by Burridge such as Xenophon, Isocrates, Satyrus, and Nepos and that they would have desired to emulate a specific Greco-Roman genre?[21] It would require, at least, direct positive evidence for the Hellenistic education of these authors to begin to reply to this point, and simply ignoring the debate about authorship will not do. Burridge gives little evidence of taking traditional authorship of Matthew and Mark or Peter's probable influence on Mark with any seriousness whatsoever. In the case of John, he ascribes it briefly to a "Johannine community" operating within the "syncretistic milieu of the eastern Mediterranean toward the close of the first century AD."[22]

This Hellenistic bias in Burridge's approach to authorship is evident when he pauses to give a little space to the question of whether the Gospel authors consciously wrote in the genre. He begins by briefly acknowledging the issue of conscious adoption of the genre:

> The question of whether Mark wrote in the genre of βίοι deliberately or whether he just fell unconsciously into a natural biographical pattern, and the suggestion made above that Matthew and Luke attempted to conform their work more closely to βίος, both raise the issue of the setting of the gospel genre in contemporary first-century society and of the level of the evangelists' education and literary awareness: would they have known some of these other βίοι and, if so, how did they meet them?[23]

---

[21] Burridge, *What Are the Gospels?*, Chapter 6.

[22] Ibid., pp. 214–215.

[23] Ibid., pp. 243–244.

An excellent question! Burridge's answer, however, is almost entirely focused on issues of *class* rather than on issues of *ethnicity* and religion. In the following pages he emphasizes, for example, the fact that slaves and servants would have had opportunity to hear after-dinner entertainments in upper-class houses, implying that these entertainments might have included literary performances. But it is not plausible that Jesus' disciples, John Mark, or indeed most Palestinian Jews would have attended after-dinner entertainments featuring readings of Greco-Roman literature in, say, Capernaum, where Peter had a house (Mark 1.29). Nor does Burridge argue for any such thing or provide any statistics to show that that would be likely. He is merely speaking of the extremely broad milieu of the Mediterranean world and the ways in which members of lower classes might have become acquainted with βίοι. He emphasizes the presence of Hellenistic "primary schools" in which teaching was carried out via excerpts from Greek literature in Greek areas such as the Decapolis, but the point there is precisely that the Decapolis *was* a Greek area, unusual in the region as a whole. Burridge even mentions that there was a conservative Jewish reaction against Hellenistic education "in the Maccabean period and later,"[24] evidence against the plausibility that Jesus' disciples received a Hellenistic education, though Burridge does not seem to recognize it as such.

The presence and nature of "Hellenistic schools" in Palestine is very much a matter of conjecture. The conclusion that there were schools in which students could learn Greek literacy (in other words, the ability to read and write Greek) in Palestine, especially in a large city like Jerusalem, is almost entirely supported by the widespread use of the Greek *language* in these areas, including among Jews, and the presence of many Greek inscriptions. But there is a vast difference between an education in which students learn to read Greek in order to get around in a world in which *koine* Greek is the *lingua franca* and an education in which they are taught from Greek exercise books, read and write about excerpts from Greek literature, and read Greco-Roman biographies of famous men. There is no good evidence that an education of *that* kind was at all common, even at the primary level, among Palestinian Jews. It would, for example, have been quite possible for Jewish boys to gain literacy in Greek from a Jewish education that used the Septuagint as a basis for the curriculum.[25]

---

[24] Ibid., p. 244.

[25] See Andrew W. Pitts, "Hellenistic Schools in Jerusalem and Paul's Rhetorical Education," *Paul's World*, Stanley E. Porter, ed. (Leiden, The Netherlands: 2008), pp. 36, 39–44. Pitts (p. 40) notes that "the level and settings of Greek education available to Jews in first-century Palestine are...difficult to assess since available rabbinical sources make no explicit reference to Hellenistic schools in Pales-

The Talmudic tractate Sotah does record a tradition that Gamaliel II, grandson of the Gamaliel under whom the Apostle Paul studied, taught many children "Greek wisdom" in his house and also taught many children Torah in his house. (Gamaliel II was the head of the reconstituted Sanhedrin after the fall of Jerusalem in A.D. 70.) The same Talmudic passage, however, interprets this tradition by saying that this was an exception made for those who would have to deal with "the authorities" and "the monarchy" and that in general Greek language is separate from Greek wisdom. The latter is prohibited for study while the former is permitted. The same passage states that in the time of the Hasmonean civil war (1st century B.C.) the sages declared, "Cursed is he who teaches his son Greek wisdom."[26]

Burridge refers to the "Cynic on the corner," but does he actually mean to suggest that there were Cynics declaiming on the corners of Jerusalem and that Jesus' disciples were listening to them and learning about Greco-Roman literature in this way? One imagines not, nor does Burridge say so. He is painting with a very broad brush indeed and, again, focusing on class, arguing that "cultural awareness was mediated down the social scale from the higher educated classes" to the lower.[27] Such considerations should do very little to satisfy us that ordinary Palestinian Jews would have been influenced by the specific conventions of Greco-Roman biography. If Burridge wishes to say that the authors of Matthew, Mark, and John definitely were either strongly Hellenized Jews or Gentiles and received a Hellenistic education and encountered βίοι in this way, he will have to make that case independently, entering the fray of the authorship debates. Conjecturing the presence of Hellenistic schools *somewhere or other* in the vicinity and pointing out that some Cynics in some cities stood on some street corners will hardly suffice. Certainly evangelicals who otherwise *accept* traditional authorship for those Gospels, and even a scholar like Richard Bauckham who believes that John was written by a different Jewish disciple of Jesus named John who was not the son of Zebedee,[28] will have little reason to accept the relevance of Greco-Roman βίοι to the Gospels without much more specific evidence that *those authors* would have known *that genre*.

These, of course, are considerations of antecedent probability. By that measure, the only one of the traditionally ascribed Gospel authors antecedently likely to have encountered Greco-Roman literature at all is Luke. Luke has long been

---

tine—though they do contain discussion on whether or not a parent should teach their child Greek."

[26] Sotah 49b.

[27] Burridge, *What Are the Gospels?* pp. 244–245.

[28] Richard Bauckham, *Jesus and the Eyewitnesses: The Gospels as Eyewitness Testimony*, 2nd ed. (Grand Rapids, Eerdmans, 2017), chapters 15, 16, 20.

thought to have been a Gentile, though that debate itself continues. If a Jew, he is a Jew of *some* degree of Greek education, given the fairly high level of his Greek writing, some of the best in the entire New Testament.[29] Craig Keener states that "the only Gospel writer likely influenced overtly by rhetorical conventions was Luke."[30] And even of Luke he says, "Though educated, Luke does not necessarily display advanced training in rhetoric."[31]

The argument is not uncommon that Luke's famous preface (Luke 1.1–4) shows acquaintance with a Greco-Roman historical convention—the convention of writing a preface to the reader—and this may well be so.[32] But if so, Luke's preface shows a connection with precisely those aspects of historical writing that seek to establish historical veracity, which I shall discuss in the next chapter. Burridge distinguishes βίος as a genre from history, though this distinction, as we shall see, does not signal that biographies were more invented than histories. Histories as well as the more focused biographies had prefaces (the next chapter will quote from several of these), and Luke's use of a preface describing his own knowledge of the events related could have alluded to historical practices generally rather than indicating an intention to follow the conventions of βίος specifically. Moreover, a preface that emphasizes the author's careful investigation into all that transpired, as told by those who "from the beginning were eyewitnesses," and the author's goal to give the reader assurance of the truth of all that he has been told, is hardly fertile ground for ultimately arguing that Luke was both aware of and making use of fictionalizing literary conventions. The next chapter will argue carefully that there is no evidence that the mere knowledge of or even influence by some broad set of Greco-Roman historical or biographical conventions conveyed an immediate sense of license to invent. Far from it. For the moment, however, I can agree that Luke's general level of Greek ability, his preface, and the plausibility that he was an educated Gentile gives us some reason to think that he may have been *acquainted with* Greco-Roman history and/or biographies and that he wished to use the convention of writing a preface to assure his readers of his historical intentions.

---

[29] Craig Keener, *Acts: An Exegetical Commentary* (Grand Rapids, MI: Baker Academic 2012), vol. 1, pp. 403–405.

[30] Craig Keener, *The Historical Jesus of the Gospels* (Grand Rapids, Eerdmans: 2009), p. 115.

[31] Ibid., p. 116.

[32] Hemer, *The Book of Acts in the Setting of Hellenistic History*, WUNT 49 (Tübingen: J.C. B. Mohr, 1989), pp. 35, 322–28. Lucian, *How to Write History*, 52–55, makes it clear that a preface is common in writing history, and he mentions that the best historians, Herodotus and Thucydides, have used prefaces to make clear the importance of the events they plan to narrate. See also Craig Keener, *Acts*, vol. 1, pp. 183–186.

In any event, being somewhat acquainted with βίοι and using specific conventions in a Gospel are different matters. Does Burridge have any more specific evidence that the evangelists were consciously writing in the genre of Greco-Roman βίος? Very little. His individual chapters on the Gospels focus chiefly on noting that they fall within the broad margins of his broad criteria. But as we have seen, this does not at all mean that it is probable that the evangelists deliberately wrote in a defined literary genre. In the case of Mark, as already noted, Burridge repeatedly raises the possibility that Mark was only accidentally "in" the genre at all. For John, he does not allege detailed features (as opposed to his broad criteria) that correspond to βίος. Indeed, he raises expressly the possibility that the author(s) of John unconsciously picked up the genre and "reinvented the wheel" either by following the Synoptics or from some now-lost source documents that were "in" the genre.[33] He turns to authorship by a "Johannine community" to insist that the Gospel has an unspecified set of "other links to Graeco-Roman...philosophical and religious ideas and literature" and that therefore "it would be strange if the author/editor(s) of the Fourth Gospel did not realize the parallels with βίοι."[34] In other words, on Burridge's own showing, the Gospel may have accidentally picked up a broad similarity to Greco-Roman biography from its sources rather than consciously being written in the genre, but the "Johannine community" would have included educated people who would have recognized such similarities after the fact. Burridge's dependence upon the denial of individual authorship by a Jewish eyewitness is rather interesting. His airy generalization about the Johannine community does not inspire confidence as a basis for strong claims like Licona's about the high prior probability that the Gospel author used specific conventions of a defined genre.

For Luke and Matthew, Burridge makes a *bit* more of an argument:

> [I]t seems that [Matthew and Luke] did recognize Mark's genre and bring it closer to other Graeco-Roman βίοι: thus the Greek style is tidied up, and ancestry, birth and infancy narratives are added, together with a clearer chronological and topical structure.[35]

These arguments do very little to bolster the case for conscious writing of βίοι by Matthew and Luke. Consider the claim that Matthew and Luke use Mark as a

---

[33] Burridge, *What Are the Gospels?*, pp. 241–242.

[34] Ibid., p. 246.

[35] Ibid., p. 241.

written source but in the course of doing so sometimes improve Mark's Greek. Suppose that we grant that for the sake of the argument. (It is certainly not implausible in the case of Luke, whose Greek is undeniably better than Mark's.) If so, it is an entirely normal human activity and tells us nothing about an attempt to write in a Greco-Roman genre. If an author of an historical work is making use of a written source, and if the source uses language that is less educated and more "clunky" than the later author's normal writing style, it is quite natural for the later writer to use his own narrative style rather than the style of his written source. If we concede that both Matthew and Luke write better Greek than Mark, this scarcely amounts to their attempting to write βίοι.

The addition of ancestry (genealogy) and birth and infancy narratives, and in Luke of a story about Jesus' boyhood, does not fare any better as an argument for deliberate adoption of the conventions of βίοι. It should go without saying that Jews were intensely interested in genealogy and especially the genealogy of a Messianic claimant. If Matthew believed that he had information about the genealogy of Jesus the Messiah he hardly required a Hellenistic model as a motive to include it. And a similar consideration applies to Luke, even if he was a Gentile author. Jesus' genealogy, either as reckoned through his mother or through Joseph, would have been important both to the authors and to their audiences. If we take at all seriously the hypothesis that Matthew and Luke had historical sources that they trusted for their genealogies, that theory is quite sufficient to explain the inclusion of the information. Similarly, if they believed that they knew something about Jesus' birth—Jesus, the Savior of the world—and especially if they believed that they had information about Jesus' virgin birth, this would be of interest in itself and would warrant inclusion. And the same for the story of Jesus' encounter with the teachers in the Temple recorded in Luke 2. No hypothesis of literary influence by Greco-Roman documents is required.

It is interesting here to see how classicist George Kennedy seems to imply that Luke was simply making up his additional material and using it to bolster the case for the value of his own Gospel. Kennedy begins mildly enough:

> What Luke promises to provide is a version of the gospel which differs from the many others...in existence by its orderly narrative...and its exactness of detail...Luke is not saying that other gospels are not true, only that he will follow a more rigorous narrative method and be more specific....[36]

---

[36] George Kennedy, *New Testament Interpretation Through Rhetorical Criticism* (University of North

Kennedy then says that Luke's genealogy, unlike Matthew's,

> performs little persuasive function in its context; it is part of his promise to provide detail and at most lends some historiographic credence to his overall narrative. Unlike the other evangelists, he claims to know something about Jesus' youth. His description of Jesus in the temple at the age of twelve (2:41–47) helps prepare the reader to understand Jesus' later skill in meeting the Pharisees....Luke is chiefly of interest here in that he shows what he thought would be meaningful to Christians a generation after Jesus' death: a more elegant presentation in better Greek, more biographical detail, and, as noted earlier, a fuller account of the period after the resurrection. Luke in the Gospel comes close to being a classical biographer, just as in Acts he comes close to being a classical historian.[37]

It is difficult not to notice Kennedy's tacit insinuation that Luke was inventing material (such as the genealogy and the story about Jesus as a boy in the Temple) in order to make his Gospel *look like* what he thought his readers wanted to see in a biography. But Kennedy provides no argument for this implication in the context beyond stating that Luke probably would not have had a source for what Elizabeth said to Mary in Luke 1 and therefore that he probably made up her words.

As a matter of fact, Richard Bauckham raises with all seriousness the possibility that Luke interviewed Mary.[38] Even if we don't think that he interviewed her directly, it is quite possible that he was using a written or oral source from Mary's family for his earliest chapters. In any event, the question of how Luke might have known what Elizabeth and Mary said to one another is scarcely sufficient to support the insinuation that Luke's preface is mere self-promotion and Luke's additional material invented to supply what was desired by an audience a generation after Jesus' death.[39] In the context of an argument over whether a) Luke was consciously adopting the genre of Greco-Roman βίος and b) whether authors of Greco-Roman βίοι routinely made up material out of whole cloth to

---

Carolina Press, 1984), p. 107.

[37] Ibid., p. 108.

[38] See Richard Bauckham, "Luke's Infancy Narrative as Oral History in Scriptural Form," in *The Gospels: History and Christology: The Search of Joseph Ratzinger-Benedict XVI*, ed. Bernardo Estrada, Ermenegildo Manicardi and Armand Puig i Tàrrech (Vatican City: Libreria Editrice Vaticana, 2013) vol. 1, 399–417.

[39] In contrast, Colin Hemer, *The Book of Acts in the Setting of Hellenistic History*, p. 99, notes Luke's comparative modesty in his preface and how well his claims stand up to examination. Similarly, Craig Keener says, "Luke follows, where we can test him..., the procedures of a good Hellenistic historian," *Acts*, vol. 1, p. 793. It is only unfortunate that Keener feels that, in this same context, he must make this compliment to Luke by way of a negative comment about John's historical care.

make their works look more interesting and detailed, such an assumption would be question begging.

Returning to Burridge, the claim that Matthew and Luke provide "a clearer chronological and topical structure" and that this is evidence of their conscious intention to write βίοι is just puzzling. The question of the relationship between Matthew's and Mark's chronology is famously difficult, and when Licona suggests, for example, that either Matthew or Mark may have changed chronology, the assertion is never that Mark's chronology is *unclear* and that Matthew's is clearer.[40] Luke's own chronology is famously vague in the central section from Chapter 9.51 through Chapter 18, a huge segment of the Gospel rife with unclear or entirely absent notes of time and place.[41] If the imposition of a clearer chronological progression on Mark is an indication of an intention to write a βίος (a questionable premise anyway), it seems that Luke and Matthew have *failed* to give such an indication.

The upshot is that Burridge's case is thin indeed for Matthew's and Luke's conscious intention to write in closer alignment with the conventions of βίοι. And as we have seen, the arguments for John's and Mark's intentions to write βίοι are even thinner. Indeed, Burridge scarcely bothers to argue that they had any such intention. The question I am examining in this chapter, again, is

> Do the Gospels belong to or resemble the genre of Greco-Roman βίος in the informative sense that the authors were probably influenced by the conventions of this genre and chose to write their Gospels according to the conventions of this genre?

Burridge's arguments are utterly unconvincing in support of a "yes" answer to this question. Taking that failure together with the antecedent improbability that the authors of Matthew, Mark, and John had encountered Greco-Roman βίοι at all, we can say that the answer to the question of influence for at least three out of four Gospels is likely "no." As for Luke, only his preface and the general possibility that he had encountered Greco-Roman literature somewhere or other supports the thesis at all, and that in a very qualified way related to a desire to assure the

---

[40] Licona, *Why Are There Differences*, p. 192.

[41] Luke 9.57, "As they were going along the road..."; 10.38, "As they were traveling along, he entered a village..."; 11.1, "It happened that while Jesus was praying in a certain place..."; 11.29, "As the crowds were increasing..."; 12.22, "And he said to his disciples..."; 13.10, "And he was teaching in one of the synagogues on the Sabbath"; 14.25, "Now large crowds were going along with him, and he turned and said..."; 15.11, "And he said..." And many more.

reader of his historical truthfulness. These conclusions are, of course, at odds with the recent confidence that the Gospels are "in" the genre of Greco-Roman βίοι in a strongly informative sense. An examination of the evidence shows that that thesis has been oversold.

Summary
Are the Gospels Greco-Roman Biographies?

- The claim that the Gospels are or have much in common with the specific genre of Greco-Roman biographies (βίοι) is widely accepted in evangelical scholarly circles today.

- Theorists such as Richard Burridge and Michael Licona believe that this genre claim supports assigning not only a minimum degree of historicity in the Gospels but also a maximum degree. The idea is that, because the Gospels are or have much in common with this genre, we should expect them to use at least some fictionalizing literary devices, since these were part and parcel of the genre.

- We need to ask whether the Gospels belong to or resemble the genre of Greco-Roman βίος in the informative sense that the authors were probably influenced by the conventions of this genre and chose to write their Gospels according to the conventions of this genre.

- We need to ask whether Greco-Roman standards of history generally and/or the practices of Greco-Roman βίος in particular support the claim that some degree of fictionalization was part and parcel of this genre.

- The question of Gospel authorship is relevant to whether or not the authors would have probably been exposed to the conventions of Greco-Roman literature. If Matthew, Mark, and John were written by their traditionally ascribed authors or by other Palestinian Jews, the answer for those Gospels is probably "no." Those arguing for a strong resemblance between the Gospels and a specific Greco-Roman genre ignore the relevance of authorship.

- The criteria used to conclude that the Gospels are in or strongly resemble the specific Greco-Roman genre of βίος are too general to yield a significant conclusion concerning the adoption of specific conventions and the document's degree of truthfulness.

- The few more specific arguments that Richard Burridge gives (such as the presence of infancy narratives in Luke and Matthew) do not support the conclusion that the authors were trying to write in this genre.

- Given the high level of Luke's Greek and the plausibility that he was a Gentile, he may have been exposed to Greco-Roman literature.

- There is nothing in Luke's Gospel that shows an intention to write in the genre of βίος in a specific sense. He does show that he intends to write according to high standards of historical factuality. This intention may have been influenced by exposure to high standards of reliability in Greco-Roman history, in which case it does not support the conclusion that Luke would have used fictionalizing literary devices.

VI

Let Ancient People Speak
for Themselves

1. The limitations of genre as a guide to historical accuracy

My previous book, *Hidden in Plain View*, was dedicated in part to the late Colin J. Hemer, in honor of his work on the book of Acts. Hemer's judiciousness on the issue of genre criticism and its relevance to the reliability of the New Testament stands in stark contrast to the overstatements I have already quoted concerning the genre of the Gospels. Hemer is quite firm that questions of actual dependence, such as we examined in the last chapter, are crucial and that their answers are probably elusive:

> It is reasonable to consider the Gospels and Acts with reference to ancient biography or historiography. But the comparisons may be disappointingly fluid. Their significance is enhanced only as we can establish resemblances as reflecting organic relationship, conscious dependence, or the like.[1]

> It is unclear to what extent any of the New Testament documents are self-conscious literature which make deliberate use of contemporary forms ....It is wholly probable that their writers, and especially one with the literary ability and aspiration of Luke, were influenced by their cultural environment and reflect its trends, but by no means certain how closely or consciously.[2]

Moreover, as Hemer points out, it is wrong headed to draw simplistic conclusions even if one thinks that an author has made deliberate use of a particular literary form.

---

[1] Colin J. Hemer, *The Book of Acts in the Setting of Hellenistic History*, WUNT 49 (Tübingen: J.C. B. Mohr, 1989), p. 42.

[2] Ibid., p. 34.

A good writer may use, perhaps deliberately, literary forms. But he will make them his servants, not his masters. He ought ultimately to be judged by what he says, rather than by an over-preoccupation with the way he says it. If he is moved by an urgent mission, he will strive to express his meaning in the most effective style. But our focus is upon the matter, not the manner.[3]

Hemer was already well aware of the suggestion that the Gospel of Luke might be considered a Greco-Roman βίος, and he cautions against thinking that such a category provides us with much information about the Gospel. His careful comments deserve to be quoted at length.

The Gospel at least is, on the face of it, a βίος. But from the perspective of our theme [of historical reliability] we need to measure Luke-Acts by a more exacting historical standard than that of Plutarch. The relevance of biography to this question is largely negative. It is another kindred strand in the ancient cultural complex. It testifies to the existence of an anecdotal or encomiastic tradition of the interest in personality....There are certainly parallels between Luke-Acts and features of history, biography and technical literature. But those parallels are neither exclusive nor subject to control. *They are fluid, relevant to the general milieu, if perhaps partly in reaction against it and hard to place accurately within it.* Most of the New Testament is perhaps best seen as a popular literature, *imperfectly representative of any defined literary type,* and motivated by a dominant theological purpose scarcely paralleled in pagan writing. If Luke is a partial exception, aspiring to a more formal style in addressing a man presumably of some literary education, his type is still somewhat free and mixed, a concisely effective vehicle for what he had to say, drawing on a flexible use of the style most natural to him. The uninitiated reader might have taken the Gospel at first sight for a biography, but soon have found it an unusual one, and then have been moved by the impact of the double work in directions other than the normal reactions to biography or history. It is my contention that one of the inevitable questions posed as a result of the document was whether it really happened. Ancient biography, no less than ancient historiography, may need to serve as a historical source. The question here is whether the work is a good source....*Rigorous concepts of history existed in Luke's world: Luke must be judged by his performance rather than on the slippery ground of parallels.*[4]

These emphatically cautious comments could not be farther from Licona's insistence that, if the Gospels even have much in common with βίοι, we should be surprised if they did *not* make use of transferral, displacement, and/or other fact-al-

---

[3] Ibid., p. 35.

[4] Ibid., pp. 93–94. Emphasis added.

tering literary devices, because these were part and parcel of that genre.[5] Licona concludes from genre identification that the prior probability for fact alteration on the part of the Gospel authors is fairly high, which runs directly contrary to Hemer's crucial cautions about the "slippery ground of parallels," the fluidity of the type, and the need to judge a work on its individual performance.[6]

In other words, even if one or more of the Gospels were consciously written as, in some sense, a Greco-Roman βίος, this would not give us much clear information in and of itself about how much historicity to expect.[7] Such a conclusion would certainly not set the sort of "ceiling" on historicity that Licona envisages, leading us positively to *expect* some alteration of facts on the part of the author.

Here we need to make a distinction between two different meanings of "flexible." Richard Burridge states repeatedly that the genre of βίος was flexible and diverse, containing works having varied relationships to historical accuracy:

> Thus βίος *is a genre capable of flexibility, adaptation, and growth,* and we should avoid facile and simplistic definitions. Furthermore, βίος nestles among neighbouring genres such as historiography, rhetoric, encomium, moral philosophy, polemic and the novel or story, with some examples tending towards overlap with one or more neighbouring borders and yet still remaining recognizably within the genre of βίος ....Therefore, it is eminently sensible to begin a search for the genre of the gospels within the sphere of βίος, *but such an attempt to consider the gospels as βίοι must always take account of this wider picture of its flexible and developing nature.*[8]

---

[5] Jonathan Peterson and Michael Licona, "Why Are There Differences in the Gospels? An Interview With Michael R. Licona," *Bible Gateway Blog*, June 27, 2017, https://www.biblegateway.com/blog/2017/06/why-are-there-differences-in-the-gospels-an-interview-with-michael-r-licona/; Licona, *Why Are there Differences in the Gospels? What We Can Learn From Ancient Biography*, (Oxford: Oxford University Press, 2017), p. 5.

[6] Strangely, in his 2010 book Licona acknowledged something close to this point himself, stating, "Because the commitment to accuracy and the liberties taken could vary greatly between biographers, identifying the canonical Gospels as *bioi* will take us only so far. Each Evangelist will need to be judged by his performance." *The Resurrection of Jesus: A New Historiographical Approach* (Downer's Grover: IVP Academic, 2010), p. 204. He even cites the passage of Hemer about judging Luke on his performance. Unless this 2010 passage includes the unstated (and unargued) assumption that every author of a βίος can be counted on to take at least *some* liberties, both Licona's practice and theory elsewhere are inconsistent with this acknowledgement. And if he is assuming that each and every author of a βίος would take at least *some* historical liberties, he is doing so without justification in Burridge's research or anywhere else.

[7] See footnote 8.

[8] Richard Burridge, *What Are the Gospels? A Comparison With Greco-Roman Biography* (Grand Rapids, Eerdmans, 2004), p. 77. Emphasis in original. Burridge's comment that some βίοι overlapped with neighboring genres, including an openly fictional genre like the novel, is interesting when we consider whether the identification of the Gospels as βίοι actually provides a "floor" of historicity. What is to

Our survey of ten works in total has provided a clear picture of the βίος genre: there is a family resemblance, yet the overall impression is of a diverse and flexible genre, able to cope with variations in any one work. The major determining feature is the subject; all these works concentrate on one individual.[9]

The word "flexible" can function in more than one way, and it is important to be clear about it. These statements seem merely to imply that the genre as a whole is "flexible," in the sense that some works within it may be more careless about facts or more inclined to invention than others. On one obvious interpretation of this concept of flexibility, it seems that even if there were a conscious decision on the part of a Gospel author to write a βίος, such an intention could be entirely compatible with inerrancy in the old sense of the word, without any deliberate fact alteration whatsoever.

Neither Burridge nor Licona has shown that documents in the βίος genre are expected, as a matter of prior probability, to be *no more* historically scrupulous or factually reliable than some upper limit. The idea that the genre itself is flexible could mean that within that genre, various individual works and authors may fall at different points on a spectrum of factual reliability. Some *given* author writing in the genre might choose to be fanciful or to intermingle fiction with his writing, or some given author might be careless about checking his facts, use poor sources, or have a bad memory. But some other author, as far as we can tell, could be extremely scrupulous and knowledgeable. This is a major reason why the genre identification is not very informative. The genre itself contains a wide range of works. This also means that the carelessness or propaganda of one author does not in and of itself mean that some *other* author, writing within such a diverse genre, did not have far higher standards for himself.

To say, then, that the *genre* is "diverse and flexible" as far as its (the genre's) relationship to historical reliability is by no means to say that every author and work *within* the genre displays a "flexible" relationship to truth and historical reliability. To apply the word "flexible" in that second way on the basis of genre identification would be to commit what philosophers call a scope error. Compare, for example, the following two statements:

---

prevent a literary device theorist from deciding that one of the Gospels (perhaps John, which is often treated as less historical than the others) exemplifies a "mixed" genre and overlaps with a less historical genre than βίος? In that case even the "floor" of historicity could be very significantly lowered. Hence even the hoped-for value of the genre identification in limiting the ahistoricity of the Gospels may be a will-o'-the-wisp. The "floor" could suddenly sink into the basement.

[9] Ibid., p. 184.

The church body of First Baptist is an ethnically diverse group.

Mr. Jones, a member of First Baptist, is an ethnically diverse individual.

Obviously these are quite different statements, and the second does not follow from the first, even if we waive the fact that it is unclear what it means to say that a single individual is ethnically diverse.

At times Licona and Burridge appear to use the word "flexible" and its cognates in the second way—implying that *each individual author* writing in the genre considered himself to have a "flexible" relationship with truth. I have given quotations in Chapter V that illustrate the way that they use the genre designation to set a "ceiling" for the reliability of the Gospels, implying that each Gospel should be expected to contain at least some fictionalization. Here I want to note in those same quotations the way that a scope error in the application of "flexible" facilitates that strong use of genre. Licona says,

> I have noted above that that there is now somewhat of a consensus…that the Gospels belong to the genre of Greco-Roman biography (*bioi*) and that this genre offered biographers a great deal of flexibility to rearrange material [and] invent speeches to communicate the teachings…of the subject.[10]

The phrase "offered biographers a great deal of flexibility" is confusing, for it implies that the mere fact that an author was writing in this genre would cause him, individually, to feel licensed to make such changes. But Licona and Burridge have not shown that at all. Similarly, Licona says,

> Authorial intent often eludes us, and the motives behind the reports are often difficult to determine ….Because *bios* was a flexible genre, it is often difficult to determine where history ends and legend begins.[11]

But this would follow only if the "flexibility" of the genre meant that it was quite plausible that *each separate author was somewhat likely to include* at least some legendary elements. If a given author took a far more historically scrupulous approach, and if we had reason to believe that he was doing so, then it would *not* be difficult to determine where history ends and legend begins. One could simply take the entire document historically, since the prior probability would be quite low that there would be *any* legend in that document, by that author, at all.

---

[10] Licona, *The Resurrection of Jesus*, p. 593.

[11] Ibid., p. 34.

Burridge makes a similar shift between the flexibility of the genre as a whole and the flexibility felt by *individual authors* in representing history, though he throws in the word "may" to qualify it:

> [T]he biographical hypothesis has some significant *historical implications* for the issues of authenticity and truth. We saw early in this study that ancient βίοι nestled between historiography and rhetorical encomium, taking from history the combining of stories and events into a written narrative, with the concentration on one person coming from encomium....Even ancient historiography had more opportunities for interpretation than modern canons of accurate reporting, but the writer of βίος appears to have more selectivity for his treatment of a subject than would be true for history. Thus, Xenophon shows that he knows, and disapproves, of certain aspects of Agesilaus' conduct...when writing his *Hellenica*, yet he suppresses these when he writes his separate account of *Agesilaus*. Even more freedom was allowed for encomium...Therefore, simply discovering that the gospels are βίοι does not answer all our questions about their historicity or truth, but it may give an indication of the freedom each of the evangelists has in constructing a portrait of Jesus.[12]

Neither the statement that Greco-Roman biography "nestles" between historiography and encomium nor the claim that some biographers seem to have shaded their pictures of their protagonists supports the conclusion that the identification of the Gospels as βίος gives us an indication of the freedom that *each individual evangelist* believed that he had to alter facts in writing about Jesus.[13]

For that conclusion we would need far stronger evidence of some kind—perhaps inductive evidence—for the conclusion that the *majority* of authors writing in the βίος genre considered themselves licensed to play fast and loose with the facts at times. If we are to make as strong a claim as Licona's that we should expect fact-altering changes, the majority in question should be a hefty one, and we should also have no evidence to the contrary concerning the Gospel authors. To put it mildly, such strong inductive evidence concerning a hefty majority of authors of βίος is lacking (despite confident scholarly generalizations with very little supporting argument), and there is plenty of reason to think, on the contrary, that the Gospel authors themselves were straightforward in their concept of truth (see Part Three).

---

[12] Burridge, *What Are the Gospels*, pp. 259–260. Emphasis in original.

[13] The idea of slanting the facts (by selection) in favor of the subject of the biography, cited here by Burridge, seems closely related to what Licona calls the "law of biographical relevance." But this is the one thing that Licona says he does *not* observe clearly in the Gospels. Licona, *Why Are There Differences*, p. 183.

2. Remaking ancient people in the image of modern professors

Burridge's reference to ancient history more broadly brings me to the next crucial point, concerning the alleged practice and mindset of "the ancients." I have argued so far that even if one or more of the Gospels were identified as Greco-Roman βίος, this would not at all mean that that author considered himself licensed, in virtue merely of the decision to write in that form, to alter historical facts.

But what if we believed that authors at the time of the Gospels *in general* considered themselves licensed to change historical facts? What if someone thought that there were evidence to this effect aside from whether or not one specifically identified the Gospels as βίοι?

One person to advocate such a sweeping view of the way "ancient people" thought is Richard Burridge himself. Here is a rather breathtaking claim about a special view of truth held by ancient people:

> We must not transfer these modern concepts to ancient texts without considering their understandings of truth and myth, lies and fiction. To modern minds, 'myth' means something untrue, a 'fairy-story'; in the ancient world, myth was the medium whereby profound truth, more truly true than mere facts could ever be, was communicated. The opposite of truth is not fiction, but lies and deception; yet even history can be used to deceive, while stories can bring truth. This issue of truth and fiction in the ancient world is too complex to cover in detail here. However, the most important point to remember is that the ancients were more interested in the moral worth and philosophical value of statements than their logical status, in truth more than facts.... Unfortunately, the debate between so-called 'conservatives' and 'liberals' about authenticity is often conducted in twenty-first-century terms. As one student asked me, 'Why does John keep fabricating material about Jesus despite his expressed concern for the "truth"?' However, the negative connotation of 'fabrication' is modern.[14]

Speaking of anachronism, this unqualified piece of psychologizing makes men of the ancient world sound an awful lot like 21st-century humanities professors influenced by watered-down postmodernism—an interesting coincidence.

In support of these large generalizations, Burridge offers the fact that the historian Tacitus appears to have invented a speech for a British chieftain named Calgacus to give to his troops before a battle.[15] Burridge then goes on to imply that the author of John literally did not really care what Jesus historically said:

---

[14] Richard Burridge, *Four Gospels, One Jesus: A Symbolic Reading* (London: Society for Promoting Christian Knowledge, 2005), pp. 169–170.

[15] Tacitus, *Life of Agricola*, 30–32.

Thus, John's stress on 'truth' is not about 'documented fact', but the 'higher truth' of who Jesus is—which is why he writes in a biographical format. For him, Jesus is 'the way, the truth and the life', so his Jesus says these words (Jn. 14:6), just as Tacitus' Calgacus condemns Roman imperialism, or Matthew's Jesus speaks from a mountain as another Moses. To ask whether Jesus or Calgacus actually spoke these words is to miss the point completely. These are not lies or fiction—they are ways of bringing out the truth about the subject which the author wishes to tell the audience.[16]

One wonders if there something so improbable about the idea that a popular teacher in the hills of Galilee would actually speak on a mountainside to a large crowd. Why should we even think that Matthew invents, for symbolic purposes, the claim that Jesus really did so? And what reason do we have to think that John had no qualms whatsoever about making up a saying of Jesus based only on his own feeling that Jesus was, "for him," the way, the truth, and the life?

I will devote an entire chapter (the next) to refuting hasty extrapolations from the fact that ancient historians sometimes did invent or partially invent speeches. For now I will simply make a few points: a) A made-up speech inserted by Tacitus in the middle of a work that does, *pace* Burridge, concern itself with boring facts (such as the specific birth and death dates of Agricola)[17] is a thin reed on which to support a wide-ranging theory that the ancients generally didn't care much about literal facts but rather about "higher truth." b) If Tacitus invented the speech to criticize Roman imperialism, as Burridge implies, it tells us very little about the character of the historical chieftain Calgacus. c) Calgacus is not the subject of the life in question; Agricola is. d) Jesus and what he really taught were *prima facie* a great deal more important to the evangelists than the historical Calgacus was to Tacitus.

Licona tells us that a feature of ancient biography is that "the main subject's character is illuminated through his words and deeds."[18] But if an *historical* person's character were illustrated merely by made-up sayings, as Burridge implies, where would the author's own knowledge of the person's character come from in the first place, and why should we believe that the main subject's character is illuminated by an invented saying? Should anyone find himself significantly more confident about George Washington's honesty after hearing the tale of the little axe and the cherry tree, though he knows that it is a pious fiction? Why should we think that the ancients were men of such fuzzy thinking that they would be influenced in that

---

[16] Burridge, *Four Gospels, One Jesus*, pp. 170–171.

[17] Tacitus, *Life of Agricola*, 44.

[18] Licona, *Why Are There Differences*, pp. 3–4.

way? At first in the passage Burridge admits that such practice would be fiction; he simply wishes to tell moderns that the ancients didn't think fiction in history was a bad thing, and he implies that neither should we. By the end he is redefining the word "fiction" to declare that non-factual invention isn't fiction at all. At least he refrains from claiming that such bald invention should be called "paraphrase."

Recall that Licona says, of John,

> John often chose to sacrifice accuracy on the ground level of precise reporting, preferring to provide his readers with an accurate, higher-level view of the person and mission of Jesus.[19]

And Licona implies that objections to his approach to the Gospels are based upon a "nineteenth century" view of truthful historical reporting:

> And why require the Gospels to have been written using literary conventions for historical reporting that were not generally accepted until the nineteenth century while eschewing attempts to understand them within the cultural and literary context of their own day?[20]

Claims like Burridge's and Licona's are not new; they were addressed eloquently by the late New Testament scholar Leon Morris. In fact, it is rather striking how well Morris is acquainted with language that sounds exactly like that of Burridge:

> John's stress on the truth serves as a warning against seeing him as an incurable theological romancer. He does not see truth as comparatively unimportant. On the contrary, for him it is of a critical importance. It is unlikely accordingly that he will tamper with the facts with a view simply to edification. It is the *truth* he is seeking. No one could make truth a central concept in a writing like this Gospel if he knew that the facts were other than he was reporting them. He must have held firmly that his writing expressed the truth as nearly as he could make it.
>
> It is, of course, possible that I have too limited a conception of truth. Certainly some recent writers think that an author might have a regard for "truth" that is perfectly compatible with a readiness to narrate "incidents" that lack factual basis. They suggest that John is like this, and that he is more interested in the truth than in the facts. They may be right; but I cannot see it that way. It is not that the idea shocks me. I see that a writer may take up such a position...What I cannot see is any real

---

[19] Licona, *Why Are There Differences*, p. 115. In support of this far-reaching claim, Licona cites the entire chapter on John in Burridge's *Four Gospels, One Jesus. Why Are There Differences*, p. 239, n. 11.

[20] Michael Licona, "Are We Reading an Adapted Form of Jesus' Teachings in John's Gospel?" *Risen Jesus*, Sept. 29, 2017, https://www.risenjesus.com/reading-adapted-form-jesus-teachings-johns-gospel.

evidence that this is what John is doing. As far as I am able I have thought through all his references to truth, and they do not seem to allow such an interpretation. He may well mean more than we normally mean by truth. I think he does. But he does not mean less.[21]

To take but one example of many, when the author of John says that the one who saw bore record and that his record is true in John 19.35, he is referring directly to something that the beloved disciple witnessed empirically—the piercing of Jesus' side and the flow of blood and water in verse 34. He goes on in verse 36 to give this event a theological significance as the fulfillment of a prophecy, but it has that theological significance only because it really happened in the world of space and time.[22]

In the remainder of this chapter I will rebut Burridge's claim that "the negative connotation of 'fabrication' is modern" by quoting some non-biblical ancient authors, including historiographers. My point is not (needless to say) that the Gospel authors had read Polybius or Thucydides, though Luke might have been acquainted with some ancient historians. My point is that Burridge's fashionably sweeping statements about how ancient people thought are simply false and that we have a large amount of evidence that ancient authors and presumably readers placed a high value upon literal truth. Burridge's implication, and at times Licona's, is that any reference to truth made by an ancient author must have a large asterisk by it. It must be reinterpreted, because those ancient folks simply meant something significantly different by "truth" than what we would mean and what we would take them to mean. I contend that such a view cannot stand up to the data and would require us to engage in an unjustified pretense of mind-reading, reinterpreting many straightforward, emphatic references to telling things as they actually happened. We would have to give such statements instead an all-too-modern (or, more precisely, postmodern) meaning that happens to be convenient to the program of literary theorists. Such an approach is far more anachronistic than the allegedly "nineteenth-century" viewpoint that Burridge and Licona are dismissing.

3. Ancient people speak

I begin with a couple of definitions of truth by two undeniably ancient authors— Aristotle and Plato. Both philosophers define "truth" in a way that anticipates and

---

[21] Leon Morris, *Studies in the Fourth Gospel* (Grand Rapids, Eerdmans Publishing Company, 1969), pp.119–120.

[22] See Lydia McGrew, "Fake Points Don't Make Points," *What's Wrong With the World*, November 8, 2017, http://whatswrongwiththeworld.net/2017/11/fake_points_dont_make_points.html. See also Chapter X, section 4.

provides the kernel of what is known in later philosophy as the "correspondence view of truth." Aristotle famously said, "To say of what is that it is not, or of what is not that it is, is false, while to say of what is that it is, and of what is not that it is not, is true."[23] Plato says something almost identical: "[A] true proposition says that which is, and a false proposition says that which is not[.]"[24] I will try to refrain from pointing out explicitly that the authors I am quoting were not writing in the nineteenth century. I ask the reader to bear that fact in mind as we go on.

From the historian Thucydides (c. 460–400 B.C.), *The History of the Peloponnesian War*:[25]

> But as to the actions of the war, I have not been content to report them on the authority of any chance informant, or from my own conception of them; but either from personal knowledge where I was present, or after the most careful investigation possible in every case where I gained my information from others. Very laborious were these inquiries; since those who were present in the several actions did not all give the same account of the same affair, but as they were swayed by favour to one side or the other, or as their memory served them. Possibly this avoidance of any fabulous embellishment may make my work less entertaining; but I shall be well content if those shall pronounce my history useful, who desire to gain a view of events as they really did happen, and as they are very likely, in accordance with human nature, to repeat themselves at some future time . . . And it is designed rather as a possession for ever than as a mere prize composition to be listened to for the moment.[26]

As in the case of Lucian, quoted multiple times below, Thucydides has a famous

---

[23] Aristotle, *Metaphysics* 4.1011b.1, as quoted in Marian David, "The Correspondence Theory of Truth," *The Stanford Encyclopedia of Philosophy* (Fall 2016 Edition), Edward N. Zalta (ed.), https://plato.stanford.edu/archives/fall2016/entries/truth-correspondence/.

[24] Plato, *Cratylus* 385b. Trans. B. Jowett (1875), https://ebooks.adelaide.edu.au/p/plato/p71cra/cratylus.html.

[25] Though I was already familiar with a number of the quotations that follow, I compiled many of them by following a conference paper given by Darrell Bock, available in audio format. Darrell Bock, "How We Can and Should Use the Historiography of the Ancient World to Think About the Gospels," presented to the 68th annual meeting of the Evangelical Theological Society meeting, San Antonio, TX, November 15, 2016, http://www.wordmp3.com/details.aspx?id=23790. After tracking down each quotation in context, I decided what to quote here, sometimes using a different translation to make it easier for readers who want to find the material publicly available. Bock's paper is a valuable compendium. In the last few minutes of the presentation, Bock turns to Licona's book and the Gospels, and he seems to imply that Licona's ideas about the Gospels match the concepts of truthful history presented in the quotations in the rest of his paper. I find this evaluation puzzling, given Licona's insistence that ancient authors considered themselves licensed to alter the facts.

[26] Thucydides, *The History of the Peloponnesian War*, 1.21–22. Translated by W. Lucas Collins, *Thucydides* (London: William Blackwood and Sons, 1878), pp. 4–5.

quotation in this same work about speeches. I will be discussing that quotation in the next chapter. Suffice it to say here that, when literary device theorists focus on a small number of quotations from ancient historiographers that allow various degrees of license in reporting set-piece speeches, they tend to miss the forest by looking at some rare trees. The historian in question (here, Thucydides) places a great emphasis upon *literal accuracy* in the reporting of events. Any license allowed in the reportage of set-piece speeches does not (as they sometimes imply), turn the robust advocacy of literal truth on its head so that it is an arcane code for, "Real facts don't matter; only higher truth matters." In this chapter, then, I mean to draw attention to the forest, or, to change the metaphor, the chorus of ancient voices advocating literal truth in historical reporting.

In the above quotation, note Thucydides' scrupulous expressions concerning the sources of his information. He actually prefers to cite incidents where he was present. Richard Bauckham has pointed out that this emphasis upon eyewitness testimony as an historical "best practice" is common in ancient historians, and this of course fits extremely well with Luke's preface to his Gospel and his claim to have talked with those who were "eyewitnesses from the beginning."[27] What it does not show at all is a general ancient feeling that literal truth was not the aim and that literal truth could be readily set aside in the service of "higher truth."

Here is Polybius (c. 200–118 B.C.) on truth in reporting history (and even speeches):

> A historian should not try to astonish his readers by sensationalism, nor, like the tragic poets, seek after men's probable utterances and enumerate all the possible consequences of the events under consideration, but *simply record what really happened and was said, however commonplace*. For the object of history is the very opposite of that of tragedy. The tragic writer seeks by the most plausible language to thrill and charm the audience temporarily; the historian by real facts and real speeches seeks to instruct and convince serious students for all time. There it is the probable that counts, even though it be false, the object being to beguile the spectator; here it is the truth, the object being to benefit the student.[28]

Here is Dionysius of Helicarnassus (fl. 20 B.C.) writing about how he gathered information about his subject. Notice the emphasis upon not having in-

---

[27] Richard Bauckham, *Jesus and the Eyewitnesses: The Gospels as Eyewitness Testimony*, 2nd ed. (Grand Rapids, Eerdmans, 2017), p. 9. See also Chapter 6 of the same work.

[28] Polybius, *The Histories*, II.56.10–12. As translated in Frank Walbank, "Polybius," Britannica.com, https://www.britannica.com/biography/Polybius. Emphasis added.

vented events and having gathered information from what he deemed to be reliable sources.

> Having thus given the reason for my choice of subject, I wish now to say something concerning the sources I used while preparing for my task. For it is possible that those who have already read Hieronymus, Timaeus, Polybius, or any of the other historians whom I just now mentioned,...since they will not have found in those authors many things mentioned by me, will suspect me of inventing them and will demand to know how I came by the knowledge of these particulars. Lest anyone, therefore, should entertain such an opinion of me, it is best that I should state in advance what narratives and records I have used as sources. I arrived in Italy at the very time that Augustus Caesar put an end to the civil war, in the middle of the one hundred and eighty-seventh Olympiad. And having from that time to this present day, a period of twenty-two years, lived at Rome, learned the language of the Romans and acquainted myself with their writings, I have devoted myself during all that time to matters bearing upon my subject. Some information I received orally from men of the greatest learning, with whom I associated; and the rest I gathered from histories written by the approved Roman authors ... With these works, which are like the Greek annalistic accounts, as a basis, I set about the writing of my history.[29]

It is difficult to imagine an approach more at odds with the dismissive attitude toward literal truth that Burridge attributes to the ancients.

Here is Cicero (106–43 B.C.) on the nature and goal of history:

> Indeed, all rules respecting it [history] are obvious to common view; for who is ignorant that it is the first law in writing history, that the historian must not dare to tell any falsehood, and the next, that he must be bold enough to tell the whole truth? Also, that there must be no suspicion of partiality in his writings, or of personal animosity?[30]

One or two quotations from Josephus (c. A.D. 37–100) are pertinent:

> There have been indeed some bad men, who have attempted to calumniate my history: and took it to be a kind of scholastic performance, for the exercise of young men. A strange sort of accusation, and calumny this! Since every one that undertakes to deliver the history of actions truly, ought to know them accurately himself,

---

[29] Dionysius of Helicarnassus, *Roman Antiquities*, I.7.1–3. Trans. Earnest Cary, 1937, http://penelope.uchicago.edu/Thayer/E/Roman/Texts/Dionysius_of_Halicarnassus/1A*.html.

[30] Cicero, *De Oratore*, 2.62. Translated by J. S. Watson, 1875, https://archive.org/stream/ciceroonoratorya00ciceuoft/ciceroonoratorya00ciceuoft_djvu.txt.

in the first place, as either having been concerned in them himself, or been informed of them by such as knew them.[31]

John Wenham gives the phrase "know them accurately himself" as "obtain an exact knowledge of them himself."[32] Again, the emphasis is upon accuracy and the preference for sources who have actually participated in the events, which again argues very strongly against an ancient ideal of "higher" rather than literal truth.

Josephus also emphasizes the dependence of the reader upon the historical author for his facts, and the burden this places upon the author to be accurate:

> But the principal scope that authors ought to aim at above all the rest, is to speak accurately, and to speak truly; for the satisfaction of those that are otherwise unacquainted with such transactions; and obliged to believe what these writers inform them of.[33]

Darrell Bock,[34] Colin Hemer,[35] and others have noted that Josephus did not live up to the standards of accuracy he professed. In a later chapter I will discuss a case in which Josephus appears to have shaded the truth to his own advantage. Propaganda and a lack of due regard for the truth were by no means unknown in the ancient world, as they are not unknown in our world. But Josephus' failure to live up to the standards he professed do not show anything remotely like the different ancient concept of truth that Burridge claims. Very much to the contrary. Josephus has to pay lip service to existing standards of historical accuracy even if he does not follow them himself at all times. Hypocrisy is the tribute that vice pays to virtue; if Josephus is sometimes a hypocrite, he knows what he is expected to aspire to. The witness of Josephus attests to the fact that deviations from truthfulness on the part of ancient authors through carelessness, bias, or deliberate distortion were instances of universal human faults, flying in the face of the best practice of their own time. As Hemer says, "Rigorous concepts of history existed in Luke's world."[36]

---

[31] Josephus, *Against Apion*, 1.10. Trans. by William Whiston, 1737, http://penelope.uchicago.edu/josephus/apion-1.html.

[32] John Wenham, "The Identification of Luke," *Evangelical Quarterly* 63.1 (1991), p. 25.

[33] Josephus, *Antiquities*, XIV.1. Trans. by William Whiston, 1737, http://penelope.uchicago.edu/josephus/ant-14.html.

[34] Darrell Bock, "How We Can and Should Use the Historiography of the Ancient World to Think About the Gospels."

[35] Hemer, *The Book of Acts in the Setting of Hellenistic History*, p. 99.

[36] Ibid., p. 94.

Hemer makes, moreover, a shrewd comment about the contrasts between Josephus and Luke:

> Josephus, then, makes strong professions of accuracy in terms reminiscent of the best standards current in antiquity....[W]e may entertain grave doubts whether he will stand the scrutiny of his own claims. Luke expresses himself briefly and with restraint in similar terms, and our brief comparison above implies a *prima facie* impression that Luke acquits himself very much better....[37]

Hemer's entire book is a testimony to the vast amount of evidence that further supports that impression of Luke's literal accuracy.

The historian Arrian (c. A.D. 86–160) gives an interesting account of how he gathered information for his life of Alexander the Great:

> Different authors have given different accounts of Alexander's life; and there is no one about whom more have written, or more at variance with each other. But in my opinion the narratives of Ptolemy and Aristobulus are more worthy of credit than the rest; Aristobulus, because he served under king Alexander in his expedition, and Ptolemy, not only because he accompanied Alexander in his expedition, but also because he was himself a king afterwards, and falsification of facts would have been more disgraceful to him than to any other man. Moreover, they are both more worthy of credit, because they compiled their histories after Alexander's death, when neither compulsion was used nor reward offered them to write anything different from what really occurred.[38]

Modern readers, obviously, are not going to share Arrian's snobbish idea that Ptolemy was more likely to be truthful because he became a king. But Arrian's aristocratic bias, despite our disagreement with it, nonetheless shows his goal—to get at the truth in a straightforward sense of "truth." Similarly, we see here again the common preference for those who actually participated in the actions recounted. In addition, Arrian considers it important to use sources who (in his opinion) are less likely to be biased, since they wrote after Alexander was dead and could not pressure them.

Plutarch (c. A.D. 46–119), who will figure so largely in a later chapter, distinguishes between what he was able to discover about events long ago and more recent events. In his preface to a life of Theseus (a dubiously historical character in Greek literature), he offers a bit of an apology:

---

[37] Ibid., p. 99.

[38] Arrian, Preface to the *Anabasis of Alexander*. Trans. by E.J. Chinnock, 1884, https://en.wikisource.org/wiki/The_Anabasis_of_Alexander.

Just as geographers...crowd on to the outer edges of their maps the parts of the earth which elude their knowledge, with explanatory notes that "What lies beyond is sandy desert without water and full of wild beasts," or "blind marsh," or "Scythian cold," or "frozen sea," so in the writing of my Parallel Lives, now that I have traversed those periods of time which are accessible to probable reasoning and which afford basis for a history dealing with facts, I might well say of the earlier periods: "What lies beyond is full of marvels and unreality, a land of poets and fabulists, of doubt and obscurity."

But, having decided to write about Theseus despite the difficulty in finding out much about him by "probable reasoning," he asks for his readers' indulgence:

May I therefore succeed in purifying Fable, making her submit to reason and take on the semblance of History. But where she obstinately disdains to make herself credible, and refuses to admit any element of probability, I shall pray for kindly readers, and such as receive with indulgence the tales of antiquity.[39]

In other words, Plutarch warns his readers explicitly that this particular life will not have the objectivity he prefers, because he cannot base it on knowledgeable, credible sources. These are partly, he warns, "tales of antiquity." The very fact that Plutarch felt the need to place such a warning into this preface indicates that, for more recent periods of time that *are* open to "probable reasoning" and "afford a basis for a history dealing with facts," Plutarch wants his readers to trust his factual accuracy.

In the introduction to his *Life of Alexander*, Plutarch makes a famous contrast between history and biography which is important not to misunderstand:

It is the life of Alexander the king, and of Caesar, who overthrew Pompey, that I am writing in this book, and the multitude of the deeds to be treated is so great that I shall make no other preface than to entreat my readers, in case I do not tell of all the famous actions of these men, nor even speak exhaustively at all in each particular case, but in epitome for the most part, not to complain. For it is not Histories that I am writing, but Lives; and in the most illustrious deeds there is not always a manifestation of virtue or vice, nay, a slight thing like a phrase or a jest often makes a greater revelation of character than battles when thousands fall, or the greatest armaments, or sieges of cities. Accordingly, just as painters get the likenesses in their portraits from the face and the expression of the eyes, wherein

---

[39] Plutarch, *The Life of Theseus*, 1. Plutarch's *Parallel Lives* will feature largely in this book. Unless otherwise noted, all translations are from the Loeb edition, translated by Bernadotte Perrin, 1914–1926, and available in the public domain at http://penelope.uchicago.edu/Thayer/E/Roman/Texts/Plutarch/Lives/. I will not give separate URLs for each of the *Lives* cited.

the character shows itself, but make very little account of the other parts of the body, so I must be permitted to devote myself rather to the signs of the soul in men, and by means of these to portray the life of each, leaving to others the description of their great contests.[40]

As Craig Keener points out, the distinction here between biography and history concerns the intimate nature of the incidents related in *Lives*. Plutarch's distinction is "in the first place an excuse for summarizing or omitting historically important facts…to focus instead on character-revealing incidents."[41] One should not, therefore, take Plutarch to mean that biography is less factually true than history. *Prima facie*, if the "slight things" recorded are to manifest the character of a real, historical individual, they should be factually true.

4. Lucian and the abuse of Lucian

By this long, largely chronological survey, we have come to Lucian of Samosata (c. A.D. 125–after 180), who has quite a lot to say about truth and history in his appropriately titled *How to Write History*. Lucian is explicit, even insistent, about the importance of factual truth:

> Now some think they can make a satisfactory distinction in history between what gives pleasure and what is useful, and for this reason work eulogy into it as giving pleasure and enjoyment to its readers; but do you see how far they are from the truth? In the first place, the distinction they draw is false: history has one task and one only—what is useful —and that comes from truth alone. As to what gives pleasure, it is certainly better if it is there incidentally, like good looks in an athlete…. So it is with history. If she were to make the mistake of dealing in pleasure as well she would attract a host of lovers, but as long as she keeps only what is hers alone in all its fullness—I mean the publication of the truth—she will give little thought to beauty.[42]

Lucian here emphatically disagrees with anyone who thinks that usefulness is best served by altering the truth. Rather, the uses of history are served only by telling the actual truth.

---

[40] Plutarch, *The Life of Alexander*, 1.1–3.

[41] Craig Keener, "Ancient Biography and the Gospels: Introduction" in Craig S. Keener and Edward T. Wright, eds., *Biographies and Jesus: What Does it Mean for the Gospels to be Biographies?* (Lexington, KY: Emeth Press, 2016), p. 14. Keener is quoting and agreeing on this point with Thomas Hägg, *The Art of Biography in Antiquity* (Cambridge, Cambridge University Press, 2012), p. 269.

[42] Lucian, *How to Write History*, 9. Trans. H. W. Fowler and F. G. Fowler, 1905, http://www.sacred-texts.com/cla/luc/wl2/wl210.htm. The translators' version of the title is *The Way to Write History*, but I have used the more widely known translation of the title in footnotes.

The historian's one task is to tell the thing as it happened. This he cannot do, if he is Artaxerxes's physician trembling before him, or hoping to get a purple cloak, a golden chain, a horse of the Nisaean breed, in payment for his laudations. A fair historian, a Xenophon, a Thucydides, will not accept that position. He may nurse some private dislikes, but he will attach far more importance to the public good, and set the truth high above his hate; he may have his favourites, but he will not spare their errors. For history, I say again, has this and this only for its own; if a man will start upon it, he must sacrifice to no god but Truth; he must neglect all else; his sole rule and unerring guide is this—to think not of those who are listening to him now, but of the yet unborn who shall seek his converse.[43]

Hemer points out the rather striking fact that Lucian's statement here sounds almost exactly like the famous dictum of the nineteenth century historian Leopold von Ranke that history seeks to show what actually happened—*wie es eigentlich gewesen.*[44] Again, these emphatic statements about sacrificing to no god but truth and telling what actually happened are light-years away from Burridge's picture of the ancient man who cares for "higher truth" rather than for mere facts.

Lucian again:

Facts are not to be collected at haphazard, but with careful, laborious, repeated investigation; when possible, a man should have been present and seen for himself; failing that, he should prefer the disinterested account, selecting the informants least likely to diminish or magnify from partiality. And here comes the occasion for exercising the judgement in weighing probabilities.[45]

What can "weighing probabilities" in one's sources possibly refer to here other than the probability of historical truth?

Lucian, yet again:

Above all, let him bring a mind like a mirror, clear, gleaming-bright, accurately centred, displaying the shape of things just as he receives them, free from distortion, false colouring, and misrepresentation. His concern is different from that of the orators—what historians have to relate is fact and will speak for itself, for it has

---

[43] Ibid., 39. Emphasis added. Michael Licona in his book on the resurrection and historiography inaccurately summarizes this paragraph as applying to "history apart from biography." *The Resurrection of Jesus: A New Historiographical Approach* (Downer's Grover: IVP Academic, 2010), p. 35 n. 24. There is not the slightest hint of such a distinction between different types of historical writing in Lucian's statement, or in its context, or anywhere else in *How to Write History*.

[44] Hemer, *The Book of Acts in the Setting of Hellenistic History*, p. 91.

[45] Lucian, *How to Write History*, 47.

already happened: what is required is arrangement and exposition. So they must look not for what to say but how to say it.[46]

Any attempt to use the reference here to "arrangement" to grant license to use fictionalizing literary devices such as Licona advocates would be extremely strained. It is obviously possible to arrange historical material without deliberately making it look like things happened in a way that is factually inaccurate. Lucian's emphasis upon factual truth is again unmistakable, and the metaphor of the mind like a mirror is one that I chose for this book even before I had read this particular quotation.

Lucian, again:

> History then should be written in that spirit, with truthfulness and an eye to future expectations rather than with adulation and a view to the pleasure of present praise. There is your rule and standard for impartial history.[47]

In other words, again and again Lucian hammers home the theme of impartiality and factual truthfulness.

What is astonishing here is that a reader of Licona's book would get a very different picture of Lucian. Licona is fond of a rather uninformative passage in this same work that does not in any way advocate the alteration of fact. Here is the quotation from Lucian that Licona cites over and over again:

> After the preface, long or short in proportion to the subject, should come an easy natural transition to the narrative; for the body of the history which remains is nothing from beginning to end but a long narrative; it must therefore be graced with the narrative virtues—smooth, level, and consistent progress, neither soaring nor crawling, and the charm of lucidity—which is attained, as I remarked above, partly by the diction, and partly by the treatment of connected events. For, though all parts must be independently perfected, when the first is complete the second will be brought into essential connection with it, and attached like one link of a chain to another; there must be no possibility of separating them; no mere bundle of parallel threads; the first is not simply to be next to the second, but part of it, their extremities intermingling.[48]

The reader will search in vain in this generalized paragraph for any reference whatsoever to an alteration of fact. Lucian is telling the writer of history to make his narrative flow well. Lucian does not say in this paragraph *how* the author is to

---

[46] Ibid., 51.

[47] Ibid., 63.

[48] Ibid., 55.

bring events into connection with one another. There are, of course, many different ways for a good writer to make one event flow well into another. One might, for example, talk about how events are causally related. Or one might group events by subject without in any way altering their chronology, showing the characteristics of an historical figure by giving multiple illustrations. Or one might give an explicit (and truthful) chronological ordering. Earlier in *How to Write History* Lucian seems to suggest narrating military campaigns and battles by alternating between reporting what is going on with each side and then giving a "bird's-eye view" of the battle as a whole. He also suggests moving from one geographical part of a campaign to another.[49] These would be ways of connecting parts of a military narrative, but of course they have nothing to do with altered fact. There is *nothing whatsoever* in the paragraph quoted by Licona or anywhere else in the whole of *How to Write History* that advocates changing chronological facts.

Yet repeatedly Licona writes as if that is what Lucian is advocating. He also quotes a passage by Quintilian (c. A.D. 35–100) that, similarly, says *not a single word* about altering any historical fact whatsoever but only about style and flow:

> History does not so much demand full, rounded rhythms as a certain continuity of motion and connection of style. For all its members are closely linked together, while the fluidity of its style gives it great variety of movement; we may compare its motion to that of men, who link hands to steady their steps, and lend each other mutual support.[50]

Licona's use of these quotations—one from Lucian and one from Quintilian—is tendentious in the extreme. Says Licona,

> The point made by Lucian and Quintilian is that historians should connect pericopes in an artistic manner by interweaving content and linking one story to another. This interweaving and linking could be especially useful when the order of events and some specific details pertaining to them are unknown. In such a scenario, we might speculate that historians were also free to create narrative details, and that this would include synthetic chronological links. Indeed, classical scholars have often suggested these types of flexibilities when the ancients wrote history. Such a practice may be why we observe so many differences, even contradictions, in the way a pericope is reported by several authors.[51]

---

[49] Ibid., 49–50.

[50] Quintilian, *Institutio Oratoria*, 9.5.129 as given in Licona, *Why Are There Differences*, p. 90.

[51] Licona, *Why Are There Differences*, p. 90.

One cannot avoid some astonishment at the suggestion out of the blue—the "speculation"—unjustified by any statement at all in the passages quoted from Lucian and Quintilian, that historians felt free to create narrative details and so-called "synthetic chronological links," by which Licona means the alteration of chronology.

Here is Licona doing the same thing again:

> In light of instructions for good literature writing by Lucian and Quintilian, we determined that historians were permitted to craft peripheral details and connect events synthetically in order to produce a narrative that flows smoothly.[52]

Licona has now moved from "we might speculate" to "we determined," despite the fact that neither the speculation nor the determination is remotely licensed by Lucian's and Quintilian's generic comments about smoothness and style.

Licona goes on using this extreme over-reading of the passage in Lucian and applying it to the Gospels. When he states that either John or Mark must have changed the day when a woman anointed Jesus' feet in Passion Week, he brings up again Lucian's recommendation about joining events like links in a chain. He suggests that John may have deliberately written as if Jesus' feet were anointed on a Saturday, though he knew that they were actually anointed the following Wednesday, in order to narrate two stories about Mary of Bethany closer together.[53] He goes so far as to say this:

> Either Mark or John appear to have changed the day, using synthetic chronological placement in order to bind the anointing explicitly to a different context than where it actually occurred. Lucian would have smiled with approval. The event is presented as historical, but the stated chronology is artificial.[54]

This is truly an amazing twisting of Lucian. It is not only that Lucian does not say any such thing in the paragraph Licona is referring to, though that is bad enough. But more: Lucian is so emphatic about historical truth, beating the drum on the matter over and over again in the very same work. Yet from his own entirely unjustified interpretation of one paragraph about connecting events smoothly, Licona concludes that Lucian "would have smiled with approval" at an alteration of chronological fact.

---

[52] Ibid., p. 110.

[53] Ibid., p. 150.

[54] Ibid., p. 191.

In *Why Are There Differences in the Gospels?* Licona does not quote *a single one* of the *five separate passages* from Lucian that I have quoted here, emphasizing the importance of historical accuracy and truthfulness. These are surely relevant to the question of whether or not Lucian "would have smiled with approval" at an historical author's deliberate change of chronological fact. But while virtually ignoring those passages, Licona refers *six separate times* to his own highly dubious interpretation of the other single paragraph.[55]

Licona does refer in passing (without quoting) to just one of these passages, paragraph 39 beginning, "The historian's one task is to tell the thing as it happened." But Licona mentions it only in a footnote and only to downplay it by emphasizing another paragraph (58) that allows license in creating speeches:

> Even in view of his statement that the only task of the historian is to relate events as they had occurred, Lucian permitted the historian to use his oratorical skills in order to improve a speech (*Hist. conscr.* 39, 58).[56]

Again, I will be quoting and discussing Lucian's paragraph 58 about speeches in the next chapter. But here again we see the attempt to dismiss or turn attention away from the *absolutely unequivocal* statements of ancient historiographers concerning historical accuracy.

Lucian's advice on how to write history weighs heavily against a Burridge-like notion of "higher truth" as outweighing literal, historical truth in ancient writing. Yet a reader of Licona's book would get the distinct and entirely inaccurate impression that Lucian is very nearly an advocate of the literary devices (transferral, displacement, and the like) listed by Licona and that he illustrates a "flexible" ancient concept of truth.

This is not letting ancient people speak for themselves.

---

[55] Ibid., pp. 90, 110, 150, 185, 191, 196. In his larger book on historiography and the resurrection, Licona sometimes mentions (briefly) Lucian's statements on historical veracity. For example, in a footnote he accurately summarizes Lucian's call for good sources in *How to Write History*, paragraph 47. Michael Licona, *The Resurrection of Jesus*, p. 35, n. 24. But he sometimes misrepresents Lucian in that larger book as well. For example, in the same footnote he summarizes Lucian's paragraph 39 thus: "For writing history apart from biography, Lucian's dictum was: 'The sole mission of the historian is this: To tell it as it occurred' (39)." Lucian *does not* distinguish history from biography in this regard at all. Licona implies that Lucian's dictum that the historian must tell the thing as it occurred is restricted by Lucian to history "apart from biography," but this is false.

[56] Licona, *Why Are There Differences*, p. 226, n. 9.

5. Julius Africanus: "Nor shall a lie be contrived for the praise and glory of Christ"

I have saved the best for last, as a reward to the patient reader who has come this far through this long chapter. Sextus Julius Africanus (c. A.D. 160–240) was a Christian historian, a convert from paganism, whose works are chiefly known through fragments preserved by Eusebius, upon whom he was an influence.[57] In his *Letter to Aristides*, Julius Africanus proposes a solution to the alleged discrepancies between Matthew's and Luke's genealogies of Jesus, based upon the Old Testament practice of Levirate marriage.

First, the very fact that Africanus is attempting a harmonization on so dry and dusty a matter as Jesus' literal genealogy already calls into question the Burridge-style dismissal of the importance of "mere facts" to the ancients, their preference for "profound truth, more truly true than mere facts could ever be," and their willingness to fabricate literal facts in the service of this alleged profound truth.

But second, Africanus expressly addresses the idea of fabrication in connection with the facts about Jesus Christ. Apparently in Africanus's time some were suggesting that perhaps the evangelists invented some of the names in their genealogies in order to make the theological point that Jesus is prophet, priest, and king. Africanus condemns their suggestion in the strongest possible terms:

> Some indeed incorrectly allege that this discrepant enumeration and mixing of the names both of priestly men, as they think, and royal, was made properly, in order that Christ might be shown rightfully to be both Priest and King; as if any one disbelieved this, or had any other hope than this, that Christ is the High Priest of His Father, who presents our prayers to Him, and a supramundane King, who rules by the Spirit those whom He has delivered, a cooperator in the government of all things. And this is announced to us not by the catalogue of the tribes, nor by the mixing of the registered generations, but by the patriarchs and prophets. *Let us not therefore descend to such religious trifling as to establish the kingship and priesthood of Christ by the interchanges of the names....The evangelists, therefore, would thus have spoken falsely, affirming what was not truth, but a fictitious commendation.* And for this reason the one traced the pedigree of Jacob the father of Joseph from David through Solomon; the other traced that of Heli also, though in a different way, the father of Joseph, from Nathan the son of David....To no purpose, then, is this

---

[57] The quotation that follows from Julius Africanus does not come from the paper by Bock, mentioned earlier. I found it while researching the church fathers' treatment of alleged Gospel discrepancies.

fabrication of theirs. *Nor shall an assertion of this kind prevail in the Church of Christ against the exact truth, so as that a lie should be contrived for the praise and glory of Christ.* For who does not know that most holy word of the apostle also, who, when he was preaching and proclaiming the resurrection of our Saviour, and confidently affirming the truth, said with great fear, If any say that Christ is not risen, and we assert and have believed this, and both hope for and preach that very thing, we are false witnesses of God, in alleging that He raised up Christ, whom He raised not up? And if he who glorifies God the Father is thus afraid lest he should seem a false witness in narrating a marvelous fact, how should not he be justly afraid, who tries to establish the truth by a false statement, preparing an untrue opinion? For if the generations are different, and trace down no genuine seed to Joseph, and if all has been stated only with the view of establishing the position of Him who was to be born—to confirm the truth, namely, that He who was to be would be king and priest, there being at the same time no proof given, but the dignity of the words being brought down to a feeble hymn,—it is evident that no praise accrues to God from that, since it is a falsehood, but rather judgment returns on him who asserts it, because he vaunts an unreality as though it were reality.[58]

Are there any questions? Julius rejects completely any notion that Jesus' symbolic value as both priest and king could be enhanced or supported by a fictional representation of his genealogy. For the Gospel authors to do so, says Julius, would have been to produce a "feeble hymn" which could bring no praise or glory to God but rather judgement upon the fabricator. Julius Africanus recognizes and emphasizes a point I shall return to in Part Three: Fake points don't make points.

Theological value does not arise from putatively historical events that did not really occur. Julius Africanus would have agreed with the following succinct statement from Leon Morris:

> In the face of those who assert that to John the spiritual significance is everything and the historicity immaterial, the question must be pressed, "What is the theological meaning of something that never happened?" The very idea of bringing out theological significance seems to imply respect for the facts. *What did not happen can scarcely be called redemptive.*[59]

Interestingly enough, quite a few other ancient people seem to have agreed. So let's let ancient people speak for themselves.

---

[58] Julius Africanus, *Letter to Aristides*, I. Trans. Alexander Robinson and James Donaldson, 1899, http://www.newadvent.org/fathers/0614.htm. Emphasis added.

[59] Morris, *Studies in the Fourth Gospel*, p. 124. Emphasis added.

Summary
Let Ancient People Speak for Themselves

- Even if an author were influenced by the genre of Greco-Roman βίος, this would be only very minimally informative about his historical intentions. We should recognize the limits of genre identification as a clue to historical reliability.

- By the theorists' own admission there is a wide range of historical accuracy among Greco-Roman βίοι, so authors will need to be judged on their own intentions and performance as we discover these independently.

- It is not true that it was part and parcel of Greco-Roman βίοι to change historical facts.

- Richard Burridge claims that ancient people generally had a different view of truth and of the legitimacy of fabrication than we do in modern times.

- Burridge's view is false. We can see its falsehood by quotation after quotation from ancient authors, such as Thucydides, Polybius, Cicero, and Lucian.

- Michael Licona misinterprets and misapplies Lucian in *Why Are There Differences in the Gospels?*

- Of particular interest to the question of ancient Christians' view of truth is a quotation from an author named Julius Africanus. He rejected in the strongest terms the idea that the Gospel writers would have changed the facts in Jesus' genealogy for theological reasons.

VII

Speeches in Ancient Historical Writing

1. How not to over-simplify about ancient speeches

There are several points that we must understand about the treatment of speeches in ancient historical writing, and simple formulas won't do the trick. In this chapter I will be making the following points:

1) It is very probable that *some* ancient historical writers made up speeches, even at times out of whole cloth.

2) Even authors who made up speeches or endorsed doing so could, and some did, draw a sharp line between the license granted to speeches and any license for reporting *other* events, having a much stricter standard for the latter. Therefore, one must not extrapolate from, "This author said it is okay to compose speeches" to "This author had a generally flexible view of truth in historical writing" or "The connotation of fabrication is modern." I have already discussed this point somewhat in the previous chapter.

3) It doesn't follow from point 1 that the Gospel authors invented speeches, nor even that they made up mere guesses of what someone *might have* said or what seemed to them "appropriate" for that person to say. Both the importance of Jesus and of his words to the early Christians make it antecedently unlikely that they would have constructed Jesus' speeches in a loose fashion.

4) The treatment of speeches varied greatly, and composing merely plausible possibilities or making ideological adaptations, much less making up whole speeches for rhetorical purposes, was *not* uniformly accepted

among secular ancient writers. Therefore, even if we were to assume some degree of influence from the "ancient milieu" upon the Gospel authors concerning their treatment of speeches, this would not be very informative, because there was no single accepted standard. Some authors were scrupulous about the need to have a good reason to think that one was recording at least approximately what a person really said on a given occasion.

5) "Speeches" are not the same thing as "speech," in the sense of "anything somebody says." Point 1 above concerns portions of a document that can be recognized *as speeches*, not pithy sayings or conversations. Therefore, beyond the fact that individual practice varied widely as far as recording set-piece speeches, it is a mistake to say that it was accepted in ancient times to compose sayings or conversations, based upon a few passages that accept composing set-piece speeches.

2. Inventing speeches

The first point—that *some* ancient authors made up speeches and *some* approved of making up speeches without reliable sources—is fairly easy to document. It is one point on which Michael Licona, Richard Burridge, Colin Hemer, and I all agree. To take but one example, Hemer points out the following concerning Josephus:

> Josephus clearly stands in a similar rhetorical tradition of history [to that of Dionysius of Helicarnassus]. Josephus' abuse of John of Gischala is borrowed from Sallust's attacks on Catiline…In his two different accounts of Herod's exhortation to his troops after the earthquake of 31 BC…Josephus offers two wholly dissimilar speeches, containing different echoes of Thucydides. Again, he presses his own viewpoint through an extraordinary two-thousand-word appeal by himself to the defenders of Jerusalem…which closely repeats some of the arguments he puts in the mouth of Agrippa II in an even longer speech at the outset of the war.[1]

As I will discuss below apropos of Burridge's use of this fact, Tacitus probably invented a high-flown speech for a Caledonian general to give before fighting the Romans.

In this area, Lucian, whom I discussed at length in the previous chapter, occupies an interesting place that shows just how careful we have to be in drawing

---

[1] Colin Hemer, *The Book of Acts in the Setting of Hellenistic History*, WUNT 49 (Tübingen: J. C. B. Mohr, 1989), p. 78. See also Michael Licona, *Why Are There Differences in the Gospels? What We Can Learn From Ancient Biography* (Oxford: Oxford University Press, 2017), p. 226, n. 9.

conclusions. In paragraph 58 of *How to Write History*, Lucian does seem to grant the right to authors to invent speeches:

> When it comes in your way to introduce a speech, the first requirement is that it should suit the character both of the speaker and of the occasion; the second is (once more) lucidity; but in these cases you have the counsel's right of showing your eloquence.[2]

Since the author is supposed to make sure that the speech he "introduces" suits the speaker and the occasion, the *prima facie* implication is that Lucian envisages and approves of the author's composing the speech for the character. The "eloquence" in question is not supposed to make the speech overly flowery if that would not suit the character delivering it. Earlier, Lucian lampoons an unnamed historical writer who included a funeral oration that Lucian considers silly, consisting as it does of "copious and remarkable" rhetoric focused on costly dinners that the deceased had given.[3] Lucian's complaint is that the speech is ridiculous, not that it is composed, and this fits well with his injunction in paragraph 58. This is not to say that Lucian suggests that an historian *ignore* sources for a speech if he has them but that Lucian does not seem to consider speech sources always necessary.

3. Speech invention cannot be extrapolated

We know from several other passages in the same work by Lucian, quoted in the last chapter, that he is extremely concerned in general with historical veracity. A reasonable conclusion, given all of the evidence, is that Lucian considers set-piece speeches to be in a different category from other events and the latter to be held to a much higher standard of care.

There are two importantly wrong extrapolations I am arguing against here. The first is a wrong extrapolation from some kind of looseness (sometimes amounting to complete fabrication) in reporting speeches to looseness in reporting events. The second is a wrong extrapolation from the fact that some authors engaged in or permitted largely un-sourced invention of speeches to the idea either that this standard of speech reporting was accepted across the board or that the Gospel authors probably accepted it.

---

[2] Lucian, *How to Write History*, 58. Trans. by H.W. Fowler and F.G. Fowler, 1905. (The translators' version of the title is *The Way to Write History*, but I have used the more widely known title in references.) <http://www.sacred-texts.com/cla/luc/wl2/wl210.htm>

[3] Ibid., 26.

The first wrong extrapolation does occasionally occur. The quotations from Richard Burridge in the previous chapter are a usefully clear example, and a longer quotation from that passage will make the error even more explicit:

> We must not transfer these modern concepts to ancient texts without considering their understandings of truth and myth, lies and fiction. To modern minds, 'myth' means something untrue, a 'fairy-story'; in the ancient world, myth was the medium whereby profound truth, more truly true than mere facts could ever be, was communicated. The opposite of truth is not fiction, but lies and deception; yet even history can be used to deceive, while stories can bring truth. This issue of truth and fiction in the ancient world is too complex to cover in detail here. However, the most important point to remember is that the ancients were more interested in the moral worth and philosophical value of statements than their logical status, in truth more than facts....Unfortunately, the debate between so-called 'conservatives' and 'liberals' about authenticity is often conducted in twenty-first-century terms. As one student asked me, 'Why does John keep fabricating material about Jesus despite his expressed concern for the "truth"?' However, the negative connotation of 'fabrication' is modern. Let us illustrate this point by looking at another ancient biography, the *Life of Agricola*, Roman governor of Britain from AD 78 to 84, written by his son-in-law, the famous historian Tacitus....While his father-in-law might have reminisced to Tacitus about his speech, the speech by Calgacus, the Caledonian chief, is clearly the 'fabrication' of Tacitus (Agricola 30–32). It is extremely unlikely that an ancient Briton would have known about half of the Roman behaviour mentioned, let alone be able to denounce it in beautifully balanced Latin rhetoric—but neither Tacitus nor his audience would have dreamt of applying the modern connotations of 'fabrication' to his work. The force of terse, pithy comments like '*solitudinem faciunt, pacem appellant*'...is true, and an ethical challenge to Tacitus' audience, even if Calgacus could never have said it. This is the important 'truth' for Tacitus, not mere 'facts', like the time or place of the battle.... Unfortunately, some modern studies assume that if there is 'fiction' in the gospels, then they are inauthentic or unreliable. However, closer attention to literary criticism shows that no-one wrote a classical biography to provide a documented historical text—but rather in an attempt to get 'inside' the person....Thus, John's stress on 'truth' is not about 'documented fact', but the 'higher truth' of who Jesus is—which is why he writes in a biographical format. For him, Jesus is 'the way, the truth and the life', so his Jesus says these words (Jn. 14:6), just as Tacitus' Calgacus condemns Roman imperialism, or Matthew's Jesus speaks from a mountain as another Moses. To ask whether either Jesus or Calgacus actually ever spoke those words is to miss the point completely.[4]

---

[4] Richard Burridge, *Four Gospels, One Jesus: A Symbolic Reading* (London: Society for Promoting Christian Knowledge, 2005), pp. 169–171.

As I already noted in the previous chapter, Burridge strongly implies that an assertion on the part of a Gospel author, like John, that he is concerned about reporting the truth needs to be radically reinterpreted as expressing a concern for "higher truth" that is "more truly true than mere facts." Burridge implies that ancient authors often sacrificed veracity in mere facts in the service of such a "higher truth." Fabrication, Burridge insists, was generally allowable in ancient historical writing but had none of the negative connotations we would attach to that concept. The last chapter refuted, via one quotation after another, Burridge's claims about views of truth in the ancient world.

For this chapter it is important to note that Burridge connects these extremely strong claims about the ancients and truth with the practice of inventing speeches. After saying that the negative connotation of "fabrication" is modern, Burridge expressly says that he will *illustrate this point* by reference to Tacitus' *Life of Agricola*, and he proceeds to argue that in all probability Tacitus invented the speech of the Caledonian general, Calgacus. Burridge argues, not unreasonably, that it is implausible that Tacitus would have known what the opposing general said to his troops, that it is implausible that Calgacus would have known of many of the imperial activities of the Romans that he criticizes, and that it is especially implausible that Calgacus would have expressed himself in the rhetorical fashion given by Tacitus.

But Burridge incorrectly uses the probability that Tacitus made up Calgacus' speech to argue for the far more sweeping claim that fabrication did not have a negative connotation in ancient historical writing. The many quotations in the previous chapter show that whatever else may be true, *that* generalization is utterly false. Burridge even uses this connection to speeches to undermine John's repeated references to truth, to undermine the historicity of a *short saying* by Jesus in John that occurs in the course of a dialogue—namely, "I am the way, the truth, and the life,"—and to question the historicity of Jesus' speaking to the crowds on a mountainside in Matthew, which is not in itself a matter only of what was said but of the setting and external facts. It is also obvious that Burridge makes the other extrapolation—namely, from the fact that *some* ancient authors invented speeches to the conclusion that inventing speeches was a generally accepted practice in ancient writing and that therefore the Gospel authors felt free to do the same.

Sometimes the connection between some degree of looseness in recording speeches and other alleged historical "flexibility" is made in a vaguer way. In a blog post about differences in Gospel accounts, Craig Keener moves rapidly from an unclear implication of dyschronological narration about the story of

Jesus cursing the fig tree in Matthew or Mark to a generic reference to different ancient standards of reportage. He includes in the latter a reference to the fact that ancient writers didn't give "anything like" a verbatim transcript of what people said.

> Did Jesus curse two fig trees over the course of two days, though each Evangelist mentions only one, with one withering at once and the other withering later but the disciples needing precisely the same lesson on faith, in very similar words, each time?
>
> But guess what? Ancient readers didn't expect ancient biographies to be in chronological order, and moving material around was considered a matter of arrangement, not of accuracy.
>
> And ancient expectations are what we need to consider: it is simply anachronistic to judge documents by standards that didn't exist in their day, or genres that didn't exist in their day, even when modern genres evolved from ancient ones with the same names. To ignore genre and the expectations that a writer could take for granted that his readers shared is like ignoring the language or culture in which a work is written. We can't speak of the "historical reliability" of parables or psalms. Readers in the early Roman empire expected history-writing and biography to be reliable in substance, but not to have anything like verbatim recall of wording.[5]

Keener's scholarly work contains a great deal of information on the subject of recording speeches in the ancient world, though the conclusions he draws from that information are open to dispute.[6] What is interesting about this statement in a popular post is that *nowhere* else in the post as a whole does Keener discuss the relaying of speeches in the Gospels. The one example discussed in the post is the cursing of the fig tree and the question of whether it withered at once or the next day—a chronological issue. Yet this discussion leads Keener directly to the mention of the recording of the spoken words. Why does a single sentence move from, "Readers in the early Roman empire expected history-writing and biography to be reliable in substance" to "not to have anything like verbatim recall of wording" in a post that isn't *at all* about how accurately speech was reported?

There are other relevant things that one could note about this short passage, in light of the distinctions I have made in earlier chapters. Keener implies a con-

---

[5] Craig A. Keener, "Differences in the Gospels, Part 2," July 23, 2018, http://www.craigkeener.com/differences-in-the-gospels-part-2/.

[6] See, for example, Keener's long section on ancient speech-recording practices in *The Gospel of John: A Commentary* (Grand Rapids, MI: Baker Academic, 2003), pp. 68ff and the similar section in *Acts: An Exegetical Commentary* (Grand Rapids, MI: Baker Academic 2012), vol. 1, pp. 258–281.

tradition between Matthew and Mark concerning whether or not the fig tree withered immediately and then dismisses it with the vague statement, "Guess what? Ancient readers didn't expect ancient biographies to be in chronological order, and moving material around was considered a matter of arrangement, not of accuracy." Readers who have gotten this far in this book will remember that I distinguished "not narrating in chronological order" in the sense of narrating achronologically from "not narrating in chronological order" in the sense of narrating dyschronologically—changing the chronology from what it really was. If Matthew knowingly, falsely narrated that the tree withered immediately when he believed that it didn't wither until the next day (or at least after the disciples and Jesus had left), he was narrating dyschronologically. He was not merely "moving material around." He would have been giving the wrong impression, not merely a rough impression. Similarly, if Mark believed that the tree withered at once and that the entire conversation about faith and moving mountains happened on the same day but for some reason deliberately "made" Jesus and the disciples come back and discuss the matter the next day, then he was not merely "moving material around" with an unclear chronology. It is extremely unhelpful to blur this distinction with statements like Keener's about the expectations of ancient readers, especially since the literary device theorists will find it much more difficult to substantiate the claim that ancient readers expected *dyschronological* narration and accordingly took the chronology in historical works with a grain of salt.

The more relevant point for my discussion in this chapter is the oddity of introducing a mention of "verbatim transcripts" immediately after the discussion of the fig tree, as if it is relevant to the question. A reader might easily go away with the vague notion that somehow the claim that the ancients didn't record things verbatim means that they *also* thought that it was okay to change chronology, because both are examples of flexibility, and the ancients had a looser and more flexible idea of historical truth and accuracy *in general* than we do. But that does not follow at all.

That there was a distinction, even a sharp distinction, between allowance for speeches and the reportage of events is evident not only from Lucian, as already discussed, but also from an interesting passage in Thucydides about speeches:

> With reference to the speeches in this history, some were delivered before the war began, others while it was going on; some I heard myself, others I got from various quarters; it was in all cases difficult to carry them word for word in one's memory, so my habit has been to make the speakers say what was in my opinion demanded

of them by the various occasions, of course adhering as closely as possible to the general sense of what they really said. And with reference to the narrative of events, far from permitting myself to derive it from the first source that came to hand, I did not even trust my own impressions, but it rests partly on what I saw myself, partly on what others saw for me, the accuracy of the report being always tried by the most severe and detailed tests possible. My conclusions have cost me some labour from the want of coincidence between accounts of the same occurrences by different eye-witnesses, arising sometimes from imperfect memory, sometimes from undue partiality for one side or the other.[7]

I quoted the latter part of this section from a different translation in the previous chapter. Notice first the distinction that Thucydides makes between the speeches and the events. Thucydides makes it clear that he made *some* allowance for the difficulty of getting good sources for speeches but that he made far less allowance for such difficulties concerning other events. He has tried to find out very exactly what happened, even to the point of undergoing labor in trying to harmonize or sift eyewitness accounts that appear to differ. I will return in a moment to the question of what the first part of this quotation is and is not saying. For now, notice that even though Thucydides allows some degree of informed reconstruction of speeches (not a loose standard in any event), he demanded even more care when it comes to other events.

An interesting similar point can be made from the treatment historians have accorded to Tacitus. In Appendix 2 I will discuss a case where Tacitus' extremely indirect dating of a trial was thought to be in error because of the discovery of a bronze inscription that some historians took to contradict it. I will argue there that Tacitus did not really change a date at all, a point recognized even by one Roman historian who used to think that he did. The interesting point for our consideration here is that this alleged alteration of fact by Tacitus was considered something of a big deal in the Tacitus scholarship of the late 1990s.

> If the trial did indeed take place towards the very end of the year, some generally held and basic assumptions about Tacitean narrative require overhauling....Such an overhaul is...a problem for those scholars who believe that Tacitus' annalistic scheme 'orders events...as they occur'.[8]

---

[7] Thucydides, *History of the Peloponnesian War*, 1.22. Trans. Richard Crawley, 1910, http://classics.mit.edu/Thucydides/pelopwar.1.first.html.

[8] C. S. Kraus, A. J. Woodman, *Latin Historians* (Cambridge: Cambridge University Press, 1997), p. 101.

What is interesting about this quotation from two scholars who think that Tacitus *did* change an implied trial date is that such a change should have been taken to be at all surprising. If, as appears likely,[9] Tacitus did invent speeches, this apparently had no tendency in itself to cause historians to take him to be loose in his treatment of detailed chronology. It was "generally held" that Tacitus was quite accurate in his chronology. It was only when scholars thought that there was a contradiction with an inscription that they rethought Tacitus' chronological accuracy. The separation between speech composition and event alteration, including chronological alteration, was taken for granted, and rightly so.

5. Wide authorial differences on speech invention

What about the extrapolation from the practice of *some* writers in inventing speeches to the practice of *other* authors concerning speeches? Here nuance is important once again. What we will find is variability, with no single "loose" standard. Thucydides' quotation has sometimes been misused to argue that ancient authors commonly invented speeches and that therefore New Testament writers probably did as well.[10] Colin Hemer is interested in the historicity of the speeches recorded in Acts, and in responding to an argument that they are not even reliable summaries, he considers this argument:

> The author, writing with ancient standards of historiography, would quite naturally have invented speeches as suited his artistic and ideological purpose.[11]

As Hemer notes, "Many inaccurate and oversimplified assumptions are current about the function of speeches in the ancient historians."[12] Scholars sometimes bring in Thucydides' preface to support sweeping claims about looseness in ancient reportage of speeches, but Hemer replies,

> The Thucydidean prologue is especially unfortunate for the objector to bring into the discussion, since (a) it is clear from that passage that Thucydides is warning readers in a way that implies one should expect the speeches to be accurate where such warnings are not placed, and (b) he maintains that even when the actual speech cannot be recalled, he has tried to remain as true as possible to the essence

---

[9] Hemer, *The Book of Acts in the Setting of Hellenistic History*, p. 76.

[10] See, both describing and dissenting from this trend, I. Howard Marshall, "The Resurrection in the Acts of the Apostles," W. Ward Gasque & Ralph P. Martin, eds., *Apostolic History and the Gospel. Biblical and Historical Essays Presented to F. F. Bruce* (Exeter: The Paternoster Press, 1970), pp. 93–94.

[11] Hemer, *The Book of Acts in the Setting of Hellenistic History*, p. 420.

[12] Ibid., p. 75 n. 42.

of the words actually spoken. And although it is true that Dionysius and Josephus treated speeches with less than Thucydidean rigour, there is reason to believe that their work, far from representing a 'universal standard', could be considered *substandard* for that reason.[13]

Remember, Thucydides says that he was present at some of the speeches and also that he attempted to adhere as closely as possible to the sense of what was really said. What Thucydides notably does not allow for is the author's use of his own eloquence, his own ideas of what *ought* to be said or, in general, his use of the speakers' words for his own ideological purposes—a point worth keeping in mind.

Hemer's implication that the practice of Josephus and others might have been deemed substandard rather than widely accepted may seem surprising, but at least we can see that the practice of inventing speeches was by no means universal. Hemer rightly cites Polybius' use of the accusation that another historian, Timaeus, invents speeches:

> It is by no means true that all ancient historians felt free to put fictitious speeches in the mouths of historical characters. There were wide variations of practice, and while some certainly did this, others are strong in their refusal to countenance such a proceeding. Should anyone defend Timaeus after Polybius' devastating exposure of his faults, there is a clinching argument: '*Timaeus actually invents speeches*'.[14]

Here Polybius' words are worth quoting directly:

> The peculiar function of history is to discover, in the first place, the words actually spoken, whatever they were, and next to ascertain the reason why what was done or spoken led to failure or success....For it is the mental transference of similar circumstances to our own times that gives us the means of forming presentiments of what is about to happen, and enables us at certain times to take precautions and at others by reproducing former conditions to face with more confidence the difficulties that menace us. But a writer who passes over in silence the speeches made and the causes of events and in their place introduces false rhetorical exercises and discursive speeches, destroys the peculiar virtue of history. And of this Timaeus especially is guilty, and we all know that his work is full of blemishes of the kind. Perhaps, therefore, some might wonder how, being such as I have proved him to be, he meets with such acceptance and credit from certain people.[15]

---

[13] Ibid., p. 421.

[14] Ibid., p. 75. Emphasis in original.

[15] Polybius, *Histories* 12.25b.1–25c.1. Trans. by W.R. Patton, 1922, http://penelope.uchicago.edu/Thayer/E/Roman/Texts/Polybius/12*.html.

In Book 2 of the same work, Polybius says,

> A historian should not try to astonish his readers by sensationalism, nor, like the tragic poets, seek after men's probable utterances and enumerate all the possible consequences of the events under consideration, but simply record what really happened and was said, however commonplace. For the object of history is the very opposite of that of tragedy. The tragic writer seeks by the most plausible language to thrill and charm the audience temporarily; the historian by real facts and real speeches seeks to instruct and convince serious students for all time. There it is the probable that counts, even though it be false, the object being to beguile the spectator; here it is the truth, the object being to benefit the student.[16]

Notice in both of these quotations Polybius' disdain for oratorical exercises and flourishes and his placing of real speeches in opposition to these. Indeed, Polybius goes so far as to say that the object of the historian is to give the reader the truth of what was said, even if it seems improbable or less interesting than what the author could make up on his own.

Polybius indicates that he will not weary the reader with his own display of talent in reporting speeches. While he acknowledges that politicians have to argue on various sides of an issue and that an historian may report what they said, he implies that even politicians should be less wordy than they sometimes are:

> [N]either do I think it is the proper part of a politician to display his ingenuity and indulge in discursive talk on any and every subject of debate that may arise, but simply to say what the situation demands, nor is it the proper part of a historian to practice on his readers and make a display of his ability to them, but rather to find out by the most diligent inquiry and report to them what was actually said, and even of this only what was most vital and effectual.[17]

When Licona refers briefly to this latter passage of Polybius in *Why Are There Differences in the Gospels*, he gives the impression that Polybius was an outlier and even rhetorically places him at odds with Thucydides:

> Although Josephus claimed great accuracy in his reporting, he felt free to invent speeches. Polybius (Hist. 2.56.10–12) had a stricter practice of reconstructing speeches than Thucydides, Plutarch, and most other historians of that era.[18]

---

[16] Ibid., 2.56.10–12. As translated in Frank Walbank, "Polybius," *Britannica.com*, https://www.britannica.com/biography/Polybius.

[17] Ibid., 36.1.6–7.

[18] Licona, *Why Are There Differences*, p. 226 n. 9.

The distance in time from Thucydides (c. 460–400 B.C.) to Plutarch (c. A.D. 46–119) is sufficiently wide that a phrase like "that era" is not very felicitous. We are not talking about any single era. But if we are to make groupings at all among ancient writers so widely spaced across time, Thucydides and Polybius belong ideologically *together* as over against Josephus. Thucydides makes it clear that he falls back on probable reconstructions only when forced to do so and that he is attempting to remain as close as his memory or sources permit to what was actually said. Moreover, the fact that in his own time Polybius was able to refer with such confidence to Timaeus' habit of speech invention as an obvious fault shows that his own view was one he expected his readers to sympathize with.

Hemer shrewdly comments that the greatest gulf in ancient historical writing lies between those who write speeches with genuine historical sources and those who write speeches without them and allude to earlier writers only to show off their own literary learning:

> There is in fact an important distinction between the two ways we find historians using their predecessors in their speeches. The use of literary reminiscence and allusion (as in Dionysius or Josephus) is quite different from the use of personal recollection and inquiry, or written sources, or possibly even an inscribed text...The difference may be variously signaled: in the difference between relative brevity and the flagrantly rhetorical, in the difference between seeking sources and unanchored literary parallels. In the former case it is not surprising if there is much unevenness of style and scale, for the sources vary. Speeches may be detailed but condensed, or brief summaries where the evidence is more limited.[19]

In other words, the greatest causes of speech report variation in conscientious writers arise from variation in their source material or memories, while the difference between them and rhetorical speech writers is that the latter are not attempting to report faithfully what was said in the first place.

An important distinction to be made here is between paraphrase (on the one hand) that is forced upon the reporter by lack of audiographic memory, technology, notes, etc., and paraphrase (on the other) that takes the opportunity to "polish up" the other person's speech or make it serve some purpose of the author's. While it is certainly true that nobody followed Jesus around with a tape recorder,[20] it does not follow that *any* of the Gospel authors felt free to manipulate either his short sayings or even his longer sermons in theoretical or ideological directions

---

[19] Hemer, *The Book of Acts in the Setting of Hellenistic History*, p. 78.

[20] Keener, *John*, pp. 55–56.

in order to make him ideologically more like themselves or to make him say what they thought he should have said.[21] Polybius' reference to "what was most vital and effectual" indicates the probability that he sometimes summarized speeches of which he had reports in the interests of brevity.[22] But once again, this has nothing to do with attempting to extrapolate what was said to some deeper meaning while putting it into the mouth of the speaker. And an author more concerned with recording a given speaker's words than with brevity, who had access to a longer speech, might well report it with even less shortening.

In the blog post mentioned above, Keener says that ancient authors were not expected to have "anything like verbatim recall of wording." What they were expected to have is one thing and what some given author may *actually* have had is quite another. Someone writing with Polybian or even Thucydidean standards who did happen to have a remarkable memory[23] might well have written down what he remembered and hence given something *closer* to verbatim recall than the phrase "anything like" would indicate. Beyond this, if we say that no ancient historians ever *attempted* to give "anything like" verbatim transcripts, we will give the false impression that all ancient historical writers thought they could insert a good deal of their own *interpretation* and put it into the mouths of historical characters.[24] Indeed, Craig Evans has strongly implied that the Gospel authors did exactly this and would have thought that it was a way of showing that they were good disciples, a surprising idea that I will discuss in a later chapter concerning ancient *chreiai* (anecdotes). We saw in Chapter II, section 2, that the term "paraphrase" can be used in confusing ways by New Testament scholars, and this is a place for caution in that regard.

The fact of the matter is that speech reporting practices varied so widely in ancient historical writings that we simply cannot make any very useful general-

---

[21] Note here the difference already noted in Chapter II, section 2, between normal witness paraphrase of the Father's words at Jesus' baptism resulting in both "This is my beloved Son" and "You are my beloved Son" and Licona's odd idea that Matthew deliberately changed the words to make the utterance seem more personal to the audience. "Bonus Episode 14: Mike Licona Answers Your Questions on the Gospels," *The Freethinking Podcast*, minute 26:30, http://freethinkingministries.com/bonus-ep-14-mike-licona-answers-your-questions-on-the-gospels/.

[22] See also Polybius, *Histories*, 29.12.10. See also Hemer, *The Book of Acts in the Setting of Hellenistic History*, pp. 75–76 on the alteration between direct and indirect quotation in Polybius.

[23] Keener (*John*, pp. 57–58) admits that remembering a teacher's words was very important to students of the time period and also mentions that Seneca boasted (whether truthfully or not) of remarkable feats of memory of dialogues heard long ago (p. 74).

[24] Ibid., p. 72, actually goes so far as to imply (without conspicuous argument) that ancient authors would not have *wanted* to record a speech verbatim even if they had it available, due to readers' literary expectations.

izations merely from the fact that the Gospel authors were in some sense "ancient men." It does not follow from that fact that they would have felt free to invent speeches for Jesus or to be quite loose in reporting. Of course, we also don't know, merely by knowing their point in time, that they would have been extremely scrupulous reporters of his speeches, trying to get as close as possible to his exact words. Nor does it follow merely from their chronological placement that they would have fallen at some identifiable, specific point in between those two at which they would desire to give neither more nor less than the "gist" of his words. One problem with the statement that the ancient "standard for accuracy was the gist"[25] is that it is all too easy for the modern theorist to decide what counts as "the gist" on the *ad hoc* basis of what the scholar wants to assert about a given passage. Sometimes what the scholar is claiming the author did is not at all what would normally be called "giving the gist," at which point the claim is positively misleading.[26] Furthermore, "ancient standards" do not tell us how close the authors would have desired to get to Jesus' exact words. We certainly don't know that they would have deliberately changed them to something *more* paraphrased, something that was a mere "gist," if they or their human sources happened to know what he said more exactly. The decision both as to what they would have done and what they did do must be judged on other bases, such as their own probable motivations and apparent performance.

6. Speeches vs. speech

Another relevant point here is that we must not blur the distinction between *speeches* in particular and *speech* of all kinds. Burridge in the quotation I have now given several times concerning Tacitus and John commits precisely this error. The statement, "I am the way, the truth, and the life," which Burridge chooses as his example, is not part of a lengthy, set speech at all. Rather, it is Jesus' reply in John 14.6 to a question from Thomas. It is followed almost immediately by a request from Philip to show them the Father, followed by Jesus' answer, which is followed shortly thereafter by a question from Judas (not Iscariot) about why Jesus is manifesting himself to them but not to the world. Burridge says, "To ask whether either

---

[25] Ibid., p. 74.

[26] Craig Keener moves from saying that "the gist" was what ancient historians attempted to retain (*John*, p. 74) to suggesting that John deliberately used Jesus' discourses as opportunities to interpret *his own* stories as he was narrating them (p. 69) and to "articulat[e]...afresh for his own generation" the implications of "historical tradition" (p. 79). Such notions of significant Johannine adaptation and manipulation of Jesus' words cast a good deal of question upon the sense in which such adaptations would retain the "gist" of what Jesus said. They illustrate the unfortunate malleability of the term "gist" in such contexts.

Jesus or Calgacus actually ever spoke those words is to miss the point completely."
He says, further, that John included this saying because this is what Jesus was "to
him." But "I am the way, the truth, and the life" is a highly memorable short *saying*
that occurs in the midst of a wide-ranging conversation placed within a realistic
setting—the Last Supper and the conversation thereafter. Burridge has no historical right to link Tacitus' invention of Calgacus' rhetorical set speech to his troops
to his own theory that John invented Jesus' short saying.

Both the comment by Lucian in paragraph 58 about an author's liberty to
"show his eloquence" and the practices noted by Josephus and Dionysius concern speeches, set speeches, not short sayings or even reported conversations. As
regards Jesus' short sayings, we have if possible even *less* reason to think that they
would have been tampered with, partly because they are so easy to remember.
Indeed it is quite possible that Jesus, as a great teacher, used such memorable aph-
orisms precisely so that they would be recalled clearly.

As regards dialogues, while we have (for example) the fairly obviously partially
fictional philosophical dialogues of Socrates written by his pupil Plato, constitut-
ing a genre of their own, these do not resemble the far shorter and less structured
conversations of Jesus, woven into a larger narrative document. These include his
discussion with his disciples in John 14, his conversations with Nicodemus and
the woman at the well in John 3 and 4, and his discussion with the disciples about
his own identity in Matthew 16. Nor do we have a statement of theory, such as
the one from Lucian, to the effect that an author has license to show his eloquence
in constructing conversations or short sayings. Indeed, as both Lucian's comment
and Polybius' strictures indicate, the whole point of being somewhat oratorical in
writing a speech was that a speech's length and structure provided a platform for
showing off. It is simply irresponsible to talk about ancient rhetorical practices of
inventing speeches as if these are relevant to reporting *speech in general*—that is,
whatever anybody says in a document.[27]

---

[27] Here one must note the odd structure of Keener's long and interesting discussion of "discourses"
in the Gospel of John (*John*, pp. 68–80). As I shall discuss at greater length in *The Eye of the Beholder*
on the Gospel of John, scholars use the term "discourse" in a confusing, specialized way that appears
unique to discussions of John. Some scholars speak of a "Johannine discourse" in a way that includes
both conversations, such as Jesus' conversation with the woman at the well, and "discourses" in the
ordinary sense of the word, such as Jesus' words at the Last Supper from John 14.23–16.16. Keener
makes it clear that he is using the term "discourses" in this specialized way (p. 68), but he then talks at
great length about ancient practices in recording speeches in the sense that I have been discussing in
this chapter—namely, structured set speeches—without acknowledging that these practices have little
or no applicability to *conversations*. His only concession to the fact that he is bringing virtually no information to light about ancient practices in recording natural conversations is to note briefly that Thu-

7. The Gospels: A *prima facie* case for accurate recording of the spoken word

With all of this in view, it may be fairly asked what the evidence *is* concerning the reporting of speeches in the Gospels. To go into that subject in detail would take a very long time. Some of that discussion will occur in my subsequent book on the Gospel of John, since John's Gospel is subject to a great deal of skepticism in this area. In Appendix 3 I will go into more detail on whether Matthew composed composite discourses in which he put together sayings that (he knew) Jesus had uttered at various other times rather than all on one occasion. Even if he did so, he might have scrupulously adhered to the information he had about what Jesus really said at some time or other. Even if the sayings were partially collected, a close adherence to Jesus' historical sayings would place Matthew toward the "conservative" end of the spectrum of speech-reporting practices. However, as Appendix 3 will argue, the evidence for composite speeches in Matthew has been overstated. At a minimum, it remains not very implausible that all of the material included in, say, the Sermon on the Mount was spoken on that occasion, though (needless to say) not recorded verbatim.

For here and now, some pertinent general considerations will suffice to support the conclusion that the Gospel authors should be located well on the conservative end of the spectrum of speech reporting practices and that their accuracy was limited most by the sheer difficulty of obtaining or retaining exact wording. In other words, they were likely not influenced by an allegedly "ancient" inclination to give *no more than* "the gist," to show eloquence, to "interpret the narrative" by putting words into someone's mouth, or in general deliberately to intermingle their own perspectives invisibly with the recorded speech of others.[28,29]

---

cydides may have reconstructed or partially invented a dialogue between envoys on different sides in a military conflict and to imply that this is somehow relevant for debates between Jesus and the Jewish leaders in John (p. 73). See Thucydides, *History of the Peloponnesian War*, 5.85–111. The reader will find upon examination that this dialogue is quite wooden and bears little resemblance to the conversations with the woman at the well in John 4 and the Jewish crowds in John 8. That point is aside from the fact have we have no reason to think that Thucydides would have been influential upon the author of John.

[28] See Keener, *John*, pp. 54, 69, 72, 79.

[29] When I speak of such limitations on the verbatim nature of the Gospel authors' reportage, I am considering it aside from the statement that the Holy Spirit would "bring to their remembrance" what Jesus had said (John 14.26). Such supernatural assistance would certainly be useful and may have been in play (perhaps especially in the case of John, who displays a remarkable memory for detail), but I am not assuming it.

Several of those who either wrote or were likely close sources for the Gospels emphasized the truth of literal events that they report. The preface in Luke 1.1–4 emphasizes Luke's careful investigation of events. There is also the insistence of the author of John's Gospel that he bore a truthful record of what he saw (John 19.35), there with immediate reference to the piercing of Jesus' side. And there is the testimony in 2 Peter 1.16 that the believers have not followed "cleverly devised tales" but rather witness testimony. I will return to these statements in Chapter X, section 2.

The reader may have some doubts about the relevance of such avowals to the reportage of speeches, however, given the fact that some historians (as we have seen) did have looser requirements for the reportage of speeches than of events. Here we should consider the special importance that Jesus himself had to the Christians, beginning with his own disciples.

A quotation from the church father Papias of Hierapolis is relevant to the question of how the original audience would have viewed both Jesus' speeches and his sayings. Papias, called by Irenaeus "a hearer of John and a companion of Polycarp,"[30] is perhaps best known as a source of information about the authorship of Mark's Gospel. Richard Bauckham has made fascinating use of Papias in discussing both authorship questions and the importance of eyewitness testimony in the early church.[31] Here is something Papias said about wanting to know the words of Jesus:

> Nor did I take pleasure in those who reported their memory of someone else's commandments, but *only in those who reported their memory of the commandments given by the Lord to the faith and proceeding from the Truth itself.* And if by chance anyone who had been in attendance on the elders arrived, I made enquiries about the words of the elders—what Andrew or Peter had said, or Philip or Thomas or James or John or Matthew or any other of the Lord's disciples, and whatever Aristion and John the Elder, the Lord's disciples, were saying. For I did not think that information from the books would profit me as much as information from a living and surviving voice.[32]

Papias, in other words, was not interested primarily in someone else's ideas of what Jesus' teachings *meant.* He wanted to know what Jesus himself (whom Papias,

---

[30] Eusebius, *Ecclesiastical History*, 3.39.1. Trans. Arthur Cushman McGiffert, 1890, http://www.newadvent.org/fathers/250103.htm.

[31] Richard Bauckham, *Jesus and the Eyewitnesses: The Gospels as Eyewitness Testimony* (Grand Rapids, Eerdmanns, 2017), Chapter 2.

[32] Eusebius, *Ecclesiastical History,* 3.39.3–4. Emphasis added.

perhaps echoing John 14.6, calls "the Truth itself") had *said*. It was for this very reason that he was so careful to try to get in contact with what he calls the "living and surviving voice" of Jesus' own followers.

Writing three centuries later and in somewhat higher-flown language, Augustine of Hippo (A.D. 354–480) says something similar:

> Herein is our liberty, when we are subject to truth. And Truth is our God, who liberates us from death, that is, from the condition of sin. For the Truth itself, speaking as Man to men, says to those who believe in him, "If ye abide in my word, ye are truly my disciples. And ye shall know the truth, and the truth shall make you free."[33]

The connection between Jesus as truth personified and our need to know Jesus' own words is the same in Augustine and Papias.

Leon Morris makes the fascinating point that John 12.49 points to authentic recording of what Jesus has said in two ways. First, since Jesus says that he does not speak on his own initiative but only as the Father has commanded him to speak, the author of John does not seem to be promoting an agenda of "high Christology" but rather reporting an authentic expression of the Son's subordination to the Father.[34] Second, if Jesus himself is recorded as saying that he speaks only as the Father has told him to speak, it is all the less likely that the author of the Gospel would have considered himself licensed to put his own words into the mouth of Jesus.

Similarly, John 14.26 makes a distinction between the work of the Holy Spirit in bringing to remembrance the words of Jesus and in teaching the disciples. Contra the use that is sometimes made of this verse,[35] the two functions are not conflated either in the words attributed to Jesus or, apparently, in the mind of the author. The verse does not speak of a function in which the Spirit gives the author license to write "as if" Jesus is teaching the theology that the author *extrapolates*

---

[33] Augustine, *On the Freedom of the Will*, xiii.37. Trans. J.H.S. Burleigh, 1953, https://archive.org/stream/AugustineCatholicAndManicheanWays_201707/Augustine_%20Earlier%20Writings%20-%20Augustine%2C%20St.%20%26%20Burleigh%2C%20Joh_4774_djvu.txt.

[34] Leon Morris, *Studies in the Fourth Gospel* (Grand Rapids, Eerdmans Publishing Company, 1969), p. 177.

[35] Craig Keener, *John*, pp. 78–79, says that one is "often scarce able to discern" in John's Gospel whether Jesus or the narrator is speaking, and adds parenthetically, "perhaps for good reason, since the narrator believes himself inspired by the Paraclete who continues Jesus' mission." It is, in fact, not true that one often has difficulty in John telling whether Jesus or the narrator is speaking. There is only one such passage, occurring in John 3. Keener is, moreover, on questionable exegetical ground in alluding to the work of the Paraclete as, in John's mind, licensing a blurred line between the thoughts of the author and the teaching of Jesus.

from Jesus' authentic statements. On the contrary, the very fact that John chooses to record a promise to bring to their remembrance what Jesus has said implies that John considers it important that they remember and relay to others what Jesus historically said.

Luke was one of two traditionally ascribed Gospel authors who was not him-self a disciple, the other being Mark. But if, as I have argued in *Hidden in Plain View*, Luke was a companion of Paul, he would have probably had opportunity to talk with multiple disciples of Jesus and other eyewitnesses, and he himself implies that he did so.[36] It is also plausible that he used the Gospel of Mark as a source. As Hemer notes, it is interesting to see how scrupulous Luke is with his (probable) speech sources:

> [T]here is a *prima facie* case for saying, whatever view one takes of the Synoptic Problem, that the 'speeches' of Luke's Gospel in particular, are largely dependent on extant or inferable sources. There is editing; there is rearrangement...but the striking thing is the extent to which Luke uses sources almost verbatim. This poses many questions about historicity and about the speeches in Acts. It may be argued that the words of Jesus were unique....But the preservation of the spoken word was not alien to the ancient world.[37]

The other traditional Gospel authors may well have had an even more direct line of access to information about what Jesus said, being either eyewitnesses them-selves or, in the case of Mark, having extensive reports of Peter to rely upon. Again, it does not follow *deductively* that the speeches of Jesus in the Gospel are reliably known and conservatively reported, but such considerations do contribute to a *prima facie* case that shifts the burden of proof either to the skeptic or to the liter-ary device theorist if he wishes to argue that they are invented or greatly adapted, especially if that adaptation is supposed to carry a theological flavoring or motiva-tion on the part of the author.

Here the "asides" in the Gospels are enlightening. In Mark 7.19, for example, the author clearly distinguishes his own editorial voice, interpreting the words of Jesus as declaring all foods clean, from the words of Jesus himself. John does something similar when Jesus says that the one who believes in him will have rivers of living water flowing from within. The narrator glosses this statement as a reference to the Holy Spirit who was not yet given (John 7.38–39). Similar asides

---

[36] Lydia McGrew, *Hidden in Plain View: Undesigned Coincidences in the Gospels and Acts* (Chilli-cothe, OH: DeWard Publishing, 2017), pp. 185, 217–218.

[37] Hemer, *The Book of Acts in the Setting of Hellenistic History*, p. 79.

by the narrator occur in John 2.18–21 and John 13.10–11. If the author felt free
to write as if his own glosses were what Jesus said originally, why bother to make
the distinction in these places? The longer discourses in John, and in general Jesus'
way of talking in John, have come under special attack, and this sociological fact
will require me to spend more space in the next volume defending Jesus' words in
John. But it is arguable that authors who were so scrupulous about distinguishing
their own voices from the voice of the Master would not be ready to make loose
adaptations, much less inventions, of his speeches or sayings.[38]

There is also the fact that none of the speeches in the Gospels, even in Luke
or John, shows signs of being written by someone who was highly rhetorically
trained. Craig Keener acknowledges, "Most Hellenistic historians had formal rhetorical training; it is not clear that Luke did....Though educated, Luke does not
necessarily display advanced training in rhetoric" and adds, "John, Matthew, and
especially Mark appear even less conversant in Greco-Roman rhetoric than Luke
is."[39] Indeed, as Appendix 3 discusses, Jesus' aphoristic style in a long discourse
like the Sermon on the Mount in Matthew is part of what has led many scholars
to think that it may be a composite of shorter segments that Jesus actually taught
at other times. As we have already seen, it was precisely in the context of showing
off oratorical skills that rhetorically trained historians were likely to write polished
speeches and insert them into historical documents.

8. Evidence about Luke as a speech recorder: Paul's speeches in Acts

Finally, consideration of the speeches by Paul in the book of Acts casts some light
on the probability that the speeches of Jesus in the Gospels are conservatively
reported, being based either directly on memory or on reliable sources. The rather
striking evidence for the authenticity of these speeches in Acts produces an *a for-
tiori* (so much the more) argument for the speeches of Jesus in all the Gospels, for
several reasons: 1) Luke is the one traditional Gospel author who might plausibly
have been exposed to higher-level Hellenistic rhetorical writing. 2) The words of
Paul would have plausibly been less urgent to retain than the words of Jesus. 3)
Luke has a number of passages that can really be called "speeches" in the sense

---

[38] This point is made by D. A. Carson, "Historical Tradition in the Fourth Gospel: After Dodd,
What?" in R. T. France and David Wenham, eds., *Gospel Perspectives*, Vol. 2: *Studies of History and Tradition in the Four Gospels* (Sheffield: JSOT Press, 1981), p. 122.

[39] Craig Keener, *The Historical Jesus of the Gospels* (Grand Rapids, Eerdmans: 2009), pp. 115–116.
See also Keener, *John*, p. 69, "[N]one of his speeches [the speeches in John] follow standard rhetorical
structures or display firsthand knowledge of rhetoric."

that they are structured, longer discourses without interruption from the audience. 4) Luke's speeches have often been questioned historically by critical scholars.

The topic of the speeches in Acts could occupy an entire chapter of its own (or more), so here I will point only to some of the most pertinent data. Colin Hemer's discussion of the topic in two sections[40] is intended, in his own words, to argue that the speeches in Acts are what he calls "Lukan summaries"—that is, that they are "historical in substance, in the sense that [they represent] what was actually said upon the specific occasion" while containing Luke's "style and vocabulary."[41] If the phrase "Lukan summaries" leads one to think that they are loose summaries, the evidence itself points to something far closer to Paul's own words on the occasions. Here are a few items from Hemer's discussion:

- While Psalm 16 is cited by both Paul and Peter to support Jesus' resurrection—both emphasizing that David's body suffered decay while Jesus' did not—the discussion of this concept by Peter in Acts 2.25–31 is arguably simpler and less rabbinic than Paul's in Acts 13.34–37.

- In both the speech to the elders of Ephesus at Miletus (Acts 20.24) and 2 Timothy 4.7, we find the reference to finishing the race as Paul's goal, and the Greek language is similar in both phrases.

- There are numerous points of contact between Paul's personal preoccupations and biography in the speech to the elders at Miletus and in his epistles. These include his desire not to be a financial burden, his desire to admonish his converts and warn them about false teaching, and his length of stay in Ephesus. In *Hidden in Plain View*, I have discussed the personality of Paul as revealed in this speech as well as an undesigned coincidence: Paul says specifically to the Ephesian elders that "they know" that he has worked with his hands to support himself (Acts 20.34). In I Corinthians, almost certainly written from Ephesus, he writes *to the Corinthians* that he is working with his own hands to support himself to that very hour (I Cor. 4.12).[42]

- In the same speech to the elders of Ephesus, Paul strikingly refers to those whom God has redeemed either "with his own blood" or "with the blood of his own," depending on how one translates the Greek (Acts 20.28). This explicit theme of redemption through Jesus' blood can hardly be said to be

---

[40] Hemer, *The Book of Acts in the Setting of Hellenistic History*, pp. 75–79, 415–27.
[41] Ibid., pp. 419–421.
[42] McGrew, *Hidden in Plain View*, pp. 181–185.

a theme on which Luke himself harps as an author, either in the Gospel or in Acts, yet it is certainly Pauline, recalling the way that Paul talks to Christians to whom he writes epistles (compare Eph. 1.7).[43]

These are just some of the examples of realism in the speeches of Paul reported in Acts.

Concerning the reports of Paul's own conversion, the non-conservative scholar E. P. Sanders has casually stated that Luke simply wrote different versions (which Sanders considers to be conflicting) because he felt like varying the story.[44] Now that we have let ancient people speak for themselves in the previous chapter, we can see that such a view hardly accords with the picture of Luke as following "the procedures of a good Hellenistic historian."[45] But someone may argue that Luke would have been more creative when he placed these accounts into the mouth of Paul as speeches. Acts 22.1–21 is Paul's speech to the angry Jewish mob in Jerusalem; Acts 26.2–23 is his self-defense before Agrippa and Festus.

Here the work of the 19th-century scholar J. S. Howson is invaluable.[46] I will not try to reproduce it all but will give some examples of the realism shown by the variation between these two speeches, realism that (in line with Paul's own desire to "be all things to all men" and his desire to tell his conversion story in ways that will be best heard by his audience) argues that they are reports quite close up to the facts.

- In both of these speeches Paul omits certain facts that might have been of interest to Luke as the narrator but would have been of less interest to Paul's audience. These include, for example, his not eating for several days after his experience on the road to Damascus and the scales that fell from his eyes when he was healed, both mentioned in the narrator's version of the story (Acts 9.9, 18–19).

---

[43] Hemer, *The Book of Acts in the Setting of Hellenistic History*, pp. 424–26. As I argued in *Hidden in Plain View*, p. 191, Ephesians was probably not written specifically to the church at Ephesus but rather is in all probability the "lost" letter to the Laodiceans, whom Paul had never met personally. I therefore am not attempting to lean here on the fact that the reference to redemption through Jesus' blood is contained in Ephesians. Probably the Ephesian church did read that letter, as it was likely passed around Asia Minor. My point here is that it is the kind of expression and thought pattern that Paul used when speaking to such an audience.

[44] E. P. Sanders, *Paul: The Apostle's Life and Letters* (Minneapolis: Fortress Press, 2015), p. 98.

[45] Craig Keener, *Acts: An Exegetical Commentary* (Grand Rapids, MI: Baker Academic 2012), vol. 1, p. 793.

[46] J. S. Howson, *The Evidential Value of the Acts of the Apostles* (New York: E. P. Dutton, 1880), pp. 105–112.

- Before the mob in Jerusalem, Paul presents himself strongly as an observant Jew and emphasizes his and others' Jewish devoutness in order to keep the mob's attention and make them more favorable to himself. He calls his audience "brothers and fathers" (Acts 22.1), emphasizes his own rabbinic education under Gamaliel (vs. 3), and emphasizes the Jewish devoutness of Ananias who came to him in Damascus, calling him not a follower of Jesus but rather "a man who was devout by the standard of the law" (vs. 12).

- Paul cleverly delays any use of the word "Gentiles" throughout his entire speech until he has had a chance to tell his story. For example, in vs. 15 he tells them that Ananias said that "the God of our fathers" has sent him to be a witness "to all men." When at last Paul has to say that Jesus sent him to the Gentiles (vs. 21), the crowd erupts in fury and will not let him continue. But at least he has had a chance to speak for some time.

- In contrast, before Agrippa and Festus, Paul omits any mention of Ananias. As Howson says, "The authority of an obscure Jew of Damascus could have no weight with Agrippa." [47]

- Before Agrippa and Festus, Paul emphasizes at the outset (Acts 26.2) and more than once (vss. 7, 21) that his opponents are Jews.

- To Agrippa and Festus, Paul speaks sympathetically of the Christians from his first mention of them, calling the Christians saints (vs. 10). He says that, in his own persecution of the Christians, he tried to induce them to blaspheme (vs. 11), a self-accusation that fits well with Paul's own self-blame in his epistles (e.g., I Cor. 15.9) but would not have gone over well with a Jewish audience.

- Paul mentions to Agrippa and Festus that the voice from heaven spoke to him "in a Hebrew dialect" (vs. 14), probably Aramaic. This is a casual indication that Paul is speaking at this moment to a Gentile audience and almost certainly in Greek. There would have been no point in mentioning a similar linguistic point to the Jewish audience in Chapter 22, where (Acts 22.2) it is mentioned that Paul is addressing the audience in "a Hebrew dialect."

These little touches are well explained by Luke's having accurate access to what Paul said on these occasions and to his being quite strikingly careful in recording it. Even though it is not by any means necessary to take Luke to be recording

---

[47] Ibid., p. 112.

the speeches verbatim, they are more detailed and Pauline even than the phrase "Lukan summaries" might be taken to indicate. Yet these are precisely the kinds of speeches in which one might expect an author like Josephus to show his own eloquence rather than recording, with a notable degree of accuracy, a speech actually given by an historical person speaking to a specific audience in a specific language.

Again, if Luke was both so knowledgeable and so conservative in recording the speeches of Paul, how much more likely is it that both Luke and the other authors of the Gospels would not heavily adapt or invent the speeches of Jesus?

Let us re-cap the major points of this chapter: First, though some ancient historical authors did indeed compose speeches and put them in the mouths of historical characters, this was neither universally accepted in their own times nor an indication of historical looseness in event reportage. Speech composition in a given author cannot and must not be extrapolated to the idea that even that author himself, much less other authors, much less "the ancients," considered fabrication in historical writing to be in general legitimate. Moreover, ancient practice for reporting speeches varied so widely that we are not justified in generalizing that ancient authors had a single, relatively loose standard for doing so—neither that they generally licensed speech invention nor that they generally licensed heavy adaptation and imaginative reconstruction, with room for the eloquence and personal agenda of the historian. The largest gap between different groups of ancient authors lies between those who reported speeches as accurately as their sources permitted and those who composed in a literary fashion.

Second, the Gospel authors in particular had reason for reporting accurately what Jesus taught, and we see them making distinctions between their own interpretations and what Jesus actually said. Moreover, they do not appear to have been highly trained rhetorically. Audience members such as Papias show the motivation of the early Christians for recording what Jesus himself taught, not extrapolations of others put into the mouth of Jesus. Papias desired to know the teachings of Jesus as "the truth itself" rather than the teaching of other men.

Third, speeches are just one kind of speech; any looseness in composing set speeches on the part of ancient authors is, if possible, even less relevant to Jesus' short sayings or conversations than to his longer speeches in the Gospels.

Fourth, the practice of Luke when recording the speeches of Paul in Acts gives us evidence that he knew what Paul actually said on real occasions and recorded it with a noteworthy degree of accuracy. This reflects well upon Luke's probable practice in his own Gospel. And it shows that the one author who was, of all the evangelists, most likely to have been exposed to a broader Hellenistic education was actually quite scrupulous in his approach to reporting speeches.

All of this is more than sufficient to block any attempt by literary device theorists to appeal to ancient speech reporting practices to support fictionalizing literary devices in *non-speeches*, whether short sayings or other events. It is, moreover, sufficient to shift the burden of proof to those who wish to argue that the content of longer speeches in the Gospels is either invented or deliberately, significantly altered by the author for his own purposes.

Summary
Speeches in Ancient Historical Writing

- It is very probable that some ancient historical writers simply made up speeches, even at times out of whole cloth.

- Some authors who made up speeches or endorsed doing so drew an explicit, sharp line between a license for composing speeches and a license for reporting *other* events, having a much stricter standard for the latter.

- Both the importance of Jesus and of his words to the early Christians make it antecedently unlikely that the Gospel authors would have fabricated Jesus' speeches or constructed them in an historically loose fashion.

- The treatment of speeches varied greatly among ancient historians, and fabricating or composing loosely was not uniformly accepted. Some rejected it explicitly. The ancient mindset does not give any single answer about the acceptability of making up speeches.

- Set-piece speeches are only one kind of speech. We do not have comparable evidence concerning short sayings or conversations.

- Specific evidence of the Gospel authors' own intentions and practice, including their separating Jesus' words from their own glosses, indicates that they did not consider themselves licensed to invent speeches and put them into Jesus' mouth.

- Jesus' discourses and teachings as reported in the Gospels do not appear to have been composed by authors highly trained in Greco-Roman rhetoric who are showing their skill by composing speeches.

- An analysis of Paul's speeches as reported in Acts provides further evidence of the conservative approach to speech reportage on the part of Luke, even though he was the one Gospel author who may have had more Greek education. Luke appears to be quite careful in reporting Paul's speeches, and he would have been at least as careful about Jesus' teachings.

---------------------------------- VIII ----------------------------------

Going Chreia-zy

1. Where we've been and where we're going

Where have we been thus far in this section? Broadly speaking, we can divide into two classes arguments for an "ancient milieu" that would have licensed factual changes in the Gospels. The first category involves claims that ancient people thought in a special way about historical truth and that, therefore, the Gospel authors probably did as well. The second type of argument is inductive. It is the claim that we *find* fictionalizing literary devices in ancient authors such as Plutarch and that, since the Gospels seem to be writing works similar to theirs, we should expect to find such devices in the Gospels as well.

In Chapters V, VI, and VII, we have been dealing with the first class of arguments, and we will be doing so in this chapter as well. The alleged background reason refuted in Chapter V is the claim that the Gospels fall into a genre called Greco-Roman βίος (biography) and that belonging to (or even "having a lot in common with") that genre is enough all by itself to mean that the authors probably considered themselves licensed to change historical facts. The background claim refuted in Chapter VI (using quotations from ancient authors themselves) is that the ancients did not disapprove of fabrication in history because they cared more for a "higher truth" that is "more truly true than mere facts." The background claim refuted in Chapter VII says that, since some ancient authors partially or entirely made up speeches in historical writing, fabrication was not considered such a bad thing in history. A corollary claim is that the Gospel authors would have considered themselves licensed to be loose in reporting the spoken word.

Looking ahead, in Chapter IX, I will refute the inductive claim that we find, by observing Plutarch and other authors, something like a baseline frequency for the use of fictionalizing literary devices listed by the theorists. I will argue there that we do not find good evidence in the secular sources cited even for the *existence* of known, acknowledged fictionalizing devices of compression, transferral, conflation, or displacement.

In this chapter I will be dealing with the last of the "background" claims, before moving to the alleged inductive case. Here, the claim is that compositional textbooks from which the Gospel authors would have been instructed directly taught students that it was legitimate to make factual alterations in history—either in reported sayings, speeches, or other aspects of events.

The way that claims about compositional textbooks function in the work of Michael Licona is instructive. It may come as a surprise to some readers to learn that Licona does not claim to have found in ancient texts any explicit discussion of several of the devices that he alleges so widely in Plutarch and the Gospels. He is quite clear on this point:

> There are many observations of differences in the pericopes [in the Gospels] that follow for which *potential devices are neither described in the compositional textbooks nor observed being employed by Plutarch*. We will keep in mind that many of the compositional devices in use by Plutarch are likewise not found in the compositional textbooks. *Nor are they taught in any of the ancient literature that has survived.* Accordingly, much of what an ancient author did and why he did it will remain in the realm of informed guesswork for modern historians.[1]

It is rather striking that Licona does not see anything historically dubious about this procedure. His interpretations of both the exercise books and the alleged ancient view of history cause him to approach Plutarch and other authors with the assumption that *some sort of* historical alteration is going on. He then infers further that several *highly specific* types of devices exist by way of conjectures about *how* Plutarch and other non-biblical authors might be altering history. He then takes these conjectures in hand and approaches the Gospels. When reading the Gospels, he sometimes claims that the Gospels are altering history by the devices he thinks he has found in Plutarch, but sometimes he makes such suggestions about the Gospels even when, by his own admission, he cannot specify a compositional device among those he has already claimed to find in Plutarch or elsewhere.

The claimed pedagogical practices and exercise books are therefore quite important, but only partly because they even allegedly support the existence of specific devices Licona names. Their greater importance lies in their alleged support

---

[1] Michael Licona, *Why Are There Differences in the Gospels? What We Can Learn From Ancient Biography* (Oxford: Oxford University Press, 2017), p. 117. Emphasis added.

for fictionalization *in general*. This background claim then kicks off a shaky chain of inference to all sorts of specific devices, once one has decided that fictionalization in history was generally taught to students.

2. Licona and Evans on ancient pedagogy and the Gospels

So what about those compositional textbooks? Do they really instruct students to modify historical facts? Both Michael Licona and Craig Evans have claimed that the pedagogy of the time at which the Gospels were written did exactly that. Evans emphatically states,

> I say this about the Gospels because we do have at hand a lot of important information about pedagogy…But more importantly listen up, about the way that a master teacher's teaching was appropriated by his disciples….The teaching was memorized, but then it was understood and could be adapted and applied. It could be expanded, it could be contracted, the wording could be altered, it could be made to fit new circumstances. It could be linked in chains together and create a discourse. This was not just allowed, it was expected, that's the way it was taught…[2]

And,

> Each evangelist presented the life and teaching of Jesus in his own fashion, using creative ways that made it understandable and relevant to different cultures and settings. The numerous differences and discrepancies we see in the Gospels are the result of the writers doing what Jesus taught—and in many ways reflect the standards of history writing current in late antiquity.[3]

When Evans speaks of "adapting and applying" Jesus' life and teaching, he refers to placing such adaptation and application into the mouth of Jesus himself and/or altering the events of Jesus' life. In a debate on the historical reliability of John, the host, Justin Brierley, asks Evans, "Is it okay for a Gospel to effectively put words into Jesus' mouth by, as it were, a kind of adapting…?"[4] Evans replies by likening an author who recorded Jesus' words verbatim to a "trained parrot" and discussing the "pedagogy of antiquity" and his concept of *chreia*, which is his idea

---

[2] Craig A. Evans vs. Bart Ehrman, "Does the New Testament Present a Historically Reliable Portrait of the Historical Jesus?" Saint Mary's University, January 19, 2012, minute 24:22, https://youtu.be/ueRIdrlZsvs?t=1463.

[3] Craig A. Evans, "Fundamentalist Arguments Against Fundamentalism," *On Faith*, https://www.onfaith.co/onfaith/2014/04/16/fundamentalist-arguments-against-fundamentalism/31725.

[4] Lydia McGrew vs. Craig Evans, "Is John's Gospel Historically Accurate?" *Unbelievable*, May 18, 2018, minute 31 and following, http://unbelievable.podbean.com/e/is-john%E2%80%99s-gospel-historically-accurate-lydia-mcgrew-craig-evans-debate/.

that the students were taught to modify historical incidents. This theory will be one of the main topics of this chapter.

Similarly, Licona states that ancient compositional textbooks taught students to change the number of people involved in an incident when reporting historical events and to create dialogue (though no dialogue actually occurred) by converting thoughts or one person's speech into dialogue.[5] He says that a number of such differences found in the Gospels occur because "this is indeed what they [the Gospel authors] were trained to do."[6]

Licona's and Evans's claims can be separated into a claim about the influence of such pedagogy on the Gospel authors and a claim about the content of the pedagogy. They are claiming both that the Gospel authors were trained according to the pedagogical methods they have in mind and also that the methods involved teaching students to alter history.[7] I shall argue that the former claim is very poorly supported and very likely false, especially (as with the claim about Greco-Roman biography) for Matthew, Mark, and John. I will argue that the latter claim (about the content of the pedagogy) is also false. It is based upon a serious misunderstanding of the rhetorical exercises in question.

3. Would the Gospel authors have studied Greek writing textbooks?

Would the Gospel authors have been trained from ancient Greek compositional textbooks similar to the *Progymnasmata* of Aelius Theon? Licona states outright that Matthew was so trained. In describing Matt. 12.9–13, where Jesus heals a man with a withered hand, Licona claims that Matthew took what were really just thoughts of Jesus' opponents and turned them into a dialogue.[8] He states, "[W]e see Matthew doing precisely what he would have been instructed to do in these compositional textbooks. It is entirely proper for him to do it."[9]

---

[5] Licona, *Why Are There Differences*, pp. 11, 42–43, 71, 128–129, 147.

[6] Michael Licona, "Gospel Differences and Compositional Textbooks," July 22, 2015, https://youtu.be/VZvwRyduNSM?t=1862.

[7] Licona and Evans are by no means the only scholars to make such claims, either implicitly or explicitly. Some of the examples I will give of misunderstanding ancient rhetorical exercises or applying the fact-altering concept of *chreia* will come from other scholars. One of the most influential works on the supposed use of fact-altering *chreia* forms by the Gospel authors is Burton L. Mack and Vernon K. Robbins, *Patterns of Persuasion in the Gospels* (1989; repr., Eugene, OR: Wipf and Stock, 2008). I am not interacting with Mack and Robbins directly both because they are not considered evangelical scholars (my focus in this book) and also because Licona himself states that Mack and Robbins go too far in their application of the concept. *Why Are There Differences*, p. 223, n. 15.

[8] Licona, *Why Are There Differences*, p. 128.

[9] Michael Licona, "Gospel Differences and Compositional Textbooks," July 22, 2015, minute

Licona makes no defense of this extremely strong statement about Matthew's education. He does not seem to think he needs to do so, nor does he mention, either in that lecture or elsewhere, the (negative) relevance of traditional Gospel authorship to his claims.

I am not saying, of course, that Gospel authorship of Matthew, Mark, and John by the traditionally ascribed Jewish authors is uncontroversial. But the issue cannot simply be brushed aside in this context. If one is going to state categorically that Matthew "would have been instructed" using Greek exercise books based on Greek literature, one can scarcely ignore the question, "Who was Matthew?" Yet that is exactly what Licona does.

Showing the same bias toward overstating Hellenization, Evans makes strong claims about rabbinic practice:

> Jewish and Greco-Roman pedagogies…were not separate and isolated from one another….Greek and Jewish memory techniques and practice overlapped. Indeed, the Greek gymnasium was present on Jewish soil, even in the vicinity of Jerusalem itself, as early as the second century BC.

He then proceeds to talk about how "young Greeks" were taught using writing exercises based upon anecdotes called *chreiai*.[10] This is an extremely strong connection to claim between Greek and Hebrew education. Evans even goes so far as to say at this same point that "most of the rabbinic rules of exegesis…were learned from the Greeks," an extravagant, insupportable statement that would doubtless surprise historians of Jewish thought.

II Maccabees 4.9 mentions the introduction by Jason, the pro-Greek high priest in the 2nd century B.C., of a gymnasium in the vicinity of Jerusalem, to which Evans alludes. But this fact does not support Hellenistic influence upon rabbinic education, for the Jews of the region strongly opposed Jason's program of Hellenization. Jason and Antiochus Epiphanes, the Greek king of the Seleucid Empire, continued attempting to enforce Greek ways on the people of Judea, and the rest, as they say, is history—namely, the Maccabean revolt. Richard Burridge refers to a Jewish reaction against Hellenistic education in precisely the time period to which Evans is referring,[11] and this is hardly surprising given the recent

---

12:58, https://youtu.be/VZvwRyduNSM?t=778.

[10] Craig A. Evans vs. Bart Ehrman, "Does the New Testament Present a Reliable Portrait of the Historical Jesus?" Acadia University, January 20, 2012, minute 18:30, https://youtu.be/UvCVnlHo-Fow?t=1110.

[11] Richard Burridge, *What Are the Gospels? A Comparison With Greco-Roman Biography* (Grand

history and Jewish sensibilities. It is astonishing that Evans would try to use the presence of a Greek gymnasium, part of what sparked such a negative reaction from the Jews, as part of an argument that rabbinic and Greek pedagogy were deeply intertwined.

As we have already seen in the discussion of Greco-Roman biography in Chapter IV, it is unlikely that a Palestinian Jewish boy would have received a Hellenistic education of the sort Evans and Licona envisage. As discussed there, the evidence that a significant number of Jewish boys in and around Jerusalem at the time of Christ received even the most basic education in being able to read the Greek language is almost entirely indirect, largely based upon the prevalence of Greek in inscriptions and other records. This leads to the reasonable supposition that, *in some fashion*, the ability to be literate in Greek must have been taught.[12] But this does not support anything like Evans's assertion that rabbinic pedagogy was strongly influenced by Greek pedagogy, much less in an ideological area such as attitudes toward reporting the life and teachings of a master. For that statement we have no evidence whatsoever and indeed evidence to the contrary.

Licona uses a different unsupported generalization to bolster the claim that the Gospel authors would have been taught from Greek compositional exercise books, quoting Gerald Downing:

> The procedures [in the exercises] are always so similar that it would be absurd to suppose without massive supporting evidence that the NT evangelists could have learned to write Greek and cope with written source material at all while remaining outside the pervasive influence of these common steps toward literacy.[13]

Downing's claim here is vastly overstated. He appears to think that he can shift the burden of proof to require "massive supporting evidence" *against* the thesis that the Gospel authors had a Hellenistic education merely by declaring that the burden has been shifted. The only point he offers in support of this statement is that the procedures *among* different surviving Greek exercise books are all quite

---

Rapids, Eerdmans, 2004), p. 244.

[12] Andrew W. Pitts, "Hellenistic Schools in Jerusalem and Paul's Rhetorical Education," *Paul's World*, ed. Stanley E. Porter (Leiden, The Netherlands: 2008), pp. 36, 39–44.

[13] F. Gerald Downing, "Compositional Conventions and the Synoptic Problem," *Journal of Biblical Literature*, 107, no. 1 (1988), p. 71. Quoted by Licona, *Why Are There Differences*, p. 14. Ironically, Downing's point in the context of his article as a whole is that these Greek exercises were so relatively simple that they give little guidance concerning complicated redactive activities on the part of the Gospel authors. Downing uses this point indirectly to support an argument he wishes to make in favor of the Q hypothesis.

similar. But what does this show? Only the unity of Hellenistic education at the primary level. It does not show that Jewish Gospel authors *received* a Hellenistic education. A phrase like "remaining outside the pervasive influence of these common steps toward literacy" simply evades stating outright that the Gospel authors had to have *actually been educated* using exercise books like those of Theon. But that has to be the claim in view.

Downing's words give the vague impression that perhaps it would have been impossible to learn to "write Greek and cope with written source material" without receiving a recognizably Hellenistic education. But that is not true. The exercises Licona and Evans are talking about are of a particular type. They use short sayings, anecdotes, and selections from Greek literature or history as "prompts" for written work. The students may be asked to paraphrase the section, disagree with what is said in it or critique it, write an essay of their own confirming a particular proverb, interweave a proverb with a Greek fable, write as if in the voice of some fictional character from Greek stories, and so forth. This is a perfectly serviceable type of curriculum, especially as a starting basis for a later career in politics or rhetoric, but it is obviously not the *only* way in which one could plausibly learn to read and write Greek and to "cope with" documents written in Greek—for example, for Matthew to learn to "cope with" Mark.

Downing's implication may be that no one at the time *would have* learned basic competence of this sort without receiving a Hellenized education using such exercise books, but this, again, is questionable, given the pervasiveness of the Greek *language* without pervasiveness of Greek *culture* in an area like Judea. As pointed out in Chapter IV, it would have been entirely possible for Jewish boys to have learned to read and write Greek by Jewish study based upon the Septuagint version of the Old Testament,[14] and in that case their fathers or rabbis could have developed their own curricular activities which, for all anyone knows, might not have resembled Theon's exercises much at all and would not have been modeled upon them.

As in the case of influence by Greco-Roman biography, so it is here: If Matthew, Mark, and John, and Peter as a major source for Mark, were indeed Jews without unusually Hellenized backgrounds, it is antecedently improbable that they received an education that used the compositional and rhetorical exercises Licona discusses. The only Gospel author who *might* have had such an education,

---

[14] A suggestion made by Pitts, "Hellenistic Schools in Jerusalem and Paul's Rhetorical Education," p. 36.

based upon the excellent quality of his Greek and other independent evidence that he may have been a Gentile physician, is Luke. But that is not because all "pedagogy of the time" was of a unified type, nor because it would otherwise have been impossible to learn to "cope with written source material."

4. Evans's eisegesis of Matthew 13.52

Evans has two more arguments that this was how the Gospel authors (and Jesus' disciples generally) would have been taught or were taught. One of these is so poor on its face that one almost hesitates to mention it. Perhaps Evans intends it to function only as a supplement or illustration after one has accepted his sweeping statements about the "pedagogy of the time." By itself it is the barest eisegesis of a Scriptural text. Evans repeatedly quotes Matt. 13.52 and insists that it refers to the modification of Jesus' own speech, putting that modification into Jesus' mouth. Here is what Jesus says, as Evans quotes it from the New Living Translation:

> Every teacher of religious law who becomes a disciple in the Kingdom of Heaven is like a homeowner who brings from his storeroom new gems of truth as well as old.

Here it is in the NASB:

> Therefore every scribe who has become a disciple of the kingdom of heaven is like a head of a household, who brings out of his treasure things new and old.

And here is Evans's interpretation:

> The scholars and lecturers of this period of time instructed their pupils in the *chreiai* of the great thinkers, teaching them how to edit, contract, or expand the *chreiai*, and to give them new application, in order to make clear to new audiences the true meaning and significance of the wisdom of the great thinkers. Creative adaptation was expected. Remaining true to the original idea was essential.
>
> This is what the writers of the New Testament Gospels did. Indeed, this is how Jesus taught his disciples when he said, "Therefore every teacher of the law who has become a disciple in the kingdom of heaven is like the owner of a house who brings out of his storeroom new treasures as well as old" (Matt. 13:52). That is, the disciples of Jesus are to pull out new lessons and applications, as well as the old, from the treasure of teaching Jesus has given them. Why should anyone be surprised that the disciples and the evangelists who followed them did what Jesus instructed them to do? Each evangelist presented the life and teaching of Jesus in his own fashion, using creative ways that made it understandable and relevant to different cultures and settings. The numerous differences and discrepancies we see in the Gospels are

the result of the writers doing what Jesus taught—and in many ways reflect the standards of history writing current in late antiquity.[15]

Evans again, this time in response to an explicit question about whether he considers it legitimate for the Gospel authors to put words in Jesus' mouth:

> Jesus' teaching has to be understood correctly, and then what is said, how he is summarized, or paraphrased, or elaborated on has to be true to the original intent and true to the entire context of his ministry and his teaching, and very true in light of the Easter event. I, as a starting place, . . . go to Matthew 13:52, where, after these parables on the kingdom of God, he asks his disciples if they understand what he's taught. And they say that they do, and then he goes on to say that the scribe, every scribe who is discipled, trained from the Kingdom of Heaven, knows how to pull out of his treasure box (literally) things that are new as well as things that are old. And I take that, in step with the pedagogy of antiquity, where you really don't know your master's teaching if you simply repeat it word for word. Anybody can do that; a trained parrot can do that. But you demonstrate your knowledge, the fact that you've been discipled, that you truly have learned your master's teaching when you are able to elaborate on it, expand it, or contract it, link different sayings together (and it's called *chreia* in the singular, *chreiai* in the plural).[16]

The verse in question is brief and aphoristic, and for this reason alone Evans's interpretation is highly questionable. What is there in that verse to make one think that Jesus is instructing his disciples to adapt his words and report their adaptations as if they are his own words, or to adapt events in his life by changing factual details? Nothing whatsoever. The context certainly does not do that. Jesus does ask them if they understand his parables, but Evans's interpretation certainly does not follow from that. There are many possibilities for the "old things" and the "new things." The "old things" might be the revelation of the Torah, while the "new things" refer to the new revelation of God in Jesus, which includes new doctrines such as the incarnation and the Trinity. The "old things" might be Jewish tradition while the "new things" refer to subsequent Christian teaching. The "old things" might be the Old Testament while the "new things" could be Christological interpretation of the Old Testament such as Jesus gives on the road to Emmaus in Luke 24. And so forth.[17]

---

[15] Evans, "Fundamentalist Arguments Against Fundamentalism."

[16] Lydia McGrew vs. Craig Evans, "Is John's Gospel Historically Accurate?" *Unbelievable*, May 18, 2018, minute 31 and following.

[17] These possible interpretations of "old things" and "new things" are not merely my own ideas, nor do they arise from some conservative bias. Similar suggestions are found in William David Davies and

Of course Jesus wanted his disciples to teach and apply his teachings in the church after his ascension. But in no way does this mean that Jesus instructed them to present their own interpretations and applications of his teachings *as if* Jesus himself *on earth* had said something that he had not actually said.[18] For such an instruction we have no evidence, and there is evidence to the contrary, as pointed out in the previous chapter, when we find the Gospel authors meticulously distinguishing their own glosses on Jesus' words from what they attribute to him.

5. The abuse of Papias and the abuse of *chreiai*

Evans's one additional attempt to argue that the Gospels are written with such adaptations, taken from compositional exercise books, is his interpretation of the word *chreiai* as found in a quotation from Papias about the composition of Mark. He gives this argument about Papias's use of *chreiai* as he introduces his interpretation of Matt. 13.52, discussed above:

> One of the first to comment on the Gospels was Papias of Asia Minor (modern Turkey). Writing near the beginning of the second century, Papias says the author of the Gospel of Mark compiled *chreiai* ("useful, instructive anecdotes") and wasn't concerned with exact sequence and chronological order. The scholars and lecturers of this period of time instructed their pupils in the *chreiai* of the great thinkers, teaching them how to edit, contract, or expand the *chreiai*, and to give them new application, in order to make clear to new audiences the true meaning and sig-

---

Dale C. Allison, *A Critical and Exegetical Commentary on the Gospel According to Saint Matthew* (London: T & T Clark, 2004), vol. 2, pp. 447–448. Davies and Allison comment, "Although we have ranked these options in what we perceive to be the order of their probability (the most probable first, the least probable last), it must be confessed that the contrast remains cryptic....All we can say with certainty is that the ability to teach things new and old rests upon the ability to understand Jesus' teaching."

[18] Aside from its being complete eisegesis, Evans's interpretation of Matt. 13.52 has a serious self-reference problem. Differences in wording could make the verse, if possible, even *more* difficult to interpret as Evans wishes. For example, if Jesus had said, instead, "The kingdom of heaven is like a treasure house filled with both old things and new," without any reference to a scribe bringing them out, it would be even more remote from Evans's ideas. And that would be a relatively minor difference compared to the extrapolations that Evans himself allows—for example, the wholesale invention of the saying, "I am the bread of life" by the Johannine community. Or if Jesus had historically said, "The kingdom of heaven is like a treasure house filled with old things and new, but let not the new things be of the scribe's own making," this would be evidence against extrapolation. Or if the saying were never uttered recognizably at all but were placed into Jesus' mouth because the author was inspired by some teaching that did not verbally resemble it, Evans would not have such a verse to work with. Given Evan's *own theory*, which he is claiming comes partly *from* this verse, how do we know that this verse *itself* is not a theological extrapolation of some kind put into Jesus' mouth? I thank Dennis Monokroussos for pointing out the self-reference issue to me.

nificance of the wisdom of the great thinkers. Creative adaptation was expected. Remaining true to the original idea was essential.[19]

Given Evans's views on the Gospel of John, quoted in Chapter III, section 2, one may well wonder what "remaining true to the original idea" even means. Perhaps it only means, as in the quotation from Evans given above, being "true to the entire context of [Jesus'] ministry and his teaching, and very true in light of the Easter event," which is hardly a ringing endorsement of historical accuracy. In any event, Evans is implying that Papias' use of the word *chreiai* with reference to Mark's Gospel means that Mark, and by extension the other evangelists, deliberately changed events and words in historical writing. This is how this theory is supposed to explain the existence of apparent discrepancies in the Gospels. Evans interprets this to be what students were instructed to do when they rewrote *chreiai* in the Greek exercise books (a point I will strongly question below), and he takes the fact that Papias uses this term to describe the incidents in the Gospel of Mark to mean that Mark was influenced by such exercises.

Evans has his own translation of Papias, and this is how he cites him:

> New Testament scholars have discovered the *chreia* form in the Gospels ....This has been much discussed in the literature of the last twenty-five years or so. Indeed, the church father Papias, who writing in the early second century wrote a large work on the teaching of Jesus..., In one of the surviving fragments...he mentions the evangelist Mark, saying that Mark "wrote down accurately everything he remembered [from Peter], though not in order ..." and that also "he followed Peter (and) adapted his teaching as *chreiai*...."[20]

A relatively small point worth making is that Evans's translation here is non-standard. While the Greek does permit one to say that Mark composed *chreiai* (anecdotes), the more common translation of Papias' remarks attributes the use of anecdotes to *Peter*. Richard Bauckham's translation of Papias is typical:

> The Elder used to say: Mark, in his capacity as Peter's interpreter, wrote down accurately as many things as he recalled from memory—though not in an ordered form—of the things either said or done by the Lord. For he [Mark] neither heard the Lord nor accompanied him, but later, as I said, [he heard and accompanied] Peter, who used to give his teachings in the form of *chreiai*, but had no intention

---

[19] Evans, "Fundamentalist Arguments Against Fundamentalism."

[20] Craig A. Evans vs. Bart Ehrman, "Does the New Testament Present a Reliable Portrait of the Historical Jesus?" minute 20:18 https://youtu.be/UvCVnlHoFow?t=1218.

of providing an ordered arrangement of the *logia* of the Lord. Consequently Mark did nothing wrong when he wrote down some individual items just as he…related them from memory. For he made it his one concern not to omit anything he had heard or to falsify anything.[21]

Since we know more about Peter than about Mark, we have (if possible) even less scope for conjecturing that Peter was rhetorically trained. Hence, Papias' saying that Peter gave his teachings in the form of *chreiai* makes it even more difficult to take this to refer to a technical, rhetorical form which Peter was taught to manipulate from Greek exercise books. Evans's translation that Mark himself *adapted* Peter's teachings as *chreiai* is one way in which his interpretation of Papias is biased from the beginning.

But the problems with Evans's use of the term *chreiai* go much deeper than a slanted translation implying that Mark rather than Peter used *chreiai*. For even if, along with Richard Bauckham, we take the word to be used broadly in the sense that an author like Theon would use it,[22] it need not at all mean that anyone involved (either Peter or Mark) was acquainted with the methods of using *chreiai* as prompts in exercise books. The term simply means "short anecdotes"—short segments of narrative about a particular person, centered on an action or saying by that person. That is all. Evans is reading into the term all of the "baggage" of the specifically curricular use of anecdotes in rhetorical exercise books (as Evans conceives of that use), but a connection with rhetorical education is quite unnecessary. For Papias to tell his readers that Peter related (or Mark related) the stories of Jesus in the form of *chreiai* tells us nothing whatsoever in and of itself about whether or not Peter or Mark had practiced rewriting anecdotes as a type of educational exercise. The term itself is simply not that heavy in meaning. Bauckham makes the point well:

> The English term "anecdote" seems the best equivalent, for an anecdote is also a brief story about a particular person, focusing on a particular action or saying or both….Greek education taught people how to use such anecdotes in argumentative rhetoric intended to persuade. Theon prescribed eight exercises for students to

---

[21] Eusebius, *Ecclesiastical History* 3.39.15, as translated by Richard Bauckham, *Jesus and the Eyewitnesses: The Gospels as Eyewitness Testimony*, 2nd ed. (Grand Rapids, Eerdmans, 2017), p. 203.

[22] Strictly literally, the word just means "uses" or "needs," and some older translators took Papias as saying that Peter taught "according to needs," in other words, as the need arose. It's worth at least knowing about this further point concerning translation, but I am willing for the sake of the argument to grant that the term here means "anecdotes" rather than "needs," while simultaneously pointing out, along with Bauckham, that this does not have the implications Evans claims.

do with *chreiai*, including memorizing *chreiai*, grammatical exercises, commenting on, confirming and refuting, all with a view to the use of *chreiai* in speeches aimed at persuading people. In order to relate the deeds and sayings of Jesus in the form of short anecdotes Peter certainly did not need to have had such rhetorical training. We simply do not know how Peter would have used such anecdotes in his preaching, if Papias is correct in implying that he did ....Peter may in fact, for all we know, simply have rehearsed the traditions. Certainly, within the Gospel of Mark, the context of the traditions is a narrative, not a speech. The Gospel doubtless aims to persuade, but only in the way that a narrative can do, quite different from the way a speech can. In my view it is therefore a mistake to apply the exercises with *chreiai* prescribed by the grammarians to analysis of *chreiai* in the Gospels. There is no reason why Peter could not have given many of the *chreiai* in Mark their basic forms in his oral rehearsing of the words and deeds of Jesus.[23]

Bauckham's point that the Gospels aim to persuade as a narrative persuades, not as a rhetorical speech does, is especially important. Theorists who wish to assimilate the Gospels to rhetorical forms persistently ignore the distinction between a persuasive speech and an historical narrative. Bauckham is also on-point in making it clear that a *chreia* is simply a short anecdote and that we should not read too much into Papias' use of the word:

[W]e should remember that the definitions and classifications of the grammarians, such as Theon, were descriptive as well as prescriptive. Essentially they were describing the various sorts of anecdotes that people, educated or not, told. In a predominantly oral culture everyone was familiar with various forms of relating short narratives or reporting sayings and would adopt such forms without needing to reflect on the matter at all. In fact, it would be difficult for anyone to tell a short anecdote that did not come within Theon's definition and qualify as one of his subtypes. Education would simply heighten self-conscious reflection on the forms of anecdote in common use and teach people effective use of anecdotes in persuasion and argumentation.[24]

Evans is simply leaning much too hard on a single word in Papias' statement about the composition of Mark.

Moreover, Evans's interpretation of the term *chreiai* in Papias goes *against* the context of Papias' discussion of Mark as well as against Papias' other statements about the importance of knowing the truth about Jesus' teaching. In the immediate context of his discussion of Mark's composition, Papias emphasizes Mark's

---

[23] Bauckham, *Jesus and the Eyewitnesses*, pp. 216–217.
[24] Ibid.

literal truthfulness: "[H]e made it his one concern not to omit anything he had heard or to falsify anything." It is quite striking that Evans takes a single word in this context to justify the idea that Mark himself deliberately "creatively adapted" Peter's teaching, expanding or contracting it or changing Jesus' words, in order to "make clear to new audiences" its significance and meaning. This appears to be precisely the sort of thing that Papias is saying Mark *did not* do. Elsewhere, as we have seen, Papias insists that he himself was not interested in hearing "someone else's commandments, but only in those who reported their memory of the commandments given by the Lord to the faith and proceeding from the Truth itself."[25] Going back to his discussion of Mark, Papias says that "Mark did nothing wrong when he wrote down some individual items just as he [Peter] related them from memory."[26] It is highly unlikely, given Papias' other comments, that Papias would have approved of Mark's procedure if he believed that Mark was engaging in the kind of creative adaptation Evans envisages.

In fact, Evans's entire interpretation is a classic case of being unable to see the forest because one is focused not even on a single tree, but on a single twig. He takes the word *chreiai* alone, gives it a heavy, rhetorical over-interpretation, and then uses it in such a way that it contradicts the very context in which it occurs and other statements by the same author. This is no basis for concluding that the Gospel authors had been educated using ancient exercise books.

6. What is a writing textbook?

But we are not yet done with the errors of the literary device theorists in their use of exercise books. The use of textbooks to support fictionalizing literary devices fails all along the line. I conceded above that, given Luke's excellent Greek linguistic ability and the possibility that he was a Gentile doctor, he *might* have encountered or even been taught from Greek exercises like those contained in Theon's *Progymnasmata*. This is somewhat plausible because these exercises were used at a lower level of rhetorical education. Even someone who was not a fully-trained rhetorician might have encountered them. It is therefore relevant at least for Luke to ask ourselves whether the theorists' portrayal of what these books taught is accurate. Did they indeed teach a theory of historiography according to which authors were encouraged to alter the words of "master teachers" to show

---

[25] Eusebius, *Ecclesiastical History,* 3.39.3–4. Trans. Arthur Cushman McGiffert, 1890, http://www.newadvent.org/fathers/250103.htm.

[26] Eusebius, *Ecclesiastical History*, 3.39.15, translated by Bauckham, *Jesus and the Eyewitnesses*, p. 203.

that they had understood them, putting those words into the mouth of the teacher in writing a memoir? Did the books indeed teach students that it is not only legitimate but expected, if they are writing a putatively historical work or a memoir, to change the order of events, to put sayings into contexts where they never occurred, and to elaborate stories fictionally?

Not at all. The extreme weakness of the theorists' arguments that all of the Gospel authors would have been influenced by Hellenistic exercise books is surprising, but it is no less surprising to see how entirely they misunderstand the exercises themselves.

Consider a modern example. Suppose that you find a high school English composition textbook lying on a table. Flipping through it idly, you find the following assignments:

- Write a speech that George Washington could have given to encourage his men at Valley Forge.

- Write a dialogue between two soldiers just before the Battle of Gettysburg. You may choose whether to use Union or Confederate soldiers.

- Here is an excerpt from Winston Churchill's *History of the English Speaking Peoples* in which he describes the Battle of Marston Moor in the English Civil War. Rewrite the account in your own words.

- Consider the proverb, "Look before you leap." Write an essay elaborating on this proverb and explaining why it is true. Then write another essay arguing against the proverb.

Do you take it from the existence of these assignments, and more like them, that high school students taught from this curriculum are learning to alter historical facts if they should become historians later in life? Of course not. These are *writing assignments*. Their intention is to give the student practice in becoming a good writer. The assignments tell you nothing whatsoever about what the students are taught about historiography and the requirements of truthfulness in recounting history. Even when an assignment tells them to imagine words that might be said by an historical character in some situation, this is just an exercise for their creativity, writing prowess, or persuasive abilities. If there is an emphasis in the curriculum upon speech writing, one might guess that politics and professional speech writing are in view as possible later careers for the students. If there is a strong emphasis upon arguing both sides of an issue, this would help to prepare students for a legal career. And so forth. None of this has anything at all to do with telling students that they are permitted or encouraged to change history if they should write history. And this is true even if the curriculum is intended for the use of, *inter alia*, future historians. Historians need to be good, vivid writers, able to carry a narrative along well, and creative writing exercises can be useful preparation to that end without in any way encouraging fictionalizing in the apparently serious presentation of facts. Nor are young people taught from such a curriculum likely to be confused on these points. They might learn to be loose in writing history if alteration of fact in historical writing is presented as normative *in some other way* in their training. But the compositional curriculum *itself* simply does not address that issue one way or the other.

This is precisely the sort of thing we find in the *Progymnasmata* of Theon and others such as Hermogenes. The writers of these rhetorical exercises simply do not address the issue of historical truthfulness. That is not their purpose, nor are their exercises even confusing on this point. Their goal is to teach students to be good at writing and rhetoric of various kinds, and that is all. I am *not* saying that Theon advocated scrupulous historical accuracy in writing putatively historical work. I *am* saying that his exercises *simply are not about that subject* and that it is not possible to tell from the exercises what he thought about that subject, any more than it would be possible to tell that about the curriculum author from the writing assignments listed above. Just as there is no reason to think that students who are taught to write from a curriculum like the hypothetical modern one just described will get the idea that creative alteration and invention of fact are welcome in serious historical writing, there is no reason to think that Theon's exercises were taken to be "instructing" students in that way either. The literary device theorists are therefore completely misinterpreting and misapplying these exercises when they imply that they provided historiographical models that instructed students to change historical facts.

This misinterpretation of the exercises is pervasive and profound. I will give a number of examples in this chapter and provide a few more similar points in an appendix. I encourage readers to see for themselves if they have doubts.[27] One can read the entirety of Theon's *Progymnasmata* (as I have done) without finding what Evans implies—pedagogy urging students to show that they are true disciples by creatively adapting and extrapolating their master teacher's words, putting those words into the mouth of the teacher, and reporting them as if they were said by the teacher himself. That is simply not the topic a writer of a rhetorical writing handbook was interested in.

---

[27] Theon's *Progymnasmata* and several other rhetorical exercise books, in the George Kennedy translation and edition cited by Licona, are available on-line at https://issuu.com/jmaksimczuk/docs/progymnasmata.

7. Misunderstanding inflection exercises

One of Licona's most striking instances of misinterpretation concerns grammatical exercises involving inflection. Greek is, of course, an inflected language. It has various cases for nouns showing whether the noun is (speaking in English grammatical terms) the subject or the object of the verb, and so forth. Greek nouns have number, as do verbs, and verbs have to agree with their subject in number. Making matters more complicated for students of classical Greek, there was a third number for verbs besides singular and plural—the dual, indicating pairs of things. Theon suggests that students vary the number of the nouns in writing various sentences so as to practice inflection. The rather dull nature of this exercise—having *nothing at all* to do with accuracy in writing history but rather having to do with grammatical fluency—is evident from Theon's description:

> Inflection takes many forms; for we change the person in the chreia into all three numbers and do this in several ways: (expressing it as) one person speaking about one or two or more; and conversely two speaking about one and two and more, and also plural persons speaking about one and two and more. If the chreia is that Isocrates the orator said that those with natural ability are the children of the gods, we inflect it as one person speaking of one other by saying, "Isocrates the orator said that the student with natural ability was a child of gods"; and as two of two, that "The twin orators Isocrates said the twin students with natural ability are children of gods"; and as plural of plural, that "The orators Isocrates said the students with natural ability are children of gods." From these examples it is evident how we shall inflect the other forms; for (the original statements) are changed into the five grammatical cases.[28]

Theon then goes on to illustrate how to have the student practice writing the different cases, such as the nominative and genitive. George Kennedy, the translator and editor, comments,

> For elementary students of Greek, a highly inflected language, practice in grammatical inflection was important. Thus they were asked to restate a chreia in a variety of grammatical forms, even though the results might seem artificial.[29]

---

[28] Aelius Theon, "The Exercises of Aelius Theon," in *Progymnasmata: Greek Textbooks of Prose Composition and Rhetoric*, trans. by George Kennedy (Atlanta: Society of Biblical Literature, 2003), pp. 19–20. I will give only the page numbers in the Kennedy translation for all citations to Theon. Licona in *Why Are There Differences* cites two different numbering systems. His second number in citations is the page number in the Kennedy translation.

[29] Ibid., p. 19, n. 78.

The results obviously *are* artificial. No student, made to carry out this exercise, could possibly conclude that he was licensed to imply in an historical work that there really once existed twin orators named Isocrates or that they spoke of twin students with natural ability. The exercise merely gives the student the opportunity to practice using the dual number.

From this type of inflection exercise Licona draws an odd conclusion:

> Theon explains that inflection can also include changing the number of persons involved. For example, we can change the number of people speaking from one to two or even more. The converse may likewise occur, changing a plurality of persons speaking to only one. The same may be said of the number of persons being addressed (101 [19]).
>
> On a regular basis, we observe Plutarch employing inflection when mentioning two or more persons speaking in one *Life* while only mentioning one speaking in another *Life*.[30]

Here Licona gives the impression that Theon is teaching students that they are permitted, in historical writing, to change the number of people who were reported to be involved on a given occasion, without historical justification. He also seems to be implying that Plutarch actually altered historical fact in this way, using the "device" or "exercise" of inflection as he had been instructed from compositional textbooks.

Can this really be what Licona means? It would be an obvious misapplication of the dull exercise in Theon's textbook. The only other option is that he merely means that Plutarch shows himself capable of the *elementary act of writing Greek* using the plural, dual, and singular, but that would be so elementary as not to merit such formal treatment, much less a label of an activity carried out by Plutarch and the Gospel writers. Anyone capable of writing Greek obviously was capable of inflecting nouns and verbs, but this has nothing to do with deliberately changing (historically) the presentation of events from one version to another version of the same event. If Plutarch sometimes spoke of one person and sometimes of multiple people, perhaps he was merely focusing on one person at one time and on a larger group at another time. No historical alteration needs to be taking place.[31]

---

[30] Licona, *Why Are There Differences*, p. 11.

[31] Licona himself (*Why Are There Differences*, p. 20) refers to this mundane reporting activity—focusing sometimes on one person who is part of a larger group—as "spotlighting," and it is a non-fictionalizing activity that Licona will sometimes discuss as if he learned it as a "literary device" from Plutarch. As already discussed in Chapter III, section 1, it was in fact known by traditional harmonizers without a special name and without reference to Plutarch long before Licona called it "spot-

But if there were any doubt about his meaning, examples actually given by Licona show that he does indeed think that historical alteration of the number of persons reportedly involved in an incident was "inflection," a known device of the time:

> [I]t is "all the others" except Cato who are assigned…the words attributed to Ahenobarbus in Pompey. Does Plutarch transfer what others were saying to Ahenobarbus (or from Ahenobarbus to others), or does he employ inflection by changing a plural in *Caesar* to a singular in *Pompey* (or change a singular in *Pompey* to a plural in *Caesar*)?[32]

In other words, Licona suggests here that Plutarch may more or less randomly change the claim that one person—Ahenobarbus—spoke the words in one biography to the claim that multiple people spoke the words in a different biography, or vice versa, just to change the number of the noun, not for an historical reason. Similarly, he writes,

> In *Cat. Min.* 30.3–4, Cato's wife and sisters (plural) were displeased when he rejected Pompey's proposal. In *Pomp.* 44.3, it was Cato's wife and sister (one). Perhaps this is a change of inflection from singular to plural or vice versa.[33]

Obviously, "sister" *is* singular and "sisters" *is* plural, so in that trivial sense (so trivial as not to deserve mention) Plutarch is inflecting the *word* differently in the different accounts. But Licona says only that perhaps this is a change of inflection. If one merely were talking about singular and plural being different, there would be no "perhaps" about the matter. Again, then, Licona must be saying that *perhaps* Plutarch changed the number of sisters *just in order to inflect the noun, without historical justification*, as though changing a singular to a plural were a thing that ancient writers randomly did in historical writing, aside from the actual number of persons involved in the incident. But Theon's dull exercise of grammatical inflection does not even remotely teach that sort of historical looseness.

8. Misunderstanding dialogue exercises

An alleged example from exercise books that Licona applies directly to the Gospels concerns the creation of dialogue. Theon uses a passage from Thucydides as an exercise prompt, as any teacher might use a passage from a modern historian to

---

lighting." But at times Licona speaks instead of "inflection" as *changing* the number of people involved.

[32] Licona, *Why Are There Differences*, p. 71.

[33] Ibid., p. 43.

give students material to work with in their writing exercises. Thucydides' passage tells how a force of Thebans entered the town of Plataea by night. Theon suggests ways to use the passage, producing variations as an exercise. One of these involves creating a sort of frame dialogue in which one person asks questions about what happened in the story, so that gradually the other person in the dialogue tells the entire story in answer to a series of questions. Theon says, "If we wish to use a dialogue form, we shall suppose some people talking with each other about what has been done, and one teaching, the other learning, about the occurrences."[34] Then he gives this example:

> A. Often in the past it occurred to me to ask you about what happened to the Thebans and Plataeans at Plataea, and I would gladly hear now if this is a good opportunity for you to give a narrative account.

> B. By Zeus, it is a good opportunity, and I shall tell you now if, as you say, you have a desire to hear about these things. The Thebans, always at odds with the Plataeans, wanted to seize hold of Plataea in peace time. A force of them, therefore, a little more than three hundred in number, went under arms about the first watch into the city, an ally of Athenians.

> A. How then did they easily escape notice, going in at night when the gates were shut and a guard posted?

> B. You slightly anticipated what I was going to say, that some men, Naucleides and those with him, opened the gates, there being no guard posted because of the peace.[35]

Theon says, "In the same way we shall continue asking and answering in accordance with the rules of dialogue." Although the short sentence that Theon actually quotes from Thucydides at the beginning of his section on narrative variation does not contain the information that Naucleides let in the Thebans, this information is found in that section of Thucydides.[36]

It is from this example that Licona concludes that someone taught from such an exercise book would have been instructed to *create* dialogue *in history*, even where no such dialogue occurred. He says, "Matthew takes the thoughts of the Pharisees and converts them into a dialogue with Jesus."[37] The passage in question

---

[34] Theon, *Progymnasmata*, p. 37.

[35] Ibid., pp. 37–38.

[36] Thucydides, *History of the Peloponnesian War*, 2.6.2.

[37] Licona, *Why Are There Differences*, p. 128.

is the healing of the man with the withered hand as recounted in Matthew 12, as compared with the same story told in Luke 6 and Mark 3. In a lecture, Licona says, of this alleged creation of dialogue, "[W]e see Matthew doing precisely what he would have been instructed to do in these compositional textbooks. It is entirely proper for him to do it."[38]

I have already dealt at some length with the dubious nature of the statement that Matthew would have been instructed from compositional textbooks like Theon's at all. Now we see that it is at least equally dubious to say that such textbooks instructed students to create dialogue when writing history or memoirs. To begin with, even in the example in Theon, the dialogue occurs in a frame story, not in the alleged historical setting. Theon's idea is to get the student to rewrite the story of the attack by imagining someone asking questions that elicit the information piece by piece. But even if Theon had suggested that students carry out an exercise in which they added dialogue to an historical setting, this would be just like creative writing exercises we are already familiar with, like asking writing students to make up a dialogue between two soldiers before the battle of Gettysburg. It would not involve suggesting to students, much less *instructing* them, that they are supposed to create similarly dramatized versions of historical events when writing works presented as history.

9. Other exercises with a narrative prompt

This point applies directly to another of Theon's suggested exercises—making a command.[39]

> If we want to treat it as a command, we shall do so as follows. At the end of the narration, after (describing) the destruction of those who entered Thebes, we shall introduce someone advising the Thebans or Plataeans as follows: "Come, O Plataeans, be worthy of your city and of your ancestors who contended with Persians and Mardonius, and of those who lie buried in your land. Show the Thebans that they do wrong in thinking you should harken to them and be slaves and in forcing those unwilling to do so, contrary to oaths and treaties, when, a little more than three hundred in number, they entered under arms during the first watch into our city, an ally of Athenians." Then we shall continue the rest as addressing Plataeans.[40]

---

[38] Michael Licona, "Gospel Differences and Compositional Textbooks," July 22, 2015, minute 12:58, https://youtu.be/VZvwRyduNSM?t=778.

[39] Theon, *Progymnasmata*, p. 35.

[40] Ibid., pp. 36–37.

This is very much like the exercise above that asks the student to write a speech (in this case a short one) for George Washington to give to encourage his troops at Valley Forge. Again, it does not recommend to students that, if they are writing actual history, they invent such dramatic commands without historical sources to back them up. I am, again, not saying that Theon would have been opposed to such invention. I am saying instead that the existence of such exercises *simply does not tell us* what he, or students trained using these exercises, would have thought about dramatizing history by putting words into the characters' mouths. As in our own time, the existence of creative writing exercises involving dramatization simply does not address common conventions for writing actual historical works, much less the standards adopted by a given author in a particular historical work.

The educational and sometimes quite artificial nature of these variation exercises is evident from the fact that one suggested assignment involves literally negating the entire story:

> Moreover, when stating the facts, sometimes we use the positive, but it is possible (as an exercise) not only to use the positive but also to produce narrations in negative form. The positive form is the way we said Thucydides produced his narration; a negative version would be, for example, "Neither did a band of Thebans, a little more than three hundred in number, go under arms about the first watch into Plataea in Boeotia, an ally of Athenians, nor did Naucleides and those with him open the gates," and so on to the end.[41]

The emphasis upon what may be done "as an exercise" supports the point I am making, as does the nature of this exercise. No schoolboy, set to rewrite a short narrative passage from Thucydides by literally negating everything that Thucydides asserts, would be under the impression that this exercise taught him that it was legitimate to change the assertion of facts into the denial of those same facts when writing history.

Theon gives a minimal dramatization exercise, somewhat similar to imagining commands uttered to the Plataeans, when he suggests that students write a slightly expanded version of a *chreia* (short anecdote) about a victorious general who died childless:

---

[41] Theon, *Progymnasmata*, p. 38. The editor, Kennedy, notes that a different scholar has suggested that this paragraph may not have been part of Theon's original text (p. 38, n. 129), though Kennedy himself chooses to include it. If this exercise was inserted by someone copying out Theon's work, it is illustrative as well of the way that these exercises were understood.

We expand the chreia whenever we lengthen the questions and answers in it, and the action or suffering, if any. We compress by doing the opposite. For example, this chreia is brief: "Epaminondas, dying childless, said to his friends, 'I leave two daughters, the victory at Leuctra and that at Mantinea.'" We expand it as follows: "Epaminadas, the general of the Thebans, was, you should know, a great man in peacetime, but when war with Lacedaimonians came to his fatherland he demonstrated many shining deeds of greatness. When serving as Boeotarch at Leuctra, he defeated the enemy; and conducting a campaign and contending on behalf of his country, he died at Mantinea. When he had been wounded and his life was coming to an end, while his friends were bewailing many things, including that he was dying childless, breaking into a smile, he said, 'Cease your weeping, my friends, for I have left you two immortal daughters: two victories of my country over Lacedaimonians, one at Leuctra, the elder, the younger just begotten by me at Mantinea.'"[42]

Some of this expansion uses known historical information, such as that Epaminadas was a Theban general. Some of it constitutes very slight dramatization, such as stating that the general smiled, that his friends were bewailing his childless death, and so forth. But again, this is a writing exercise given to students. Nowhere does Theon suggest that even this extremely minimal degree of dramatization is particularly recommended to historians writing as historians. Similarly, an author of a modern compositional curriculum who told students to fill out and slightly dramatize a briefly-described historical scene would not be making any recommendation one way or another concerning the propriety of this activity when writing actual historical work.

If it is replied that I am making too much of an analogy between modern and ancient historical conventions, I suggest that the reader remember an important point: These writing exercise books are supposed to be an important part of the *evidence* for a *difference* between ancient and modern historical conventions. Yet it turns out that we have similar compositional exercises in our own time and that they mean nothing in and of themselves about historiographical convention. All of the past three chapters have gone to show that the claims of large differences between ancient and modern attitudes toward historical truth are either exaggerated or false. Without other evidence that *writing textbooks* constitute, in and of themselves, *historiographical advice*, there is no reason to think that they do. Any good teacher in *any* age might teach his students to write using such exercises, and unless he also tells them that they are to expand actual historical events in

---

[42] Ibid., pp. 21–22.

this same way, the schoolboy exercises themselves simply do not tell us what the students were being taught about accuracy in writing history. Indeed, we can see again and again that these exercises were artificial and mundane.

10. Misunderstanding elaboration exercises

"Elaboration" sounds like it might be a fertile field for finding advice or a device for altering history, but the same type of misunderstanding of Theon occurs there. Licona says,

> Writers can add to the original words or thoughts for clarification, further description, or artistic improvement. Theon is thinking in terms of only a very few additional words. However, he follows up his section on "Paraphrase" with one on "Elaboration," in which a text is expanded in order to add what was lacking in thought and expression.[43]

At Jesus' crucifixion, Matthew includes some additional words from the crowd that are not recorded in the other Gospels, and Licona refers to these as Matthew's "elaborating":

> The logia of the Jewish leaders at Golgotha differ slightly. In Mark 15:31b–32 they say, "He saved others; he is not able to save himself. [He is] the Messiah, the King of Israel! Let him come down from the cross now, in order that we may see and believe." Matthew 27:42–43 is similar to Mark with only slight alterations but then elaborates, "He saved others; he is not able to save himself. He is the King of Israel. Let him come down from the cross now and we will believe in him. He has trusted in God. Let God rescue him now if He wants. For he said, 'I am God's Son.'"[44]

Is Licona suggesting that the additional taunts in Matthew did not occur historically, that Matthew put them into the mouths of the Jewish leaders as a rhetorical "elaboration"?

Keener suggests that perhaps Jesus' connected discourses in the Gospel of John are the result not of John's having an excellent memory for what Jesus historically said or even of his passing on additional tradition (not found in the Synoptics) about what Jesus said but rather of John's "developing his material" in the way that Greco-Roman authors did who were using the "rhetorical technique of elaboration" in order to "expound the meaning" of his tradition "for his own gen-

---

[43] Licona, *Why Are There Differences*, p. 13.

[44] Ibid., p. 164.

eration."[45] Keener portrays the "technique of elaboration" as adding non-factual material to putatively historical documents in such a way that it appears factual.

But once again, Theon never enjoins students to do anything of the kind. In fact, the misunderstanding in this case is particularly striking since the exercise in Theon does not even involve anything like creative writing in which the student adds something to a narrative. In the passage of Theon cited by Licona, Theon compares two orators who both praise the Athenians for a noble act of returning good for evil to a city that had been the cause of harm to them. One orator states the praise of the Athenians more briefly while the other states it at greater length and with more structure. I quote the entire section to make it obvious that Theon is not talking about changing history at all. Nor is he talking about putting words in anyone's mouth. He is talking about writing something like a speech or what we might call an editorial and improving upon a different author's way of making the same point. Historical elaboration is not even in the picture, nor anything that looks at all like it.

> Elaboration (*exergasia*) is language that adds what is lacking in thought and expression. What is "lacking" can be supplied by making clear what is obscure; by filling gaps in the language or content; by saying some things more strongly, or more believably, or more vividly, or more truly, or more wordily—each word repeating the same thing—, or more legally, or more beautifully, or more appropriately, or more opportunely, or making the subject pleasanter, or using a better arrangement or a style more ornate.
>
> Consider the words about the Euboeans in Aeschines' *Against Ctesiphon* and Demosthenes' *On the Crown*. The Athenians had gone to their aid, even though the Euboeans had been the cause of wrong to them, and had saved them and restored their cities. Aeschines says: "You righteously and justly restored the cities themselves and their constitutions to those who had entrusted them to you, not thinking it right to remember your anger when they had put faith in you." And Demosthenes: "You, on the one hand, did a noble thing in saving the island, but it was a yet nobler thing by far, that when their lives and their cities were absolutely in your power, you gave them back, as it was right to do, to the very men who had offended against you, and made no reckoning, when such trust had been placed in you, of the wrongs which you had suffered." Because Demosthenes' version is heavier in sound Aeschines' version can seem in contrast solid, firm and simple, and because those who understand such things can perceive that Demosthenes repeats sounds, let us, when teaching, examine and discuss the details. Aeschines simplified in combining the good deeds into one; Demosthenes made them into two things, presenting

---

[45] Craig Keener, *The Gospel of John: A Commentary* (Grand Rapids, MI: Baker Academic, 2003), p. 54.

separately the act of saving and the act of restoring, and at the same time he has amplified the second act with the addition of "a yet nobler thing by far." Moreover, Aeschines spoke of the state of mind in which the Athenians acted; Demosthenes described it more fully: "You, on the one hand, did a noble thing," brings credibility by adding "on the one hand."[46]

A later rhetorical exercise book attributed to Apthonius the Sophist (4th century A.D.) illustrates the same point. Apthonius gives a full illustration of "elaborating the *chreia*" where the *chreia* in question, in this case a short, proverbial saying that Apthonius calls a "verbal *chreia*" is attributed to Isocrates: "Isocrates said [that] the root of education is bitter but the fruits are sweet." What Apthonius calls an "elaboration" of this saying is what we would call a short essay, using the saying as an essay prompt. I will not weary the reader by quoting the entire sample essay that Apthonius writes. The elaboration exercise consists of first praising Isocrates, then putting the saying into the writer's own words (in clearly indirect speech and without the slightest pretense that Isocrates said it in this way), and then arguing in various ways that this saying is true and wise. The essayist talks about the rigors of education, in which boys may be beaten by their pedagogues, followed by the reward of virtue in their adulthood, the harm that comes to boys who run away from education and lose its value, makes a comparison with sowing seeds in the earth and reaping the crop, and so forth. The summing-up sentence in the illustrative essay is, "Looking at all this, one should admire Isocrates for his wise and beautiful speculation about education."[47]

This cloying little example essay has nothing whatsoever to do with altering an historical report. Again, elaboration, like all the other types we have looked at, is a rhetorical exercise, not an historiographical method.

11. Misunderstanding paraphrase exercises

Finally, let us consider the rhetorical exercise of paraphrase. We have already seen repeatedly that "paraphrase" is an important term for literary device theorists and that they sometimes use it in surprising ways. As mentioned in Chapter II, section 4, Licona has suggested that perhaps Jesus did not utter "Before Abraham was, I am" in an historically recognizable form but rather John created that saying as an "adaptation" of more implicit indications of Jesus' deity in

---

[46] Theon, pp. 71–72.

[47] Apthonius the Sophist, "Preliminary Exercises of Apthonius the Sophist," in *Progymnasmata: Greek Textbooks of Prose Composition and Rhetoric*, trans. by George Kennedy (Atlanta: Society of Biblical Literature), pp. 98–99.

completely different scenes. He suggests that, if John engaged in this activity, it should be called a "loose paraphrase."[48]

Evans has insisted that, as part of ancient pedagogy, disciples were instructed to report their teacher's words in a different form from that in which he uttered them, in order to show their understanding. As I have quoted before, when asked, "Is it okay for a Gospel to effectively put words into Jesus' mouth by, as it were, a kind of adapting...?" Evans replied,

> Jesus' teaching has to be understood correctly, and then what is said, how he is summarized, or paraphrased, or elaborated on has to be true to the original intent and true to the entire context of his ministry and his teaching, and very true in light of the Easter event....I take that, in step with the pedagogy of antiquity, where you really don't know your master's teaching if you simply repeat it word for word. Anybody can do that; a trained parrot can do that. But you demonstrate your knowledge, the fact that you've been discipled, that you truly have learned your master's teaching when you are able to elaborate on it, expand it, or contract it....[49]

And he followed this up by challenging me as his opponent in the debate, asking if I "allow for paraphrase."

Similarly, Evans says,

> This is what the writers of the New Testament Gospels did. Indeed, this is how Jesus taught his disciples when he said, "Therefore every teacher of the law who has become a disciple in the kingdom of heaven is like the owner of a house who brings out of his storeroom new treasures as well as old" (Matt. 13:52). That is, the disciples of Jesus are to pull out new lessons and applications, as well as the old, from the treasure of teaching Jesus has given them. Why should anyone be surprised that the disciples and the evangelists who followed them did what Jesus instructed them to do? Each evangelist presented the life and teaching of Jesus in his own fashion, using creative ways that made it understandable and relevant to different cultures and settings. The numerous differences and discrepancies we see in the Gospels are the result of the writers doing what Jesus taught—and in many ways reflect the standards of history writing current in late antiquity.[50]

---

[48] Michael Licona, "Are We Reading an Adapted Form of Jesus' Teachings in John's Gospel?" *Risen Jesus*, Sept. 29, 2017, https://www.risenjesus.com/reading-adapted-form-jesus-teachings-johns-gospel. "Bonus Episode 14: Mike Licona Answers Your Questions on the Gospels," *The Freethinking Podcast*, minute 23:30 and following, http://freethinkingministries.com/bonus-ep-14-mike-licona-answers-your-questions-on-the-gospels/.

[49] Lydia McGrew vs. Craig Evans, "Is John's Gospel Historically Accurate?" *Unbelievable*, May 18, 2018, minute 31 and following.

[50] Evans, "Fundamentalist Arguments Against Fundamentalism."

Notice that, in Evans's view, the creative alterations and "paraphrases" made by the Gospel authors account for discrepancies in the Gospels. He is not envisaging the authors' reporting their own application of Jesus' teachings in their *own* voices, as (e.g.) a narrative gloss. Doing so would not create even an apparent discrepancy. Rather, he envisages them as changing Jesus' words and the details of Jesus' actions in such a way that it creates discrepancies among the narratives.

Craig Keener seems to conceive of the ancient exercise of paraphrase in a somewhat similar way, though perhaps with less radical results than those Evans envisages:

> [P]araphrase of sayings—attempts to rephrase them without changing their meaning—was standard rhetorical practice, as evidenced by the school exercises in which it features prominently. Such paraphrase provided a degree of rhetorical freedom, and in the case of familiar lines would prove more aesthetically appealing than verbatim repetition.
>
> Thus even writers intending to write accurate history could "spice up" or "enhance" their narratives for literary, moralistic, and political purposes.[51]

At a minimum, we can say that all of these scholars think of paraphrase in the ancient world as involving deliberately putting words into the mouth of an historical figure that one knows he did not say, in a putatively historical work, *not* merely because one can get the wording only approximately, *not* merely because one has to select or abbreviate in the interests of space and time, but because one considers it more enlightening, interesting, or applicable to one's audience to change the words and attribute this adaptation to the original speaker. The scholars attribute the writers' sense of freedom to do this in part to their being trained in rhetorical exercises. On this point, Evans is the most emphatic, insisting that those who solely report their teacher's words as closely as possible to what he actually said would not have been well-trained disciples.

Just as in the other cases, there is no evidence in the exercise books of recommending historical alteration when using paraphrase as an exercise. Both moderate paraphrase and interpretive extrapolation (though different things) have roles to play in education and elsewhere. But neither of these amounts in itself to the deliberate reporting of one's own words in an historical work as if they are the words of another. Literary device theorists like Evans repeatedly blur the distinction between paraphrasing or interpreting for *some purpose or*

---

[51] Keener, *John*, pp. 19–20.

other and putting words into the mouth of an historical figure in an allegedly historical work.

A good educator will often ask a student to paraphrase a passage from a document or even a speech. There are multiple points to doing this. One point is to make sure that the student is able to assimilate a source of factual information while not plagiarizing it. While this might seem like a modern preoccupation, Lucian actually makes a rather modern-sounding complaint about historians who borrow Thucydides' exact words in describing a plague or military event and use them for a completely different event in their own histories. According to Lucian, such historians wrongly think that this makes them good historians like Thucydides. Lucian has contempt for such writers because they have not bothered to develop their own style and think they can ride on the coattails of a greater author.[52] In contemporary pedagogy, we tell students that they cannot quote the exact words of an author unless they explicitly cite, so in most cases they must take notes and paraphrase the source in their own words. This, of course, has *nothing whatsoever* to do with historical alteration, either of reported events or of the spoken word. The student is to use factual information in the source accurately, but he is to state that information in his own words when writing in his own voice. This is nothing like putting words into the mouth of an historical character.

Another use of both paraphrase and further interpretation is, as Evans indicates, to show that one has understood. A good educator may use this approach with literature, with poetry, with speeches, and with Scripture. "What do you think this poem is saying?" "Explain in your own words what you think is the point of Jesus' words here." And so forth. Educationally, such use of paraphrase is most useful when there is a better-informed teacher on hand to correct the paraphrase, interpretation, or application if it goes far astray. But a teacher who asks a student to explain in his own words the meaning of the Gettysburg Address is, *of course*, not telling the student to take his own interpretation and substitute it for the actual Gettysburg Address in a work of history, giving the impression that Lincoln spoke the student's version instead of the version we have from more accurate historical sources. And the more interpretive a student's words are and the farther they are from a minimal paraphrase, the more potentially controversial it would be for him to report them in an historical work as if they were actually said by the person in question.

The Greek exercise books do recommend paraphrase as an exercise but make no statement whatsoever about the degree of freedom allowed or encouraged in

---

[52] Lucian, *How to Write History*, 15.

reportage of the spoken word *in history*. That is simply not the point of the exercises. Here is a discussion of the value of paraphrase in Theon:

> Despite what some say or have thought, paraphrasis (paraphrase) is not without utility. The argument of opponents is that once something has been well said it cannot be done a second time, but those who say this are far from hitting on what is right. Thought is not moved by any one thing in only one way so as to express the idea…that has occurred to it in a similar form, but it is stirred in a number of different ways, and sometimes we are making a declaration, sometimes asking a question, sometimes making an inquiry, sometimes beseeching, and sometimes expressing our thought in some other way. There is nothing to prevent what is imagined from being expressed equally well in all these ways. There is evidence of this in paraphrase by a poet of his own thoughts elsewhere or paraphrase by another poet and in the orators and historians, and, in brief, all ancient writers seem to have used paraphrase in the best possible way, rephrasing not only their own writings but those of each other.[53]

Here are examples that Theon goes on to give: He talks about a saying found in the poet Homer, "Such is the mind of men who live on earth, as the father of men and gods grants it for the day"—a line spoken by the fictional character Odysseus.[54] Theon then points out that other people have adapted this same proverb. One author used a version of it in a letter to a friend, for example. Similarly, he talks about how various orators have envisaged the miseries of a sacked city by paraphrasing a line from the *Iliad*. He talks about how Thucydides has a proverbial line in a speech (attributed in Thucydides to Pericles of Athens), stating that the dead are not envied. Theon points out that Demosthenes paraphrases this short saying and uses it in his own speech "On the Crown." Demosthenes is making the same point and makes no pretense to be giving an historical record of the words of Pericles. He is not writing an historical record at all but making a speech to the Athenians, at a later time, about a later subject. In the course of it he finds the saying in Thucydides useful and gives his own version of it, saying, "The dead are not disliked, even by their enemies." Theon, reasonably enough, takes this to be an allusion to the line attributed to Pericles in a speech in Thucydides' *Peloponnesian War*.[55]

Theon's point is that it is possible to say the same thing at least equally well on different occasions for different purposes and sometimes to improve rhetorically

---

[53] Theon, *Progymnasmata*, p. 6.

[54] Homer, *Odyssey* 18.136–137. As translated in the Kennedy edition of Theon, p. 6.

[55] Demosthenes, "On the Crown," 18.315.

upon an earlier statement. He is not even remotely addressing the question of the propriety or proper degree of elasticity of paraphrase in historical reportage. He even emphasizes that sometimes good writers and orators rephrase their own sayings at different times, which obviously has nothing to do with historical alteration.[56]

Elsewhere Theon gives an example in which the teacher might illustrate paraphrase by drawing out the meaning (perhaps a political meaning) of a line from the orator Demosthenes:

> We should not attempt to paraphrase everything, only what lends itself to a good restatement. For example, a thought like the following: "Although recognizing that it is legal to accept the gifts offered, you indict as illegal the return of gratitude for them" ... might be paraphrased by a teacher as, "If you recognize that it is legal to accept the gifts offered, you cannot say that gratitude for them is illegal."[57]

This saying is related to public policy, where a politician's engaging in a tit-for-tat activity is considered to be corrupt while offering the bribe in the first place is not regarded as corrupt. The paraphrase has nothing whatever to do with historical alteration, pretending that Demosthenes wrote something other than he wrote. It is rather the teacher's attempted explanation.

Theon continues,

> Begin with the simplest thing, for example, with exercise of memory, then pass to paraphrasing some argument in a speech, then to paraphrasing some part of the speech, either the prooemion or narration. Thus our young men will gradually become capable of paraphrasing a whole speech, which is the result of perfected ability.[58]

---

[56] One of the strangest claims made by Evans is that Jesus taught his disciples in accordance with Evans's concept of *chreia* by giving his own words in somewhat different forms at different times. Obviously, Jesus' making the same statement in multiple forms teaches nothing of the kind. How does the fact that Jesus sometimes taught the same content in somewhat different words license the disciples to put words in Jesus' mouth if they later write memoirs about him? This argument makes no sense at all. "And so, there is some creativity [in John], much more creativity than we see in Matthew, Mark, or Luke. So, when we look at the handbooks of education in antiquity and historiography, we realize that that fits within it, even if it's at the edges of it. So, I would have to ask Lydia, does she allow for paraphrase? Jesus seems to be teaching his disciples that way in his own example where he repeats parables and other things in various ways in various settings, and they're a little bit different. And so, Jesus seems able to restate his own teaching, paraphrase his own teaching. Matthew 13:52 seems to be an instruction that his disciples do that." Lydia McGrew vs. Craig Evans, "Is John's Gospel Historically Accurate?" *Unbelievable*, May 18, 2018, minute 51:56.

[57] Theon, *Progymnasmata*, p. 71.

[58] Ibid.

Aha! The literary device theorist might think that here at last we have found a rec-ommendation of paraphrase in reportage as superior to the mere "parroting" in-volved in reporting what was really said. See, the exercise of memory is the simplest thing, while the ability to paraphrase a whole speech is the result of perfected ability.

But Theon is simply talking, again, about an exercise in learning rhetoric and persuasion. He says nothing whatsoever to indicate that these student paraphrases are to be presented as the historical words of a particular person. The student per-forms these exercises for his teacher, to see how well he can do in persuasion. The evaluating teacher, of course, realizes quite well that these are paraphrases carried out as exercises. Once again, this is exactly like having students restate the Get-tysburg Address or some other famous speech of old in their own words. Nothing whatsoever follows concerning historical representation.

Theon also suggests that the teacher might compose a model argument for students to imitate. But this is not a matter of treating the teacher as a sage. The student is not showing his understanding by paraphrasing the speech and putting it back into the teacher's mouth in a memoir. Rather, again, this is an exercise in good writing, as the context makes clear. A model for imitation may be useful to get the student started, so the teacher writes a model speech so that the student can imitate good rhetorical style.

> Thus, in addition to what has been said, the teacher himself must compose some especially fine refutations and confirmations and assign them to the young to re-tell, in order that, molded by what they have learned, they may be able to imitate. When the students are capable of writing, one should dictate to them the order of the headings and epicheiremes and point out the opportunity for digression and amplification and all other treatments, and one must make clear the moral character (*êthos*) inherent in the assignment (*problêma*). And one should show concern for the arrangement of the words, teaching all the ways students will avoid composing badly...[59]

I note again here that amplification, digression, etc., occur in the student's own composition. They are amplifications *on the subject of the essay or speech*, not ampli-fications added to someone else's words and placed into his mouth.

I will not weary the reader with more examples at this time. Suffice it to say that it is like this all the way through. The authors of the exercise books are writing curricula in rhetoric, and those curricula are not teaching the ethics of truthfulness in reporting history, one way or another.

---

[59] Ibid., p. 13.

12. Writing skills in ancient professions

The literary device theorist has another passage he can try to use. Theon promotes his work by mentioning various professions for which it is useful, and "historian" is among those listed:

> Now I have included these remarks, not thinking that all are useful to all begin-
> ners, but in order that we may know that training in exercises is absolutely useful
> not only to those who are going to practice rhetoric but also if one wishes to un-
> dertake the function of poets or historians or any other writers. These things are,
> as it were, the foundation of every kind ... of discourse, and depending on how one
> instills them in the mind of the young, necessarily the results make themselves felt
> in the same way later.[60]

The important phrase here is "or any other writers." Theon is pointing out that, while future rhetoricians are the most obvious consumers of his curriculum, *all* future writers can profit, including poets and historians. But this, again, does not mean that he is giving advice or opinions concerning the degree of factuality that an historical narrative should have. He is plainly not doing so, and it is interesting to note that these sentences occur immediately before the passage just quoted about how a teacher should compose writing and rhetoric models for the students. Historians among others are indeed writers, and Theon's exercises are intended to teach good writing, which of course will be useful to historians *inter alia*. Theon is advertising the broad usefulness of his writing curriculum. That is all.

At one point Licona comes close to acknowledging this point. But if he fully acknowledged it, it would undermine his entire use of the exercise books to bolster the idea that fact-changing literary devices were taught in antiquity. If one once really acknowledges that the exercise books are *merely* teaching writing and rhetoric, like English composition textbooks in our own day, then what becomes of the claim that a Gospel author would have been instructed from such textbooks to turn the thoughts of the Pharisees into dialogue in writing a memoir of Jesus? Licona therefore immediately tries to deflect his own semi-acknowledgement:

> The compositional textbooks of antiquity provided exercises meant to assist as-
> piring writers in the development of their writing skills. In these exercises, stu-
> dents improved their skills by altering the wording of their sources. Although the
> textbooks do not specifically state this was the manner in which they handled

---

[60] Ibid.

their sources when writing professionally, it is a very small step of faith to surmise they would employ such alterations.[61]

This is merely confused. Licona creates a false dichotomy: Either the students would later use what they had learned "when writing professionally" (which he implies would involve historical alteration) or they would not use the skills they had learned in their professional work. The latter would seem strange. Why are they bothering to do all of this training, or why are their parents bothering to have them receive this education, if it will have no relevance to their later professional work? But the erroneous implication is that the sort of "writing professionally" in which they would use what they learn from rhetorical exercise books would be a) writing history while b) altering historical fact. Licona also speaks in this quotation of the prompts used by Theon in the exercises as "their sources," which is confusing. A saying of Odysseus in a fictional tale by Homer (for example), a fable, or a proverb is not an historical source at all.

There is no indication whatsoever that Theon views himself as teaching students how to use historical sources *qua* sources—that is, as factual sources. Again, the topic of how one should use historical sources factually is not even in view. Note that this is the case even when the exercise prompt happens to be a passage from Thucydides' history. Remember that in one exercise Theon even suggests that a student might negate the entire passage from Thucydides. This is obviously just an exercise in writing negations, not a license to turn historical facts upside down.

If a student ended up being an historian, he would need to be able to write well. In that sense, of course an historian would use the skills learned from a good writing curriculum in his "professional writing," and he would do so even if he never bent a single fact. Moreover, there were many other professions (as Theon himself indicates) to which these skills would apply. The most obvious career would be the professional rhetorician, who both gives speeches and teaches speaking and speech-writing for a living. Another profession would be that of politician. There were also at that time professional speech writers—logographers. They would (as in our own time) write speeches for others to deliver.

Here we may note an interesting remark by Diodorus of Sicily (1st century B.C.). Diodorus was not entirely opposed to composing set speeches in historical writing. As discussed in the last chapter, some historians did allow this, and Diodorus was one of them, though he thought that such speech composition could

---

[61] Licona, *Why Are There Differences*, p. 14.

get out of hand and overshadow the narrative. When discussing historians who, in his opinion, invented too many speeches or speeches that were too long, he says,

> [S]urely there is opportunity for those who wish to display rhetorical prowess to compose by themselves public discourses and speeches for ambassadors, likewise orations of praise and blame and the like; for by recognizing the classification of literary types and by elaborating each of the two by itself, they might reasonably expect to gain a reputation in both fields of activity. But as it is, some writers by excessive use of rhetorical passages have made the whole art of history into an appendage of oratory.[62]

In other words, Diodorus points out that a rhetorician had ample opportunities for using rhetorical skills in his professional writing, other than speech composition *within history*.

Hence, contra Licona, it is a rather *large* step of faith to "surmise" that those taught using the *Progymnasmata* of Theon would have considered themselves thereby licensed to make factual alterations when writing history.

Licona concludes his chapter on compositional exercise books by saying, "We will not be disappointed when a careful viewing of ancient literature bears out our hunch."[63] That is to say, the hunch that ancient writers used the exercises as models of and permission for historical alteration. Here Licona refers to his following chapter on Plutarch and other historical authors. The examples there often concern the other fictionalizing literary devices Licona has defined, such as displacement, compression, etc. As I noted at the outset of this chapter, Licona admits that some of the most prominent devices he claims to find in Plutarch are never discussed in ancient historiography nor in writing textbooks. Licona's discussion of the compositional exercise books is supposed to set the stage by implying that young students were taught by the exercises that alteration of history *in general* was legitimate.

The next chapter examines the attempted inductive case concerning Plutarch and other authors. Licona's idea is that we simply *do find* such fact-altering literary devices as displacement, transferral, and compression with some frequency in these authors of biographical and historical work and therefore must accept that they really existed and were accepted. This inductive case is supposed to bear out the "hunch" that they had been taught to make such changes in their education. I will argue that we find nothing of the sort.

---

[62] Diodorus Siculus, *Library of History*, 20.1.2–3. Trans. Russel M. Geer, 1954, http://penelope.uchicago.edu/Thayer/E/Roman/Texts/Diodorus_Siculus/20A*.html.

[63] Licona, *Why Are There Differences*, p. 14.

Summary
Going Chreia-zy

- Both Michael Licona and Craig Evans have claimed that the Gospel authors were influenced by ancient Greek rhetoric textbooks and that these textbooks encouraged students to change facts in historical writing.

- By the same considerations discussed in Chapter V, it is unlikely that Matthew, Mark, and John would have been exposed to Greek exercise textbooks. Once again, theorists ignore authorship in this discussion and hastily assume exposure to a particular type of Greek curriculum if an author writes in the Greek language.

- The Jews made a distinction between knowledge of the Greek language and Greek literature. It would have been entirely possible for someone to be literate in the Greek language without being taught from Greek literature or exercise books.

- Craig Evans engages in significant eisegesis when he interprets Matt. 13.52 to mean that Jesus instructed his disciples to alter his words when reporting them.

- The church father Papias uses the term *chreiai* to describe the way that Peter told his stories as Mark heard them. The best explanation of this word in the context is something like "short, instructive anecdotes." This does not mean that either Peter or Mark was influenced by writing exercises from Greek rhetoric textbooks.

- To interpret Papias as endorsing the alteration of events or of Jesus's words on the basis of the single word *chreiai* is to tear that word out of context. On the contrary, in this very passage Papias emphasizes Mark's factual accuracy.

- Writing textbooks are not giving advice on how much factual alteration is allowable in history. They are just trying to teach students how to write well. An exercise in which a student makes up dialogue or dramatizes an historical event is not an endorsement of fictionalization when writing a work that presents itself as historical. It is just an interesting exercise for the student.

- The writing exercise books, such as the *Progymnasmata* of Theon, do not recommend making factual alterations in writing history. The exercises do not address that question. The theorists misunderstand many different types of exercises when they try to use Theon to argue that ancient authors took a loose approach to historical reportage.

IX

Devices, Discrepancies, or (Just) Differences?

1. Horses, not zebras: Literary device theories and the burden of proof

A proverb says, "When you hear hoof beats, think horses, not zebras." The saying encapsulates wise advice to look for explanations common to experience before one looks for uncommon, convoluted explanations. That is, of course, assuming that the common explanation accounts for the evidence at least equally well. Uncommon things *do* happen, and we should be able to recognize evidence for them. But when a perfectly ordinary explanation will account perfectly well for the evidence at hand, we have no need to "think zebras" and look for something more complex. This principle, a version of what philosophers call Occam's razor, says that, all else being equal, simpler explanations are to be preferred over more complex explanations. We should not "multiply entities without necessity."

In this chapter and succeeding ones, these types of principles will come up again and again, because it is an unfortunate habit of some academic disciplines to turn these principles on their heads and to prefer uncommon, convoluted, literary explanations over simpler, ordinary ones. As the examples will show, there is a persistent failure even to think of more obvious explanations that reflect our daily experience of human behavior. This leads to a persistent failure to recognize the weight of the burden of proof that a complex hypothesis bears.

When it comes to hypothesizing that a given author has used a fictionalizing literary device, this failure takes the form of leaping to that conclusion while overlooking much simpler explanations of the data.

To understand the difficulty in showing that a literary device is present, we should review what a fictionalizing literary device is. To recap from Chapter I, a fictionalizing literary device has the following features:

1) What is presented in a seemingly realistic fashion in the work is actually contrary to fact. The real facts have been altered.

2) The alteration of fact was made by the author deliberately.

3) The alteration of fact is invisible within that work itself.

Here I want to emphasize one more feature of a fictionalizing literary device, which is important from the perspective of literary device theorists:

4) The alteration of fact was accepted by the original audience, not in the sense that the original audience could recognize by reading the work that the device is present in that location (see #3), but in the sense that the original audience understood and accepted that factual changes of this general type might be made as part of the literary conventions that governed the work in question.

Condition #1 means that the theorist has to argue something more than merely that there are differences between two accounts or that one author has narrated somewhat quickly or briefly. The theorist must argue that the author's narrative contains material that is contrary to fact. (See the discussions in Chapter II of different senses of "compression," "transferral," "paraphrase," and so forth.)

Condition #2 makes the thesis even stronger. It is not enough to show that the author made a mistake or was careless, or even that there is an irresolvable discrepancy between two accounts (or between an account and other known historical fact). One must argue that the author *knew* that his account was contrary to fact and that he chose to write as he did with this understanding.

Condition #3 goes further and makes it quite difficult to show that a literary device is present merely from the text of the work. By the hypothesis in question, there is (as noted in Chapter I, section 3) no "tag in the text" to show that what is coming up or has just been stated is ahistorical or altered. There is nothing akin to "once upon a time" or "there once was a man" that acts as a conventional signal of a parable or legend. That invisibility rules out one way in which a theorist might otherwise justify the belief that a literary device or ahistorical narrative is present.

It is condition #4 that is supposed to save the author who uses such devices from the charge of deception, but that condition adds even more to the burden of proof. Because such changes were allegedly accepted at the time, part of the literary norms of the genre, we too are called upon to find them acceptable and not to consider them to be misleading or even erroneous. Michael Licona says,

In order to accomplish his objective, Plutarch occasionally bends the facts to support the portrait he is painting—a portrait that is largely true though not always entirely so in the details. He does not bend to mislead his readers but rather to emphasize an important *deeper truth* about his main character that readers can now grasp more fully and emulate. Like every biographer of his day, he had no commitment to present the facts with photographic accuracy or legal precision; nor would his intended readers have expected that of him or of any biographer. Accordingly, Plutarch's commitment to the truth in his *Lives* is genuine but qualified. Like most other historians of his day, Plutarch takes liberties with his sources that would make us uncomfortable in modern biography, adding details or scenes in order to reconstruct what must have happened, or to emphasize a quality that may not have been as matured in the main character as he portrays, or to improve the story for the delight of his readers.[1]

As we saw in Chapter III, section 1, the statement that Plutarch "does not bend to mislead his readers" is itself somewhat misleading. Licona states elsewhere that Plutarch "gives the reader the impression that" events took place in a way contrary to fact,[2] and he repeatedly says that Plutarch and other authors using literary devices "narrated as though" or "describe as though" things happened in a way contrary to fact.[3] He even says that the author of John "appears deliberate in his attempts to lead his readers to think the Last Supper was not a Passover meal," contrary to fact.[4] Needless to say, these changes are also more than just failing to write with legal precision. If we take Licona to be consistent throughout all these passages, the phrase "does not bend to mislead" can only mean, at most, that if readers *are* misled about the facts by such narration (as they may indeed be), that is not the *ultimate point or purpose* of the factually altered narration; rather, some sort of edification or delight brought about by "emphasizing deeper truth" is the ultimate goal. Moreover, if readers are savvy enough, and if these norms of truth-bending are widely enough accepted, readers will hold many of the facts in Plutarch's (or John's) narrative with a sufficiently light touch that they will not be misled. But that is not because the narrative makes it clear when something is not historical. Rather, it is because readers will know to put a question mark over *so much* of the factual material that seems to be asserted that they will, hopefully,

---

[1] Michael Licona, *Why Are There Differences in the Gospels? What We Can Learn From Ancient Biography* (Oxford: Oxford University Press, 2017), pp. 17–18. Emphasis in original.

[2] Ibid., p. 50.

[3] Ibid., pp. 39, 46, 55, 157, 177.

[4] Ibid., pp. 156, 163

withhold actual belief in the truth of the propositions that are fabricated or altered, among others. Hence, audience acceptance of the devices and audience expectation that the author will sometimes alter the facts or add scenes (even if they don't know which ones those are) are crucial to absolving the author of the charge of merely engaging in ordinary fabrication, propaganda, or deception.

Here is another statement affirming the importance of condition 4, from William Lane Craig:

> What I've said is that I don't think by the standards of that day for John to move the cleansing of the temple to early in Jesus' ministry rather than during Passion Week is an error. This by the standards of that day would be permitted by ancient standards of historiography and therefore this is not incompatible with the reliability of the Gospels.[5]

I have addressed in Chapter II, section 4, the incorrect claim that, if an alteration of fact was "permitted by ancient standards," this means that such a change would not constitute an error and would be fully compatible with the historical reliability of the documents. Here I am stressing the importance of societal *acceptance* to the entire approach. For an author to move an event chronologically, to change details, to add scenes, and so forth counts as a device, in the view of these scholars, rather than *ordinary* disregard for truth, only because it was accepted in its own time, because audiences wouldn't have minded, and because it was generally understood that this type of fictionalization might crop up at unpredictable moments in historical narratives.

What the theorists do not seem to realize is that this condition for a literary device adds substantially to the burden of proof. With this condition included, it is not even enough to show (if they can) that a given author did deliberately make something up or deliberately change a fact. They must also show that his audience would have expected him to do that kind of thing from time to time and would have accepted and understood that doing so was a literary convention applicable to the kind of work he was writing. In order to argue that he was not trying to deceive, they must at least show that he *believed* that about his audience. In other words, they must show that he was not just a garden-variety liar, propagandist, or inventive raconteur with little concern for historical fact.

It is fairly obvious that saving the author from the charge of mere deception or disregard for truth is important for those who wish to apply these theses to the Gospels. If we have any respect for the Gospel authors at all, we do not wish to

---

[5] William Lane Craig, May 6, 2018, "An Objection to the Minimal Facts Argument" https://www. reasonablefaith.org/media/reasonable-faith-podcast/an-objection-to-the-minimal-facts-argument/>

accuse them of being *ordinary* fabricators, much less deceivers. Presumably Christian scholars would acknowledge that the prior probability that the evangelists were just ordinary deceivers is low, which is why they insist that these devices do not count as deception.[6] But by piling up all of these conditions, they make it more and more difficult to justify their own conclusions in concrete cases.

The past three chapters refute several attempts to lighten this epistemic burden. The theorists hoped to make a background case by arguing for a general ancient atmosphere or a general nature of the genre that permitted and encouraged factual alterations. Background information is certainly relevant to such a determination. To go back to the example in Chapter I, section 2, we approach a movie like *Chariots of Fire* knowing full well that it may contain partial fictionalizations, and the movie fulfills those expectations, as we discover when we check it by other sources. But the three previous chapters have refuted the idea that alteration of fact was "part and parcel" of the genre in which the Gospels were written[7] or that there was a general ancient acceptance of altering historical fact.

Now we turn to the attempted inductive case from non-biblical sources, and we will see that that fails as well. Once the claim that such devices as displacement, transferral, etc., occur in Plutarch and others is shown to be unsupported, the case from ancient practice is undermined at every step. At that point we are justified in strongly suspecting that those literary devices are a figment of the imaginations of modern professors. In other words, we may justly doubt whether these devices were real things *at all*. And in that case, there is no reason to approach the Gospels with a high prior probability, based on their alleged genre or the literary conventions of the time, that the evangelists engaged in such practices.

2. From differences to devices: A flowchart

A flowchart (Figure 1) illustrates the various steps that one should go through in thinking carefully about whether differences between two historical documents lead to the reasonable conclusion that a fictionalizing literary device is present.

---

[6] Most or all of the evangelical literary device theorists are also publicly committed to inerrancy; baldly saying that Matthew or John lied about the facts concerning Jesus is impossible to square with any notion of inerrancy whatsoever. Even the theorists themselves realize this and hence commit themselves, presumably sincerely, to a more convoluted claim about genre, literary devices, and so forth. This also makes it possible to promote their views to others committed to inerrancy by saying that we must understand inerrancy relative to genre and that their theories simply involve more fully understanding the Gospel authors as they understood themselves.

[7] Jonathan Peterson and Michael Licona, "Why Are There Differences in the Gospels? An Interview With Michael R. Licona," *Bible Gateway Blog*, June 27, 2017, https://www.biblegateway.com/blog/2017/06/why-are-there-differences-in-the-gospels-an-interview-with-michael-r-licona/.

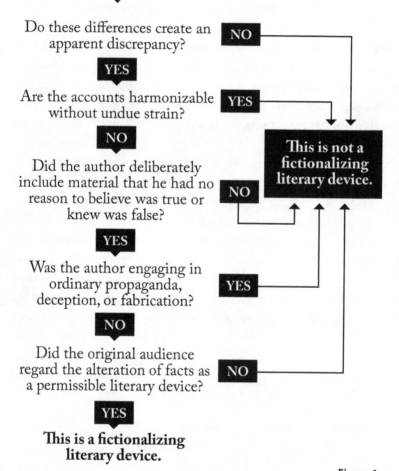

The accounts contain differences

Do these differences create an apparent discrepancy? — NO

YES

Are the accounts harmonizable without undue strain? — YES

NO

Did the author deliberately include material that he had no reason to believe was true or knew was false? — NO

YES

Was the author engaging in ordinary propaganda, deception, or fabrication? — YES

NO

Did the original audience regard the alteration of facts as a permissible literary device? — NO

YES

This is not a fictionalizing literary device.

This is a fictionalizing literary device.

Figure 1

Suppose that we notice that there are differences between two accounts, either by the same author or by different authors. These are accounts of the same event or time period, occurring in works that appear in some significant sense to be otherwise historical. We may not be sure just how historically reliable they are, but they are not obviously fiction. They present themselves as if they are narrating historical events.

The first question we should ask is whether these differences even amount to an *apparent* discrepancy. Literary device theorists sometimes rather surprisingly declare a fictionalizing literary device to exist when the only difference between two accounts is that one account contains a particular detail, saying, or incident and another account does not. I call these utterly unforced errors. In New Testament studies such utterly unforced errors seem to crop up most often in critics' discussions of the Gospel of John. Hence, for example, there is not even an apparent discrepancy between Jesus' utterance, "I thirst" and any aspect of the Synoptic accounts of the crucifixion, yet theorists have suggested that "I thirst" was invented as a "dynamic equivalent transformation" of "My God, why have you forsaken me."[8] There is not even an *apparent* discrepancy between the fact that Mark quotes the phrase from Isaiah about the voice crying in the wilderness and applies it, as the narrator, to John the Baptist and the fact that John says that John the Baptist himself said that he was the voice crying in the wilderness. One could even argue plausibly that these are mutually confirmatory; the author of the Gospel of Mark may have directly or indirectly associated these words with John the Baptist because John the Baptist quoted this portion of Isaiah and applied it to himself. Yet, even in the absence of any apparent discrepancy, Licona has suggested that perhaps John transferred the words to the lips of John the Baptist though he never historically said them.[9] So it is important to stop and ask ourselves first whether there is even any apparent discrepancy. It is particularly poor reasoning to leap from the mere presence of *differences* between accounts to the theory that an author has deliberately changed history. Differences between accounts do not *per se* render either account historically improbable. And the other questions make no sense until we answer this first question. If there is no apparent discrepancy to harmonize, it makes no sense to ask whether it can be harmonized without undue strain.

Suppose that, upon examination, you think that the differences amount to at least an apparent discrepancy, though possibly one that, with some thought, can be harmonized. At this point it is important to ask whether harmonization is both possible and plausible. It should go without saying that people will disagree a great deal about the answer to this question. New Testament scholars, for example, are extremely averse to thinking that events that are even somewhat similar have happened on more than one occasion. This can take them past the first two steps of the flowchart in a single bound. Where someone without such a sensitivity would think that there was not even an apparent discrepancy, that it merely looks like

---

[8] Licona, *Why Are There Differences*, p. 166; Daniel B. Wallace, "*Ipsissima Vox* and the Seven Words From the Cross," unpublished paper presented to the Society for Biblical Literature Southwest Regional meeting, March 5, 2000, pp. 4–9.

[9] Licona, *Why Are There Differences*, p. 121.

something broadly similar happened on more than one occasion (which is quite normal in daily life), a New Testament critic and perhaps some classicists would think not only that there is an *apparent* discrepancy but that it is *irresolvable*, unharmonizable, that the accounts of the two events are in *irreconcilable conflict*, since it is *so* improbable that something similar happened twice.

But despite the fact that there will be inevitable disagreements, it is very important to pause at this node of the flowchart, asking if the accounts are harmonizable without undue strain, because harmonization is not a religious enterprise. It is not contrary to the objective study of history, nor is it a desperate last-ditch effort to "save" documents to which we have some arational commitment. As emphasized throughout this book, harmonization should be regarded as simply good historical practice. If two different accounts of the same event or an overlapping time period have any decent claim to be regarded as historical in nature, it is reasonable and important to consider whether they can be harmonized. Nor is this a matter of fudging and going to wild lengths. It is normal for truthful witness testimonies to differ and even at times to contain some apparent discrepancies but to be able to be harmonized, and the use of intelligent imagination for this purpose is not in itself an *ad hoc* move, motivated by religious dogma, but rather a healthy way to approach historical investigation. Very often, too, the harmonization is quite plausible once considered and is not difficult to see if one simply puts one's mind to it. This question is therefore important and logically comes prior to the question of whether an author deliberately (as opposed to accidentally) included information he knew to be false, which is the next question after it. For if there is no false information in either report, there is no need to ask whether that false information was included deliberately. And if there is a completely plausible harmonization available, then there is no need to conclude, on the basis of the differences, that there is false information in either account.

As we shall see in this chapter, harmonizing accounts is as relevant to studying secular history as it is to studying the Gospels. If one suggests that Plutarch's two accounts of some events are not really in conflict with one another and that the literary device theorist is reading in a conflict where none exists, this suggestion can hardly be motivated by a commitment to the inerrancy of Plutarch. Very much to the contrary; as we shall see at the next step of the flowchart and by application in the examples, it is the literary device theorist who is often overly reluctant to think that any author, even a secular author, has made a simple error and concludes quite unjustifiably that he has *deliberately* changed the truth. Thus we have the following strange spectacle: The theorist declares a real discrepancy where none exists, because the theorist resists or does not even contemplate entirely plausible harmonizing moves. This seems to place the author (say, Plutarch) in the position of having committed an error. The theorist then rescues Plutarch from this quite unnecessary danger of ordinary error by hypothesizing further that Plutarch inserted the false information deliberately and hence cannot be accused of simple error. This is not responsible historical practice.

As we have seen before, Licona has made the rather astonishing statement that, in interpreting the Gospels, he tries to think of a literary device *before* seeking to harmonize the accounts:

> Where I differ [from most evangelicals] is, I place a priority on genre over harmonization. So, *before seeking to harmonize Gospel texts*, one should read the Gospels in view of their biographical genre, which includes their authors' use of the various compositional devices commonly used when writing history and biography.[10]

This is an extremely poor methodology, and indeed one wonders (given the variety and flexibility of literary devices Licona claims to have identified) how or why one would ever get around to harmonizing two accounts at all if one followed this method. How would one know that an attempt to find a literary device had failed and that one was forced, as it were, to fall back upon harmonization? The question is especially worth asking given that Licona will sometimes suggest that an author "crafted" an account or a part of an account without even using any more specific literary term.[11]

The last several chapters have removed a great deal of the claimed justification for the prior assumption that the Gospels contain fictionalizing devices. In this chapter, it is important to stress that Licona's inductive work in Plutarch and other ancient authors is supposed to give us a baseline for the frequency and categories of these devices. This work in Plutarch is supposed to be part of what justifies him in seeking literary devices in the Gospels before seeking to harmonize. On pain of circularity, then, he cannot enter his study of Plutarch *assuming* that Plutarch must exhibit (somewhere or other) transferral, displacement, and so forth. He is supposed to be *finding* those devices in Plutarch, *finding out* how often Plutarch and other secular ancient authors use them, and then using that as a basis upon which to expect them in the Gospels.

---

[10] Ibid. Emphasis added.
[11] Ibid., p. 184.

Therefore, for the study of these secular authors, the question must be asked: Can the accounts be harmonized by normal means without undue strain? The order of the flowchart must be observed rather than being turned on its head, or else the argument that such devices exist in the secular authors is circular—one finds what one assumed was there before even starting out to look.

Another reason for stressing the importance of this node of the flowchart is that apparent discrepancies are normal in witness testimony and in historical accounts throughout history, right up to the present. The results of mere discrepancy hunting *cannot* be sufficient grounds for hypothesizing a literary device, or else we should, to be consistent, erase all discrepancies in all testimony and in all history, relabeling them as literary devices. In an interview, cold-case detective J. Warner Wallace emphasizes this important point concerning the analysis of witness testimony:

> I see people now, even people who are in the Christian camp, our brothers and sisters who are theologians or historians or textual critics....They compromise something on the part of the author.... "Oh, this is a form of biography in which it was not unusual in the first century to exaggerate certain details." Really? I mean, if you took that approach with the cases I work, you'd never solve a case. Because you will see differences between authors, and unless you think there's some genre of eyewitness testimony that's offered in 1975 when this thing was written, and there isn't. This is just what eyewitness testimony looks like. So I'm always careful not to jump into some theory that a historian or a theologian is offering about why there might be differences. Because I'll bet you that guy has never interviewed eyewitnesses. And if you have done that for a living you'll realize that...there is no reason to jump to other explanations. This is just what reliable eyewitness testimony looks like.[12]

Here we return to the proverb at the beginning of the chapter: When you hear hoof beats, think horses, not zebras. If a perfectly ordinary harmonizing explanation will do a good job accounting for the differences in the documents, there is no need to hypothesize that this is an instance of an esoteric, ancient literary device. There is nothing particularly "ancient-looking" about finding an apparent discrepancy between two accounts concerning chronology, or a saying attributed in different places to different people, or the other types of differences that Licona and others discuss. These are the normal variants of historical accounts in every age. The very question at issue is whether there even *existed* such an ancient literary

---

[12] J. Warner Wallace, interview on *The Rational Rise* with James Fox Higgins, May 30, 2018, minute 1:02:00, https://www.youtube.com/watch?v=iywQ_gyaDrU&feature=youtu.be&t=29m37s.

device as "displacement" in which an author engaged in a widely accepted practice of deliberately writing (in the "world" of his document) as if an event took place at a time when it did not take place. If one can simply harmonize accounts—for example, by pointing out that the times or dates given are actually far more non-specific than the theorist thinks or even suggesting that a generally similar event might have happened on more than one occasion—then the difference is satisfactorily accounted for by the normal mechanisms of human experience. Given the prevalence of differences and even apparent discrepancies throughout history, it is methodologically more reasonable to make use of such categories when interpreting Plutarch, Tacitus, or the Gospel of Matthew than to hypothesize a specialized type of device that was particular to that era and culture.

A similar point applies in a slightly different way to the next node of the flowchart, where one pauses to ask whether the author deliberately altered fact. The alternatives there, again, are the extremely common human experiences of variation of memory, memory error, not looking things up in one's notes, receiving new information, and the like. It is rather surprising to notice how seldom Licona hypothesizes that Plutarch or another secular author committed a normal error. He does do so just occasionally,[13] but time and again that hypothesis cries out for consideration *even if* there is a real discrepancy, yet Licona does not so much as consider it. It is difficult to see why this should be. After all, no one (presumably) is committed to the inerrancy of Plutarch, even under a redefined definition of "inerrancy." Besides, Licona occasionally (very occasionally) does say that perhaps Plutarch made an error. But why so seldom? Below I will discuss one unconvincing argument that Licona makes to the effect that Plutarch composed several of his *Lives* at about the same time, but this is hardly a sufficient basis for not even considering the idea that he might have made an error in one of them but not in another, especially on some of the tiny details in question. New information can be gained in a short time, and keeping trivial details in one's mind among several different accounts would be very difficult. Licona also fails to consider the possibility of normal error or receiving new information even between *Lives* that do not fall into that group. He also fails to consider the possibility of error when two completely different authors, writing at far greater differences of time, are in question.

One can only conjecture what might be influencing the theorist when he does not consider ordinary error as an explanation, but one plausible conjecture is that it would seem boring or disparaging to think that an ancient historian might have

---

[13] Licona, *Why Are There Differences*, pp. 54, 57, 93–94.

made a garden-variety error, might simply not have had his notes or another account open in front of him at every moment, might have misunderstood an earlier source, and so forth. It seems more interesting and perhaps more complimentary to the author to think that he deliberately changed the facts for a literary or ideological reason. But that is not good historical reasoning. Minor error and natural witness variation are known causes of apparent discrepancy and even of real discrepancy. Think horses, not zebras.

So even if one decides that the differences between the accounts rise to the level of an apparent discrepancy, even if one decides that the discrepancy cannot be plausibly dealt with by normal means of harmonization, one must still ask what the evidence is that there was a *deliberate* as opposed to an *accidental* report contrary to fact. But even if we answer "yes," that the alteration was deliberate, the flowchart is not done yet. At the next node of the flowchart, we consider *why* an author might have inserted incorrect information deliberately.

The next question is this: Was the author engaging in *ordinary* propaganda, deception, or fabrication? This is a very important question. Liars are known in all ages. Another common category is the accomplished raconteur who does not much care about truth, who likes to make an impression and knowingly exaggerates or embellishes because he feels like it. One may justly consider him a type of liar, though perhaps not a malicious one. Or again, "fake news" is a phrase we hear often in our own time, and it is a truism that various news outlets bend and shade the facts for their own political or ideological ends. Or a man writing his memoirs might deliberately write deceptively because some event in his past was embarrassing or could hurt his political career if known; it is therefore to his advantage to whitewash the event many years later, to put his own false "spin" on it.

None of these constitutes a literary device. Not one. It is worth pausing and pondering that point. There is *nothing* particularly ancient about propaganda or fictional embellishment by those who are not historically scrupulous. These are common human activities and faults. But as discussed above, the theorists are not attributing ordinary deception or fabrication to either the secular or Gospel authors they discuss. Rather, they are attributing something more esoteric: An accepted *device* in the time of the author. So before thinking that an author who falsified his story used a literary device, we should first ask whether he was doing something far more common than that.

This node is particularly difficult to get past, as we shall see when we discuss some of the differences below in secular literature. The theorists often seem to have a very peculiar view of an author like Plutarch, Josephus, or Tacitus. On this view, the author must be viewed as so honorable and scrupulous that he would never *just* bend the truth because he was writing a type of propaganda or following a raconteur's whim. Nor would he simply be careless, not looking up his sources at every point. The author is to be regarded as in some way more high-minded than that, though *why* we should think of secular historians as above such things is never explained. However, on these theories, the author is *not* too high-minded to write deliberately in such a way that his readers, if they take his narrative at face value, will be confused about the literal historical facts. He is not too high-minded to set aside the consideration that he *may* be misleading his readers. He thinks it more important to delight them, to improve them morally, or even just to make his story flow better (according to some unpredictable, private conception of "better") than to tell the historical truth on some factual point. And he expect or hopes that his readers will be savvy enough to take enough of his factual narrative with a grain of salt; then, perhaps, they won't be misled after all. All of that the theorists are quite happy to attribute to ancient authors, but not ordinary deception or happy-go-lucky disregard for truth. This is an utterly unjustified approach. Indeed, it is anti-historical. We learn what authors are like in part by watching what they do, and if there is reason to believe that an author is deliberately writing in such a way that his readers may well be confused about historical facts, it is an entirely live option that he is the kind of misleading person that we ourselves encounter all the time. It is not an historical axiom that one must always *compliment* Plutarch or Josephus. And it is not clear that the elaborate literary device view of an author as using potentially misleading literary devices is all that complimentary anyway.

It is an unsavory thought but one that must be faced: If the theorists are so insistent that Matthew, Mark, Luke, and John sometimes *deliberately* changed historical fact while writing in historically realistic ways, why *don't* they conclude that they were, to some extent or other, deceptive? Supposedly it is because the theorists have independently established the existence of real, accepted literary devices permitting such changes. But again, the work on secular authors is part of what is supposed to establish that point. The existence of those devices cannot be presupposed in approaching the secular authors. And if the secular authors could (for all we can tell to the contrary) just be ordinary deceivers or propagandists, then we are left, once more, with no reason to absolve the Gospel authors of deception, *if* we insist that they deliberately changed the facts in their narratives. So this node of the flowchart must be squarely faced.

I will not always mention, in every example I discuss, that this especially diffi-cult hurdle would remain at the end for the literary device theorist even if he got over all of the others. That should be taken as read, even when I argue that the difference in question does not get past some earlier point in the flowchart.

Of course people will disagree, perhaps even strongly, about the "yes" or "no" answers at different points on the flowchart. Do not mistake a disagreement with me about some particular case for the conclusion that the heuristic of the flow-chart is misguided in the first place. The questions need to be faced even if people differ as to their correct answers. The problem is that the literary device theorists are moving far too quickly and not stopping to ask important questions along the way. The flowchart requires us to slow down. If the literary device theorists would follow it, it would induce them to consider possibilities they are dismissing with-out due thought and to acknowledge the weight of the burden of proof they have taken on.

Sometimes the answer to a given question is quite easy. Consider, for exam-ple, *Chariots of Fire* and the portrayal there of Jennie Liddell as a young woman in the United Kingdom arguing with her brother over his running, when the historical Jennie Liddell was at that time a child in China. (I discussed this inci-dent in Chapter I, section 2.) The question of whether that alteration of fact was deliberate or not on the part of the movie makers receives an easy "yes" answer. Jennie Liddell herself was still alive at the time that the movie was made. Modern methods of communication and investigation were available. The makers of such movies do research such matters in order to decide how to portray events. And so forth. It is enormously improbable that the makers of the movie mistakenly believed that such a conversation really took place between brother and sister.

There is one other node of the flowchart, which I have inserted for the sake of completeness, though I will not be discussing any examples that fail at just this point. Would the audience, *as distinct from the author*, have regarded this as an accepted literary device? That is, could the author have been *mistaken* about the social conventions surrounding his work? It would be in theory possible that the author would *regard* himself as using a literary device rather than engaging in ordinary fabrication (a "no" answer at the node that asks if he was engaging in ordinary deception or fabrication) but that he would be mistaken about what his audience knew or believed (a "no" answer on the last question). Evidence for such a disconnect between author and audience could arise if the author later said that he "thought people would understand" that he felt free to intermingle fiction with fact but if a large proportion of his audience was actually confused. Of course, one would have to decide in such a case whether the author was merely fudging in order to save face when he was caught fabricating, but external evidence might cause one to conclude that he was sincere. If the author were sincere, one could consider this a failed but genuine *attempt* to use a fictionalizing literary device. Generally, however, if I consider something to be a deliberate fabrication but not a literary device, I will be considering it to be an instance of ordinary falsification.

This version of the flowchart has been developed specifically in response to instances like those discussed by Licona in which the "kickoff" fact—the thing to be explained—is a difference between two accounts of the same events. Other facts could kick off such an inquiry instead. For example, one might argue that, strictly speaking, the conclusion that there is a literary device (an invented dialogue between Jennie and Eric Liddell) in *Chariots of Fire* is not an explanation of differences between two *accounts* of the *same* event. Rather, it explains a discrepancy between the events portrayed in the movie and independently known facts about Jennie Liddell's life. No such conversation *could have* occurred, given the timeline of her life. Or, as in the case of the speech of Calgacus discussed in Chapter VII, section 3, the "thing to be explained" could be the apparent improbability of Tacitus's knowing what Calgacus said and of Calgacus's uttering such words. Variations of the flowchart can be devised for cases where someone's allegation of a literary device arises in the first place from something other than differences between two accounts. In those cases, as well, various analogues to the other questions will arise: Can the alleged historical problem be resolved? This would be analogous to asking whether harmonization is possible and plausible. Would the author have been putting in this ahistorical or erroneous material *deliberately*? And so forth. Licona's book is about why there are differences in the Gospels, and his section on Plutarch is based on differences between Plutarch's accounts of events. In some cases he considers differences between other ancient authors' accounts of the same events. So I have developed the flowchart with that type of case in mind.

3. Sallust and the Catiline conspiracy

With a fuller understanding of the flowchart in hand, let us move on to a detailed consideration of some alleged examples of literary devices in Greco-Roman authors. Licona gives two examples from the Roman historian Sallust (c. 86–35 B.C.) in which Sallust allegedly changes the time at which an event took place for rhetorical or thematic effect. One of Sallust's works is a fairly lengthy account of an ultimately unsuccessful conspiracy by a Roman senator named Catiline in the first century B.C. Licona, following classicist John Ramsey, claims that Sallust deliberately moved a meeting between Catiline and his fellow conspirators and a "speech" he gave to his followers at that meeting back a year in time in order to portray Catiline as a revolutionary at an earlier time than he actually was. I put the word "speech" in quotation marks, because I deny that Sallust recounts a speech at all.

Licona compares Sallust's account of what Catiline was saying to prospective fellow conspirators in 64 B.C. with an account by Cicero of a meeting between Catiline and his followers in 63 B.C.:

> A fourth example of historical displacement is furnished by Sallust's account of an impassioned speech of Catiline to his supporters, which Sallust claims was delivered about 1 June 64 (*Cat.* 17.1). That speech, scholars conclude, was almost certainly modeled on a revolutionary speech that Catiline is alleged to have delivered to his supporters shortly before the July elections in 63 BCE (Cicero, *Mur.* 50). The two occasions bear a striking resemblance to each other in both the content and physical setting of the speech itself. Sallust tells us that Catiline delivered his remarks in June 64 at a meeting of his followers behind closed doors, with all outsiders excluded, whereas Cicero describes the meeting in July 63 as a "*contione domestica*," a "harangue to his private circle" (*Mur.* 50). Sallust chose to place Catiline's revolutionary speech of 63 one year earlier, at the time of his first failed candidacy for the consulship because, as Ramsey comments, Sallust decided to present Catiline as a wild-eyed revolutionary as early as the elections of 64. We know, however, that at that time Catiline was far from being the down-and-out, desperate politician he is made out to be in the Sallustian speech. Rather, in 64 he stood a good chance of being elected consul for 63 and had the backing of senior political figures like Marcus Crassus and even Julius Caesar. Sallust distorts the true picture to cast Catiline as a villain even before he resorted to desperate measures after his second defeat, at the election in 63, more than one year later.[14]

It is quite unconvincing, to begin with, to argue that Catiline would not have planned a conspiracy while still running for legitimate office. He could easily have been exploring both possible paths to power in 64. Second, the fact that both sets of comments were given behind closed doors is extremely poor as an argument that Cicero and Sallust recount the same event. This is, after all, a conspiracy. Conspirators presumably meet behind closed doors, excluding non-conspirators, more often than once. This does not constitute a striking resemblance of physical setting.

---

[14] Licona, *Why Are There Differences*, pp. 188–189.

But Licona argues further that Sallust has moved the speech by alleging a "striking resemblance" between Sallust's and Cicero's accounts, the intended conclusion being that they must recount the same "speech" and that, therefore, the differences in time frame must mean that one or the other has moved the "speech." When one turns to the passages Licona cites, one finds nothing of the sort. In Sallust one quite literally finds no account of a meeting (only a brief mention that a meeting did take place), much less any account of a speech, much less any account of a speech in which Catiline gives remarks that "bear a striking resemblance" to the remarks attributed to him by Cicero. Here is the passage Licona cites from Sallust, plus much more afterwards, so that the reader can see that I am not cutting off the passage too soon:

> Accordingly, towards the first of June in the consulate of Lucius Caesar and Gaius Figulus, he addressed his followers at first one by one, encouraging some and sounding others. He pointed out his own resources, the unprepared condition of the state, the great prizes of conspiracy. When he had such information as he desired, he assembled all those who were most desperate and most reckless. There were present from the senatorial order Publius Lentulus Sura, Publius Autronius, Lucius Cassius Longinus, Gaius Cethegus, Publius and Servius Sulla, sons of Servius, Lucius Vargunteius, Quintus Annius, Marcus Porcius Laeca, Lucius Bestia, Quintus Curius; also of the equestrian order, Marcus Fulvius Nobilior, Lucius Statilius, Publius Gabinius Capito, Gaius Cornelius; besides these there were many men from the colonies and free towns who were of noble rank at home. There were, moreover, several nobles who had a somewhat more secret connection with the plot, men who were prompted rather by the hope of power than by want or any other exigency. The greater part of the young men also, in particular those of high position, were favourable to Catiline's project; for although in quiet times they had the means of living elegantly or luxuriously, they preferred uncertainty to certainty, war to peace. There were also at that time some who believed that Marcus Licinius Crassus was not wholly ignorant of the plot; that because his enemy Gaius Pompeius was in command of a large army, he was willing to see anyone's influence grow in opposition to the power of his rival, fully believing meanwhile that if the conspirators should be successful, he would easily be the leading man among them.[15]

One sentence near the beginning of this passage tells us what Catiline said when sounding out potential conspirators one by one. This is not even an account of remarks given at a meeting. Sallust then says that Catiline gathered together those

---

[15] Sallust, *The War With Catiline* 17.1–7. Trans. J. C. Rolfe, revised John T. Ramsey, 1931, http://penelope.uchicago.edu/Thayer/E/Roman/Texts/Sallust/Bellum_Catilinae*.html.

whom he had decided to include, and he lists many names of those involved in the plot. But neither here nor later does Sallust give an account of what Catiline said to that gathering of the conspirators.

The content of the remarks attributed to Catiline even in sounding potential followers bears no "striking resemblance" to anything in Cicero, in part because it is not particularly striking or unusual. The so-called "speech" that supposedly bears a "striking resemblance" to Cicero's report is described by this *single sentence* in Sallust: "He pointed out his own resources, the unprepared condition of the state, the great prizes of conspiracy." This is the kind of thing anyone organizing a conspiracy might say. It is hardly distinctive.

Here is Cicero's relatively detailed account of what Catiline supposedly said behind closed doors to his fellow conspirators a year later:

> All this you yourselves recollect; for you remember, when the expressions of that wicked gladiator got abroad, which he was said to have used at a meeting at his own house, when he said that it was impossible for any faithful defender of the miserable citizens to be found, except a man who was himself miserable; that men in an embarrassed and desperate condition ought not to trust the promises of men of a flourishing and fortunate estate; and therefore that those who were desirous to replace what they had spent, and to recover what they had lost, had better consider what he himself owed, what he possessed, and what he would dare to do; that that man ought to be very fearless and thoroughly overwhelmed by misfortune, who was to be the leader and standard-bearer of unfortunate men.[16]

There is not much resemblance at all between the two descriptions of the remarks, even waiving the fact that Sallust does not say that the remarks he mentions so briefly were given to a group. In the passage in Sallust, Catiline emphasizes his own resources, whereas in the remarks recorded by Cicero he emphasizes his own desperation and misery. Sallust recounts his talking about the unprepared condition of the state, but there is no mention of that in the remarks that Cicero summarizes. The only extremely vague resemblance lies in the phrase in Sallust "great prizes of conspiracy" and the parallel one might draw to "replace what they had spent, and to recover what they had lost" in Cicero's description, but this is not striking at all. Any conspiracy leader is going to suggest to his followers, no doubt multiple times, that they have something to gain by following him. In short,

---

[16] Cicero, *For Murena*, 50. Trans. C. D. Yonge, B. A. London. Henry G. Bohn, 1856, http://www.perseus.tufts.edu/hopper/text?doc=urn:cts:latinLit:phi0474.phi014.perseus-eng1:50. Later citations of this work are to the same translation, available and indexed at Perseus, though they may be found at different specific URLs.

Licona's statement that there is a striking resemblance of content is flatly false. These could easily be two different occasions, not only because in Sallust there is no account of remarks actually presented to the gathered conspirators but also because the accounts of the remarks are not notably similar.

Licona writes as though the differences between these two accounts amount to an apparent discrepancy, as though there is no resolution to this discrepancy, and as though the only plausible reason for the discrepancy is a deliberate change of fact on the part of Sallust. But in point of fact, the example fails at the very first step. There is not even an apparent discrepancy. The accounts do not even appear on their faces to describe the same event. Any scholars who conclude that Sallust is describing a speech and that that speech was "almost certainly modeled" on the account in Cicero are going far beyond the evidence.

I note, too, that the alleged reason for Sallust's change would, if it were correct, appear to render his activity propagandistic, a point that does not even seem to have occurred to Licona. Licona says, "Sallust distorts the true picture to cast Catiline as a villain even before he resorted to desperate measures…" But such a distortion would not succeed unless the audience accepted this picture of Catiline, in which case this would be ordinary truth distortion, not a literary device.

The next example, also from Ramsey, concerns the same plot by Catiline. Here the question concerns when Catiline uttered a certain threat or whether he uttered it twice. The alleged literary device is, again, chronological displacement. The claim is that Sallust moved the threat later in time by about five months in order to make a bombastic climax to Catiline's last meeting with the senate before leaving Rome to join his own soldiers.

Here is Cicero's account:

> Accordingly, the next day, in a full meeting of the senate, I addressed Catiline himself; and desired him, if he could, to [give] some explanation of these reports which had been brought to me. And he—for he was not much addicted to disguising his intentions—did not attempt to clear himself; but openly avowed and adopted the statements. For he said then, that there were two bodies of the republic,—the one weak with a weak head, the other powerful without a head,—and that, as this last had deserved well of him, it should never want a head as long as he lived. The whole senate groaned at hearing itself addressed in such language, and passed a resolution not severe enough for such unworthy conduct; for some of them were against too rigorous a resolution, because they had no fear; and some, because they had a great deal. Then he rushed forth from the senate, triumphing and exulting,—a man who never ought to have been allowed to leave it alive, especially as that very same man

in the same place had made answer to Cato, that gallant man who was threatening him with a prosecution, a few days before, that if any fire were kindled against his own fortunes, he would put it out not with water, but by the general ruin.[17]

Cicero dates the account of the confrontation between the full senate and Catiline to the day when the *comitia* (the election in which Catiline was running for office) was to have been held. Cicero says that he asked the senate to postpone the election in order to investigate these matters. This would have been in the summer of 63 B.C. in an election for a term to begin in 62 B.C. Catiline's utterance about the fire and the general ruin, then, would have been "a few days before" the originally scheduled election for consul and hence also in the summer. Licona erroneously says that the threat by Catiline took place (according to Cicero) *on* the day when the consular elections were to have been held, a point I shall return to shortly. In any event, Cicero is here describing apparently two meetings in the summer of 63. At one of them Cato, Catiline, and some others were present; another meeting occurred a few days later, involving the full senate. In both cases, says Cicero, Catiline was defiant. In the meeting with the smaller group, according to Cicero, he uttered a threat about bringing general ruin if a fire were kindled against his own fortunes.

Sallust gives an account of a different meeting, in November of that same year, when (he says) Catiline uttered a threat about opposing the fire against him by bringing about general ruin:

> When he took his seat, Catiline, prepared as he was to deny everything, with downcast eyes and pleading accents began to beg the Fathers of the Senate not to believe any unfounded charge against him; he was sprung from such a family, he said, and had so ordered his life from youth up, that he had none save the best of prospects. They must not suppose that he, a patrician, who like his forefathers had rendered great service to the Roman people, would be benefited by the overthrow of the government, while its saviour was Marcus Tullius, a resident alien in the city of Rome. When he would have added other insults, he was shouted down by the whole body, who called him traitor and assassin. Then in a transport of fury he cried: "Since I am brought to bay by my enemies and driven desperate, I will put out my fire by general devastation."[18]

Sallust notes that at this same meeting Cicero presented a "brilliant speech," which we know as the first oration against Catiline and can independently date to November 7 or 8 in 63 B.C. So Sallust is speaking of a meeting in November,

---

[17] Cicero, *For Murena*, 51.

[18] Sallust, *The War With Catiline*, 31.7–9.

and Sallust also makes it clear in the context that this meeting is occurring some time later than the election in the summer.[19]

So it is true that Sallust and Cicero are referring to different meetings of the senate with Catiline and are placing this similar utterance at those different meetings. Whether or not this causes the differences in the accounts to clear even the first node of the flowchart depends a great deal upon one's estimate of the probability that Catiline would have said something like this twice. If one thinks it entirely plausible without further reflection that he would have said something similar on two occasions, one will deem this not even to amount to an *apparent* discrepancy. But, since Licona gives several arguments against his having uttered it twice, suppose that we grant that these two records of a similar threat may be said to amount to an *apparent* discrepancy, while keeping in mind that, at the next node (the question of harmonization) we may conclude that it is plausible that something like this was uttered twice after all.

Licona says that it would have been very "tempting" to Sallust to "shift" these words to the later meeting (for rhetorical reasons) and quotes Ramsey on the subject:

> Sallust…can't resist postdating Catiline's threat from July to make it fall precisely on November 8th so that it will have the greatest impact…by having Catiline utter his chilling threat as his last, parting words. Sallust as a creative writer saw the possibility of making a good story better by tweaking it. What harm is done, he could argue. Catiline did in fact utter a threat likening an attack by a political enemy to "fire" which he would extinguish not with water but by means of general destruction (*ruina*, the word found in both Cicero's and Sallust's version). Further, he made that threat at a meeting of the senate in 63 BCE, in response to a threat from a political enemy (Cato/Cicero).[20]

I cannot help noting that the conjectures about Sallust's motives for moving events are *ad hoc*, even to the point of being in tension with each other. On the one hand, in the previous example Sallust is supposed to have moved a story of Catiline's conspiracy *earlier* in time by a year in order to portray Catiline as a wild-eyed rebel all along. On the other hand, in this example he is supposed to have moved Catiline's threat *later* in time by about five months in order to make a splashy climax to Catiline's last meeting with the senate. But if Sallust wanted to portray Catiline as villainous even when he was pretending to be an ordinary

---

[19] Ibid., 26.5.

[20] Licona, *Why Are There Differences*, p. 188.

politician running for office (the first conjecture), it would have made more sense for Sallust to have left the threat at the time when, according to Cicero, it was actually uttered—namely, a few days prior to an election in which Catiline was running for consul.

Licona's arguments that Catiline did not utter this threat twice are not very strong. He says that the threat "is such a unique formulation that it does not lend itself to repetition. It was undoubtedly highly effective the first time it was uttered for its shock value. The same effect would not have been achieved if it were uttered more than once."[21] But would Catiline have agreed? We have all known people who are fond of a particular phrase they have devised and use it on more than one occasion, even if other people may feel that it loses its force by repetition. If anything, the later meeting was a more perfect time for the threat than the earlier meeting. According to Cicero, the summer occasion on which Catiline uttered the threat was even before the election was to be held. Though Cato was threatening to prosecute him, Catiline at that time still had some hopes of winning the election, a point that Cicero himself emphasizes.[22] In November, Catiline has lost the election, and the senate is unimpressed by his protestations of innocence. Thus a threat to bring down Rome in general ruin, given his own desperate situation, makes even more sense in November than in June. If it were Cicero rather than Sallust who were being accused of moving the saying, these points would probably be brought up to argue for that opposite point. It is therefore entirely plausible all by itself that Catiline did utter the threat at the end of his last meeting with the senate in November, before leaving the city and joining his troops in open rebellion. In fact, the same considerations of rhetorical bombast that are supposed to have tempted Sallust to move the threat literarily to make a dramatic climax may well have inclined the historical Catiline to re-use it on that occasion.

Licona also makes an argument from silence that shows a failure to understand Cicero's speech.

> If Sallust's context (at the meeting on 8 November) were the correct one, it would have played into Cicero's hands when he was defending his client Murena just a week or two later. Cicero would undoubtedly have seized upon those words, holding them up to the jury as the last, mad words of the villain Catiline before he stormed out of the senate and left Rome to join his rebel army.[23]

---

[21] Ibid., pp. 187–188.

[22] Cicero, *For Murena*, 50.

[23] Ibid., p. 188.

This argument is entirely out of touch with the way that Cicero uses Catiline's threat in his defense of Murena. Murena ran against Catiline in the election that summer and won. He was then accused (before taking office) of electoral bribery—that is, influencing people to support him in the election by bribery. Cicero's argument in his defense is that, *at the time of the election in the summer,* the Roman people were rightly frightened by Catiline's wild behavior and by the thought that he might win the election. Cicero argues that they swung over to support Murena for this reason, not because Murena committed bribery:

> I need not remind you with what terror all good men were seized in consequence of these occurrences, and how entirely they would all have despaired of the republic if he had been made consul....Therefore, as...men...saw Catiline inflamed with hope and desire, all who wished to repel that pest from the republic immediately joined the party of Murena.[24]

It is in this context that Cicero recounts Catiline's threat to Rome in the summer. Telling about a repetition of the threat several months after the election was over would not have served the argumentative purpose of defending Murena from the charge of bribery in the summer. Licona does not seem to understand what Cicero is doing at this point in his speech.

It is therefore quite plausible that Catiline did utter the threat twice and therefore that the accounts are harmonizable without difficulty. But suppose that, for some reason, one considers it too improbable that Catiline would have said something so similar twice. There are plenty of other questions to consider before concluding that Sallust has moved the threat, much less that Sallust was using an accepted literary device in so doing. Most notably, Licona never even considers the possibility that Sallust might have simply become confused about which meeting with the senate was the occasion of the threat.

This point deserves stress: Literary device theorists, and biblical scholars generally, have an extremely bad habit of assuming that, if A is a source for B, then B must have had A's manuscript open in front of him at the very moment of writing, must have understood A's manuscript perfectly, and must have had quite clearly in mind every detail pertaining to the point in question. On the basis of these strong assumptions about the process of composition, scholars will immediately conclude that any discrepancy and perhaps even any difference between B's account and A's must be the result of a *conscious decision* on the part

---

[24] Cicero, *For Murena,* 50–52.

of B to depart from what A says. This is far too strong a set of assumptions to be sustained.

Consider how complicated the events were in this case: By Cicero's own account, there were at least two meetings with Catiline in the summer of the election. One involved a smaller group of senators and one was with the full senate. Then, by the independent dating of Cicero's first oration against Catiline and by Sallust's account, there was yet a *third* meeting in November, at which the senate again challenged Catiline with accusations of conspiracy against Rome. He was defiant in all three cases and left the senate in anger in all three cases without any resolution of the charges against him. Ramsey and Licona do not deny this. One can't help thinking that the meetings are so similar in their broad outline that, if we did not have the evidence from Cicero for all three of them, it is quite likely that some scholar would say that Sallust moved an *entire* meeting of the senate, not just Catiline's threat. After all, it would just be *too much to believe* that members of the senate had *three* similar meetings with Catiline. Yet, apparently, they did.

Bearing in mind that there were three similar meetings, one can see quite a plausible way in which Sallust might have made a mistake. Suppose that Sallust knew independently of the November meeting with the senate, perhaps by having read Cicero's oration against Catiline given on that occasion. If Sallust also read Cicero's speech in defense of Murena hastily and/or did not remember it clearly, if he then wrote about a meeting of Catiline with the senate, he might readily become confused about which meeting Cicero is referring to when he describes Murena's threat.

In support of this point I return to something rather remarkable that I noted above: *Licona himself* makes a mistake about which meeting of the senate Cicero is talking about when he describes Catiline's threat to bring down Rome. Licona says,

> When Catiline stood for a consulship in 63, at a meeting of the senate that took place about mid-July, *on the day on which the consular elections were originally to have been held*, Catiline uttered an ominous and memorable threat, warning that he would bring about general destruction if Cato carried out his intention to indict and prosecute him.[25]

And Licona attributes this timing to Cicero. But here is what Cicero actually says, after recounting the meeting on the day when the consular elections were to have been held:

---

[25] Licona, *Why Are There Differences*, p. 187. Emphasis added.

[T]hat very same man [Catiline] in the same place had made answer to Cato, that gallant man who was threatening him with a prosecution, *a few days before*, that if any fire were kindled against his own fortunes, he would put it out not with water, but by the general ruin.[26]

In other words, Cicero actually locates the threat several days before (*paucis diebus ante*) the day on which Licona thinks he does.

In our own time, one can have Cicero's oration in defense of Murena open in a computer tab, translated into English, at the very moment that one is writing about these historical events on the same computer. Licona was attempting to discuss precisely when Cicero dated Catiline's threat. Yet even with all the advantages of 21st-century technology, he made a small slip about what Cicero was saying. My point is simply that this is an excellent illustration of the complexity of the events involved and of how easy it is to make a mistake. How much easier would it be to make a mistake in a time when one had to work with scrolls, notes taken from scrolls, or one's memory? Even if we assume (reasonably enough) that Cicero's defense of Murena was one of Sallust's sources for these events, it is hardly beyond the realm of plausibility that he assigned Catiline's threat to the November meeting as a sheer error, with no intention of moving it.

Finally, there is the question of whether Sallust would have been engaging in ordinary fabrication rather than some special literary device if he actually did deliberately move the threat. We must remember that a literary *motivation* is not the same thing as a literary *device*. As already discussed, for an author to be using a literary *device*, he should believe that what he is doing is an acceptable form of factual alteration, that his audience will understand that he may, in writing the type of work in question, make such factual changes from time to time, and therefore that his audience will (if they take enough of his narrative with the proper number of grains of salt) not be misled about the factual matter in question. Ramsey, as quoted by Licona, does not even *claim* this. He merely claims that Sallust was motivated by the desire to give a chilling conclusion to the November senate meeting and that he would have rationalized the change to himself as not doing any "harm," given that Catiline did utter the threat at some time. But rationalization for altering facts is not the same thing as a conviction that one is using a societally accepted literary device. People rationalize in every age, and surely gifted storytellers do so in order to salve any twinges of conscience they might feel about bending the facts. Even if one became convinced that Sallust deliberately moved

---

[26] Cicero, *For Murena*, 51. Emphasis added.

Catiline's threat, there is no reason to think he was using a literary device as opposed to simply disregarding literal truth for his own casual reasons.

Given all of the other evidence, however, it seems highly likely that Sallust was either recounting a second threat that really occurred or else that he merely made an error.

4. Plutarch: Pompey brings back Cicero

For the next several examples, we turn to Plutarch. Plutarch's *Lives of the Noble Greeks and Romans* are paradigmatic Greco-Roman βίοι, and Licona's claim is that we find various categories of literary devices in Plutarch's *Lives* that cast light upon differences in the Gospel narratives. While he uses other ancient authors as well (such as Sallust), and while his general method is the same no matter what author he is discussing, he spends the most time on Plutarch. At the end of his study, he concludes,

> Our analysis of thirty-six pericopes that appear on two or more occasions in Plutarch's *Lives* supports the conclusions of classical scholars that the type of compositional devices we have identified were standard practice in writing biographical literature in that era. When this background knowledge is added to the fact that the Gospels share close affinity to Greco-Roman biography, the same genre in which Plutarch's *Lives* fit, and that a significant amount of the differences in the Gospels can be easily understood in light of this background knowledge, it becomes quite plausible that the evangelists were aware of and made use of many of the compositional devices we inferred from Plutarch's *Lives* as well as those prescribed in the compositional textbooks. Thus, the suspicions of many New Testament scholars that the evangelists used compositional devices similar to those we have identified in this book are correct. Accordingly, we now have some more clearly defined and assured ideas pertaining to how the flexibility of ancient biography impacts our understanding of the Gospels.[27]

If one is bound and determined to make such an argument, the attempt to use Plutarch's *Lives* is at least an understandable strategy. Since the accounts were written by the same author, there is at least *some* plausibility to the idea that the author would have known what he had written elsewhere and that discrepancies were deliberate. But as I shall argue, even that should not be taken as a given, considering the minuscule nature of many of the details in question and the cumbersomeness of having more than one document open at the same

---

[27] Licona, *Why Are There Differences*, p. 200.

time. It is also entirely possible that Plutarch came across different information in between writing his accounts.

Plutarch does give us a chance to compare different accounts of the same events and time periods, because he often will tell about the same events in different *Lives* with an emphasis upon a different character involved.[28] But Licona's conclusion from an analysis of Plutarchan examples that the devices he has named and defined were "standard practice in writing biographical literature of that era" is vastly under-supported by his arguments and by the text of Plutarch.

In our next example, Licona alleges that Plutarch compresses and conflates events. (As discussed in Chapter III, section 1, Licona defines compression and conflation in terms that, by the definition I have given, are fictionalizing devices.) The section of Plutarch in this example concerns a time period in the 50s B.C. when Cicero had been exiled from Rome. The military leader and politician Pompey, portrayed by Plutarch as indecisive, was deciding that he needed to change his political focus and support having Cicero's banishment reversed. Licona says that Plutarch, in his biography of Pompey, compresses and conflates the account of the events leading up to the vote to have Cicero returned.[29]

In *Cic.* 33.1–5, Pompey's actions to recall Cicero from banishment occurred in three stages: (1) Pompey and Cicero's friends attempted to have Cicero returned, but Clodius opposed them. (2) After Clodius's time in office expired, violence occurred in the Forum on 23 January 57 where Cicero's brother (among others) was injured and believed to have been killed. (3) In response, one of the tribunes prosecuted Clodius for violence, and many people began changing their minds and came from the cities surrounding Rome to join Pompey. With these, Pompey drove Clodius from the Forum and summoned the people for a vote, which occurred on 4 August 57. However, when Plutarch tells the same story in *Pomp.* 49.1–4, he compresses and conflates the action into one stage: Pompey escorted Cicero's brother with the people into the Forum, where some were wounded, others killed, and Clodius was defeated.[30]

A point to be made at the outset and borne constantly in mind in our discussions of Licona's examples is that none of these dates occurs explicitly in

---

[28] I have placed several additional examples concerning Plutarch and one concerning Tacitus into Appendix 2 for those who want to see more.

[29] When a name or abbreviation of a name appears in italics, it refers to a Plutarchan biography named for that person. E.g., *Pompey* and *Pomp.* both refer to Plutarch's *Life of Pompey*. When a name is not italicized, it refers to the person by that name.

[30] Licona, *Why Are There Differences*, pp. 51–52.

the Plutarch passages cited. Licona repeatedly writes of highly specific dates *in Plutarch* as though they are stated *in the text*, but they are not. It may be that the inference that those dates were intended or implied by Plutarch is historically secure in some fashion, but it has to be an inference, and Licona does not always give the argument. This point is important, since in many cases a crucial question at issue is whether there is a discrepancy between two of Plutarch's *Lives*, and the case for the discrepancy sometimes depends upon the claim that Plutarch puts an event on a certain date.

When one turns to *Pompey* and *Cicero*, one is hard-pressed to find the compression and conflation Licona claims. In fact, it is arguable that this example fails at the very first node of the flowchart—that there is not even any apparent discrepancy between the two works. The narrative in Pompey is shorter and less detailed concerning these events, but the accounts appear to be entirely compatible.

To take the relative brevity of the narrative in *Pompey* to mean that Plutarch is deliberately writing of different events as if they were the same event and/or deliberately writing of a series of events as if they take place over a shorter period of time than they really took requires woodenness and over-reading. These are themes that will come up more than once in my analysis of these examples and of the Gospel examples. While literary device theorists apparently believe that anyone who criticizes them "from the right"—that is, who criticizes them because he believes that the Gospel authors did not deliberately alter facts—is rigid and wooden, what we will find again and again is that it is the literary device theorists themselves who read texts rigidly. This leads them to assume, for example, that a brief narration means a brief time period in the narrative world, to assume that narrative order is chronological order within the narrative, and to exaggerate every nuance that one might indirectly infer from the text into a deliberate, positive implication of the text. They then place the documents side by side and "find" discrepancies between them—unsurprisingly, given the methods employed. It is perhaps a little surprising to see this method used even in the interpretation of non-biblical literature.

Here is the narrative in *Cicero* of Cicero's exile and recall. Clodius is a lowlife politician Plutarch despises, with whom Pompey had previously made a regrettable alliance.

As for Clodius, after driving Cicero away he burned down his villas, and burned down his house, and erected on its site a temple to Liberty; the rest of his property he offered for sale and had it proclaimed daily, but nobody would buy anything. Being therefore formidable to the patricians, and dragging along with him the people, who indulged in great boldness and effrontery, he assailed Pompey, attacking fiercely some of the arrangements made by him on his expedition. The disgrace which this brought upon Pompey led him to reproach himself for his abandonment of Cicero; and changing front he used every effort to effect Cicero's return, and so did his friends. But since Clodius opposed himself to this, the senate decided to ratify no measure that came up in the mean time and to do no public business, unless Cicero should be permitted to return. During the consulship of Lentulus, however, when the disorder went on increasing, so that tribunes were wounded in the forum and Quintus the brother of Cicero lay unnoticed for dead among the slain, the people began to change their minds, and Annius Milo, one of the tribunes, first ventured to prosecute Clodius for violence, and many joined themselves to Pompey both from the people and from the surrounding cities. With these Pompey came forth, drove Clodius from the forum, and summoned the citizens to the vote. And it is said that the people never passed any vote with such unanimity.[31]

Here is the narrative in *Pompey* that, according to Licona, compresses and conflates events:[32]

And finally, when Pompey appeared at a public trial, Clodius, having at his beck and call a rabble of the lewdest and most arrogant ruffians, stationed himself in a conspicuous place and put to them such questions as these: "Who is a licentious imperator?" "What man seeks for a man?" "Who scratches his head with one finger?" And they, like a chorus trained in responsive song, as he shook his toga, would answer each question by shouting out "Pompey." Of course this also was annoying to Pompey, who was not accustomed to vilification and was inexperienced in this sort of warfare; but he was more distressed when he perceived that the senate was delighted to see him insulted and paying a penalty for his betrayal of Cicero. When, however, it had come to blows and even wounds in the forum, and a servant of Clodius, stealing along through the crowd of bystanders towards Pompey, was found to have a sword in his hand, Pompey made this his excuse, although he was also afraid of the insolent abuse of Clodius, and came no more into the forum as long as Clodius was tribune, but kept himself continually at home, where he was ever debating with his friends how he might appease the anger

---

[31] Plutarch, *Life of Cicero*, 33.1–5. Plutarch's *Parallel Lives* will feature largely in this book. Unless otherwise noted, all translations are from the Loeb edition, translated by Bernadotte Perrin, 1914–1926, and available in the public domain at http://penelope.uchicago.edu/Thayer/E/Roman/Texts/Plutarch/Lives/. I will not give separate URLs for each of the *Lives* cited.

[32] The reference to divorcing Julia arises from the fact that Julius Caesar had given Pompey his daughter in marriage as a way of cementing their alliance. Caesar and Cicero are political enemies, and those who want Pompey to align himself with Cicero and the senate therefore urge Pompey to divorce Caesar's daughter.

of the senate and the nobility against him. To Culleo, however, who urged him to divorce Julia and exchange the friendship of Caesar for that of the senate, he would not listen, but he yielded to the arguments of those who thought he ought to bring Cicero back, who was the greatest enemy of Clodius and most beloved in the senate, and he escorted Cicero's brother, who was a petitioner for his return, with a large force into the forum, where, though some were wounded and some killed, he nevertheless got the better of Clodius.[33]

Though *Pompey* expands upon Clodius's insults, adds the fact that there was an assassination attempt against Pompey, and brings up the suggestion that Pompey divorce Caesar's daughter as a way of placating the senate, the passage in *Pompey* does give less detail about the attempts to have Cicero recalled. But this does not mean that Plutarch is conflating events or implying that events took less time than they did. The implication that there was some violence in the forum even before the expiration of Clodius's time as tribune is of course compatible with growing violence after that. *Pompey* does not happen to state at exactly what point in all of this Clodius's term in office expired.

In fact, contra Licona, in *Pompey* the whole series of events clearly takes some time. *Pompey* adds the claim that someone was trying to approach Pompey with a sword and that Pompey made this his excuse for not coming into the forum for a while. Instead, he stayed at home and debated with his friends what he should do, though resisting the suggestion that he should divorce Julia. So, just as in *Cicero*, there is some period of time between Pompey's first disaffection with Clodius and the final ousting of Clodius's sympathizers. Eventually, in *Pompey*, Pompey went into the forum with a large force, had a skirmish with Clodius, and was victorious in getting a law passed for the recall of Cicero. This is all completely consistent, even easily consistent, with the events related in *Cicero*. There are merely somewhat differing details about different portions of the entire series of events. The reference in *Cicero* to "driving" Clodius from the Forum, for example, fits perfectly with the reference to some being wounded and killed in that confrontation in *Pompey*.

As for Cicero's brother, Quintus, one guesses that perhaps Licona's case for "conflation and compression" into "one stage" (which Licona does not explain in any detail) is based in part on the fact that the account in *Cicero* mentions the brother in reference to the earlier violence in the forum, whereas the account in *Pompey* mentions his being escorted into the forum by Pompey as part of the

---

[33] Plutarch, *Life of Pompey*, 48.7–49.3.

later, violent confrontation with Clodius and his followers. But this is an extremely poor argument, if that is what Licona is implying. Why should Cicero's brother not have been in the forum both times? He could have been wounded in general violence one time and then escorted safely later when there was a stronger force supporting the bid for Cicero's return. After all, *Pompey* even says that there was fighting and danger in the Forum while Clodius was tribune, so it's not as though all was serene in the forum before the final confrontation. And if Quintus were deeply involved in advocating a vote for Cicero's return, his presence in the forum on more than one occasion is highly plausible. In one case he is said to have been wounded in the course of mob violence, while in the other he is said to have been escorted in (presumably safely) with a large, ultimately successful force, so there is every reason to think that these refer to two entirely different occasions on which he was in the forum.

The ostentatious act of "escorting" Quintus would actually make sense if he had been injured earlier. He would presumably have been a sympathetic figure to Cicero's supporters, both as Cicero's brother and as someone who was hurt in a riot earlier. The previous violence is apparently being attributed to the absence of Cicero himself. The account in *Pompey* simply does not mention Quintus's having been injured earlier. One could even argue that this is an undesigned coincidence connecting the two accounts. The account in Pompey mentions his being escorted into the forum, while the account in *Cicero* provides a possible explanation (in addition to his being Cicero's brother)—namely, his having been injured earlier and hence becoming a symbol to the sympathetic crowd of the violence in Cicero's absence.

The fact that Licona makes no argument but simply asserts the presence of literary devices forces one to try to construct an argument for some sort of tension between the two accounts. Could the supposed problem be that *Pompey* does not bring up Pompey's decision to try to have Cicero returned until *just before* the narrative of the successful confrontation with Clodius? But that would be a weak argument based on a wooden reading. It would require interpreting Plutarch to imply in *Pompey* that Pompey decided to cooperate with Cicero's supporters and then *instantly* went out, got together a force of people, and marched into the forum. But the exact time relation between his decision to support Cicero's return and the final confrontation in the forum is left unspecified in *Pompey*, while the *Life of Cicero* states, giving more detail on this point, that Pompey made ineffective political efforts in that direction while Clodius was still tribune. His decision to support Cicero's return could have been a gradual one, and he might have made some political efforts to that end and then eventually, when he considered the measure to have enough popular support, acted physically and decisively at last. Alternatively, one can take the reference to his yielding "to the arguments of those who thought he ought to bring Cicero back" to refer only to his specific decision to take stronger action when he saw the people on his side.

One even wonders if Pompey's earlier efforts (however ineffective) to have Cicero recalled could have been what occasioned the assassination attempt against him, mentioned in *Pompey*. Otherwise it is a little odd that Clodius would have tried to assassinate Pompey when he seems merely to have despised him and to have enjoyed insulting him. This would constitute another undesigned coincidence of sorts, in which the reference in *Cicero* to earlier efforts by Pompey on the side of Cicero occasioned the assassination attempt described only in *Pompey*.

The ways in which the accounts fit together are so natural, uncontroversial, and even complementary that it is difficult to see why one would think that there are fact-changing compositional devices of compression and conflation in *Pompey*. Plutarch seems to have told the same events consistently but with different emphases in terms of length and detail, sometimes being non-specific as to the amount of time involved. (See the discussion in Chapter II, section 1, of two different concepts of "compression.") At the most, if one insists on thinking that the later initial reference to Pompey's decision to support Cicero's return in *Pompey* creates an apparent discrepancy of some sort with *Cicero* (which describes earlier attempts on his part in that direction), such a minor tension is easily harmonizable in one or more of the ways just suggested. This is a case of creating and exaggerating differences between two accounts that vary in a normal historical fashion and then solving the artificial problem using the artificial machinery of literary devices.

5. Plutarch: Who called Caesar a robber?

Licona alleges that Plutarch has engaged in both conflation and transferral when it comes to some insults against Julius Caesar in the Roman senate. These occurred after the events in the previous example, during the time when Caesar and the senate were increasingly at odds. Pompey took the side of the senate.

> In *Caes.* 30.2, Scipio introduced a motion that Caesar be declared a public enemy if he did not disarm by a certain date....In *Caes.* 30. 3, Lentulus the consul said there was a need for arms against a bandit....In *Pomp.* 58.4, Marcellus called Caesar a bandit and urged that he be declared a public enemy if he refused to lay

down his arms....Plutarch appears to conflate the logia uttered against Caesar by Scipio and Lentulus and transfer them to Marcellus.[34]

Licona does not even suggest any particular reason, either literary or thematic, for Plutarch to make Scipio and Lentulus say certain things in one *Life* and to have Marcellus say them in a different *Life*. The alleged devices appear to be random and pointless. Is Plutarch supposed to have made these deliberate changes merely for the sake of variety?

The occasion in question appears to be very similar, and plausibly the same senate sitting, in both *Lives*, but that gives us no reason to think that the statements in question were "logia" that could not have been said or suggested by more than one person on that occasion. The word "logia" conveys a false air of technicality, as though these are highly specific sayings that must have been uttered only once by only one person. Here is the passage in *Caesar*:

> However, the demands which came from Caesar certainly had a striking resemblance of fairness. He demanded, namely, that if he himself laid down his arms, Pompey should do the same, and that both, thus become private men, should find what favour they could with their fellow citizens; arguing that if they took away his forces from him, but confirmed Pompey in the possession of his, they would be accusing one of seeking a tyranny and making the other a tyrant....But in the senate, Scipio, the father-in-law of Pompey, introduced a motion that if by a fixed day Caesar did not lay down his arms he should be declared a public enemy. And when the consuls put the question whether Pompey should dismiss his soldiers, and again whether Caesar should, very few senators voted for the first, and all but a few for the second; but when Antony again demanded that both should give up their commands, all with one accord assented. Scipio, however, made violent opposition, and Lentulus the consul cried out that against a robber there was need of arms, not votes; whereupon the senate broke up, and the senators put on the garb of mourning in view of the dissension.[35]

And here is the passage in *Pompey*:

> And yet the requests and demands which Curio made in behalf of Caesar seemed to be very popular in their character. For he demanded one of two things: either that Pompey also should be required to give up his soldiery, or else that Caesar's should not be taken away from him; for whether they became private persons on just and equal terms, or remained a match for each other with their present forces,

---

[34] Licona, *Why Are There Differences*, pp. 64–66.

[35] Plutarch, *Life of Caesar*, 31.1–6.

they would make no disturbance; but he who weakened one of them doubled the power of which he stood in fear. To this Marcellus the consul replied by calling Caesar a robber, and urging that he be voted a public enemy unless he should lay down his arms; nevertheless, Curio, aided by Antony and Piso, prevailed so far as to have the opinion of the senate taken....[A strong senate majority approves of the proposal that both give up their commands.] Marcellus, however, rose and declared that he would not sit there listening to speeches, but since he saw ten legions already looming up in their march over the Alps, he himself also would send forth a man who would oppose them in defence of his country. Upon this, the city went into mourning, as in the presence of a public calamity....[36]

These descriptions of events are remarkable for their similarities. Is there any discrepancy, even an apparent discrepancy, in saying that Marcellus called Caesar a robber (not reported in highly specific words) and also that Lentulus said that he was a robber and urged the use of arms against him? Not in the slightest. This is, by Plutarch's own description, a high-tension senatorial debate with feelings running high on both sides. It is entirely likely that more than one person would refer to Caesar in such derogatory terms in such a discussion. The references need not even have been independent. Caesar's opponents could all have been referring to him as a robber among themselves, and Lentulus and Marcellus would, if they were both present, doubtless have heard each other's remarks. Have literary device theorists never heard of "talking points"? Those who are on the same side of a political debate *often* level the same insults against their opponents.

Consider as well the statement that Scipio introduced a motion that Caesar be declared a public enemy if he did not lay down his arms by a certain date and the claim that Marcellus urged that such a motion be adopted. Does this pair of historical claims, found in different *Lives*, provide evidence of "transferral"? Of course not. If this is transferral, then we have "transferral" going on every time one senator introduces a motion and another senator supports it! As the theorists must know, that is the kind of thing that happens in senate meetings. One person introduces a motion and others express support for it. We certainly do not need to suspect a literary device if Plutarch reports Scipio's introduction in one account and Marcellus's support in another.

This example does not even get past the first node of the flowchart. There is not even an apparent discrepancy concerning who called Julius Caesar a robber and who urged that he be declared a public enemy. A simple understanding of

---

[36] Plutarch, *Life of Pompey*, 58.1–59.1.

the most common behavior of political bodies and political enemies explains the varied names.[37]

But let us suppose that someone is (unreasonably) dissatisfied with any of these arguments and insists, strangely enough, that there is an irresolvable contradiction at this point: In *Caesar* it is Lentulus who calls Julius Caesar a robber, but in *Pompey* it is Marcellus, and this is a contradiction with no solution. I raise this hypothetical position in order to discuss Licona's odd habit of (usually) ignoring the possibility that Plutarch may have made an error. As already noted, Licona occasionally will raise this possibility, but most of the time (as here) he does not even mention or to attempt to refute it before alleging a compositional device.

One wonders why. One possibility that would account for some of these instances concerns Licona's dating of the *Lives*. Licona briefly talks about dating and follows classicist Christopher Pelling in placing six of the *Lives* into a group that, he says, were probably composed around "110 CE and perhaps a bit later."[38] Licona continues,

> Since Plutarch's biographical project took approximately three decades, there is a possibility, even a likelihood, that he discovered more reliable data that he used when writing the set of six than what he had before him a few years earlier when writing *Lucullus* and *Cicero*. This could, though not necessarily, account for some of the differences between the accounts. Accordingly, we are able to detect Plutarch's use of compositional devices with greater confidence when identifying how he tells the same story differently within the set of six *Lives*.[39]

---

[37] The alleged transferral of the insults against Caesar is not the only device Licona alleges in these passages, but I am not taking the space to address all of them in the main text. For example, in the elided verses in the quotation from *Caesar*, it says that the people feted Curio with garlands when he told them of Caesar's proposals. In *Pompey*, the people throw garlands at Curio when he rushes out and tells them prematurely that the senate and Caesar have reached a compromise. Licona takes this to indicate both a time displacement and an alteration of the content of Curio's message to the people (*Why Are There Differences*, p. 65). But the statement in *Caesar* 30.2 about Curio and the people is simply non-specific about the *precise* order of events that all took place at this time, and the narration of Curio's being pelted with garlands emphasizes how reasonable Caesar's proposals appeared and how popular they were, which Plutarch also emphasizes in *Pompey*. Curio obviously could have described Caesar's proposal that both should lay down arms at the same time that he (hastily) told the crowds that this was now settled with the senate. Licona also takes Plutarch's reference to Lentulus as consul elect in one account and as consul in another account to mean that Plutarch was probably dislocating the events in one account (p. 65). But this is wooden. Lentulus would take office very soon thereafter and had already been elected. Referring to him as "consul" a month or less before he actually took office would be a natural, if slightly imprecise, manner of speaking and need not indicate any dating intention on Plutarch's part.

[38] Licona, *Why Are There Differences*, p. 19.

[39] Ibid.

In the case of an alleged discrepancy and hence (in Licona's view) "compositional device" between *Caesar* and *Pompey,* both of which are included in what Licona calls the "set" of six that he believes were composed within a period of a year or two around A.D. 110, it may be that Licona does not even consider it necessary to *discuss the possibility* that Plutarch forgot something or gained additional information. They are to be treated as parts of a "set," he may think, based upon the same information, in such a strong fashion that any discrepancies between them *must* be deliberate and, moreover, the result of factual alteration.

This still does not explain all the places where Licona ignores the possibility of accidental discrepancy. In the previous example, the alleged "conflation and compression" lies between *Pompey* and *Cicero.* But Licona and Pelling believe that *Cicero* was composed some time between A.D. 100 and 110, while *Pompey* was one of the six composed around 110 or a little later—a wide time period in which to gain information or forget what one had already written elsewhere. Yet not only does Licona not consider the harmonization I gave in the previous section, he also does not even bother to say why he is confident that Plutarch is engaging in "compression and conflation" rather than simply learning more about Pompey's earlier efforts to recall Cicero from banishment.

But what about the argument that six of the *Lives* were all composed at the same time and that this precludes error or gaining new information between any of those? First, Licona's own account of Pelling's reasoning makes it clear that the dating of Plutarch's *Lives* is a chancy, troublesome business. Licona himself admits that "the chronology in which Plutarch penned them is difficult to establish."[40] While Pelling's conjecture that the six biographies listed were conceived of together, during a relatively brief period of time (perhaps a year or two) may be correct, it is far from certain. Classicist J. L. Moles is inclined to accept Pelling's argument from cross-references among the *Lives* for the conclusion that Plutarch prepared material for more than one *Life* at a time and in that sense that multiple *Lives* were "composed together." But Moles's discussion of the difficulties besetting such theorizing shows that highly specific dating conclusions should be held lightly.[41] Moles also emphasizes the crucial distinc-

---

[40] Ibid.

[41] J. L. Moles, *A Commentary on Plutarch's* Brutus (Newcastle Upon Tyne: *Histos* Supplement 7, 2017), pp. 8–11. Moles does believe that Plutarch sometimes changed chronology for literary or thematic motives (pp. xi, 4, 80), so his comment cited here does not serve any agenda to the contrary. He does at one point (p. 199) state that there is an error causing a discrepancy between two of the *Lives* contained in Licona's and Pelling's suggested "set," so he does not take the dating of those *Lives* to

tion between Plutarch's having in some sense composed several *Lives* around the same time and his having *written* them at the same time.[42]

Indeed, I would add this: The fact that Licona is talking about *six* biographies, together with the sheer technological aspects of writing, makes it obvious that the writing itself must have taken some significant time period. We should also remember the great difficulties in comparing large scrolls in a world without even the convenience of large writing tables.[43] It is *highly* unlikely that Plutarch would have gone to the trouble to do a careful, visual comparison of all overlapping event accounts among six different *Lives* in order to ensure that either no discrepancies had crept in or that all discrepancies were deliberately introduced rather than accidental. This is especially relevant when, as is so often the case, the matters in question are bewildering or trivial or both—a name here, a difference of one or two days there, a statement uttered on one of two or more similar occasions, back-and-forth wrangling in the Roman senate, etc.

As for gaining new information, as I will emphasize again below when discussing a recalcitrant discrepancy between two of the *Lives*, there is no historical rule against gaining new information within a short period of time. If one begins reading a different source or if one remembers something one had forgotten, one may gain information within a single day. The vague grouping of Plutarch's composition of six *Lives* within a period of a year or two (even if that conjecture were more secure) scarcely means that we should *discount* the possibility that Plutarch got something clarified or learned something new between the writing of one biography and the writing of another in that time period. This is all the more important given that gaining new information is a common human occurrence, whereas we have no independent evidence for the compositional devices Licona is alleging. Think horses, not zebras.

In short, if Pelling's dating conjecture is all that Licona has to offer in defense of utterly ignoring the possibility of Plutarch's producing discrepant accounts through ordinary means such as forgetfulness or new information, it is weak indeed.

6. Plutarch: Were Antony and Octavian in the battle?

After Julius Caesar was assassinated, his friend Antony and his heir Octavian made war together against the forces of two of the conspirators involved in the

mean that Plutarch could not make an error in one of them on a point that he got right in another.

[42] Ibid., p. 11.

[43] Lydia McGrew, "What Was Writing Like in the 1st Century," *Extra Thoughts*, April 1, 2015, http://lydiaswebpage.blogspot.com/2015/04/what-was-writing-like-in-1st-century.html.

assassination, Brutus and Cassius. Licona alleges a discrepancy and some kind of deliberate alteration (though he does not give it a device name) concerning whether or not Antony and Octavian were personally present in one of the battles. Licona says,

> There is a difference pertaining to whether Antony and Octavian were present at the first battle. In *Brut.* 41.1 and 42.2b–3a, neither Antony nor Octavian were with their armies in the first battle. At the beginning of the battle, Antony went away to a marshy area, and Octavian was nowhere to be seen after his friend Marcus Artorius described to him a dream in which Octavian was commanded to leave the camp. However, in *Ant.* 22.1–4, Antony was victorious everywhere (22.1), and Caesar (the name given here rather than Octavian) narrowly escaped secretly when his camp was overrun by Brutus.[44]

What is particularly striking about this claim of discrepancy about Antony is that Plutarch *expressly states*, in the *very account* where Licona says that Antony was present in the battle, that some sources have claimed that Antony was *not* present. (And something similar is true concerning Octavian.) Nor does Plutarch reject this claim; he reports it in a neutral fashion that appears to qualify carefully any impression that Antony was definitely present at this victory.[45] Hence, the text of the very document Licona cites refutes his claim of a discrepancy.

The phrase "Antony was everywhere victorious and successful" in *Antony* 22.1 means, one eventually sees, that the Antony "team" or forces were successful in the first encounter. Plutarch makes it clear that it does *not* necessarily mean that Antony was personally present in the battle.

> However, after they had crossed the sea, taken up war, and encamped near the enemy, Antony being opposed to Cassius, and Caesar to Brutus, no great achievements were performed by Caesar, but it was Antony who was everywhere victorious and successful. In the first battle, at least, Caesar was overwhelmingly defeated by Brutus, lost his camp, and narrowly escaped his pursuers by secret flight; although he himself says in his Memoirs that he withdrew before the battle in consequence of a friend's dream. But Antony conquered Cassius; although some write that Antony was not present in the battle, but came up after the battle when his men were already in pursuit.[46]

---

[44] Licona, *Why Are There Differences*, p. 106.

[45] Octavian's and Antony's forces were fighting different forces on the opposite side. Octavian's forces were fighting Brutus's forces and lost their portion of the battle.

[46] Plutarch, *Life of Antony*, 22.1–4.

The only difference with the report in *Brutus* is a very slight one of emphasis; there Plutarch goes into somewhat more detail about Antony's absence:

> Neither of the generals was with his men; for Antony, we are told, turned aside from the attack at the outset and withdrew into the marsh, and was nowhere to be seen after he had forsaken his camp....[47]

There simply is no discrepancy here at all, since both accounts indicate that Antony may not personally have been present during the victorious battle against Brutus's forces. If one wished to strain to make some sort of contrast, one might say that "some write" in *Antony* (concerning the report that he was not present) is somewhat more distancing than "Neither of the generals was with his men, for…we are told," etc., in *Brutus*, but this really would be a stretched attempt to place the documents in conflict. Plutarch certainly does not say in *Antony* that what "some write" is false nor indicate that he thinks it is false.

Making matters strange indeed, Licona actually acknowledges in passing that Plutarch reports the possibility of Antony's absence in *Antony*:

> He adds that some assert that Antony was also absent from that battle but came afterward while his soldiers were chasing the enemy (*Ant.* 22.3; cf. *Brut.* 42.2b–3a).[48]

But just a few sentences later, Licona returns once again to asserting a discrepancy:

> In *Brutus*, Plutarch says Antony and Octavian were absent from the first battle, whereas they were present in *Antony*.[49]

If Licona realizes that Plutarch acknowledges in *Antony* that Antony may have been absent, why does he continue after that to insist that Antony was definitely present in that account? There literally is not even the appearance of any contradiction concerning Antony.

The claim that Octavian was definitely present in the first battle (an ignominious defeat for his forces) has little more to be said for it, since Plutarch also explicitly states *in both versions* that Octavian might not have been personally present. Concerning Octavian's defeat in the first battle, Plutarch says in *Antony*,

> In the first battle…Caesar was overwhelmingly defeated by Brutus, lost his camp, and narrowly escaped his pursuers by secret flight; although he himself says in his Memoirs that he withdrew before the battle in consequence of a friend's dream.[50]

---

[47] Plutarch, *Life of Brutus*, 42.2–3.

[48] Licona, *Why Are There Differences*, p. 106.

[49] Ibid., pp. 106–107.

[50] Plutarch, *Life of Antony*, 22.2.

This hardly amounts to a clear statement that Octavian (whom Plutarch calls "Caesar" here) was personally present in the battle in which his forces were defeated. Caesar's personal presence in the battle is left unclear in this passage. The "although" need not mean that the two possibilities are in conflict. Again, it can be a clarification of the preceding sentences. His forces (the "Caesar team") *were* overwhelmingly defeated. That much is definite and is asserted. *Where* Octavian was when he barely escaped his pursuers is not clear. Since he "lost his camp," it is possible that he was in the camp during the battle and escaped from there—a possibility that is borne out in *Brutus*. Withdrawing before the battle need not be incompatible with narrowly escaping by secret flight, and if there is any tension between the two (if, e.g., one thinks of narrowly escaping by secret flight as necessarily occurring later), Plutarch presents both possibilities.

In *Brutus*, Plutarch is quite definite that Octavian was not personally in the battle and refers to two reasons for him not to be there: First, he was sick and had to be carried about in a litter, so he could not have been fighting anyway, and second, the friend's vision warned him to flee, which he did from the camp.[51]

Licona says that Plutarch "provides the competing report in *Brutus* that casts the main character's antagonist in a negative light," suggesting that not only is there a discrepancy about the presence of Octavian in the battle but that it is caused by Plutarch's greater desire to cast him in a negative light in *Brutus*—in other words, some kind of thematic literary device.[52] Strangely, Licona has just cited a theory of Pelling's that the removal (in report or rumor) of a general from a battle in which he was victorious was meant to denigrate the general's achievement, and Licona seems to think that this is relevant to this alleged discrepancy concerning Octavian.[53] But this does not make sense, since Octavian's forces *lost* this battle. There was no achievement of Octavian's to deprecate. They lost. Octavian himself might have been somewhat relieved to report that he wasn't personally present, so that his military leadership on the field could not be blamed for the defeat.

In any event, since Plutarch reports in *both* lives Octavian's claim that he was not personally present (a point Licona does not mention), since he does not reject

---

[51] Plutarch, *Life of Brutus*, 41.2, 7. The only hint of a difference is that, in *Antony* 22.2, Plutarch says that Octavian says in his memoirs that he escaped before the battle by heeding his friend's vision. In *Brutus* 41.7, Plutarch says that Octavian says in his memoirs that he "barely succeeded in having himself carried forth," which has a more rushed appearance and which one might think occurred later rather than before the battle. In both cases, Plutarch is attempting to present (perhaps from memory) what *Octavian* says in his memoirs. In either case, Octavian is not in the battle.

[52] Licona, *Why Are There Differences*, p. 107.

[53] Ibid.

that report in *Antony*, and since the thoroughness of Octavian's defeat is just as clear in both accounts, there is neither any discrepancy nor any "better" or "worse" portrayal of Octavian in the two accounts.

7. Plutarch: Did Pompey personally deliver an illegal encomium?

Up until now my examples have followed a roughly chronological order in Roman history. Here I am stepping out of that order (backwards a bit in time) in order to discuss a case where Licona has noted what appears to be a genuine discrepancy between two of Plutarch's *Lives*. This will provide an opportunity to emphasize once again the crucial point: A discrepancy is not *ipso facto* a literary device. Therefore, mere discrepancy hunting, and even discrepancy finding, does not by itself justify jumping to the conclusion that the author was using a fictionalizing literary device.

In *Pompey*, Plutarch says quite explicitly that Pompey broke his own laws by coming personally into court and giving an illegal encomium for one of his friends who was a defendant. By a law that Pompey himself had supported, the jury was not supposed to hear an encomium in favor of the defendant.

> Once more, therefore, Pompey was in ill repute, and this was still further increased because, although he had put a stop by law to encomiums on persons under trial, he himself came into court to pronounce an encomium on Plancus. Cato, who happened to be one of the jurors, clapped his hands to his ears and said it was not right for him, contrary to the law, to listen to encomiums.[54]

This is unambiguous. Notice that Plutarch does not say something that could mean simply that Pompey was "behind" the encomium. This does not sound at all like the saying, "George is building a house," discussed in Chapter II, section 3, which in some contexts could mean that George is having a house built by contractors. Plutarch emphasizes Pompey's personal activity—"He himself came into court to pronounce an encomium."

But in *Cato Minor*, in what certainly appears to be a description of the same event, Plutarch is fairly explicit that Pompey wrote the encomium and sent it to the court for someone else to read:

> Moreover, though Pompey himself had made illegal the customary panegyrics upon men under trial, he wrote a panegyric upon Munatius Plancus and handed it in at his trial; but Cato (who chanced to be one of the jurors) stopped his ears with his hands and prevented the reading of the testimony.[55]

---

[54] Plutarch, *Life of Pompey*, 55.4–5.

[55] Plutarch, *Life of Cato the Younger*, 48.4.

Unlike the majority of the examples discussed by the theorists, this appears to be a genuine case of a discrepancy. The contrast between Pompey's personal action in coming into court and his turning in something to be read certainly rises to the level of an apparent discrepancy, and it is difficult to think of any plausible harmonization. As things stand, it is quite difficult to harmonize the two accounts.

But what is the next node? Did the author *deliberately* include material that he had no reason to believe was true or knew was false? And here we have no reason to believe that Plutarch deliberately falsified in either account. But Licona does not pause even for a moment before claiming a literary device:

> Plutarch reports the reading of Pompey's encomium differently. In *Cat. Min.* 48.4, Pompey wrote the encomium and had it read at the trial but was not present. This is confirmed by other historians. Therefore, it is interesting to observe that in *Pomp.* 55.5, Plutarch reports that Pompey himself appeared in court and delivered his encomium. Plutarch transfers the action of reading the encomium from Pompey's emissary to Pompey himself, since Pompey was ultimately behind it.[56]

Licona does not offer an argument that Plutarch's change here between the two *Lives* is a deliberate deviation from truth. Having claimed a discrepancy, he asserts a literary device, taking several stages of conjecture in one flying leap. He does not argue, for example, that Plutarch *must have known while writing Pompey* that Pompey did not personally come into court. Indeed, it would be very difficult to argue any such strong thesis.

It is not enough to show that Plutarch knew or believed this at *some time*, which is evident from *Cato Minor*. One should provide some good reason to think that he knew it at the time when writing the portion of the document that asserts the contrary and therefore that his change must have been a deliberate abandonment of fact. Otherwise, the difference can be quite readily and more simply explained by his remembering the story wrong on one occasion or gaining new information in between writing the two documents.

Licona might move the argument forward a bit if he were to argue definitely that *Cato Minor*, which gives the more accurate information, was written first and that it is unlikely that Plutarch, having once understood that Pompey was not

---

[56] Licona, *Why Are There Differences*, p. 60. Here Licona alleges that Plutarch has transferred, *since* Pompey was ultimately behind the action. But by no means does he restrict transferral to such situations, as was evident above concerning Lentulus and Marcellus. There he alleged that Plutarch transferred the condemnation of Caesar as a robber from one to the other, even though no one claimed that one person was behind the insult and that the other was stating it on his behalf.

personally in court, would have become confused about this matter in a relatively short time before writing *Pompey*. One would also have to rely upon the claim that *Pompey* was written rather close to the time when *Cato Minor* was written. But he does not provide any argument about the precise *order* of the *Lives*, probably because no such precise information is available given the difficulty in dating them. The most that Licona can rely on is the fact that these two *Lives* are both in what he calls the "set" of six that were composed at about the same time—a period of a year or two.[57] But that tells us nothing about the order within that group and also would not preclude Plutarch's getting clearer information on the subject in between the actual writing of the two works.

One conjecture that seems fairly plausible is that Plutarch heard or read something that was unclear on the matter, perhaps saying that Pompey "gave" an encomium for Plancus. Such a report would be ambiguous as between his delivering it personally and turning it in. If Plutarch misinterpreted such a statement, he might have written as he did in *Pompey* in good faith and then might have obtained information that clarified the matter before he wrote *Cato Minor*. Even reading the same source more carefully and thoroughly could account for the difference. This theory cannot, of course, be proven, but it is the kind of misunderstanding that happens quite commonly in daily life and therefore has more to commend it than the far more elaborate theory that Plutarch knowingly stated an explicit falsehood about Pompey's personal action in one of the *Lives*.

If Plutarch did do so, of course, that *still* does not mean that he was engaging in a literary device, for his fabricating such a detail need not mean that he believed that this was a societally accepted device and that his audience would not be misled. Indeed, if he wanted (for example) to make Pompey look especially bad by saying that he came into court personally, thus violating his own law in a brazen fashion, such propaganda would work only if the audience *did* believe it.

8. Josephus bends the truth

For this example I move forward in time to the first century after Christ's birth and to a different author, Flavius Josephus (c. A.D. 37–100). John Jordan Henderson suggests that Josephus is probably bending the truth in his autobiography concerning the reason for his own assignment to Galilee by the Jewish authorities before the destruction of Jerusalem.[58] Henderson may well be right

---

[57] Ibid., p. 19.

[58] John Jordon Henderson, "A Comparison of Josephus' Life and Jewish War: An attempt at Establishing the Acceptable Outer Limits of Biographies' Historical Reliability," in Craig S. Keener

about that, but the further conclusion he draws shows some confusion, which we can pinpoint using the heuristic of the flowchart.

In discussing Josephus, Henderson often does use categories that resemble those of the flowchart. For example, he sensibly attributes apparent discrepancies in numbers and minor details to Josephus' probable reliance on memory and not looking up all such matters in his sources, rather than to special rhetorical purposes. It is especially laudable that Henderson does not hypothesize deliberate alteration if he does not have a clear, credible motive to suggest.[59] Henderson also rightly points out that the mere presence of material in one narrative that is absent in another is no reason to question the veracity of the unique material, since the choice of what to narrate depends on what is pertinent in one context rather than another.

There is some unclarity in Henderson's discussion of chronology. As is all too common, he suggests that chronological discrepancies or apparent discrepancies might be the result of the fact that writers of ancient biography felt free to rearrange their material topically, without specifying whether he is attributing achronological or dyschronological narration to Josephus.[60] Since he does not discuss the chronological examples in detail, it is difficult to know precisely what he is suggesting in that area.

The issue in question here, however, does not concern chronology but rather the purpose of Josephus' mission to Galilee at the beginning of the Jewish revolt against Rome in A.D. 66. In his writings, Josephus gives two widely different accounts of the purpose for which the Jewish leaders in Jerusalem sent him to Galilee. In the *Jewish War*, he states (writing of himself in the third person) that he went to help the Jews of Galilee prepare to defend themselves against Rome. His discussion is quite explicit and extensive, and even a partial quotation shows how clearly he is saying that he prepared the Jews in Galilee to fight the Romans:

> ...[W]hen they were returned back to Jerusalem, they overbore some of those that favored the Romans by violence, and some they persuaded to join with them, and got together in great numbers in the temple, and appointed a great many generals for the war....But John, the son of Matthias, was made governor of the toparchies of Gophnitica and Acrabattene; as was Josephus, the son of Matthias, of both the Galilees. Gamala also, which was the strongest city in those parts, was put under his command.

---

and Edward T. Wright, eds., *Biographies and Jesus: What Does it Mean for the Gospels to be Biographies?* (Lexington, KY: Emeth Press, 2016), pp. 269, 273–274.

[59] Ibid., pp. 272–273.

[60] Ibid., pp. 269, 272.

So every one of the other commanders administered the affairs of his portion with that alacrity and prudence they were masters of; but as to Josephus, when he came into Galilee, his first care was to gain the good-will of the people of that country, as sensible that he should thereby have in general good success, although he should fail in other points....Josephus also,...betook himself to make provisions for their safety against external violence; and as he knew the Romans would fall upon Galilee, he built walls in proper places about Jotapata, and Bersabee, and Selamis; and besides these, about Caphareccho, and Japha, and Sigo, and what they call Mount Tabor, and Tarichee, and Tiberias....He also got together an army out of Galilee, of more than a hundred thousand young men, all of which he armed with the old weapons which he had collected together and prepared for them.

And when he had considered that the Roman power became invincible, chiefly by their readiness in obeying orders, and the constant exercise of their arms, he despaired of teaching these his men the use of their arms, which was to be obtained by experience; but observing that their readiness in obeying orders was owing to the multitude of their officers, he made his partitions in his army more after the Roman manner, and appointed a great many subalterns....He also taught them to give the signals one to another, and to call and recall the soldiers by the trumpets, how to expand the wings of an army, and make them wheel about; and when one wing...had success, to turn again and assist those that were hard set, and to join in the defense of what had most suffered. He also continually instructed them...what concerned the courage of the soul, and the hardiness of the body; and, above all, he exercised them for war, by declaring to them distinctly the good order of the Romans, and that they were to fight with men who, both by the strength of their bodies and courage of their souls, had conquered in a manner the whole habitable earth.[61]

If Josephus really engaged in these war-like activities, it is virtually impossible that he would have forgotten them even thirty years later when writing his autobiography. Yet here is the very different account he gives there:

So when Gessius had been beaten, as we have said already, the principal men of Jerusalem, seeing that the robbers and innovators had arms in great plenty, and fearing lest they, while they were unprovided of arms, should be in subjection to their enemies, which also came to be the case afterward; and, being informed that all Galilee had not yet revolted from the Romans, but that some part of it was still quiet; they sent me and two others of the priests, who were men of excellent characters, Joazar and Judas, in order to persuade the ill men there to lay down their arms, and to teach them this lesson, That it were better to have those arms reserved

---

[61] Josephus, *The Jewish War*, II.20.3–7. Trans. William Whiston (1737), https://www.gutenberg.org/files/2850/2850-h/2850-h.htm#link22HCH0020.

for the most courageous men that the nation had [than to be kept there]; for that
it had been resolved, That those our best men should always have their arms ready
against futurity; but still so, that they should wait to see what the Romans would do.

When I had therefore received these instructions, I came into Galilee, and found
the people of Sepphoris in no small agony about their country, by reason that the
Galileans had resolved to plunder it, on account of the friendship they had with
the Romans, and because they had given their right hand, and made a league with
Cestius Gallus, the president of Syria. But I delivered them all out of the fear they
were in, and persuaded the multitude to deal kindly with them ... [62]

In other words, Josephus says here that he went to Galilee not as a general to get
the people ready to fight the Romans but rather as a peacekeeper with the goal
of urging the hot-headed Galileans not to act hastily and to wait and see what
the Romans would do. He also notes (which may be true) that he protected the
people of Sepphoris from Galilean revenge for their (the Sepphorans') support
for Rome. This is woven into the picture of himself as going to Galilee merely as
a peace-keeping governor, with no intent to make preparations for revolt against
Rome as described in the *Jewish War*.

In his autobiography, Josephus describes the anarchic state of Galilee at that
time and the activities of various robbers, and he gives the impression that his
fortification of the cities was to protect them against these men. He describes with
frustration how a leader of "a seditious tumult of mariners and poor people" went
with some Galileans and burned the palace at Tiberias and how he (Josephus)
went and salvaged what valuables could be gotten out of the wreckage. He then
describes some of his own conflicts with John of Gichala, a Galilean leader who
was in favor of revolt against Rome. He follows this up with,

But when I had dismissed my fellow legates, and sent them back to Jerusalem,
I took care to have arms provided, and the cities fortified. And when I had sent
for the most hardy among the robbers, I saw that it was not in my power to take
their arms from them; but I persuaded the multitude to allow them money as
pay, and told them it was better for them to give them a little willingly, rather
than to overlook them when they plundered their goods from them. And when
I had obliged them to take an oath not to come into that country, unless they
were invited to come, or else when they had not their pay given them, I dismissed
them, and charged them neither to make an expedition against the Romans, nor

---

[62] Josephus, *The Life of Flavius Josephus*, 7–8. Trans. William Whiston (1737), https://www.gutenberg.org/files/2846/2846-h/2846-h.htm.

against those their neighbors that lay round about them; for my first care was to keep Galilee in peace.[63]

The very strong implication is that the fortification of the cities and provision of arms were carried out because of Galilean plunderers and that his only care was peacekeeping.

There is really no getting around the contradiction here. If one of these accounts of Josephus' motives and mission is right, the other is wrong. It is not even that the external facts described in his autobiography must be invented. For example, he really apparently did have a conflict with John of Gichala for the control of Galilee, and he may well have salvaged valuables from the palace at Tiberias and protected the people of Sepphoris. The point, rather, is that, if the account in the *Jewish War* is correct, then Josephus in the *Life* must either be suffering unaccountable amnesia on a large scale or else deliberately suppressing and concealing the fact that he presented himself to the people of Galilee as being there *to prepare them for war with Rome*. Even if one attempts to harmonize the accounts using the phrase "wait to see what the Romans would do," concluding that Josephus was telling the people of Galilee to hope for the best and prepare for the worst (war with Rome), this does not really amount to a harmonization. For in the *Jewish War* he is a general *of* the revolting Jewish people, present in Galilee on the assumption that war with Rome is coming and explicitly preparing his people to fight the Romans. The very strong impression given in the *Life* is completely to the contrary, and the suppression of his warlike intentions (if the account in the *Jewish War* is correct) must be judged to be prevarication.

Here we can pass rather easily over the node concerning the deliberate nature of the change. If Josephus was mentally capable of writing his autobiography, he must have remembered whether or not he was in Galilee for the purpose of preparing his people for war with Rome, whether or not he gave them stirring talks on the subject of Roman methods of warfare, whether he had them gather arms and fortify cities merely against local robber bands or against the Romans, and so forth. That is hardly the sort of thing one would be likely to forget, nor is it a matter of having to look up some obscure fact in a cumbersome scroll.

Very well, then. We have an apparent discrepancy that is, as far as we can tell, impossible to harmonize, and the change of fact appears to be deliberate on the part of the author. But now we come to the question: Was the author engaging in

---

[63] Ibid., 14.

ordinary propaganda, deception, or fabrication? And here Henderson's *own* plausible account of Josephus' motives amounts to a decisive "yes." Henderson suggests,

> While Josephus' earlier account in *War* of having been a *strategos* sent to fight the Romans did not presumably bother Vespasian and Titus, to whom he also accounted in the same work his pledge of loyalty, he would have had reason to fear that Domitian would not have been so understanding...Although Josephus makes a point to note Domitian's kindness to him at the conclusion of *Life*, I believe this justifiable fear of Domitian caused him to rewrite the story of his role in the Jewish rebellion three decades before, changing the motivation of his initial arrival in Galilee from resistance fighter to pacifist.[64]

While "peacekeeper" might be a more perfect word choice than "pacifist," Henderson's theory seems quite viable. This may indeed have been Josephus' motive for revising history. It is undeniable that the account in the *Life* appears less likely to upset a Roman audience than that in the *Jewish War*.

But if he did change history in this way for this reason, that is *nothing remotely like* an accepted literary device. Indeed, this has nothing whatsoever to do with literature. It is not about rhetoric or literary pretensions, much less societally agreed-upon devices, but about political and personal survival in the reign of Domitian. This is a human pattern we are familiar with. It happens quite often (and perhaps all the more so when tyrants are on the throne) that people in political positions need to whitewash their pasts for the current administration. And such a change would scarcely be likely to work unless Domitian believed the *Life* rather than the *Jewish War*. In other words, so far from being an accepted literary device intended to deceive no one, this act of self-preserving revisionism would have been a *direct and express* attempt to mislead for one's own benefit.

Yet Henderson then moves to talking about what may have been "accepted in the genre" of biography:

> One could even argue that no contradiction occurs in the Synoptic Gospels comparable to Josephus' contradictory claims about the aim of his own mission to Galilee.
> Josephus' work therefore stands as an example of the range of variation that might have been accepted in the genre of ancient biography, though we cannot say for certain whether he would have been seen to exceed the limits of this range.[65]

---

[64] Henderson, "A Comparison of Josephus' Life and Jewish War," p. 274.
[65] Ibid., p. 275.

Henderson shows commendable caution in wondering whether Josephus might have exceeded the limits of the range of variation (i.e., fabrication) accepted in the genre. What is odd is that he should raise the question at all with reference to this particular change. Is there any useful sense in which one could speak of what Henderson hypothesizes as "accepted"? What would that even mean? At the most, it might mean that some people who realized that Josephus changed history might feel sympathy for him. Perhaps one might say to another, "Yes, old Josephus really had to be shifty there, but can you blame him? The poor fellow had to cover his tail. We're talking about Domitian here, after all!" And so forth. But this is not what is normally meant by "accepted in the genre." The notion of an activity "accepted in the genre" is supposed to have something to do with literary norms. For an alteration to be "accepted in the genre" must mean that such truth alteration is expected by the audience and taken to be normal for that genre and hence (as already discussed) that such partial fictionalization does not count as deceit.

But that is *not* what Henderson himself conjectures about Josephus. On the contrary, he conjectures that Josephus may have changed his own past history in his *Life* precisely in order to make at least a portion of his audience (specifically, the Romans and especially Domitian) believe that he *was not* a fighter against Rome earlier in his life. This has nothing whatsoever to do with genre norms. It assumes that Josephus was hoping that the Roman audience would take the document to be historical and hence would *accept as factual* his self-representation in the *Life*. In other words, Josephus's alteration here (if something like Henderson's theory is right) fails to be an ancient literary device because it is a case of ordinary propaganda and fabrication, an activity known throughout human history. It seems that Henderson feels that he must, in the last paragraph of his essay, connect all of Josephus's variations (including this one) to the "range of variation that may have been accepted in the genre of ancient biography," without realizing that his own theory precludes that possibility.

9. Accepted literary devices in Greco-Roman biography and history: A failed argument

Why do all of these examples fail to make it through the filter of the flowchart? The answer is fairly straightforward: The claim that an author is using an accepted fictionalizing literary device is an extremely strong one. It contains sub-claims not only about what is found in the text but also about the author's knowledge, his intentions, the culture of his audience, and what he believed about the culture of his audience. Mere differences and discrepancies between accounts have so many simpler explanations—horses, not zebras. For analyses of more examples in Greco-Roman literature, see Appendix 2.

The literary device theorists needed far more background data to make it plausible in the first place that such literary devices existed *at all* in biographies or histories in the time period in question. If we are thinking about biopics in our own time, we have interviews with directors and screenwriters, news stories about how movie-makers changed the historical stories, statements from living historical people presented, "making of" documentaries, and so forth. We have a wealth of explicit, independent data supporting the existence of the historical novel and the partially fictionalized movie. There are also sometimes disclaimers written by authors at the beginning of their own memoirs about which portions have been changed. In other words, we do not need to rely on the mere existence of differences and discrepancies between apparently historical accounts in order to conclude that certain types of works are partially fictionalized.

This is why the previous chapters are important. The literary device theorists need, and claim to have, background information showing that there were known fictionalizing devices at the time and/or that generally historical documents were expected to be factually altered at unexpected moments. The generalizations about the different view of truth held by "ancient people" were to play that role in the argument, as were generalizations about the nature of Greco-Roman biographies, speech reportage, and exercise books. All of this was supposed to provide a cumulative background case. Then the only remaining question supposedly concerned how to *label and classify* the fictionalizing alterations one already expected to find when approaching authors like Sallust, Plutarch, and Josephus.

But that background case failed, as argued in earlier chapters. This left only an attempted inductive case from the works themselves, discussed in this chapter. And when we turn to the documents, we do not find esoteric patterns supporting arcane devices. Instead, we find mundane, often pointless variation of precisely the sort that history and witness testimony in all ages abounds in. Indeed, if we were to apply consistently the methods used by Licona and some classicists, we would virtually erase normal variation and discrepancy due to human limitation, varied interests, and error. Again and again the conclusion that an author was using a literary device depends upon jumping ahead in line, neglecting far simpler explanations arising from daily human experience. Even in the very few cases where sensible harmonization fails and there is also strong reason to think an alteration was deliberate, we must remember that human experience includes the fact that people sometimes lie.

At this point, there is no reason left to believe that audience-accepted fictionalizing literary devices of transferral, displacement, compression, and fabrication of details existed *at all* in the time of Plutarch, Josephus, and the Gospels. That case has been refuted. We can now approach the Gospels and see them more clearly, unencumbered by a distorting prior expectation that they, being ancient works, manifest an alien concept of what counts as truthful reportage.

Summary
Devices, Discrepancies, or (Just) Differences?

- The claim that an author used fictionalizing literary devices has a heavy burden of proof, since the claim is highly complex and unusual.

- When confronted with differences in two reports, we should "think horses, not zebras." We should try to use a simpler, more common explanation rather than an elaborate, uncommon explanation for which we have no independent evidence.

- We can understand the burden of proof for fictionalizing literary devices by means of a flowchart showing the questions that a scholar should ask himself before concluding, based on differences between accounts, that an author has used a fictionalizing literary device.

- No one is committed to the inerrancy of Plutarch or some other non-biblical author. When considering their works, we must explicitly consider the possibility of a normal error or even of ordinary deception or propaganda. These are not the same as accepted literary devices.

- There is not good evidence that ancient authors such as Sallust and Plutarch used the fictionalizing literary devices of displacement, transferral, compression, conflation, or fabrication of a context. Repeatedly, when scholars claim such devices, there are better, simpler explanations for differences between accounts. The chapter gives several examples.

PART THREE

The Mirror:
The Gospels as
Historical Reports

X

The Evangelists as Honest Reporters

1. The reportage model: What it is and what it isn't

One of the greatest gifts that the art of writing has given to mankind is the ability to connect mind with mind. By reading, I can listen to the voice of a man who died long before I was born. To some degree, I can learn what he was like. When a work presents itself as telling an historical story, and when I find it confirmed repeatedly, I gain confidence in the author's reliability. I learn to trust him.

In just this way, the research for my previous book, *Hidden in Plain View*, gave me a new level of respect for the evangelists—the authors of the Gospels and Acts. By seeing how casually-mentioned details in their accounts fit together beautifully, I learned to trust them not to tamper with the facts. As I wrote there,

> The argument from undesigned coincidences tells us something about what the authors of these documents were like. What picture of the author of the Gospel of John emerges from what we have seen? It is a picture of a careful recorder with a vivid and meticulous memory, someone with his own, independent, close access to the facts, someone who is not inventing, massaging, or exaggerating his data. Even within fairly conservative scholarly circles, it is sometimes too readily suggested that John took a loose approach to facts about time and place, redacting earlier sources to fit some agenda—that he relocated the cleansing of the Temple to early in Jesus' ministry as opposed to shortly before the crucifixion, that he altered the day of Jesus' crucifixion for theological reasons, and so forth. I submit that this is not the John who emerges from the study in this book and that the argument from undesigned coincidences pulls strongly in a different direction. These authors have primarily a *testimonial* project rather than a literary or redactive one. They are honest witnesses giving their reports and honest historians relating witness reports— emphasizing and mentioning different details, to be sure, but ultimately aiming to tell what really happened. The providential provision of four Gospels gives us a three-dimensional view of the events.

Or what of the author of Acts? Given the minute, one might even say boring, details in Acts of Paul's life and travels corroborated by this study, some of which the author of Acts himself does not seem to have fully understood at the time, the idea that he was writing in any sense a work of fiction can be readily dismissed. The picture of that author, who is also the author of Luke, comes shining through as exactly what Christian tradition has always held him to be—a close companion of Paul, a man who knew the apostles and had access to eyewitnesses, and a careful, conscientious historian.[1]

What is the reportage model of the Gospels that I am advocating here? It is nothing esoteric or technical. It is simply the idea that the Gospels are what they appear to be *prima facie*—namely, memoirs of Jesus and his disciples, told with the intention to present historical truth. The reportage model says that the narrative of the Gospels is meant to be factual in the ordinary sense of that word.[2]

Here are several of the most important characteristics of the reportage view of the Gospels and their authors:

- The authors were trying to tell us what really happened, not deliberately altering or embellishing the facts, not even details, for literary or theological reasons.[3]

---

[1] Lydia McGrew, *Hidden in Plain View: Undesigned Coincidences in the Gospels and Acts* (Chillicothe, OH: DeWard Publishing, 2017), pp. 225–226.

[2] It should go without saying that parables are not a problem for this model. When someone within the work tells a fictional story (e.g., when Jesus tells parables), the audience knows that these are just stories. Jesus left his audience in no doubt about this, and the authors of the Gospels leave the reader in no doubt.

[3] I emphasize "not even details," here and elsewhere, because at times literary device theorists will imply that their theories should not concern anyone because they concern mostly "peripheral details" or "minor details," as though this did not matter. See Michael Licona, *Why Are There Differences in the Gospels? What We Can Learn From Ancient Biography* (Oxford: Oxford University Press, 2017), pp. 20, 184, 200, 258. As we will see in the examples in Part Four and have already seen in the list given in Chapter I, section 4, the theories repeatedly call larger matters into question. See also Chapter XI, section 6, where I discuss the use of the word "details" as if large portions of the infancy narratives were mere "details." Sometimes a claim that only a "detail" is altered involves essential changes to the story. For example, if Luke geographically moved the first appearance of Jesus to his disciples from Galilee to Jerusalem, this means that the first meeting was not unexpected, which is relevant to the evidence for the resurrection; it also would make it virtually impossible to accommodate the doubting Thomas sequence, which is evidentially important. But even when a theory implies that an author did nothing more than (e.g.) deliberately add a small amount of ahistorical dialogue, change the date of an event by a few days, or change the number of people present, this does amount to deliberate factual alteration. It would mean that the author was a person who thought little of writing in a way that would confuse his readers about what happened. Hence, I emphasize without apology that, even when the word "details" is used in a way that is not misleading, the reportage model is incompatible with an author's *deliberately* altering details. The next chapter will discuss at much greater length why even things that would be

- The authors tried to record what various people said in a way that would be recognizable if you were present and understood the relevant language(s).
- The authors were highly successful in gathering and conveying true factual information.

The first two points emphasize that the authors are attempting to write historically rather than ahistorically. They do not consider themselves licensed to alter history. The third point emphasizes that they succeeded in producing documents that are highly reliable in a literal, historical sense.

A further understanding of the reportage view comes from recognizing what it is not.

- The reportage model of the Gospels does not mean that we must have a tape-recorded version of the words of Jesus or others.
- The reportage model does not mean that we have answers to all questions about what happened in the events recorded in the Gospels.
- The reportage model does not mean that the authors of the Gospels never narrated achronologically.

Opponents of the reportage view sometimes try to counter it by straw man tactics, and this matter of paraphrase and "tape-recorded" or "verbatim" reportage has proven to be a point of attack. An example of this straw man fallacy occurred in an interview with Craig A. Evans in which he said,

> My critics, and there aren't too many, but there are a few out there, they say, "If it's not tape-recorded, word-for-word, what Jesus said, then John is being false. You're saying John isn't true. John is misrepresenting Jesus." And that's the kind of, I don't know if you want to call it fundamentalism, or rigidity, that's the part that I find problematic.[4]

There is, as far as I know, no critic of Evans who says that, if we do not have a tape-recorded version of what Jesus said, the evangelist is misrepresenting Jesus. I certainly do not say this and have emphasized repeatedly, in a debate with Evans himself prior to this interview, that this is not my position.[5]

---

naturally called "details" really do matter.

[4] "Gospel Reliability," *Veracity Hill*, minute -43.20, https://www.veracityhill.com/episodes/episode-112-gospel-reliability.

[5] I was the only critic of Dr. Evans discussed in this interview, though my name was not explicitly introduced until several minutes later. Evans provided no citation for this claim about what his critics say; he named no critic who says this. Not only is this not my position, I emphasized *four times* to Evans that it was not my position when I debated him prior to this interview. See the transcript of my

The distinction already made in Chapter II, section 2, between normal para-phrase and the radically redefined concept of "paraphrase" used by literary device theorists will help to counter this straw man. *Recognizable* paraphrase, without the intent to manipulate what was said in order to make some point of the author's own, is not the same thing as verbatim tape-recording.[6] Moreover, limitations caused by the absence of audiographic memory and modern technology are differ-ent from a deliberate *preference* for changing someone's words. Evans's own view (as discussed in Chapter VIII, sections 2 and 4) is that the Gospel authors measured their own discipleship by their willingness to *alter* Jesus' words, restate them in their own words, then put them back into Jesus' mouth in their reports. And as we have seen (see Chapter III, section 2), Evans himself postulates the invention of entire sayings of Jesus with no historically recognizable basis whatsoever. These approach-es are obviously at odds with the reportage model, while normal paraphrase is not.

The second point—that the reportage model does not say that we must have answers to all our questions—is worth mentioning, since I have emphasized from the beginning of this book the importance of knowing Jesus through the Gospels. I will discuss further in the next volume what I call a high-resolution Jesus as opposed to a "fuzzy" or "foggy" Jesus. I want to head off any misun-derstanding to the effect that I am saying that the Gospels leave no questions unanswered. There are places where the Gospel authors themselves may not specify a chronological order (see next point) and other places where we may not be sure of the correct harmonization between two accounts. So I am not saying that there is *per se* something wrong with a scholar's methodology if he admits

---

debate with Evans here, https://drive.google.com/file/d/1DRVsnODNLh_U2d-2ZY5MXJ3B4zcN-JqZ7/view. (Search for the word "verbatim" in the transcript to find my statements on this subject.)

[6] I discuss the matter of possible composite discourses in Appendix 3 rather than in the body of this chapter. If an audience of the time would understand that an author was likely to include *some* material that was uttered at another time within a "bracketed" discourse in a thematic manner, or *if* the author was making a knowledgeable attempt to place material at a particular time by serious plau-sibility, then some degree of composite discourse construction is not incompatible with the reportage model. Moreover, honest reporters may simply not have access to the precise *order* in which a speaker addressed certain topics in a longer discourse, while having good reason to think that the material was all uttered on that occasion. Again, this is compatible with their giving a version of what was said that is historically recognizable. Finally, at times the "placement" of spoken material by an honest, reporting author is so chronologically vague that it does not count as the composition of a discourse at all. E.g. Luke 11.5 is translated, "Then he said..." in the NASB, but the first word is the Greek καὶ, which does not indicate temporal order. Luke need not be indicating that what Jesus says in verses 5–12 was stated on the same occasion as what he says in verses 1–4. This is simply a case of achronological narration of sayings material. For a more detailed treatment of alleged composite discourses in Matthew, see Appendix 3.

at some points in the Gospels that he does not know precisely what happened. Such an admission is sometimes unavoidable.

The difference between the reportage model and the literary device model is that the latter introduces vastly greater, and entirely unnecessary, sources of confusion about events than does the former. By approaching the documents with a high prior probability that the authors made factual alterations according to unpredictable and undetectable algorithms, the literary device theorist has to say that he does not know what happened at multiple points where the texts themselves, taken at face value, are quite clear. Consider again the sample list in Chapter I, section 4, of passages that the literary device theorist questions. The literary device theorist introduces questions about historicity even when no apparent contradiction is present, creates "tensions" that are figments of his own imagination, and refuses to accept entirely reasonable historical harmonizations when these are available. This leaves him more and more uncertain about more and more passages, and gratuitously so, even when the Gospels provide a clear account. As John Wenham says of New Testament studies generally,

> Forced harmonizing is worthless. The tendency today, however, is the opposite—to force the New Testament writings into disharmony, in order to emphasize their individuality. The current analytical approach to the gospels often has the effect of making scholars more and more uncertain at more and more points, till eventually their view of Jesus and his teaching is lost in haze.[7]

While the reportage model will still inevitably (and rightly) acknowledge the presence of unanswered questions in the Gospels, it does not multiply these indefinitely. The authors are taken, at a minimum, to believe what they say rather than secretly and invisibly writing as if things happened in a way that they themselves do not believe.

The third point, about achronological narration, is especially important. To recap from Chapter II, section 1, achronological narration is narrating while not being specific about chronological order. If I simply say, "We did this, and we did that," I am not necessarily indicating that we did the second thing after we did the first thing. Everyone narrates achronologically at times, especially when describing events that happened around the same time. Dyschronological narration, in contrast, is *changing* the chronology in a narrative from what is factually true to what is factually false. If I said, "First we did this, and then we did that," when I

---

[7] John Wenham, *Easter Enigma* (Eugene, OR: Wipf and Stock, 1992), p. 128.

knew that the second event really occurred before the first, that would be dyschronological narration—a form of fictionalizing the time scheme.

Repeatedly, literary device theorists will try to support dyschronological narration by saying that ancient people did not require narration to be chronological. But this could refer merely to achronological narration. Craig Keener suggests that John changed the time of Jesus' cleansing the Temple from late in his ministry (when, according to Keener, it actually occurred) to make it appear that it occurred early in his ministry. Keener claims that this dyschronological change would be compatible with ancient narrative practices. After suggesting that John moved the Temple cleansing, he says, "As noted in the introduction, ch. 1, ancient readers did not expect ancient biographies to adhere to chronological sequence."[8]

In his introduction, Keener does make the statement that "ancient biographers did not need to follow a chronological sequence; most felt free to rearrange their material topically."[9] But this statement is ambiguous. It does not distinguish achronological from dyschronological narration. In support, Keener cites examples that are achronological. For example, he cites the fact that Plutarch accidentally narrates the same incident twice in his *Life of Alexander*.[10] In this little anecdote, one of Alexander's followers says that those Greeks were deprived of great pleasure who died without seeing (as he saw) Alexander sitting on the throne of Darius. (The reference is to a long-standing hatred between the Greeks and the Persians and to Alexander's conquest of Persia.) But the repetition is not dyschronological. Plutarch merely drops in this short anecdote in two different places without at all implying that it happened at different times.[11]

Keener also cites St. Augustine in support of his claims about the ancients and chronology. Given Keener's use of these principles when it comes to the Temple cleansing, he seems to be implying that Augustine's views bolster the case that ancient readers accepted dyschronological narration:

---

[8] Craig Keener, *The Gospel of John: A Commentary* (Grand Rapids, MI: Baker Academic, 2003), p. 518.

[9] Ibid., p. 12

[10] Plutarch, *Life of Alexander*, 37.7, 56.1.

[11] Note how easy it was even in the very same *Life* for Plutarch to forget (apparently) that he had narrated the same little anecdote already and to mention it again. Though such an accidental repetition is not an error, the point is relevant to the discussion in the previous chapter of the possibility that Plutarch made an error on some minor point. Looking backward and forward in one's own manuscript and in the scrolls of others was a time-consuming and cumbersome business; it is not at all improbable that one would forget precisely what one had written even in the very same work, much less in a different work composed within the same two-year period.

Nor did early Christians expect the Gospels to reflect chronological sequence; Augustine suggested the evangelists wrote their Gospels as God recalled the accounts to their memory.[12]

This is particularly confused, because Augustine is explicitly talking *only* about achronological narration in the passage Keener cites from the *Harmony of the Gospels*. Here is Augustine:

Matthew proceeds in the following terms: And when Jesus had come into Peter's house, He saw his wife's mother laid, and sick of a fever. And He touched her hand, and the fever left her: and she arose, and ministered unto them. *Matthew has not indicated the date of this incident; that is to say, he has specified neither before what event nor after what occurrence it took place.* For we are certainly under no necessity of supposing that, because it is recorded after a certain event, it must also have happened in actual matter of fact after that event. And unquestionably, in this case, we are to understand that he has introduced for record here something which he had omitted to notice previously. For Mark brings in this narrative before his account of that cleansing of the leper which he would appear to have placed after the delivery of the sermon on the mount; which discourse, however, he has left unrelated .... For of what consequence is it in what place any of them may give his account; or what difference does it make whether he inserts the matter in its proper order, or brings in at a particular point what was previously omitted, or mentions at an earlier stage what really happened at a later, provided only that he contradicts neither himself nor a second writer in the narrative of the same facts or of others? ... [I]t is reasonable enough to suppose that each of the evangelists believed it to have been his duty to relate what he had to relate in that order in which it had pleased God to suggest to his recollection the matters he was engaged in recording. At least this might hold good in the case of those incidents with regard to which the question of order, whether it were this or that, detracted nothing from evangelical authority and truth .... For this reason, therefore, *when the order of times is not apparent, we ought not to feel it a matter of any consequence what order any of them may have adopted in relating the events. But wherever the order is apparent, if the evangelist then presents anything which seems to be inconsistent with his own statements, or with those of another, we must certainly take the passage into consideration, and endeavour to clear up the difficulty.*[13]

---

[12] Keener, *John*, p. 13. Keener's lack of clarity concerning achronological and dyschronological narration stands in contrast with the clarity of Allan Chapple noted earlier in Chapter II, section 1, on this very point concerning the Temple cleansing. As Chapple says, if John moved the Temple cleansing, he did not give merely a rough idea of when Jesus cleansed the Temple; he gave a *wrong* idea. Allan Chapple, "Jesus' Intervention in the Temple: Once or Twice?" *JETS* 58:3 (2015), p. 551.

[13] St. Augustine, *The Harmony of the Gospels*, II.21.51–52. Trans. S. D. F. Salmond (1888), http://

Augustine thus provides evidence *against* the idea that Christians of his own time accepted dyschronological order. On the contrary, Augustine emphasizes that an apparent discrepancy between chronologies, when the order is apparent, *does* require harmonization. This is a rejection of dyschronological narration. Augustine says that it is only when the author does not specify the order that we can sometimes conjecture that one author or the other was narrating achronologically, so there is no contradiction between two accounts. Augustine's discussion here is utterly at odds with the idea that John would have thought himself licensed to change the year of the Temple cleansing,[14] and Augustine himself expressly held that Jesus cleansed the Temple twice, stating that two cleansings were "evident."[15]

As the example of Augustine shows, the fact that narrative order is not always chronological order—in other words, that authors sometimes narrate achronologically—has been known to traditional harmonizers for centuries. Nor have modern inerrantist harmonizers of a highly conservative stripe lost sight of that possibility. Vern Poythress, for example, explicitly introduces the idea of achronological narration as a tool of Gospel harmonization,[16] as does John Wenham when he harmonizes the Easter narratives.[17]

Here, too, literary device theorists sometimes succumb to the temptation to characterize those who disagree as naïve and ignorant. Craig Evans, for example, characterizes the "extreme on the right" in Gospel interpretation thus:

> One extreme (…let's call it the extreme "on the right") tends to think that every verse and every word in the Gospels are historical, that the words of Jesus have been recorded word for word, the events described are described exactly and in precise chronological sequence. Folk who see the Gospels this way often place a priority on the historical, or at least on what is perceived to be historical. If it is historical, then we know it is true. So goes the reasoning.[18]

---

www.newadvent.org/fathers/1602221.htm. Subsequent citations of this work are to the same translation, available and indexed at New Advent, though they may be found at different specific URLs. Emphasis added.

[14] I note, too, that St. Augustine was highly trained in Greco-Roman rhetoric prior to his conversion.

[15] St. Augustine, *The Harmony of the Gospels*, II.67.129.

[16] Vern Sheridan Poythress, *Inerrancy and the Gospels: A God-Centered Approach to the Challenges of Harmonization* (Wheaton, IL: Crossway, 2012), Chapter 17.

[17] Wenham, *Easter Enigma*, pp. 77–78, 107.

[18] Craig A. Evans vs. Bart Ehrman, "Does the New Testament Present a Historically Reliable Portrait of the Historical Jesus?," Acadia University, January 20, 2012, minute 7:26, https://youtu.be/UvCVnlHoFow?t=445.

Although Evans claims that he has had many students over the years who think this way (until he reeducates them), he does not name a single living scholar, not even a very conservative scholar, who does. On the contrary, highly conservative harmonizers make frequent use of the fact that narrative order may *not* be chronological order to produce traditional harmonizations on chronological matters.

The shoe is very much on the other foot. It is the literary device theorist who repeatedly forgets that narrative order does not automatically imply chronological order and who then insists that an author has *changed* chronology when it is quite plausible that the author has narrated achronologically. We have already seen in the discussion of Plutarch that literary device theorists read woodenly concerning chronology, insisting that an author is indicating that events took a short period of time or occurred in a given order when the author is not clearly specifying those matters one way or another.[19] The same issue will arise repeatedly in Part Four when we discuss Gospel examples. The reportage view of the Gospels, in contrast, in no way means that the authors always narrated in chronological order.

2. The evangelists and their witness sources in their own words

At various points in this book I have mentioned statements that the Gospel authors and apostles made about themselves and their message and purposes. It will be useful here to collect several such quotations. In Part Two I cleared away any worry that statements about testifying to the truth and similar concepts should have an asterisk next to them. We should not qualify them by a footnote reading, "This statement must be interpreted only by professional New Testament scholars. Do not interpret at home." Or, "The concept of truth used here must be understood in a special, ancient fashion. Do not take this statement to refer to literal historical truth." With the attempted postmodernization of the evangelists and apostles thoroughly debunked, we can read these statements and receive their impact fully. I give them, with relatively little comment but with some added emphasis, in the order in which they occur in the New Testament.

> Inasmuch as many have undertaken to compile a narrative of the things that have been accomplished among us, *just as those who from the beginning were eyewitnesses and ministers of the word have delivered them to us*, it seemed good to me also, having followed all things closely for some time past, *to write an orderly account for you*, most excellent Theophilus, *that you may have certainty concerning the things you have been taught.* (Luke 1.1–4, ESV)

---

[19] Chapter IX, section 4, see also Chapter IX, footnote 36.

Ample evidence, both internal and external, indicates that Luke succeeded in this endeavor in an entirely literal sense.

Here is the author of John's Gospel, emphasizing the empirical nature of his witness:

> So the soldiers came, and broke the legs of the first man and of the other who was crucified with Him; but coming to Jesus, when they saw that He was already dead, they did not break His legs. But one of the soldiers pierced His side with a spear, and immediately blood and water came out. *And he who has seen has testified, and his testimony is true; and he knows that he is telling the truth, so that you also may believe. For these things came to pass* to fulfill the Scripture, "Not a bone of Him shall be broken." And again another Scripture says, "They shall look on Him whom they pierced." (John 19.32–37)

John clearly emphasizes that the witness testifies truthfully to physical facts—that Jesus' legs were not broken, that his side was pierced, and that water and blood came forth. The beloved disciple does not say that he is attesting to a "higher truth" that is "more truly true than mere facts." He is emphatic that he is attesting to real events that he has seen with his own eyes. And, as I emphasize below, it is the actual occurrence of these events that fulfills Scripture. It is the historical reality that has deep significance. The deep significance does not reside in a fictional tale or a fictional aspect of the story.

Immediately after relating the events surrounding Thomas and his doubts, John says,

> Therefore many other signs Jesus also performed *in the presence of the disciples,* which are not written in this book; but these have been written so that you may believe that Jesus is the Christ, the Son of God; and that believing you may have life in His name. (John 20.30)

Note the emphasis upon the fact that signs were performed in the presence of the disciples. The author makes it clear that he is focusing on signs to which the disciples themselves can attest, incidents that *really happened* in historical fact, and incidents, therefore, that the reader/hearer can rely upon in deciding whether or not to believe on Jesus.

Here is another emphatic declaration of the beloved disciple's historical truthfulness:

> Peter, turning around, saw the disciple whom Jesus loved following them; the one who also had leaned back on His bosom at the supper and said, "Lord, who is the

one who betrays You?" So Peter seeing him said to Jesus, "Lord, and what about this man?" Jesus said to him, "If I want him to remain until I come, what is that to you? You follow Me!" Therefore this saying went out among the brethren that that disciple would not die; yet Jesus did not say to him that he would not die, but only, "If I want him to remain until I come, what is that to you?" This is the disciple who is testifying to these things and wrote these things, and *we know that his testimony is true*. (John 21.20–24)

There is some controversy over whether the last verse, verse 24, may have been written as a sort of "afterword" by some person other than the author of the Gospel itself. Richard Bauckham has an interesting argument from the use of what he calls the "'we' of authoritative testimony" that it is still the author himself speaking.[20] Even if the last two verses of the Gospel were added as a small coda, that does not mean that the book as a whole was written by a "community," that the last chapter was written by someone else, or (most importantly) that the beloved disciple had merely a vague role somewhere "behind" the Gospel. Here Bauckham's argument is quite convincing that "wrote these things" may include a scenario where the beloved disciple used an amanuensis, but that there was no greater distance than that between him and the work—not that he was only an influence or the source of "traditions lying behind" the work.[21] The emphasis in verse 24 upon his truthfulness is therefore pertinent to the book as a whole.

In the book of Acts, there is a fascinating reflection of Jesus' own words in Peter's criteria for a replacement for Judas Iscariot. When setting up the lot-drawing for a replacement, Peter says,

"Therefore it is necessary that of the men who have accompanied us all the time that the Lord Jesus went in and out among us—beginning with the baptism of John until the day that He was taken up from us—one of these must become a witness with us of His resurrection." (Acts 1.21–22)

This fits well with what Jesus had said to the disciples only a few weeks earlier on the night of his betrayal, as recorded in John.

"When the Helper comes, whom I will send to you from the Father, that is the Spirit of truth who proceeds from the Father, He will testify about Me, and you will testify also, because you have been with Me from the beginning." (John 15.27)

---

[20] Richard Bauckham, *Jesus and the Eyewitnesses: The Gospels as Eyewitness Testimony* (Grand Rapids, MI: Eerdmans, 2017), pp. 371–380.

[21] Ibid., pp. 358–361.

Jesus had told the disciples that the coming of the Holy Spirit would coincide with a special mission to testify about Jesus, because they had personally been present with him in his ministry. When Peter formally calls upon the gathered disciples to appoint a replacement for Judas, he says that it should be someone who has been with them from the beginning (just as Jesus had said). Peter interprets this rather stringently as referring to accompanying the other disciples and Jesus from the time of John the Baptist.[22] The disciples are at this time waiting for the promised coming of the Holy Spirit, emphasized by Jesus shortly before his ascension (Acts 1.8), with a further emphasis there upon being his witnesses. They are concerned to appoint a qualified successor before that special event occurs.

This concept of being eyewitnesses from the beginning also occurs in Luke's own preface to Theophilus, quoted above (Luke 1.2). John and Luke are perfectly complementary here,[23] and the emphasis in Peter's words upon the on-going *physical* presence of the witnesses with Jesus shows that the concept of "testifying" or "being witnesses" was first and foremost one of empirical testimony. Such empirical testimony needs to be truthful in the historical sense or it does not serve its purpose.

Also in Acts, we find Peter and John speaking to the Jewish leaders, who tell them to stop preaching in the name of Jesus. Papias indicates that Peter was a principal verbal source for Mark's Gospel,[24] and John the Son of Zebedee is an excellent contender for the author of John, though of course this authorship claim is contested. (I accept the authorship of John's Gospel by John the son of Zebedee and will be discussing authorship in *The Eye of the Beholder.*) So what Peter and John say is relevant to the truthfulness of the Gospels. What is Peter and John's view of their mission?

> And when they had summoned them, they commanded them not to speak or teach at all in the name of Jesus. But Peter and John answered and said to them, "Whether it is right in the sight of God to give heed to you rather than to God, you be the judge; for *we cannot stop speaking about what we have seen and heard.*" (Acts 4.18–20)

Their emphasis is not upon teaching some "higher truth" nor even, just here, explaining the meaning of Jesus' teachings. Expounding Jesus' teachings is not out-

---

[22] It is possible that Matthew, though one of the twelve, did not meet the criterion of having accompanied the disciples during the ministry of John the Baptist. See Matt. 9.1–13, Matt. 10.2–4, Mark 2.14–19.

[23] A point emphasized by Richard Bauckham, *Jesus and the Eyewitnesses*, p. 116.

[24] Eusebius, *Ecclesiastical History*, 3.39.15–16.

side of the scope of their mission, but further teaching is not what they are talking about here. Their burning mission is to speak of what they have heard and seen— to be empirical witnesses.

Here is Peter emphasizing both the non-fictional nature and the empirical nature of the disciples' witness:

> *For we did not follow cleverly devised tales* when we made known to you the power and coming of our Lord Jesus Christ, *but we were eyewitnesses of His majesty*. For when He received honor and glory from God the Father, such an utterance as this was made to Him by the Majestic Glory, "This is My beloved Son with whom I am well-pleased"— and *we ourselves heard this utterance made from heaven when we were with Him on the holy mountain*. (2 Peter 1.16)

While I realize that the Petrine authorship of 2 Peter is contested, I do not intend here to go into the debate over that authorship. I consider Petrine authorship to be quite secure. If you absolutely insist upon doubting Petrine authorship of 2 Peter, ponder this, at least: These verses indicate a stress among the earliest Christians upon *non-fictional teaching* about Jesus coming from *eyewitnesses to the events*, such as the Father's endorsement of the Son at the Transfiguration. In this context, it is an extremely modest and entirely justified conclusion that the original audience of the Gospels considered them to be reportage.

The words "heard and seen," already noted in Acts 4, come up again in I John.

> What was from the beginning, *what we have heard, what we have seen with our eyes, what we have looked at and touched with our hands*, concerning the Word of Life—and the life was manifested, and we have seen and testify and proclaim to you the eternal life, which was with the Father and was manifested to us—*what we have seen and heard we proclaim to you also*, so that you too may have fellowship with us; and indeed our fellowship is with the Father, and with His Son Jesus Christ. (I John 1.1–3)

Concerning these verses, Bauckham comments,

> [I]t should surely be clear (though not admitted by all scholars) that the language of 1:1–3 is designed to include, even to emphasize apprehension by the physical senses…What was seen may go beyond what could have been empirically observed by anyone present, but it is hard to see how the author could have referred more clearly to apprehension by the physical senses.[25]

---

[25] Bauckham, *Jesus and the Eyewitnesses*, p. 377.

John and Peter in Acts emphasize truthful reportage of empirically observed data. And one epistle attributed to Peter and one attributed to John stress the same theme.

Here I would just again remind readers of the statements by Papias and Julius Africanus discussed earlier. (See Chapter VI, section 5, and Chapter VII, section 7.) Papias' emphasis upon the "living and surviving voice" and the words that go back to Jesus as "the truth itself" are beautifully consonant with the emphasis in passages from Luke, John, Acts (Peter and John), 2 Peter, and I John. Papias says,

> Nor did I take pleasure in those who reported their memory of someone else's commandments, but *only in those who reported their memory of the commandments given by the Lord to the faith and proceeding from the Truth itself.* And if by chance anyone who had been in attendance on the elders arrived, I made enquiries about the words of the elders—what Andrew or Peter had said, or Philip or Thomas or James or John or Matthew or any other of the Lord's disciples, and whatever Aristion and John the Elder, the Lord's disciples, were saying. For I did not think that information from the books would profit me as much as information from a living and surviving voice.[26]

Julius Africanus cites Paul's dictum that it is a terrible thing to be a false witness for God by testifying that God did something that he did not do (I Cor. 15.15) and uses it to condemn the theory that the Gospel authors invented a fictional genealogy for Jesus:

> Nor shall an assertion of this kind prevail in the Church of Christ against the exact truth, so that a lie should be contrived for the praise and glory of Christ. For who does not know that most holy word of the apostle also, who, when he was preaching and proclaiming the resurrection of our Saviour, and confidently affirming the truth, said with great fear, If any say that Christ is not risen, and we assert and have believed this, and both hope for and preach that very thing, we are false witnesses of God, in alleging that He raised up Christ, whom He raised not up? And if he who glorifies God the Father is thus afraid lest he should seem a false witness in narrating a marvelous fact, how should not he be justly afraid, who tries to establish the truth by a false statement, preparing an untrue opinion? For if the generations are different, and trace down no genuine seed to Joseph, and if all has been stated only with the view of establishing the position of Him who was to be born—to confirm the truth, namely, that He who was to be would be king and priest, there being at the same time no proof given, but the dignity of the words being brought down to a feeble hymn,—it is evident that no praise accrues to God from that, since it is a

---

[26] Eusebius, *Ecclesiastical History,* 3.39.3–4. Emphasis added.

falsehood, but rather judgment returns on him who asserts it, because he vaunts an unreality as though it were reality.[27]

Again and again, the literary device view would require us to reinterpret radically the Gospel authors' and apostles' own explicit statements of what they were attempting to do and to ignore clear statements by other early Christians about the importance of truth. The reportage model does not require these exegetical gymnastics.

3. How does fiction teach?

When I was studying English Literature in graduate school in the early 1990s, postmodernism was already sweeping all before it. There were only a few of us left, whether professors or students, who believed in the intrinsic value of a work of literature, independent of our own subjective manipulations. Those of us who did believe in outdated things like objective meaning used to spend time discussing Art with a capital A, and one of the topics of conversation on occasion was the question of how fiction teaches truth. Is there some special way in which fiction, as opposed to history, science, or philosophy, teaches? If so, what is it?

I think that I am now in a somewhat better position to answer that question, having studied epistemology for a few decades and having put that philosophical training together with my knowledge of literature. It has been said that the philosopher tells us that what is true of the postman is true of all men and that the novelist tells us that what is true of all men is true of the postman. That maxim, though no doubt oversimplified, provides a key to the question of fiction's unique contribution and how it differs from the way that history teaches.

The philosopher, when he is thinking about human nature (as not all philosophers do), tries to find universal truths. He is delving into metaphysics. In contrast, the novelist or playwright takes things that we know in the abstract as truths of human nature and makes them concrete, showing vividly that they are true of individual people. It could happen to you or to me.

Hence, perhaps we know in principle that jealousy destroys lives, but it is in watching *Othello* that we find that truth brought home with horrible vividness. Perhaps we realize at some theoretical level that people are more complex than they appear and that the outwardly hardened sinner may be harboring a repentance we cannot see, but it is when one reads Marilynne Robinson's novel *Gilead* that one comes to understand that at a heart level, and many other truths as well.

---

[27] Julius Africanus, *Letter to Aristides*, I.

A philosopher might say that literature shows us the conceivability of particular states of affairs. And that is true. If you thought it too psychologically implausible that a person could romantically love two people at once, a novel may show you that it isn't that implausible after all, by realistically portraying such a situation and making it vividly imaginable. But literature goes beyond that. It brings things home. It forces us to pause, ponder, and meditate on truths that we know otherwise but perhaps would rather not think about or simply don't otherwise take the time to think about.

In this sense, fiction *qua* fiction does not teach *brand-new* things. Some fiction, in fact, attempts to teach falsehoods—that sex outside of marriage has no negative consequences as long as everyone involved is reasonable and as long as the adulterers are in love, that things always turn out well for good people, or (more pessimistically) that the world is devoid of meaning and that ugliness is the ultimate truth. When these falsehoods in works of fiction come up against our independent knowledge of the truth, we rightly reject the falsehood. A novelist may attempt to teach falsely about an historical character. If a novel were to attempt to rehabilitate Nero and turn him into a sympathetic figure, an historically savvy reader would remain unconvinced. When, on the other hand, a work of fiction teaches things we independently know to be true, and importantly true, our hearts rise up and confirm the knowledge our minds already possessed. We understand more deeply and emotionally what we already knew intellectually. The function of fiction is to remind and to clothe the truth appropriately. The *justification* for believing that truth propositionally should come from elsewhere.

The teaching we receive from historical facts is otherwise. It bears its evidential value in itself. This is true even before we bring God into the matter. The existence of Stonehenge, and its artifactual nature, really mean that mankind *can build* a Stonehenge. The stones are there—hard and incontrovertible. Stonehenge in a story would be science fiction. Stonehenge in England is archaeological fact.

If a hard-hearted man of your acquaintance *really does* shed a sincere tear over a touching human event, and if you witness his weeping, that is historical evidence that he has an unsuspected soft spot. In contrast, if a mutual friend writes a work of fiction, putting the hard-hearted acquaintance into the work, and sends a tear sliding down his face, you will be understandably skeptical. You will rightly consider your friend's vivid imagination to provide little evidence of a real soft spot in the historical Scrooge's heart.

Consider the difference between the way that history teaches and the way that fiction teaches with reference to a biblical passage—Jesus blessing the children, telling the disciples to let the children come to him (Mark 10.13–16). This is not, I wish to make clear, a passage that (to my knowledge) has been specifically called into question yet by evangelical literary device theorists. But I think it makes the point quite well.[28] Suppose that you seriously questioned whether this Gospel incident happened in an historically recognizable fashion. But suppose that you wanted to emphasize to an audience the proposition, "Jesus loves little children."

The passage in which Jesus takes up the children in his arms is ideally suited for teaching this proposition. It asserts that Jesus really showed love to little children in the real world, while he was walking around on the soil of that strip of land next to the Mediterranean Sea. It is ideally suited because it asserts that Jesus really uttered, recognizably, the injunction to allow little children to come to him.

If this incident never happened, and if you knew that, then the passage doesn't provide you with any significant evidence that Jesus loves children. It "teaches" that Jesus loves the children only as an apocryphal story "teaches" that. It may make us meditate on the love of God for all men. Little children are part of mankind. It may give us some *extremely* weak reason to think that maybe, somewhere, some time, Jesus said or did *something* nice about little children that got converted, or translated, or retold in legendary fashion, as this story. But *ex hypothesi*, if this event was not historical, it wasn't *this* event. If the story of Jesus and the little children is just a pious, devotional insertion into the Gospels, its independent, historical, evidential value for "Jesus loves the little children" is virtually nil.[29] As a fictional story, it is not evidential.

It may be said in response to my argument thus far that an authoritative teacher *can* use fiction as a way of teaching a brand-new truth. Jesus may be using the parable of the Prodigal Son (Luke 15.11–32) to teach the new truth that the Gentiles will be received fully into the church. If so, the teaching is cryptic, and the disciples

---

[28] I also note that, if invisible literary devices, including fabrication of some incidents, were really "part and parcel" of the Gospels' genre, as literary device theorists have claimed, we have some reason to question the incident right there. A large question mark hangs over many incidents in the Gospels. The theorists do not have the luxury of confining our skepticism only to those passages that they personally have chosen to question so far, since the devices they advocate would leave no clear tag to mark them out in the text itself.

[29] While this particular example is hypothetical, it is analogous to examples that are not hypothetical. Evangelical scholars have questioned the historicity of the incident in which Jesus breathes on his disciples and says, "Receive the Holy Ghost." (John 20.22–23) Both Craig Keener and Mike Licona

required further revelation (as narrated in the book of Acts) to make it clear. If that is the meaning of the parable, then we can say that fiction was a vehicle of new teaching, teaching that the hearers would not have already known. This is correct. But that does not contradict my argument thus far. For in that case, the fictional story is only a vehicle of the teaching. The epistemic force comes entirely from the authority of Jesus, the teacher, who could have chosen to communicate that truth by bare statement. The story itself does not convey *extra* epistemic force in favor of the proposition that the Gentiles are to be received equally with the Jews into membership in the church. It is not the fiction that is teaching; it is the authority figure who is teaching and clothing his teaching openly in a fictional garb.

Moreover, Jesus was in no way ambiguous about the fact that he was using a fictional story. Both the Gospel authors and his audience recognized that he was teaching in parable and that parables are fiction. A teacher who knowingly blurs the distinction between fact and fiction in an attempt to induce his readers to believe things calls his own authority into question by such a dubious method.[30] This is something that Jesus never did, and we have no reason to believe that his apostles ever did so either.

It is important for scholars to bear in mind that fiction does not teach in the same way that fact teaches. Fiction *qua* fiction has no inherent force in support of

---

do so. Craig Keener, *The Gospel of John: A Commentary* (Grand Rapids, MI: Baker Academic, 2003), pp. 1196–2000; Craig Keener, *Acts: An Exegetical Commentary* (Grand Rapids, MI: Baker Academic 2012), vol. 1, pp. 790, 793; Licona, *Why Are There Differences*, p. 180. At most, Keener acknowledges that there might have been some event or other (he does not seem at all sure what it was like) that lay behind the record in John. See further discussion in Chapter XVI, section 7. Yet strangely, the fact that Keener questions the historicity of the event does not prevent him from writing a devotional on the incident in which he writes *as though* it is historical, telling readers that this passage teaches that Jesus equipped his disciples with power for their mission and equips us as well. The date of the devotional blog post is about ten years after the publication date of the John commentary and two years before that of the Acts commentary. This represents a rather significant confusion about how history and fiction teach, and it is also quite likely to confuse readers about Keener's own confidence in the historicity of the event. Craig Keener, "As the Father sent me, I send you—John 20:21," September 21, 2013, http://www.craigkeener.com/as-the-father-sent-me-i-send-you-john-2021/.

[30] As pointed out in Chapter VIII, footnote 18, there is also a self-reference problem inherent in the claim that the Gospel authors used their own authority to teach by putting their own words into Jesus' mouth. The alleged excuse for such an idea is a (mis)interpretation of verses such as John 14.26 concerning the Paraclete's guidance. But if the authors believed they were licensed to put their own extrapolations into Jesus' mouth, with no way of distinguishing which utterances were really made by Jesus from their interpretive glosses, then that verse itself, allegedly conferring apostolic authority, might not have been recognizably uttered by Jesus. Thus the argument undermines itself. Of course, the verse does *not* teach that they have the authority to put their own interpretations into Jesus' mouth. On the contrary: The ministry of the Holy Spirit in teaching them is expressly *distinguished* from his ministry in bringing to their remembrance what Jesus has historically said.

a factual or theological conclusion. It merely darkens counsel to imply that Jesus' "I am" sayings *teach* that he is God if, in fact, he never uttered them in an historically recognizable fashion. In other words, as the next section will argue, fake points don't make points.

4. Fake points don't make points

There are a number of places in the Gospels where literary device theorists are under the impression that an author changed or shaded facts (or that it is quite plausible that he did so) in order to make a theological point. Craig Keener calls this "narrating theologically" and says that it was particularly characteristic of John:

> John takes significant liberties with the way he reports his events, especially in several symbolic adaptations in the passion narrative ...[31]

> A close examination of the Fourth Gospel reveals that John has rearranged many details, apparently in the service of his symbolic message. This is especially clear in the Passion Narrative, where direct conflicts with the presumably widely known passion tradition (most notably that Jesus gives the sop to Judas, is crucified on Passover, and carries his own cross) fulfill symbolic narrative functions.[32]

Keener not only suggests (in the second of these quotations) that John exaggerated or invented Jesus' carrying his own cross, that John moved the day of Jesus' crucifixion, and that in some way John has invented or exaggerated Jesus' giving the sop to Judas. He also suggests that John moved the Temple cleansing to place Jesus' entire ministry metaphorically "within" Passion Week and also that the incident of Jesus' breathing out and saying, "Receive the Holy Ghost" may not be recognizably historical.[33] Michael Licona has suggested that perhaps John invented the doubting Thomas sequence as a rebuke to those who do not believe in Jesus' resurrection, though ultimately he does not conclude that this is the case.[34]

In the Synoptic Gospels, Craig Evans's theory is that Matthew invented the involvement of the mother of James and John in asking for a place at Jesus' right

---

[31] Craig Keener, *Acts: An Exegetical Commentary* (Grand Rapids, MI: Baker Academic 2012), vol. 1, p. 593.

[32] Keener, *John*, pp. 42–43. For the phrase, "theologizing narrative," see p. 520.

[33] Licona either follows Keener or leans strongly in the same direction as Keener on several of these points. On the alleged moving of the Temple cleansing, see *Why Are There Differences*, pp. 195–196; the alleged changing of the day of the Last Supper and crucifixion, pp. 155–156, 163–164; Jesus breathing on the disciples after his resurrection, pp. 180–181.

[34] Ibid., p. 177.

and left hands, in order to cast James and John in a better light.[35] Another suggestion concerning the Synoptic Gospels is that Matthew may have invented the healing of two blind men early in Jesus' ministry as a "doublet," so that Jesus can (fictionally) refer to his own healing of the blind as proof of his Messiahship when messengers come from John the Baptist.[36] And Licona has suggested that perhaps Mark deliberately suppressed the conversion of the thief on the cross in order to portray Jesus as "rejected by all."[37]

In all of these cases, the idea is that the author was making some point—a theological or ideological point—by making his narrative factually false. There is simply no way of getting around it. The theorists are saying that the Gospel authors thought the true facts would not make their points well enough or vividly enough. The disciples wouldn't appear in a good enough light if Matthew told only the true facts; Jesus wouldn't appear strongly enough to be "rejected by all." Jesus' ministry wouldn't have enough of a tragic feeling (in the Gospel of John) of being overshadowed by his final hour unless John made an elaborate, symbolic use of a factual falsehood about when Jesus cleansed the Temple. Jesus wouldn't look enough like the Lamb of God in the story unless he died on the day that the Passover lambs were sacrificed. And so forth. The true facts were not, according to these theories, enough. The Gospel authors felt moved instead to invent things that never occurred, to suppress things that did occur, or to exaggerate, in order to make a point. And they did it quite realistically. On these theories, the Gospel authors believed that fake points do make points—that greater theological significance would arise within their narratives if they deliberately made their realistic narratives *false*.

It is rather astonishing that biblical scholars could place such a mindset into the heads of the evangelists in light of the passages quoted in the last section. It is, in fact, difficult to explain, and it would take us afield into the sociology of the discipline of New Testament studies even to attempt to conjecture how scholars come to think that the evangelists thought this way. It should be evident from the previous quotations that these theories are grossly anachronistic and diametrically opposed to the perspective of the evangelists. To the Gospel authors, the revelation of God in Christ was first, foremost, and centrally an historical revelation. The enormous thing that had happened, that they had to convey to the world, was

---

[35] Craig A. Evans, *Matthew* (New Cambridge Bible Commentary) (Cambridge: Cambridge University Press, 2012), p. 353.

[36] Licona, *Why Are There Differences*, p. 135.

[37] Ibid., p. 165.

that God became flesh, that he came down from heaven, and that here on earth he fulfilled all the prophecies of the Messiah and brought salvation, in his own person. It is because these things *happened* that they can have significance. If they did not happen, they cannot have significance. To quote Leon Morris, explaining the mindset of the author of John,

> In the face of those who assert that to John the spiritual significance is everything and the historicity immaterial, the question must be pressed, "What is the theological meaning of something that never happened?" The very idea of bringing out theological significance seems to imply respect for the facts. What did not happen can scarcely be called redemptive.[38]

This is why the beloved disciple so strongly emphasizes that these things really happened to fulfill the Scripture. Jesus' bones were *not* broken, so Scripture was fulfilled (John 19.36). If his bones *had been* broken, that particular Scripture (Psalm 34.20) *would not* have been fulfilled by that event. Fake points don't make points. Jesus' garment was *not* torn, and instead the soldiers cast lots for it. This really happened, and that is how Psalm 22.18 was fulfilled (John 19.24). If John simply made up the casting of lots, it would not have fulfilled Scripture. Fake points don't make points.

When Matthew narrates the flight to Egypt, he says (Matt. 2.15) that this event "fulfilled" Hosea 11.1, "Out of Egypt have I called my son." You may certainly puzzle over Matthew's application of Hosea 11.1. You can worry about double fulfillment. You can ask what Matthew means by "fulfillment" in this passage. You can wonder about what sort of parallel he is drawing between the events in Jesus' life and the events in Israel's history. But what you cannot doubt, if you are a reasonable person at all, is that Matthew is *saying to his readers* that the flight to Egypt and the return from Egypt really happened in the life of the infant Jesus, and that this *event* fulfilled something written in the Old Testament.[39]

Douglas Moo comments trenchantly concerning Matthew and the Christian worldview:

> [Matthew] writes from the conviction that the decisive revelation of God had recently been manifested in the historical actualities of Jesus' life and teaching.

---

[38] Leon Morris, *Studies in the Fourth Gospel* (Grand Rapids, Eerdmans Publishing Company, 1969), p. 124.

[39] In a written debate with Bart Ehrman, Licona speculates that both Luke and Matthew may have invented all of the non-overlapping portions of their infancy narratives in order to make a more interesting story. This would include the star, the shepherds, the flight to Egypt, the slaughter of the inno-

To say...that "'Jesus said' or 'Jesus did' need not always mean that in history Jesus said or did what follows"... attributes to Matthew an unconcern with history that seems to me at odds with one of the most distinctive features of the Christian message....I am suggesting that concern for historical actualities, which is the essential byproduct of the incarnation, kept [Matthew] from combining history and nonhistory....[40]

For Matthew, as for John, theological significance and literal events are inextricably woven together. Fake points don't make points.

The same argument applies to matters other than prophecy. D. A. Carson observes that the Apostle Paul emphasizes specific historical sequence when drawing theological conclusions. For example, in Galatians 3.17, Paul emphasizes that the Mosaic law came *after* the promise to Abraham. Similarly the author of Hebrews (Heb. 4.2–9) emphasizes that the psalmist wrote Psalm 95 *after* the entry into the promised land and argues on this basis that the psalmist must be referring to some other "rest" that is still to come. The hermeneutical reliance upon historical sequence is striking. Says Carson,

> The point is that these (and numerous other) New Testament readings of the Old Testament Scriptures turn on historical distinctions (not least sequence in time to establish continuity and discontinuity) in order to establish theological instruction....Theological interpretation is here tightly intertwined with subtle historical reading of biblical texts.[41]

The evangelists and the early Christians understand that God dips his pen in history and writes his story using realities, not literary inventions.

---

cents, etc.—anything that is not overlapping propositional content. While Licona stresses that he does not affirm this hypothesis, he also implies a major problem of some kind with the infancy narratives in Matthew and Luke, saying that he does not "know what's going on" with the infancy stories and that they "include the most profound and difficult differences in the Gospels." He states that "one can provide some plausible" but "speculative" solutions. The idea of entire invention of the non-overlapping portions is the only speculation he brings forward. "Licona Responds to Ehrman on New Testament Reliability," 2016, https://thebestschools.org/special/ehrman-licona-dialogue-reliability-new-testament/licona-detailed-response/. Licona then claims, incorrectly, that even if Matthew and Luke invented to this large extent, the overlapping content would nonetheless be firmly established merely by the fact that they both narrate it, making it "multiply attested." This argument embodies a serious misunderstanding of the probabilistic nature of multiple attestation. See Lydia McGrew, "Finessing Independent Attestation: A Study in Interdisciplinary Biblical Criticism," *Themelios* 44.1 (2019), pp. 89–102, http://themelios.thegospelcoalition.org/article/finessing-independent-attestation-interdisciplinary-biblical-criticism.

[40] Douglas J. Moo, "Matthew and Midrash," *JETS* 26 (1983), pp. 38–39.

[41] D. A. Carson, "Theological Interpretation of Scripture: Yes, But...," in R. Michael Allen, ed., *Theological Commentary: Evangelical Perspectives* (London: T & T Clark, 2011), p. 191.

5. The artless author

We have, then, evidence for the reportage model both in the statements that the evangelists and their sources made about their intentions and in the way that they argued from events and from Scripture.

It should be evident by this time that the reportage model and the literary device model are incompatible, because they give us different concepts of what the authors of the Gospels were attempting to do. On one model, the authors were sincerely attempting to report what they knew to be true and were reporting *because* they believed in the truth of what they narrated. On the other model, the authors were sometimes or even frequently altering the truth on purpose, while narrating realistically, in order to make a theological point or an artistic improvement—to make their version of the story "better" than fact. These are conflicting psychological portraits. In the next chapter I will be showing how these conflicting models make for incompatible approaches to evidence. The reportage model allows us to see evidence for historicity clearly, while the literary device model buries and negates such evidence by attributing it, without justification, to the authors' complex fictionalizing activities.

A useful word to describe the author in the reportage model is the term "artless" as used by 19th-century authors like John James Blunt and J. S. Howson. Both of these men, expanding upon the work of William Paley in the 18th century, talk about how various kinds of evidence show that the authors were not "up to" something contrived but rather were reporting what they justifiably believed to be true. Says Blunt,

> The general drift of our argument is this, that when we see the writers of the Scriptures clearly telling the truth in those cases where we have the means of *checking* their accounts,—when we see that they are artless, consistent, veracious writers, where we have the opportunity of examining the fact,—it is reasonable to believe that they are telling the truth in those cases where we have not the means of checking them,—that they are veracious where we have not the means of putting them to the proof.[42]

Howson uses the term when discussing the different accounts of Paul's conversion given in Acts. He points out that the alleged discrepancies between them show that the author was not attempting to manipulate his sources of information, not even to "improve" them by smoothing away these difficulties:

---

[42] J. J. Blunt, *Undesigned Coincidences in the Writings Both of the Old and New Testament: An Argument of Their Veracity* (London: John Murray, 1863), p. 3. Emphasis in original.

These apparent discrepancies are a very small matter; and it is to be observed that they occur within the limits of the same document, and for this very reason furnish a testimony to the *artless simplicity* with which it is written.[43]

Howson goes on to argue that Paul's own accounts of his conversion are particularly well-suited to the settings in which they are placed, a topic we discussed already in Chapter VII, section 8. Howson continues,

> If these…things can be established, without at the same time any suspicion of artifice being excited, the trustworthiness of the Biblical history of this Apostle receives some appreciable support.[44]

The artlessness of the author, as Howson and Blunt use that term, is thus the opposite of artfulness or artifice, where the latter refer to cunning or craftiness. The artless author is truthful in a plain and unvarnished sense. He is not trying to manipulate either his facts or his audience's perceptions.

Having introduced the term "artless," I hasten to correct a possible misinterpretation, which should be added to my comments above on what the reportage view is not. The concept of artlessness used here has to do with an author's relationship to *truth*. It does not imply that the author was crude, disorganized, uneducated, or lacking in talent. By speaking of the artless author and saying that the Gospel authors were artless in Blunt's and Howson's sense, I do *not* mean to say that the authors of the Gospels did not have themes, that they did not select material that was especially relevant to those themes, or that they did not write their narratives with skill.

It is unfortunate that literary device theorists have abused the term "artistry" to mean fabrication and alteration of fact,[45] either by inventing, changing, or suppressing facts. Factual alteration is not an inevitable result of artistry. On the

---

[43] J. S. Howson, "Appendix II: The Three Accounts of St. Paul's Conversion," in William Paley, *Horae Paulinae*, edited by J. S. Howson, (London: Society for Promoting Christian Knowledge, 1877), p. 400. Emphasis added.

[44] Ibid., p. 401.

[45] Licona, *Why Are There Differences*, pp. 117, 137, 161, 184–185, 193, 195. On p. 262, n. 37, Licona says that "literary artistry does not require the events to be fictitious." In the context in the main text, pp. 195–196, he is referring to Jesus' cleansing the Temple and (apparently) the day of his crucifixion. By saying that literary artistry does not require that the events are fictitious, Licona means only that these events have not been *entirely invented*. Jesus really did cleanse the Temple on *some* occasion and was really crucified. But John's supposed "literary artistry" would be fact-altering and hence fictional as defined in Chapter I, since it would involve invisibly changing the day and/or time at which these events took place in his Gospel.

contrary, the idea of an authorial theme and selection of material is valuable for *defending* historicity when we note that the inclusion of an incident, saying, or discourse in only one Gospel does not in any way call its historicity into question. This point will be especially relevant in thinking about the Gospel of John. An author can select true, historical material that shows a particular aspect of Jesus' character or a theological truth, bringing out information that other authors have not chosen to include, while not repeating material already available elsewhere. Both John 20.30 and 21.25 emphasize the obvious—that it would be impossible for one book to record everything about Jesus and that the author has selected his material. But selection, even motivated by a theme and/or the author's own interest, does not imply fictionalization of any kind whatsoever, including the kinds postulated by the literary device theorists. Artlessness in the sense that Howson and Blunt use the term does not prevent an author from telling his story in a manner that is non-fictionally artistic.

As we will see in the next chapter, the artlessly veracious author tells what he believes to be true, and in so doing he furnishes opportunities for his narrative to be confirmed.

Summary
The Evangelists as Honest Reporters

- The reportage model of the Gospels means that the authors were trying to tell us what really happened.

- The reportage model of the Gospels means that the authors tried to record what was said in a way that was recognizably historical.

- The reportage model of the Gospels means that the authors were highly successful at conveying true factual information, even in details.

- The reportage model of the Gospels does not mean that we must have a tape-recorded version of the words of Jesus or others. This is a straw man that literary device theorists sometimes use against those who disagree with them.

- The reportage model does not mean that we can answer all questions about what happened in the events recorded in the Gospels.

- The reportage model does not mean that the authors of the Gospels never narrated achronologically (without indicating a chronology). This is a straw man used by literary device theorists, who also sometimes use evidence of achronological reporting as if it supported changing chronology (dyschronological narration).

- The evangelists and the apostles stated clearly their commitment to factual truth. We must not ignore or set aside this evidence.

- Fictional stories and details about the life of Jesus would not provide evidence for theological truth. Fake points don't make points.

- The author who is carefully attempting to tell the factual truth has fundamentally different motives from an author who considers himself licensed to invent and change facts in historical writing.

XI

Evidence and the Artless Author

1. Undesigned Coincidences vs. literary devices

What is an undesigned coincidence? My previous book, *Hidden in Plain View: Undesigned Coincidences in the Gospels and Acts*, was entirely about this topic. Briefly, an undesigned coincidence is an incidental interlocking between two accounts that points to the truth of both. We find repeatedly in truthful historical accounts—whether secular or religious—that a comment made casually in one account fits together with something mentioned in another account, confirming both. Very often, these connections concern incidental details.

Suppose that one morning your co-worker comes in to work a bit late. He comments that a local intersection, which he names, was partially closed due to a traffic accident and that he had to wait for police to direct him through the slowdown. Several hours later a second co-worker comes in. He says that he was delayed due to a flat tire, which he got at the same intersection because there was glass in the road. He does not mention that the intersection was partially closed. He says nothing else about an accident. The two statements complement each other quite well, but at the same time they vary in ways that make it seem unlikely that the two people have deliberately colluded. If there was indeed an accident at that intersection, it is plausible that there would be glass in the road at least for a few hours until it could be cleaned up. But the second co-worker does not mention any other signs of an accident, and the first co-worker does not mention glass in the road. The testimony of one (to the accident) explains the testimony of the other (concerning the glass and the flat tire).

This is an undesigned coincidence. The narratives fit together like puzzle pieces in a way that provides a more complete picture of what happened to both people, but they do not appear to be the result of contrivance on the part of the people involved. Hence, they appear undesigned. It would be quite an elaborate scheme for the two co-workers to plan this as a hoax and for each to restrain himself carefully, giving only part of the information, in order to produce the appearance of casualness and absence of design. Under ordinary circumstances, without independent information to indicate that the people involved are clever hoaxers of an unusual kind, the coincidence between their testimonies is strong evidence that they are both telling the truth.

These sorts of coincidences arise often among the Gospels and also between Acts and Paul's epistles. William Paley, Anglican clergyman and justly famed apologist, originated the argument from undesigned coincidences and coined the phrase in the 18th century;[1] the Anglican clergyman J. J. Blunt and others took up the argument and expanded its application in the 19th century.[2] It fell into obscurity during the 20th century before being brought back to the attention of scholars and Christian apologists in the early 21st century. The work of philosopher and apologist Timothy McGrew[3] and my book *Hidden in Plain View* have been part of that revival, as has the work of apologist and cold-case detective J. Warner Wallace[4] and New Testament scholar Peter Williams.[5]

Here is one example (out of many) of an undesigned coincidence discussed in *Hidden in Plain View*.[6] When we read of the feeding of the five thousand in the Gospel of John, we notice that it mentions in passing that Jesus turned to Philip and asked, "Where are we to buy bread, so that these may eat?" (John 6.5) Of course, Jesus does not actually intend that the disciples will buy bread to feed the multitude. He is, in a sense, teasing Philip and the other disciples. Philip immediately rises to

[1] William Paley, *Horae Paulinae*, edited by J. S. Howson (London: Society for Promoting Christian Knowledge, 1877, first published 1790); *A View of the Evidences of Christianity: In Three Parts*. (Murfreesboro, TN: Dehoff Publications, 1952, first published 1794).

[2] John J. Blunt, *Undesigned Coincidences in the Writings Both of the Old and New Testament, an Argument of Their Veracity* (Birmingham, UK: The Christadelphian. 1965 reprint of 1847 edition).

[3] See, for example, the discussion by Timothy McGrew on *Evidence4Faith*, April 24, 2011, http://www.evidence4faith.com/shows/e4f-042411.mp3. See also Timothy McGrew's talk "Undesigned Coincidences in the Gospels," given at First Baptist Church, Kenner, LA, January 9, 2011, https://first-kenner.org/audio/jan2011/010911A%20.mp3. See also a six-part series of posts by Timothy McGrew on undesigned coincidences in Acts, published by the *Christian Apologetics Alliance*, September 1–November 16, 2013. Links to all posts in the series available at https://apologetics315.com/2013/11/undesigned-coincidences-series-by-tim-mcgrew/.

[4] J. Warner Wallace, *Cold-Case Christianity: A Homicide Detective Investigates the Claims of the Gospels* (Colorado Springs, CO: David C. Cook), pp. 183–187.

[5] Peter J. Williams, *Can We Trust The Gospels?* (Wheaton, IL: Crossway, 2018), Chapter 4.

[6] Lydia McGrew, *Hidden in Plain View: Undesigned Coincidences in the Gospels and Acts* (Chillicothe, OH: DeWard Publishing, 2017), pp. 107–113.

the bait, objecting that they cannot possibly buy enough bread for the crowd. But a question arises: Why did Jesus ask Philip, in particular, where to buy bread?

This is the sort of question to which we might never get an answer. Very often we have no idea why, in the hurly-burly of real life, some particular person was chosen for a given task or question. It is possible that Jesus just asked Philip at random, as the person who happened to be standing at his elbow at the moment. But *if* the story is true, it is plausible that there is some more definite reason for directing the question to Philip and therefore possible that we could *discover* that reason by comparing this account with other facts. Thus the details of this story in John's Gospel become what probability theorists call somewhat dependent with the details that we might find elsewhere, on the hypothesis that the documents are telling the truth.[7] Put in informal terms, if the authors are telling the truth, we have some reason to think that what they report will be confirmed elsewhere, including the details. The idea that there is "some reason" need not rise as high as a confident expectation. Indeed, we often have only one true account of a given incident and no independent confirmation of that incident or of its details. But empirical truth is available to more than one person, and if an account is true, its separate confirmation is at least a real possibility on the table. Undesigned coincidences give us such confirmations from other documents, and the confirmation is indirect and subtle, making it more likely to be a result of truth than of artifice.

So why Philip? He is not as prominent as Peter, James, and John, so someone contriving the detail wouldn't be especially likely to mention him on the grounds of his great importance among the disciples. He isn't said to carry the money bag, like Judas (John 12.6). Perhaps someone inventing the tale might make Judas the person consulted, but that reason does not apply to Philip. As it turns out, the Gospel of Luke mentions briefly that the feeding of the five thousand took place near the town of Bethsaida (Luke 9.10). But Luke says nothing about Philip in connection with the feeding. (John's Gospel mentions Philip more often than any other Gospel, though still only a few times.) But when we turn back to John, we find the statement in totally unrelated contexts that Philip was from the town of Bethsaida (John 1.44, John 12.21). These references to Bethsaida in John are not connected in any way whatsoever with the feeding of the five thousand. John does

[7] For a detailed analysis of the probability-theoretic basis for undesigned coincidences, explained in secular terms, see Lydia McGrew, "Undesigned Coincidences and Coherence for an Hypothesis," *Erkenntnis*, On-Line First, August 6, 2018, https://doi.org/10.1007/s10670-018-0050-4. Author's accepted manuscript version archived with publisher's permission at http://lydiamcgrew.com/UndesignedCoincidencesErkenntnis.pdf.

not mention that the feeding of the five thousand took place near Bethsaida. For that matter, John's references to Bethsaida are not connected with much of anything. John mentions in passing that Philip is from that town. In the next chapter, I will discuss unnecessary details that have no apparent literary or theological significance, and the way that in themselves they are a signal of literal historicity. In this instance we can see that unnecessary details in one document may fit into an undesigned coincidence with another document.

With all of these references in hand, we can see that a reasonable explanation for Jesus' asking Philip where to buy bread is the fact that Philip was "a local" in that region, and that the other disciples knew it. As Jesus, with a twinkle in his eye, asks where they can buy bread to feed the crowds, he turns to a man from the nearby town and poses the question to him. This conclusion is not certain, but it is both plausible and highly suggestive. It is therefore also evidence of truth in the various narratives—in John's narrative of the feeding of the five thousand, in Luke's mention that it occurred near Bethsaida, and in John's other passing references in different contexts to the home town of Philip. Had John contrived the detail of Jesus' asking Philip and intended to connect it with the feeding near Bethsaida, it is likely that he would at least have mentioned that the feeding took place near Bethsaida and probably also would have mentioned *in that context* that Philip was from that town. Otherwise any such connection was far more likely to be lost on his readers. Indeed, many if not most Christians who are highly familiar with *all* of the Gospels have overlooked the connection.

Notice that this coincidence concerns what is undeniably a *detail* of John's story about the feeding of the five thousand. Now let us consider even a relatively "moderate" literary device view: On such a view, it is quite plausible antecedently that the Gospel authors "crafted" various details of their stories to make them more vivid and interesting. In other words, we should not expect the mere details to be true but only the big picture or "core story."[8] Remember that "expansion of narrative details" is one of the literary devices that Michael Licona claims was accepted at the time that the Gospels were written. Says Licona,

If minor details were unknown, they could be invented to improve the narrative while maintaining historical verisimilitude.[9]

---

[8] See Michael Licona, *Why Are There Differences in the Gospels? What We Can Learn From Ancient Biography* (Oxford: Oxford University Press, 2017), pp. 147, 170. In fact, as documented at multiple points throughout this book, evangelical literary device theorists do sometimes question the historicity even of events and scenes, which most ordinary readers would consider to be "big picture" items.

[9] Ibid., p. 20.

Licona further explains this alleged device by quoting classicist Christopher Pelling, who refers both to "the fabrication of circumstantial detail" and the "fabrication of a context."[10] Remember, too, that Licona insists that we "should be surprised" if the evangelists *did not* employ such "compositional devices,"[11] since they were "part and parcel" of the genre to which he believes the Gospels belong or at least bear a significant similarity.[12] This amounts to a fairly high expectation that the Gospel authors sometimes simply fabricated at least the details of their stories. Remember, too, that Licona believes that the Gospel authors sometimes created dialogue that never occurred and that in so doing they were following the advice of compositional textbooks.[13]

But in that case, why should we suspect in the first place that there was any reason for Jesus' question to Philip or that the bit of dialogue even happened? John could have fabricated that detail in order to improve his narrative by throwing in some more random details. On the literary device view of the Gospels, John may well have made up the short dialogue with Philip altogether. On the literary device view, the details of John's narrative may very well not arise from other facts in the *real world*, such as Philip's real town of origin or anything else. In a work of fiction, we realize that it is often entirely meaningless to ask why so-and-so did precisely *that*, or who *that* passing person was, because we realize that the author has probably not fleshed out that aspect of his fictional "world." Similarly, if the details and dialogue of John's Gospel are quite plausibly made up, it may be not merely *difficult* to find out why things happened that way in the story but also literally *meaningless*. If we regard it as quite plausible that Jesus didn't ask Philip that question *at all*, then there is, on that hypothesis, no reason *why* he did so. The reason for Jesus' question to Philip may have no place in reality any more than does Hamlet's shoe size. The higher we consider the antecedent probability that John made up bits of his narrative, the less reason there is to think that there is any explanation for Jesus' question to Philip in the real world.

This principle is true in general of undesigned coincidences and also (as we will see later in this chapter) coincidences between biblical narratives and external data. In fact, those external incidental confirmations can be thought of as

---

[10] Ibid., p. 228, n. 34.

[11] Ibid., p. 5.

[12] Jonathan Peterson and Michael Licona, "Why Are There Differences in the Gospels? An Interview With Michael R. Licona," *Bible Gateway Blog*, June 27, 2017, https://www.biblegateway.com/blog/2017/06/why-are-there-differences-in-the-gospels-an-interview-with-michael-r-licona/.

[13] Licona, *Why Are There Differences*, pp. 13, 128.

undesigned coincidences of a different type, though usually I reserve the term for coincidences between biblical documents. If we think that the statements we find in the biblical narratives are plausibly or even probably fabricated, even in part, we have no reason to think that there may be other confirmation of them, since they are not literally true in the first place. And if we think that such fabrication applies especially to details, then we should not look for the details to be confirmed. This theory makes it much more difficult to see such confirmations clearly when they *do* arise. The bias in favor of fictionalizing literary devices thus carries a great danger of blinding the theorist to the actual evidence for historicity.

The epistemology in this area is actually rather fascinating, though there is no need to understand it in technical terms in order to see how the assumption that the Gospels contain fictionalizing literary devices biases the theorist and obscures the evidential value of historical confirmation.

Consider a concrete example: Suppose that I have frequently found Jack to be a practical joker, so that any extraordinary story he tells me is likely to be false. If Jack tells me that he has learned important secrets of foreign policy and that his life is now in danger, I will be inclined to take this as another one of Jack's jokes. If Jack were a different person, his testimony would have more weight in favor of even such an unusual claim, but my previous experience downgrades the value of his testimony. Now suppose that Jack is subsequently found dead in a car accident. While this may cause me to wonder briefly if he was telling the truth in this one case, like the boy who cried wolf, I am more likely to reflect that car accidents do happen and continue to think that the whole thing is a mere coincidence. This is a result of my high prior probability that any unusual, dramatic story Jack told was embellished or invented. Similarly, when the literary device theorist approaches the Gospels with a fairly high antecedent probability that a Gospel passage contains at least embellished details if not entirely invented contexts or scenes, then the theorist is more likely to overlook or explain away evidence *against* that proposition, such as the discovery of external confirmation of a detail in the story or an undesigned coincidence.

It might be tempting to believe that one can take a smorgasbord approach to undesigned coincidences and literary devices—a little bit of this and a little bit of that. When one is struck by the "coolness" of an undesigned coincidence, one will accept it. But when one has trouble harmonizing an alleged contradiction between two Gospel accounts, then one might think it expedient to jump to the literary device school of thought and claim that a literary device (say, dyschronological displacement) was "accepted at the time," explaining the Bible difficulty in that way. One might think that one could do this at any time, taking the Gospel authors to be truthful when that is useful and taking them to be using fact-changing literary devices when that seems useful.

The *ad hocness* and epistemic lack of principle in such an approach is evident when one asks this question: What kind of author is one creating in such a process? Not a psychologically coherent author. If one actually believes that the literary device view of the Gospels is correct, that such fact-changing devices were "part and parcel" of the Gospels' genre, and if one interprets the Gospels consistently in this way, then to be consistent one should have a high probability from the outset that what appear to be undesigned coincidences are *unlikely* to be correctly explained by the activities of literally truthful authors. After all, *highly scrupulous, literally truthful authors*, giving us what they believe to be historically accurate reports even in matters of detail, are precisely what the literary device view tells us we do *not* have. The smorgasbord approach is untenable.

In the entire previous section of this book, I have argued that there is no good reason to think that fictionalizing literary devices of displacement, compression, transferral, etc., were accepted at the time of the Gospels' writing. In the first chapter of this section I have argued that it is highly unlikely that the Gospel authors or their audiences envisaged the Gospels in that way. Now we will see that the evidence of undesigned coincidences and the evidence of external incidental confirmations also goes directly contrary to the idea that the Gospel authors are writing their accounts using such devices. If we find again and again that there is good reason to believe that the authors *have been* historically truthful in their accounts, then this disconfirms the literary device picture. It confirms, instead, the reportage view.

If one assumes the literary device picture at the outset, one will find it difficult to appreciate accurately the value of this evidence while being consistent. But this mental bind can be broken if one recognizes the failure of the argument for a high antecedent probability that the Gospel authors used fictionalizing literary devices. Someone who previously accepted these literary devices can thus re-evaluate, take seriously the possibility of artless evangelists, and give due appreciation to the evidence for the literal historicity of the Gospels without epistemic inconsistency.

2. How did John the Baptist know that Jesus was the Son of God?

While virtually any undesigned coincidence or incidental external confirmation could be called into question or overlooked by applying the methods of the literary device theorists, this possibility is not just hypothetical. There are actual cases where a literary device theorist has overlooked an undesigned coincidence by his focus on a redactive thesis.

One of the undesigned coincidences discussed in *Hidden in Plain View* concerns John the Baptist's statement that he bore record that Jesus was the Son of God when he saw the Spirit descend on him like a dove. As I wrote there, there is a gap in the description of John the Baptist's testimony:

> John the Baptist as quoted in John is explicit: He discovered who Jesus was at the time of his baptism because of a combination of factors—an interior revelation to himself from God and the visible sign of the Spirit descending like a dove. So far, so clear.
>
> Those of us who are familiar with the baptismal accounts in Matthew, Mark, and Luke are apt to overlook, however, what John the Baptist leaves *unexplained* in this account of the baptism. He does not say why he bore witness that Jesus is the Son of God. There is no statement here that John the Baptist received a revelation that the one he was waiting for was the Son of God....John the Baptist seems to be referring to some further knowledge that he gained at the time of the baptism from something specific that occurred then. He says that he has "seen and borne witness that this is the Son of God." But why would the sight of the Spirit descending like a dove tell him that? What he recounts as a personal revelation is that the person on whom the Spirit descends is the one who will baptize with the Holy Spirit. Nothing about being the Son of God.
>
> The answer is found in a well-known detail of the baptism of Jesus, but one that is not told in the Gospel of John. Here it is from Matthew:
>
> > And when Jesus was baptized, immediately he went up from the water, and behold, the heavens were opened to him, and he saw the Spirit of God descending like a dove and coming to rest on him; and behold, a voice from heaven said, "This is my beloved Son, with whom I am well pleased." (Matt 3.16–17)
>
> Mark 1.11 and Luke 3.22 are similar. Now John's words are explained: John the Baptist and all who witnessed the scene at the baptism had reason to think that Jesus was the Son of God because a voice from heaven *said* that he was the Son of God. If we take it that the events recounted in the other Gospels actually occurred, this explains the words of John the Baptist in the Gospel of John.[14]

I further noted in *Hidden in Plain View* the rather remarkable fact, especially in such a theological Gospel as John's, that the voice from heaven is entirely omitted. If we are merely thinking in terms of John's desire to teach theological truth, this is

---

[14] McGrew, *Hidden in Plain View*, pp. 35–37.

striking. If John the evangelist invented the words of John the Baptist, inspired by the earlier accounts, why did he not include the voice from heaven and thus make his account more complete? It would have taken only a single sentence in John the Baptist's mouth. Something like, "And I heard the mighty voice from heaven that said, 'This is my beloved Son.'" If John were putting words into John the Baptist's mouth, why would he leave that out? The obvious answer is that it is *just wrong* to think that John put words into people's mouths for theological reasons. John the evangelist doesn't have John the Baptist mention the voice because, on this particular occasion when recalling Jesus' baptism, John the Baptist didn't mention the voice. At the same time, John the Baptist's reference to seeing and bearing record that Jesus was the Son of God is well explained by the combination of his seeing the dove-like form and his hearing the voice from heaven. What he saw fit together with the information he received from the Father's voice. But such simple explanations rarely occur to literary device theorists.

Licona seems to think it fairly plausible that the evangelist put words into John the Baptist's mouth. To begin with, he suggests that John may have invented John the Baptist's self-identification as the voice crying in the wilderness, a reference to Isaiah 40.3. Although Licona acknowledges that it is quite possible that John the Baptist actually said this, he claims that it is "impossible to know" whether John the evangelist transferred the words of Isaiah to the mouth of John the Baptist—in other words, made up that saying of John the Baptist.[15] This is a completely unforced error. There is no contradiction between the Synoptics and John on this point, not even an apparent one. In fact, if John the Baptist called himself the voice of one crying in the wilderness, this may have been in the minds of the Synoptic authors and may have resulted in their quoting the passage with reference to John the Baptist. Yet Licona has such a high prior probability for John the evangelist's fictionalizing activity that he says it is "impossible to know" whether he reported this saying of John the Baptist without historical warrant. (I will discuss this utterly unforced error again in Chapter XIII, section 2, and relate it there to the issue of reliability.)

When it comes to John the Baptist's statement that he bore record that Jesus is the Son of God, Licona sees in John the Baptist's words not a confirmation of the historicity of the Gospel's record, given its question-answer fit with the Synoptic accounts. Rather, he sees a tension.

> In all three Synoptics (Mark 1:11; Matt. 3:17; Luke 3:22b), God's voice testifies that Jesus is his Son. However, in John 1:32–34, there is no mention of a voice

---

[15] Licona, *Why Are There Differences*, p. 121.

from heaven (nor is there a mention of heaven being opened). Instead, John the Baptist says God told him he would provide him with a sign. The Spirit would descend and remain upon the one he had chosen to baptize others with the Holy Spirit. And it is John the Baptist rather than God who directly testified that he saw the sign and testified that Jesus is God's Son. Therefore, in the Synoptics, the voice from heaven directly testifies that Jesus is God's Son, whereas in John, it is John the Baptist.[16]

Though Licona does not say in so many words that there is a contradiction between John and the Synoptic Gospels here, his repeated use of contrastive terminology—"instead," "rather than," "whereas"—strongly implies a tension. The idea appears to be that *either* John the Baptist "directly" testifies that Jesus is God's Son or else God the Father does so, but not both. This sort of invented conflict between the Gospels, so unfortunately typical of New Testament scholarship, obscures the actual explanatory relationship between them. There is no statement in John's Gospel that John the Baptist "directly testifies" that Jesus is the Son *as opposed to* learning from the voice from heaven. Rather, the audible testimony of the Father provides an excellent *explanation* for John's ability to testify to the theological fact that Jesus is the Son of God. But the literary, redactive approach creates such a fog that the theorist does not see the undesigned coincidence between the Gospels.

3. The wicked tenants

In all three Synoptic Gospels, Jesus tells a parable, shortly before his crucifixion, about wicked tenants who beat the owner's servants and kill his son. The three versions contain various minor wording differences, and I do not intend to discuss all of them. These wording differences fall easily within the realms of both moderate, recognizable paraphrase and additive harmonization. For example, in Mark 12.5 Jesus says that the owner sent many other servants, in addition to the three that Jesus has listed in a series. Luke 20.9ff simply records the three servants sent and does not mention the many others. Obviously, Luke does not have to record every word exactly the same as Mark in order to give a fully and equally historical account of the parable.

One difference in particular attracts Licona's attention, and he attributes it to Matthew's redacting Mark to create a dialogue. Here Licona shows a tendency that we will see again in Part Four—a tendency to ignore the possibility that Matthew

---

[16] Ibid., p. 124.

was a witness of these events or that he had some other independent access to the events besides Mark's account. Repeatedly Licona will operate under narrow, redactive constraints. In this approach, the only explanation considered is that Matthew changed Mark's account without independent factual warrant. This limits explanatory options and sometimes even begs the question against normal reportage.

In this case, Licona's tendency to treat Matthew as entirely dependent on Mark concerning this event is further exacerbated by the fact that he thinks, incorrectly, that Matthew would have learned from compositional textbooks to create fictitious dialogues in history—dialogues that never happened in the scenes where they are set. (See Chapter VIII, section 8.) So that is what he hypothesizes immediately:

> In Mark 12:9 and Luke 20:15–16, Jesus asked what the owner of the vineyard would do. He then answered his own question, saying the owner would kill those tenants and give the vineyard to others. However, Matt. 21:41 takes Jesus's statements and creates a dialogue with his interlocutors, adding words for effect: "They said to him, 'He will put those evil men to a miserable death and will rent the vineyard to other tenants who will give to him what he is due at the appointed time!'" In doing so, Matthew transfers the answer from Jesus to the chief priests and Pharisees and adds for effect.[17]

Here Licona combines the idea of creating a dialogue with his broad concept of transferral.

The only alternative theories he contemplates are that the difference "could result from the flexibility allowed within the handing on of oral tradition" or that "only the core of the story was known to one or more of the evangelists who then creatively reconstructed the scene, each differently."[18] The latter of course would mean that *all* of the evangelists invented portions of the scene without historical warrant. Licona prefers the redactive hypothesis that Matthew and Luke altered Mark over the other theories. He does not seriously consider the possibility that more than one Synoptic author had access to independent information about what *actually occurred*.

But as it happens, there is an undesigned coincidence in this parable between Luke and Matthew that supports such independent information. Luke ends the account of the parable with Jesus asking and answering a question about what will happen to the wicked tenants:

---

[17] Ibid., p. 147.
[18] Ibid.

"What, then, will the owner of the vineyard do to them? He will come and destroy these vine-growers and will give the vineyard to others." When they heard it, they said, "May it never be!" (Luke 20.15–16)

Why do the people exclaim, "May it never be"? Remember that at this point in Luke's account, Jesus has given no interpretation of the parable. Moreover, the wicked tenants have been described solely in a negative light. Even if one takes it that the hearers had already gotten Jesus' drift and figured out that this parable was meant to apply to them, it seems a little hasty, almost self-damaging, for them instantly to apply it to themselves, sympathize with the villains of the piece, and express horror at the fate that befalls them. After all, in the story Jesus is telling, the tenants deserve all they get. This is hardly a pacifist society in which the hearers would be upset by the owner's draconian actions. The wicked tenants have killed his son and are receiving their just punishment. Why, then, the haste to identify with the bad guys?

Matthew explains this by showing that Jesus expressly applied the parable to the people of Israel or, at least, to the religious leaders:

"Therefore when the owner of the vineyard comes, what will he do to those vine-growers?" They said to Him, "He will bring those wretches to a wretched end, and will rent out the vineyard to other vine-growers who will pay him the proceeds at the proper seasons." Jesus said to them, "Did you never read in the Scriptures,

'The stone which the builders rejected,
This became the chief corner stone;
This came about from the Lord,
And it is marvelous in our eyes'?

Therefore I say to you, the kingdom of God will be taken away from you and given to a people, producing the fruit of it. And he who falls on this stone will be broken to pieces; but on whomever it falls, it will scatter him like dust." (Matt. 21.40–44)

The very aspect of the text that Licona thinks Matthew may have created—the short back-and-forth between Jesus and some in the crowd—follows a more natural sequence than the portion that is given in Luke. The first reaction of the audience is, as one might expect, to side with the owner of the vineyard and to express support for justice *against* the wicked tenants. But then Jesus turns the tables on them when he interprets the parable, explaining that the kingdom of God will be taken from them and given to a different people. This is shocking and angering. Matthew and Mark indicate that, when the religious rulers knew that Jesus' parable was directed at them, they were all the more determined to seize him (Matt. 21.45–46, Mark 12.12). In Luke we find the horrified exclamation of some in the crowd—"May it never be!"—which is well explained by the additional information contained in Matthew. This exclamation probably occurred in response to what Jesus said about God's taking the kingdom away and giving it to others. Luke may just not have heard that bit of the story, and neither did Mark. But Matthew, having independent access to the circumstances, knew that Jesus made this pointed application.

Once we put on the table the hypothesis that Matthew was not merely redacting Mark but actually knew something of his own about what happened, we gain new light on the passage. Licona, by using only redactive hypotheses involving a "flexible" relationship to truth or "creative reconstruction," does not even consider this explanatory relationship between the passages.

As for the alleged conflict between Jesus' answering his own question and the crowd's answering his question, that is hardly difficult to resolve. Critics typically overlook the possibility that multiple people spoke at once or that people repeated things that each other said, yet this happens all the time in real life. One possibility is that Jesus paused for a moment and that some in the crowd spoke up at approximately the same time that Jesus decided to go ahead and answer his own question. Another possibility is that someone in the crowd spoke up and answered the question approximately as given in Matthew and that Jesus affirmed, "That's right, he'll come and destroy those tenants," or words to that effect, remembered and recorded by Peter as told to Mark. This sort of natural harmonization hardly stretches the bounds of credibility. In fact, it describes quite a common interactive teaching situation.

There remains some ambiguity about the precise *order* of what Jesus said. Did he quote Psalm 118 about the stone that the builders rejected before or after the people said, "May it never be"? Luke quotes these words of Jesus after the people's exclamation (Luke 20.17–18), whereas, if Jesus combined that citation with his explicit interpretation of the parable as in Matthew, it would seem more likely that the exclamation came after the reference to the Psalm. But this ambiguity concerning exact order is entirely consonant with normal memory variation among truthful witnesses giving recognizable paraphrases of what Jesus said on that occasion.

Most importantly, these variations and the undesigned coincidence are well explained by there being more than one witness reporting the event, giving us more information than we would have from just one. Literary device theorists make it unnecessarily difficult for themselves to see this evidence.

4. The foot washing and the dispute

In *Hidden in Plain View*, I pointed out that there are two undesigned coincidences connecting the foot washing on the night in which Jesus was betrayed (the Last Supper) with a dispute among the disciples. This sometimes happens between two Gospels: There will be an undesigned coincidence in which Gospel A explains Gospel B and, in the same passage, a coincidence in which Gospel B explains Gospel A. These cases are particularly satisfying.

Here, one coincidence concerns the question of why Jesus washed the disciples' feet on that particular night, as reported in John 13. As I acknowledged in *Hidden in Plain View*, it is possible that Jesus washed the disciples' feet on that night for no special reason except, at most, the thought of his own impending death. Perhaps he simply wanted to teach this lesson about mutual service and humility before his death, as he instituted the Lord's Supper on that same night. Still, one cannot help wondering why he washed their feet and drew the moral from it *just then*. If we could find an explanation in another Gospel, this would be interesting and satisfying. In the case of Philip and Jesus' question before the feeding of the five thousand, we wondered whether there was some specific reason why he asked Philip. Here, too, if the event took place in the real world, the possibility of clearer motivations becomes a live option.

And as it turns out, Luke provides a very interesting candidate for such an explanation, for Luke 22.24ff says that a dispute arose among the disciples on that night about who would be the greatest in Jesus' kingdom. According to John 13, Jesus rose from supper, took off his outer garments, and literally took on the lowliest servant's role. This would be a visible rebuke to the disciples' bickering.[19]

The undesigned coincidence has another side: Not only does Luke 22 mention that the disciples were arguing about who would be the greatest, it also says that Jesus rebuked them with reference to his own servanthood:

And there arose also a dispute among them as to which one of them was regarded to be greatest. And He said to them, "The kings of the Gentiles lord it over them;

---

[19] Richard Bauckham discusses the extremely menial nature of this task. It was so lowly a job, Bauckham says, that if there were servants in a household who were not slaves, the task would devolve upon the slaves as lower members of the household hierarchy. Richard Bauckham, "Did Jesus Wash His Disciples' Feet?" in *Authenticating the Activities of Jesus*, ed. by Bruce D. Chilton and Craig A. Evans (Boston, MA: Brill, 1999), p. 412.

and those who have authority over them are called 'Benefactors.' But it is not this way with you, but the one who is the greatest among you must become like the youngest, and the leader like the servant. For who is greater, the one who reclines at the table or the one who serves? Is it not the one who reclines at the table? But I am among you as the one who serves." (Luke 22.24–27)

This response is interesting for two reasons. First, it provides a second undesigned coincidence with John 13. In what sense is Jesus "among them as the one who serves"? We, who are used to hearing sermons on the servant leadership of Jesus, may not think to ask the question. But Jesus seems to have something quite clear in mind here, and there is no obvious referent in the immediate context in Luke alone. Here Jesus is contrasting the usual status of the one who serves at the table with the one who reclines at the table. (At that time, people reclined at low eating tables rather than sitting on chairs.) And he is saying that he is among them as a servant. Since Jesus apparently *is* reclining at the table with them in Luke, it's odd that he seems to *contrast* himself with the one who reclines at the table.[20] This statement is well explained by the foot washing in John's Gospel, though Luke does not mention the foot washing at all and thus leaves Jesus' statement unexplained.

The second reason that this rebuke is interesting is that the first part of it bears verbal similarities to Jesus' response on an earlier occasion, possibly only about a week or two before, when the disciples were arguing about the same topic. In Mark 10.35ff, we learn that James and John came to Jesus and asked that they might sit on each side of him in his kingdom—places of high status. Matthew 20.20ff adds that their mother was involved in the request and does not mention James and John's initial question to Jesus. I will be discussing the alleged transferral of the request from the mother to James and John in Chapter XIV, section 5. I have already mentioned several times Craig Evans's theory that Matthew simply made up the mother's involvement.[21] Here I want to focus on Jesus' words of rebuke when the other disciples were angry with James and John. This is how Mark records them:

Hearing this, the ten began to feel indignant with James and John. Calling them to Himself, Jesus said to them, "You know that those who are recognized as rul-

---

[20] This way of explaining the oddity in Luke in terms of the appearance that Jesus *is* reclining at table and the contrast Jesus seems to be drawing between himself and one who reclines at the table came to my attention from J. Wesley Price, "Incidental Coherence in the Gospels," *Muse Accordingly*, November 19, 2018, https://youtu.be/vHz6Tadvk1s?t=1063.

[21] Craig A. Evans, *Matthew* (New Cambridge Bible Commentary) (Cambridge: Cambridge University Press, 2012), p. 353.

ers of the Gentiles lord it over them; and their great men exercise authority over them. But it is not this way among you, but whoever wishes to become great among you shall be your servant; and whoever wishes to be first among you shall be slave of all. For even the Son of Man did not come to be served, but to serve, and to give His life a ransom for many." (Mark 10.41–45)

Undeniably the first part of this is quite similar to the first part what Jesus says in Luke 22. But the latter part is different, for in Mark Jesus emphasizes his death as his way of serving, whereas in Luke he talks about reclining at the table (which fits with the supper context) and does not otherwise specify in what sense he is among them as the one who serves.

The undesigned coincidence between Luke and John concerning the foot washing, together with the smooth movement in Jesus' words in Luke from discussing the kings of the Gentiles to his own role as a servant, is evidence that Jesus in fact said something recognizably like what Luke 22 records on the night of the Last Supper. Both of these factors locate Jesus' words in Luke quite firmly in the actual context of the Last Supper. The undesigned coincidence does not look like something Luke did to make Jesus appear to say it that night (contrary to fact), since Luke makes no mention of the foot washing and leaves Jesus' words about being among them as one who serves unexplained.

It would be hyper-subtle for Luke to put those words into Jesus' mouth in his narrative to allude to the foot washing when the connection might be so easily overlooked. The 19th-century English clergyman J. S. Howson emphasizes this important point: "An intentional and contrived coincidence must be of such a character as to *strike* the reader. Otherwise it fails of its purpose. If it was kept latent for the intelligent…critics of a later age to find out, it has not attained the end for which it was meant at the time of its contrivance."[22] This point is extremely important to bear in mind when considering the undesigned appearance of a coincidence; it is a point that New Testament critics, including literary device theorists, rarely think of.

Unsurprisingly, when Licona discusses these passages, he does not see the undesigned coincidences at all. He does not even consider them. Instead, he strongly suggests that Luke has non-factually transferred the entire dispute among the disciples and Jesus' response to the context of the Last Supper, where it did not occur:

---

[22] Paley, *Horae Paulinae*, p. 25 n. 2.

Luke omits the request of James and John. However, he appears to have taken Jesus's statement pertaining to Gentile rulers lording it over others, that the disciples are rather to exercise humble servant leadership, and that he has set the example by coming to serve and give his life as a ransom for many, and has situated it in the first occasion described above, although that occasion occurs in a different context (Last Supper), perhaps a week later than we find in Mark // Matthew. Of course, it is possible that Jesus addressed a similar dispute pertaining to which of the disciples was the greatest on multiple occasions. However, there are enough verbal similarities between Jesus's answer in Mark and Luke to suggest Jesus's reply could derive from the same tradition....The final portion of Jesus's logion preserved by Luke may also suggest familiarity with Jesus's act of foot washing, which John also narrates during the Last Supper (John 13:3–16).[23]

The reference both to Luke's "preserving" a "logion" of Jesus—namely, "I am among you as the one who serves"—and to a reflection of *Luke's familiarity* with the foot washing is merely confusing. Why say that this "suggests familiarity with Jesus's act of foot washing" if the saying is authentic? Luke's recording it suggests familiarity with what Jesus actually *said* on that night, *regardless* of whether Luke knew about Jesus' act of foot washing. The connection with the foot washing lies in the meaning of the words, if they were actually uttered on that night. That is to say, the connection with Jesus' act of washing the disciples' feet lies in reality, not in Luke's mind.

When Licona says that "it appears" that a Gospel author has done something, this is fairly definite in his rhetoric. He does not even bother to say here merely that "perhaps" Luke moved the dispute and Jesus' response, though as I have discussed before, even those statements indicate a certain evaluation of plausibility on the part of the scholar. Here he says that it appears that Luke *has* invented by "situating" Jesus' words and the dispute in a different context. Licona even goes so far as to draw a little moral for his reader:

> If Mark is Luke's source for this tradition, Luke's redaction of and displacement of the tradition to a different context gives us an idea of the extent of Luke's flexibility with the tradition.[24]

Instead, it tells us something about the degree of flexibility in relation to truth that Licona *attributes* to Luke. This, once again, illustrates the incompatibility between literary device views and the robust historical reliability of the Gospels.

---

[23] Licona, *Why Are There Differences*, pp. 141–142.

[24] Ibid., p. 141.

Licona's theories not only overlook but actually would require us to *dismiss* any evidential value in the two undesigned coincidences between Luke and John concerning the foot washing. For according to Licona's theory, the dispute didn't take place on that night. Luke moved it there from a different context. In that case, the dispute cannot be the real explanation for the foot washing. Moreover, if Jesus didn't utter the rebuke to his disciples ending with "I am among you as the one who serves" on that night, then that utterance *cannot have really referred*, as uttered by Jesus, to his act of foot washing as *recently witnessed* by his disciples. The apparent undesigned coincidences must, on Licona's theory, be misleading when they seem to support the historicity of Jesus' words and the dispute on that night. The appearance must be a result of mere coincidence and of Luke's hyper-subtle "displacement." Jesus just happened to wash their feet that night; there was no real connection to a dispute. Luke also made it appear that Jesus *may* have been referring to the foot washing by his redaction of Jesus' words. But inexplicably, Luke didn't narrate the foot washing in order to complete the allusion.

The contrast between the undesigned coincidences in these passages and Licona's redactive theories provides a clear instance of the incompatibility between the literary device approach and the picture of the artless author that is supported by undesigned coincidences. It also illustrates the way in which the blinkered, hasty assumptions of anti-realistic redactive criticism cause scholars to overlook genuine evidence for the historicity of the Gospels.

5. The women from Galilee

The coincidence I will be describing here is of a slightly different type from the others. Here, the incidental interlocking that points to truth takes the form not of a question and answer but of a consistent picture supported by casual details in multiple documents. The picture looks like this: There was a group of women who followed Jesus from Galilee and who were present both at the cross and at the empty tomb. These included Mary Magdalene, Joanna, another woman named Mary, and others. Their names are spread across several different Gospels. The angel at the tomb reminded this group of women of what Jesus had said to them while he was in Galilee *because* they really had been with Jesus in Galilee.

But this picture does not emerge all at once. It is not described in any one place in any one Gospel. Rather, it emerges in a natural way when we put together different passages, some in the same Gospel and some in different Gospels. We could consider these passages in any order, but an interesting way to look at them is to start with the words of the angel at the tomb as found in Luke:

> While they were perplexed about this, behold, two men suddenly stood near them in dazzling clothing; and as the women were terrified and bowed their faces to the ground, the men said to them, "Why do you seek the living One among the dead? He is not here, but He has risen. Remember how He spoke to you while He was still in Galilee, saying that the Son of Man must be delivered into the hands of sinful men, and be crucified, and the third day rise again." And they remembered His words … (Luke 24.4–8a)

Luke has previously described these women as "the women who had come with him out of Galilee," who were present at the crucifixion (Luke 23.49) and at the burial (Luke 23.55). In those passages he did not name any of them, though he will do so a bit later in Luke 24. What is interesting is that the angel seems to know that these very women to whom he is speaking are from Galilee and can be expected to remember what Jesus said to them while he was in Galilee, predicting his own death and resurrection. Luke records that they actually do remember Jesus' prediction when reminded by the angel.

Richard Bauckham notes that the angel seems to assume that the women were present when Jesus told his disciples in Galilee what was going to happen to him, as in Luke 9.22, 43, where Jesus predicts both his death and his resurrection.[25]

So far, this shows that this passage in Luke presents a consistent picture with other passages in Luke's passion narrative. But this picture can be confirmed when we look at a completely unrelated passage in Luke's Gospel:

> After this, Jesus traveled about from one town and village to another, proclaiming the good news of the kingdom of God. The Twelve were with him, and also some women who had been cured of evil spirits and diseases: Mary (called Magdalene) from whom seven demons had come out; Joanna the wife of Chuza, the manager of Herod's household; Susanna; and many others. These women were helping to support them out of their own means. (Luke 8.1–3)

Luke here names Mary Magdalene, Joanna, and Susanna, while stressing that there were "many others" in the group.

This short mention of the women in Luke 8 is *itself* confirmed in an entirely independent way by its beautiful fit with unique information in Matthew 14.2.

---

[25] Richard Bauckham, *Jesus and the Eyewitnesses: The Gospels as Eyewitness Testimony*, 2nd ed. (Grand Rapids, MI: Eerdmans, 2017), p. 130.

When a superstitious Herod Antipas was musing on who Jesus might be and worrying that he might be the resurrected John the Baptist (whom Herod had executed), he spoke "to his servants." The obvious question, "How could Matthew have known what Herod was saying to his servants?" is answered by the appearance, in a completely different context in Luke 8 (in the list just quoted), of Joanna, the wife of Chuza, Herod's household manager. This particularly lovely undesigned coincidence between Matthew and Luke provides a plausible source for Matthew's information about Herod's thoughts. That is, it does so if we do not cut ourselves off from that confirmation by taking it as highly likely that Matthew simply made up the detail that Herod was speaking "to his servants" to make his story more interesting. The assumption that Matthew was likely to fabricate details would make it more difficult to notice that this small detail is realistically explained by an unrelated passage in Luke.

So Luke's mention that there was a group of women who had been with Jesus in Galilee at the crucifixion and empty tomb fits with his own earlier mention of such a group of women, but it does so in an off-hand way. Luke is very casual about this connection. It does not appear to be something Luke is trying to make deliberately. When he finally does get around to naming the women who found the tomb empty, he does *not* mention Susanna (though she is in the list of Galilean women in Chapter 8) and does mention Mary the mother of James (though she is not in the list in Chapter 8):

> Now they were Mary Magdalene and Joanna and Mary the mother of James; also the other women with them were telling these things to the apostles. (Luke 24.10)

This does not look like a contrived, literary attempt on Luke's part to connect the list of resurrection witnesses here with his own list earlier in his own Gospel. If it were, one would expect him to give the same names rather than a set of names that only partially overlaps. Bauckham also notices the absence of Susanna from the list of witnesses to the empty tomb in Luke 24 and suggests that perhaps Luke did not know whether she was present on Easter.[26] This, of course, is a real-world suggestion; Luke intends his account of the events on Easter morning as a report of what really happened, making him scrupulous about not including the name of a witness if he did not have evidence that she was really there. It also enables us to see the connection *within* Luke's Gospel between the reference to the women from Galilee in Chapter 8 and Chapter 24 as a result of reality rather than literary contrivance.

---

[26] Ibid., p. 50.

Mark and Matthew also mention the women from Galilee at the cross. Mark says,

> There were also some women looking on from a distance, among whom were Mary Magdalene, and Mary the mother of James the Less and Joses, and Salome. When He was in Galilee, they used to follow Him and minister to Him; and there were many other women who came up with Him to Jerusalem. (Mark 15.40–41)

Notice that Mark's list here contains the names Salome and Mary the mother of James, which do not occur in Luke 8. Luke never mentions Salome at all and mentions Mary the mother of James in connection with the resurrection, but not earlier. Luke seems to know something of his own about the women who followed Jesus from Galilee, including (in Luke 8) Joanna the wife of Chuza and Susanna, unmentioned by Mark and Matthew at all. In Luke 24, he connects Joanna with the group of women who told the disciples about the message of the angel. So Luke is not simply following Mark, but Mark provides apparently independent confirmation for the existence of this group of women who ministered to Jesus in Galilee and followed him from there. What is more, Mark's confirmation that this group of women, who later came to the tomb, were from Galilee and had known Jesus there fits quite well with Luke's unique mention of the words of the angel to the women, telling them to remember what Jesus said to them while he was in Galilee. If they really were with him in Galilee, they could have had opportunity to hear his predictions of his death in that region.

But now let us see how literary device approaches to the resurrection accounts would undermine the undesigned coincidence. Licona insists that Luke compresses (in the dyschronological sense) the events after Jesus' resurrection to make it appear that they all occurred on a single day.[27] Since this makes it impossible for the disciples to travel to Galilee and meet Jesus (the walk to Galilee from Jerusalem would take too long), Licona further claims that Luke deliberately moved a Galilee appearance of Jesus geographically to Jerusalem in order to allow everything to happen on a single day.[28] This theory, in turn, leads him to argue that Luke had to remove the angel's instruction in Mark 16.7 to meet Jesus in Galilee after the resurrection. Luke therefore "morphed" the angel's mention of Galilee from an instruction to *meet* Jesus in Galilee into a reference

---

[27] Licona, *Why Are There Differences*, pp. 177, 180. Licona, *The Resurrection of Jesus: A New Historiographical Approach* (Downer's Grover: IVP Academic, 2010), p. 596, n. 449

[28] Bart Ehrman vs. Michael Licona, "Are the Gospels Historically Reliable," Kennesaw State University, February 21, 2018, minute 1:46:20, https://youtu.be/qP7RrCfDkO4?t=1h46m20s.

to what Jesus *previously said* in Galilee. In other words, the angel didn't really say to the women what Luke records.

Licona sets up an alleged tension between Mark's and Luke's mentions of Galilee in the angel's words:

> In Luke, Galilee is mentioned as the place where Jesus had predicted his betrayal, crucifixion, and resurrection, whereas it is where the disciples are to go promptly in Mark and Matthew.[29]

At the same time, he rejects "conflating" (by which he means combining) the different accounts of what the angel said by additive harmonization, expressly referring to the entirely plausible example of such a combination carried out by John Wenham in his harmony of the resurrection narratives.[30] Licona's argument against the angel's having said everything found in both accounts is quite weak:

> It would seem odd, however, that Luke or his source would report only that which Mark and Matthew have omitted, since there is little overlap between them.[31]

Actually, that doesn't seem odd at all. The statement by the angel recorded in Matthew and Mark and the statement in Luke are quite brief, taking only a few seconds to say. They overlap at precisely the obvious point—the assurance that Jesus' body is not there, for he is risen. This is exactly the sort of variation that one does find among different witnesses, whose accounts often supplement one another.[32] It is especially noteworthy here that Luke is the only Gospel to mention Joanna at all, in any location, so it is not implausible that Joanna was an important source for Luke. If the words of the angel reported in Luke were the ones that happened to strike Joanna, and especially if she wanted to add information that Luke had not received from others, this is exactly what we would find.

Licona then presses further the claim that the differences concerning the words of the angel about Galilee are part of a "larger picture" of Luke's redaction:

> It is noteworthy that while in Mark // Matthew the disciples are instructed to go to Galilee where they will see Jesus, in Luke, Galilee is mentioned only as the

---

[29] Licona, *Why Are There Differences*, p. 175.

[30] Ibid., pp. 175, 255 n. 133. Contrast John Wenham, *Easter Enigma: Are the Resurrection Accounts in Conflict* (Eugene, OR: Wipf and Stock, 1992), p. 88.

[31] Licona, *Why Are There Differences*, p. 175.

[32] Sometimes they even supplement deliberately, if they realize that another witness has not mentioned something. See J. Warner Wallace, *Cold-Case Christianity: A Homicide Detective Investigates the Claims of the Gospels* (Colorado Springs, CO: David C. Cook), pp. 80–84.

location where Jesus had predicted his betrayal, crucifixion, and resurrection. *This is not as insignificant as it may appear at first look but is only one element of a larger picture involving redaction in the Synoptics.* As we observed above, Luke compresses all of the appearances and the ascension to have occurred on the same day as Jesus's resurrection. So there is no time to have the disciples go to Galilee. Thus, Luke may have redacted the message of the angel in Mark // Matthew by eliminating a trip to Galilee.[33]

The implication is that the reference to what Jesus said in Galilee in Luke 24.6, found in the angel's mouth, is Luke's *redaction* of the *completely different* mention of Galilee by the angel in Mark, where Galilee is the place where Jesus will be meeting his disciples. Instead of Luke's having information that this is what the angel *really said* to the women, Licona treats the difference in the angel's message as a result of Luke's partially fictional redaction of Mark. The idea, apparently, is that Luke decided to have the angel say *something or other* about Galilee, but to change the angel's message to make it consistent with his own intention to eliminate the trip to Galilee and have all of Jesus' post-resurrection appearances occur on Easter Day.[34]

These theories blind Licona to the possibility that these are confirmed as historical words of the angel. While Licona refers briefly to the possibility that Mark and Luke had different sources for the words of the angel, his rejection in the very same context of *putting together* the contents of the angel's message means that he actually does not think that the information in such varying sources should be historically combined into a single, coherent account of what the angel said.[35] And his suggestion that Luke redacted the angel's words to eliminate the reference to a meeting in Galilee, in order to accommodate his intended geographical alteration, means that he views the angel's words about Galilee in Luke with historical suspicion. Once again, the literary device approach blocks the appreciation of real evidence for historicity.

---

[33] Licona, *Why Are There Differences*, p. 180. Emphasis added.

[34] Licona suggests quite a few fictionalizing changes in the resurrection accounts, several of which I will discuss in Chapter XVI. When it comes to changing the words and messages of those involved in the resurrection, Licona also suggests that John invented Jesus' mention of the ascension to Mary Magdalene (John 20.17) in order to "weave mention" of the ascension into his Easter narrative, since he had decided not to narrate the ascension (*Why Are There Differences*, p. 181). Licona is therefore not particularly hesitant to suggest that the Gospel authors simply made up parts of what was said to the women at the time of the resurrection.

[35] Ibid., pp. 174–175.

6. The evidence of Archelaus

The next several sections concern places where incidental *external* confirmations of the Gospels' historical accuracy support the historical intention of the authors. If the fictionalization theories were true, we should not expect to find details of these incidents confirmed. Yet we find that they fit very well with incidental details of culture and history known from extra-biblical sources. This, in turn, disconfirms fictionalization.

The first of these examples is about Jesus' infancy. Matthew records that Joseph and Mary returned with the child Jesus from Egypt after the death of Herod the Great. This occurred (we know independently) in 4 B.C. According to Matthew, when Joseph heard that Archelaus had taken Herod the Great's place in Judea, he settled with his family in Galilee instead:

> But when Herod died, behold, an angel of the Lord appeared in a dream to Joseph in Egypt, and said, "Get up, take the Child and His mother, and go into the land of Israel; for those who sought the Child's life are dead." So Joseph got up, took the Child and His mother, and came into the land of Israel. But when he heard that Archelaus was reigning over Judea in place of his father Herod, he was afraid to go there. Then after being warned by God in a dream, he left for the regions of Galilee, and came and lived in a city called Nazareth. (Matt. 2.19–23)

If one didn't know much more about the background, one might assume that Galilee was better than Judea because someone other than a son of Herod the Great was ruling in Galilee. But that is not the case. Herod Antipas, also a son of Herod the Great, received the rule of Galilee and Perea, and this is why he is referred to as "Herod." He ruled Galilee for the rest of Jesus' life e.g., Luke 23.7–15). So what was so especially worrisome about Archelaus that Joseph, even prior to receiving information in a dream, was afraid to go to Judea after hearing that Archelaus was in charge there?

That information comes to us from Josephus, who records a dramatic series of events before and after the death of Herod the Great. Herod the Great ordered some men put to death by being burned alive shortly before his own death, because they had cut down an image of an eagle in the Temple. Just after his death, some supporters of those he had executed began mourning loudly in the Temple. Archelaus had been promised the rule of Judea after Herod's death, though it had not yet been officially confirmed by Caesar Augustus, and he assumed that it was his job to keep order in the Temple precincts. He sent Roman soldiers to quiet the crowds who were loudly bewailing the deaths of those executed by Herod the Great, but matters escalated, and the people eventually stoned some of the soldiers to death. The crowd was especially large because it was the time of Passover. At this point, Archelaus decided to put down decisively what he saw as an incipient rebellion. He sent a much larger army, including cavalry, into Jerusalem and even into the Temple precincts. They killed three thousand Jews in Jerusalem and scattered more. Archelaus' heralds went abroad telling the people that Passover was canceled and that they were to go home immediately.[36] This extreme reaction brought Archelaus into danger of not being confirmed as tetrarch of Judea at all (because he had allegedly treated the Jews too harshly and presumed too far on the promise of ruling Judea), but he journeyed to Rome and convinced Caesar Augustus to give him the position.

It is quite plausible that Joseph, returning from Egypt to Bethlehem, heard a frightening story of bloodshed from some of the people fleeing from Jerusalem just after Passover time. Having escaped one homicidal madman who reacted with mass violence to a perceived threat to his authority, Joseph was naturally reluctant to bring his child, prophesied to be the "king of the Jews," to live under the rule of another. Since Mary herself was from Galilee (Luke 1.26) and since he and Mary had been there before traveling to his ancestral town of Bethlehem at the time of Jesus' birth, Joseph decided to go back to Nazareth instead. (The fact that Joseph probably reasoned this way does not, of course, preclude his receiving a warning in a dream as well.) This all fits together well; the confirmation from outside information about Archelaus is evidentially satisfying.

But if one believes that the Gospel authors felt free to craft or alter details, why think that Joseph really was afraid to settle in Judea when he heard of Archelaus? Perhaps Matthew just made that up to explain how Jesus was born in Bethlehem (as prophesied) but ended up growing up in Galilee. But on the other hand, if that detail were invented, it would be surprising to find that it fits so well with what we know independently about Archelaus.

In response to challenges to the infancy narratives from skeptical scholar Bart Ehrman, Licona has declared that the infancy narratives in Matthew and Luke "include the most profound and difficult differences in the Gospels." He implies that there is a major problem with them, that they are extremely difficult to harmonize, and says that he does not "know what's going on" with them. He says that "one can provide some plausible solutions" to the alleged problem but that

---

[36] Josephus, *Jewish War*, Book II, chapter 1.

they are "speculative." At that point Licona suggests, "Let's just speculate for a moment" and proceeds to put forward the following:

> Matthew and Luke both agree that a Jewish virgin named Mary who was engaged to a Jewish man named Joseph gave birth to Jesus in Bethlehem. The early Christians all knew this much. However, little else was remembered about this event. So, Matthew and Luke added details to their account to create a more interesting narrative of Jesus's birth, a type of *midrash*.[37]

This extreme suggestion is all that Licona offers in response to Ehrman's attacks on the infancy narratives. He also refers to the overlap between the accounts as the "core" of the story and to the rest, not attested by both accounts, as "details." This therefore amounts to suggesting the fictional creation of all of the non-overlapping material in Luke's and Matthew's narratives, since on this theory only the overlapping material (Jesus' being born to a virgin espoused to Joseph, etc.) and "little else" was known at the time that the evangelists wrote.

Without discussing all of the challenges that have been brought against the infancy narratives, I will say here only that Licona's evaluation of their differences is vastly exaggerated. With only one exception, the differences between the infancy narratives of Matthew and Luke do not even amount to apparent discrepancies. The accounts have much non-overlapping content, but there is not even an apparent discrepancy between, e.g., the coming of the Magi and the coming of the shepherds. It is just that Luke narrates the latter and Matthew the former. There is not even an apparent discrepancy in the mere silence of Matthew about the journey from Nazareth to Bethlehem, though Ehrman tries artificially to create one.[38] The

---

[37] Michael Licona, "Licona Responds to Ehrman on New Testament Reliability," 2016, https://thebestschools.org/special/ehrman-licona-dialogue-reliability-new-testament/licona-detailed-response/. As N.T. Wright has pointed out, the use of the term "midrash" to describe wholesale invention of stories about recent past events is an abuse of the term. N.T. Wright, *Who Was Jesus* (Grand Rapids: Eerdmans, 1992), p. 95. Robert Gundry suggested that Matthew's infancy narrative was an elaborate "midrash" in this same sense and that the slaughter of the innocents and other events unique to Matthew were invented. For example, Gundry suggests that the slaughter of the innocents is a "midrash" on the sacrifice of the turtledoves recorded in Luke. Gundry, however, is suggesting that Luke's infancy narrative represents a portion of an "expanded Q" that was at least presumptively historical. Gundry applies the claim of free invention only to Matthew's Gospel. The point concerning Archelaus would thus apply to Gundry as well, but it is interesting that Licona's speculation extends the suggestion of "midrash" (meaning complete invention) to Luke. Robert H. Gundry, *Matthew: A Commentary on His Literary and Theological Art* (Grand Rapids, MI: Eerdmans, 1982), pp. 26–60.

[38] Bart Ehrman, "Bethlehem and Nazareth in Luke: Where Was Jesus Really Born?" March 6, 2015, https://ehrmanblog.org/bethlehem-and-nazareth-in-luke-where-was-jesus-really-born/. Ehrman here claims falsely that Bethlehem was Joseph and Mary's "home town" *according to Matthew.*

only thing that amounts even to an *apparent* discrepancy between the two accounts is Luke's writing in a way that can be plausibly interpreted to mean that Joseph and Mary went immediately back to Nazareth after Mary's purification rites were completed (Luke 2.39). But even if the wording of this verse indicates that Luke was unaware of the flight to Egypt and events surrounding it, such as the slaughter of the innocents, Luke's account does not explicitly say that they returned *immediately* to Nazareth, so it is not obvious that there is, strictly speaking, an error in Luke's account at this point. In any event, *one single apparent discrepancy* indicating (plausibly) simple lack of information on the part of one of the evangelists is a far cry from the "profound and difficult" differences alleged by Licona.[39]

If the differences between the infancy narratives are so "profound and difficult" that the only plausible solution one can think of involves radical fictionalization by both Luke and Matthew, then of course one will not expect to find the details of the return from the flight to Egypt to be confirmed. Indeed, the *entire flight to Egypt*, on this hypothesis, is a "detail" vis-à-vis the so-called "core" which is just the overlap between Luke and Matthew. If the flight to Egypt did not occur at all, then of course the return from Egypt didn't occur, and Joseph's fears about Archelaus when deciding where to settle did not occur. If Joseph and Mary (for example) returned immediately to Nazareth after the purification in the Temple, prior to the death of Herod the Great, Joseph did not need to think about Archelaus when deciding where they should live.

He says that they were "originally from Bethlehem" and went to live in Nazareth only later, after Jesus' birth. He is not referring to the idea that Bethlehem was the ancestral home of Joseph, which is not mentioned in Matthew. Rather, he is using Matthew's mere silence about the journey from Bethlehem to Nazareth just before Jesus' birth (discussed by Luke) to justify the claim that Matthew and Luke contradict each other concerning when Mary and Joseph first lived in Nazareth. This is an entirely artificial "contradiction."

[39] Licona, *Why Are There Differences*, pp. 262–263 n. 5, further implies some serious problem with the infancy narratives by quoting (out of context) a statement by Jonathan Pennington that we would not know that the two stories referred to the same person if we read them without the name of the same child attached to them. But see Jonathan T. Pennington, *Reading the Gospels Wisely: A Narrative and Theological Introduction* (Grand Rapids, MI: Baker Academic, 2012), p. 56. In context, Pennington is merely setting up an alleged problem with the infancy narratives for discussion; a few pages later he makes it clear that he considers the problems to be exaggerated and thinks that "reasoned harmonization" between the narratives is quite possible. "The stories they tell about Jesus' early earthly days entail different perspectives on the events but are not contradictory," p. 61. The method of asking whether one would know that the same person were in view if one attached different names to different accounts is an extremely poor way of judging historicity. One can easily use this method to create "contradictions" between real aspects of the same person's life. See Lydia McGrew, "The Extreme Improbability of One's Own Life," *What's Wrong With the World*, June 27, 2016, http://whatswrongwiththeworld. net/2016/06/the_extreme_improbability_of_o.html.

But the return from Egypt *is* confirmed in a fashion akin to an undesigned coincidence with external information. Matthew mentions Joseph's fears about Archelaus very much in passing. He does not say why Joseph thought it better to take his family to live under the rule of Antipas than that of Archelaus. He makes no mention of anything specific that was worrisome about Archelaus. Moreover, the mention of Archelaus is "extra," from a theological and narrative point of view, since Matthew also says that Joseph was warned at that time in a dream. The dream could have accomplished the goal of taking Mary and Joseph back to Nazareth, if Matthew invented this part of the story. Why mention Archelaus at all? The simplest explanation is that it is *true* that Joseph was afraid of Archelaus (probably because he heard of his recent bloodshed) and that Matthew in some manner learned about this aspect of Joseph's thoughts.

Licona is explicit that he is not absolutely affirming his speculation. He says, "I'm not saying this is what Matthew and Luke did. I don't know what's going on with the infancy narratives."[40] But, once again, it is the only suggestion he makes, after saying that he "think[s] one can provide some plausible solutions" to the allegedly hard problem of the infancy narrative difficulties. This so-called solution is a non-starter for multiple reasons. We have every reason to think that Matthew and Luke would not have considered themselves free to invent whole incidents about the birth of Jesus. The suggestion also runs counter to the subtle and interesting external confirmation of Matthew's narrative of the return from Egypt. But fictionalizing device theories take no account of such evidence and indeed lead the theorist to bypass that evidence.

6. The Temple cleansing and forty-six years

I have already discussed the Temple cleansing, arguing in Chapter IV, section 3, that there is nothing particularly implausible about Jesus' having carried out this type of protest on two different occasions. (See further discussion in Chapter XIV, section 2.) Several evangelical New Testament scholars believe that John dyschronologically moved the Temple cleansing to the beginning of Jesus' ministry, though in reality it occurred only once—during Passion Week, as narrated in the Synoptic Gospels.[41] Here I want to note a particular detail in John's account

---

[40] Michael Licona, "Licona Responds to Ehrman on New Testament Reliability."

[41] William Lane Craig, "Biblical Inerrancy," *Reasonable Faith*, December 24, 2014, https://www.reasonablefaith.org/podcasts/defenders-podcast-series-3/s3-doctrine-of-revelation/doctrine-of-revelation-part-7/; William Lane Craig, "An Objection to the Minimal Facts Argument," *Reasonable Faith*, May 6, 2018, https://www.reasonablefaith.org/media/reasonable-faith-podcast/an-objec-

that, taken together with external information and also with information from Luke, confirms the historicity of a Temple cleansing early in Jesus' ministry.

After Jesus cleanses the Temple as recorded in John, the indignant leaders ask him what authority he has to do such a thing. Jesus replies cryptically, "Destroy this Temple, and in three days I will raise it up." (John 2.18–19) The leaders, interpreting him literally, reply, "It took forty-six years to build this Temple, and will you raise it in three days?" The narrator explains that Jesus was speaking of his body.[42, 43] The interesting and seemingly random phrase is the reference to forty-six years.

Historically, this reference to forty-six years points quite strongly to the *beginning* of Jesus' ministry. A location in time at the Passover of the year A.D. 28 is the most common scholarly estimate based on this statement by the Jewish leaders, calculating from the time when Josephus records that Herod began to rebuild the Temple, probably some time between 20 and 19 B.C.[44] If one counts parts of years as years (e.g., parts of the years of Herod's reign or parts of the Jewish year), the reference to forty-six years would place the conversation even earlier.

The reference to forty-six years also fits well with Luke's statement that John the Baptist came baptizing "in the fifteenth year of the reign of Tiberius Caesar" (Luke 3.1). There are two different ways of estimating this year referred to in Luke, depending upon whether or not one accepts a co-regency of approximately two years between Tiberius and Caesar Augustus. Accepting a co-regency puts

---

tion-to-the-minimal-facts-argument/; Craig Keener, *The Gospel of John: A Commentary* (Grand Rapids, MI: Baker Academic, 2003), pp. 518–519; Licona, *Why Are There Differences*, p. 195.

[42] This is one of several places in the Gospel of John where the narrator inserts his own interpretations into the narrative, but he is careful to do so *in his own voice*, making it clear that this is his own gloss on what Jesus said. If the authors (especially John) were as ready as the literary device theorists claim to put their own words into Jesus' mouth, why is John so scrupulous in making this distinction?

[43] In *Hidden in Plain View* (pp. 70–73) I discuss an undesigned coincidence involving this comment by Jesus. By the time of Jesus' trial before the high priest recorded in the Synoptic Gospels, this saying had become garbled and was treated as a threat to destroy the Temple and raise it in three days. Such a confusion makes more sense if Jesus' comment really occurred several years earlier rather than only a few days before his arrest. Craig Blomberg notes that this point tends to confirm the early Temple cleansing. Craig Blomberg, *The Historical Reliability of John's Gospel* (Downers Grove, IL: Intervarsity Press, 2001), p. 89.

[44] See Duane W. Roller, *The Building Program of Herod the Great* (Berkeley, CA: University of California Press, 1998), p. 67, which estimates that Herod began building the Temple in late 20 B.C. or early 19 B.C. See also John F. McHugh, *John 1–4: A Critical and Exegetical Commentary* (London: T & T Clark, 2009), p. 208; Charles Ellicott, *Commentary for English Readers, in loc.* at John 2.20; William Sanday, *The Authorship and Historical Character of the Fourth Gospel* (London: Macmillan & Co., 1872), pp. 64–67.

Luke's date for the beginning of John the Baptist's ministry between A.D. 26 and 27, making A.D. 28 just right for the first Passover of Jesus' ministry recorded in John. There is evidence from coins that Tiberius did consider himself co-regent with Caesar Augustus from A.D. 12 or 13.[45] If one rejects counting the fifteen years from a co-regency, one is forced to push the *entire* ministry of Jesus, as represented in Luke, two years later. This move does nothing to date the Temple cleansing recorded in John to the *end* of Jesus' ministry. Therefore, while there is more than one way of putting together Luke's reference to the fifteenth year of Tiberius and the Jewish leaders' reference in John to forty-six years, it is extremely difficult to get the reference in John to describe a date any later than A.D. 29, and 28 is more likely.[46]

Craig Blomberg briefly considers the possibility of achronological narration of the Temple cleansing in John—in my opinion, an untenable theory in this case, even though not a fictionalization theory.[47] But he does not fully accept achrono-

---

[45] See William Sanday, *The Authorship and Historical Character of the Fourth Gospel*, pp. 64–67 and the twelfth coin shown at http://www.romanemperors.com/augustus.htm.

[46] Andreas Köstenberger is unusual among scholars in that he places this first Passover of Jesus' ministry, recorded in John, as late as in A.D. 30. Köstenberger gets this year by reckoning the forty-six years from eighteen months after Herod actually began building the Temple, when the initial part of the building project was completed, according to Josephus. This would begin the forty-six year count at about 17 B.C. Andreas Köstenberger, *John: Baker Exegetical Commentary on the New Testament* (Grand Rapids: Baker Academic, 2004), p. 109. This is quite a strained interpretation of what the Jewish leaders say to Jesus. On the face of it they appear to be contrasting the total amount of time that the Temple complex has been under construction with his statement that he can raise it in three days. Köstenberger's estimate of such a late date for the first Passover of Jesus' ministry also requires stretching (even on his own account) of the ministry of John the Baptist, a later-than-necessary start for the ministry of John the Baptist, or a longer gap between the beginning of John the Baptist's ministry and Jesus' first Passover. All of these moves are probably bound up with his confidence that Jesus was crucified in A.D. 33. See "April 3, A.D. 33: Why We Believe We Can Know the Exact Date Jesus Died," *First Things*, April 3, 2014, https://www.firstthings.com/web-exclusives/2014/04/april-3-ad-33. Köstenberger *does not* take his late dating of this Passover to point to the end of Jesus' ministry. On the contrary, he is convinced that John firmly places this Temple cleansing at the *beginning* of the ministry, and, based upon both this and his rejection of a co-regency between Tiberius and Augustus, he dates Jesus' entire ministry from 29 and 33 A.D.

[47] Some additional reasons against an achronological interpretation of John at this point: 1) The conversation with Nicodemus in John 3 clearly occurs in Jerusalem, near the beginning of Jesus' ministry. In addition to the explicit chronological indicator in 3.22 (see the next reason), the fact that this conversation does not occur in Holy Week is also clear from Nicodemus's own trajectory of discipleship. Later in Jesus' ministry (John 7.50–51) he is sympathetic to Jesus. He is called a secret follower by the time of the crucifixion (John 19.39–42). John 3 records his first conversation with Jesus; it begins a progress of gradual, developing interest in and sympathy for Jesus. Since John normally narrates Jesus' travels to and from Jerusalem quite explicitly, it would be unusual for the Passover trip in Chapter 2 to describe a much later visit while the conversation with Nicodemus occurs during some earlier visit to Jerusalem for which Jesus' travel is completely unmentioned. By a large margin the most reasonable

logical narration and argues that two Temple cleansings are quite possible, in part because of this reference to forty-six years:

> I remain intrigued by the unusually precise reference to forty-six years since Herod began to have the temple rebuilt (John 2:20). Unless it has actually been at least forty-eight years since the start of the rebuilding of the temple when the unnamed Jews spoke these words, it cannot be any later than AD 28, two years too early for the temple cleansing in the last week of Jesus's life, even on the earlier of the two options for dating the crucifixion (30 and 33). Nor does forty-six appear to be a round number or an approximation, or to have any symbolic significance. The Jewish leaders could have erred in their calculation, and John could have accurately reported their errant statement, but how likely is this here? Heavily desirous of a finally and fully rebuilt temple, the temple leaders—of all people—most likely kept an accurate count of how long they had been waiting.[48]

Blomberg rightly rejects the poor argument that no single Gospel presents more than one Temple cleansing, pointing out that such a method would have absurd consequences:

> [A]re we thereby establishing a historiographical criterion that when two Gospels each have partially similar incidents appearing once and once only in their narratives, even if in entirely different contexts, we may never assume that more than one such episode occurred? By this logic, the curing of the paralyzed man in Mark 2:1–12 in Capernaum must be a variant of the curing of the paralyzed man in Jerusalem in John 5:1–15, since each of these two Gospels narrates only one miraculous cure of a paralyzed man.[49]

---

inference is that Jesus speaks with Nicodemus while in Jerusalem during the same trip described in John 2. 2) The Judean ministry of baptizing described in John 3.22ff occurs after Jesus' conversation with Nicodemus and at a time when John the Baptist is still alive. This *must* be early in Jesus' ministry and also places the conversation with Nicodemus firmly in a very early period. Again, it is quite implausible to suggest that this time in Judea occurs at some entirely separate period from the Passover described in Chapter 2. John describes Jesus as journeying to Jerusalem in John 2.13, as remaining in Judea for a time in John 3.22ff, and as journeying back north to Galilee through Samaria in John 4. The geographical indicators work strongly here as chronological indicators, fixing the Temple cleansing at an early Passover and making achronological narration hard to maintain. In the face of all the evidence from natural readings of multiple texts placing this cleansing early in Jesus' ministry, there is no reason even to consider achronological narration unless one unnecessarily resists two Temple cleansings. See also the undesigned coincidence mentioned in note 43 in this chapter.

[48] Craig Blomberg, "A Constructive Traditional Response to New Testament Criticism" in James K. Hoffmeier and Dennis R. Magary, eds., *Do Historical Matters Matter to Faith* (Wheaton, IL: Crossway Books, 2012), p. 361.

[49] Ibid., p. 362.

The reference to forty-six years is a strong argument against achronological narration of the Temple cleansing in John, and by the same token it is an argument against a literary device of dyschronological narration. To begin with, the allusion to forty-six years is subtle. John could hardly be confident that his readers would count backwards in Herod's reign and infer from this reference (which would be fictional if John were narrating dyschronologically) that he was "placing" this Temple cleansing early in Jesus' ministry. In other words, if he were trying to make his fictional placement more realistic, this passing bit of dialogue might be overlooked and not serve that purpose. Still less would they be likely to compare it to Luke 3.1 and fix the time even more firmly at the beginning of Jesus' ministry by noting the coherence with the fifteenth year of Tiberius mentioned there.

Thus far, the argument here is similar to the usual argument for undesigned coincidences, discussed above: Such subtle allusions do not serve the ends of an author who is inventing his facts and wishes to make his invention appear realistic. They are too easy to overlook. Therefore, they are evidence that things really happened as the author tells them. But the problem for the literary device theorist is even greater. For we must remember that the literary device theorist *does not* wish to characterize the author as a deceiver. The author is supposedly using accepted devices, and this use exempts him from being considered deceptive. Here the theorist is in a cleft stick of his own making. He wants to say that the author's use of devices is invisible and realistic. After all, the author is supposedly making things happen at a time in his narrative when they did not really happen. But he doesn't want to say that the author is *misleading* his readers. Yet the more the theorist attributes effort and cleverness to the author in placing hyper-realistic indicators into his text to try to make the event happen at a particular time in his narrative world, the harder it becomes to absolve the author of the charge of attempted deception. Perhaps the readers wouldn't have noticed the implication of this allusion to forty-six years. But if John went out of his way to invent it and insert it into the narrative *in the hopes that they would*, how can we continue to say that John was not trying to mislead? Presumably the whole point of such an addition would be to try to make it look to the readers as though Jesus really did cleanse the Temple at the outset of his ministry.

The literary device theorist does not think that the Gospels, even John, are *entirely* fictional. They supposedly contain *some* literal historical information. If the reader cannot take the chronology of Jesus' Temple cleansing in John as intended to convey historical information when there are so many indicators of chronology, including one that would have to be invented with a great deal of forethought, when *can* he take John to be historical? Again, we must ask: If the readers of John's Gospel noticed the reference to forty-six years and were also familiar with the Synoptic accounts, why would they *not* think that there were two Temple cleansings? Why would they have concluded instead that John was dyschronologically placing the Temple cleansing early in an ultra-realistic fashion? If John narrated dyschronologically, why would they not have been misled? Here the literary device theorist finds it difficult to have it both ways—to make his author extremely good at crafting realistic literary worlds while absolving him of the intention to deceive.

7. The fish and the stater

In Matt. 17.24–27 we find the story of the Temple tax and the coin in the fish's mouth. The collectors of the two-drachma tax for the Temple come to Peter and ask if his master pays the tax. Peter answers that he does. When he enters the house in Capernaum where Jesus is staying, Jesus implies that they should not have to pay the tax. But he then says this:

> "However, so that we do not offend them, go to the sea and throw in a hook, and take the first fish that comes up; and when you open its mouth, you will find a shekel. Take that and give it to them for you and Me." (Matt. 17.27)

The narrative ends there, and some question has been cast on the claim that Peter actually did do this and that the miracle occurred as one might naturally infer from Jesus' words. This question provides another opportunity for seeing how incidental external evidence can confirm events in the Gospels unexpectedly.

I want to be clear that the hypothesis I am discussing here is *not per se* a literary device theory. Craig Blomberg, who has questioned whether Peter actually went and found a coin in a fish's mouth, is not suggesting any ahistoricity in the narrative itself. Rather, he suggests that Jesus was in some way being facetious or metaphoric (which presumably Peter could tell from Jesus' manner) and that Peter never really *expected* to find a coin in the mouth of a fish. What is actually narrated—the conversation—would still be fully historical given this suggestion.

The reason for Blomberg's doubt is somewhat subjective—namely, that the miracle seems to him, as to other scholars, theologically unworthy, a "trivial and unnecessarily spectacular method for Jesus to pay a simple tax."[50] Hence, although the theory itself is not a literary device or fictionalization theory, it casts doubt on

---

[50] Craig Blomberg, "New Testament Miracles and Higher Criticism: Climbing Up the Slippery Slope," *JETS* 27/4 (December, 1984), p. 433.

the occurrence of a miracle that one would otherwise infer from the narrative and doing so for theological reasons.[51] It is therefore interesting to see how external evidence confirms Jesus' seriousness in giving this instruction to Peter.

The Temple tax, as already mentioned, was two drachmas per person and is literally called the "two-drachma tax" in the Greek (Matt. 17.24). Jesus tells Peter to go and catch a fish, finding in its mouth a coin. Different translations render the word for the coin differently. Some, like the NASB, call it a shekel, others (such as the NIV) call it a "four-drachma coin." The actual word is "stater." The word "stater" had indeed come to be used for a coin worth four drachmae.[52]

The point that springs to the eye here is that Jesus expressly tells Peter that he will find a stater and should use it to pay the tax for himself and for Jesus. In other words, Jesus predicts that Peter will find a coin of just exactly the right denomination to pay the tax for the two of them and instructs him to use it for that purpose so as not to offend the officials. This does not look like a metaphorical or facetious comment. One theory Blomberg treats as somewhat plausible is that Jesus was suggesting in a roundabout way that Peter should go fishing and catch fish which can be sold to pay the tax.[53] But this procedure would not produce precisely the amount of tax for the two of them, which Jesus specifies. Jesus also does not refer merely to some fabled fish with some coin or other in its mouth but rather to a

---

[51] In general, the methodological approach in this article is somewhat different from that in Blomberg's other work. Contrast, for example, his excellent comments on not testing every pericope separately in *The Historical Reliability of John's Gospel*, p. 63. In the 1984 article, Blomberg takes each of several miracles of Christ and asks whether it is theologically meaningful enough to be regarded as probably historical. This approach is questionable, especially insofar as it takes incidents one at a time and doubts them rather than looking (as Blomberg does elsewhere) at evidence that supports the reliability of a given document overall and allowing this to support the historicity of individual incidents, even if they fulfill no other special "criteria of historicity." In other cases discussed in the 1984 article, such as changing water into wine (Ibid., p. 429–430), the Gospel *does* narrate the miracle; it would be impossible to deny the occurrence of the miracle without denying the historical truth of the narrative. Blomberg does conclude in the article that this miracle and all those narrated are historical. The only miracle Blomberg ends up questioning in the end is the one that (as it happens) the Gospel does not explicitly narrate. The criterion of theological significance is two-edged, since a critical scholar not only could but often would argue from the theological significance of an event to its *non-historicity*—arguing that it was invented to make a theological point. (Indeed, this happens often even with non-miraculous parts of the Gospels.) It seems arbitrary to argue for historicity *from* theological importance. Finally, the miracle of the coin in the fish's mouth is *prima facie* less showy and unnecessary than Jesus' cursing of the fig tree, for which Blomberg finds a theological rationale (pp. 428–429) or inviting Peter to walk on the water (Matt. 14.22–23).

[52] "Stater," *International Bible Encyclopedia Online*, https://www.internationalstandardbible.com/S/stater.html.

[53] Blomberg, "New Testament Miracles and Higher Criticism," p. 434.

specific coin of the time period with a value exactly equal to the tax for two people. If Jesus is merely being facetious or metaphoric, the specificity of the money amount is surprising. Here, then, the sort of precision that catches Blomberg's attention in the forty-six years discussed in the last section supports Jesus' literal prediction of a miracle in the case of the fish and the coin.

As for theological significance, while we should hesitate to lay much stress on such a criterion in the Gospels anyway, it is fairly easy to see the miracle as teaching an important lesson. Most of us know of anecdotes from fellow Christians (especially missionaries) in which God's servants need a specific sum of money and receive it from someone who could not have known of that need. These coincidences are interesting and are often understandably taken as special providences, signs that, as Jesus says, we are of more value to the Father than many sparrows (Matt. 6.8, 10.31). Such events represent God's personal knowledge of our needs and his care for us. If the person who gave the command to catch a fish were Jesus himself, finding the coin would bring home this truth even more forcefully.

Moreover, this miracle resembles others, such as the great catches of fish in Luke 5.1–11 and John 21.1–9, where Jesus gives a sign to his disciples by producing a surprising result under naturally unpropitious circumstances. Of course, a skeptic will deny the occurrence of *all* of these, but Blomberg's purpose is not to question Jesus' miracles in general. If we are allowed (as we should be) to draw some conclusions about Jesus' personality, one reasonable inference is that Jesus was sometimes playfully specific in setting up a miracle, as when he tells the disciples in John 21.6 to cast the net on the other side of the boat. The specific order and prediction to Peter fits this pattern well.

8. Pilate's wife

Pilate's wife makes a brief appearance in the crucifixion narrative in the Gospel of Matthew (Matt. 27.19). She sends a message to Pilate, warning him to have nothing to do with condemning Jesus, whom she refers to as a "righteous man," because she has suffered greatly in a dream the previous night because of Jesus. The Gospels don't contain any information that tells us whether she had ever heard of Jesus prior to the trial, but even if she had not, she could have had a dream which she interpreted (upon hearing about the trial) to be about Jesus.

This brief story of Pilate's wife is ripe for questioning by skeptical New Testament scholars and/or literary device theorists. It is attested only in a single verse in Matthew. As mentioned in the previous paragraph, it requires a certain amount of imagination to give a fully natural explanation of her dream, and it seems somewhat unlikely that God would have miraculously sent her such a dream, even if one is open to the miraculous. Jesus was supposed to die for the sins of the whole world at this time. Jesus himself knew that he must suffer crucifixion under Pilate, especially after his prayer in the Garden of Gethsemane (compare Mark 14.36 and John 18.11), and he makes no attempt to induce Pilate to release him when they talk. Why would God send a dream to Pilate's wife to try to save Jesus?

Making the case even more tempting to someone who admits fictionalization in the Gospels, Pilate's wife's dream bears some similarity to the dream of Julius Caesar's wife, Calpurnia, before Caesar's assassination in the forum. As Plutarch tells the story, Calpurnia warns Caesar not to go to the forum that day because she has had a bad dream.[54] Caesar does not heed her warning and, of course, is murdered. If one thinks that the authors of the Gospels crafted details for dramatic effect, and if one also thinks that they were aware of Roman literature, this would seem like a place to question historicity.

Craig Evans does not explicitly question the historicity of the event, though he does rather significantly raise the parallel to Calpurnia's dream:

> In the infancy narrative of Matthew, dreams play an important role in disclosing the divine will…, as they do here. If Pilate knows what is good for him, he'll find Jesus innocent and release him. The story could not fail to impress readers in the Roman world, who well knew the story of the death of Julius Caesar a century earlier: "Now Caesar's approaching murder was foretold to him by unmistakable signs…. In fact the very night before his murder he dreamt now that he was flying above the clouds, and now that he was clasping the hand of Jupiter; and his wife Calpurnia thought that the pediment of their house fell, and that her husband was stabbed in her arms…." (Suetonius, *Julius* 81.1, 3).[55]

Actually, this verse in Matthew easily *could* fail to impress Jewish readers in the Roman world, if they did not happen to know the story of Caesar's wife, as many Jews might not (*pace* Evans). And Matthew does not generally go out of his way to impress a Gentile, Roman audience. Moreover, as already pointed out, it isn't at all clear that it was the "divine will" that Pilate should listen to his wife and release Jesus. Evans's suggested parallel to the function of the dreams in the infancy narratives is strained, and it casts an unnecessary doubt upon the historicity

---

[54] Plutarch, *Life of Caesar*, 63.8–11.

[55] Craig A. Evans, *Matthew* (New Cambridge Bible Commentary) (Cambridge: Cambridge University Press, 2012), p. 453.

of the dream here. Is the implication that Matthew invented the dream of Pilate's wife to fit with a Matthean theme of dreams as "disclosing the divine will"? Evans does not clearly say.

This somewhat cryptic passage in Evans's commentary is accompanied by a footnote in which Evans blandly suggests that the reader can see the work of F. M. Gillman for a "critical assessment of the story."[56] That article *does* suggest that the story of the dream of Pilate's wife was developed from the story of Calpurnia's dream.[57]

But here, once again, there is external evidence for a confirmatory fact—namely, that Roman governors often did bring along their wives on their tours of duty to the provinces, even though this practice was against an old regulation. By the middle of the first century A.D., this old rule was either unenforced or set aside. Caesar Augustus had been quite strict about such things, allowing his generals to visit their wives only in the winter.[58] The old, stoical Roman way was for wives of high officials to remain in the safety and civilization of Italy rather than following their husbands on deployment.

Tacitus tells about a debate in the senate, which occurred in A.D. 21, on this very subject.[59] An old-fashioned senator, Caecina Severus, launched into a speech in which he moved that no magistrate in charge of a province should be permitted to take his wife along when he went to manage the province. He urged various arguments in favor of this revival of the older regulation, including reports of wives' excessive meddling in the affairs of governance and their encumbering their husbands with a large retinue. He said that he himself voluntarily left his beloved wife behind in Italy when his duties took him to the provinces. But the practice of taking one's wife along to the provinces was evidently quite popular among the senators, who wanted to have that option should they be appointed. Other senators, including the popular and respected Drusus, opposed Severus's motion, and it was eventually "evaded"—presumably, tabled without a vote and allowed to fall into oblivion.[60]

If Matthew invented the incident of Pilate's wife and her dream, he must have known in some other way or luckily guessed that a Roman governor like Pilate might well have brought his wife along on his tour of duty in the province during

---

[56] Ibid., p. 486 n. 549.

[57] F. M. Gillman, "The Wife of Pilate (Matthew 27:19)," *Louvain Studies* 17 (1992):152–65.

[58] Suetonius, *Life of Augustus*, 24.1.

[59] Anthony A. Barrett, "Aula Caecina Severus and the Military Women," *Historia* 54/3 (2005), p. 301.

[60] Tacitus, *Annals*, III.33–34.

that time period. While this practice may seem obvious to modern Americans, accustomed as we are to military bases abroad where families often live, it apparently was not obvious to all Romans. A Jewish author might or might not have known whether Pilate's wife could have been with him. An author who did not live at that time and place would have had no way to look up the practice and be sure that the detail was realistic. We sometimes forget that there were no easy ways in the 1st century to research social customs one did not happen to know about. If, for example, the Gospel of Matthew were written after the destruction of Jerusalem in A.D. 70, and if the author had not lived in the 30s in the province where Pilate was governor, he would have had few resources for finding out how likely it was that Pilate would have had his wife with him. Given the strictness of Augustus and the apparent change under Tiberius, it would be quite possible for someone trying to invent things to get it wrong—to assume, for example, that wives were not allowed with their husbands. Even some skeptics have been mistaken on this point and have used the supposed prohibition on wives accompanying husbands as an argument against the historicity of the incident.[61]

The idea that Matthew or some pre-Matthean written source is alluding to Caesar's wife is questionable. Matthew's narrative does not emphasize this little detail about Pilate's wife in any other way. Matthew does not even say what Pilate thought of the message from his wife, and he seems to indicate that Pilate would have preferred to release Jesus anyway, aside from her dream. He does not narrate any dramatic evil that befalls Pilate as a result of not following her advice. He does not *do* anything with the dream.[62] He just mentions it in passing, exactly as an author would do if he were honestly passing on something he had reason to believe was true, not trying to make a literary point. Any similarity to the incident of Caesar's wife may reflect the fact that Romans in general took dreams seriously and were superstitious about them, making Pilate's wife more likely to send him a message about her dream. If anyone was thinking about Calpurnia, it was likely Pilate's wife, not Matthew.

While the confirmation from customs during the reign of Tiberius is indirect, it is relevant. It certainly forms part of a cumulative case for Matthew's historicity, at least for scholars who are not looking for heavy literary parallels rather than

---

[61] Arthur J. Yates, "Some Intrinsic Evidences of the Gospels' Genuineness," *The Month: A Catholic Magazine and Review* 243 (September, 1884), p. 224. George R. Dekle, Sr., *The Case Against Christ: A Critique of the Prosecution of Jesus*, (Newcastle Upon Tyne: Cambridge Scholars Publishing, 2011), p. 197.

[62] Timothy McGrew brought this point to my attention while I was writing this section.

sober facts. If we put the reportage view of the Gospels on the table as a live option, we can place the confirmation concerning the wives of Roman provincial governors into its proper place rather than leaping to assume a literary motive for Matthew's account.

9. Jesus carries his cross

A surprising instance of the way that literary assumptions about the Gospels blind one to the true force of external evidence occurs in Craig Keener's treatment of Jesus carrying his cross in the Gospel of John. Repeatedly, in various works, Keener speaks of John's narrative about Jesus carrying his cross as though it bends the historical facts for theological reasons and is in conflict with Mark's. In fact, there is no contradiction between them, and Keener himself admits that John's narrative of Jesus carrying his cross is both supported by external historical evidence and harmonizable with Mark. Yet he does not see that this counteracts his own implication that John is "narrating theologically."

The verse in question is John 19.17:

> They took Jesus, therefore, and He went out, bearing His own cross, to the place called the Place of a Skull, which is called in Hebrew, Golgotha.

This verse, read in isolation, could understandably be interpreted to say that Jesus carried his cross all the way to Golgotha. It does not at all follow that John was *attempting* to make it look like Jesus carried his cross the whole way *instead of* receiving help or that John was attempting to deny or suppress the involvement of Simon of Cyrene, narrated in Mark:

> And they led Him out to crucify Him. They pressed into service a passer-by coming from the country, Simon of Cyrene (the father of Alexander and Rufus), to bear His cross. (Mark 15.20–21)

We must recall again that harmonization is a normal and justified historical practice, not a religious enterprise. Mark's "led him out to crucify him" fits well with John's "he went out, bearing his own cross." D. A. Carson has reasonably suggested that the reference to Simon as "coming from the country" may indicate that Jesus carried his cross as far as the city gate, at which point he was unable to go further.[63] Certainly Mark does not say or imply that Jesus was not compelled to carry his cross *at all*, and it would be very surprising if any such thing occurred.

---

[63] D. A. Carson, *The Gospel According to John* (Grand Rapids, MI: Eerdmans, 1991) p. 609.

Mark's narrative alone, together with knowledge of customs of crucifixion (discussed below), yields the picture of Jesus as beginning to carry his own cross and being replaced by Simon, pressed into service by the soldiers, somewhere along the *Via Dolorosa*. This is easily compatible with John, who may have been especially struck by the picture of Jesus, beaten and bleeding, forced to bear his own cross.

Yet Keener repeatedly suggests a conflict between Mark and John:

> A close examination of the Fourth Gospel reveals that John has rearranged many details, apparently in the service of his symbolic message. This is especially clear in the Passion Narrative, where *direct conflicts* with the presumably widely known passion tradition (most notably that Jesus gives the sop to Judas, is crucified on Passover, and carries his own cross) fulfill symbolic narrative functions.[64]

> John takes significant liberties with the way he reports his events, especially in several symbolic adaptations in the passion narrative ... [65]

In a footnote to this second claim of John's "significant liberties" in reporting events, Keener lists the fact that Jesus carries his own cross in John as an example.[66] Here is Keener's discussion in his commentary on John:

> More significantly from the standpoint of Johannine theology, John is emphatic that Jesus carried "his own" cross .... [J]ust as Jesus "laid down his life" (10:18) and "delivered up" his spirit (19:30) ... so here he remains in control in the narrative. A condemned criminal normally carried his own *patibulum*, or transverse beam of the cross, to the site of the execution, where soldiers would fix the *patibulum* to the upright stake ... that they regularly reused for executions ....
>
> In the Synoptic tradition and probably the broader passion tradition, Jesus is too weak to carry his cross, and it is carried by Simon of Cyrene. Given the unlikelihood that the soldiers would simply show mercy to a condemned prisoner, scholars are probably correct to suppose that Jesus was too weak to carry the cross and that his executioners preferred to have him alive on the cross than dead on the way ....
>
> That the Synoptic report is undoubtedly historical does not render impossible a historical basis for John's account: it is in fact most likely that the soldiers would have sought to make Jesus carry his own cross at the beginning, following standard custom, until it became clear that he could not continue to do so. But merely reporting (or inferring) those initial steps is hardly John's point; by emphasizing Jesus'

---

[64] Keener, *John*, pp. 42–43. Emphasis added.

[65] Craig Keener, *Acts: An Exegetical Commentary* (Grand Rapids, MI: Baker Academic 2012), vol. 1, p. 793.

[66] Ibid., p. 793, n. 105.

carrying his own cross, he emphasizes Jesus' continuing control of his passion. Just as condemned criminals must bear their own instrument of death, Jesus chose and controlled his death.[67]

As is unfortunately often the case with New Testament scholars, it is a little difficult to figure out *precisely* what Keener is suggesting John has done. As noted, he says that in this passage John is in "direct conflict" with Mark and "takes significant liberties" in reporting. Yet he admits here that John and Mark are harmonizable at this point and even seems inclined to accept historically both that Jesus and Simon of Cyrene carried the cross for some distance or other. So how does John take "significant liberties"?

One begins to get an inkling of Keener's thesis in the artificial tension that his wording creates between John and Mark. By saying that "in the Synoptic tradition," Jesus is too weak and Simon carries the cross, Keener gives the vague impression that in the Synoptic tradition, Simon carries the cross for *virtually all of the way*, though actually none of the Synoptics is that specific. He then writes as though there is something *antecedently* probable about Mark's account, though in point of fact there isn't. Without Mark's account, we would have no reason whatsoever to think that the soldiers impressed *any* person to carry Jesus' cross. If we knew the usual custom and did not have Mark, we would assume that Jesus carried the crossbeam himself. Of course, *if* Jesus was too weak to do so, then it is somewhat more likely that the soldiers would force someone else to do it than that they would take the risk of killing Jesus on the way by continuing to drive him, much less carry the crossbeam themselves. But we discover that Jesus had to have such help only by reading Mark. I say this not to cast any doubt on Mark's account but merely to point out that Keener's way of writing of Mark's account as "undoubtedly historical" gives the incorrect impression that the Synoptic account is probable on *independent* grounds, whereas in fact we accept what Mark says simply because we treat Mark as historical, not because there is independent reason to think that soldiers regularly impressed bystanders to carry crosses. The reference to Mark's account as "undoubtedly historical" in contrast with the *extremely* tentative reference to John's historicity—"does not render impossible an historical basis for John's account"—merely illustrates the scholarly bias against John after the scholar creates a vague and quite unnecessary tension between John and the Synoptics.

Second, the use of the phrase "initial steps" for the amount of carrying that Jesus probably did historically is unjustified by anything either in history or in

---

[67] Keener, *John*, pp. 1133–34.

either of the texts and merely insinuates that John is bending the truth. It could easily have taken more than a few "initial steps" for the soldiers to decide that they were in danger of killing Jesus on the way if they continued to drive him to carry his cross and for them to decide to force a bystander to carry it. In fact, this is quite probable. And as already mentioned, if the phrase "coming from the country" in Mark indicates that Simon was encountered somewhere near the city gate, then Jesus carried the cross for more than a few "initial steps."

Third, the use of "or inferred" downplays the probability that John provides eyewitness testimony about the *Via Dolorosa*. This is particularly surprising given the beloved disciple's statement (John 19.35) that he witnessed the breaking of the other prisoners' legs and the piercing of Jesus' side at the crucifixion. If he was there at that point in the crucifixion, why should he not have seen Jesus carrying his cross earlier? Moreover, other followers of Jesus who were witnesses (such as the women mentioned in all four Gospels) would certainly have talked about what they saw. Luke expressly refers to women weeping for Jesus on the *Via Dolorosa* (Luke 23.27). Luke has just mentioned Simon of Cyrene in the previous verse (Luke 23.26), but if Jesus did carry his own cross part of the way, as is both antecedently likely and narrated in John, the women would have seen that as well. Why suggest that John merely "inferred" that Jesus carried his own cross? This suggestion further distances John's narrative from historical reality, implying that John may have exaggerated a purely inferred possibility for his own theological purposes. Note, too, the distinction Keener makes between "reporting" and "inferring" and his definite statement that John is not "merely reporting" what happened to Jesus. Why should we *not* think that John is "merely reporting"? The language of this passage quite unjustifiably, and indeed *against* external evidence, treats John's narrative as something other than reportage.

Though it is hard to pin down what Keener is implying, it seems to be something like this: John knew that Simon of Cyrene really carried Jesus' cross almost all the way to Golgotha. But he wanted to make a theological point about Jesus as "in control of his death," so he deliberately suppressed all of the involvement of Simon of Cyrene and deliberately wrote in such a way that his own narrative *makes it look like* Jesus carried the cross *all the way* to Golgotha. Hence, in the narrative world of John's Gospel, Jesus carries his cross all the way, whereas in the Synoptic tradition, Simon carries it most of the way. Hence, there is a "direct conflict" from which we can see that John has taken "significant liberties" with the historical facts at this point. Note that, while Keener is unclear in his exposition about *how* John took "significant liberties" or *why* one should think there is a "direct conflict" between John and the Synoptics, forcing the reader to infer what, precisely, he is getting at, he states quite definitely and clearly that both of these are true.

The idea that Jesus' carrying his cross is a symbol of Jesus' control of his death is anachronistic to the point of being ludicrous. It cannot possibly have looked that way to any contemporary bystander. For a blood-covered prisoner to be forced to carry his own crossbeam after having been kept up all night, dragged from one tribunal to another, brutally flogged, and tortured with a crown of thorns, would have been a *further form of torment and degradation*. An audience and/or author who had actually seen crucifixions would be overwhelmingly unlikely to think of the prisoner's carrying his own cross as a symbol of his control.

One can more easily make up a theological meaning for the involvement of Simon of Cyrene: Jesus tells his disciples in Mark that they are to take up their crosses and follow him (Mark 8.34). Simon's act in Mark symbolizes the fact that we need to be willing to carry the cross ourselves. So Simon is a symbol of the ideal Christian, carrying the cross for Jesus. See how easy it is to develop such theories? This theory is much more reasonable *as symbolism* than the claim that Jesus' carrying his own cross symbolizes control of his death. But of course that is no reason to doubt the historicity of Mark's story, nor am I raising it for that reason. My point is only that symbolic interpretations can be developed *ad infinitum* and that it is even easy to think of theories that make more sense than Keener's suggestion about John.

What is perhaps most striking of all in Keener's treatment of this passage is his failure to recognize the full relevance of the external evidence. Keener himself gives several references to the fact that it was a normal practice to force prisoners to carry their own crosses. In his *Moralia*, Plutarch wrote,

> …whereas every criminal who goes to execution must carry his own cross on his back, vice frames out of itself each instrument of its own punishment…[68]

The 2nd-century diviner Artemidorus wrote, "He who is nailed to the cross first carries it."[69] And in the Greek romance novel *Chaereas and Callirhoe*, when sixteen men are sentenced to be "suspended" (most probably crucified), the narrator says, "They were brought out chained together by feet and neck, and each of them

---

[68] Plutarch, *Moralia*, 554.

[69] Artemidorus, *On the Interpretation of Dreams*, 2.56.

carried the pole."[70] Keener himself asserts definitely that "a condemned criminal normally carried his own *patibulum,* or transverse beam of the cross, to the site of the execution" and that this was "standard custom."

This constitutes external confirmation of John's narrative on *precisely the point* where Keener says that John takes "significant liberties" in reporting events. It is disturbing that an extremely learned scholar, confronted with the fact that a Gospel is externally confirmed on a specific point in the narrative, would assert that *that very point* constitutes a significant historical liberty on the part of the evangelist. But such is the strength of theory over straightforward evidence that this is precisely what Keener does, speaking *instead* of Mark's narrative as "undoubtedly historical," even though there is no similar external confirmation for a common practice of impressing a bystander to help a condemned man carry his cross. (Roman soldiers could press people to carry things in general, e.g., Matt. 5.41.) Keener's reasoning concerning Mark *assumes* the background fact that it was normal to force a prisoner to carry his own cross, so that *if* the prisoner became unable to do so, the soldiers might be expected to press someone else into service. They certainly would not carry it themselves. But this relationship between the external evidence and Mark is indirect and only highlights the confirmation of John. That is to say, even in interpreting Mark correctly in light of cultural evidence we must assume what is expressly stated in John—namely, that Jesus was forced to carry his own cross. Again, that is not to say that there is the slightest problem with Mark's historicity. It is merely to emphasize that external information confirms John's narrative rather than Mark's in a direct and specific way. Keener's treatment of this incident provides a classic example of the way that literary theories distort one's ability to appreciate the impact of external confirming evidence.

Both internal undesigned coincidences and external incidental confirmations show us that the Gospels are reportage rather than partially fictionalized stories. Again and again, literary device theorists miss this evidential support because they assume that the Gospel authors did not have independent information about what really happened or were modifying the facts for literary or theological reasons. The literary device view of the Gospels is incompatible with taking seriously their status as reportage, and the reportage view fits better with the evidence. If we do not assume that the Gospels are heavily manipulated literary artifacts, we can accept confirmatory evidence and put it in its proper place rather than explaining it away.

---

[70] Chariton, *Chaereas and Callirhoe,* 4.2.6–7.

Summary
Evidence and the Artless Author

- Undesigned coincidences depend upon connections between details of stories. If we think that Gospel authors were licensed to manufacture or change details, we shouldn't expect to find undesigned coincidences in the Gospels. But we do find them. An author who produces documents with many undesigned coincidences does not look like the kind of author who was altering or inventing details of his stories.

- Repeatedly, a literary device theorist is blind to the internal evidence of an undesigned coincidence because he approaches that passage with a high prior probability that one or both of the authors was licensed to invent.

- Repeatedly, a literary device theorist is blind to external incidental support for a Gospel passage because he approaches the passage with a high prior probability that an author was licensed to invent.

- The specific evidence of the ways in which the Gospels' details fit together both with each other and with external evidence supports the reportage model of the Gospels rather than the literary device model.

XII

Still More Evidence for the Reportage Model

1. Unexplained allusions

Several more classes of evidence besides undesigned coincidences and external confirmations support the conclusion that the Gospels are honest historical reports, though some of these confirmations are virtually unknown in the current apologetic literature. One of these is the argument from unexplained allusions.

Repeatedly in the Gospels (and in Acts and the Pauline epistles) we find "dangling" comments. These are allusions to cultural practices, to events, or to aspects of an event that have no clear explanation and that do not appear to advance either the narrative or any theological or literary purpose. Their contribution to the verisimilitude of the accounts is striking once one's attention is drawn to them, for the creator of a highly crafted literary document would have no reason to include them and indeed would have reason to leave them out. This is the kind of thing that one finds in oral history when the narrator artlessly recounts what he remembers. The inclusion of such a pointless, puzzling detail constitutes evidence of historicity in and of itself.

While it is always possible, with enough ingenuity and determination, to make up a theory about some theme or other that an author *might* try to advance by an unexplained allusion, this merely testifies to the interpreter's powers of conjecture. The hallmark of an unexplained allusion is that any suggestion concerning a theme or theological purpose for invention is severely underdetermined by evidence and obviously *ad hoc*. The fact that we can't find any point for the comment *just is* the point. The author didn't include the detail in order to make a point. He included it in passing because he believed that it was true.

Interestingly, in many cases a single half of an undesigned coincidence would be an unexplained allusion if we did not have the other text. For example, at Jesus' trial the witnesses say that Jesus said he would destroy the Temple and raise it again in three days (Mark 14.58). If we did not have John 2.19, in which Jesus says, "Destroy this Temple, and in three days I will raise it up," the account of the testimony in the Synoptics would be an unexplained allusion to something Jesus supposedly said. We might wonder what that was all about, but we would never know. As things stand, the testimony at the trial is obviously a garbled version of Jesus' earlier prediction. So we may explain an unexplained allusion if we gain other information. In that case, the undesigned appearance of the coincidence lies in the absence of any obvious explanation *in the immediate context* of the text that raises the question. That is, the best explanation for the details is the larger picture of reality, which we gain from both accounts, not the artistic genius of either author. The connection is not obvious and becomes clear only when we have some distant and apparently unrelated passage in hand.

There is thus a close connection between undesigned coincidences and unexplained allusions, and it is fascinating to realize that the sheer oddity and "dangling" nature of the question side of an undesigned coincidence is evidence in and of itself for historicity. The fact that the Synoptics record an odd and (in the Synoptics) unexplained accusation against Jesus is some evidence that they are reporting what witnesses actually said at the trial. An artful author, inventing the accusation, would be more likely to invent a reason for it so as to advance his theme clearly.

Similarly, Jesus' phrase "I am among you as the one who serves," discussed in the previous chapter, is an unexplained allusion within the Gospel of Luke alone. It seems to refer to some particular way in which Jesus is among them as a servant at that particular time, but Luke leaves the reference unexplained. If Luke had wanted to allude to the foot washing, he should have mentioned the foot washing. The foot washing explains the allusion in Luke, but *within Luke*, the allusion is left dangling. Undesigned coincidences often contain unexplained allusions as one portion. In this sense, undesigned coincidences have evidential force on multiple levels.

Here are a few unexplained allusions that do not participate in known undesigned coincidences. One of these occurs in Mark 3.17:

And He appointed the twelve: Simon (to whom He gave the name Peter), and James, the son of Zebedee, and John the brother of James (to them He gave the name Boanerges, which means, "Sons of Thunder"). (Mark 3.16–17)

No other Gospel mentions that Jesus called James and John the Sons of Thunder. Nowhere, not even in Mark, do we find a story about the origin of this nickname. There is not so much as an explanatory phrase to tell us how Jesus came to give James and John the nickname "Boanerges."

We may guess that something related to "Boanerges" is found in Luke 9.53–54, where James and John suggest calling down fire on a Samaritan town after the people there refuse to receive Jesus. Perhaps this is an indication of their personalities. But that, though interesting, is probably not the original explanation of the nickname, which Jesus plausibly gave earlier. (That incident does not occur until Jesus is leaving Galilee for the last time to journey south, which may have been about six months before his death.)

There could be many possible reasons for Jesus to give the nickname, and these are not mutually exclusive. One must consider that the disciples were probably quite young at the time. Anyone who has worked with young men can think of plenty of reasons for calling a pair of brothers the Sons of Thunder. Maybe they were especially loud and boisterous. Maybe they were especially argumentative. Or maybe, as in the case of the Samaritan city, they were inclined to be harsh in their judgements.

The fact is that we simply don't know. But that itself is a fascinating point. The passage in Mark is a list of the names of Jesus' disciples. That's it. It's just a list. In its very bareness lies its verisimilitude. What other reason than the desire to report truth, truth remembered by one in a position to know, could there be for telling us *in passing* that Jesus nicknamed James and John Boanerges, the Sons of Thunder? The detail serves no apparent literary purpose. It serves no theological agenda. Of course there must have *been* a reason, maybe several reasons, for the bestowal of this nickname, but Mark, following his source (e.g., Peter), feels no compulsion to tell us what that reason is. Perhaps Mark never found out. He considers the detail worth mentioning, but only as a small part of the list of the disciples' names. This is who they were. This was what Jesus, the Master, called them.

Luke's Gospel has two unexplained allusions in a teaching about repentance. In this case, the unexplained nature of the allusions arises from the fact that Luke is recording what Jesus said. It is clear that the audience of Jesus' original teaching knew what events he was referring to. In fact, someone in the crowd brought up one of them to Jesus. But Luke's own audience may well *not* have known what these events were.

Now on the same occasion there were some present who reported to Him about the Galileans whose blood Pilate had mixed with their sacrifices. And Jesus said to them, "Do you suppose that these Galileans were greater sinners than all other Galileans because they suffered this fate? I tell you, no, but unless you repent, you will all likewise perish. Or do you suppose that those eighteen on whom the tower in Siloam fell and killed them were worse culprits than all the men who live in Jerusalem? I tell you, no, but unless you repent, you will all likewise perish." (Luke 13.1–5)

Luke makes not the slightest attempt to explain these references. Nor does he emphasize them. The allusions are fairly precise—eighteen people who died in the fall of the tower and Galileans (as opposed to those from some other region) whom Pilate killed. Is it likely that Theophilus, Luke's high-placed and probably Gentile immediate audience (Luke 1.3), would have known about these news items in Jesus' lifetime? Luke probably did not record these references in particular for the benefit of his own readers. Rather, it is Jesus who is discussing current events with *his* audience, using them as illustrations; Luke records what his human sources have told him. The touch of realism is unmistakable.

There are several unexplained allusions in the Gospel of John, and I will be mentioning these again in the companion volume, *The Eye of the Beholder*. One allusion occurs in John 2.12, where the evangelist says briefly that, after the miracle at Cana, Jesus went with his mother, brothers, and disciples down to Capernaum and stayed there a few days. John gives no explanation whatsoever for this trip to Capernaum. The very next verse takes us to the time of Passover and begins to tell about the cleansing of the Temple. Verse 12, about the visit to Capernaum, is left dangling, serving no narrative, theological, or thematic purpose.

Mentioning pointless details like this simply because they are true confirms very strongly the quality of artlessness in the Gospels' reports. We must bear in mind that this artless mention of irrelevancies is a *positive* quality. This is not simply an argument from our own ignorance of any special purpose these details serve. Rather, the argument from unexplained allusions springs from our knowledge of *how witnesses actually talk*. If you have spoken with a person remembering events from a long time ago, the tendency to make parenthetical digressions or to mention small details simply because they interest the speaker or occur to his mind is a real quality of such oral history. We therefore make an inference to the best explanation that this is why we find such unexplained allusions in the Gospels—because their authors were artless reporters and were close to the facts. This is a far better explanation than a "literary theory of the gaps" approach in which we hold out indefinitely for *some* deep, complex theological or literary explanation of such details rather than accepting their artless quality at face value.

Something that we need to recover in biblical scholarship is the notion of *chance variation* in accounts. Sometimes a variation is just a variation. If two authors report an event in different words, this does not have to have any special meaning. If two authors report the words of God the Father at Jesus' baptism slightly differently, this does not have to have any theological purpose. And if one author reports a detail just because it occurred to him to mention it, this does not have to have any deep meaning. Normal witness testimony has a chance quality about it, as do reports that use witness testimony. We can imagine John himself, remembering, mentioning that they went down to Capernaum and stayed several days, in just the way that a witness will sometimes throw in something otherwise irrelevant to the story. We can imagine Luke, having a witness report about Jesus' teaching on repentance in hand, reporting what (according to the witness) occasioned the remarks. No further explanation is needed, yet a fictionalizing author would be far more likely to give a lead-in or explanation that most readers would understand rather than an allusion to events that readers would probably not be familiar with.

Here is another. John's Gospel tells about a baptizing ministry early in Jesus' ministry in which his disciples baptized while John the Baptist was still free:

> After these things Jesus and His disciples came into the land of Judea, and there He was spending time with them and baptizing. John also was baptizing in Aenon near Salim, because there was much water there; and people were coming and were being baptized—for John had not yet been thrown into prison. Therefore there arose a discussion on the part of John's disciples with a Jew about purification. And they came to John and said to him, "Rabbi, He who was with you beyond the Jordan, to whom you have testified, behold, He is baptizing and all are coming to Him." (John 3.22–26)

This short passage contains a curious unexplained allusion: What was the dispute between John the Baptist's disciples and another Jew about purification? The passage gives us absolutely no idea, and it seems unlikely that we will ever know. In general terms we can say that baptism probably had some original connection with Jewish purification rituals, but that does not explain this specific allusion. For some reason, the disciples of John the Baptist came to John to ask him to resolve this dispute. But John the evangelist records only their expression of concern that Jesus was baptizing more people than John the Baptist was. (The narrator is careful to clarify in 4.2 that Jesus himself did not personally baptize anyone but delegated baptism to his disciples.) How does the complaint relate to the dispute that occasioned it? One can guess that *perhaps* Jesus' disciples carried out baptism in some different form or under some different set of ritual requirements than did John the Baptist and that the disciples of the Baptist had been debating the relative merits of these practices with an unnamed follower of Jesus. But this is entirely conjectural and gives us no idea what the difference or differences might have been. It is obviously not important to the evangelist to clarify. He reports the dispute with the Jew about purification in passing, exactly as an artless reporter would do, as the lead-in to the complaint and John the Baptist's famous declaration of his own subordination to Jesus, culminating in verse 30 with, "He must increase, but I must decrease." That is where the evangelist is going in the narrative, but he felt no need to explain the dispute with the Jew. For the purposes of the narrative and John the Baptist's declaration, there was no need even to *mention* the dispute. John could have started out with the complaint that Jesus' disciples are baptizing so many. The mention of the dispute with the Jew is just by the way. What could be more like truth?

The historicity of Acts is not the main theme of this book. If it were, it would make this an even longer book than it is. But it is relevant to give one example of an unexplained allusion in Acts that has this same wonderful quality of artlessness:

> Paul, having remained many days longer, took leave of the brethren and put out to sea for Syria, and with him were Priscilla and Aquila. In Cenchrea he had his hair cut, for he was keeping a vow. (Acts 18.18)

The author of Acts writes in the brief manner of a man who simply reports something that happened by the way and does not bother to explain it for his readers. That the nature of Paul's vow and the connection with cutting his hair is an unexplained allusion becomes evident simply by reading the commentaries on the passage. Here, for example, is the Pulpit Commentary (*in loc.*):

> As regards the nature of the vow, it is not quite clear what it was. It was not the simple Nazaritic vow described in Numbers 6:18–21; nor is the word here used by St. Luke (κειράμενος) the one which is there and elsewhere employed by the LXX., and by St. Luke himself in Acts 21:24 of that final shaving of the hair of the Nazarite for the purpose of offering it at the door of the tabernacle (ξυράω).

It seems rather to have been of the nature of that vow which Josephus speaks of as customary for persons in any affliction, viz. to make a vow that, for thirty days previous to that on which they intend to offer sacrifice, they will abstain from wine and will shave off...their hair... But it further appears, from certain passages in the Mishna, that, if any one had a Nazarite vow upon him outside the limits of the Holy Land, he could not fulfill such vow till he was come to the Holy Land, to Jerusalem; but it was allowable in such case to cut his hair short (κείρεσθαι τὴν κεφαλήν), and as some say to take it with him to Jerusalem, and there offer it at the same time that he offered his sacrifice and shaved his head (ξυρήσασθαι). It would seem, therefore, that either in a severe illness or under some great danger (ἀνάγκη) St. Paul had made such a vow; that he had been unwilling to cut his hair short at Corinth, where he was thrown so much into the society of Greeks, and therefore did so at Cenchreae just before he embarked for Syria....

My point here is not to endorse this explanation of Paul's vow but rather to point out the complexities involved in figuring out exactly why he might have shaved his head at the town of Cenchrea in fulfillment of a vow. This does not fit with anything else in Luke's narrative, nor is it clear enough to assist any theological theme. We are not even given any story about *why* Paul took a vow. Luke mentions it so hastily that, as mentioned in various commentaries, some have been unsure whether the one who had the vow was actually Aquila rather than Paul! The best explanation for the inclusion of this pointless and somewhat puzzling detail is simply that the author believed it to be true and decided to write it down while he was telling the events—a classic case of an unexplained allusion.

2. Unnecessary details

Unnecessary details are similar to unexplained allusions in that both confirmations of artlessness serve no apparent literary or theological purpose within the document in which they occur. The unnecessary details I will discuss in this section are not especially puzzling. They do not allude to an explanation that is missing from the passage.

Again, undesigned coincidences rely upon numerous unnecessary details of this sort, as discussed in *Hidden in Plain View* and in the previous chapter. Here are a few of the many unnecessary details that participate in undesigned coincidences: Mark mentions that the grass was green at the time of the feeding of the five thousand.[1] John mentions that Jesus asked Philip where they could buy

---

[1] Lydia McGrew, *Hidden in Plain View: Undesigned Coincidences in the Gospels and Acts* (Chillicothe, OH, DeWard, 2017), pp. 66–67.

bread, and John mentions that Philip was from the town of Bethsaida.[2] Matthew says that Herod mused to his servants about who Jesus was.[3] John mentions that the name of the servant whose ear Peter cut off was Malchus.[4] Luke mentions that the feeding of the five thousand took place near Bethsaida.[5] And so forth. Again and again, we find that these little details dovetail beautifully with comments made in other accounts. Thus undesigned coincidences show that such pointless little details (pointless from the perspective of heavy themes) are exactly what they appear to be—historical notes of veracity, mentioned by the way. We have unnecessary details in the Gospels because they are historical reports, not literarily massaged documents in which the authors alter or fabricate even peripheral details, much less larger incidents.

Notice, too, that these unnecessary details occur in Luke and Matthew as well as in Mark. I point this out because so often, redactive critics assume that Luke and Matthew merely add to or redact stories in Mark without factual justification. But as I pointed out in *Hidden in Plain View*,[6] undesigned coincidences challenge this assumption. There are specific places where Matthew or Luke appears to be telling the same story found in Mark but add some small detail, not in Mark, that participates in such a coincidence.

Unnecessary details can also participate in incidental external confirmations, as when the Jewish leaders in John say that the Temple has been in the process of being built for forty-six years. As noted in the previous chapter, Craig Blomberg refers to this number as "unusually precise" and notes the lack of any apparent symbolic significance.[7] In other words, it looks like reportage on John's part, and as a matter of fact it fits together quite well with Luke's time references in Luke 3.1. Similarly, John mentions that there were five porticoes at the Pool of Bethesda (John 5.2), and archaeology has confirmed this otherwise pointless detail.[8]

---

[2] Ibid., pp. 107–110.

[3] Ibid., pp. 87–89.

[4] Ibid., pp. 118–120.

[5] Ibid., pp. 89–91, 107–110.

[6] Ibid., pp. 28, 87–88, 93, 95.

[7] Craig Blomberg, "A Constructive Traditional Response to New Testament Criticism" in James K. Hoffmeier and Dennis R. Magary, eds., *Do Historical Matters Matter to Faith* (Wheaton, IL: Crossway Books, 2012), p. 361

[8] Joachim Jeremias, *The Rediscovery of Bethesda*, New Testament Archaeology Monograph, no. 1 (Louisville, KY: Southern Baptist Theological Seminary, 1966), p. 31. "The Bethesda Pool: Site of One of Jesus' Miracles," *Bible History Daily*, 4/24/2018, https://www.biblicalarchaeology.org/daily/biblical-sites-places/jerusalem/the-bethesda-pool-site-of-one-of-jesus%E2%80%99-miracles/.

There are many unnecessary details that do not participate (as far as we have yet found) in undesigned coincidences or external confirmations, but their narrative quality is the same as those that do. An unnecessary detail appears to be there for no special reason; it is there just because the author believed it was true. It lends verisimilitude to the account precisely by being so pointless, and in some cases (though not always) vivid. Such details are thus plausible marks of witness testimony—either from the author himself or from one or more of his human sources. There are so many of these in John's Gospel—especially passing notes of time and quantity—that I will not try to give them all here.

In John 1.39, the narrator notes the hour when the disciples of John the Baptist went with Jesus to his lodging—about the tenth hour. While commentators have disagreed as to whether we should interpret this time note according to the Roman or the Jewish use of hours, my point is its specificity and the lack of necessity for it in the narrative. The author says that they stayed with Jesus that day, but (without knowing which system of hours he is using) we can't be sure whether this refers to a long day beginning about 10 a.m. or merely to the remainder of the day from about 4 p.m. Either way, there is no special literary or other symbolism implied whatsoever for the hour of the day. John merely notes it realistically in the narrative.

Similarly, John mentions with pointless precision both the number and size of the water pots at the marriage at Cana in John 2.6. There were, he says, six of them, each containing about twenty or thirty gallons. In very *general* terms, one can say that the number and size of the water pots help to emphasize the quantity of wine that Jesus miraculously produced. But there was no reason to be so precise to achieve that effect. Indeed, if John had invented the number of jars for that reason, one might have expected it to be even larger—ten, say. The number six and the almost intrusive estimated number of gallons bespeaks rather the eye of the beholder. While one can strain to make up some symbolic reason for *any* number or other detail given in the Bible, and while the minds of critics are endlessly inventive, such an exercise is merely multiplying theories without necessity and without any objective control. We find such artless precision in real reportage when a witness has an excellent memory, and on the face of it, that is what these examples appear to be, unless they are the result of a deep type of deceptiveness that deliberately covers its fictions in pointless, invented details for the very purpose of lending them verisimilitude—an option I will discuss below.

When Mark describes the stilling of the storm in Chapter 4, he notes in passing that Jesus was not merely asleep in the boat but was "in the stern, asleep on the cushion" (Mark 4.38). The fact that Jesus was asleep is all that Mark need for the narrative. The further details of the stern and the cushion add nothing to the story but specificity itself.

The Gospels distinguish the feeding of the five thousand and the feeding of the four thousand by two unnecessary details, found in multiple Synoptic Gospels. I will take them from Mark. First, the number of loaves differs specifically—five loaves in the feeding of the five thousand and seven in the feeding of the four thousand. Mark mentions this both when he tells the events and later when Jesus is reminding the disciples (Mark 6.38, 8.5–6, 8.18–21). Mark specifies the number of fish as two in the feeding of the five thousand and says only "a few" in the feeding of the four thousand. It is interesting that Mark does not give a different specific number for the fish in the four thousand feeding; perhaps his source did not know or remember a specific number for that incident, and if so Mark did not invent one. Jesus is discussing bread with his disciples in the later passage, where he chides them for not trusting him after seeing the miracles, so he emphasizes the numbers of loaves. These numbers would have stuck in their minds. While the number seven, of course, can be given many alleged symbolic meanings, any such attempt for five would be more contrived, and Jesus contrasts the numbers as he simply describes the literal differences between the two events.

J. J. Blunt has a similar and even more interesting comment on the consistent distinction maintained between both the numbers *and kinds* of baskets of leftovers taken up in the two events:

> [T]here was, no doubt, a marked difference between these two vessels, whatever that difference might be, for κοφίνος is invariably used when the miracle of the five thousand is spoken of; and σπυρίς is invariably used when the miracle of the four thousand is spoken of. Moreover, such distinction is clearly suggested to us in Matt. xvi. 9, 10, where our Saviour cautions his disciples against the "leaven of the Pharisees and Sadducees" and in so doing, alludes to each of these miracles thus: "Do ye not understand, neither remember the five loaves of the five thousand, and how many baskets (κοφίνους) ye took up? neither the seven loaves of the four thousand, and how many baskets (σπυρίδας) ye took up?" though here, again, the distinction is entirely lost in our translation, both [words] being still rendered "basket" alike.[9]

---

[9] J. J. Blunt, *Undesigned Coincidences in the Writings Both of the Old and New Testament: An Argument of Their Veracity* (London: John Murray, 1863), p. 264.

The distinction Blunt notes between the words for "basket" also occurs in Mark's account of Jesus' rebuke to the disciples. Blunt shrewdly notes that translators who do not maintain the distinction were not witnesses and hence are less likely to think it important. (Of course some modern translators do make a distinction in the words for the baskets.)

> [S]uch uniformity mark[s] very clearly the two miracles to be distinctly impressed on the minds of the Evangelists, as real events; the circumstantial peculiarities of each present to them, even to the shape of the baskets, as though they were themselves actual eye-witnesses: or at least had received their report from those who were so.
>
> It is next to impossible that such coincidence in both cases, between the fragments and the receptacles, respectively, should have been preserved by chance; or by a teller of a tale at third or fourth hand; and accordingly we see that the coincidence is in fact entirely lost by our translators, who were not witnesses of the miracles; and whose attention did not happen to be drawn to the point.[10]

Although Blunt is careful to note that we do not have absolutely clear independent information about the meanings of the words, he also points out that the word used for "basket" in the feeding of the four thousand, where they take up fewer baskets full of leftovers, is the same as that used in Acts 9.25 for the container in which the believers let Paul down over a wall when he needed to escape from Damascus. This supports the idea that the baskets used to pick up leftovers after the feeding of the four thousand were fairly large, which would explain why there were fewer of them than the twelve taken up in the feeding of the five thousand.

I note how these simple, real-world observations render, if possible, even sillier than usual any attempts to find symbolic numerological significance in the numbers "twelve" and "seven" for the baskets of leftovers collected.

Another unnecessary (and vivid) detail occurs in Mark 10.50. A blind man, named here as Bartimaeus, has been calling out to Jesus to help him. When Jesus orders them to bring Bartimaeus to him and Bartimaeus hears this message, Mark's Gospel says, "Throwing aside his cloak, he jumped up and came to Jesus." The small detail that he threw his cloak aside is unnecessary for furthering the story itself. We can only guess that perhaps the cloak was heavy or that Bartimaeus thought that it might trip him or just that he wanted to go to Jesus quickly, unencumbered. The detail is realistic, credible, and bespeaks the eye of one who saw the event.

---

[10] Ibid., p. 265.

At about this same point in Jesus' life, while he is passing through Jericho, Luke narrates the calling of Zacchaeus the tax collector. When Zacchaeus climbs a tree in order to see Jesus, he chooses a sycamore tree (Luke 19.4). Luke distinguishes this word from the slightly different word used by Jesus when he says in Luke 17.6 that those with enough faith can remove a sycamine tree (probably the black mulberry) and cast it into the sea. There is no need for Luke to be so precise about these kinds of trees. Almost any reasonably tall tree will do to help a short man to see over a crowd, and uprooting any tree and casting it into the sea is a good metaphor for strong faith. The best explanation is that Luke's sources (most likely human sources) specified these trees in these places and that he faithfully reported them, maintaining the distinction between the similar words.

A bonus in this case is that, as Peter Williams points out, the sycamore tree did not grow in northern Mediterranean countries at the time but did grow in Jericho. Thus, external information confirms Luke's unnecessarily specific botanical detail about Zacchaeus.[11]

As the time of the Triumphal Entry nears, Jesus sends his disciples to find a colt on which he will ride. Mark relates, "They went away and found a colt tied at the door, outside in the street" (Mark 11.4). Only Mark is so specific, almost emphatically so, about where they found the colt. The colt was not in a courtyard but outside. It was, even more specifically, outside at the door, in the street. None of these specifics are necessary to the story, and Matthew and Luke do not bother to include them. These unnecessary details present, once again, the picture of a vivid scene, witnessed by someone who was present and remembered exactly where the colt was tied.

Finally (of the instances I am discussing here), John 21 contains a wonderful little unnecessary detail in the scene at the Sea of Galilee after Jesus' resurrection. Jesus appears on the shore in the dawn, and the beloved disciple is the first to recognize him. When he exclaims to Peter, "It is the Lord!" Peter dives into the water, not waiting for the boat to land. I will return below to the topic of Peter's personality, but here I want to draw attention to one small thing: John says, "When Simon Peter heard that it was the Lord, he put on his outer garment, for he was stripped for work, and threw himself into the sea" (John 21.7). As Leon Morris notes, this is a surprising detail. "When we reflect on it, it is a little strange that a man about to cast himself into the sea should put on a coat. This can scarcely be an invention."[12] The fact that Peter was stripped might explain his action; perhaps

---

[11] Peter J. Williams, *Can We Trust the Gospels* (Wheaton, IL: Crossway, 2018), p. 82.

[12] Leon Morris, *Studies in the Fourth Gospel* (Grand Rapids, MI: Eerdmans, 1969), p. 206.

he wanted to cover himself out of respect for Jesus. But this is quite roundabout. We conjecture a psychological reason for his donning the outer garment only after reading that he did so. It would not have been particularly surprising if Peter had not bothered to put anything on, leaving himself more free for swimming. During Jesus' ministry these men must have been around each other frequently in various states of undress for bathing and changing as they traveled together. The question of precisely how much clothing Peter was wearing at the moment is not germane to the story anyway. John mentions that he was stripped only because he has seen fit to mention that he put a coat *on* before diving in. This little sequence—Peter, in haste, grabs a coat to cover his nakedness and then jumps in—is beautiful in its unnecessary specificity and realism.

Richard Bauckham, though convinced that three of the Gospels (Mark, Luke, and John) do reflect witness testimony, appears ambivalent about vivid detail as evidence of witness testimony. On the one hand, he makes explicit comments to the effect that vivid details do not support witness testimony. On the other hand, he finds such details interesting and treats them as relevant in practice:

> An imaginative and skilled storyteller can also write with vivid detail, and so this feature of Mark's narratives may be evidence only of his own artistry. On the other hand, eye-witness testimony need not necessarily include vivid detail.... Whether or not Mark's vivid detail comes from his eyewitness sources, we can observe how readily Luke and especially Matthew, in the interests of abbreviating Mark's narrative, dispense with it. This suggests that in no more than one step, from the vivid details as told by an eyewitness to the text of an author incorporating that testimony in a written work, vivid detail could easily disappear. So vivid detail has no probative force—for or against—in an argument about eyewitness testimony.
>
> That said, it is at least interesting that some of the stories we have suggested come from those who are named in them are among the most vividly told. This is true of the raising of Jairus's daughter (Mark 5:22–24a, 35–43), the healing of Bartimaeus (Mark 10:46–52), the story of Zacchaeus (Luke 19:1–10), and the story of Cleopas and his companion (Luke 24:13–35). The last three of these four stories are certainly told from the perspective of the named characters. In fact, if the details in these stories really are recollected, rather than the product of storytelling imagination, they can only have been recollected by, respectively, Bartimaeus, Zacchaeus, and Cleopas (or his anonymous companion). The recollection of the raising of Jairus's daughter, if that is indeed the basis of the story, could be that of Peter, James, John, or the girl's mother, but could at any rate plausibly be that of Jairus.[13]

---

[13] Richard Bauckham, *Jesus and the Eyewitnesses: The Gospels as Eyewitness Testimony* (Grand Rapids, MI: Eerdmans, 2017), pp. 54–55.

Of course, the vivid detail in Mark can scarcely be used as evidence of Mark's close-ness to eyewitness testimony, since a good storyteller (whether Mark or his oral source) can create vivid detail…[14]

In response to this, I note first that not all unnecessary details are vivid and that Bauckham's focus in these passages is upon vividness. This is especially true of several of the unexplained allusions mentioned in the last section and also of several of the unnecessary details mentioned in this section. It is simply not true that a good storyteller would be likely to include all of these. The statement that Jesus and his mother and brothers went to Capernaum and stayed there a few days (John 2.12) is not part of any particular story and *interrupts* the flow of John's narrative. The statement that Philip was from Bethsaida, made by John in the course of describing how some Greeks came to Philip at a feast and wanted to see Jesus (John 12.20–21), is also an interruption. There may be some reason why Philip's being from Bethsaida in Galilee seemed relevant to the narrator, but it is obscure if so, and there is no reason to think that the first audience would have found it any clearer. Galilee was not a Greek region. Again, in John 2.6 the hyper-precision concerning the number of water pots at the marriage at Cana and their approx-imate size is almost a distraction. A lively storyteller would probably emphasize that they were *large* water pots, but it is not good storytelling practice to get into the nitty-gritty of how many gallons each one held.

But even when it comes to vivid details (such as Bartimaeus's throwing off his cloak), Bauckham underrates their relevance when he says that we cannot use them as evidence merely because a good storyteller *can* create vivid detail fictionally. From a probabilistic perspective, the fact that someone engaging in fakery *can* do some-thing does not mean that the presence of such a feature is not *evidence* for reportage. If the mere possibility of a logically possible alternative explanation were enough to destroy evidential relevance, rational empirical and historical inference would be impossible.[15] A fictional storyteller includes vivid detail *precisely because* such details make his story *look true*. He may do so in an openly fictional work, like a novel, but the Gospels are certainly not novels. Not even the literary device theorists consider them to be so. Or a storyteller may do so in the service of trying to deceive his read-ers into thinking that he knows more about what happened than he does or that he is telling an entirely factual story when he is partially making it up.

---

[14] Ibid., p. 343.

[15] Lydia McGrew, "The World, the Deceiver, and The Face in the Frost," *Quaestiones Disputatae*, 7:2 (2017), pp. 112–146.

Here, as in the case of the forty-six years and the Temple cleansing, discussed in the last chapter, the literary device theorist would be in a cleft stick if he tried to dismiss the relevance of vivid details on the grounds that they *might* be fabricated to make a story interesting. As we saw there, the literary device theorists wish to say both that the Gospels are to some extent historical documents and that the authors are not deceivers since their alterations were considered acceptable at the time. But the entire previous section of this book has refuted the claims that the Gospels belonged to a specific genre that was a mixture of fact and fiction. If Mark, in an uncanny anticipation of much later literary realism,[16] invented the detail that Bartimaeus flung off his cloak to come to Jesus or the unnecessary specifics about where the colt was tied in order to make the stories more credible, he was trying to make it look like he knew something that he did not know. If this were true, we could not easily absolve Mark of the charge of deception.

Bauckham tacitly acknowledges this point concerning the Gospel of John:

> Thirdly, the occasions on which the Beloved Disciple appears in the narrative are marked by observational detail. As Tovey puts it, "at every point where the beloved disciple appears . . . the narrative includes items of close detail which suggest 'on the spot,' eyewitness report." Lincoln objects to this claim: "Vivid details are part and parcel of an omniscient narrator's perspective in good storytelling and in this narrative are also found at points where the Beloved Disciple does not appear." Of course, the presence of such narrative detail cannot prove that the Gospel really does embody eyewitness reporting, but that is not what is being claimed here. The point is rather that the Gospel portrays the Beloved Disciple as one qualified to give eyewitness reports of the occasions on which he was present. Although there is observational detail in other passages of the Gospel, what is notable is how consistently the appearances of the Beloved Disciple are accompanied by such detail.
>
> Thus, in 1:39, there is the "seemingly unmotivated detail" of the specific time: "about the tenth hour," that is, four o'clock in the afternoon. In 13:26, the Beloved Disciple, from his position next to Jesus at the table, observes Jesus dip a piece of bread and give it to Judas. In 18:18 (relevant if the "other disciple" of vv. 15–16 is the Beloved Disciple) there is considerably more vivid detail about the fire than in the Markan parallel (14:54). According to 19:33–35, the Beloved Disciple observed that Jesus' legs were not broken and that the thrust of the sword into his side pro-

---

[16] C. S. Lewis makes a similar point about John. Fictional realism in minute and vivid detail is anachronistic as ascribed to a work of this period; nor does it become common shortly after the writing of the Gospels. Hence, Lewis says that John would have "anticipated the...technique of modern...realistic narrative" "without known predecessors or successors" if he invented the vivid stories of Jesus. C. S. Lewis, "Modern Theology and Biblical Criticism" in *Christian Reflections*, edited by Walter Hooper (Grand Rapids, MI: Eerdmans, 1967), p. 155.

duced flows of blood and water. In the empty tomb, Peter "saw the linen wrappings lying there, and the cloth that had been on Jesus' head, not lying with the linen wrappings but rolled up in a place by itself" (20:6–7), and the Beloved Disciple shares this observation (20:8). Finally, ch. 21 has the detail about Jesus' preparing breakfast (21:9) and the exact number of the huge catch of fish (21:11). Such evidence should not be misused. On the one hand, in many cases the detail is, of course, significant detail, with a clear role in the narrative, while, on the other hand, vivid detail is the stock-in-trade of a skilled storyteller, such as the author of this Gospel most certainly was. *All the same, these details do help to give readers the impression that the Gospel portrays the Beloved Disciple as an observant witness of what happened.*[17]

If the Gospel is *not* dependent on real memories of the beloved disciple, it is *pretending* to be precisely that, which is not something that literary device theorists want to admit.

Indirectly, disconfirming a particular alternative to truthful reportage helps to confirm reportage.[18] As we whittle down the alternatives, reportage gets a boost. If there were lots of plausible ways for the Gospels not to be reportage that would explain the facts, this would increase the probability that they are not reportage. The genre suggested by the literary device theorists is one proposed alternative, and the considerations given here disconfirm it. If we must choose between their being extremely clever deception and their being reportage, this consideration moves us in the direction of reportage.

The more we learn about the Gospels, the more we realize how difficult it would be for their authors to create such an appearance of verisimilitude by mere cleverness and therefore how improbable *that* option is. Deception is not the simplest explanation for the appearance of verisimilitude and witness testimony. Once we admit that the Gospels *look like* witness testimony, the burden of proof has shifted, and it would require other evidence to cause us to conclude that appearances are deceiving. The presence of undesigned coincidences and incidental confirmations supporting otherwise irrelevant details is strong evidence *against* deliberate deception.[19] Other unnecessary details are likewise *prima facie* evidence of genuine testimony.

---

[17] Bauckham, *Jesus and the Eyewitnesses*, pp. 398–99. Emphasis added.

[18] As a probabilistic matter, it is not *invariably* true that disconfirming one explanation of the data helps to confirm another possible explanation. That is a matter of the specific evidence and hypotheses involved. In this case, it is correct to say that disconfirmation of the literary device view confirms the reportage view, since the evidence in question shows that the documents appear to be realistic.

[19] Peter Williams discusses some wonderful external incidental confirmations in his chapter "Did the Gospel Authors Know Their Stuff?" in *Can We Trust the Gospels*, pp. 51–86. These include, among

Bauckham's own cited memory studies indicate that both vivid and irrelevant detail are indeed characteristic of what he calls "recollective memory" of real events:

> Recollective memories are usually characterized by visual imagery. Brewer reports an experiment that showed that "most recollective memory gave rise to reports of visual imagery. Accurate recollections tended to show stronger imagery than inaccurate recollections."
>
> …As we have noted already, Brewer has argued that recollective memories frequently include irrelevant details, and this is an argument for a copy component in recollective memory. Such details have been especially associated with flashbulb memories; in fact, they are not peculiar to flashbulb memories but are found also in other recollective memories.[20]

In other words, both vivid and irrelevant details are characteristic of many eyewitness memories—a point certainly relevant to the probabilistic evaluation of such features in the Gospels.

Bauckham states that "there is little irrelevant detail in the Gospel narratives," though he admits that such a perception may be an artifact of the "deep-rooted desire" of Gospels scholars to "explain all details as significant."[21] This is certainly true, especially since the significances that scholars attribute to narrative details are often highly speculative and could be arbitrarily different if the scholars happened to think of something else. Bauckham rightly notes that the stories in the Gospels (perhaps especially the Synoptics) may have already been boiled down somewhat for ease of memory and repetition, which would tend to eliminate irrelevant details. Nonetheless, there remain quite a number of irrelevant details in the Gospels, carrying valuable evidential significance.

3. Reconcilable variation

The 19th-century Anglican scholar T. R. Birks, editor of William Paley's work, coined the phrase "reconcilable variation" or "reconcilable diversity" for the evidence from Gospel harmonization. Birks intended "reconcilable variation" to be

---

others, the fact that the Pharisees really did debate about tithing dill and cumin (p. 81, compare Matt. 23.23), the inclusion of obscure towns in Palestine such as Chorazin and their location in relation to each other (p. 60, compare Luke 10.13), the fact that Luke, who was probably not from Galilee, refers to the Sea of Galilee as a mere "lake" (p. 58, Luke 5.1–2, 8.22, 23, 33), the artlessly accurate use of names in their proper frequencies, and, perhaps even more fascinating, the use of disambiguating phrases by speakers precisely when using the most common names, including "Jesus" (pp. 69–75).

[20] Ibid., p. 332.

[21] Ibid., p. 343.

an umbrella term, covering undesigned coincidences as well as the possibility of plausible harmonization where there is no undesigned coincidence.[22]

> The entire sameness of the narrative, in two or three distinct works, would weaken, and almost destroy the authority of all, except the earliest, since it would be a strong proof that they were mere copies, and that the writers had no independent means of information. On the other hand, positive contradictions would prove that one or other work was inaccurate, and if very numerous and important, would go far to convict them of utter and wilful falsehood. And hence the very test of historical truth, in such cases, is found in the substantial unity of the various narratives, their partial diversity, and the reconcileable nature of that diversity, when due allowance is made for the purpose of each writer, and the individual character of their separate works.[23]

By the "purpose of each writer and the individual character of their separate works," Birks does not mean any sort of fictionalization but rather the normal selectivity of different factual reporters—for example, the fact that John reports more of Jesus' early Judean ministry and more events in Judea than the Synoptics do.[24]

Whether and in what senses harmonizability is evidence of historicity is a fascinating question, which I can address here only relatively briefly. Because Birks includes undesigned coincidences (and even in some cases external confirmations[25]) under the heading of reconcilable variation, it will be helpful to break the concept down a bit. I have already said enough both here and in *Hidden in Plain View* about the evidential value of undesigned coincidences and have published technical work on the subject.[26] When one narrative contains casual details that explain something different stated or implied in another narrative, we have evidence of both independence between the two narratives and the truth of both.

But what about harmonizability when there is no such explanatory relationship? Is that evidence in itself of the truth of the narratives? Well, that depends. First, harmonization plays a major evidential role in answering objections to historicity based on alleged contradictions. In that sense, harmonization has evidential value as a defensive move. The skeptic or literary critic of the Gospels

---

[22] T. R. Birks, *Horae Evangelicae, or The Internal Evidence of the Gospel History* (London: Seeleys, 1852), pp. v, 269–271.

[23] Ibid., pp. 269–270.

[24] Ibid., pp. 273ff.

[25] Ibid., p. 287.

[26] Lydia McGrew, *Hidden in Plain View*, pp. 11–20, 225–226; Lydia McGrew, "Undesigned Coincidences and Coherence for an Hypothesis," *Erkenntnis*, On-line First, August 6, 2018, https://doi.org/10.1007/s10670-018-0050-4.

alleges a tension or contradiction; the advocate of a reportage model points out that this is not really the case and explains why.

This book is full of such examples, and Part Four will contain even more. One that we have discussed recently concerns the alleged tension between John and Mark about whether or not Jesus carried his own cross. Noting that John's claim that Jesus did carry his own cross is not really in conflict with Mark's account (besides being confirmed by the external evidence of Roman custom) is evidentially valuable insofar as it teaches the habit of commonsense hermeneutics, reminding scholars and readers not to run after literary themes and tensions unnecessarily. Similarly, pointing out that Jesus would not have historically appeared "in control" of his death by being forced to carry his cross and emphasizing the anachronistic nature of such an "explanation" of John's narrative helps to activate real-world understanding. Pointing out that a witness may have been especially psychologically impressed by the sight of the bleeding Jesus, forced to carry his cross to the city gate until he was unable to go on, brings in the real-world conditions of human testimony, too easily forgotten in the world of scholarly theorizing.

Evidentially, the value of noting reconcilable variation is thus defensive, but in the best of senses. Considered in this defensive role and applied to just one pair of narratives of one incident, such harmonization does not give us more reason than we had at the outset to consider the documents to be historical. But it answers an objection and teaches a habit of mental toughness in the face of poor methodology that will stand us in good stead when considering questions of historicity. Reasonable harmonization serves to remind us of evidence we already have in the form of common sense. When we recognize that two Temple cleansings aren't as implausible as the theorists are telling us, we have gained something in our conscious understanding both of the world and of the Gospels. When we think about the fact that a woman who was with a group (e.g., Mary Magdalene with the women who went to the tomb in Matt. 28.1) may *leave* that group, and that people in real life often leave groups that they are with, or go away from and return to certain locations, we are poised to give a robust and reasonable answer to alleged contradictions in the resurrection narratives. When we remember that sometimes one person hears something that another person does not hear, and when we apply this real-world insight to the crucifixion narratives, we are armed against attacks on Jesus' words from the cross that attempt to "whittle down" the total number of his sayings. Such a re-introduction of common sense into biblical interpretation will correspond to a raised evaluation of the Gospels' historicity for those who might have been inclined to waver on these points and therefore needed to have them stressed. For someone who already had a robust sense of these points, it will not add any new evidence.

But now consider a different type of example: Suppose that John is accused of a crime that occurred at a particular time at a particular address. Police begin to check out John's movements on that day. Mary tells the police that she saw John at the gym at a time that would give him an alibi. Jill tells the police that she ran into John at a friend's house on that same day. Jill gives a time for John's presence at the friend's house just twenty minutes after the time when Mary said she saw him at the gym. As it turns out, the friend's house is just ten minutes away by car from the gym. Both locations—the house and the gym—are a good forty minutes away from the location of the crime, even in the best traffic conditions. Hence, both Jill's and Mary's evidence contribute to John's alibi. They also exhibit a rather special kind of reconcilable variation. While they place John at different locations within a relatively short span of time, it is quite possible for John to have been in each of those places at the stated times. Moreover, it would have been quite easy for either Jill or Mary to have said something that *contradicted* the other's alibi for John. Suppose that Mary had said that she saw John at the gym just twenty minutes later. Then it wouldn't have been possible for both her and Jill to be right. At a minimum, one of them would have to be somewhat mistaken about the time. Or suppose that Jill had said that she saw John at the friend's house just fifteen minutes earlier. In that case, too, a contradiction would have resulted. On the other hand, if Jill and Mary were colluding to give John an alibi, it is more likely that they would both have said that they saw him in the *same* location rather than working out an elaborate alibi that required him to drive from one place to another in a short and rather precise period of time. But if either Jill or Mary lied and they did *not* collude, it is rather surprising that one of them did not contradict the other, since the time periods involved are so close. Hence, in a situation like this where it is especially easy for two narratives to contradict one another if not based on fact, even a single harmonization provides positive evidence of trustworthiness. Non-contradiction is more probable here given truth than given independence and invention, and the variation of the stories is evidence of independence. The fact that Jill's and Mary's stories are compatible with each other makes them stronger together than the two alibis would be separately, since their compatibility is difficult to explain aside from truth.

An example of this kind of reconcilable variation, which I have called elsewhere an undesigned coincidence, concerns Aquila and Priscilla in Acts and in Paul's epistles. I give a detailed discussion in *Hidden in Plain View*.[27] The short version is this: Paul sends greetings *from* Aquila and Priscilla to the Corinthians in I Corinthians (when he is apparently writing from Ephesus) but *to* Aquila and Priscilla in the book of Romans (which he appears to have written from Corinth). This must mean that Aquila and Priscilla were with him in Ephesus when he wrote I Corinthians but that he expected them to be in Rome when he himself was in Corinth writing Romans not very long afterwards. These locations for Aquila and Priscilla are possible given what else Acts says about them, though Acts does not affirm either claim directly. However, if the author of Acts were writing fictionally or partially fictionally, and if he "had" Priscilla and Aquila leave Ephesus too soon in Acts 19 or stay with Paul in his travels at the beginning of Acts 20, a contradiction would have resulted. They needed to be with Paul when he wrote I Corinthians (as I argue in *Hidden in Plain View*, almost certainly during the time period described in Acts 19.21–22); there also needed to be time for them to separate from Paul after that and travel to Rome and for Paul reasonably to believe that they had arrived there. This, of course, is a whirlwind description of the coherence of the documents, but it should be sufficient to show that this case resembles the case of the alibis outlined above.

We find another application of the notion of being consistent and harmonizable when we think of the Gospels as a whole. Here I am coming closest to stating in probabilistic terms what Birks says in the quotation above. Consider large portions of, say, the Gospels of Matthew and John. While a *single* harmonization of an alleged tension merely removes the objection and returns us to an independent estimation of the historicity of the documents, the observation that again and again the documents survive such challenges while including great variation about the life of Jesus has a further, positive effect. Put simply, what sort of documents *are* these, that they manifest variation showing independent information about the events, and different emphases, and yet manage to cover the life of the same person while being reconcilable with each other again and again? If the authors were frequently inventing material, but were not dependent, we would expect *more* intractable apparent contradictions than (upon a fair and careful examination) we find. If, on the other hand, they were dependent (either upon each other or upon a common source), we would not find so many variations and even apparent contradictions requiring harmonization in the first place. This is not to deny that there remain some recalcitrant alleged contradictions—places where even the careful and just examiner may not be able to find a satisfactory, plausible harmonization.

---

[27] Lydia McGrew, *Hidden in Plain View*, pp. 175–181.

But there are not a great many. For the most part, the variations are what we would expect to find among truthful, knowledgeable witnesses giving different but complementary information. Thus, the fact that the Gospels are harmonizable *so often* and across such a *wide variety of narratives* means that they are consistent when consistency on that scale would be hard to come by if the authors were not historical in intention and knowledgeable about the facts.

4. Peter's Personality

This section is about Peter's personality, but this is just one example of its kind. In *The Eye of the Beholder* I will illustrate the unity of the personality of Jesus in all four Gospels and the "high-resolution" picture of Jesus himself that we obtain from the Gospels' honest reporting. I am postponing that discussion to that volume, because the attacks on John have so often taken the form of claiming that Jesus talks and acts in a radically different way in the Gospel of John than he does in the Synoptic Gospels. Demonstrating the remarkable unity of the personality of Jesus in the Gospels is an important part of defending John's historicity. The evidence from unity of personality in Scripture is one type of argument that 19th-century writers used and that has fallen out of vogue. We would do well to revive it.

Jesus' personality is not the only one to stand out in sharp relief throughout the New Testament. Acts, for example, displays Luke's gifts as a reporter when he portrays Paul's personality, which is obviously the same as that in Paul's epistles. Yet the similarities are subtle and indirect. They consist in traits such as Paul's touchiness about money and his tendency to "guilt trip" his converts and followers.[28] In *The Eye of the Beholder*, I will show how Mary and Martha's different personalities in Luke and John intersect realistically with Jesus' love and understanding.

Christians have heard so many sermons about Peter that by this time they may take for granted the Gospels' consistent portrayal of him. But it probably does not occur to all those who preach on the subject to point out that this consistency is an argument for historicity. The subject could receive a much longer treatment, but a few points will suffice to sketch the case.

The most noteworthy characteristic of Peter is his impulsive, emotional, and at times boastful nature. I categorize these three traits together because they are so closely related that it would be difficult to illustrate them separately. Though his emotion sometimes takes the form of expressions of humility as well as boasting, his extravagance is the same across all the stories.

---

[28] Ibid., pp. 182–183.

322 | *The Mirror or the Mask*

Sometimes this trait takes the form of physical action. E.g., Peter flings himself at Jesus' feet after the first great catch of fish, imploring him to leave him, for he is a sinful man (Luke 5.8). (This incident is unique to Luke.) Peter's impulsive nature reveals itself often in words as well. In his study of Peter's character, J. S. Howson comments,

> Most men find it difficult to be silent at critical moments of their lives. And all this is particularly true of vehement and impulsive natures. Such persons speak promptly, and speak unaffectedly, when they are under emotion. And such a character was St. Peter's.[29]

Naturally, it is Peter and not any other disciple who asks Jesus to invite him to come to him on the water—an aspect of the scene unique to Matthew (Matt. 14.28–31). Nor does this seem to be *just* showing off, though perhaps it is that as well. Such an impulse to go to Jesus on the water flows naturally from Peter's ardent nature. Says Howson,

> He is prompt and forward alike on the good side and on the bad side. On the one hand, a strong impulse of vigorous faith is displayed; on the other hand, he manifests a very wilful presumption.[30]

At the scene of the Transfiguration, Peter bursts out with the suggestion that they construct three tabernacles for Jesus, Elijah, and Moses. Mark says that Peter didn't know what to say, because they were all terrified. It is characteristic of Peter, when he does not know what to say, that he says something extravagant (Mark 9.6–7). Howson remarks pointedly, "[W]e cannot imagine this utterance coming from any other of the Twelve Apostles."[31]

It is Peter who boasts on the night of the Last Supper that, even if all of the other disciples fall away from Jesus, he never will (Mark 14.29). Howson comments, "We remember, as we ought to remember, the sin which followed this presumption. But we ought not forget the true, honest, ardent faith which inspired his rash promise."[32] When Jesus says that he is going away and that Peter cannot follow him now but will follow later, Peter asks touchingly, "Lord, why can I not follow you right now? I will lay down my life for you" (John 13.37), a comment

---

[29] J. S. Howson, *Horae Petrinae, or Studies in the Life of St. Peter* (London: The Religious Tract Society, 1883), p. 141.

[30] Ibid., p. 145.

[31] Ibid., p. 7.

[32] Ibid., pp. 147–148.

reported only in John. It is characteristic of Peter at this stage in his life that he does not really know himself, believing that he has more strength of purpose than he really has. It is Peter who strikes off the ear of the high priest's servant in defense of Jesus (John 18.10, Mark 14.47, Matt. 26.51, Luke 22.50).

When Mary Magdalene reports that the tomb is empty, it is Peter who rises up with the beloved disciple and runs to the tomb (John 20.3). When Jesus appears on the shore of the Sea of Galilee and the beloved disciple recognizes him, it is Peter who leaps into the water, not waiting for the boat to land (John 21.7). We have discussed this point above because of the unnecessary and unusual detail that he first put on his outer garment. Throughout all of these varied incidents, some unique to just one Gospel, the warmhearted though sometimes unwise and undisciplined personality of Peter comes through as clearly as possible.

Closely connected to Peter's impulsive and emotional character, though not mentioned as often, is his tendency to argue.[33] There is nothing remotely literary about this aspect of Peter's personality. We feel that we know him in this respect. He is like the annoying student who so often thinks he knows better than the teacher. In Peter's case, this touch of arrogant aggressiveness is intertwined with his overwhelming love for Jesus. The combination is unmistakable, unique to Peter, and (again) consistent across all the Gospels.

Several of the incidents already named exhibit this trait. Before the great catch of fish in Luke, Peter protests, "Master, we worked hard all night and caught nothing," though he immediately adds, "but I will do as you say and let down the nets" (Luke 5.8). One can sense that Peter does not think that Jesus knows much about fishing. No doubt the memory of his own earlier comment is part of why Peter feels such awe and embarrassment after the miracle of the great catch.

But though Peter is overawed for the moment in Luke 5, in some later incidents he is even more pushy. When Jesus begins teaching the disciples plainly that he is going to be killed, Peter has the effrontery to take him aside and rebuke him (Mark 8.32). Matthew gives his words at this point as, "God forbid it, Lord! This shall never happen to You" (Matt. 16.22), illustrating yet again the combined forwardness and affection in Peter's nature. This incident comes after Peter's confession of Jesus, and Matthew introduces the incident in verse 21 with the phrase "from that time Jesus began to show his disciples" that he must die. When Peter rebukes Jesus, then, he has recently confessed that Jesus is the Messiah. It seems that Jesus began right away to attempt to correct false ideas of imminent messianic earthly reign,

---

[33] Howson refers to this characteristic as Peter's impatience. Ibid., pp. 7, 144–147.

but Peter would not accept this. Jesus' breathtakingly stern rebuke, "Get behind Me, Satan; for you are not setting your mind on God's interests, but man's" (Mark 8.33) may have dampened Peter's tendency to argue for a while, but not for long.

When Jesus wants to wash Peter's feet on the night of the Last Supper, he first protests that Jesus must never wash his feet (John 13.8) and then tries to induce Jesus to wash his hands and head as well. He cannot simply allow Jesus to do to him what Jesus is doing to everyone else. Peter has his own ideas and presses them.

Even his boast that he will never forsake Jesus, though all the rest do, is an instance of his contrariness. For Jesus has just predicted that they *will* "all fall away" (Mark 14.27). Peter's loving heart is hurt at the implication that he will do anything of the kind. It does not seem to occur to him that Jesus knows more about the matter than he does. By this time he seems willing to consider that Jesus might die, but he insists (contrary to Jesus' own prediction) that in that case he will die with him (Mark 14.31).

Peter's forwardness, though somewhat tempered after his own great failure when he denied Jesus, is visible even in the scene where Jesus calls forth Peter's humility at last—the famous commission to feed the sheep in John 21. Peter no longer boasts that he loves Jesus more than the others. He simply tells Jesus that, as Jesus knows, he loves him. He is learning.[34] But even then, when he turns and sees the beloved disciple following, he gets curious and cannot forbear asking, "Lord, and what about this man?" (John 21.21–23) Jesus has to take him down a peg yet again, reminding him that his plans for the other disciple are not really Peter's business. Though Peter is not precisely arguing with Jesus here, the scene does seem to manifest the pattern in which Peter puts himself forward with an inappropriate question, argument, rebuke, or suggestion and has to be reined in.

It would be incredible if the Gospel authors had contrived to portray Peter again and again in ways that show such consistency of personality across such a variety of incidents. It is one thing to copy a story from someone else. It is another thing for several different authors to make the reader feel that he recognizes the character portrayed in entirely different scenes. This is the mark of historical memoirs. It places a stamp of truthfulness upon the reports. Howson comments,

> This study, short and scanty as it has been…contains evidence of the truth of the Gospel narratives. A certain very remarkable aspect of character in the case of St.

---

[34]There is an undesigned coincidence here, since the Gospel of John never mentions that Peter has boasted that he loves Jesus more than the other disciples. Hence, Jesus' line of questioning is unexplained in John alone. *Hidden in Plain View*, pp. 57–60.

Peter has been brought to view from an examination of several passages. It is the self-same aspect which comes to view in all of them; and the passages relate to scenes very various in their circumstances and details. Such uniformity with diversity cannot be the result of accident. Still less can it be the result of fraudulent design. No one can suppose that in any degree these passages are copied from one another, so as to produce the impression of identity in the personality of St. Peter. And let it here be added that, without exhausting the instances that might be adduced, examples have been purposely taken from all the four Gospels. If the...reader of Holy Scriptures will look into all this closely, he will see that it contains an evidential argument of no inconsiderable weight.[35]

Two more points concerning Peter are worth mentioning here, as they contribute to the case for the historicity of the Gospels. First, the Gospels and Acts show a remarkable consistency in their connection of Peter with John. On three occasions in the Synoptic Gospels, Jesus singles out Peter with the two sons of Zebedee, James and John, to be present while others are left behind. These are the raising of Jairus's daughter (Mark 5.37), the Transfiguration (Mark 9.2), and Jesus' agony in the Garden of Gethsemane (Mark 14.32). The author of Luke records in Acts a completely different set of scenarios where Peter and John are the most prominent leaders of the early church and are confronted by the Jewish leaders (Acts 3.1–4.21). Luke makes no attempt to include James the son of Zebedee in these scenes, showing once more his care in specifying what happened. If he did not know that all three—Peter, James, and John—were together in a particular incident, he was not going to bring in James.

The noteworthy coherence of John with the Synoptics on this point (Peter's special relationship with John) depends on whether one is prepared to grant on other grounds that the beloved disciple is John the son of Zebedee. Recently, Richard Bauckham has argued strenuously that he is not, though he is (on Bauckham's view) an eyewitness—a different John who was a disciple of Jesus but not one of the twelve.[36] That the Gospel of John associates the beloved disciple strongly with Peter is beyond question, and this happens in incidents independent of the Synoptics. Peter asks the beloved disciple by signals to try to find out who will betray Jesus (John 13.23–24). The beloved disciple (here called the "other disciple") obtains permission for Peter to enter the high priest's courtyard (John 18.15–16). Peter and the beloved disciple are apparently lodging together when Mary Mag-

---

[35] Howson, *Horae Petrinae*, p. 148.
[36] Richard Bauckham, *Jesus and the Eyewitnesses*, chapters 15, 16, 20.

dalene brings the news of the empty tomb early in the morning, and they run together to investigate (John 20.1–10). The beloved disciple tells Peter when he recognizes Jesus on the shore (John 21.7). Peter and the beloved disciple are close to one another in the scene in John 21, prompting Peter's question to Jesus, "What about this man?" (John 21.20–21) In fact, the close association of the beloved disciple with Peter, and the parallel this forms to Peter's close association with John the son of Zebedee in the Synoptics and Acts, provides one of many good arguments for the identity of the beloved disciple with John the son of Zebedee. I believe that the arguments as a whole are extremely strong for that identity, but the question of John's authorship is beyond the scope of the discussion here. If one is prepared to grant on independent grounds that the beloved disciple is John the son of Zebedee, then John's Gospel becomes part of the same pattern concerning Peter—namely, that he had an especially close relationship with John.

The second additional point concerning Peter in the Gospels concerns the little-noticed evidence that other Gospel authors *besides Mark* had independent contact with Peter. Our survey above has implied this already, since there are unique incidents there about Peter in other Gospels, but it is good to make it quite explicit. Mark was, by patristic evidence, the disciple of Peter, and parts of Mark's Gospel seem to come from Peter's perspective,[37] but we hear far less about the fact that there is unique Petrine information in the other Gospels. In addition to the unique scenes already mentioned in John, only John reports the earliest meeting between Jesus and Peter. This is the first time that Jesus gives Peter his nickname (John 1.40–42). John records what is probably a unique Petrine confession to Jesus' Messiahship (John 6.67–69). This incident, containing the famous words, "Lord, to whom shall we go?" illustrates yet again Peter's warm-hearted, expressive personality. It is difficult to imagine any other disciple uttering those words. Matthew has a few unique items: Peter's walking on the water in Chapter 14 and his specific words of rebuke to Jesus in Chapter 16. Interestingly, Mark does *not* report that Peter went out and wept bitterly after he denied Christ and the cock crowed. That item is found only in Matthew and Luke (Matt. 26.75, Luke 22.62).

Only Luke records the great catch of fish early in Jesus' ministry, with its enormous significance to Peter. This is the place where Jesus tells Simon Peter that from now on he will be a fisher of men (Luke 5.11). Even more subtly, only Luke records that Jesus looked at Peter just before Peter went out and wept (Luke

---

[37] See, e.g., Richard Bauckham, *Jesus and the Eyewitnesses*, Chapter 7.

22.61). Given Luke's scrupulous use of his sources, this provides interesting evidence that Luke had personal contact with Peter.

Further evidence of Luke's contact with Peter comes from a fascinating study by Colin Hemer of small differences in the Transfiguration scene between Luke and Mark. Mark says that this scene occurred six days after Jesus' previous sayings (Mark 9.2). Luke says that it occurred "some eight days" after the same sayings. Hemer comments on this, "It may be the mark of a careful writer to be *imprecise* where definiteness is not warranted: he is unwilling to press the current hesitancy of an informant into the convenient mould of other tradition."[38] In other words, if Peter was less precise about exactly when the Transfiguration occurred when talking with Luke than he was when Mark heard him, Luke was not going to substitute Mark's precision, even if he had access to Mark. Instead, he represented accurately his own independent evidence.

Hemer also notes the following points of difference: Only Luke points out that Jesus went up to the mountain for the purpose of prayer and that the Transfiguration occurred while he was praying (Luke 9.28). In fact, Luke specifies that the appearance of his face began to change during his prayer. Luke's account mentions the visually notable fact that there were two men with Jesus before it gives their identities as Moses and Elijah (vs. 30). The subject of the conversation (Jesus' death) is mentioned only in Luke (vs. 31). Only Luke notes that the disciples were extremely sleepy, but he carefully says that they were fully awake when they saw Jesus' glory and the two men with him (vs. 32). One can imagine that perhaps they had become sleepy as Jesus prayed for a long time but awoke just before the Transfiguration itself began. Only Luke notes that Peter made his suggestion of three tabernacles at the moment when the other two were parting from Jesus (vs. 33). Only Luke specifically notes that the disciples were afraid as they entered the cloud that overshadowed Jesus (vs. 34).

Hemer takes the statement that the disciples told no one right away about the Transfiguration to be unique to Luke (vs. 36). This may be the case, though it depends upon how one translates the Greek at the beginning of Mark 9.10. If one translates it as the NASB does, speaking of Jesus' words to them concerning his death, "They seized upon that statement," then the claim that they did not tell anyone what had happened is indeed unique to Luke. If, on the other hand, one interprets Mark 9.10 as saying that they "kept the matter to themselves," as

---

[38] Colin Hemer, *The Book of Acts in the Setting of Hellenistic History*, WUNT 49 (Tübingen: J. C. B. Mohr, 1989), p. 358.

the ESV translates it, then it is possible that Luke could be getting the idea of the disciples' subsequent silence from Mark. If this detail is unique to Luke, it forms part of an undesigned coincidence, since Luke does not record (as Mark does) that Jesus told them not to tell anyone what they had seen until his resurrection (Mark 9.9), though Luke does record that they kept silent at that time. In any event, Hemer has listed a wide array of highly specific and often emotionally or visually vivid details of the Transfiguration that are unique to Luke.[39]

Several of these details and differences from Mark are unnecessary. The designation of approximately eight days is a seemingly unmotivated departure from Mark, as already mentioned. The progress from the sight of two men (some men or other) with Jesus to their identities bespeaks the perspective of someone who saw what happened and only gradually decided who these men were. The statement that the disciples had been sleepy but were awake to see Jesus' glory is an interruptive aside, rather embarrassing to the disciples, and could even cast doubt upon the truth of their narrative. It is difficult to see what motive Luke could have in including it except a belief that it was true. The information about their sleepiness could well have come from Peter.

Hemer makes the fascinating observation that we can think of these details as answers to questions that someone might pose directly to a participant. "How long after?" "What was the first thing you saw?" "Did you hear what they said?" "If you were so sleepy, are you really sure about what you thought you saw?" And so forth. He also points out that, even if Mark's Gospel was available to Luke before the final version of his Gospel was written, Luke could easily have been gathering materials for his own Gospel before he read Mark's.[40] And he conjectures that Luke could have come into personal contact with Peter during Paul's imprisonment at Caesarea in approximately A.D. 57–59.[41]

This analysis of the differences between Luke's and Mark's Transfiguration scenes simultaneously supports Luke's personal access to Peter and warns against the facile critical assumption that differences between Luke and Mark in the same scene are factually unsupported alterations of Mark. Hemer, keeping his real-world imagination alive and not forgetting the possibility that Luke is a reporter rather than an inventor, sheds a light on the Transfiguration that lies beyond the scope of the literary critic with his feeble redactive candle.

---

[39] Ibid., pp. 356–357.

[40] Ibid., p. 358 n. 85.

[41] Ibid., pp. 354–55, 362.

Many individual examples and whole classes of evidence confirm the reportage model, but modern New Testament critics commonly leave these out of account. These documents do not look like literary constructs. They look like the work of artless reporters whose goal is to tell us about Jesus of Nazareth and his companions.

Summary
Still More Evidence for the Reportage Model

- Unexplained allusions confirm the reportage model of the Gospels. In an unexplained allusion, an author includes a reference to an aspect of the world that the document itself does not describe any further, leaving an unanswered question.

- Unnecessary details confirm the reportage model of the Gospels. Unnecessary details are pointless in the story. They appear to be reported simply because they are true.

- Some unnecessary details in the Gospels, though not all, are especially vivid.

- Reconcilable variation confirms the reportage model. When we find that different accounts are plausibly harmonizable, this strengthens our ability to resist claims of contradiction. Reconcilable variation is especially helpful when it would be easy for the reporters to contradict each other if they were not telling the truth, e.g., when it occurs in a large variety and number of cases.

- The unity of personalities, across multiple Gospels and various scenes, confirms the reportage model. A case study of Peter's personality illustrates this type of evidence.

PART FOUR

The Mirror or the Mask in Gospel Examples

Introduction to Part Four

At last, we have come to a major section of this book devoted *entirely* to Gospel examples. In Part Three, Chapter XI, I examined some Gospel examples and showed how they support the reportage model. We saw there that undesigned coincidences and external confirmations provide evidence for the reportage model but that literary device theorists blind themselves to this evidence by hypothesizing that details of the texts (or even whole incidents) are the result of fictionalizing change.

Part Four will systematically survey many passages that even evangelical scholars have said exhibit deliberate, fact-altering changes. For each passage discussed, I will show how scholars overlook simpler, alternative explanations.

Parts One, Two, and Three have set up this discussion so that the reader is well equipped to see these passages in a just light. Part One has provided background evidence that helps to make clear what the theorists are saying when they use certain terms (e.g., "displacement" or "compression"). The crucial distinctions made there allow us to keep our eye on the ball and not to be confused by equivocal and shifting word usage. Part One also explains what is at stake in the debate, allowing readers to recognize the importance of keeping fictionalizing change distinct from non-fictionalizing change and to understand the impact of fictionalization upon meaningful reliability. Traditional inerrantists can also understand the gutting of inerrancy that results if one redefines the term so as to accommodate fictionalization. This argument shows that any prior commitment to inerrancy does not *support* the acceptance of fictionalizing literary devices.

Part Two systematically refutes the claim that there is independent evidence that the Gospels are likely to contain fictionalization because of the kind of documents they are and the literary influences upon their authors. This should do away with any *antecedent* expectation that one will find such changes in the Gospels. The fact that they present themselves as historical in nature thus should influence us in a straightforward way as we interpret them. That appearance of historicity, *pace* the literary device theorists, is not undermined or qualified by alternative ancient views of truth or considerations of genre or compositional techniques that the Gospel authors would have known and used. This clearing-away operation in Part Two allows the Gospels to speak for themselves.

Part Three presents further *positive* evidence of the historical intention and success of the Gospel authors, concentrating on lines of support that the apologetics literature does not often survey. Part Three also shows in concrete cases how the literary device views and redactive-critical assumptions distort the theorist's approach to such positive evidence so that he has difficulty seeing it clearly. Among other things, Part Three shows that, if the evangelists did *not* believe what they wrote, they are attempting to lead their readers to think that they are writing historically. This means that the literary device theorist cannot carve out the niche into which he wants to place the Gospels—a niche for works that are only partially historical but are also non-deceptive.

Part Four will build on the previous sections by taking us to the Gospels themselves and allowing us to see that there is no *inductive* case there for fictionalizing literary devices. As when we were surveying Plutarch and other secular authors, we should use the heuristic of the flowchart for inferring fictionalizing literary devices on the basis of differences (see page 180).

Again and again we find that the New Testament critics who advocate a fictionalizing change do not satisfy the relevant burden of proof. They jump the line by postulating a fictionalizing alteration without giving due consideration (or *any* consideration) to far simpler hypotheses that explain the differences well. In some cases, they suggest a possible fictionalization even when there is no apparent discrepancy.

The theorists' haste to suggest fictionalizing changes is puzzling unless we remember that they are approaching the Gospels with a strong prior assumption that they will find them. They are thus inclined to regard harmonization as suspect and *ad hoc* while considering unnecessary, hyper-complex literary theories to be the results of objective scholarship. Michael Licona has gone so far as to say that he looks for literary devices *before* attempting to harmonize the Gospels.[1] He has also indicated that he hypothesizes literary devices by observing the Gospels even when he does not believe that he has independent evidence for the existence of a particular device:

---

[1] Jonathan Peterson and Michael Licona, "Why Are There Differences in the Gospels? An Interview With Michael R. Licona," *Bible Gateway Blog*, June 27, 2017, https://www.biblegateway.com/blog/2017/06/why-are-there-differences-in-the-gospels-an-interview-with-michael-r-licona/.

There are many observations of differences in the pericopes that follow [from the Gospels] for which *potential devices are neither described in the compositional textbooks nor observed being employed by Plutarch.* We will keep in mind that many of the compositional devices in use by Plutarch are likewise not found in the compositional textbooks. Nor are they taught in any of the ancient literature that has survived.... We must keep in mind that since we cannot enter a time machine, return to the first and early second centuries, and interview the evangelists and Plutarch pertaining to their compositional practices, I am only surmising some of their compositional techniques, given what we learn from the compositional textbooks, a few other sources, and the rare opportunities where we can compare how an ancient author redacted the source we know he used.[2]

When Licona claims the existence of a literary device in the Gospels though he has no specific device to name, he falls back upon a category such as "artistry" or "crafting."[3] In one of the very places where he *does not even claim* that he is applying a specific, named literary device that he has found in Plutarch or elsewhere, Licona draws a moral for the reader: "This shows the extent to which at least one of the evangelists or the sources from which he drew felt free to craft the story."[4] What it shows, rather, is the extent to which Licona feels free to *attribute* "crafting" to the authors. It therefore shows the extremely high prior probability he is giving to the existence of such alteration, which in turn causes him again and again to "find" fictionalization when he reads the Gospels. Given such broad categories as "expansion of inadequate material," "fabrication of a context,"[5] "literary artistry,"[6] "redacting the tradition,"[7] "adapting the tradition,"[8] and "crafting,"[9] it is hard to see why a theorist who prioritizes devices over harmonization would engage in harmonization at all.

---

[2] Michael Licona, *Why Are There Differences in the Gospels? What We Can Learn from Ancient Biography* (Oxford: Oxford University Press, 2017), p. 117. Emphasis added.

[3] Ibid., pp. 184–185. Further examples include the suggestions that John invented the incident in which Jesus breathed on the disciples, pp. 180–181, and that Matthew has invented Jesus' early healing of two blind men as a "doublet," pp. 131, 135. Licona does not say that these correspond to *specific* literary devices that he claims to have found in Greco-Roman literature.

[4] Ibid., p. 176.

[5] Ibid., p. 228, n. 34.

[6] Ibid., pp. 117, 137, 161, 184–185, 193, 195.

[7] Ibid., pp. 118–119.

[8] Michael Licona, "Are We Reading an Adapted Form of Jesus' Teachings in John's Gospel?" *Risen Jesus*, September 29, 2017, https://www.risenjesus.com/reading-adapted-form-jesus-teachings-johns-gospel.

[9] Licona, *Why Are There Differences*, pp. 161, 175–176, 177–178, 184.

Once we clear out of the way the claimed support for viewing the Gospels as Licona does, based on claims about ancient views of truth, genre, and compositional devices, and once we realize that we have solid grounds for treating the Gospels as historical in intention, we can use knowledge of human experience and considerations of simplicity to evaluate claims of Gospel fictionalization with care and rigor.

I will discuss the Gospel examples in Part Four under broad headings that (for three of the chapters) indicate the kind of error the literary device theorists commit. Utterly unforced errors are suggestions of fictionalization "out of the blue." In this category there is often not even an apparent contradiction between the Gospel accounts. Or the suggestions of fictionalization that the critic places (apparently) on a par with an obvious harmonization are so strained that the disproportion between evidence and theory is particularly strong. These suggestions are especially indicative of a low view of reliability. After all, if you thought that an author was historically reliable, why would you suggest out of nowhere that he made up a scene or fictionally altered a detail when there is not even an apparent conflict with some other information? The first question of the flowchart is, "Do these differences create an apparent discrepancy?" and the second is, "Are the accounts harmonizable without undue strain?" Claims of fictionalization in this category fail even to get past the first question of the flowchart, or they epistemically downplay an extremely simple harmonization and artificially raise the probability of a bizarre suggestion of fictionalization.

The next category, which I call "fictions only need apply," refers to cases where there is at least some (perhaps weak) appearance of tension between the Gospels or between a Gospel and some external fact, but theorists simply disregard or too lightly dismiss hypotheses that do not involve deliberate alteration of fact. Claims of fictionalization in this category fail at a later point in the flowchart—usually at the second question.

The third category is over-reading. These are cases where there may be some appearance of tension between two accounts but where this tension arises from reading one or more of the documents too rigidly—for example, assuming that narrative order is chronological order. The reasonable harmonization at the second question of the flowchart takes the form of pointing out that it is not necessary to read so much into the text. As pointed out in Chapter X, section 1, very often it is the traditional harmonizer who recognizes the possibility of achronological narration and the literary device theorist who reads with too much rigidity and then jumps to the conclusion that the author must have made a deliberate change of fact.

The last chapter of this book will focus on suggestions of fictionalization that all concern the resurrection of Jesus, regardless of what error they exemplify. It's rather striking to see how often in the resurrection narratives scholars suggest such alterations, sometimes saying that the "device" in question is something vague like "crafting." The cluster of suggested fictional alterations surrounding the resurrection also illustrates the importance of these issues. The resurrection is the central miracle of Christianity. Widespread claims that the authors of the resurrection accounts changed the facts in their stories would, if justified, undeniably undermine the strength of the evidence for Christianity itself. It is not possible to defend the resurrection strongly while simultaneously casting great doubt on the historicity of the resurrection accounts and their coming from witnesses who were in a position to know what happened.[10]

The categories of errors are, of course, not mutually exclusive. For example, a case in which a critic is considering only fictional theories may also involve over-reading. Sometimes there is a judgement call involved. Given the flexibility of what counts as an unforced error, one could reasonably argue that the Temple cleansing should be placed in that chapter rather than in the chapter called "Fictions Only Need Apply." Or one might think that the entirely unnecessary suggestion that Matthew invented multiple demoniacs or multiple blind men should go into a different chapter rather than "Utterly Unforced Errors," since that suggestion arises in the context of the apparent discrepancy over the number of demoniacs healed.[11]

The precise categorization of the examples is far less important than the cumulative case that emerges from considering a wide variety of proposed fictionalizations. Again and again, the claim or suggestion of fictionalizing change arises from an epistemically insupportable preference for complex theories. Sometimes these arcane theories involve invisible theological or literary motivations rather than normal variations in witness testimony. After we have seen this pattern often enough, we should come to realize that the case for fictionalizing literary devices in the Gospels is extremely weak, and we should reject the conclusion that they are there.

---

[10] Lydia McGrew, "Minimal Facts vs. Maximal Data Approaches to the Resurrection," *Apologetics Academy,* April 12, 2018, https://www.youtube.com/watch?v=RUt3r3dXBr4.

[11] The blog posts that I originally wrote on these Gospel examples include one entirely devoted to the error of "Making Things Complicated." I have decided not to have a chapter by that title in this book and have distributed examples from that post to other categories, which has sometimes made categorization slightly less precise. "Licona Examples V: Making Things Complicated," What's Wrong With the World, November 28, 2017, http://whatswrongwiththeworld.net/2017/11/licona_gospel_examples_v_makin.html.

Appreciating the argument here does not require specialized knowledge that New Testament scholars possess and laymen lack. On the contrary, the problems arise from the confusions of over-specialized scholars who apparently have been trained to make systematic epistemic errors, errors that laymen and those in other fields may have better hope of avoiding.[12] The repeated failure of New Testament critics to make a cogent case for the evangelists' fictionalizing change should bolster our confidence in the historicity of the Gospels, allowing the reportage model to continue to guide both scholarly interpretation and personal application.

---

[12] Lydia McGrew, "Six Bad Habits of New Testament Scholars and How to Avoid Them," *Apologetics Academy*, January 8, 2018, https://www.youtube.com/watch?v=_9fUKdpP16k.

Utterly Unforced Errors

1. Reliability and unforced errors

In Chapter II, section 4, we discussed the concept of meaningful reliability. There we saw that meaningful reliability means, at a minimum, that a statement made by a witness or other source gives us *some* reason to think that what it says is true. More robustly, if a source has high reliability, it gives us quite strong reason to think that what it states is true. While there might be countervailing considerations that would force us to conclude that a given statement from an otherwise reliable source is not true, a highly reliable source is one that provides weighty evidence in favor of its claims. If we believe that we always have to double-check what someone says, we are not treating him as reliable. We are treating him as if his testimony has virtually no force for what it attests. If we think that we can dismiss his testimony on a whim, conjecturing at the drop of a hat that he might have just made something up, we are also not treating him as significantly reliable.

Utterly unforced errors by New Testament critics dismiss Gospel narratives in exactly this light fashion. The theorists conjecture or claim that something was invented even when there is no reason to do so. Or they lay out a menu of possible explanations of the passage that put fictionalizations on a par, epistemically, with factual reportage, even when they give nothing like a good reason to think that the author may have fictionalized. In practice, this amounts to taking a *low* view of the historical reliability of the document.

The sorts of considerations given in Part Three, which are of course only some of the arguments in favor of the Gospels' historical reliability, should force a critic to do more than just dream up the idea that a Gospel author *might have* made up a detail or an entire scene. When we have reason to think that a witness is truthful, we need to have some grounds for thinking that he is inventing. Utterly unforced errors show the epistemic recklessness of literary device theorists.

2. Did John the Baptist call himself the voice of one crying in the wilderness?

The rate at which critics commit utterly unforced errors about the Gospels is higher in the Gospel of John than it is in other Gospels. This is a result of a bias against John's full historicity that I will be refuting at length in *The Eye of the Beholder*. We have had a taste of this bias in examples discussed earlier, and several of the utterly unforced errors in this chapter also concern John.

Michael Licona says that "it is impossible to know" whether John the Baptist called himself the voice of one crying in the wilderness, even though John's Gospel says that he did. John tells us that the Jewish leaders in Jerusalem sent messengers to ask John the Baptist who he was. When he denied that he was the Messiah, Elijah, or "the prophet," they continued to press him to identify himself. He answered, "I am a voice of one crying in the wilderness, 'Make straight the way of the Lord,' as Isaiah the prophet said." (John 1.23) This is a quotation of Isaiah 40.3. The Synoptic Gospels do not recount this scene in which the messengers press John about his identity, and hence they do not quote the response in which he applies Isaiah to himself. The Synoptic Gospels do, however, quote the verse from Isaiah in reference to John the Baptist (Mark 1.3, Matt. 3.3, Luke 3.4). This, of course, in no way constitutes a contradiction or a tension between John and the Synoptics. On the contrary, the Gospels all fit together quite nicely. If John the Baptist really quoted this verse in relation to himself, that could well be part of the reason for the Synoptic authors' association of the verse with him.

But, while Licona admits that there is no reason why John the Baptist could not have made such a statement himself, he declares it impossible to know whether he said it:

> Whereas the Synoptic authors tell their readers that John the Baptist is the messenger of whom Isaiah spoke, John 1:23 narrates John the Baptist claiming he is the messenger of whom Isaiah spoke. All four Gospels give the same message while John offers it as the words of John the Baptist. Perhaps John transferred the message of Isaiah to the lips of John the Baptist. *It is impossible to know.* And there is no reason why John the Baptist could not have made such a claim about himself and the Synoptics chose to communicate the role of John the Baptist by citing the Scriptures he allegedly fulfilled.[1]

---

[1] Michael Licona, *Why Are There Differences in the Gospels What We Can Learn from Ancient Biography* (Oxford: Oxford University Press, 2017), p. 121. Emphasis added.

If there is no reason against the historicity of this saying of John the Baptist, why does Licona say that it is impossible to know whether John the evangelist transferred the message to the lips of John the Baptist? Why even raise such a possibility, much less raise it to such a high status that it becomes literally impossible to know whether the event happened or not? This serious suggestion of a fictionalizing literary device does not even begin to get past the first node of the flowchart.

The disturbing implication of even this relatively moderate example is that Licona functionally treats the Gospel of John as lacking minimal reliability as an historical source. John's narrative that John the Baptist made this claim for himself apparently counts for little or nothing. Here is a non-miraculous event—John the Baptist's applying Isaiah 40.3 to himself. It is an event that is not particularly improbable on any other grounds. It is an event that, rightly considered, is even slightly confirmed by the Synoptic Gospels' association of the verse with John the Baptist. It occurs in a scene (the questioning by the messengers) that doesn't occur in the Synoptic Gospels anyway. These words of John the Baptist do not appear to be contradicted by anything in any of the Gospels. But the mere fact that the Synoptics do not *also* recount the event and that Licona can *conceive* of the idea that perhaps John invented these words of John the Baptist is apparently enough to throw the incident into significant doubt.[2]

Here the "device" of transferral looks very much like a solution in search of a problem.

3. Doubling up on demoniacs and blind men

In this pair of examples, the suggestion of a fictionalization comes up in response to an alleged discrepancy—that Mark reports only one person healed in a story while Matthew reports two. But there is an extremely easy harmonization available, which Licona himself brings up. He then puts this harmonization into a menu of possible explanations in a "choose your own solution" format. The other suggestions are so extreme as to be wildly out of proportion to any alleged discrepancy in the documents.

The difference in question is of the same general type in two places: Mark 5.1–17 tells about a demoniac whom Jesus healed. He lived among the tombs and was impossible to control, even with chains. Jesus cast out the demons into a herd

---

[2] In Chapter XI, section 2, I discuss another artificially created doubt about this same section of John—whether John the Baptist said that he saw and bore record that Jesus was the Son of God. In that case, the saying actually participates in an undesigned coincidence.

of swine, and the man was restored to his right mind. Matthew 8.28–34 tells what certainly seems to be the same story, though in less detail, but says that there were two demoniacs.

In Mark 10.46–52, we have the story of the healing of blind Bartimaeus when Jesus is entering Jericho shortly before his death. Mark is the only Gospel who names a blind man healed at this point in Jesus' ministry. Matthew 20.29–34 again seems to be telling the same story of healing the blind in Jericho, though somewhat more briefly. But Matthew mentions two blind men.

In both of these cases, Licona conjectures quite legitimately that Mark may be "spotlighting." As discussed in Chapter III, section 1, "spotlighting" is just talking about one person in a story and not mentioning the larger number of people present. It is a standard proposal in traditional harmonizations of Gospel accounts and is not particularly a literary device nor a device taken from Greco-Roman literature. It is extremely likely that this is the correct explanation for the differences in the number of men healed in the two incidents. In the case of Bartimaeus, the fact that Mark knows the name of the man healed makes it even more likely that he would focus on that particular person. I have noted in Chapter XII, section 2, the vivid detail of Bartimaeus casting aside his cloak when he comes to Jesus. Mark's human source (possibly Peter) may have focused especially on the more forward of the two blind men.

But, although Licona does raise the possibility of "spotlighting" in both cases, he presents the reader with an entire menu of other options, as if these are on a par with the harmonization. These are *far* more farfetched. For the demoniacs, here are the options:

> In Mark 5:9, when Jesus asked the demoniac to tell him his name, he replied, "My name is Legion, for we are many." Matthew does not include this element. The verbal agreement between Matthew, Mark, and Luke in this pericope is not nearly as close as we find in many other pericopes. Was Matthew using a different source? Or did he seek to illustrate multiple demons by adding a second demoniac? …There is another possible solution. Matthew is prone to abbreviate stories found in Mark….Perhaps Matthew has doubled up the demoniac in order to compensate for not telling the story of Jesus healing another demoniac mentioned earlier in Mark 1:21–28.[3]

> Matthew may have used a different source or illustrated multiple demons through creating an additional person or conflated two stories. However, it could also be

---

[3] Licona, *Why Are There Differences*, pp. 131–132.

that Mark, followed by Luke, has shone a literary spotlight on the main demoniac whom Matthew reveals.[4]

So Licona is suggesting the obvious harmonization as just one possibility among several and is casually listing along with it the truly strange suggestion that Matthew may have made up multiple demoniacs in this story to "compensate" for not telling about an entirely different demoniac whom Mark tells about in a different incident. He also suggests that Matthew may have invented a second demoniac to "illustrate multiple demons." Nowhere does Licona so much as suggest a Greco-Roman literary device in which one makes up a second person in a story in order to "compensate" for not telling an entirely different story. Perhaps his use of the word "conflated" in the second quotation above means that he is attempting to shoehorn this suggestion into the category of "conflation."

The whole notion of compensation here makes very little sense and involves treating those whom Jesus heals as impersonal types or game counters rather than as real people. If Jesus really healed a demoniac as recounted separately, in a completely different context, in Mark 1, that was a *different person* from the demoniac healed in Mark 5. So it makes no sense to think that Matthew would think he could compensate for not telling the story in Mark 1 by inventing a second demoniac in his own story that parallels Mark 5. Suppose that I tell you a story in which I claim that two men, Jim and Bob, were on a long journey together and had a flat tire. I know that someone else has told a different story about how someone named George had a flat tire on a completely different journey going to a completely different location. This same person has *also* told a story that sounds like it is the *same* as my story of Jim and Bob, only he didn't happen to mention Bob. Suppose that there was no one named Bob present with Jim at all. I am just making up Bob and putting him into the "Jim" story. How would I be *compensating* for not telling about George's flat tire, on a completely different trip to a completely different destination, by *inventing Bob* and putting him into the story with Jim? Who does such a thing?

It is difficult to see how even an author who thinks little of inventing would have such a convoluted motivation. Why would even a fabricator think that he was compensating for not telling an *entirely different story* by "doubling up" on the number of people involved? Certainly such a suggestion (as well as the suggestion of inventing demoniacs willy-nilly to "illustrate multiple demons") is incompatible with any concept of Matthew as an historically reliable author.

---

[4] Ibid., p. 132.

Licona does the same thing when it comes to the healing of the blind in Jericho:

> As we observed in the preceding pericope, Matthew, who was given to abbreviating Mark, may have doubled up on the number of blind men in order to include another story from Mark 8:22–26 of Jesus healing the blind that Matthew will not otherwise mention.[5]

Licona also suggests here that Mark may be "spotlighting" and focusing on Bartimaeus, since he provides his name. As in the case of the demoniacs, he leaves the choice between these options up in the air.

Licona is apparently following Craig Keener, whom he cites, in suggesting these "compensating" moves. Keener does not even discuss the possibility that there were really two blind men and two demoniacs and that Mark is "spotlighting"; he says that Matthew *probably* invented additional people healed in these stories. Keener believes that Matthew *both* duplicated the entire episode of the blind men within his own Gospel (see the next section) *and* doubled up on the number of blind people healed as "compensation." Keener says,

> [Matthew] probably doubles the healings of the blind men for the same reason that he doubled the demoniacs delivered in 8:28 ....; he had omitted one elsewhere (Mk 8:22–26) as part of his abbreviating technique and so compensates by simply adding one in this story.[6]

> Matthew doubles Mark's demoniacs (Mt 8:28//Mk 5:2), as he later doubles his blind men...In both other instances of doubling he has omitted one of Mark's accounts (the demoniac of Mk 1:23–26; the blind man of Mk 8:22–26), hence he feels justified compensating here....[7]

---

[5] Ibid., p. 135.

[6] Craig S. Keener, *The Gospel of Matthew: A Socio-Rhetorical Commentary* (Grand Rapids, MI: Eerdmans, 2009), pp. 306–307. See a similar statement concerning Matt. 20 on p. 282.

[7] Ibid., p. 282. At this point Keener goes so far as to add, "[S]uch a literary practice would not have been unusual in his day." In support of this bold assertion, he cites only other New Testament critics rather than any 1st-century examples. Upon investigation, it turns out that these citations do not support this claim at all. One of them does not even address the issue of the numbers of demoniacs and blind men and seems utterly irrelevant. A. B. Bruce, *The Miraculous Element in the Gospels* (New York: A. C. Armstrong and Son, 1895), p. 145. The other two sources cited contain merely bare assertions that Matthew engaged in elaborate redactive activities. Robert H. Gundry, *Matthew: A Commentary on His Literary and Theological Art* (Grand Rapids, MI: Eerdmans, 1982) p. 158; M. D. Goulder, *Midrash and Lection in Matthew* (Eugene, OR: Wipf and Stock, 1974), p. 45. Neither of these goes so far as to claim that there was a "not unusual literary practice," current in Matthew's day, that involved doubling up on people in one story to compensate for not telling another story, nor do they provide independent evidence for that assertion. Goulder does make a baseless and implausible assertion that the author of 2 Chronicles has combined two stories. He says that 2 Chronicles 28.5–18 is an amalgam of 2 Kings

Of course, if Matthew did not want to use the space to include the other stories, the obvious "abbreviating technique" is just leaving out the other stories, not inventing non-existent persons in other incidents. And as a matter of fact, Matthew *has* left out these other healing stories. It is no part of an "abbreviating technique" to make up fictional people and put them into different stories.

This notion of doubling up people to compensate is an unforced error, showing a preference for hyper-complexity that is unjustified by any evidential considerations.

4. Did Matthew invent an entire incident of healing the blind?

In the course of discussing various possible explanations for the one blind man at Jericho in Mark 10 and the two blind men at the same point in Matthew 20, Licona raises a different issue: He suggests that perhaps Matthew has deliberately duplicated the entire incident of the blind men within his own Gospel, placing the invented "doublet" healing early in his own Gospel so that it can serve as a sign to John the Baptist:

> But Matt. 20:29–34 may have a doublet in 9:27–31. In that context, Jesus healed a leper (8:1–4), healed a paralyzed man (8:5–13), healed others and cast out demons (8:14–17), healed two demoniacs (8:28–34), healed another paralytic (9:1–8), raised a dead girl (9:18–26), healed two blind men (9:27–31), and healed a demoniac who was mute (9:32–34). John the Baptist was imprisoned and appeared to be in doubt about Jesus. So he sent a few of his disciples to ask Jesus, "Are you the one who is to come, or should we wait for another?" (11:3). Jesus told them, "Go and report to John what you hear and see: the blind receive sight and the lame are walking, lepers are cleaned and the deaf hear, even the dead are raised, and the poor have the good news proclaimed to them" (11:4–5). John the Baptist could thus be assured Jesus was the Messiah, since he was doing the very things expected of the Messiah (Isa. 61:1). Accordingly, Matthew may have included the doublet (although with variations) he would repeat later in 20:29–34 to provide an example of Jesus healing the blind as evidence for Jesus being the Messiah. If the healing of two blind men

---

16.5–6 and the story of a completely different incident in 2 Kings 6.19–23. Goulder then claims that Matthew similarly creates "omnibus" miracles, borrowing little bits and phrases from other miracle stories in Mark; he even tries to say that Matthew is amalgamating the healing of a leper (Mark 1.44) with the healing of two blind men (Matt. 9.30–31) because in both cases Jesus enjoins those he heals not to tell anyone. A wild and baseless conjecture about the Old Testament hardly supports a wild and baseless conjecture about the New Testament. All the less so does it support Keener's assertion that doubling up to compensate was a "literary practice" that "would not have been unusual" in Matthew's day. Keener's statement to this effect is just another unfortunate illustration of the way that one scholar will echo and even extrapolate from other scholars' poor arguments and bare assertions, leaving a reader who does not have time to follow up on the references to assume that an almost certainly false assertion about what was "accepted in the day" has been established by specialized scholarship.

in Matt. 9 is a doublet, it could weaken the proposal that Matthew added another blind man to Bartimaeus in order to account for another story of Jesus healing the blind man mentioned in Mark but not covered in Matthew. But there was no need to do so if Matthew twice narrated this story of Jesus healing two blind men.[8]

Licona defines a doublet (a concept that is not his invention but is common in New Testament studies) like this:

> One original tradition appears in two different settings within the same book as though occurring on separate occasions.[9]

Both this definition and Licona's discussion of how the concept would apply to Matthew make it clear that "doublet" as he is using it is a fictionalization.[10] As Licona casts the matter, the theory that Matthew has a "doublet" in 9.27–31 would tend to undercut the idea that Matthew doubles up the blind men in Matt. 20, since he would already have *enough* blind men healed (somewhere or other) in his Gospel to compensate fully for not narrating the different incident in which Jesus heals a blind man in Mark 8. If one thinks that there is an invented incident (a "doublet") in Matt. 9, then one should, as Licona ranks things, be more inclined to accept "spotlighting" by Mark as the explanation for the difference between Mark 10 and Matt. 20. One would then take the two blind men in Matt. 20 to be

---

[8] Licona, *Why Are There Differences*, p. 135.

[9] Ibid., p. 267.

[10] In principle it would be possible for an author quite accidentally to narrate the same saying or event twice, as Plutarch does in the *Life of Alexander* (see the discussion in Chapter X, section 1). This would not be either fictionalizing or erroneous if one or both of the narratives are achronological. A slightly different concept of a "doublet" is sometimes used as an argument for the use of both Q and Mark as sources for Matthew and Luke, the idea being that Matthew and Luke copied a different variant of a story, once from each source, generating two versions. See Daniel B. Wallace, "The Synoptic Problem," *Bible.org*, June 2, 2004, https://bible.org/article/synoptic-problem. Even the theory of accidental repetition (without intending to make it appear that the event occurred twice) should not be used uncritically, since most "doublets" conjectured by scholars are sayings of Jesus, and it is extremely likely that Jesus, like all good teachers, repeated the same sayings on multiple occasions. The best explanation for the occurrence of a merely somewhat similar incident or saying twice in the same Gospel is that the Gospel author had reason to believe that something similar happened twice. At times the concept of a "doublet" is used in an unambiguously fictionalizing way, as Keener and Licona use it here. The author is supposedly deliberately making it look like the event or saying occurred twice, perhaps for some thematic reason. This is known as a "redactional" doublet. See Bob Welch, *Repetitive Prophetical and Interpretive Formulations in Luke's Gospel of Codex Bezae: An Analysis of Readings in D*, PhD dissertation for the School of Philosophy and Religion (Bangor, Wales, UK: 2015), p 57. Such a fictionalization claim bears a significant burden of proof that New Testament scholars scarcely even attempt to meet. They treat it as sufficient argument to notice the general similarities between the sayings or incidents, however weak these may be.

historical, having concluded that the two blind men in Matt. 9 are *not* historical. So on this view either Matthew invented a non-existent blind man healed in Jericho or he invented *two* non-existent blind men healed earlier in Jesus' ministry, but probably not both.

Let's look at the theory about a "doublet" in Matt. 9.27–31. On this theory, Matthew deliberately invented a story that Jesus healed two "extra" blind men early in his ministry. Moreover, on this theory Matthew must have deliberately introduced additional variations (which Licona lists in a footnote)[11] that appear to distinguish this healing from the one in Jericho, though he knew that one of them was his own invention. Matthew's purpose in this wholesale fabrication, on this theory, was to provide a fulfillment of the prophecy in Isaiah that the blind would be healed when the Messiah came, and to make this fulfillment occur *before* the messengers come from John the Baptist to ask Jesus if he is the Messiah.

This entire suggestion proceeds from a failure to understand that fake points don't make points (see Chapter X, section 4). Licona even refers to this made-up incident as "evidence for Jesus being the Messiah." But if Jesus did not really heal the blind before the messengers from John showed up, then there simply was not a real fulfillment of that prophecy in that context. A made-up healing is not evidence that Jesus is the Messiah. For Matthew to invent such a fulfillment and try to make it look like it happened at a certain point in time would be both deceptive and theologically forceless, since a fictional event cannot be a real fulfillment of prophecy. If messengers came to Jesus from John the Baptist in the real world and there was no healing of the blind to refer them to, the messengers would have not been convinced of Jesus' Messiahship on the grounds (*inter alia*) that he healed the blind.

This theory would also seem to imply that Jesus' statement in Matt. 11.5 that the blind had received their sight was fictional, for why would Jesus have said such a thing if, as yet, he hadn't healed any blind people? If he had healed blind people by this time, Matthew could have referred to *those* healings and wouldn't have needed to invent a "doublet" incident. Luke 7.18–23 confirms Matthew on this point, for Luke records the incident of the messengers from John and the same statement by Jesus in response. Luke also says that at that time Jesus was healing *many* who were blind. If Luke is right, the entire elaborate invention attributed to Matthew is quite unnecessary, unless we assume that Matthew *did not know* that Jesus was healing many blind people at the time and *mistakenly* thought that he had to invent an earlier "doublet" healing—a complicated hypothesis indeed.

---

[11] Licona, *Why Are There Differences*, p. 244, n. 49.

If Jesus was healing many other blind people, this could easily have included the blind men mentioned in Matt. 9. If Jesus was a miracle-worker, why should he not have healed the blind both early and late in his ministry?

Keener endorses the theory that the earlier story is a "doublet" by Matthew. He thinks Matthew did it in addition to inventing an extra blind man in the Jericho incident to "compensate" for not telling a different story in Mark. Just before the quotation given in the previous section, Keener says,

> This account in Matthew [9:27–29] occurs at a different point in the story in Mark (10:46–52); Matthew preserves that story in the appropriate place as well (Mt 20:29–34...), but repeats it here to list it among Jesus' ten signs. This repetition, like Matthew's others, reinforces the point he wishes to make.[12]

The arbitrariness of these theories is illustrated by the fact that Licona thinks that there would have been "no need" for Matthew to "compensate" by inventing an extra blind man in the later incident in Jericho if he introduced a "doublet" earlier in his Gospel. But Keener thinks that Matthew did both. Once one starts suggesting such unprecedented authorial behaviors, one has to make up subjective rules that govern when the author will feel a need to invent in one way as opposed to another.

Keener's confident statement that "this account occurs at a different point in the story in Mark" ignores the fact that the two do not appear to be the same account at all. Why call the story in Mark 10 (paralleled in Matt. 20) "this account," meaning the *same* incident found in Matthew 9? Matthew 9 says that this event occurred "as Jesus went on from there" after raising Jairus's daughter, placing it in an obviously different temporal location in Jesus' ministry. In Matthew 9, in contrast with both Matthew 20 and Mark 10, Jesus is in a house when he heals the men. Matthew 9 says that Jesus told the men not to talk about the event (though they disobeyed). For the event at Jericho, such an order would not have made sense, since Jesus is accompanied by crowds at the time of the healing and since it occurs shortly before his Triumphal Entry. In Matthew 9 the two blind men follow Jesus and eventually talk with him in the house. In Matthew 20 they are sitting by the side of the road and hear that he is passing by. There is not any reference in Matthew 9 to their being rebuked by the crowd as Bartimaeus is rebuked before the healing at Jericho. Matthew's presentation undeniably treats the two healings as different accounts.

The only similarity is that there are two blind men involved and that they cry out to Jesus calling him "Son of David" and asking him to "have mercy on us."

---

[12] Keener, *The Gospel of Matthew*, p. 306.

This is hardly a basis for declaring that Matthew has invented the earlier incident. Of course the people were conjecturing at the earlier point in Jesus' ministry that he might be the Messiah. John the Baptist himself obviously thinks that Jesus is probably the Messiah, which is why he sends his disciples to Jesus. The Messiah would naturally be referred to as the Son of David. Matthew says that the crowds were wondering if Jesus was the Son of David in Matt. 12.23. Asking him to "have mercy" would be a natural way to ask for him to perform a miracle. "Son of David, have mercy on me" is the same cry for help that Matthew records for the Canaanite woman in 15.22, but that story is obviously not a "doublet" with the healing of the blind men. As with "transferral" as discussed in section 2, the very concept of a "doublet" here is a solution in search of a problem, and its application is an utterly unforced error. There is not the remotest appearance of contradiction between the Gospel accounts concerning whether or not Jesus healed two blind men early in his ministry. Matthew tells about Jesus healing two blind men in a way that has a couple of extremely minor similarities to the Jericho incident later in his own Gospel, and that is all.

This claim of fictionalization does not even get past the first node of the flow-chart.

5. Did Matthew deliberately move Jesus' saying from one healing to another?

Unforced errors in New Testament studies are sometimes the result of the grip that redaction criticism and rigid assumptions about the authors' use of sources have upon the minds of New Testament scholars. In this instance, the suggestion in question does not even follow the usually suggested redactive-critical line of influence, since the fictionalizing theory in question has Matthew fictionally re-dacting a story that is unique to Luke, even though Luke is not supposed to have been a source for Matthew. This theory requires the further hypothesis that Matthew had some source *like* Luke's version of the story, which we no longer possess. The imagined source cannot even be the hypothetical Q, since that supposedly contained material common to Luke and Matthew, not material unique to Luke.

Despite the roundabout nature of such a theory, even by redaction critics' own lights, and despite the fact that there is *no contradiction whatsoever between any documents*, nor any other reason to think that Matthew has fictionalized, Licona concludes that it is "difficult if not impossible to discern" what has really happened. The theory concerns something Jesus said in Matthew's account of the man with the withered hand:

Luke reports this story [of the healing of the man with the withered hand] as well as a different one in Luke 14:1–6, although there are similarities between both. In the second story Jesus was dining at the house of a ruler of the Pharisees on a Sabbath. Because there was a man with dropsy in attendance, they watched Jesus closely to see if he would break the Sabbath and heal the man. Jesus asked the lawyers and Pharisees who were present, "Is it lawful to heal on the Sabbath?" When they were silent, Jesus healed the man, sent him away, and said to them, "Which of you having a son or an ox that has fallen into a well on a Sabbath will not immediately pull him up?" (Luke 14:5). Matthew provides a similar logion of Jesus in our earlier pericope [about the man with the withered hand]: "What man among you who having only one sheep and it falls into a pit on the Sabbath will not take hold of it and lift it out?" (Matt. 12:11).

It could be that Matthew knew of both stories and, given his tendency to abbreviate, redacted portions of Luke's second story and then conflated those portions with the first story. Consider this logion from the first component in Luke (the healing) when compared with the pericope in Matthew:

> Which of you having a son or an ox that has fallen into a well on a Sabbath will not immediately raise him up...? (Luke 14:5)

> What man among you who having only one sheep and it falls into a pit on the Sabbath will not take hold of it and lift it out...? How much more value is a man than a sheep! So it is lawful to do good on the Sabbath. (Matt. 12:11–12)

> However, teachers in antiquity as well as today often vary an illustration, anecdote, parable, or fable. *Accordingly, as is often the case, it is difficult if not impossible to discern whether an author is reporting a separate event or has heavily redacted an existing one.*[13]

Put more explicitly, the fictionalizing theory in question is this: Matthew knew of both the story of Jesus healing the man with the withered hand on the Sabbath and (from some now-lost source) the story of Jesus healing the man with dropsy. Jesus didn't really say anything about lifting a sheep out of a pit when he healed the man with the withered hand. But Matthew decided, given the very general similarities between the stories otherwise (healing on the Sabbath, confounding the Pharisees), to take the saying attributed to Jesus about pulling an ox out of a well on the Sabbath, alter it to refer to lifting a sheep out of a pit, and attribute it to Jesus in his own version of the story of the man with the withered hand.

---

[13] Ibid., pp. 128–129. Emphasis added.

Licona freely admits that Jesus might have said something similar on more than one occasion. Indeed, a reasonable inference is that this shows the similarity of Jesus' personality and ways of speaking as portrayed in Matthew and Luke. Jesus also makes comments about leading an animal out to water on the Sabbath in Luke 13.15–16 when he heals the woman who was bent over—another story unique to Luke. Jesus appears to have been fond of pointing out that the rabbinic interpreters of the Sabbath rules were more considerate of animals than of humans. And Jesus refers in yet another, completely different passage to the hypocrisy connected with the Sabbath in John 7.32–33 when he contrasts healing on the Sabbath with circumcising a baby boy on the Sabbath. In all of these places a real-world hypothesis is that this was what Jesus was like. He skewered hypocrisy and lack of compassion concerning the Sabbath rules whenever the religious leaders told him that he should not heal on the Sabbath, and he did so by a variety of contrasts between what they did not allow and what they did allow, often concerning animals. It shows a lack of contact with historical reality to take broad similarities between two of the sayings about animals to mean that they are variants of something Jesus said only once.[14]

Yet even after his admission about teachers, Licona says, "Accordingly, as is often the case, it is difficult if not impossible to discern" whether Matthew is really reporting something Jesus said when healing the man with the withered hand or whether he invented the saying in that context. How is this "accordingly"? Surely the fact that teachers *often* vary an illustration and that we have no other reason to think that Matthew often (or ever) made such fictionalizing change should lead us to accept without hesitation that Matthew intends to report this saying as historical in its own context.

Other than the broad similarity between the sayings, the only argument that one might try to bring forward is the fact that Luke does not happen to mention that Jesus said anything about pulling an animal out of a well or pit in his own account of the man with the withered hand (Luke 6.6–11). This would just be a weak argument from silence; it does not constitute a contradiction or tension. But Licona seems to think that the mere fact that critics can generate the fictionalizing

---

[14] Licona takes the trouble to note the specific Greek words used for "lifting" in the two sayings—*anaspasei* in Luke and *egerei* in Matthew. But since these are not even the same Greek word it is difficult to see why he bothers to mention the Greek. One can see from a good English translation that both sayings are about lifting up an animal out of a difficult spot. Citing the Greek only reveals *differences* between the sayings as quoted, not further similarities. It certainly does nothing to support the idea that one saying is a fictional redaction and displacement of the other.

theory makes it "impossible to discern" what Jesus said. In examining these utterly unforced errors, one can scarcely avoid the conclusion that literary critics are giving epistemic force to the fecundity of their own imaginations.

6. "Except for immorality"

The example in this section does not come from a scholar who claims to be applying Greco-Roman literary devices to the Gospels. In that sense one can say that Robert Stein, the evangelical scholar in question, is not strictly speaking a literary device theorist. In fact, Stein has recently argued that Licona's and Burridge's thesis that the Gospels are Greco-Roman biography is unsupported, though at the same time commending Licona for not accepting what Stein views as too many traditional harmonizations.[15] But the resemblance to the methods used in other examples in this chapter should be clear—the conjecture of redactive adaptation based upon nothing but differences between accounts without even any apparent contradiction. This resemblance helps to clarify that, when a scholar puts the label of a literary device onto such a change, this is not an objective discovery bolstered by independent research into the conventions of the time. The literary device theorist merely adds an assertion about alleged literary conventions. But the method for "finding" such changes by the evangelists predates the claims concerning Plutarch or Greco-Roman biography.

Robert Stein,[16] followed by Daniel Wallace,[17] concludes that Jesus did not actually utter the famous "exception clause" in his teaching on divorce—"except for immorality." Matthew attributes this exception to Jesus in both of the places where he gives Jesus' teaching on divorce—once apparently early in Jesus' ministry in the Sermon on the Mount (Matt. 5.31–32) and also later in Matthew 19.3ff.

---

[15] Robert Stein, Review of *Why Are There Differences in the Gospels? What We Can Learn from Ancient Biography*, *JETS* 61, no. 1 (March, 2018), pp. 180–184.

[16] Robert Stein, "Is It Lawful for a Man to Divorce His Wife?" *JETS* 22, no. 2 (June, 1979), pp. 115–121; Studying *the Synoptic Gospels: Origin and Interpretation* (Grand Rapids, MI, Baker Book House, 2001), pp. 163–165.

[17] Daniel B. Wallace, "An *Apologia* for a Broad View of *Ipsissima Vox*," unpublished paper presented to the 51st annual meeting of the Evangelical Theological Society, November 18, 1999, p. 12. Wallace's main point is that Stein's view must be compatible with the ETS's stance on inerrancy, since Stein is a member of the Society, but Wallace also appears to endorse Stein's view. Wallace and Stein both treat this change as an example of giving the "very voice" (*ipsissima vox*) of Jesus and thus as a kind of paraphrase, because (according to Stein) Matthew was guided by the Holy Spirit to realize that Jesus was being hyperbolic when he left out any divorce exception. But the addition of the exception clause is a significant change to Jesus' teaching; if he did not utter it historically, to add it to his teaching and put it into his mouth with no historical justification in his historical teaching is quite a stretched notion of "paraphrase" or *ipsissima vox*. See Chapter II, section 2.

The latter of these appears to be the same incident recorded in Mark 10.2ff. It is unclear whether the earlier occasion in Matthew's Sermon on the Mount is recorded anywhere else. The teaching found in Matthew in the Sermon on the Mount *may* be recorded separately in Luke 16.18; Stein insists that this is "Q material" common to Matthew and Luke but adapted by Matthew, but it could well be that Luke is giving a version of the later teaching recorded in both Mark and Matthew. Luke 16 places the saying vaguely at a time when the Pharisees were listening (Luke 16.14), and there is more than one verbal difference from the teaching in Matthew 5, as I will discuss below. Or Luke could be reporting yet a third occasion on which Jesus addressed this subject.

Stein repeatedly emphasizes that Matthew was inspired by the Holy Spirit in putting these words into Jesus' mouth.[18] This theological claim is supposed to mitigate any concern about stripping away the historicity of the clause as an utterance of Jesus himself. A Christian struggling in a practical way with the issue of divorce may beg to differ on whether it matters if Jesus himself said this or if Matthew merely thought that it was what Jesus really meant. The "exception clause" makes quite a large difference to the content of the teaching. Merely asserting that we should continue to accept the inspiration of the Gospels and the authority of the teachings attributed to Jesus while undermining their historical factuality is a dubious procedure for deriving Christian doctrine and practice.[19] In fact, if Matthew and the other evangelists made *deliberate*, invisible factual alterations to the life and teaching of Christ, one may reasonably question whether their documents are inspired at all.

The main factor that Stein emphasizes in his argument is that Matthew alone, in both of his records of Jesus' teaching on this subject, has the clause "except for immorality." Neither Mark nor Luke has it. Stein takes this to mean that Matthew has added this clause, putting it into Jesus' mouth, as an interpretation of Jesus' teaching, since Matthew took Jesus' no-exception words to be hyperbolic. It is important to emphasize here that the presence of the clause in Matthew

---

[18] Stein, "Is It Lawful for a Man to Divorce His Wife?" pp. 115, 120.

[19] Licona does this repeatedly as well. While defending the idea that John may have heavily "adapted" Jesus' teaching, he simultaneously insists that we must "accept the Gospels as God has given them to us." See Michael Licona, "Are We Reading an Adapted Form of Jesus' Teachings in John's Gospel?" *Risen Jesus*, Sept. 29, 2017, https://www.risenjesus.com/reading-adapted-form-jesus-teachings-johns-gospel. In other words, even if we decide that the evangelists made significant ahistorical alterations, we should treat the Gospels as God-given in a partially fictionalized form. One cannot help wondering on what basis one could legitimately ask anyone to take such a stance given such a loose view of the Gospels' historical truthfulness combined with their appearance of historicity.

alone *does not constitute a contradiction* between Matthew and either of the other Gospels. It is merely a difference. Matthew records the exception clause; Luke and Mark do not. But why should this lead us to conclude that Matthew added the clause though Jesus never said it?

Stein's argument explicitly follows strong redaction critical assumptions. Stein says, "[I]f Matthew did in fact use Mark, then preference should be given to the earliest Gospel,"[20] bolstering this with citations concerning Markan priority. But this wording implies that Matthew and Mark are in conflict at this point, when in fact they are not. There is no need to talk about "giving preference" to one Gospel over another if there is no contradiction between them.

Stein further argues that, if Jesus really did utter the exception clause and Luke and Mark do not record it, then they were deliberately omitting it. "It is far more likely therefore that Matthew would have sought to explain what Jesus meant by adding the 'exception clause' than that Mark would have made the saying more difficult by omitting it."[21] He even goes so far as to say that such an omission would "appear more like a rejection" of part of Jesus' teaching.[22]

The problems with this reasoning are numerous and show why Stein's conclusion is an unforced error. First, Stein assumes tacitly an extremely rigid notion of the Matthean use of Mark according to which Matthew is not permitted to have his own knowledge of what Jesus said or did, independent of Mark. If Matthew is following or using Mark at all, then on this theory he knows nothing *beyond* what Mark says about that incident, and anything added to Mark must be added without factual justification. This extreme, rigid notion of so-called "Markan priority" (which does not follow from a more minimal concept of Markan priority) is quite unjustified and a serious cause of error in New Testament scholarship. To give just one counterexample, when Matthew tells of the death of John the Baptist, though he looks like he may be following Mark in much of the passage, he uniquely adds that Herod spoke to his servants when musing on who Jesus might be, and this unique phrase in Matthew is confirmed by an undesigned coincidence.[23] If we leave "on the table," as we certainly should, the possibility that Matthew was an eyewitness of much of Jesus' ministry and/or that he had access to eyewitnesses independently of Mark and

---

[20] Stein, "Is It Lawful for a Man to Divorce His Wife?" p. 117.

[21] Ibid., p. 118.

[22] Ibid., p. 116, n. 5.

[23] See Chapter XI, section 5, and Lydia McGrew, *Hidden in Plain View: Undesigned Coincidences in the Gospels and Acts* (Chillicothe, OH: DeWard Publishing, 2017), pp. 87–89.

"Q material," then we must allow the variations between Matthew and other accounts to have their own evidential weight. The narrow assumption that Matthew knows nothing on his own (except perhaps in "special M" material) is a straitjacket upon historical inquiry, yet it is all too typical of New Testament criticism, unfortunately including that of evangelicals.

Something similar applies to Q. Having declared the saying of Jesus on divorce in Matthew 5 to be "Q material," Stein is concerned only to reconstruct what was really in Q and then concludes that any divergence in Matthew from this conjecturally constructed Q must be Matthew's ahistorical addition.[24] Although Matthew had probably not yet joined the twelve disciples at the time of the Sermon on the Mount, that does not preclude his having his own sources of information (the other disciples, for example) about what Jesus said. Or he might have been in the crowd even though Jesus had not yet called him. We must keep our real-world imagination engaged in order to do good historical work, but the assumptions of redaction and source criticism stifle such realistic hypotheses, artificially treating them as if they do not exist.

Second, the extremely strong claim that Luke and Mark would have to be deliberately suppressing the exception clause if Jesus really said it goes far beyond the evidence. Here we must remember that sometimes a variation is just a variation. Witnesses frequently vary in whether or not they report every word of what a teacher says and in what they report. Sometimes one witness remembers a phrase that a different witness does not include. Why assume that Luke and Mark must have known of the exception clause and suppressed it if it really occurred?

Stein's argument that Matthew is adding to Jesus' words recorded in Mark may seem strengthened if we take it that Luke does not have the clause in a separate teaching incident, making it seem that Matthew is suspiciously adding the clause on two separate occasions where parallel passages in other Gospels do not have it. Even if this were the case, it is not terribly implausible that Luke's and Mark's sources for the two teachings on divorce just happened to recount the teaching without the clause while Matthew knew that it was included both times. But further, it is not at all clear that Luke 16.18 is the same teaching incident recorded in the Sermon on the Mount. The absence of the exception clause itself makes it possible that Luke is attempting to record the incident in Mark 10 instead and basing his work on Mark, though giving an abbreviated version thereof. There are other verbal differences between Luke 16.18 and Matt. 5.32 that make this

---

[24] Stein, "Is It Lawful for a Man to Divorce His Wife?" p. 118.

plausible. For example, Matt. 5.32 says that whoever divorces his wife except for immorality "causes her to commit adultery." Luke 16.18 says at the same point, "Whoever divorces his wife and marries another commits adultery." This resembles Mark 10.11 more than Matt. 5.32. And Luke's statement a few verses earlier that the Pharisees were listening may be an indication that he is referring to the later teaching instead. It is even possible that Luke is recording yet a third teaching on divorce. Both Stein's assumption that the teaching on divorce in Luke 16 is "Q material" shared with the Sermon on the Mount and his implication that the only notable difference from Matthew 5.32 is Matthew's addition of the exception clause are on shaky ground.[25]

Stein also argues that the incredulity of the disciples concerning Jesus' teaching is evidence that Jesus did not utter the exception clause, since his speaking as if divorce is prohibited without exception would make his teaching sound harder to obey. If his teaching included the exception clause, Stein argues that it would have been concurrent with a known rabbinic position held by the school of Shammai. The idea seems to be that the disciples would not have been surprised by Jesus' teaching if it were part of a known rabbinic line of thought. But this is doing *a priori* history with a vengeance. The disciples say (only in Matthew) that if this is the way things are, and divorce is so difficult to obtain morally, it is better not to marry (Matt. 19.10). If indeed the teaching of Jesus as given in Matthew was a known rabbinic position, it appears that they *did* find it excessively strict. Perhaps they had hoped that Jesus would allow a greater range of exceptions, leaning toward the more lenient rabbinic school (usually identified with the teaching of Hillel), or to "triangulate" between the two. Perhaps a more lenient position was more common. Stein himself conjectures that Jesus was teaching in a Jewish context of "easy divorce" for the husband.[26] If that is true, the disciples might well have been

---

[25] Stein also brings forward Paul's discussion of divorce in I Cor. 7.10–11 and the absence of any exception clause there as further evidence against the historicity of the exception clause in Jesus' literal teaching (Ibid., p. 118), but this is misguided. Paul does not describe any particular incident or scene in which Jesus made statements about divorce. The existence of the accounts in Mark and Luke shows that versions of Jesus' teaching on this subject that did not record the exception clause were available; that is not in question. Even if Paul is referring to a tradition about Jesus' teaching on earth (as opposed to a personal revelation to him as an apostle), he must be referring to something he knows derivatively, since he (unlike Matthew) could not have been an eyewitness. It is quite likely that any knowledge Paul had of Jesus' teaching on this subject is entangled with the testimonial evidence behind Luke's and Mark's accounts and hence is not independent. Treating the absence of an exception clause in Paul's teaching as independent evidence that Jesus did *not* utter an exception clause is methodologically flawed.

[26] Ibid., p. 117.

influenced by that cultural background. The fact that a position on divorce is held by some religious sub-group does not prevent people who do not identify with that group from finding it overly strict and expecting that their spiritual mentor will not take that position.

Stein does not seem to realize that the presence in Matthew itself (and only in Matthew) of the disciples' statement that in that case it is better not to marry is evidence that they *did* find the teaching recorded in Matthew problematic. He says,

> The reaction of both the opponents of Jesus as well as his disciples is one of great surprise and doubt over the wisdom of marrying at all if divorce is prohibited. Even in the Matthean account the reaction of the disciples seems best understood in the light of a total prohibition on divorce (see Matt 19:10–12). Such a reaction would be surprising if Jesus had uttered the "exception clause" ....[27]

The first sentence is a confusing representation of the Synoptic texts. No one in either Mark or Luke says that it is better not to marry if divorce is prohibited. Luke records no discussion at all, and Mark says only that the disciples were questioning Jesus again about the subject in the house (Mark 10.10). The opponents ask about Moses and the writing of divorce (in both Matthew and Mark) but say nothing about the wisdom of marrying. The disciples' "surprise and doubt over the wisdom of marrying at all" are described only in Matthew, which is also the only place where the exception clause is found. To use the disciples' reaction, found only in Matthew, as evidence that Jesus did *not* utter the exception clause, also found only in Matthew, is a poor inference. The far more reasonable conclusion is that this *was* the disciples' reaction to the teaching *with* the exception included. Matthew completes Mark at this point, telling us more about both what Jesus said to the Pharisees and what the disciples said when they questioned him further in the house.

Once again, there is no contradiction among the Gospels concerning whether Jesus uttered the exception clause. To treat the absence of a portion of Jesus' teaching in one Gospel as significant evidence against its historicity, and thus to pit mere absence against the positive testimony of a Gospel that includes it, is to treat the latter Gospel as having no individual credibility. To conclude on such grounds that an evangelist made up Jesus' words and put them into his mouth is an utterly unforced error.

---

[27] Ibid., p. 118.

7. "I thirst" and "It is finished"

Two of the most creative unforced errors Licona endorses come from the work of Daniel Wallace and concern Jesus' words on the cross. Licona and Wallace propose that Jesus did not historically say either "I am thirsty" (John 19.28) or "It is finished" (John 19.30). On their theory, instead of the first of these he said, "My God, why have you forsaken me" (Mark 15.34). Instead of the second he said, "Father, into your hands I commit my spirit" (Luke 23.46). According to the theory, the sayings in John are John's "dynamic equivalent transformations" of the sayings in Mark and Luke.[28]

It is important to stress several things. First, Licona does not even claim that these extreme changes correspond to some specific, independently established Greco-Roman literary devices. Given that he is following Wallace, who claims that these are examples of *ipsissima vox* (the very voice, though Wallace calls it a "broad" use of *ipsissima vox*), one guesses that Licona would say that they constitute paraphrase, but he does not claim to have evidence that wholesale substitution of words that do not, on their face, appear to say the same thing *at all* corresponds to a special ancient type of paraphrase. Second, these are obviously not what anyone in Licona's audience, using the word normally, would call "paraphrase," so to call it that would be misleading. The meaning of "I thirst" is on the face of it completely different from, "My God, why have you forsaken me?" Licona goes so far as to say that by inventing "I thirst"

---

[28] An anonymous questioner in a webinar has pressed the point that early in his unpublished paper on the words from the cross, Wallace says that (by analogy with the ratings given to textual readings) he gives his confidence in his theories in the paper a C or a C+ rating, thus indicating some doubt about them, and adds that the paper is offered "in the spirit of cooperative inquiry..." Daniel B. Wallace, "*Ipsissima Vox* and the Seven Words From the Cross," unpublished paper presented to the Society for Biblical Literature Southwest Regional meeting, March 5, 2000, p. 2. The idea seems to be that I, as a critic of the views, should not even *attribute* these theories to Wallace, simply because he makes this qualification, despite his arguing for them at length. As pointed out in Chapter I, section 4, merely saying that one is not certain of one's conclusions does not exempt a scholar from criticism for granting them much more plausibility than they deserve. Moreover, Wallace's stance in the paper itself is not really tentative in practice. Wallace refers to these ideas as "the thesis of this paper" (p. 6), "the thesis of this essay" (p. 7, n. 16), "the heart of my paper" (p. 4), and even "my thesis" (p. 12). He argues for these ideas at length and with apparent scholarly seriousness. He says, "My proposal is this: the Johannine Jesus' 'I thirst' (John 19:28) is a dynamic equivalent transformation of 'My God, my God, why have you forsaken me?'" (p. 4) He says explicitly that "there is good evidence, coming from several arenas" for his proposal about "I thirst" (p. 10). He even refers to the theory about "It is finished" as "my view" (p. 11). He states positively that John "transforms" Luke's last word from the cross into "It is finished" (p. 11). If Wallace can refer to this as *his view*, presumably it is legitimate for me to do so as well when disagreeing with it. Licona, who *agrees* with Wallace's claim about "I thirst," says that Wallace "proposes" it, and Licona himself endorses both of these ideas with more confidence even than he usually expresses, as noted in this analysis. I therefore make no apology for saying that both Wallace and Licona *propose* these ideas and for speaking of these as *their views*.

John has "retained [the] meaning" of "My God, why have you forsaken me?" This is patently false. Similarly, Licona claims that "It is finished" "maintains the gist" of "Father, into your hands I commit my spirit."[29] This is a severely misleading use of the term "gist." The two sayings, again, do not appear to say the same thing at all. If this is what Licona means by "retains the meaning" and "maintains the gist," readers should exercise great caution when reading his assurances that the Gospel authors maintained the gist of Jesus' words when "adapting" them.[30]

Third, these theories are utterly unnecessary. There is no contradiction or problem in the documents that these extreme theories solve. They are utterly unforced errors.

Here is what Licona says concerning "I thirst":

> In Jesus's next-to-last statement on the cross, Mark // Matthew have Jesus say, "My God! My God! Why have you forsaken me?" But John appears to substitute "I am thirsty." In Jesus's final statement on the cross, Mark // Matthew report that Jesus then cried out loudly and died; Luke reports that Jesus cried out loudly, "Father, into your hands I entrust my spirit," then died; and John reports that Jesus said, "It is finished," then died. These are quite different renditions. Since Luke does not provide a next-to-last statement from Jesus on the cross and one could quite plausibly suggest Mark // Matthew simply did not provide the words of Jesus's final statement when he cried out loudly, the differences could be said to appear between Mark // Matthew and John in Jesus's next-to-last statement and between Luke and John in Jesus's final statement....For the next-to-last logion, it appears that John has redacted "My God! My God! Why have you forsaken me?" (Mark // Matthew) to say, "I am thirsty." Daniel Wallace proposes that since every occurrence of "thirst" in John carries the meaning of being devoid of God's Spirit, the evangelist has reworked what Jesus said "into an entirely different form." It is "a dynamic equivalent transformation" of what we read in Mark // Matthew. Accordingly, in John, Jesus is stating that God has abandoned him. In Mark 15:34, Jesus quotes Ps. 22:1: "My God! My God! Why have you forsaken me?" Thus, John can write, "Knowing that everything had now been accomplished, *in order that the Scripture may be fulfilled* [i.e., Ps. 22:1], Jesus said, "I am thirsty" (John 19:28 ...). John has redacted Jesus's words but has retained their meaning.[31]

When one reads that passage carefully, one should be struck by how little it contains in the way of argument. Once again, Licona treats John's historicity so lightly

---

[29] Licona, *Why Are There Differences*, pp. 165–166.

[30] Ibid., pp. 17–18, 115, 117.

[31] Licona, Why Are There Differences, pp. 165–166. Emphasis in original.

that he sets it aside on a whim, because Wallace happens to have thought of a convoluted and implausible fictionalization theory. John's attestation to Jesus' words from the cross apparently counts for nothing as an historical record. If this can be called an argument, Licona implies that we should count backwards from Jesus' death in both John and the Synoptics in order to pair up the sayings and decide which one is a fictionalized alteration of the other, even if they appear facially utterly different. This is hardly a good method. The use of the term "logion" creates a false air of technicality for this dubious procedure and is particularly strange in this context, since the term is usually used even by New Testament scholars only when there is some *appearance* that the sayings are similar. Here all that is needed in order to claim that something is the same "logion" is to count backwards, noting which is the "next-to-last" saying in John or in the Synoptics before Jesus' death.

One might attempt to create an (artificial) tension between John and the Synoptics at this point by arguing that the bystanders offer Jesus wine after he says, "I am thirsty" in John (19.29) and after he cries out, "My God, why have you forsaken me?" in the Synoptics (e.g., Mark 15.34–36). But this is strained. Each sentence takes mere seconds to utter. If we assume that this offering of wine is the same incident, Jesus could have cried out quoting Psalm 22.1, "My God, why have you forsaken me?" and could also have said, "I am thirsty," both within a very brief space of time. In fact, one could argue quite plausibly that the Gospels are complementary here, since it is unclear precisely why a bystander would offer Jesus wine if he cried out only, "My God, why have you forsaken me?" Even the misunderstanding in the Synoptics that he was calling for Elijah (in Aramaic) would not naturally lead to offering wine, except perhaps as a general act of pity. The action makes more sense if Jesus also said, "I am thirsty" at that time.

The only other argument Licona gives (taken from Wallace) is that everywhere else where the word "thirst" is used in John it is used in a metaphoric, spiritual sense.[32] This is supposed to lend significant support to the idea that John has invented the attribution of literal thirst to Jesus in an entirely realistic setting while secretly, invisibly intending it in a spiritual sense. It is difficult to express how poor an attempt at argument this is. For one thing, it overlooks the fact that Jesus was almost certainly suffering from dehydration on the cross and that the original audience (familiar with crucifixions) would have been aware of this fact. So here an historically independently *probable* event is treated as fictional for entirely literary reasons. Are we really to think that Jesus' use of thirst as a metaphor elsewhere in

---

[32] Wallace, "*Ipsissima Vox* and the Seven Words from the Cross," p. 6.

John's Gospel means that he was never really thirsty and never literally expressed thirst? Or that John would not record it if he did? Why would anyone think such a thing? Tacitly, Jesus indicates thirst when he asks the woman at the well for a real drink of water (John 4.7), though he goes on in the discussion to use thirst and water metaphorically in addition. There is literal water in Jacob's well. Jesus in John says that he is the bread that came down from heaven (John 6), but that does not mean that there is no literal bread in John's Gospel. In John 6, Jesus has just fed five thousand people with literal bread. To take "I am thirsty" uttered on the cross to be ahistorical on the grounds that the term "thirst" is used only met-aphorically elsewhere in that Gospel is historically absurd. Licona's and Wallace's claim undermines not only the historicity of John, on the flimsiest of grounds, but also the humanity of Jesus in his sufferings on the cross.

In the unpublished paper that Licona is following, Wallace offers a bit more in the way of attempted argument, if something simultaneously so subjective and so psychologically convoluted can be called an argument. Wallace emphasizes John's literary themes and the fact that John portrays Jesus' crucifixion as his glorification. Hence, an historical record of physical thirst is allegedly out of place.[33] Richard Bauckham answers this sort of one-sided, anachronistic view of the "Johannine Jesus" and the crucifixion with straightforward historical information:

> That the Johannine passion narrative could be read as a triumph *rather than* as a narrative of abject humiliation is intrinsically very unlikely. Everyone in the ancient world knew that crucifixion was an excruciatingly painful way to die, and ... —even more important for the social values of the time—the most shameful way to die, the fate of slaves, enemies of the state and others who were treated as subhuman, deserving of this dehumanizing fate. This is why none of the Gospel narratives need to say explicitly that Jesus suffered physical pain or to point out the humiliation of such a death. The mere telling of the familiar tale of events entailed in death by cru-cifixion—familiar to people from observation, though rarely recounted in ancient literature—was more than enough to convey the agony and the shame. There are in fact as many references to physical violence against Jesus in John as in the Synop-tics (a little noticed fact which betrays how easily a prejudice about the difference between John and the Synoptics can blind readers to what the texts themselves say). However, John also has a more powerful means of stressing the humiliation of the cross. His passion narrative begins with Jesus' washing of the disciples' feet. No action was more characteristically and exclusively that of a slave. Jesus adopts the role of a slave on the way to his death by the form of execution reserved for

---

[33] Ibid., pp. 6–10.

slaves. The footwashing signifies the voluntary self-abasement that took Jesus to the ultimate humiliation of the cross. Of course, John has Jesus ironically proclaimed king, in the title on the cross, at the same time as he dies like a slave, while after his death he receives a burial fit for a king. But the irony does not mean that the glory cancels the shame.[34]

But Wallace believes that John would not have accurately recorded an historical expression of physical thirst from Jesus. Acknowledging that several scholars considering his thesis have pointed out that there is nothing unlikely about an expression of thirst from the cross, Wallace counters that the "issue in my mind is whether in *John's* portrait of Jesus such would be likely."[35] Faced with the undeniable fact that John's narrative records *precisely that*, Wallace develops the strange, blatantly *ad hoc* theory that John was willing to write that Jesus expressed thirst *only because it did not really happen*. Throughout this section of his paper, Wallace speaks of Jesus as if he is a mere literary figure to be manipulated by John.[36] The theory about John's psychology starts with the assumption that John *would not* have recorded a real, historical statement of thirst. That would have been at odds with his literary themes. John also, according to Wallace, would not have recorded what sounds like a cry of abandonment as given in the Synoptics—"My God, why have you forsaken me?" So, if Jesus said only what is recorded in the Synoptics at approximately this point in the crucifixion, John could not record that in line with his themes; he had to replace it with something else. (One wonders why he could not simply have left it out *without* replacing it, if he were really in the grip of such a thematic obsession.) But it was, on Wallace's view, consonant with John's themes for John to *appear* to record an expression of thirst and even to record it as occurring just before a bystander gives Jesus wine, as long as the evangelist himself knew privately that he had in mind an invisible, spiritual meaning rather than a recognizable, historical

---

[34] Richard Bauckham, "The Johannine Jesus and the Synoptic Jesus," pp. 10–11, https://web.archive.org/web/20140826114112/http://richardbauckham.co.uk/uploads/Accessible/Johannine%20Jesus%20&%20Synoptic%20Jesus.pdf.

[35] Wallace, "*Ipsissima Vox* and the Seven Words," p. 7, n. 16. Emphasis in original. Representative quotations both from this unpublished paper and from the unpublished 1999 paper by Wallace have been posted by theological blogger Steve Hays, with trenchant commentary. For quotations from the 1999 paper see Steve Hays, "A Broad View of *Ipsissima Vox*," *Triablogue*, April 18, 2018, http://triablogue.blogspot.com/2018/04/a-broad-view-of-ipsissima-vox.html. For quotations from Wallace's paper on the words from the cross, see Steve Hays, "Silly Putty Jesus," *Triablogue*, April 19, 2018, http://triablogue.blogspot.com/2018/04/silly-putty-jesus.html. I have both papers in my possession and have read them in their entirety.

[36] A point made by Steve Hays, "Silly Putty Jesus."

expression of physical thirst. On Wallace's view, it is "Johannine" for Jesus to express thirst on the cross only if John's record is secretly ironic.[37]

When it comes to the parallel suggestion concerning "It is finished" as a replacement for "Father, into your hands I commit my spirit," the attempted argument is even shorter and no more plausible. Licona scarcely bothers to argue, contenting himself with the count backward method, bare assertion, and a list of irrelevant references about Jesus' mission on earth and his return to the Father:

> Jesus's final logion in Luke 23:46, "Father, into your hands I entrust my spirit"…, becomes "it is finished" in John 19:30. What is finished? John says Jesus had come to "take away the sin of the world" by laying down his life for it (John 1:29; cf. 3:17; 10:15, 17; 12:47). His redemptive work on the cross was now complete (John 19:28, 30), and he could return to his Father (John 7:33; 14:12, 28; 16:5, 10; 20:17). John redacts Jesus's words, and although he maintains their gist, he adds some theological flavoring that is consistent with the portrait of Jesus he has painted from the very beginning: Jesus is the Lamb of God, sacrificed for the sins of others.[38]

Again, the phrase "final logion" gives an air of scholarly technicality to an overwhelmingly implausible conjecture. Licona simply states (in what is, for him, surprisingly definite language) that Luke 23.46 *becomes* John 19.30 and that John "redacts" Jesus' words, which in this case means that he alters them beyond all recognition. Licona does not even bother to say "maybe" or "perhaps." He covers the paucity of argument for so extreme a claim by the blatantly inaccurate statement that John "maintains the gist" of Luke 23.46 but merely "adds some theological flavoring."

What possible argument could be made for such a substitution? There is no contradiction between Jesus' saying, "Father, into your hands I commit my spirit" and his saying, "It is finished." As with the other pair of sayings, the obvious question is this: Why could he not have historically said both? Again, the one implicit argument (from phrases like "final logion") seems to be the mere proximity of other events. Each of these sayings is the last saying *recorded* in Luke and John, respectively, before Jesus dies. In John, immediately after, "It is finished" we read, "And He bowed His head and gave up His spirit" (John 19.30). Luke has,

> And Jesus, crying out with a loud voice, said, "Father, into Your hands I commit My spirit." Having said this, He breathed His last. (Luke 23.46)

---

[37] Wallace, "*Ipsissima Vox* and the Seven Words From the Cross," pp. 6–10.

[38] Licona, *Why Are There Differences*, p. 166.

But does this amount to a contradiction, or even an apparent one? Not at all. If Jesus called out to the Father in a loud voice (as Luke says) but said, "It is finished" more quietly just as he "breathed his last," someone farther from the cross could have heard the louder but not the quieter saying. The author of John, who expressly says (John 19.35) that he witnessed the soldier thrust a spear into Jesus' side shortly thereafter, could have been standing close and thus would have been able to supply the supplementary information. Once again, each item takes only a second or two to say, and the smallest amount of real-world imagination combines them easily. Referring to both of these sayings as "the final logion" locks one into a literary-critical box.

As in the case of "I am thirsty," Wallace provides a bit more than Licona in the way of attempted theoretical justification for the invention of "It is finished." Needless to say, he does not bother to consider seriously that Jesus might have uttered both "It is finished" and "Father, into your hands I commit my spirit." Instead, he grapples with the purely literary question of why, if Jesus just before dying said, "Father, into your hands I commit my spirit," John did not record that rather than fabricating something else in its place. Wallace even admits that on the face of it, the saying given in Luke meets his own notion of John's literary themes. He notes that it would seem to fit with John 2.24, where Jesus does not entrust himself to men. In Luke 23.46 he does entrust himself to the Father.[39] One might also mention (if we must speak of John's alleged literary themes) the connection with Jesus' statement in John that he lays down his own life (John 10.18).

Faced with a problem even on his own hyper-literary terms, Wallace comes up with a misguided and once more blatantly *ad hoc* theological argument: "[T]he Spirit is given to the *disciples* in John, not to God. And the Spirit could not be given until Jesus was glorified ....Thus, the glorification of Jesus ...is the very thing that permits the release of the Spirit." Wallace continues, "This theme would seem to be a sufficient deterrent from adopting the wording used by Luke as Jesus' last statement."[40] One cannot help noticing that Wallace appears to be straining to justify a predetermined conclusion. In Jesus' teaching in John, the Spirit is clearly portrayed as a personal entity, in some sense separate from himself. The Paraclete will testify of Jesus (John 15.26), and he will teach the disciples (John 14.26). Jesus speaks of the Spirit in the third person and promises that the Father will send him at Jesus' request (John 14.16, 26). The Spirit as spoken of in John is

---

[39] Wallace, "*Ipsissima Vox* and the Seven Words from the Cross," p. 11.

[40] Ibid. Emphasis in original.

not Jesus' own personal spirit, which he commits to God in Luke 23.46. It is not as though the Holy Spirit is trapped inside the body of Jesus and cannot get out until he dies.[41] To attribute such a view to John is an utter misunderstanding of the theology Jesus teaches in John's Gospel itself. To use such a misunderstanding as a basis for saying that John himself would not have recorded what is reported in Luke 23.46 and that he therefore invented "It is finished" as a *replacement* is to heap unforced error upon unforced error. Once again, such assertions scarcely merit the term "argument."

Wallace, later followed by Licona, then insists, "[I]f we accept John's radical repackaging of the dominical material so that it no longer looks like the original saying, we must with equal force say that it *means* the same thing."[42] Wallace appears unaware that saying something in a forceful manner doesn't make it true. Obviously, these "radical repackagings" do not remotely appear to mean the same thing as the words in the Synoptics. Wallace's wild speculations about John's secret motives and invisible authorial activities are unconvincing, and in the highly unlikely event that they were correct, the words as recorded in John would still not mean the same thing *to the audience* as the Synoptic sayings.

This is not good historical investigation. This is just poor literary criticism. Yet this sort of unsupported conjecture, rather than rigorous, objective, scholarly argument, is the basis upon which theorists dehistoricize the Gospels.

I have begun Part Four with utterly unforced errors in order to give the reader a sense of the methodology of those who claim fictionalization in the Gospels. It is important to realize, and I will no doubt mention it again, that *no new discovery* justifies this method. Neither Licona nor any other scholar has read Plutarch nor any other ancient author and found a new key to special ancient literary devices, permitting him to recognize the fictionalizations claimed in these examples. Rather, New Testament scholars go on, as they have been doing for many years, creating tensions between the Gospels that do not exist and conjecturing non-factual invention on the basis of flimsy argument, if any argument. The lightness with which they make such claims shows that they are not treating the Gospels (especially the less favored Gospels such as Matthew and John) as credible sources of historical information.

---

[41] This point is raised by Steve Hays, "Silly Putty Jesus."

[42] Wallace, "*Ipsissima Vox* and the Seven Words from the Cross," p. 12. Emphasis in original.

Summary
Utterly Unforced Errors

- Literary device theorists make utterly unforced errors when they conjecture "out of the blue" that a Gospel author made up or changed some aspect of the Gospels, even when there is no appearance of discrepancy between accounts.

- Utterly unforced errors reveal a low view of the reliability of the Gospels in practice, for one would not conjecture fictionalization on such flimsy grounds if one thought that the individual documents were reliable sources.

- Literary device theorists make utterly unforced errors when they suggest that

  - John the Baptist never called himself the voice of one crying in the wilderness,

  - Matthew added blind men and demoniacs to healings where they were not present in order to "compensate" for not telling other healing stories,

  - Matthew invented an entire incident of healing the blind early in Jesus' ministry in order to provide a reference for Jesus' claims of fulfilling Messianic prophecy,

  - John invented the sayings from the cross "I am thirsty" and "It is finished,"

  - and more.

- No discovery in ancient Greco-Roman literature supports these fictionalization theories.

Fictions Only Need Apply

1. Jumping the line

As I will mention more than once in this book, if the mere appearance of discrepancy between two accounts of an event were sufficient to justify the conclusion that an author has used a fictionalizing literary device, we would have no more ordinary apparent discrepancies or even ordinary, good-faith errors in history or modern testimony. We would always assume that one or both of the authors or speakers must have *deliberately* changed the facts for some reason, never that the apparent discrepancy arose from different witness perspectives, different witness interests and information, or variations in memory. All of the normal causes of apparent discrepancy, known to historians and detectives alike,[1] would be swept aside in favor of literary theories. This, of course, is quite unreasonable and shows that a mere appearance of discrepancy is *not* sufficient to justify a conclusion of deliberate fictionalization.

But when literary device theorists are not making utterly unforced errors, as discussed in the previous chapter, they are doing the next thing—making hasty judgements of fictionalization based upon little or nothing more than some initial appearance of a discrepancy. The appearance of a discrepancy takes us only past the very first node of the flowchart for finding literary devices based upon differences. There are many other possibilities, well supported by our normal experience of human interactions, that deserve consideration.

Even an honest error in one account or another is a *simpler* explanation of a mere apparent discrepancy than an elaborate plan on an author's part to write "as if" something happened when he knew quite well that it did not really happen

---

[1] See the relevant remarks of cold-case detective J. Warner Wallace, quoted in Chapter IX, section 2. J. Warner Wallace, live interview, *The Rational Rise* with James Fox Higgins, May 30, 2018, minute 1:02:00, https://www.youtube.com/watch?v=iywQ_gyaDrU&feature=youtu.be&t=29m37s.

that way. This is true from a purely historical point of view, and a commitment to inerrancy should not cause one to overlook this important epistemic point. Indeed, as discussed at length in Chapter IV, the inerrantist has a great deal to lose and nothing to gain by concluding that the Gospel authors altered facts on purpose. Inerrancy does not in any way, shape, or form support the conclusion of fictionalizing literary devices. The two are completely at odds.

If literary device theorists wish to claim the freedom as historians, unfettered by theological considerations, to conclude that the authors of the Gospels changed the facts deliberately, they would do far better epistemically, as historians, to consider the possibility of a good-faith error. Licona has explicitly claimed that scholarly integrity without theological prejudice may require the adoption of literary device views, even if they seem to be at odds with biblical inerrancy. He says,

> It is important to know that I am a historian. When the practice of history is conducted with integrity, the historian does not permit himself or herself to allow their theological presuppositions to weigh in to their investigation....[I]f I as a Christian historian want to conduct an investigation in the Gospels with integrity, I cannot bring a theological conviction that the Bible is God's infallible Word to that investigation. Historians who practice with integrity must come to an investigation being as open as possible to what it may yield....[2]

This statement of principle leaves him without any reason as an historian for not considering good-faith error as a possibility in discussing biblical examples (much less Plutarch), yet repeatedly he jumps to the conclusion of a literary device, dismissing harmonization and not even considering the possibility of good-faith error.

The examples I will discuss in this chapter all show evidence of haste in concluding fictionalization, using Licona's treatment as a foil for the most part. In most cases discussed in this chapter, scholars alleging a literary change of fact do not even consider non-fictionalizing alternatives. In some cases, they reject alternative theories almost out of hand, with very little consideration or on the basis of *a priori* historical assertion. This sort of haste shows the pattern: Fictions only need apply.

2. The Temple cleansing once more

I have repeatedly addressed in this book the claim that John moved Jesus' cleansing of the Temple several years earlier in his ministry, and I will not rehearse all of

---

[2] Michael Licona, "Are We Reading an Adapted Form of Jesus' Teaching in John's Gospel," *Risen Jesus,* September 29, 2017, https://www.risenjesus.com/reading-adapted-form-jesus-teachings-johns-gospel.

those points here.[3] Since I have refuted the claim that there was a known, accepted literary device of narrating dyschronologically and that John would have been influenced by such a literary norm, an obvious question arises: Why should we think that John has moved the Temple cleansing?

In this section I will address a few more of the flimsy arguments that John has dyschronologically moved the cleansing. Examples in this chapter are supposed to arise from at least an apparent discrepancy; in the case of the Temple cleansing there is an apparent discrepancy only if one insists that Jesus did not or would not have cleansed the Temple twice. If there was only one Temple cleansing, which John places firmly early in Jesus' ministry, while the Synoptics place it firmly at the end of the ministry, there is an apparent discrepancy. But why insist that there were not two Temple cleansings?

As noted in an earlier chapter, William Lane Craig is quite dismissive of the idea of two cleansings, calling it an "artificial harmonization." Craig's main reason for this swift dismissal, though briefly stated, is apparently the resemblance between the two accounts:

> [W]e don't have to have recourse to any such artificial harmonization which really doesn't do justice to the fact that the story is told in the same terms. It is the same story. It is not a second incident. Rather, we can simply say that the evangelists didn't aim always to tell a chronology—in the same order—and therefore could move the events about as suited their literary purpose.[4]

Here again there is a potential confusion about what it means for the evangelists not always to "aim to tell a chronology." The unwary reader might assume that Craig is merely describing achronological narration. But Craig is explicit elsewhere that he intends to endorse dyschronological narration of this incident.[5] Aside from the mistaken notion that there is evidence for an accepted ancient device of dyschronological narration, Craig relies on the claim that the story is "told in the same terms." Presumably he is referring to similarities such as the fact that in both incidents Jesus drives out those who are selling doves,

---

[3] See Chapter III, section 2, Chapter IV, section 3. See also Chapter X, section 1, on Craig Keener's confusion between dyschronological and achronological narration and the application of this to the Temple cleansing, and Chapter XI, section 6, on external confirmation for John's narrative at this point.

[4] William Lane Craig, "Biblical Inerrancy," *Reasonable Faith*, December 24, 2014, https://www.reasonablefaith.org/podcasts/defenders-podcast-series-3/s3-doctrine-of-revelation/doctrine-of-revelation-part-7/.

[5] William Lane Craig, "An Objection to the Minimal Facts Argument," May 8, 2018, https://www.reasonablefaith.org/media/reasonable-faith-podcast/an-objection-to-the-minimal-facts-argument/.

that he overturns tables, and that he rebukes the sellers by saying that they are misusing his Father's house.

But is this really so uncanny a set of resemblances that it makes it "artificial" to consider that there were two incidents and to say with such definiteness, "It is the same story"? Such an insistence reckons without the differences in the narratives even *aside from* the chronological placement. Here are just some of those:

- John, but not the Synoptics, mentions that Jesus made a whip of cords (John 2.15).

- John, but not the Synoptics, mentions that Jesus drove out sheep and oxen as well as doves (John 2.15).

- The Synoptics, but not John, say that Jesus quoted apparently from Is. 56.7, "My house shall be called a house of prayer for all the nations."

- John says (2.16) that Jesus rebuked them by saying that they have made his Father's house a place of business, while the Synoptics say that he rebuked them by saying that they have made it a robbers' den (e.g., Mark 11.17), an apparent allusion to Jer. 7.11.

- The Synoptics (e.g., Mark 11.16) but not John mention that Jesus would not permit anyone to carry merchandise through the Temple.

- John says (2.18) that the Jewish leaders challenged Jesus about his authority to do this (there is some implication that they asked immediately) and asked for a sign. Jesus answered by saying, "Destroy this Temple, and in three days I will raise it."[6] The Synoptic Gospels (e.g., Mark 11.18) say that the leaders were afraid of Jesus and sought ways among themselves to destroy him. Mark says that they asked about his authority on the next day (Mark 11.28) but says nothing about asking for a sign. Jesus answers there by his counter-question about whether or not the baptism of John the Baptist was from heaven.

If we had strong independent reason to think that these were the same event, these differences *could* be combined in various ways into one event. But when the

---

[6]This leads to an undesigned coincidence. See Lydia McGrew, *Hidden in Plain View: Undesigned Coincidences in the Gospels and Acts* (Chillicothe, OH: DeWard Publishing, 2017), pp. 70–73. Craig Blomberg also notes that this coincidence between Jesus' words in John and an accusation at his trial tends to confirm the occurrence of an historical early Temple cleansing. There would have been more time for Jesus' words here to become distorted if this cleansing occurred several years before Jesus' trial. Craig Blomberg, *The Historical Reliability of John's Gospel* (Downers Grove, IL: Intervarsity Press, 2001), p. 89.

firm chronological placement by the evangelists already suggests two events, these differences form part of a case for two events. All the evidence points in the same direction. And these differences strongly rebut any claim that the descriptions of the events are just too similar for there to be two of them. Just as one would expect if Jesus made two such protests at the Temple, the general description is similar, but the specific details differ.[7]

Here a comparison to a contemporary scenario is in order. I have stood in front of the same abortion clinic in my town, holding the same type of sign from the organization 40 Days for Life, on more than one occasion. People in passing cars have also thrown insults at those holding signs on more than one occasion. If one described the events at that general level, one might think that they were the same incident. If someone read in one author that one such vigil took place in November, while another author reported that something like it took place in February, a clever critic might argue that an author had chronologically displaced the narrative. But that difference of date would be a hint that these were different occasions, and further details would tend to confirm that conclusion further—descriptions of the weather, the specific insulting words or gestures, the number and names of other people holding signs, and so forth.

It is hardly an artificial harmonization to suggest that Jesus protested in this way twice, separated by three years or more. It is not even a case where truth is stranger than fiction. If the sellers of merchandise returned to their previous activities after the first such demonstration (as they no doubt would do), and if Jesus were moved with zeal for his Father's house later, just before his death, he might well have protested again in a similar fashion.

It would be difficult to improve upon the words of one of those wonderful writers of the 19th century, T. R. Birks:

> The evangelists mention a double cleansing of the temple by our Lord, once at the very beginning, and one just before the close, of his public ministry. The later event is recorded by St. Matthew, St. Mark, and St. Luke, but the earlier by St. John only. They have so great a resemblance in their general character, that some critics, in defiance of the clear statements of the gospels, and with a strange sacrifice of common sense to rash hypothesis, have maintained them to be the same. Yet, amidst the resemblance, there is a minute difference, which suits well the difference of the circumstances, and shows the historical accuracy of either narrative. In St. John, at the first occurrence, the rebuke is couched in a general admonition. "Take these things

---

[7] Allan Chapple makes the same point. "Jesus' Intervention in the Temple: Once or Twice?" *JETS* 58:3 (2015), pp. 547–550.

hence: make not my Father's house *a house of merchandize.*" But on the repetition of the offence, and the second exercise of authority, the rebuke becomes a cutting and severe denunciation of their aggravated sin. "It is written, My house shall be called the house of prayer; but ye have made it a *den of thieves.*" This minute, but appropriate difference, will go far, with thoughtful minds, to confirm the historical accuracy of the evangelists in their report of each event.[8]

Another line of argument, also weak, used against two Temple cleansings is what I call *a priori* history. In doing *a priori* history the critic decides ahead of time what would *not* have happened and uses his own perception of such matters to discount the positive testimony of an historical source close to the time of the alleged event. Craig Keener provides a good example of the use of *a priori* history to discount the historicity of John's placement of the Temple cleansing. In his commentary on this passage in John, he says,

> It is historically implausible that Jesus would challenge the temple system by overturning tables yet continue in public ministry for two or three years afterward, sometimes even visiting Jerusalem (although in John's story world, Jesus does face considerable hostility there: 7:30–52; 8:59; 10:20–21, 31–39; 11:46–57).[9]

He concludes immediately that it is "more than likely" that John moved the cleansing. The footnotes to this section contain similar expressions of confident *a priori* history:

> Jesus' freedom for long after challenging the establishment does not comport well with what we know of municipal elites.[10]

> Augustine, by contrast, argues for two cleansings—as if historically the Sadducees would have allowed his survival during any subsequent visits to Jerusalem![11]

It is rather striking that Keener makes these pronouncements as part of an argument for the elaborate theory that John moved the Temple cleansing within his "story world" in order symbolically to place the entirety of Jesus' ministry "within" his Passion.[12] Keener further implies that John was counting on readers or hearers

---

[8] T. R. Birks, *Horae Apostolicae*, appended to William Paley, *Horae Paulinae*, edited by T. R. Birks (London: Religious Tract Society, 1850), pp. 394–395. Emphasis in original.

[9] Craig Keener, *The Gospel of John: A Commentary* (Grand Rapids, MI: Baker Academic, 2003), pp. 518–519.

[10] Ibid., p. 518, n. 240.

[11] Ibid., p. 518, n. 241.

[12] Ibid., p. 519.

of his Gospel, merely in virtue of their familiarity with the Synoptic placement, to realize that there was only one cleansing and to divine his theological symbolism. Does this theory "comport well" with *anything else* in our experience of historical authors and readers? Keener apparently considers that his own idea about what *would not* have happened is so self-evidently true that it allows him to enter the realms of highly speculative, not to say anachronistic, literary conjecture about John's private symbolic intention rather than accepting the testimony of this early author at face value about what *did* happen.

This is hasty indeed. One way to see the insufficiency of such *a priori* claims about what "would not" have been allowed is to consider Mark's Gospel itself. For in Mark, Jesus returns to the Temple the very next day after the cleansing and continues to teach there for several days. He is not stopped. He is not prevented from entering. One might even say that he enters insouciantly (Mark 11.27). The Jewish leaders are angry, not only because he cleansed the Temple but also because of his parables directed at them and his ability to deal easily with their attempted verbal traps, but they fear the people and are not able to arrest him until Judas betrays his location at night with only his disciples around him. This is an entirely plausible story, and it occurs in Mark's Gospel alone. Why then should *John* be considered ahistorical for portraying Jesus as able to re-enter the Temple later after having cleansed it the first time? If anything, we do not even know whether he re-entered the Temple as soon in John's Gospel after the cleansing incident as he does in Mark's.

It would be historically insensitive to think that, according to the Synoptics, Jesus' death shortly thereafter is determined by the Temple cleansing all by itself. There are several other fairly obvious reasons why Jesus is captured and killed within a few days of the cleansing in the Synoptics. The Triumphal Entry is even more salient than the Temple cleansing. It alarms and angers the religious leaders. The children cry out, "Hosanna to the Son of David" within the Temple precincts, and Jesus refuses to silence them when asked to do so. His citation of Psalm 8 in this context, with its resonances of claims to deity, is calculated to anger the leaders (Matt. 21.15–16). In the Synoptics, Jesus' parable of the vineyard is another inciting event (Mark 12.12). Judas's decision to cooperate with the leaders is a major reason for Jesus' death during that Passover. And John gives still further relevant information about why Jesus was arrested at that time (John 11.45–53). The raising of Lazarus inflamed messianic hopes still further, the people were following Jesus in large numbers, and the Jewish leaders met to discuss their fears that Jesus would start a revolution and that the Romans would destroy the Jewish nation. It is not as though there were some historical law that Jesus must automatically die within a certain number of days after *any* Temple cleansing, regardless of whether there were any other factors in play.

One can even argue that there is a significant coincidence between an early Temple cleansing and the curious fact, noted in both Mark 3.22 and Mark 7.1–13, that "teachers of the law" came to Galilee from Jerusalem and criticized Jesus. Why were religious leaders from Jerusalem so set against Jesus, given only the events recounted in Mark? But if Jesus had already engaged in such a provocative action in Jerusalem early in his ministry, as told in John, this could certainly explain their seeking him out again both to oppose him and to find further grounds on which to accuse him.[13]

Or consider the matter from the perspective of reading John's Gospel alone. Keener is forced to admit that in John's so-called "story world," Jesus *does* face great opposition in Jerusalem on subsequent occasions. Once again, let us ask simply as a matter of plausibility: Does John present us with a narrative, a "story world," that hangs together, or does he not? Yes, he does. Jesus, in John as in the Synoptics, is a highly charismatic leader, able to move crowds and enormously popular because of his miracles. Early in his ministry, he engages in an act of semi-violent protest that shocks the religious sensibilities of the leaders. They question his authority immediately, and he gives them a cryptic and unsatisfactory answer. But just as in Mark, he is allowed to go away unscathed. In John he then moves about the country, sometimes visiting Jerusalem relatively briefly, where he causes controversy repeatedly and is twice almost stoned to death (John 8.59, 10.31, 11.8), sometimes returning to the hills of Galilee (John 4.3, 7.1) or to the Transjordan (11.54). On one occasion the people know that the leaders would like to kill him and speculate about why they do not stop him from teaching (John 7.25). He is so impressive to the Temple guards that they do not arrest him during that feast when the religious leaders send them to do so (John 7.45–46). Just before his last Passover he is especially popular because of the raising of Lazarus, and the people (who know that the leaders would like to kill him) ask among themselves whether he will come to the feast (John 11.56–57). Eventually (as in the Synoptics) he is trapped at night by the betrayal of one of his disciples and, finally, crucified by the Romans at the insistence of the Jewish leaders.

---

[13] Allan Chapple makes the same point. "Jesus' Intervention in the Temple: Once or Twice?" p. 556. A similar point is made by Leon Morris concerning additional visits to Jerusalem reported in John, *Studies in the Fourth Gospel* (Grand Rapids, Eerdmans Publishing Company, 1969), p. 49.

A reasonable person reading John does not find himself spontaneously saying, "This would *never* happen. He would have been arrested quicker, sooner. His ministry could not have continued after that early Temple cleansing." John, like the Synoptics, presents a believable picture of a tempestuous, bold, and canny rabbi whose popularity, *chutzpah*, and frequent movement allow him to get away with repeatedly frustrating the elites of his day until they finally manage to get hold of him, bring bogus charges against him, and have him executed. I would venture to guess that there would be far fewer scholars arguing that that Jesus' continuing ministry after an early Temple cleansing "would not" have been allowed to happen if it were not for the presence of a later Temple cleansing in the Synoptics. Yet on its own terms, this objection is supposed to challenge the reasonableness of John's narrative *all by itself.* To say that the ministry arc that John narrates so plausibly "would not" have happened because of the propensities of "municipal elites" is, rightly considered, nothing more than scholarly foot-stomping.

The treatment of this incident by too many New Testament critics shows the low credibility granted to individual Gospels, especially John, as historical sources and the haste to adopt fictionalizing theories on the basis of weak arguments.

3. Did the centurion personally come to Jesus?

The incident of the centurion who wanted Jesus to heal his servant can too easily serve as a kind of gateway to the acceptance of fictionalizing literary devices in the Gospels. It serves this function well rhetorically for several reasons. First, the change that Matthew has allegedly made seems so minor that a reader confronted with the suggestion that Matthew did so may believe that nothing is lost if he concedes it, even if it is a fictionalization. Second and even more important, the distinction between a fictionalizing change and a non-fictionalizing change is easy to miss in this case, since the most common harmonization of the accounts of this miracle makes use of a non-fictionalizing concept of transferral. At the same time, however, there are some difficulties with this non-fictionalizing harmonization, and the literary device theorist can thus discuss the passage with the intention of attributing fictionalizing transferral to Matthew. Given the popularity of the traditional harmonization, the unwary reader may not notice at first that this is what is going on, not realizing the problems with the non-fictionalizing transferral that are motivating the literary device theorist. If these difficulties come to the fore, someone who has previously accepted the non-fictionalizing transferral may think that he is *forced* to accept a fictionalization in Matthew. These issues need to be untangled so that we can make a clear-eyed evaluation of this minor Bible difficulty.

The apparent discrepancy about the centurion concerns the question of whether the centurion approached Jesus personally to ask him to heal his slave. Luke is quite explicit and goes into a certain amount of detail. The centurion heard about Jesus and sent Jewish messengers to appeal to Jesus on his behalf. They mention his friendliness to the local Jews and tell Jesus that he is worthy to have a miracle performed for him (Luke 7.3–5). When Jesus has begun to walk to the centurion's house, the centurion (according to Luke) sends further messengers to tell Jesus that he is not worthy for Jesus to come under his roof and that he knows that Jesus can heal the servant with just a word (Luke 7.6–9). Jesus compliments the centurion's faith, and when the messengers return to the house, they find the slave healed.

Matthew, who is clearly telling the same story, certainly *appears* to be saying that the centurion personally came to Jesus:

> And when Jesus entered Capernaum, a centurion came to Him, imploring Him, and saying, "Lord, my servant is lying paralyzed at home, fearfully tormented." Jesus said to him, "I will come and heal him." But the centurion said, "Lord, I am not worthy for You to come under my roof, but just say the word, and my servant will be healed. For I also am a man under authority, with soldiers under me; and I say to this one, 'Go!' and he goes, and to another, 'Come!' and he comes, and to my slave, 'Do this!' and he does it." Now when Jesus heard this, He marveled and said to those who were following, "Truly I say to you, I have not found such great faith with anyone in Israel.... And Jesus said to the centurion, "Go; it shall be done for you as you have believed." And the servant was healed that very moment. (Matt. 8.6–13)

The passage says that the centurion came to Jesus and implored him. When Jesus answers, the passage says that Jesus said "to him" that he would come and heal the servant. Most notable of all, Jesus gives his final order to go "to the centurion," and the word "go" is in the singular in the Greek. In other words, Jesus gives this final order to return home to the centurion personally as an individual, not to (plural) messengers acting on his behalf.

The most common traditional harmonization of this passage with the account in Luke attributes a non-fictionalizing transferral to Matthew, such as I discussed in Chapter II, section 3. If I say, "George asked me to lend him fifty dollars," this may be a brief way of describing a scenario in which George sent Jack to ask me to lend him fifty dollars. While the statement is somewhat ambiguous, it may not be intended to give the impression that George came to me personally. Similarly, if I say that Bill is building a house, in a cultural context where contractors usually do the actual building, this may just mean that Bill has commissioned the building of a house. St. Augustine gives a good representation of the traditional, non-fictionalizing type of transferral that is allegedly happening in this passage:

[I]f this was the manner in which the incident took place, how can Matthew's statement, that there came to Him a certain centurion, be correct, seeing that the man did not come in person, but sent his friends? The apparent discrepancy, however, will disappear if we look carefully into the matter, and observe that Matthew has simply held by a very familiar mode of expression. For not only are we accustomed to speak of one as coming even before he actually reaches the place he is said to have approached, whence, too, we speak of one as making small approach or making great approach to what he is desirous of reaching; but we also not unfrequently speak of that access, for the sake of getting at which the approach is made, as reached even although the person who is said to reach another may not himself see the individual whom he reaches, inasmuch as it may be through a friend that he reaches the person whose favour is necessary to him. This, indeed, is a custom which has so thoroughly established itself, that even in the language of everyday life now those men are called *Perventores* who, in the practice of canvassing, get at the inaccessible ears, as one may say, of any of the men of influence, by the intervention of suitable personages ....Consequently it is nothing out of the way for Matthew, a fact, indeed, which may be understood by any intelligence, when thus dealing with an approach on the part of the centurion to the Lord, which was effected in the person of others, to have chosen to express the matter in this ... method, "There came a centurion to Him." ... And now, as regards the rest of this paragraph, it would be a superfluous task to go over in detail the various matters which are recounted by the one and omitted by the other. For, according to the principle brought under notice at the outset, there is not to be found in these peculiarities any actual antagonism between the writers.[14]

In contrast, Licona's treatment of the same incident proposes a fictionalizing use of transferral by Matthew:

There is one major difference between the accounts. In Luke, the centurion sent elders and friends to Jesus but never saw him. Matthew brushes out the elders and friends from his narrative and instead has the centurion go to Jesus in person. Because Matthew tends to present abbreviated versions of stories paralleled in Mark and Luke, this is likely an example of Matthew compressing the narrative and trans-

---

[14] Augustine, *The Harmony of the Gospels*, Book II, 20.49. Trans. S. D. F. Salmond (1888), http://www.newadvent.org/fathers/1602220.htm.

ferring what a messenger had communicated to the literal mouth of the one who had sent the messenger....Matthew compresses the story and transfers via substitution.[15]

Licona says that Matthew "has the centurion go to Jesus in person" and transfers the message "to the literal mouth" of the centurion. This is *not* the same solution that Augustine presents, though it might be easy to overlook the crucial difference. Augustine is saying that Matthew merely gives (at most) an *accidental* impression that the centurion was present in person but was not intending to make it look like the centurion spoke personally to Jesus. On this view, Matthew merely used language that was potentially ambiguous, as if I said that George asked me to lend him fifty dollars when in fact George did so by sending Jack. It is extremely important to remember that the existence of non-fictionalizing transferral does not support the existence of fictionalizing transferral. The two are completely different. If I go out of my way to make it look like George was present, deliberately transferring the message "to the literal mouth" of George, perhaps making explicit reference to how George looked on that occasion in order to make the transferral realistic, I have engaged in fictionalization. No such misleading activity is a common and accepted device in our own time, nor do we have evidence that anything of the kind was a literary device at the time of the Gospels.

Licona treats this difference briskly and does not even consider the non-fictionalizing transferral option. There are difficulties with that option, as I have implied above and will discuss more in a moment, but Licona does not say what they are or why he opts for the idea that Matthew "has" the centurion go to Jesus "in person." It is likely that Licona knows that non-fictionalizing transferral is a very common traditional harmonization of this difficulty,[16] yet he does not discuss it. This is in keeping with his usual *modus operandi* of not distinguishing fictionalizing from non-fictionalizing concepts that could go under the same heading. He moves immediately and confidently to asserting a fictionalizing transferral. One gets the impression that Licona does not understand the importance of the distinction.

At this point Licona compares the device that he claims Matthew is using to the case I have discussed in Chapter IX, section 7—Pompey's illegal encomium in

---

[15] Michael Licona, *Why Are There Differences in the Gospels What We Can Learn from Ancient Biography* (Oxford: Oxford University Press, 2017), p. 130.

[16] See, for example Norman Geisler and Thomas Howe, "Is There a Mistake in the Accounts Concerning Jesus and the Centurion?" *Defending Inerrancy*, http://defendinginerrancy.com/bible-solutions/Matthew_8.5-13_(cf._Luke_7.2–10).php; Troy Lacey, "Centurion Contradiction," *Answers in Genesis*, Sept. 1, 2015, https://answersingenesis.org/contradictions-in-the-bible/centurion-contradiction/.

Plutarch.[17] There Licona alleges that Plutarch knowingly transferred the illegal encomium from a messenger to Pompey himself, having Pompey come in person into court to deliver the encomium, even though Plutarch knew that he did not do so. As argued in Chapter IX, Licona's argument at this point skips over several stages at which he would need to give stronger evidence that Plutarch is changing the facts deliberately; indeed there is no discernible motive for Plutarch to do so, especially since he says quite clearly in a different *Life* that Pompey did not come into court personally. So comparing the passage in Matthew to Plutarch here is not helpful; it merely compares one case where Licona jumps to conclusions to another case where he does so. Plutarch could easily have just made a mistake in one of his *Lives*, either by forgetting something or by misunderstanding what had happened and subsequently receiving more precise information—hardly a shocking conclusion.

Licona refers repeatedly in the book to Matthew's habit of abbreviating accounts, as we will see again when we come to the account of Jairus's daughter. There is sometimes an unstated implication that the Gospel authors cannot abbreviate without changing the facts, but this is untrue. In this case, for example, if Matthew merely wanted to write more briefly but knew of the Lukan information, he could simply have omitted both the fact that the messengers were Jewish and the reasons they gave. He could have written something to the effect that a centurion sent messengers to Jesus asking him to heal his servant. Then, when Jesus was on his way, the centurion sent additional servants saying, "I am not worthy that you should come under my roof," and so forth, just as already recounted in Matthew. Such an account would have been about the same length as the current account. The main difference in initial length is in the specific words of the Jewish messengers. In fact, it is not entirely clear that Matthew is motivated to abbreviate *per se*, since he includes further words from Jesus, not found in Luke, to the effect that many (obviously Gentiles) will come and sit down at the table in the kingdom with Abraham while the sons of the kingdom are cast into darkness. This could have been left out as well if Matthew's intent were to abbreviate. In fact, the case for a consistent tendency to abbreviate in Matthew is not nearly as strong as many New Testament critics believe. We should not allow ourselves to be hermeneutically trapped into thinking that fictionalization, deliberately making it look like things happened in a way contrary to reality, is the only way to write briefly.

There are, however, puzzles for the traditional harmonization of Matthew and Luke. Matthew's narrative is quite unified in its appearance that the centurion is

---

[17] Licona, *Why Are There Differences*, p. 130.

personally present. The final statement that Jesus said, "Go, it shall be done for you as you have believed" *to the centurion*, where the command is in the singular, is particularly hard to square with the Augustinian solution. If the centurion were back at his house sending messengers to Jesus, he would not need to go anywhere. And if Jesus were speaking to the messengers, he would not have used the singular.

A slightly better harmonization is the theory that the centurion sent messengers at first but later came to join the crowd as they neared the house and that Jesus, knowing who he was, spoke just the very last words recorded in Matthew directly to him. As an interpretation of Matthew, however, this breaks up Matthew's account in a way that seems quite artificial. The statement that Jesus said something to the centurion early in the passage would then mean something different from the final statement that Jesus said something to him.

This is therefore one of the places where, as mentioned in Chapter IV, I am inclined to think that the best explanation is simple memory variation among witnesses. If narrative order among incidents happens to follow chronological order in this case, Matthew may not have been called as a disciple at this point in Jesus' ministry. (The calling of Matthew is found in Matthew 9.) The differences between the accounts in Luke and in Matthew are evidence of some degree of testimonial independence between them—in other words, that they are ultimately relying on different human sources for the story. If Matthew were getting the story at second hand or even further removed, he could have gotten the impression that Jesus and the centurion were talking personally with one another. This would be technically an error on Matthew's part, if we assume that Luke's information about the messengers is correct. But, as discussed in Chapter IV, such a good-faith error would be far less destructive of the reliability of the Gospel than an intention on Matthew's part to narrate falsely and invisibly.

If those who accept Licona's view are going to rely upon the appearance that the centurion is present to reject traditional harmonizations, they should not jump to the conclusion that Matthew *deliberately* made the centurion come to Jesus personally, *knowing* that he did not. If we are going to insist that the passage in Matthew strongly makes it appear that the centurion is personally present, the simplest explanation of that appearance is that Matthew *believed* that the centurion was present. Literary device theorists repeatedly forget this basic principle: As a matter of historical inquiry, it is a dubious method to assume that the author of a supposedly historical work put in material that he himself did not even believe to be true. A simpler hypothesis, almost always sufficient to explain the data, is that the author at least believed what he said. This is no less true when there is an apparent contradiction between two accounts than when there is not. Yet as we will see throughout this part of the book, literary device theorists jump again and again from either the appearance of a discrepancy or even from mere differences to the conclusion that an author has deliberately portrayed events in a way that he does not believe himself.

4. What did Jairus say about his daughter?

The rather simple apparent discrepancy to be dealt with here is a difference between Matthew, on the one hand, and Mark and Luke, on the other, concerning what Jairus said when he came to Jesus and asked him to heal his daughter. Mark tells us that Jairus said this,

> My little daughter is at the point of death; please come and lay your hands on her, so that she will get well and live. (Mark 5.23)

Luke says, as narrator, that Jairus "began to implore Him to come to his house; for he had an only daughter, about twelve years old, and she was dying." (Luke 8.41–42) Both Mark and Luke then have a separate incident (after the healing of a woman with an issue of blood while Jesus is on his way to Jairus's house) in which messengers come from the house to tell Jairus not to bother Jesus, because the child is dead. Jesus then assures Jairus that he should have faith, and he continues to the house and raises the girl from the dead.

Matthew differs in that he records the initial words of the father to Jesus as stating that the girl is dead: "My daughter has just died; but come and lay Your hand on her, and she will live." (Matt. 9.18) The rest of the account in Matthew is quite similar to that of Mark and Luke; Matthew records the interruption in which Jesus heals the woman with the issue of blood and the subsequent raising of the girl. He does not, however, record the coming of the servants with the message that the child is dead. This, of course, fits very well with the record of the father's initial words.

Licona is very definite that Matthew has changed the facts in his story, by making it the case that the girl *is* already dead when Jairus comes to Jesus. But as far as Matthew knew, this was not really the case, since the father had really said only that she was dying, as recorded in Luke. Then, allegedly, Matthew changed the initial words of Jairus to correspond to these changed external facts in his narrative:

In Mark and Luke, Jairus's daughter apparently died sometime after Jairus left his house to find Jesus. However, in Matthew, Jairus was aware that she had already died when he left his house to find Jesus...Matthew compresses his account and narrates Jairus's daughter as already dead when Jairus comes to Jesus.[18]

More traditional harmonizers such as Augustine and Vern Poythress have also harmonized this apparent discrepancy by saying that Matthew was trying to compress his account, but Poythress, following Augustine, adds an interesting "mind-reading" twist to the explanation. Here is Augustine:

> For what Matthew directs our attention to, is not the mere words spoken by the father about his daughter, but what is of more importance, his mind and purpose. Thus he has given words calculated to represent the father's real thoughts. For he had so thoroughly despaired of his child's case, that not believing that she whom he had just left dying, could possibly now be found yet in life, his thought rather was that she might be made alive again. Accordingly two of the evangelists have introduced the words which were literally spoken by Jairus. But Matthew has exhibited rather what the man secretly wished and thought. Thus both petitions were really addressed to the Lord; namely, either that He should restore the dying damsel, or that, if she was already dead, He might raise her to life again.[19]

The obvious problem with this approach is that it is difficult to see how Matthew could have known, in the normal course of events, that this was the father's secret thought. If Jairus said nothing to Jesus about the girl being dead, how would Matthew, even if he witnessed the scene, have known or guessed that Jairus had despaired of her case and privately thought that she was already dead? One *might* argue that, if Jesus (who would have known Jairus's thoughts) or Jairus himself literally told Matthew what his thoughts were at the time, it would not be fictionalization for him to attribute these words to Jairus at the time. This seems a bit strained. Or perhaps we might hypothesize that the Holy Spirit gave Matthew a special revelation about what Jairus was thinking, though it is difficult to see why the Holy Spirit would give a special revelation about such a detail. And if he did, it is surprising that he would inspire Matthew to report that revelation as the *words* of the father rather than his thoughts. But why think that Matthew had access to that private information? This solution of the minor

---

[18] Licona, *Why Are There Differences*, p. 133.

[19] Augustine, *The Harmony of the Gospels*, Book II, 28.66. Vern Poythress, *Inerrancy and the Gospels: A God-Centered Approach to the Challenges of Harmonization* (Wheaton, IL: Crossway, 2012), pp. 206–207.

apparent discrepancy seems quite implausible, and it does not entirely solve the discrepancy anyway.

But having gone so far as to suggest that Jairus may have believed that his daughter was dead, due to the gravity of her condition when he left, one can readily go a step further and consider a much better harmonization. If the girl's breathing were slowing and she scarcely seemed to be breathing at all when he left, Jairus may have left his house in a great hurry, hoping to catch Jesus before her death. As Augustine suggests, he may have been mentally despairing. Or he may have been wavering between believing that she was dead and believing that she was not dead yet. This is, after all, a world without stethoscopes or other ways to check vital signs. It is not especially implausible, given the two accounts, that in his mentally agitated state he may have actually said something like this, "My daughter is dying. She's probably just now died! But if you come and lay your hands on her, she will live." In that case, both Matthew's and Mark's versions of his words would fall well within the range of normal paraphrase, and the differences can easily be attributed to the variations of truthful witness memory. It is interesting that both versions say that the girl will live if Jesus lays his hands on her. A harmonization of this kind takes account of this: If Jesus comes and touches her, she will live, whether she has died already, as Jairus in his fear and grief is inclined to believe, or is alive, as he still partly hopes.[20] This harmonization is one that Licona does not consider.

Whether or not Matthew knew (either from witnessing the scene and/or from Mark's account) that the servants came later and told Jairus that the girl was dead, simply not including that part of the story is not the same thing as deliberately suppressing it to try to make it look like she was dead before Jairus left the house. Omitting that part of the story could be a matter of benign compression—merely telling a story more briefly, without altering facts.

There is, again, the tacit idea here that it would be impossible for Matthew to leave out the subsequent coming of the servants without altering Jairus's initial words, as if he had to fictionalize what Jairus said in order to shorten the account. But this is not true. If he believed that Jairus definitely said that his daughter was dying but *did not* say that she was already dead, he could easily have reported his initial words as found in Mark, left out the coming of the servants, and then simply added a brief phrase upon their arrival at the house. Both Matthew and Mark report that they found the people mourning loudly. Matthew could have added to that verse (8.23), "For the girl was dead," as an explanation for the presence of the mourners.

---

[20] I owe this additive harmonization suggestion to Timothy McGrew.

Moreover, if abbreviating were that important to Matthew, one wonders why he did not leave out the entire incident of the woman with the issue of blood, which he does report. That seems an obvious place to compress, in the non-fictionalizing sense, since it interrupts the story of the raising of Jairus's daughter. Matthew abbreviates in some ways but not in obvious other ways, which calls into question the strength of his commitment to shortening and certainly serves as a counterexample to the claim that he had to put words into Jairus's mouth in order to compress.

Again, this is an extremely minor example. Indeed, even if one suggested (which Licona does not consider) that Matthew supplied Jairus's words somewhat incorrectly from his own or someone else's honest memory, that would be an extremely minor error. But we need to hold up to the light and consider more carefully the hasty treatment of biblical people as if they are literary characters. In the previous chapter we saw what this is like on full display when applied to the "Johannine Jesus" and the "Synoptic Jesus." Because "John's Jesus" supposedly would not cry out, "My God, why have you forsaken me?" John allegedly has him say, "I am thirsty" instead, while intending this as an invisible literary metaphor for spiritual abandonment. Similarly, various blind men healed by Jesus become mere counters, like pieces on a game board. If Matthew leaves out one healing of a blind man he may "double up" on featureless blind man tokens elsewhere in order to "compensate." Jairus was a real person who said real words. We should require more evidence than this apparent discrepancy to envisage Matthew as treating him more as his own literary construct than as a man of flesh and blood whose daughter Jesus raised to life.

5. James, John, and their mother

A minor apparent discrepancy, easily solved in a non-fictionalizing fashion, arises between Mark's and Matthew's accounts of the request made by James and John and their mother—that they may sit on Jesus' right and left hands in his kingdom (Matt. 20.20–23, Mark 10.35–40). The minor apparent discrepancy is simply that Mark says that the sons of Zebedee themselves came to Jesus and made this request, even including an initial part of the dialogue in which they ask him first that he will do whatever they ask, while Matthew says that their mother came with them and knelt before Jesus. Matthew attributes the words of the request itself to her. Matthew mentions that the sons were present, though Mark does not mention the presence of the mother.

There is really no great difficulty here. The commentary by 18th-century theologian John Gill surveys several normal harmonizing options:

> The matter may be reconciled thus. These two disciples...move [their mother], to use her interest with Christ, in their favour:...accordingly, she agreeing to the motion, they all three came, as Matthew relates, and the mother is the mouth, and speaks for her sons; so that they may be said to make such a request by her, she representing them; or they joined in the petition with her; or as soon as she had made it, they seconded it, and made it their own.[21]

Matthew expressly mentions that the mother *came with her sons* (Matt. 20.20) when she was about to make the request. This certainly sounds like an indication that they were involved in the request with her. Mark and Matthew are parallel in the latter part of the discussion, where Jesus talks directly with James and John (Matt. 20.22ff, Mark 10.8ff). These points make this scenario a good candidate for non-fictionalizing transferral. There are various ways this could have gone, as Gill indicates. The disciples came with their mother and were obviously in agreement with her request. Their body language, if nothing else, and the fact of their coming together in a somewhat formal fashion probably indicated that she was their spokesman. Perhaps she, kneeling, literally uttered the initial words given in Mark 10.35, "We want you to do for us whatever we ask of you" as well as the subsequent request. With her sons literally present, perhaps standing right behind her, it is a clear instance of non-fictionalizing transferral to attribute these statements to them. Or perhaps they made the kick-off request that Jesus would do whatever they all were about to ask him, while their mother knelt before Jesus, with their mother following up in the conversation with the specific request. Or perhaps at some points various people talked at the same time or one person spoke while others nodded. There are multiple, totally non-fictionalizing options here, since they were all present and making the request as a group. Jesus, of course, spoke straight to James and John themselves and asked if they were able to drink his cup, as recounted in both Gospels. It is unclear whether they knew what this question meant, but they answered confidently that they were able.

When we activate our real-world imagination, we can envisage these possibilities quite clearly. It is plausible that Peter, remembering chiefly the boldness of James and John and how he was indignant along with the rest of the disciples (Mark 10.42, Matt. 20.41), may simply not have bothered to mention to Mark

---

[21] John Gill, *Exposition of the Entire Bible*, 1746–63, https://www.studylight.org/commentaries/geb.html, *in loc.* at Matt. 20.20.

the involvement of the mother in the scene. But this would not be because Peter was trying to suppress the mother's involvement, transfer her words to the literal lips of her sons, or make it look like she was not present. It is extremely important to remember what literary critics of the Gospels too often forget: An author or witness who does not mention something need not be suppressing it. If an author does not mention an incident, this need not mean that he was trying to make it look like that incident didn't happen. If an author does not mention the involvement of a particular character, we should not assume that he was aware of that character's involvement and trying to brush the character out of the scene, to make it look like he was not there. We must avoid the temptation to treat every omission as a heavy literary decision, much less a fictionalizing one.

Despite the ease with which this minor apparent discrepancy can be traditionally harmonized, Michael Licona and Craig Evans consider *only* fictionalizing explanations. Evans's idea is the most striking. He suggests that Matthew invented the mother's involvement out of whole cloth:

> Because the request arouses the indignation of the other disciples (v. 24), we should not be surprised that the scene is mitigated by Matthew, who in various ways seeks to put the disciples in a better light. According to vv. 20–21, it is the *mother* of James and John who makes the request. But it is clear that Matthew knows Mark's version, for he has Jesus reply: "You [pl.] do not know what you [pl.] are asking" (cf. Mark 10:38). The use of "they" in the next sentence clearly indicates that the "you" in Jesus' response is plural – that Jesus was addressing James and John, not their mother.[22]

Evans thinks that a mere literary idea that Matthew seeks in various ways to cast the disciples in a better light should be enough to make us *unsurprised* if Matthew realistically invented an entire character's involvement in a scene. Apparently we are to view Matthew as far more committed to his *Tendenz* to mitigate the negative portrayal of the disciples (James and John) than he is to anything like historical truth. In pursuit of some slight mitigation, he will conjure up an entire character (their mother) and place her in a scene in which she did not really participate. The suggestion is all the more remarkable since Matthew expressly states that James and John were present, obviously approving of the request. He even tells us that they boldly answered that they were able to drink Jesus' cup when Jesus, no doubt with an air of sorrow and warning, asks them if they are able. How

---

[22] Craig A. Evans, *Matthew* (New Cambridge Bible Commentary) (Cambridge: Cambridge University Press, 2012), p. 353–354.

"mitigated" is their pride in asking for places on Jesus' right and left hand? Moreover, the jealous indignation of the ten other disciples is just as prominent in both accounts, which does not place *them* in a good light. It is difficult to see how such an invention does any significant work to cast the disciples in a better light. And, as noted in Chapter III, section 2, it is impossible for Evans to claim credibly that such a change would be non-deceptive, since any intended effect of casting James and John in a better light by inventing the mother's role requires the audience to accept her existence and participation.

Evans is quite unaware of the evidential import of the fact that Matthew says that James and John were present. He notes it but says only that it means that "Matthew knows Mark's version." Evans does not see this as evidence that Matthew and Mark are both describing *reality* and *agreeing* about it. Rather, as he sees it, there are two different versions of the story, and Matthew has added a mother in his version for thematic reasons. But the fact that Matthew says that James and John were present and conversed with Jesus about the request strongly undermines Evans's claim about trying to cast them in a better light and suggests various plausible harmonizations of the accounts.

Licona presents us with only two options, both of them fictionalizations. One is fictionalizing transferral. He does not even consider any of the non-fictionalizing transferral possibilities; as usual he seems uninterested in observing a distinction between fictionalizing and non-fictionalizing transferral. And he presents Evans's view as the only other option, though not the one he most prefers:

> Mark may have brushed the mother out of the story and transferred the request to her two sons since they were present and perhaps motivated their mother to ask Jesus on their behalf. However, it could instead be that Matthew added the mother in order to cast James and John in a better light.[23]

So according to Licona, either Mark deliberately suppressed the involvement of the mother ("brushed the mother out of the story") or Matthew *invented* her. Licona's word "added" is commendably clearer than Evans's passage about the mother; Licona cites Evans as a source for the theory. Licona parallels these two as the only options at the end of the chapter in his summary as well:

> Mark transfers the mother's request to her sons, since they were probably the initiators or Matthew adds her in order to cast James and John in a better light.[24]

---

[23] Licona, *Why Are There Differences*, p. 141.
[24] Ibid., p. 142.

In a footnote we learn that Licona prefers the transferral option, on the grounds that elsewhere the evangelist does not hesitate to portray the disciples in a negative light.[25] While Licona is certainly right to question the generalization that Matthew tries to downplay the negative portrayal of the disciples, it is worth noting that he never says anything about the extreme nature of Evans's theory, nor does he use the magnitude of such an invention as an argument against it. Indeed, he treats it as much more probable than any more traditional harmonization and apparently rejects it chiefly or only because he questions the premise that Matthew usually seeks to mitigate the disciples' bad behavior.

Licona's own preferred theory—that Mark "brushed the mother out"—is an unnecessary hypothesis, as already discussed. The sons were literally present, as Mark and Matthew agree. Matthew says that they came with their mother, which seems to indicate that the three came as a group to make the request. And they verbally showed their approval of the request and their desire for the positions of honor as the conversation continued, as Mark and Matthew agree. Hence, it was not necessary for either Mark or Peter as his source to "brush the mother out" in order to say that James and John made the request. Mark just doesn't mention her. But neglecting to mention her involvement is not the same thing as suppressing it, "brushing her out," in an effort to make it look like she was not there.

That Licona's theory is a fictionalizing version of transferral is even more evident in a lecture in which he uses this example. He precedes it with the example from Plutarch concerning Pompey's illegal encomium. He gives this as a paradigm case of transferral in Plutarch, and he then proceeds to say immediately that the evangelists used transferral, thus defined and illustrated, in the Gospels.[26] Since Plutarch is quite explicit that Pompey "himself came into court" to deliver his illegal encomium,[27] this would be a fictionalizing change if Plutarch did it on purpose (see Chapter IX, section 7). I have pointed out that the mere discrepancy in Plutarch's *Lives* on this point does not provide sufficient evidence for deliberate falsehood by Plutarch, but the point here is simply that such a deliberate change could not be non-fictionalizing transferral. Licona also says, "It's obvious that either Matthew or Mark has altered the details. And if I had to

---

[25] Ibid., p. 245, n. 57. In this footnote Licona says that Mark does not hesitate elsewhere to portray the disciples negatively, but by the logic of the argument he must mean Matthew. In a lecture he makes this same argument and says "Matthew" at this point in the argument. Michael Licona, "Why Are There Differences in the Gospels," April 19, 2014, https://youtu.be/xtemSTrkogE?t=2105.

[26] Licona, "Why Are There Differences in the Gospels," https://youtu.be/xtemSTrkogE?t=1977.

[27] Plutarch, *Life of Pompey*, 55.4–5.

guess I'd say it was probably Mark that altered it and brushed the mother out of the account."[28] Hence, Licona's comparison of the case of the sons of Zebedee to his view of the Plutarch case, as well as his wording, makes his meaning clear. He treats it as obvious that one evangelist or the other has deliberately altered the facts. Fictions only need apply.

6. On what day in Passion Week were Jesus' feet anointed?

In *Hidden in Plain View* I note that John says that Jesus came to Bethany six days before the Passover in the week in which he died (John 12.1ff). John does not try to narrate Passion Week day by day thereafter, but he says that the Triumphal Entry took place "on the next day" after Jesus came to Bethany and after Mary of Bethany anointed his feet at a dinner in his honor (John 12.12). In John's Gospel, then, the anointing occurs on the day before the Triumphal Entry. It is fascinating to compare the reference in John to "six days before Passover" with Mark's telling of the events of Passion Week, in which he mentions repeatedly how many days before Passover particular events took place. If we kick off the countdown according to John and follow Mark's count from then on, we do indeed find six days before Passover, which I consider to be an undesigned coincidence confirming both documents.[29]

But we can see the independence of John's and Mark's accounts from the presence of an apparent discrepancy concerning the anointing of Jesus' feet. I think that it is difficult to doubt that the two events are the same. The anointings in Mark and in John are similar not only in outline but in specific aspects of the dialogue between Jesus and others. And they take place very close together in time and both in Bethany.

Here is the beginning of Mark's account. (I am numbering the verses here, contrary to my usual practice, because the verse numbering will come up in the exposition that follows.)

> 1 Now the Passover and Unleavened Bread were two days away; and the chief priests and the scribes were seeking how to seize Him by stealth and kill Him; 2 for they were saying, "Not during the festival, otherwise there might be a riot of the people." 3 While He was in Bethany at the home of Simon the leper, and reclining at the table, there came a woman with an alabaster vial of very costly perfume of pure nard; and she broke the vial and poured it over His head. (Mark 14.1–3)

---

[28] Licona, "Why Are There Differences in the Gospels," https://youtu.be/xtemSTrkogE?t=2068.
[29] McGrew, *Hidden in Plain View*, pp. 113–118.

Mark 14.1 says that the Passover was two days away and then, only two verses later, begins to tell about the dinner and the anointing. Mark therefore seems to locate this event on a different day in Passion Week than John does. Certainly John, who rather firmly locates the anointing the evening before the Triumphal Entry, has taken no trouble to smooth away this apparent discrepancy; John was not altering his own account to make it tally with Mark's, and he was probably not relying upon Mark's account nor upon a tradition that "lies behind" Mark for his information. John is also unique in that he alone names the woman, Mary of Bethany, who anointed Jesus' feet and also associates Martha and Lazarus with the dinner. The independence is a clue that John had his own knowledge of events. This makes the dovetailing concerning the number of days before Passover when Jesus arrived in Bethany all the stronger as a confirmation of John's interest in historical accuracy. But it does create a puzzle concerning the day of the anointing.[30]

Craig Blomberg suggests that Mark is narrating achronologically at this point for thematic reasons, simply telling about the anointing closer to Jesus' death. Mark's reason for doing so is, on Blomberg's view, that Jesus says that the anointing is for his burial.

> Mark 14:3 ... is linked with verse 2 merely by a *kai* (and) and goes on to describe an incident that takes place at some unspecified time while Jesus 'was in Bethany'.... [O]ne can understand why Mark would insert the story immediately preceding a description of other foreshadowings of his death ....[31]

Blomberg has pointed out elsewhere that *kai* can simply be an indefinite connector and hence is sometimes used in achronological narration.[32]

Theological blogger Steve Hays has made a complementary suggestion that I find somewhat helpful—that Mark may have narrated achronologically here accidentally as an artifact of the process of composition. The idea is that Mark might have written 14.1–2 and then might have broken off writing, returning to write about the anointing at Bethany as another event that took place during Passion Week but not intending to connect it to the reference to the Passover as two days

---

[30] Both Licona (*Why Are There Differences*, p. 149) and Craig Blomberg (*The Historical Reliability of John's Gospel*, p. 176) take it that the anointing in Luke 7 is an entirely different incident. On this point I agree with both of them.

[31] Blomberg, *The Historical Reliability of John's Gospel*, p. 175.

[32] Craig Blomberg, *The Historical Reliability of the New Testament* (Nashville: B & H Academic, 2016), pp. 62–63.

away.[33] This ingenious suggestion is commendable in that it explicitly activates realistic imagination concerning how Mark might really have written his Gospel without any attempt to change events.

Ultimately, though, I am not fully convinced by the achronological suggestion. If Mark were narrating achronologically in verse 3, I would have expected him to put more content concerning Wednesday prior to that, in verses 1–2, after stating that the Passover and the Feast of Unleavened Bread were two days away. Mark narrates almost nothing immediately after that careful time designation and before the dinner at Bethany and the anointing. Mark says that the chief priests were trying to figure out how to destroy Jesus but feared the people. But he already told us that much in 12.12, with apparent reference to Monday. The only additional information here, apparently on Wednesday, is that they explicitly decided that they would put off trying to seize Jesus during the feast, lest there be a riot. This resolution seems to have changed abruptly when Judas came to them in 14.10 with the offer to betray Jesus. Since Mark introduces the day in 14.1, he presumably intends to narrate some substantial events that happened *on that day*. Why would he make such an explicit time reference in 14.1, narrate only the decision of the Jewish leaders on that day, break off abruptly to tell about something that happened several days earlier, and then return in verse 10 to the narrative of events on Wednesday? This would be an extremely choppy composition process indeed, almost as if he did not even read what he had last written when he began narrating the dinner at Bethany. And even if that were the case, why would he not make some better time indicator when returning to Wednesday in verse 10? Mark has been indicating the days in his narrative of Passion Week from Sunday to Wednesday fairly clearly (Mark 11.11–12, 19–20, 13.1–3, 14.1). It would be surprising if he suddenly began narrating achronologically in 14.3, even as an artifact of breaking off and resuming writing. It is far simpler to take it that Mark intends all of the events at the beginning of Chapter 14 to occur on Wednesday.

For this reason, though I have presented the achronological options as worth consideration, I am inclined to think that this is an instance in which either Mark or John has simply made a minor, good-faith chronological error, and one that would be quite easy to make. Mark's Gospel makes it clear that Jesus stayed for the night in Bethany more than once while he was in Jerusalem for this Passover (Mark 11.11,19). In fact, on the first occasion when he does not do so (Thursday night),

---

[33] Steve Hays, "Projecting Contradictions," *Triablogue*, January 11, 2018, http://triablogue.blogspot.com/2018/01/projecting-contradictions.html.

he is captured in the Garden of Gethsemane. If John is correct that Jesus stayed in Bethany for one night before the Triumphal Entry, then it appears that there were at least five evenings on which Jesus was in Bethany. Given his closeness to the family of Mary and Martha, confirmed by both John and Luke (see Luke 10.38–42), and given that Lazarus had recently been raised from the dead, it is not at all unlikely that Jesus ate with Mary, Martha, and Lazarus on more than one occasion. He may have done so on every evening from Saturday through Wednesday. Though Mark recounts that at this dinner they were officially at the home of Simon the Leper (Mark 14.3) this does not preclude the presence of the now-famous Lazarus and his sisters, as mentioned in John 12.2. With several of the same people present at dinner with Jesus on multiple evenings during the same week, in the same small town, it would be extremely easy for an honest witness (perhaps Peter or John), recalling the dinner some years later, to misremember on which night Jesus' feet were anointed. I lean slightly toward the conclusion that it was John who misremembered in this case. Here I would consider the probability that John was recollecting the events later, perhaps considerably later, than the time when Mark was written.

There is also the fact that, if the author of Matthew was a disciple, he made no attempt to correct Mark's apparent chronology (Matt. 26.1–7) even though he would have been present. Matthew includes an additional prediction by Jesus of his own death, with specific reference to the fact that the Passover is coming in two days (Matt. 26.1–2). If Jesus gave the Olivet Discourse of the previous chapters late on Tuesday, ending after sundown, he might have made this prediction after sundown on that night, as they walked back to Bethany, which would have been considered on the Jewish reckoning to be the beginning of the next day. The meeting of the chief priests and elders, said by Matthew to have gathered together in the court of the high priest (Matt. 26.3), would have probably happened during the day on Wednesday, with the anointing of Jesus' feet occurring at dinner in Bethany that evening.

As discussed at length in Chapter IV, section 4, an understandable good-faith error is far less detrimental to a witness's reliability than deliberate change. Whom should you trust more, a witness who years later makes a slip between Saturday and Wednesday, when the people involved were engaged in similar activities on Saturday and Wednesday, or a witness who testifies that an event occurred on Saturday when he knows quite well that it really happened on Wednesday?

This brings us to Licona's approach to this apparent discrepancy, which follows the same pattern we have seen elsewhere. Licona presents the reader with two and only two options: Either Mark or John has narrated dyschronologically. Licona says that this apparent discrepancy constitutes perhaps the "best candidate" for what he calls "synthetic chronological placement," by which he means dyschronological narration. He is quite explicit that either John or Mark has changed the day on which Jesus' feet were anointed, not that one or the other of them has narrated achronologically. He says that Mark "locates...the anointing two days prior to Passover" but that John "says it occurred six days before Passover." Licona's conclusion is that one or the other of them has altered the day:

> *Either Mark or John appear to have changed the day*, using synthetic chronological placement in order to *bind the anointing explicitly to a different context than where it actually occurred*....The event is presented as historical, but *the stated chronology is artificial*.[34]

Licona states definitely that "either Mark (followed by Matthew) or John [has] displaced the event." He seems inclined to think that it is John who has done so, partly because he thinks that John "probably" dyschronologically moved the Temple cleansing.[35,36] Thus one fictionalization theory begets another.

---

[34] Licona, *Why Are There Differences*, p. 191. Emphasis added. "Synthetic chronological placement" is a kind of literary device, according to Licona. Hence, based on his approach to compositional devices generally, it is not supposed to count as an error. Licona generally maintains a careful distinction between errors and compositional devices. See, for example, his discussion of a handful of places that might be errors on his view *because* he cannot account for them as compositional devices. Bart Ehrman vs. Michael Licona, "Are the Gospels Historically Reliable," Kennesaw State University, February 21, 2018, minute 1:45:36, https://youtu.be/qP7RrCfDkO4?t=6336. In the context of this discussion with Ehrman Licona is both explicit and emphatic that a compositional device does not count as "inaccurate," though Ehrman presses the point. In an odd and apparently isolated departure from this distinction in a recent publication, Licona lists the possibility that Mark moved the day on which Jesus' feet were anointed among other items as a possible "error," an item that has "a reasonable chance of being incorrect," in Mark. It is not clear why he does this, if he believes it would have been a compositional device, since he usually considers compositional devices to be (emphatically) not errors. Michael Licona, "Are the Gospels 'Historically Reliable'? A Focused Comparison of Suetonius's *Life of Augustus* and the Gospel of Mark," *Religions*, February 28, 2019, p. 15, https://www.mdpi.com/2077-1444/10/3/148.

[35] Ibid., p. 150.

[36] In a footnote (p. 247, n. 69), Licona says that Blomberg "prefer[s] John's chronology over Mark's," citing the same passage from Blomberg that I cited earlier. Licona appears unaware of or unconcerned with the fact that Blomberg's proposal is quite clearly that Mark narrates achronologically, *not* dyschronologically. This footnote in Licona's book follows immediately after Licona says that either John or Mark has displaced the event (dyschronologically) and raises the possibility that Mark may have done so in order to "bring the symbolic anointing of Jesus for his burial closer to the event itself" (p. 150). Blomberg thinks that Mark may have narrated achronologically for such a thematic reason, but not dyschronologically. A reader combining Licona's exposition with his note to Blomberg might well be confused into thinking that Blomberg endorses dyschronological narration. This is just one more example of the way that the failure to maintain this crucial distinction creates confusion.

At no point in his discussion does Licona consider achronological narration (by Mark, for example, as suggested by Blomberg). Nor, despite his avowed commitment (quoted earlier) not to be constrained by theological presuppositions, does he even briefly consider the possibility of good-faith error by either Mark or John. He leaps over all intermediate stages and goes directly for dyschronological narration by Mark or John, telling us that it is either one or the other.

As discussed in Chapter VI, section 4, Licona misapplies the ancient author Lucian at this point in his argument. As I explained there, Licona severely over-reads a bland passage from Lucian about making one's narrative flow well. Licona speaks as if this passage endorses dyschronological narration.[37] He treats this highly questionable interpretation of the passage in Lucian as established beyond question[38] and applies it to John's allegedly moving the day of the anointing, even going so far as to say that Lucian "would have smiled with approval" at John's dyschronological narration.[39] Licona seriously misrepresents Lucian's historical emphasis, for he repeats over and over again in *Why Are There Differences in the Gospels?* his own eisegesis of the passage on narrating smoothly while neglecting to mention multiple passages in which Lucian insists upon the importance of literal historical truth in narrating events. These are the types of claims about ancient authors that could lead a reader to think that there is objective, strong evidence for the existence of accepted ancient fictionalizing literary devices and to believe that the Gospel authors would have considered themselves to be doing the right thing literarily by changing facts.

According to Licona, John's reason for dyschronologically moving the anointing by Mary is to place it next to the raising of Lazarus (in John 11), so that two stories about Mary of Bethany are narrated close together. Licona says that John tells the story of the raising of Lazarus "just prior to the anointing in John" and that moving the anointing thus fulfills the norm of joining the parts of one's narrative like links in a chain, using "overlapping material."[40] But if telling two stories about Mary close together were really important to John, he could have done that much better than he does here. It simply isn't true that John narrates the story of Lazarus' resurrection just prior to the story of the anointing. If John wanted to link those two like "links in a chain," he would have introduced the story of the foot anoint-

---

[37] Ibid., p. 90.
[38] Ibid., p. 110.
[39] Ibid., pp. 150, 191.
[40] Ibid., p. 150.

ing much *closer* to the story of the raising of Lazarus. As it is, in between the two stories he takes ten verses to tell of a conspiracy of the Jewish leaders to kill Jesus, Jesus' going away to the wilderness, and the musings of the people about whether or not Jesus will come to the Passover (John 11.47–57). The intervening verses not only separate the two stories about Mary in the narrative but also emphasize John's intention to narrate chronologically. Because of the plot to kill him, Jesus removes himself from the immediate vicinity of Jerusalem for an unspecified time period and returns only six days before Passover at the beginning of John 12. So there is both geographical movement and a chronological gap between the narrative of the raising of Lazarus and the dinner on the day before the Triumphal Entry. Licona's theory not only misrepresents Lucian and gratuitously treats John as deliberately fictionalizing, it also does not explain the data well on its own terms.

Moreover, if John merely wanted to place the narration of the anointing nearer to the story of Lazarus' resurrection, he could have done so achronologically, using some phrase like, "And when Jesus was in Bethany again." And he could have left out the statement that the Triumphal Entry occurred "on the next day" (John 12.12). There was no need to put in chronological markers if narrative closeness were the motivation. As we have seen before, Licona's procedure assumes that there was no way for an author to accomplish some harmless narrative goal like abbreviating or telling about two events near one another without changing the facts. The far more reasonable conclusion based on the text is that John *believed* that the event took place the evening before the Triumphal Entry. Whether one concludes that perhaps Mark was narrating achronologically or that one or the other author made a minor, good-faith error, fictionalization is an entirely unnecessary hypothesis.

As the flowchart illustrates, it is crucial to look at simpler, more common possibilities before concluding that an author has fictionalized. Think horses, not zebras. Literary device theorists often seem unaware that their theories, being highly complex, have a heavy burden of proof. Accepting that burden means asking oneself carefully why one should *not* adopt explanations that accord better with our regular human experience. Too often, the theorist seems to turn methodological common sense on its head, giving preference to more creative, literary theories. This leads to false dichotomies, such as the claim that either *this* author deliberately changed the facts or *this* one did, with no other options considered. Good readers of the Bible, not to mention good historians, can do better, and they should.

Summary
Fictions Only Need Apply

- Literary device theorists often make hasty judgements that an author has deliberately changed the facts. These judgements involve ignoring or dismissing plausible harmonizations.

- Sometimes even in the Gospels an historian should be willing to consider the possibility of a minor error as, at a minimum, a simpler and hence more plausible alternative than deliberate fictionalization.

- Theorists apply the "fictions only need apply" approach when they suggest that

  - John moved the Temple cleansing back by three years,
  - Matthew made up the involvement of James and John's mother in asking Jesus to let them sit on his right and left hands,
  - either John or Mark deliberately moved the day when Jesus' feet were anointed in Passion Week,
  - and more.

Over-reading

1. Over-reading as wooden reading

All of the Gospel examples in this chapter illustrate the literary theorist's tendency to over-read historical works, a tendency also evident in rigid readings of Plutarch. Over-reading might be considered a kind of eisegesis, but I have chosen the more specific term "over-reading" because "eisegesis" can mean any highly implausible interpretation imposed on the text. I use the term "eisegesis" elsewhere in this book for Craig Evans's extremely odd interpretation of Matt. 13.52. Over-reading, as I intend it, refers specifically to a type of interpretive woodenness. It includes arguments from silence, as when a critic argues that one text "says" or "implies" that something did not happen, reasoning from the mere fact that the text does not mention that detail or event. It also includes treating narrative order as chronological order when achronological narration is entirely plausible in the passage. Some of the examples already touched on involve over-reading. In the previous chapter I discussed Michael Licona's claim that Mark "brushes out" the mother of James and John when they come to ask for special positions in Jesus' kingdom. But all that we really know is that Mark *does not mention* the mother. It does not follow that he has brushed her out. As mentioned in the introduction to Part Four, the categorizations used for these chapters are not mutually exclusive.

Before we examine specific examples of over-reading, it will be useful to return to the matter of achronological narration, already discussed in Chapter II, section 1, and Chapter X, section 1. It is particularly ironic that literary device theorists will sometimes accuse a critic who accepts a reportage model of the Gospels of being "rigid" and rejecting achronological narration. As noted in Chapter X, Craig Evans creates a straw man by saying that those who disagree with him "on the right" insist "that the words of Jesus have been recorded word for word, the events described are described exactly and in precise chronological sequence."[1]

The facts are precisely the opposite. Achronological narration—meaning narrating without intending to indicate a specific chronology by narrative order—is well-known to traditional harmonizers. It is, rather, the literary device theorist who will read a document rigidly as saying or implying that Event A happened before Event B or that Event A took a certain span of time. The theorist thus creates an unnecessary contradiction between documents. Then the theorist attributes fictionalizing displacement or compression to the author.

It is very important to remember that the first impression one would get from a document or the impression one would get if an account were read in isolation is not necessarily the *best* interpretation, much less the true account of events. Nor does the reportage model commit one to a stubborn insistence on one's first interpretation as the only good interpretation. Far from it. The reportage model reminds us that truthful witnesses are *often* incomplete or ambiguous and therefore that it is especially valuable to have multiple accounts. Our interpretations should be based on the total evidence available, and this may include other accounts of the same event that help to clarify matters and that lead to a different reading from one's first impression. It is a terrible historical method to interpret two accounts of the same event in a way that seals them off from one another and then to declare that there is an irresolvable tension or contradiction. The fact that one's first, spontaneous, independent interpretations do not mesh well with one another does not mean that there is an irreconcilable discrepancy between the accounts. Interpreting documents in isolation is not a good way to do history; it inevitably leads to an overestimate of the number of contradictions in either secular historical documents or in the Bible.

Skeptical scholar Bart Ehrman expressly insists upon such a method, ridiculing harmonization as "fundamentalist gymnastics" and "writing one's own Gospel":

> I should stress that some of these differences can scarcely be reconciled unless you want to do a lot of imaginative interpretive gymnastics, of the kind fundamentalists love to do, when reading the texts. For example, what does one do with the fact that the women apparently meet different persons at the tomb? In Mark it is one man, in Luke it is two men, and in Matthew it is one angel. The way this discrepancy is sometimes reconciled, by readers who can't believe there could be a genuine

---

[1] Craig A. Evans vs. Bart Ehrman, "Does the New Testament Present a Historically Reliable Portrait of the Historical Jesus?," Acadia University, January 20, 2012, minute 7:26, https://youtu.be/UvCVnlHoFow?t=445.

discrepancy in the text, is by saying that the women actually met two angels at the tomb. Matthew mentions only one of them, but never denies there was a second one; moreover, the angels were in human guise, so Luke claims they were two men; Mark also mistakes the angels as men but mentions only one, not two, without denying there were two. And so the problem is easily solved! But it is solved in a very curious way indeed. This solution is saying, in effect, that what really happened is what is not narrated by any of the Gospels: for none of them mentions two angels! This way of interpreting the texts does so by writing a new text that is unlike any of the others, so as to reconcile them to one another. You are certainly free to write your own Gospel if that's what you want to do, but I wonder if that is the best way to interpret the Gospels that you already have.[2]

This is nothing more than pseudo-scholarly bullying. There is nothing "gymnastic" about suggesting that angels look like men when they bring messages to human beings. That idea comes up quite independently in other biblical texts (e.g., Gen. 18.2, cf. Heb. 13.2), and Ehrman has no knowledge to the contrary about what angels look like. No one who harmonizes the resurrection accounts is saying that either Luke or Mark "mistook" the angels for men but merely that they were reporting their appearance. And it is entirely normal in truthful reportage to mention one person or aspect of an event but not another. That is not "gymnastic," either. Ehrman's "writing your own Gospel" line is a contentless rhetorical flourish. Any good historian who puts together multiple, non-identical historical accounts using reasoned conjecture is going to come up with a suggestion about reality that does not represent what just one of the accounts said. That is the beauty of having more than one account of an event: We can get a bigger picture than we could if we had only one account. What really happened is *normally* more than what only one witness reports. *Pace* Ehrman, this is the only responsible way to use historical sources that have a claim to credibility.

One way of engaging in reasonable conjecture is to consider that one author might be writing achronologically, when the text warrants that theory. We certainly do engage in achronological speech and writing even now. This seems to occur somewhat more often in verbal exposition than in writing and somewhat more often in children than in adults. If a child says, "We went to the museum, and we went to the park, and we talked to Jim," you don't get a very good idea of whether these three events happened in the order narrated or not. Further questioning will be required to find out whether Jim was at the park or the museum (or somewhere

---

[2] Bart Ehrman, "Fuller Account of Resurrection Discrepancies," *The Bart Ehrman Blog*, April, 2013, https://ehrmanblog.org/fuller-account-of-resurrection-discrepancies/.

else) and whether the visit to the park took place before the visit to the museum. At most, in this sort of "and ... and" narration, one might make a readily defeasible supposition that the events took place in the order narrated, but it should be held lightly and quickly corrected in light of additional information.

It may well be true that ancient writers wrote achronologically somewhat more frequently than do writers in modern times, and this is especially true when it comes to events that all happened around the same time. Craig Blomberg discusses achronological narration in Scripture with reference to specific Greek words used to connect parts of the narrative. As Blomberg notes, when an author uses merely the Greek conjunctions *kai* or *de*, this need not be taken to imply a chronological order, though of course one may infer chronological order from other contextual clues in addition to narrative order. Blomberg applies these points to the order of the temptations in the wilderness, which are narrated in a different order in Luke than in Matthew. "[L]ike so many places in the Gospels ... where the order of events varies, at least one of the divergent accounts does not make any claims to being in chronological order."[3] Based on the Greek, Blomberg leans toward the conclusion that it is Luke who is narrating achronologically in this case, though it is not impossible that Matthew is doing so. With all of this in mind, we should be careful about assuming that mere narrative order automatically equals chronological order. Therefore we should hesitate even more to attribute a *change* of chronological order to an author.

The attribution of achronological narration can, like anything, be used too often or in an implausible way. In the previous chapter I discussed one case (the anointing of Jesus' feet in Passion Week) where I am unconvinced by harmonization suggestions involving achronological narration. One need not accept every such suggestion. But if some traditional harmonizers make this suggestion too often, literary device theorists undeniably consider it too seldom. Even worse, the latter blatantly ignore the distinction and thus make confusion worse confounded when they make vague claims that the ancients were not very concerned about chronological narration. One must always ask (and scholars should be more careful to ask themselves), "What do you mean by that?" In many cases, some of which we have already discussed, literary device theorists will fail to distinguish achronological from dyschronological narration and insist quite definitely that an author has narrated dyschronologically, after having introduced the matter with generic claims about the ancients and chronology.

---

[3] Craig Blomberg, *The Historical Reliability of the New Testament* (Nashville, TN: B & H Academic, 2016), pp. 62–63.

This matter of chronology is just one way in which we must beware of over-reading, as we shall see in the examples. Rightly considered, the examples do not make it past the second question in the flowchart. Even if they did, there would be many other steps to be navigated before concluding that the author was using an accepted fictionalizing literary device. But we have no need to go any further in the flowchart when, as prudent historians, we use legitimate harmonization so that different documents can shed light upon each other.

2. Did the Pharisees stay silent?

As mentioned in Chapter VIII, sections 3 and 8, Michael Licona thinks that the episode in which Jesus heals a man with a withered hand exemplifies the creation of dialogue by Matthew. Chapter VIII has already refuted the claim that Matthew would have been instructed by Greek exercise books to invent dialogue in historical writing. Here I will discuss the alleged discrepancy that gives rise to this claim in the first place.

The alleged discrepancy in the accounts concerns whether the Pharisees ask Jesus a question early in the encounter. Matthew records that they did:

> Departing from there, He went into their synagogue. And a man was there whose hand was withered. And they questioned Jesus, asking, "Is it lawful to heal on the Sabbath?"—so that they might accuse Him. And He said to them, "What man is there among you who has a sheep, and if it falls into a pit on the Sabbath, will he not take hold of it and lift it out? How much more valuable then is a man than a sheep! So then, it is lawful to do good on the Sabbath." Then He said to the man, "Stretch out your hand!" He stretched it out, and it was restored to normal, like the other. (Matt. 12.9–13)

Mark's version of the story records no question asked by Jesus' opponents, but he does not deny such a question, either:

> He entered again into a synagogue; and a man was there whose hand was withered. They were watching Him to see if He would heal him on the Sabbath, so that they might accuse Him. He said to the man with the withered hand, "Get up and come forward!" And He said to them, "Is it lawful to do good or to do harm on the Sabbath, to save a life or to kill?" But they kept silent. After looking around at them with anger, grieved at their hardness of heart, He said to the man, "Stretch out your hand." And he stretched it out, and his hand was restored. (Mark 3.1–5)

Here we must remember that the interpretation of a text in isolation must not be rigidly binding. While one would *guess* from Mark's account all by itself that the opponents of Jesus did not speak first, Mark does not *say* so. His statement that they were watching Jesus to see if he would heal the man is not, in fact, incompatible with Matthew's claim that someone or other asked Jesus an explicit question. And Mark says that they were silent when Jesus asked *them* a question. He does not say that they were silent all along. I will return momentarily to this point.

Luke's account, if read in isolation, contains the strongest "flavor" of entire silence on the part of the opponents, though Luke is still not explicit on this point:

> On another Sabbath He entered the synagogue and was teaching; and there was a man there whose right hand was withered. The scribes and the Pharisees were watching Him closely to see if He healed on the Sabbath, so that they might find reason to accuse Him. But He knew what they were thinking, and He said to the man with the withered hand, "Get up and come forward!" And he got up and came forward. And Jesus said to them, "I ask you, is it lawful to do good or to do harm on the Sabbath, to save a life or to destroy it?" After looking around at them all, He said to him, "Stretch out your hand!" And he did so; and his hand was restored. (Luke 6.6–10)

Luke differs slightly from Mark here in his emphasis upon the fact that Jesus knew their thoughts while they were watching him, which Mark does not say. This may suggest (though this is a guess) that Luke himself believed that they remained entirely silent and that Jesus knew what they were thinking only because of his ability to read hearts. One can certainly picture the scene that way, with a great deal of dramatic tension and eloquent looks and facial expressions, if one reads Luke alone. But Luke is not entirely explicit.

When Licona interprets these passages, he is quite definite that Mark and Luke both say that the opponents of Jesus were completely silent throughout:

> [I]n Mark 3:2–5 and Luke 6:7–10 the Pharisees are portrayed as being silent throughout the entire event while observing Jesus to see if he would heal the man, thereby breaking the Sabbath and providing them with grounds to accuse him. But Jesus knew their thoughts and asked them whether it was lawful on the Sabbath to do good or to save a life. In Matt. 12:10–13, the Pharisees were not silent. Instead, Matthew takes the thoughts of the Pharisees and converts them into a dialogue with Jesus[.] ...Matthew converts Jesus's one-sided address to the Jewish leaders into a dialogue with them.[4]

---

[4] Michael Licona, *Why Are There Differences in the Gospels? What We Can Learn from Ancient Biog-*

Licona's failure here even to consider additive harmonization arises in no small part from his confidence that Mark and Luke definitely portray the opponents of Jesus as silent "throughout the entire event." But if we allow Matthew to have value as a source in his own right, we have reason to note that Mark and Luke do not actually say this. Mark, in particular, says that the opponents were silent, but he mentions this silence *after* Jesus asks them a question. It is over-reading to interpret Mark's reference to silence as if it applied to the entire encounter. The emphasis in Mark is upon their recognition that Jesus has asked them a question that they cannot answer without looking bad.

This exchange follows a pattern we see in other parts of the Gospels, including Mark. In Mark 11.27–33 Jesus puts the leaders to silence by asking if the baptism of John the Baptist was from heaven or of men. They tell him that they cannot answer, and he therefore refuses to answer their question about his own source of authority. But they were not silent throughout. In fact, they asked him a question first. In Matthew 22.34–46 the Pharisees ask Jesus about the greatest commandment. He answers them but then goes on to ask the famous questions about whose son the Messiah is and why David calls the Messiah "Lord." They are unable to "answer him a word" (Matt. 22.46), and after that, no one asks him any further questions. Mark's noting that the Pharisees are silent after Jesus asks them a "gotcha" question does not, contra Licona, amount to an assertion that they are silent throughout the incident. Moreover, though Mark may not have known of an initial question, it would fit with the pattern of the other passages if the encounter began with an opponent's asking Jesus a question and continued with his outwitting them. Jesus' opponents were often over-confident, and he turned the tables on them more than once.

It's possible that Luke may have read Mark's account and guessed that the opponents did not speak throughout the entire incident. This might mean that Luke did not have access to Matthew's version and/or that he preferred to follow what he inferred from Mark. But this theory is not even really necessary to explain Luke. Jesus could very well have guessed at their thoughts before they spoke, so that even if someone did eventually speak up after a dramatic pause, there is no error in what Luke wrote. Moreover, we should not think of people as literally acting like a chorus—either all speaking or all remaining silent. One can well imagine that most of the people involved did remain silent, leaving Jesus to guess their thoughts, while just one person spoke aloud. The statement in Matthew that

raphy (Oxford: Oxford University Press, 2017), pp. 128–129.

"they" asked him should not be taken in a wooden way to mean that all of Jesus' opponents spoke simultaneously. One could have spoken for the group.

A little real-world imagination lets us see how it might have gone. The man with the withered hand is in the synagogue. Perhaps the opponents of Jesus edge him forward while Jesus is teaching. Jesus takes in the scene. There is a pause, during which Jesus knows full-well what they are up to. Then one person, perhaps to break the tension, speaks up, asking him if it's lawful to heal on the Sabbath. Jesus does not answer directly but tells the man to come forward. He asks his opponents which of them will not lift a sheep out of a pit on the Sabbath. He asks them, "Is it lawful to do good or harm on the Sabbath?" They are silent, knowing that there is no good answer they can give. Jesus looks at them with anger, tells the man to stretch out his hand, and heals him. There is nothing implausible about this harmonization of the three passages. Licona's failure even to suggest it arises because he amalgamates Luke and Mark, over-reads Mark's statement that "they were silent" as if it applies to the episode from beginning to end, and then jumps to the conclusion that Matthew has created dialogue.

Licona has two other reasons for reading this passage in this way: He claims that Matthew would have been taught to create dialogue by studying Greek exercise books; this was already dealt with in Chapter VIII. He also claims that Matthew creates a dialogue in the parable of the wicked tenants. I rebutted this claim in Chapter XI, section 3. Thus, once again, the theorist takes various fictionalization conjectures to reinforce one another.

There is another factor in play here as well—the persistent refusal to give Matthew any independent weight as an historical source when he is taken to be following Mark. This issue came up when discussing the parable of the wicked tenants and Jesus' discussion with the crowds. There as well, Licona does not even consider the possibility that different Gospel authors, including Matthew, may have had additional knowledge of the events. He considers only hypotheses that involve adding material to Mark without historical justification. Why?

A major problem in New Testament scholarship, which has now apparently spread to evangelical scholarship, is an overly rigid understanding of Markan priority and the two-source hypothesis. The general idea of the two-source hypothesis, stated in neutral terms, is that Mark wrote before Matthew and that, when a story is found with closely similar wording in both Matthew and Mark (even if it is also found in Luke), Matthew probably used Mark as a written source. Material found in Luke and Matthew but not in Mark is taken to be "Q material," with the theory that in these places Matthew and Luke used a now-lost source known as Q.[5]

The major problem arises not with a generic version of this hypothesis but with using it to lock out any consideration of independent information in places where Matthew is supposedly following Mark or Q. It cannot be said too often: It *does not follow* from the general idea that Mark wrote first and that Matthew used Mark that Matthew does not have his own memories or other sources of information, even in places where he is similar to Mark. "The two-source hypothesis" and "Markan priority," and their wide acceptance by scholars, should not be used to deny the possibility of independent Matthean information. We should not accept a false dichotomy according to which Matthew or Luke must be entirely independent of Mark or else entirely dependent upon Mark for some incident. Yet often, this is precisely what happens.

In a lecture on the deity of Jesus, Licona explains to the audience how he is using the concept of Gospel sources.[6] It is interesting to see how he explains the two-source hypothesis. First, he introduces the idea that Mark may have been a source for both Luke and Matthew. He then raises the question of why, if Matthew really was a disciple, Matthew would have used Mark. He answers this question by mentioning both Mark's probable connection to Peter, a leading apostle, and the fact that there were some incidents (like the Transfiguration) at which Peter was present but Matthew was not present. He then gives the following summary:

> Here's the thing: If the story is in Matthew, Mark, and Luke, then scholars say, "Well, it probably comes from Mark as a source." If it's in Matthew, Mark, but not in Luke, they say that Matthew got the story from Mark. If it's in Luke and Mark but not in Matthew, Luke got the story from Mark.

He continues by describing what Q is (a hypothetical source thought to lie behind similarly worded material common to Matthew and Luke), but in the present instance we are not concerned with alleged Q material. In *Why Are There Differences in the Gospels?*, Licona says that he "assume[s] Markan priority" and "hold[s] the two-source hypothesis with the majority of scholars."[7] Given both his practice and his

---

[5] We saw in an earlier section (Chapter XIII, section 6), that even if one grants the existence of Q it can be difficult to be sure when something is "Q material." Sometimes Matthew and Luke may actually be describing different sayings or incidents that were similar.

[6] Michael Licona, "Did Jesus Claim to be God?" July 8, 2017, minute 37:47, https://youtu.be/gT2TN6kA5kY?t=2267.

[7] Licona, *Why Are There Differences*, pp. 117–118. On p. 211 he considers the possibility that Mat-

lecture comments about scholarly consensus on these matters, one can reasonably assume that the summary he gives in the lecture fairly represents his approach to Synoptic issues. But notice how rigid that theory is. Having explained to his audience that Matthew could have been a disciple and could still have had reason to use Mark, Licona proceeds apparently to endorse a scholarly approach that *cuts out Matthew* as an *additional* source of independent information if the story he tells is found in Mark. This is remarkable, especially since Licona has said that Matthew might use Mark because there were events at which Peter was present and Matthew was not. But what about events where Matthew *was* present? Or what about events for which Matthew got information from disciples other than Peter in *addition* to what is found in Mark? Ignoring these possibilities, Licona tells his audience only that scholars say that the story "probably comes from Mark as a source" or that "Matthew got the story from Mark" if it is in both Mark and Matthew. Suddenly Matthew has become a non-entity as a witness to any incident where he appears similar to Mark.[8]

If we are genuinely to be open to reasonable historical hypotheses, we have to resist this urge to erase Matthew as a potential historical source of information in his own right. This is not a crazy idea, unworthy of consideration, simply because too many New Testament scholars wrongly believe that they must cut out Matthew as a witness in order to be faithful to a consensus view. Indeed, the very variations of wording and detail that scholars persistently use to argue that Matthew redacted Mark are in many cases evidence instead of at least some independent information in those places. It is not good historical practice to treat this possibility as a non-starter when interpreting a story like the man with the withered hand, especially since we have cases where Matthew's unique information is confirmed by undesigned coincidences and external confirmations. (I discuss some of these in Chapter XI, sections 3 and 5.)

---

thew may have "heard directly from" one of the female witnesses at the cross, the mother of the sons of Zebedee. That is a highly unusual instance where Licona seriously suggests that Matthew may have been in touch with an eyewitness and may have supplied unique material on that basis. For the most part, treating Matthew as an independent source is not his practice when the incident is also found in Mark.

[8] In Chapter VIII, section 3, I noted the oddity that Licona says that Matthew "would have been instructed" from Greek exercise textbooks. Licona does not address the question of who Matthew was. It seems highly unlikely that, if Matthew was Matthew (so to speak), he would have been taught from such textbooks. This raises a real question about whether Licona does think that the author of Matthew was a Palestinian Jewish tax collector who was a disciple of Jesus. In the lecture on the deity of Christ, he seems to be at least granting traditional Matthean authorship for the sake of the argument, in order to explain to his audience why they should be open to the version of Markan priority he is presenting even if they accept Matthean authorship.

The obvious application in the present case is that Matthew may have recalled that someone in the synagogue spoke up and asked Jesus if it was lawful to heal on the Sabbath, even if everyone else remained silent. But Licona never considers this possibility. What starts with over-reading of Mark (that Mark portrays the opponents as remaining silent throughout the incident) concludes with a fictionalizing literary device (that Matthew created dialogue) by way of rigid redactive-critical assumptions.[9]

3. Luke's "editorial fatigue"

In the previous chapter, we discussed a case where John is supposed to have displaced the anointing of Jesus' feet, knowingly putting it on a day in Passion Week when it did not actually occur. In that case, it certainly *appears* that both John and Mark are being explicit about chronology, giving rise to a puzzle about when the event occurred. While, as discussed there, achronological theories are possible (for Mark, not for John), these have a bit of an uphill climb given that Mark refers to "two days before Passover" just two verses before narrating the foot anointing.

But everything is grist to the literary device theorist's mill, and that degree of chronological explicitness is not required for a theorist to claim chronological displacement. A theorist may quite easily make that claim when the context in one account is left vague, as in the example in this section. The supposedly displaced teachings are Jesus' warning to the one by whom offense comes and his curse upon anyone who causes a little one who believes in him to stumble.[10]

The difference between Luke, on the one hand, and Matthew and Mark, on the other, arises like this: Mark 9.33–42, Matt. 18.1–6, and Luke 9.46–48 all tell about a time when the disciples were arguing about who would be the greatest in the kingdom. To rebuke them, Jesus took a child and set him among them, telling the disciples that whoever receives such a child in his name receives Jesus himself. Matthew also includes the statement that they must humble themselves and

---

[9] Chapter XIII, section 5, discusses another fictionalizing theory that Licona raises about this passage. That is the utterly unforced error that Matthew may have known of the story of the man with dropsy as told in Luke (even though that is neither Markan nor "Q material"), redacted Jesus' saying there about pulling an ox out of a well into the saying about pulling a sheep out of a pit, and placed it without historical warrant into the story of the man with a withered hand. Licona rates this unforced error so highly that he says that it is "difficult if not impossible" to tell if the saying about the sheep actually occurred in the healing of the man with the withered hand or whether Matthew has "heavily redacted" something from another incident (*Why Are There Differences*, p. 129). The presumption against Matthean reliability and independent knowledge is so strong that the theory in that case is not even based upon the usual source-critical lines of influence.

[10] Licona, *Why Are There Differences*, p. 244 n. 46.

become as children in order to enter the kingdom of heaven. And Matthew and Mark both include (though Mark has it a few verses later than Matthew does) the famous statement that, if someone causes one of these little ones who believe to stumble, it would be better for him to have a millstone tied around his neck and to be thrown into the sea.

Luke, like Matthew and Mark, says in Chapter 9 that Jesus put a child in their midst and said that whoever receives the child receives him. Luke then follows the immediate order of Mark by including an apparently irrelevant comment from John about how they tried to stop someone who was casting out demons in Jesus' name; Jesus disagrees with this procedure (Mark 9.38–41, Luke 9.49–50). Luke ends the scene at that point, while Mark moves on to the statement about the millstone and the little ones who believe on Jesus. It's entirely possible that for some reason John made such a comment on that very occasion, perhaps wanting to change the subject, and that Jesus, after answering him, came back to say more about the little ones who believe on him, still in the presence of a child. But it's noteworthy that Mark himself does not give the saying about millstones *immediately* after the rebuke to the disciples with the child in their midst and that Luke resembles Mark in this respect. Perhaps Luke was using Mark and simply did not continue following Mark after noticing that things went "off-topic" with the reference to the person casting out demons in Jesus' name.

The oddity is that in Luke 17.1–2, many chapters later, Luke *does* relate a very similar saying about a millstone and little ones. He also relates a saying found in the earlier immediate context in Matthew, calling down woe upon the one by whom stumbling blocks come. Licona claims that Luke has displaced the sayings and put them into a different context.

To see why this does not even look like a different historical context, it's useful to know a little bit more about Luke 17, other than that no children are mentioned. (That is the only thing Licona mentions about that chapter.[11]) Other facts are relevant to deciding how to understand chronology in relation to Luke 17. These verses come in the midst of a large section of Luke that is rather famously difficult in New Testament studies: Luke 9.51 through the middle of Luke 18 or the beginning of Luke 19 (depending on how one reckons). The difficulty arises in part because Luke keeps referring to Jesus as traveling to Jerusalem, though Jesus seems to take far too long to get there and seems to be taking a circuitous route, if

---

[11] Ibid.

this is just one journey.[12] It also arises from the fact that Luke does not appear to be following along with the order in Matthew or Mark during these chapters, so we can't track what is going on from those Gospels to infer a chronology. A related issue is the "heaped" nature of the material in this central section, often containing little or nothing in the way of chronological or contextual indicators.[13] Some of this material resembles sayings or events found in Matthew or Mark, but some of it is found only in Luke.

In Luke 16, just before the sayings we are considering, Jesus has just told the parable of the rich man and Lazarus, which is unique to Luke. The nearest indicator of a possible context for *that* parable comes several verses earlier, when it says that the Pharisees were lovers of money and were listening to Jesus and scoffing at him (Luke 16.14). Perhaps that is the context for the parable of the rich man. There is no transition whatsoever *after* the parable of the rich man and Lazarus into the sayings at the beginning of Luke 17. Consistent with the choppy nature of these chapters, Luke 17 just begins, "He said to his disciples..." (Luke 17.1). Whether Jesus said what follows to his disciples on *anything like* the same occasion on which he told the parable of the rich man and Lazarus is not at all clear. All things considered, it seems most probable that it was a different occasion, occurring at some unspecified time when only the disciples were present.

With all of that in mind, here is the beginning of Luke 17:

> He said to His disciples, "It is inevitable that stumbling blocks come, but woe to him through whom they come! It would be better for him if a millstone were hung around his neck and he were thrown into the sea, than that he would cause one of these little ones to stumble. Be on your guard! If your brother sins, rebuke him; and if he repents, forgive him. And if he sins against you seven times a day, and returns to you seven times, saying, 'I repent,' forgive him." The apostles said to the Lord, "Increase our faith!" And the Lord said, "If you had faith like a mustard seed, you would say to this mulberry tree, 'Be uprooted and be planted in the sea'; and it would obey you." (Luke 17.1–6)

---

[12] For a suggestion about Jesus' overly long "journey to Jerusalem" in the large central portion of Luke, see Lydia McGrew, "A Possible Solution to a Long-Standing Puzzle," *What's Wrong With the World*, February 15, 2018 http://whatswrongwiththeworld.net/2018/02/a_possible_solution_to_a_longs.html.

[13] Here are just some of the vague connecting phrases in this section of Luke: Luke 9.57, "As they were going along the road..."; 10.38, "As they were traveling along, he entered a village..."; 11.1, "It happened that while Jesus was praying in a certain place..."; 11.29, "As the crowds were increasing..."; 12.22, "And he said to his disciples..."; 13.10, "And he was teaching in one of the synagogues on the Sabbath"; 14.25, "Now large crowds were going along with him, and he turned and said..."; 15.11, "And he said..." And many more.

If this is not part of a "sayings section" of Luke, what would a sayings section look like? There is simply *no context given* for any of this material. Do the disciples (as represented here in Luke) ask Jesus to increase their faith at the same time that he makes the comment about millstones? Are we to take it that Jesus (according to Luke) made the statement about millstones at the same time that he made the statement about forgiving your brother? Who knows? Most of these statements by Jesus are not even on the same topic, with the exception of the reference to stumbling blocks in general and causing little ones to stumble in particular. Other than that, this is a hodge-podge.

Nor (and this is important) is there an uncanny, verbatim resemblance between this set of miscellaneous remarks in Luke and the context of Jesus' comments recorded earlier in Matthew and Mark. Here's how that goes: Jesus' statement that it is inevitable that offenses come, but woe to him by whom they come is found in Matthew just *after* the saying about little ones and millstones (Matt. 18.6–7). It is not recorded at all in Mark, and the two sayings are given in the opposite order in Luke 17.1–2. The saying about forgiving your brother if he sins occurs in the same chapter of Matthew as the story about the argument over status and the little child, but many verses later, and *not* as part of the same story. In Matt. 18.21, Peter *comes to* Jesus and asks how often he should forgive his brother. The "seventy times seven" response, and an entire parable, are found at that point in Matthew. The very fact that Peter comes to Jesus is a *prima facie* indicator that Matthew is not placing this discussion on the same occasion when Jesus set a child among them. Mark 9.33–35 is explicit that Jesus called the twelve to him when he placed the child among them. Presumably Peter was there among the others on that occasion and would have had no need to come to Jesus to ask a further question about forgiveness. Luke randomly drops a similar saying about forgiveness and sinning seven times in a day into the pile in Luke 17.1–3 with no question from Peter, no parable, and an added warning to be on your guard thrown in for good measure. The request from the disciples to increase their faith is not found in Mark or Matthew; the saying about faith like a mustard seed and uprooting a tree is vaguely similar to but also different from a saying that occurs in a quite different context in Matt. 17.20, well *before* the narrative of the controversy over status in the kingdom.

In other words, Luke is just "chunking in" a collection of Jesus' sayings at this point, and we cannot even tell with any justified confidence where he is getting them from. Did he have Matthew available to him in the form in which we have it or not? What independent source might he have had for the saying about faith as small as a mustard seed? Why does he record the sayings about the millstone and offenses along with these other sayings but with no surrounding story? Is he recounting the same teaching or a different one? We simply do not know.[14]

Licona gives a very different impression when discussing this part of Luke:

> Moreover, we can sometimes observe Luke breaking up tradition and placing portions in a different context (e.g., cf. Mark 9:33–49 // Matt. 18:1–22 with Luke 9:46–50 and 17:1– 4). That Luke has done this here is evident from the editorial fatigue present in Luke 17:2, where Luke mentions "one of these little ones." However, there are no "little ones" in this context. In fact, the closest references to a child are in Luke 11:11–13; 18:15.[15]

This is a bit cryptic as it stands. Licona gives more analysis in a lecture. There he first talks about the incident of the foot anointing at Bethany, calling it a case of displacement. He likens this case in Luke to his claim about the foot anointing, saying, "Let's look at another example of displacement." In other words, Luke's action is supposed to be like the action that Licona attributes to John—narrating dyschronologically, making it look like something happened at a time and in a context where it did not historically happen. Licona describes the scene that is common to all the Synoptic Gospels—the dispute over who will be the greatest, Jesus' placing the child in the midst, and Jesus' saying that whoever receives such a child receives him. Then he says,

> Now, the Gospels include other teachings within the context in which this story appears. Temptations will come, but woe to the person who tempts. If a body part causes you to sin, cut it off. If your brother sins, rebuke him, if he repents, forgive him, even if he sins and repents many times. Now, of the three Gospels, Matthew provides the fullest version. Luke provides almost as much. However, he displaces portions of the story to a different context. Luke Chapter 9 reports their argument about who is greatest amongst them, and Jesus places a child before them and tells them if they receive a child in his name they receive him and the Father, and the least among them is the greatest. But then Luke displaces the rest of those teachings, the remainder of the story, eight chapters later, in Luke Chapter 17. "Temptations will come, but woe to the person who tempts. It would be better if a millstone were hung about his neck and he were cast into the sea than that he should cause one of these little ones to sin." Now, this is interesting. It would be easy to say, "Well, Jesus was just saying the

---

[14] D. A. Carson makes similar comments about Luke's central section and chronology in his commentary on Matthew. *Matthew (The Expositor's Bible Commentary)* (Grand Rapids, MI: Zondervan, 2010), p. 462.

[15] Licona, *Why Are There Differences*, p. 244 n. 46.

same teaching on a different occasion." And no doubt Jesus taught the same thing many times. Agreed. But is this a different occasion? I don't think so, and here's why. Listen to what he says. "Temptations will come, but woe to the person who tempts. It would be better for him if a millstone were hung around his neck and he drowned in the sea than he should cause one of these little ones to stumble." What little ones? This is Luke 17 we're talking about now. When you look at Luke 16, no little ones, no children are mentioned. There are no children mentioned in Luke 17 other than this little reference. And there are no children mentioned in Chapter 18 until about halfway through. So what little ones [is] he mentioning? Now of course we would look at it and say, well, of course he's referring to that teaching of putting the little one, the child in front of them and saying that. But that's because we read that in the other Gospel. When we read it in Luke we don't see that, because it's not until eight chapters later. What Luke has done here is he's displaced the story, this teaching here, and he didn't kind of clean it up. This is what some scholars like Mark Goodacre refer to as editorial fatigue. And this is just wonderful for us to see this, because it tells us, this is a very clear example of Luke displacing the story.[16]

My detailed analysis above reveals several ways in which this description is simply inaccurate. The teaching about forgiving your brother does *not* occur in the same context in Matthew as the teaching about a child. On the contrary, the twelve are already present in Matthew when Jesus teaches them about the little child, whereas Peter *comes to* Jesus, as told much later in the chapter, with a question about forgiving your brother. Worse still, the teaching about cutting off a member that causes you to stumble occurs in Matthew and Mark but *does not occur in Luke*, so it is flatly inaccurate to list that teaching with others and then to say that Luke "displaces the rest of those teachings" to another location in his Gospel.

Third, Luke 9.49–50 (when Jesus places a child among them) reports a teaching that Licona does not mention, just as Mark does, right along with the placement of a little child—namely, Jesus' response to John's question about someone else who was casting out demons. At that point one might say that Luke seems to be following Mark. He does not break off abruptly immediately after the mention of a little child and "displace the remainder of the story." He even includes a teaching found in the immediate context in Mark that is not thematically related to the controversy among the disciples.

Licona is overly rigid in any event concerning the phrase "these little ones" in Luke 17. It is entirely possible to use the word "these" to refer to a group or

---

[16] Michael Licona, "Why Are There Differences in the Gospels," April 19, 2014, minute 47:35, https://youtu.be/xtemSTrkogE?t=2855.

type of people who are not physically present. A popular speaker might say to a friend, "These kids who come to my talks are looking for answers." He does not have to be literally pointing to anyone when he makes the comment.[17] He does not have to be in the presence of any of "these kids." We have an instance that appears to be exactly of that kind in Matt. 10.42, which says that if anyone gives a cup of water to "one of these little ones" (the Greek is the same as Matt. 18.6) in the name of a disciple, he will have a reward. But there are no little ones present in that context. Nor does that saying about a cup of water appear in any other context in Luke or Mark; it certainly does not appear in any context in another Gospel where actual little ones are present. So even if one believes (see Appendix 3) that the comments in Matthew 10 are part of a composite discourse, one has no argument that Matthew is "displacing" the teaching from another context where little ones are present and has forgotten to erase the little ones through "editorial fatigue."[18] If Jesus did say something about "these little ones" and millstones more than once, he may have done so when no actual little ones were present, and Luke could have heard of that occasion.

Most importantly, there *is no story whatsoever* in Luke 17.1–3 surrounding the saying about a child and a millstone, so Licona's statement that Luke moves "portions of the story" and "the remainder of the story" is misleading. We may never know where Luke got the sayings he reports in a heap at the beginning of Chapter 17 or why he relates them at that point in his Gospel, but whatever his reason for reporting them there, it was not the one Licona gives—"displacing the rest of the story." If it were, he would have bothered to relate some other *story*. If he were moving the sayings to a different context, he would have given a different *context*. Ironically, no small part of the reason for thinking that Luke is reporting a saying that came from the earlier dispute is the fact that he provides no different context at all.

The theory of "editorial fatigue" is not "wonderful" but hyper-complex. It amounts to the claim that Luke was *trying* to make it look like Jesus said this at some other time but did not succeed in making it look that way, because he forgot

---

[17] See also John 7.49, where the Jewish leaders refer to "This crowd which does not know the law...," though no crowd is present.

[18] Mark 9.41 does not count as a place where Jesus speaks in the presence of a literal child about giving one of "these little ones" a cup of water, since that verse refers instead to giving a cup of water to "you"—presumably to the adult disciples. If Matt. 10.42 were "moved" from the context of Mark 9.41, Matthew would be gratuitously *introducing* "little ones" into the saying without any little ones present, which is highly implausible.

to erase the reference to "little ones." Apparently he also forgot to include any other context—a rather large amount of fatigue.

It is over-reading to take Luke to be narrating a chronological placement in Chapter 17 when that passage gives no chronological indicators. It is extreme over-reading to take him to be attempting to move a saying of Jesus to a different context and to suffer from "editorial fatigue." Without that over-reading we can recognize that Luke tells, with no contradiction, the same story in his Chapter 9 that Matthew and Mark tell and that he later records other teachings of Jesus, including a warning about causing little ones to stumble, in an unordered "sayings" section.

4. When did Jesus predict that Peter would deny him?

The example in this section could have been covered in the previous chapter, "Fictions Only Need Apply," but it also involves over-reading. Licona uses the question of exactly when Jesus predicted that Peter would deny him to support the conclusion that the evangelists sometimes "crafted or creatively reconstructed" certain aspects of their stories. The idea is that different authors crafted a specific placement for Jesus' prediction within the night of the Last Supper where they found it "most appropriate or desirable," without historical justification.[19] This claim of factually unsupported crafting is a result of both over-reading and refusing to consider a harmonization in which Jesus emphasizes the prediction by making it twice. The latter is fairly well-supported by the accounts, with two of them plausibly narrating the earlier prediction on that night and two narrating the later.

All four Gospels report that Jesus predicted, on the night of the Last Supper, that Peter would deny him three times. Matthew's and Mark's accounts are very similar both in wording and in narrative placement. Luke's record is different from either Matthew's or Mark's, containing significant unique statements by Jesus, but it may be narrated achronologically. John's is different from the others as well, containing unique dialogue between Peter and Jesus placed with some degree of chronological firmness prior to the departure from the upper room. Here are all four:

> After singing a hymn, they went out to the Mount of Olives. And Jesus said to them, "You will all fall away, because it is written, 'I will strike down the shepherd, and the sheep shall be scattered.' But after I have been raised, I will go ahead of you to Galilee." But Peter said to Him, "Even though all may fall away, yet I will not." And Jesus said to him, "Truly I say to you, that this very night, before a rooster crows twice, you yourself will deny Me three times." But Peter kept saying

---

[19] Licona, *Why Are There Differences*, p. 258, n. 61.

insistently, "Even if I have to die with You, I will not deny You!" And they all were saying the same thing also. (Mark 14.26–31)

After singing a hymn, they went out to the Mount of Olives. Then Jesus said to them, "You will all fall away because of Me this night, for it is written, 'I will strike down the shepherd, and the sheep of the flock shall be scattered.' But after I have been raised, I will go ahead of you to Galilee." But Peter said to Him, "Even though all may fall away because of You, I will never fall away." Jesus said to him, "Truly I say to you that this very night, before a rooster crows, you will deny Me three times." Peter said to Him, "Even if I have to die with You, I will not deny You." All the disciples said the same thing too. (Matt. 26.30–35).

These two versions are verbally nearly identical. One of the slight verbal differences between them is the emphasis in Mark on Peter's repetition. He "kept saying insistently" that he would never deny Jesus. Here are Luke's and John's:

"Simon, Simon, behold, Satan has demanded permission to sift you like wheat; but I have prayed for you, that your faith may not fail; and you, when once you have turned again, strengthen your brothers." But he said to Him, "Lord, with You I am ready to go both to prison and to death!" And He said, "I say to you, Peter, the rooster will not crow today until you have denied three times that you know Me." And He said to them, "When I sent you out without money belt and bag and sandals, you did not lack anything, did you?" They said, "No, nothing." And He said to them, "But now, whoever has a money belt is to take it along, likewise also a bag, and whoever has no sword is to sell his coat and buy one. For I tell you that this which is written must be fulfilled in Me, 'And He was numbered with transgressors'; for that which refers to Me has its fulfillment." They said, "Lord, look, here are two swords." And He said to them, "It is enough." And He came out and proceeded as was His custom to the Mount of Olives; and the disciples also followed Him. (Luke 22.35–39)

Therefore when he [Judas] had gone out, Jesus said, "Now is the Son of Man glorified, and God is glorified in Him; if God is glorified in Him, God will also glorify Him in Himself, and will glorify Him immediately. Little children, I am with you a little while longer. You will seek Me; and as I said to the Jews, now I also say to you, 'Where I am going, you cannot come.'" ... Simon Peter said to Him, "Lord, where are You going?" Jesus answered, "Where I go, you cannot follow Me now; but you will follow later." Peter said to Him, "Lord, why can I not follow You right now? I will lay down my life for You." Jesus answered, "Will you lay down your life for Me? Truly, truly, I say to you, a rooster will not crow until you deny Me three times. (John 13.31–33, 36–38)

At this point in John there follows a chapter of dialogue and Jesus' teachings, and in John 14.31, Jesus says, "Get up, let us go from here," and they go out to the Garden of Gethsemane.

From these variations Licona moves quickly to suggest the conclusion that the authors felt free to craft details without historical warrant:[20]

> [T]hese sorts of discrepancies could suggest the event itself was remembered while some of the peripheral details were not. As a result, ancient authors, including the evangelists, may have reported the peripheral details either as they or their sources recalled them, crafted them, or even creatively reconstructed them as part of their literary artistry in writing a quality narrative.[21]

That the evangelists crafted or creatively reconstructed some peripheral details on occasion seems likely. One may…compare the location where Jesus informs Peter he will deny him three times before the night is over. In Mark 14:26–32 // Matt 26:30–36, Jesus and his disciples had left the room where they had just eaten the Last Supper and went to the Mount of Olives. It is there and before they entered

---

[20] Licona draws the same conclusion about Peter's denials themselves—that the denials "were remembered" while details were not (Ibid., p. 161). In this case the passive "were remembered" is especially striking, since one might expect Peter himself to remember such details. I am not discussing the puzzles surrounding the details of Peter's denials at length here, but I recommend a harmonizing approach. Nor should harmonization of Peter's denials be derided as requiring that he denied Jesus six times. We should use reasonable imagination to attempt harmonization, coupled with mental flexibility. Craig Blomberg shows these qualities in his discussion of the issue. "You Asked: Are the Differing Narratives of Peter's Denials Reconcilable?" *The Gospel Coalition*, December 12, 2011, https://www. thegospelcoalition.org/article/you-asked-are-the-differing-narratives-of-peters-denials-reconcilable/. For example, Blomberg points out that the Greek word for "another" servant who challenged Peter is grammatically masculine but that a masculine can be inclusive of the feminine. He points out that multiple people could have spoken to Peter at once. He also points out that the reference to "the maid-servant" in Mark 14.69 does not have to mean the same servant girl who spoke to Peter before. It is also obvious that one person could have said multiple things, speaking to Peter and then turning to those around and speaking to them. Concerning the fire and precisely where Peter was located at the time of Peter's second denial, we do not know whether there may also have been a second fire in the porch or whether Peter moved out to the porch and then returned to the fire in the courtyard a little later when he hoped that the girl who was previously questioning him might have gone away. These are the sorts of considerations that are entirely legitimate in dealing with historical documents and complex events. And they fall within the normal range of human testimony. In contrast, the hypothesis that otherwise reliable authors invented when they did not know what happened is dubious. Contra the implication Licona makes (p. 158), we do not face a choice between hypothesizing that Peter denied Jesus six times and jumping to the conclusion that the Gospel authors invented details. Indeed, if we assume that Luke and Matthew had access to Mark (and the literary device theorists themselves assume this), we would expect them to *follow* Mark if they had no additional, independent information, rather than inventing details without warrant. That they have differing details is some evidence that they had other sources of information about Peter's denials.

[21] Licona, *Why Are There Differences*, p. 184.

Gethsemane that Jesus informs Peter he will deny him three times. However, in Luke 22:31–39, it occurs before they go to the Mount of Olives. And in John 13:33–38; 18:1, it is while they are eating the Last Supper. It may be that the relative rather than the specific time was remembered when Jesus predicted Peter would deny him thrice and the evangelists felt free to locate it where they thought most appropriate or desirable.[22]

Here is a now-familiar pattern: While the placement of Jesus' prediction in Matthew and Mark is fairly explicit,[23] it is not nearly so explicit in Luke. Licona over-reads both Luke and John not only to be placing the prediction prior to their leaving the upper room but even at particular points within the Last Supper, so that his exposition gives the impression that even Luke and John are in tension with each other. That is, he suggests that in John the prediction occurs specifically while they are eating. He then suggests as an explanation that the authors crafted or creatively constructed (contradictory) details because they did not really know when in the course of the evening the event took place.

John does not at all say that the dialogue between Jesus and Peter took place while they were eating. The nearest reference to food occurs before Judas Iscariot leaves the room, when Jesus gives him the sop as an indicator that he is the one who will betray him (John 13.30). After Judas leaves, Jesus begins to address the group, saying that he gives them a new commandment that they should love one another. At some point here, Peter asks Jesus where he is going, but there is nothing that places this definitely "while they are eating."

Moreover, Luke doesn't imply that there was no food around anymore by the time of Jesus' prediction. There is no particular reason to think that they *stopped* eating at some specific moment prior to singing a hymn and leaving the upper room, so even if one takes Luke to be placing Jesus' prediction in the upper room, there is nothing there that makes Luke's account conflict with John's. Any contrast between Luke's and John's timing of the prediction is a major over-reading of both, though of course the specifics of the dialogue are unique to each. One would do better to say that Luke and John appear to agree (though Luke is less clear) that Jesus predicted Peter's denial once before they left the upper room than to try to divide the four accounts (as Licona does) into three different placements.

---

[22] Ibid., p. 258, n. 161.

[23] This is the case not only because of the explicit time reference to their going out after singing a hymn but also because Matt. 26.31 says, "Then Jesus said to them, 'You will all fall away...'" using the word *tote* for "then." While that word can be used for logical rather than chronological order, there is no reason to think that it is being used in that way here.

Luke's language even allows for the possibility that he is narrating the prediction achronologically. Luke 22.39, where Luke says that Jesus went out to the Mount of Olives with the disciples, begins with the temporally non-committal word *kai*. Licona does not appear to have a category for narrating achronologically because one does not know specifics. In other words, if Luke happened not to know precisely when in the evening the dialogue took place between Jesus and Peter, he may have deliberately narrated it without specific temporal terminology in order *not* to place it firmly in any one place. This is all the more likely since what Luke relates is importantly different from what Mark and Matthew record. If Luke had access to Mark (for example), he would have recognized that he had more to tell, presumably from some human source. Namely, Luke had heard about Jesus' statement to Peter that Satan has desired to sift all of the disciples (the "you" at first is plural) but that he has prayed for Simon (the "you" there is singular). Jesus then tells Simon to strengthen his brothers when he has turned—a prophecy of Peter's later restoration. This unique information is further evidence of a point discussed in Chapter XII, section 4. Luke appears to have had some special access to information about Peter, possibly from talking with Peter himself. Luke, recognizing that this dialogue and the related prediction that Peter would deny Jesus *might* not be the same as the incident related by Matthew and Mark, may have narrated it earlier while delicately refraining from being linguistically definite about when it occurred, thus leaving open the alternate possibility that Jesus said it later in the evening at the same time as the prediction narrated in Matthew and Mark. This nuanced suggestion is importantly different from the idea that he definitely *placed* it at a time for which he lacked historical warrant, as suggested by Licona's wording.

A reasonable additive harmonization here would be the suggestion that Jesus in fact predicted Peter's denial twice (but not three times) on that evening. This may (though this is conjectural) explain the emphatic nature of Peter's insistence that he will never deny Jesus on the later occasion, as recorded in Mark. If Jesus had made this unflattering prediction earlier in the evening as well, Peter may have been especially insistent in rejecting it the second time. Notice, too, that neither Luke nor John records a prediction that the other disciples will forsake Jesus on that night, though in Luke Jesus says that Satan has desired to have all of them. Perhaps Jesus initially predicted Peter's denial in the context of a conversation focused on Peter (though in the presence of the others) in the upper room, prompted by Peter's questions, "Where are you going?" and "Why can I not follow you now?" At that point, perhaps all of the dialogue between Jesus and Peter contained in John and Luke occurred. Then, after they left the upper room, Jesus predicted that they would *all* fall away that night, citing the prophecy about smiting the shepherd and scattering the sheep. At that point, despite Jesus' prediction about him earlier that night, perhaps Peter spoke up to argue further, insisting that even if all the rest were to fall away, he would not do so.[24] Jesus then stated again that indeed Peter would deny him that very night.

If it seems improbable that Jesus would make the same prediction about Peter twice in the same night, we should reflect on how often those of us who are parents have had to say the same (sometimes unflattering) thing to a child who insists on arguing the point. Sometimes these repetitions occur quite close to one another, even within the same conversation. If a young person (or even an employee) insists on protesting a negative comment or correction, the person in authority is sometimes forced to insist upon it even if he would have preferred not to say it explicitly again. For Peter to jump on Jesus' general statement that all of them will fall away and argue, despite Jesus' earlier prediction about himself, would fit well with Peter's personality as discussed in Chapter XII, section 4. Peter was not one to accept Jesus' predictions meekly if he disagreed with them.

A word here is in order about my own suggested harmonizations. It may well be that particular readers find a harmonization suggestion to be implausible. It is at least worth reconsidering in that case whether one has been influenced by the extraordinary resistance in New Testament scholarly circles to thinking that something broadly similar happened more than once. We should reflect on how often we repeat ourselves in daily life and how often broadly similar things happen to us before we impatiently dismiss such a proposal.

But beyond that, we must keep in mind that there are multiple nodes to the flowchart even *after* we ask whether two accounts can be harmonized without undue strain. Perhaps it seems to a reader that Jesus would not have predicted Peter's denial twice in the same evening and therefore that there is a remaining tension between John (at least) on the one hand and Matthew and Mark on the other. But even if you are not satisfied with my suggested harmonization or with any that you can think of, it *does not follow* that the Gospel authors considered themselves licensed to craft details out of their own heads. One must, next, ask if this tension

---

[24] This specific boast of Peter's, comparing himself with the other disciples, is not narrated in John, which gives rise to an undesigned coincidence with John 21. See Lydia McGrew, *Hidden in Plain View: Undesigned Coincidences in the Gospels and Acts* (Chillicothe, OH, DeWard Publishing, 2017), pp. 57–60.

arose from any author's *knowingly* inserting factually inaccurate information. Further, one must ask why we should think that there was an accepted "literary device" that allowed them to do so. Remember: The earlier chapters, long and detailed as they were, argued that we do not have independent evidence for accepted fictionalizing literary devices—e.g., "crafting peripheral details."

5. Did Luke or Mark change the facts about the thief on the cross?

A well-known Bible difficulty about the crucifixion concerns whether a thief, singular, or thieves, plural, mocked Jesus when they were crucified with him. Mark notes in just a few words, "Those who were crucified with Him were also insulting Him" (Mark 15.32, with a similar statement in Matt. 27.44). Luke tells of a dialogue among the three:

> One of the criminals who were hanged there was hurling abuse at Him, saying, "Are You not the Christ? Save Yourself and us!" But the other answered, and rebuking him said, "Do you not even fear God, since you are under the same sentence of condemnation? And we indeed are suffering justly, for we are receiving what we deserve for our deeds; but this man has done nothing wrong." And he was saying, "Jesus, remember me when You come in Your kingdom!" And He said to him, "Truly I say to you, today you shall be with Me in Paradise." (Luke 23.39–43)

If we knew that this was the *only* interaction between Jesus and the thieves, there could be a minor apparent discrepancy, since Luke would be implying that only one of them insulted Jesus while the other rebuked him, whereas Mark says that "those" crucified with Jesus were insulting him.

A fairly obvious solution is simply that these represent two different times during the crucifixion and that one thief had a change of heart.[25] An alternative, suggested by Augustine, is the use of a manner of speaking wherein one uses the plural for the singular. (Sometimes this is referred to as synecdoche—substituting the whole for the part.) Augustine gives a good example from Hebrews 11.33, "They shut the mouths of lions," when probably the author has only Daniel in mind.[26] In our own time we can think of a use of the word "people," as in, "It's so annoying when people on Facebook say that," even if one is thinking of only one person on Facebook who has made the statement. Augustine explicitly states that

---

[25] This is a fairly standard resolution. See "Matthew 27:44—Did Both Robbers Revile Christ, or Did Only One Do this?" http://defendinginerrancy.com/bible-solutions/Matthew_27.44.php.

[26] Augustine, *The Harmony of the Gospels*, Book III, 16.53.

this solution would not work if Matthew and Mark said that "both of" those who were crucified within Jesus insulted him.[27]

I find the latter of these an elegant solution and the former entirely plausible. It is on the former that I will be focusing most attention in this section, since Licona addresses it and since rejecting it involves over-reading Mark's and Luke's time placements. (Licona does not address the plural-for-singular suggestion at all.)

Licona does consider a harmonization momentarily, but he then sets it aside and in the end presents the reader with only two fictionalizations as alternatives:

> Does Mark // Matthew or Luke or both preserve the true account of the thieves? The tension vanishes if we propose that both thieves initially reviled Jesus but one later had a change of heart and repented. Such is plausible given deathbed conversions. On the other hand, all three Synoptics place the response of the thieves in the same location of their narrative: The three have just been crucified, lots were cast for Jesus's clothing, the Jewish leaders are mocking him, and even one or both thieves mock him. This is immediately followed by darkness covering the land beginning at noon. Thus, Luke appears to be reporting the same incident as Mark // Matthew. Luke may have displaced the act of the repentant thief from a later time that day, or Mark—followed by Matthew—left the thief unrepentant in order to highlight Jesus being rejected by all. As a historical question, it is impossible to determine what occurred with the available data. Accordingly, it would appear that either displacement or the altering or omission of narrative details has occurred.[28]

The speed with which this analysis moves from "the tension vanishes if we propose..." to "it is impossible to determine what occurred" to "accordingly, it would appear that either displacement or the [deliberate, thematically motivated] altering or omission of narrative details has occurred" is breathtaking. While Licona admits the availability of a harmonization, he rejects it instantly. He then declares it impossible to determine what occurred as an historical matter. But he does not leave it at that. He tells the reader that "it would appear" that one type of fictionalization or another has taken place. Apparently that much *is* possible to determine, on his view.

---

[27] In saying this, Augustine is scrupulous to distinguish something that would be fictionalizing from something that is not. The use of a mere fuzzy manner of speaking—"those who were crucified did this," "people do this," "they shut the mouths of lions," etc., when there is only one in view—is not *per se* an attempt to *make it look like* a plural number is literally acting. In contrast, the use of the term "both," would be an unambiguous attempt to convey that both of the thieves insulted Jesus. This kind of careful linguistic distinction is too often missing in the work of New Testament critics.

[28] Licona, *Why Are There Differences*, p. 165.

Let us be clear about what the "omission of narrative details" is that Licona suggests for Mark: It is a deliberate attempt to *leave the thief unrepentant* in order to make Jesus appear to be "rejected by all," even though he was not, in fact, rejected by all if one of the thieves repented. Mark on this theory would be attempting to *make it look like* neither thief repented, even though he *knew* that one of them did. As for Luke, the conjecture is that he was attempting to make it look like the thief repented at an earlier time in the day than the historical repentance ("may have displaced the act of the repentant thief from a later time that day"), though Licona suggests no motive at all for this. And at the end of the analysis, these are the only two options Licona leaves us: It "appears" that one or the other of these is taking place. This either/or is also visible in his summary at the end of the chapter: "Either Luke displaces an event or Mark // Matthew alter details."[29]

So what is the argument for rejecting the idea that one thief had a change of heart? It is a classic example of over-reading. "[A]ll three Synoptics place the response of the thieves in the same location of their narrative" and "Luke appears to be reporting the same incident." As with the rigid claim that John reports that Jesus predicts Peter's denial "while they are eating the Last Supper," so here: Licona treats the reports about the thieves as if they occur at an extremely specific, single time during the crucifixion, when the narratives imply nothing of the kind. This case provides an even more glaring instance of over-reading than the one in the previous section. Here, at more length, are Mark's and Luke's accounts. (Matthew's is very similar to Mark's.)

> Then they brought Him to the place Golgotha, which is translated, Place of a Skull. They tried to give Him wine mixed with myrrh; but He did not take it. And they crucified Him, and divided up His garments among themselves, casting lots for them to decide what each man should take. It was the third hour when they crucified Him. The inscription of the charge against Him read, "THE KING OF THE JEWS."
>
> They crucified two robbers with Him, one on His right and one on His left. And the Scripture was fulfilled which says, "And He was numbered with transgressors." Those passing by were hurling abuse at Him, wagging their heads, and saying, "Ha! You who are going to destroy the temple and rebuild it in three days, save Yourself, and come down from the cross!" In the same way the chief priests also, along with the scribes, were mocking Him among themselves and saying, "He saved others; He cannot save Himself. Let this Christ, the King of

---

[29] Ibid., p. 167.

Israel, now come down from the cross, so that we may see and believe!" Those who were crucified with Him were also insulting Him.

When the sixth hour came, darkness fell over the whole land until the ninth hour. (Mark 15.22–33)

When they came to the place called The Skull, there they crucified Him and the criminals, one on the right and the other on the left. But Jesus was saying, "Father, forgive them; for they do not know what they are doing." And they cast lots, dividing up His garments among themselves. And the people stood by, looking on. And even the rulers were sneering at Him, saying, "He saved others; let Him save Himself if this is the Christ of God, His Chosen One." The soldiers also mocked Him, coming up to Him, offering Him sour wine, and saying, "If You are the King of the Jews, save Yourself!" Now there was also an inscription above Him, "THIS IS THE KING OF THE JEWS."

One of the criminals who were hanged there was hurling abuse at Him, saying, "Are You not the Christ? Save Yourself and us!" But the other answered, and rebuking him said, "Do you not even fear God, since you are under the same sentence of condemnation? And we indeed are suffering justly, for we are receiving what we deserve for our deeds; but this man has done nothing wrong." And he was saying, "Jesus, remember me when You come in Your kingdom!" And He said to him, "Truly I say to you, today you shall be with Me in Paradise."

It was now about the sixth hour, and darkness fell over the whole land until the ninth hour. (Luke 23.33–44)

Licona's over-readings are extreme and even in tension with the text. He argues that the Gospels imply only one interaction between Jesus and the thieves, occurring when "the three have just been crucified" and that it is "immediately followed by darkness covering the land." This set of statements does not fit with Mark's report, which says that it was the third hour when Jesus was crucified but the sixth hour when darkness set in. So how could it be that, in Mark, the three have *just been* crucified when the thieves insult Jesus and that this "incident" is "immediately followed" by darkness over the land, since there were three hours from the beginning of the crucifixion to the darkness?

Indeed, the term "incident" is quite inappropriate, given that Mark's Greek imperfect verb tense for their insulting Jesus is progressive in meaning. Mark indicates that at some time or other they, like others, "were insulting" Jesus. He does not narrate a single incident in which they insulted him. In this regard Mark's reference to the thieves is similar to what he says about the bystanders and the chief priests. Insulting is not the sort of thing that has to happen at just one time. The thieves could have insulted Jesus at one time in the three hours and one of them could have resumed doing so later on, before the darkness.

Luke's use of, "It was now about the sixth hour" is quite naturally taken to mean that the darkness began after all of the things he has just narrated have happened. Luke here agrees with Matthew and Mark that *time has passed* in the crucifixion between its beginning and the beginning of the darkness, and that these various events have taken place during that period of time. Three hours is a long time for the thief to be hanging on the cross, easily allowing him to join in insulting Jesus at first and to have second thoughts later on. If one were to strain to find temporal indicators in Luke concerning the repentant thief, the fact that the statement, "It was now about the sixth hour" comes immediately after Jesus' dialogue with the thief might place their discussion toward the *end* of the first several hours of the crucifixion rather than when "the three have just been cruci- fied." (The word translated "now" is *édé*, which can also be translated "already.") If Luke is saying that the thief repented after several hours of the crucifixion had passed, this time indication would *support* the natural harmonization that Licona is resisting. But even that conjecture probably attributes more precision to Luke than he intended.

Here, as in the attempt to change "My God, why have you forsaken me?" into "I thirst," we see the curiously wooden mindset of the redactive critic. The words from the cross must be made to match up in number (last, second-to-last) be- tween John and the Synoptics, even at the cost of developing wild theories about John's invention of words that bear no resemblance to the Synoptic sayings and insisting that they mean the same thing. Here, the interactions with the thieves are assumed to take place all at the same time, a single incident reported in all three Synoptic Gospels, when there is not the slightest reason in the accounts to make that assumption.

The conjecture that Mark suppressed the conversion of the thief shows this same absence of flexibility and real-world imagination. It is entirely conceivable that some people at the crucifixion heard things that others did not hear. Peter, probably one of Mark's major human sources, was not present himself. It is quite plausible that Mark and Matthew simply never heard about the conversion of the second thief but that Luke, doing more interviews, did get this account. Per- haps one of the women standing near to the cross heard the exchange and told Luke about it. Why would one suggest that Mark deliberately suppressed the repentance of the thief for theological reasons, trying to make it look like Jesus was rejected by all, rather than adopting the far simpler theory that he simply did not hear about it in the first place?

As for Luke, without a severe over-reading, there is not the slightest reason to say that he places Jesus' conversation with the thief earlier in the crucifixion than the time when it occurred. Luke's narrative is quite easily consistent with the theory that one of the thieves had a change of mind.

Whether one accepts Augustine's theory that Mark and Matthew made a non-fictionalizing use of the plural for the singular or whether one holds that both thieves insulted Jesus at first and one repented later, there is nothing in this Bible difficulty that supports a fictionalization theory of any kind. We are certainly not justified in accepting the false dichotomy that either Luke has dyschronologically moved the repentance of the thief or Mark has deliberately suppressed it.

Over-reading is a bane of New Testament studies. We should scrupulously avoid it when an author is obviously indefinite on some point. Even when there is some plausible first impression, it must be subject to correction by comparison with other information. When there is a plausible range of meanings, it is simply poor hermeneutics to insist on one's first impression as the only possible meaning the passage can bear and to pit such interpretations against one another. Over-reading does not become more justified when one places a literary device label on one's conclusion. That only adds further methodological errors to the first one. Skeptical scholars will always use over-reading to cast doubt upon the truthfulness of the Gospels' accounts. It is important for Christian scholars to be sounder historians. We must resist over-reading from the outset rather than building theoretical castles on such a shaky foundation.

Summary
Over-reading

- Many unnecessary claims of contradiction in the Gospels arise from over-reading.

- Over-reading includes taking an author to be trying to suppress an event if he merely doesn't mention it, incorrectly taking an author to be indicating chronological order by narrative order, and taking an author to be saying something more specific than he actually says.

- Over-reading involves taking one's first impression of a passage in isolation and remaining tied to this interpretation rather than qualifying it in the light of information from other sources.

- Qualifying one's initial impression of a passage in light of other evidence is not religiously motivated gerrymandering but responsible historical practice.

- Literary device theorists often over-read, insist that the Gospels cannot be harmonized, then claim a fictionalizing literary device.

- Examples of over-reading rebutted in this chapter include the claims that

  - Mark and Matthew contradict Luke and John about when Jesus predicted that Peter would deny him,
  - either Luke or Mark changed the facts about the thief on the cross,
  - and more.

XVI

Fictionalizing Literary Devices and the Resurrection Accounts

1. Once again: Why does all of this matter?

When we think of the resurrection of Jesus, we come back full circle to the question asked in the first section of Chapter I: "Why does all of this matter?" Evidential Christian apologetics has focused strongly on the resurrection, and rightly so, for it is the central sign by which God confirmed that Jesus is Lord and God incarnate, raising him from the dead. It is God's seal of approval set upon the teachings of Jesus. We can infer that what Jesus taught is true, both about himself and about many other subjects, if he was raised from the dead. The resurrection also confirms that God exists—the God of Abraham, Isaac, and Jacob, whom Jesus said that he came to reveal.

But what happens when we start to theorize quite seriously that the Gospel authors put words into Jesus' mouth, invented scenes, and altered and invented times and myriad other details in the Gospels, including parts of the resurrection stories? One immediate consequence is that the value of the resurrection for confirming specific doctrine via the teaching of Jesus is greatly reduced. If we must seriously question whether the Gospels record Jesus' historical teaching in *historically recognizable* form, then how much good does it do to believe that God endorsed Jesus' teaching? Why should we think that the evangelists' unrecognizable extrapolations represent what he really taught?

As for the resurrection itself, one cannot confirm the *implications* of the resurrection appearances while simultaneously undermining the reliability of the accounts of those appearances. Take, for example, the idea that Jesus rose from the dead physically. Suppose that one quite seriously thinks that the Gospel authors may have "crafted" the details of the resurrection appearance accounts or may have altered them at will for literary or theological purposes. That could readily mean that, for example, Luke added the claim that Jesus ate with his disciples (Luke 24.40–42). If Luke is the kind of author to alter such matters, he may have done this for theological or literary reasons. Such a suggestion is no more radical than others that I will discuss in this chapter—suggestions that have been made with all seriousness by evangelical scholars. If Jesus' eating with his disciples in Luke 24 were merely Luke's apologetic embellishment, then it would do little or nothing to confirm the physicality of the resurrection. (New Testament scholar Dale C. Allison makes this very suggestion.[1]) To say that it is multiply attested that Jesus' resurrection was physical while simultaneously raising the probability that the details that lead to that conclusion were invented undermines the basis of the conclusion. As noted in the case of the infancy narratives in Chapter XI, section 6, variations that arise merely from the authors' vivid imaginations are the wrong kind of variations for supporting independent attestation to the *truth* of the overlapping content.

Michael Licona's major book on the resurrection gives the impression that we can throw the *specific* post-resurrection appearances into historical doubt while remaining rationally confident that the group of disciples had *some* post-resurrection appearance experience. The far vaguer claim is supposed to be able to bear the weight of the argument that Jesus really rose from the dead, even if the specific appearance accounts are dubious:

> What may we conclude about the appearances to the disciples? A similarity exists with the miracles of Jesus. Bracketing the issue of the nature of the event itself— that is, was it a divine act, magic, psychological delusion or trickery—a paucity of evidence should deter us from affirming the historicity of particular miracles of Jesus. Historians may conclude that Jesus performed acts that he and others interpreted as miracles and exorcisms and that these acts caused many onlookers to drop their jaws in amazement. However, it is difficult to award historicity with a great deal of certainty to any particular miracle or exorcism reported in the Gospels. In a similar manner, historians may conclude that, subsequent to Jesus' death by crucifixion, a number of his followers had experiences in individual and group settings that convinced them that Jesus had risen from the dead and had appeared to them. We may affirm with great confidence that Peter had such an experience in an individual setting, and we will see that the same may be said of an adversary of

---

[1] *Resurrecting Jesus: The Earliest Christian Tradition and Its Interpreters* (New York: T. & T. Clark, 2005), pp. 278, 292.

the church named Paul. We may likewise affirm that there was at least one occasion when a group of Jesus' followers including 'the Twelve' had such an experience. Did other experiences reported by the Gospels occur as well, such as the appearances to the women, Thomas, the Emmaus disciples, and the multiple group appearances reported by the tradition in I Corinthians 15:3–7 and John? Where did these experiences occur? Historians may be going beyond what the data warrants in assigning a verdict with much confidence to these questions.[2]

It is important to notice that all that Licona is affirming is that there was *some occasion or other* on which the disciples had an experience as a group that convinced them that Jesus was risen. There is no one specific appearance that he is saying historians are warranted in affirming *as described in the Gospels in detail*, only the generic description of some group experience or other. But if historians would be "going beyond what the data warrants" in being confident about *specific* post-resurrection appearances, as opposed to a generic summary, why should Christians be rationally confident that Jesus appeared to his disciples at all, even as a conclusion? This approach encourages a troublingly fideistic dichotomy in which we believe some things "as Christians" and other things "as historians," where the latter is far more limited. How strong is the evidence, then, for our beliefs as Christians?

It would be a weak argument indeed for the resurrection—certainly nothing that anyone should risk his life for—to say that Luke must have *believed* that the resurrection was physical or he would not have made up certain *particular* details, and that Luke's belief that the resurrection was physical probably reflects the disciples' own *belief* that it was physical. If we want to defend the proposition that Jesus really was physically raised from the dead, and if we are asking people to believe that and to commit their lives to God on the basis of that claim, we want to know *why* the disciples believed that he arose, not merely *that* they believed it on some basis or other. If they did not believe it on the basis of the actual experiences we find in the resurrection accounts, and if we don't know what they claimed in any detail, there is a large epistemic problem. Was their belief rational? Could it have been a mistake? Was it based on enthusiasm or wishful thinking? Just how clear were their experiences? There are excellent answers to these questions, but they come from pointing out what the original witnesses claimed *in detail*, and we know that only from the resurrection accounts. If the resurrection narratives do not at least tell us what the disciples claimed they saw and heard, as opposed to

---

[2] Michael Licona, *The Resurrection of Jesus: A New Historiographical Approach* (Downer's Grover: IVP Academic, 2010), p. 371–372.

someone's embellished or invented version of those claims, it becomes much more difficult to give an evidentially robust defense of the resurrection.

Dale Allison, who regards himself as a Christian though he does not affirm the physical resurrection, has pressed hard on such matters. In a symposium between Allison (on the one side) and several evangelical scholars (on the other), Allison implies that the detailed resurrection stories are historically shaky and that this makes it difficult to present a strong evidential argument for the resurrection. "As for the accounts of Jesus being touched and eating food—again, can we really establish the origin of those stories, even if they did in fact happen? Many scholars ... regard the texts as legendary, and I cannot see how [Christians] can argue anything much from them without making a case to the contrary. But how can it be done?"[3]

It is therefore quite important to see whether theories of non-factual alteration in the resurrection narratives hold up to examination. It is interesting to see how widespread and even radical these suggestions are, even from evangelical scholars.

The explosion of more radical theories when we come to the resurrection stories is partly a function of the variation and independence among them, coupled with the general tendency in New Testament scholarship to over-read and to dislike additive harmonization. It is also partly a function of the fact that several unique resurrection accounts appear in the Gospel of John, and (as we have already seen) the Gospel of John comes in for a double dose of doubt from New Testament scholars. Though I plan to deal with these matters again in *The Eye of the Beholder*, I will be considering several of the doubts cast upon John's resurrection accounts in this chapter, especially since most of these arise from alleged discrepancies with one or more of the Synoptics.

We will see as we have seen throughout this book that these suggestions are not based upon an objective recognition of signs in the text that the author is using a specialized, accepted literary device. Instead, we will find merely the same errors of literary criticism that have created unnecessary tensions and cast unnecessary doubts upon the Gospels' reliability for a long time. These claims are not the result of new discoveries from Greco-Roman literature. Instead, this is just the old debate in which anti-harmonizers insist upon problems in the documents without sufficient justification. What is new is the attempt to claim that none of this matters because we can refer to the non-factual parts of the stories as "literary devices" rather than erroneous tales or legends. But that sort of reassuring word

---

[3] Dale C. Allison, Jr., "Response to Gary Habermas," *Philosophia Christi* 10:2 (2008), pp. 331–332.

magic does not make the documents, viewed through the literary device lens, any more objectively reliable than they would be if more dismissive terms were used.

Let us then ask once more whether these claims stand up to scrutiny. I will argue that they do not.

2. Did John or Matthew "relocate" Jesus' appearance to Mary Magdalene?

Each of the previous chapters in Part Four has ordered the examples roughly according to their placement in the life of Jesus. Analogously, I discuss the examples in this chapter beginning from the morning of Easter Day and moving forward on Easter. Since chronology is sometimes precisely what is in question, this organization will be necessarily approximate, but an obvious place to begin is the women's visit to the tomb on Easter morning.

The question of where Mary Magdalene first saw Jesus after his resurrection and the interweaving of the appearances to the women presents a famously difficult crux in harmonization. It is just as well to go directly to the cause of the alleged discrepancy, which we can see most efficiently by looking at Matt. 28 and comparing it to John 20.

Matt. 28.1 names only two women who came to the tomb, though it does not exclude the possibility that more women were present:

> Now after the Sabbath, as it began to dawn toward the first day of the week, Mary Magdalene and the other Mary came to look at the grave.

From that point on, the narrator refers to "the women" and "they," without any names. In vs. 5, the angel speaks to "the women," telling them that Jesus has risen and to go and report to the disciples. In vs. 8, "they" leave and go quickly to report. In vs. 9, Jesus meets "them," they worship him, and he speaks to them and sends them again on their way with a message for his brothers, which could include disciples beyond the eleven.

If you read this portion of Matthew in isolation, you would indeed get the *impression* that Mary Magdalene was with the other women all the time, and this is what creates the alleged contradiction with John. For if Mary Magdalene were with the other women the whole time in Matthew, then she saw Jesus first under quite different circumstances from those narrated in John 20. But it is important to note that Matthew never *says* that all the women stayed together and may not be attempting to give that impression. There is certainly no reason to think that Matthew is trying to imply that the women stayed together contrary to some other fact that he knows.

Matthew also does not say that there were only two women to begin with. If Matthew said that only two women came, and if we said (per John 20) that Mary Magdalene left the group (see below), there would be a conflict with Luke 24.10 and Mark 16.1. If there were only two women to begin with, there could not be a plural number of women who spoke to the angel and to Jesus after Mary Magdalene left. But Matthew simply lists two by name, not saying that these were the only women. Mark and Luke make it quite clear that there were more than two, making it possible for a plurality of women to see the angel and Jesus even if Mary Magdalene left the scene quickly.

If we turn to John 20.1–2, we find that John says that Mary Magdalene saw the stone taken away from the tomb and ran to tell the disciples (Peter and the beloved disciple, specifically) that "they" have taken away Jesus and that "we" do not know where they have laid him. The "we," of course, implies that there were multiple women present initially, though John does not name any others, and John does not say or imply that the others were physically with Mary when she spoke to Peter. In John, the two disciples then go to the tomb and find it empty. Mary Magdalene returns either with them or just behind them and is weeping by the tomb, still believing that Jesus' body has been taken away. Then comes one of the most lovely scenes in all of Scripture:

> But Mary was standing outside the tomb weeping; and so, as she wept, she stooped and looked into the tomb; and she saw two angels in white sitting, one at the head and one at the feet, where the body of Jesus had been lying. And they said to her, "Woman, why are you weeping?" She said to them, "Because they have taken away my Lord, and I do not know where they have laid Him." When she had said this, she turned around and saw Jesus standing there, and did not know that it was Jesus. Jesus said to her, "Woman, why are you weeping? Whom are you seeking?" Supposing Him to be the gardener, she said to Him, "Sir, if you have carried Him away, tell me where you have laid Him, and I will take Him away." Jesus said to her, "Mary!" She turned and said to Him in Hebrew, "Rabboni!" (which means, Teacher). (John 20.11–16)

It is quite plain here that Mary Magdalene does not know that Jesus is risen, indeed, has no notion of such a thing, until she realizes that the "gardener" is actually her beloved teacher. F. L. Godet comments,

> Mary remains and weeps, and as one does when vainly seeking for a precious object, she looks ever anew at the place where it seems to her that He should be.... She perceives the two angels at the moment of their appearance. This fact does not

contradict the earlier appearance of an angel to the women who had first visited the tomb. The angels are not immovable and visible after the manner of stone statues.—Mary answers the question of the celestial visitors as simply as if she had been conversing with human beings, so completely is she preoccupied with a single idea: to recover her Master. Who could have invented this feature of the story?[4]

The scene is noteworthy not only for its beauty but also for its vividness and realism. The alleged discrepancy with Matthew, again, is this: If we were to take Matthew in isolation and draw the conclusion that Mary Magdalene first saw Jesus with the other women while running away from the tomb, this would directly contradict the scene in John, where she first sees him apparently alone and at the tomb, believing at first that he is the gardener who knows where the body has been taken. The two scenes are quite different. Mary Magdalene in John 20 gains no joy (in contrast to the women in Matt. 28.8) from conversing with the angels, still believes that Jesus is dead at first, and implies to the disciples that Jesus' body has been stolen. She does not realize that Jesus is alive until later, *after* she has recognized Jesus. She is certainly not on her way to give the disciples a message at that time. Mary Magdalene cannot have first met Jesus in both of these ways.

A great variety of suggestions have been made to resolve this apparent discrepancy, some convoluted and unconvincing.[5] By a margin, the simplest harmonization is this: Mary Magdalene came at first with the other women, but she left the group quickly when she saw the stone already taken away from the tomb, jumping to the conclusion that Jesus' body had been removed. Perhaps there were a few exclamations among them about the possibility that the body had been stolen. She left the other women and ran back to tell Peter and the beloved disciple what had happened. Matthew, who may or may not have known that Mary Magdalene separated herself from the group, narrates without pause what happened to the rest of "the women"—their approaching the tomb, their encounter with the angel, their going on their way to tell the disciples, and their

---

[4] Frédéric Louis Godet, *Commentary on the Gospel of John, with an Historical and Critical Introduction*, translated by Timothy Dwight (New York, NY: Funk & Wagnalls, 1886), vol. II, p. 416.

[5] See, for example, Darrell Bock's survey of some suggestions, *Baker Exegetical Commentary: Luke 9:51–24:53* (Grand Rapids, MI: Baker Academic, 1996), pp. 1886–1888. The suggestion I prefer is nearest to Bock's suggestion #1, which he attributes to John Wenham among several others. However, Bock's summary is not an entirely correct description of Wenham's view. Bock summarizes view #1 as taking Matt. 28.9 and John 20:11ff to describe the same event, which is emphatically not Wenham's view. Trying to make Matt. 28.9–10 describe the same meeting with Jesus as John 20.11ff creates many unnecessary problems that Wenham's view avoids. See John Wenham, *Easter Enigma: Are the Resurrection Accounts in Conflict* (Eugene, OR: Wipf & Stock, 1992), pp. 82–83, 94–95.

meeting with Jesus on the road. John, in contrast, stays consistently with the perspective of Mary Magdalene and tells about how she returned alone to the tomb, saw the angels briefly, and met Jesus there after the two male disciples had come to the tomb and had gone away. This is extremely close to the solution given by John Wenham in his fascinating and solid harmony of the Easter accounts, with one exception: Wenham places a break, to my mind unnecessarily, between Matt. 28.8 and 28.9, suggesting that the women who met Jesus on the road to tell the disciples had, in between those two verses, met up with Mary Magdalene and heard of her experiences.[6] His suggestion is that they were then going to some other location where the remaining disciples were lodged. I see no reason for the supposition of a long break between these verses. The other women's meeting with the angel at the tomb would have taken only a few minutes as described in the Synoptics. Jesus' meeting with them on the way to tell the disciples (whichever disciples they had in mind) is also brief as Matthew describes it. The byways of Jerusalem are varied, as Wenham himself notes.[7] They could have simply gone away and not happened to run into Mary Magdalene; they could have met Jesus before they ever saw anyone else, as indeed Matthew seems to imply. This could have happened either before or after Jesus spoke briefly to Mary Magdalene. (That scene, too, is quite short, and Jesus after his resurrection apparently had the ability to move from place to place very quickly.) I'm inclined to think that Jesus met the other women before meeting Mary Magdalene. Eliminating Wenham's suggestion of a gap between Matt. 28.8 and 9 allows one to read Matthew quite smoothly as following the perspective of the rest of the women.[8]

This harmonization resolves many alleged difficulties in one fell swoop. For example, there is no reason to try to compare what the angels said to Mary Magdalene with what they said to the other women, or what Jesus said to her with what he said to the other women. These were different meetings altogether, as indeed the texts imply. It also permits us to read both Matthew and John in their internal sequences in a natural way, the only *caveat* being that Matthew writes as if he may be unaware that Mary Magdalene left before the women saw the angel and Jesus. We must not adopt a rigid mindset according to which people are stone statues (as Godet warns against doing with angels) and can never leave a group.

---

[6] Ibid., pp. 94–97.

[7] Ibid., pp. 82–83.

[8] The summary in the (probably non-canonical) long ending of Mark says that Jesus appeared first to Mary Magdalene on Easter, and Wenham is attempting to accommodate this claim (Ibid., pp. 46, 95), but even so, it is not necessary to place a lengthy pause in between Matt. 28.8 and 28.9.

In contrast, Michael Licona rejects harmonization and presents the reader with a pair of fictionalizing theories as the only options. His conclusion is that either Matthew or John has "relocated" Jesus' first appearance to Mary Magdalene, and he does not hesitate to draw a moral for his readers:

> At minimum, it appears that either Matthew or John has relocated the appearance to Mary Magdalene. This shows the extent to which at least one of the evangelists or the sources from which he drew felt free to craft the story.[9]

It is especially noteworthy that Licona himself states that this alleged change does not correspond, even in his own reckoning, to any specific literary device that he believes he has found in Plutarch. He says that "the location of Jesus' post-resurrection appearance to Mary Magdalene" is one of the differences that "cannot be plausibly understood in light of the specific compositional devices we are considering." [10] In other words, he is developing an idea that Matthew or John literarily "relocated" this scene, even when by his own admission he has no independent evidence for the accepted existence of such a device. He bases his conclusion solely on the fact that he is dissatisfied with any of the suggested harmonizations. Therefore, since he already believes that the Gospel authors made factual alterations, he concludes that either Matthew or John must have done so here. Yet despite the fact that this conjecture is based upon nothing but his own dissatisfaction with available harmonizations, he tells his readers to take note of it as evidence of just how far the authors felt free to go in altering the facts—"crafting the story."

And how far would that be? In the case of Matthew, it would mean that Matthew knew that Mary Magdalene was not present with the women who saw the angel and Jesus but that he deliberately wrote as if she was, contrary to fact. Matthew would be "locating" Mary Magdalene's first meeting with Jesus in not just a different physical place but in an entirely different type of scene. It is an extremely strange habit of literary device theorists to write as if authors are literally omniscient about every factual background element of the story. If they do not mention something that happened, the literary theorist takes it that they must have been deliberately suppressing it to change the facts for some complex reason. My own guess is that Matthew had simply not heard that part of the

---

[9] Michael Licona, *Why Are There Differences in the Gospels? What We Can Learn from Ancient Biography* (Oxford: Oxford University Press, 2017), p. 176.

[10] Ibid., p. 184.

account (the meeting between Mary Magdalene and Jesus as found in John 20), not that he is relocating anything.

In the case of John, the "crafting" would be even more extreme. For the appearance to Mary Magdalene is not simply physically located differently from the appearance in Matt. 28, as though John moved the same scene a few yards to the south. On the contrary, as already discussed, John writes an entirely separate scene, and a very important and moving one at that. What Mary knows, sees, and believes is entirely different from what the women experience who meet him on the road. Her interaction with Jesus is quite different from theirs. The bland term "relocates" sounds better than saying, "Perhaps John invented the entire scene between Jesus and Mary Magdalene in the garden of the tomb as a piece of pious fiction," but that is what such "relocating" would amount to. Terminology should not be allowed to obscure the radical nature of this suggestion. This would amount to major invention by John, which Licona treats as just one of two options, not even deciding between them. This is not the last time we will see a suggestion that John may have invented an entire scene in the resurrection narratives.

It would certainly be possible, even if one were dissatisfied with extant harmonization suggestions, to hold out for one that has not yet been suggested or to keep thinking about the matter. Once again, this is not a matter of some new, technical discovery concerning Greco-Roman literature that "solves" the alleged discrepancy about where Jesus first appeared to Mary Magdalene by attributing a specialized convention to John or Matthew as indicated in their texts. Rather, it is a matter of the long-standing difference between those who accept harmonizations (or hold out for further ones) in the resurrection accounts and those who think there are embellishments instead.

What are the grounds for Licona's rejection of harmonization in this case? In a footnote, Licona rejects both Wenham's suggestion and a similar theory from Craig Blomberg that Mary Magdalene may have gone ahead of the other women and run back to the disciples after seeing the stone moved:

> Yet these scenarios are not at all the impression readers receive when reading Matt. 28:1–10. Moreover, it does not square with Luke 24:1–12, since Peter ran to the tomb when the women (including Mary Magdalene; vv. 9–10) made the announcement to the disciples.[11]

---

[11] Licona, *Why Are There Differences*, pp. 255–256, n. 144. See Craig Blomberg, *The Historical Reliability of John's Gospel* (Downers Grove, IL: Intervarsity Press, 2001), p. 261.

Licona's definiteness in interpreting Matt. 28 is evident in the main text as well:

> The story differs in Matt. 28:8–10 in which upon hearing the message of the angel at the tomb, the group of women, which included Mary Magdalene, left quickly with fear and trembling and ran to tell Jesus's disciples. Jesus met them along the way...Thus, in Matthew, Mary Magdalene first encountered Jesus when she was running away from the tomb to deliver the angel's message to the disciples, whereas in John it was at the tomb.[12]

Licona bases his rejection explicitly on the fact that Mary Magdalene's absence isn't the impression we would receive from Matt. 28 *taken alone*. It would be difficult to exaggerate how misguided this is as a method of historical investigation. If we want to find out what really happened, we must be open to putting documents together rather than reading them in isolation. Very often we learn something new by listening to a different witness of an event. It needs to be possible to learn different things from different accounts without resisting new information on the grounds that the total picture isn't "the impression we would receive" from just one of the accounts in isolation. No one who suggests the harmonization given here is saying that we would receive, from Matthew alone, the impression that Mary Magdalene left the group.

Licona commits the error of over-reading when he refers to "the group of women, which included Mary Magdalene" in Matt. 28. If one did not go back to Matthew and read carefully, one might think from Licona's wording that Matthew literally names Mary Magdalene as present in the group later on in the passage. But the idea that the group "included Mary Magdalene" is an indirect inference. Lack of information on Matthew's part is not the same thing as error in what he wrote. Here, John supplements the information and corrects what might have been our erroneous first impression from Matthew (that Mary Magdalene did not leave the group). As discussed earlier, interpreting passages in isolation and refusing to harmonize is the methodology that Bart Ehrman attempts to foist upon New Testament readers, deriding anything more nuanced and flexible as "fundamentalist." Responsible historical investigation and responsible harmonization follow a better procedure, taking all evidence into account.

The other argument is that this harmonization is in conflict with Luke 24.1–12, in which (allegedly) Peter goes to see the tomb only after being informed of the resurrection by *all* of the women. On the harmonization suggested here, Peter and

---

[12] Ibid., pp. 175–176.

the beloved disciple went to the tomb after hearing from Mary Magdalene, but the other women had not yet spoken to them at that time. If Luke definitely said that Peter heard from all of the women together *before* he went to the tomb, this harmonization would face a problem. But this claim about Luke is another case of over-reading. Here is Luke, beginning with the last words of the angel at the tomb:

> "Remember how He spoke to you while He was still in Galilee, saying that the Son of Man must be delivered into the hands of sinful men, and be crucified, and the third day rise again." And they remembered His words, and returned from the tomb and reported all these things to the eleven and to all the rest. Now they were Mary Magdalene and Joanna and Mary the mother of James; also the other women with them were telling these things to the apostles. But these words appeared to them as nonsense, and they would not believe them. But Peter got up and ran to the tomb; stooping and looking in, he saw the linen wrappings only; and he went away to his home, marveling at what had happened. (Luke 24.6–12)[13]

Several indicators in this hurried passage from Luke show that he is not attempting or pretending to give a blow-by-blow description of what happened in chronological order. "Were telling" in verse 10 is imperfect in tense, indicating on-going action. Of course the women did not tell these things only once. They must have told their story several times just on that first day. The indefinite phrase "all the rest," beyond "the eleven," refers to an unspecified group who would likely not all have been gathered together in just one place at just one time, very early in the morning. Their telling "all the rest" must have taken place over the course of hours on that first day alone. And if, as John 20.2 may well indicate, Peter and the beloved disciple were separate from the rest of the eleven on Easter morning, the women would have told different groups of the eleven at different times. Similarly, the initial skepticism of the disciples—"these words appeared to them as nonsense"—was not something that happened at just one time but was an on-going phenomenon until various male disciples came to believe through their own experiences.

Verse 12, beginning, "But Peter got up" starts with the non-committal Greek *de;* we have learned already from Craig Blomberg that this is a chronologically indefinite term. In this context in particular its relation to what comes before has

---

[13] We will recall from Chapter XI, section 5, that the phrase "they remembered his words" and the reference to what Jesus said in Galilee participate in an undesigned coincidence concerning the women from Galilee, though Licona treats the angel's words in Luke as part of a redaction of the quite different message of the angel in Matthew and Mark.

a reasonable logical rather than chronological interpretation. All of the disciples, including Peter, were skeptical about what they heard from the women, but Peter at least was willing to go and investigate. This does not have to mean that Peter had heard from all of the women *at the same time before* leaving for the tomb. In multiple ways the terminology of this paragraph is generic, rushed, and chronologically loose. Luke is "chunking things in," describing events that happened at around the same time within the same eventful and vital day, but without being highly specific about when they happened. At some time or times the women named were reporting and the male disciples were dismissive. But at some point in all of this Peter got up (instead of just sitting around being skeptical) and ran to the tomb, saw it empty, and went to his home marveling. We must not over-read, especially not when we have evidence in the form of a plausible harmonization of John with the Synoptics that Peter went to the tomb after hearing Mary Magdalene's story but probably heard from the other women later that day.

The rejection of harmonization here is a result of rigid reading coupled with the hasty suggestion that the authors deliberately and knowingly altered the facts.

3. Were angels present at the tomb when the women first arrived?

The question in this section brings us back to Godet's important point that angels are not stone statues and to my corollary that neither are human beings. To change the metaphor, the literary New Testament critic sees life as a series of snapshots, frozen in time. Luke and Mark must be narrating the "same incident" at the same point in the crucifixion when they talk about a thief or thieves insulting Jesus. John and the Synoptics must be talking about the same saying when they report the "second-to-last logion" that Jesus says on the cross. Mary Magdalene must stay with the group she came with when they are at the tomb. A woman or group of women must report what they have seen at the tomb at one time only, before Peter goes to the tomb. But real life is not a series of snapshots but a moving picture. People go to different places. They repeat themselves. They hear and see different things at different times. They do not always remain in the same groupings. And angels, supposing them to exist at all, may be even more mobile and unpredictable.

The claim I will refute in this section is so puzzling that I cannot even set it up by stating an apparent discrepancy, because there isn't one. It therefore counts as an utterly unforced error. Licona claims that there is an apparent discrepancy between John and the Synoptics concerning whether or not angels were present when the women first visited the tomb:

The narratives differ pertaining to whether an angel was at the tomb during the initial visit of the women. Whereas all three Synoptics report the presence of one or more angels at the empty tomb when the women arrived, John's account suggests no angels were present until Mary's second visit.[14]

This statement is unequivocally false. John's account suggests nothing of the kind. It does not address in any way, shape, or form whether or not angels were present at the tomb when Mary Magdalene arrived at the tomb the first time. Here is all that John's account says about her first visit to the tomb:

> Now on the first day of the week Mary Magdalene came early to the tomb, while it was still dark, and saw the stone already taken away from the tomb. So she ran and came to Simon Peter...(John 20.1–2)

Where in this brief statement about Mary Magdalene's first glimpse of the tomb is there the slightest implication that "no angels were present"? There is no description of Mary's going and examining the tomb. Nothing about these two verses resembles the women's approach to the tomb described in the Synoptics. All that John says Mary Magdalene saw is that the stone was already taken away. Then she ran to Peter.

The most that can be said about angels in these two verses is that perhaps these verses indicate that Mary Magdalene didn't see (or didn't take note of) any angels before she ran off. Her first thought seems to have been to go to the disciples and tell them her surmise that Jesus' body has been taken away. Why should she have seen angels at all at this point, even if they were present inside or in the vicinity of the tomb?

If the complaint is that an angel or angels would have been *outside* of the tomb if angels were present at all and that in that case John should have mentioned them, that objection must be taken up with Mark and Luke. They both imply that the women saw angels only *after* they entered the tomb (Mark 16.4–5, Luke 23.2–4).[15] If anything, John's failure to mention any angels visible outside the tomb when Mary first arrives (if it means anything at all) is in agreement with the implication

---

[14] Licona, *Why Are There Differences*, p. 176.

[15] In fact, Licona notes precisely this point as a difference *among* the Synoptics, claiming that Matthew portrays the angel as talking to the women outside and is thus at odds with Mark and Luke. Ibid., p. 172. Wenham deals with that claim of discrepancy by explaining the probable use of the simple Greek past to indicate the pluperfect in the passage about the angel. The angel *had* rolled away the stone and had sat upon it, but he need not have been still outside when he spoke to the women. *Easter Enigma*, pp. 76–78.

of Mark and Luke—that angels appeared to the women only inside the tomb. If Mary didn't approach or enter the tomb when she came first (a very natural reading of John), we would not expect her to have the type of experience of angels that Mark and Luke describe as occurring *inside* the tomb. Even in John itself when she eventually does see the angels (20.12), she sees them only when she looks inside.

Perhaps part of Licona's unstated argument is the fact that Peter and the beloved disciple do not see angels when *they* come and look in at the grave clothes (John 20.5–8). But this would not be good reasoning. If anything it would prove too much—namely, that no angels were present on Mary Magdalene's second visit either, since the male disciples were there at about the same time and didn't see them. The impression given in John's narrative is the uncanny ability of the angels to show up unexpectedly, to appear in precisely the place where someone else failed to see them just a little while ago. The two male disciples look into the tomb and see no angels. Mary looks in just four verses later, probably only a short time later, and there sit the angels. It is not as though we should expect to see them slowly descending from heaven or walking toward the tomb from a distance. Nor do we, in any Gospel. They are just…there. In this portrayal of the angels, too, John is at one with Luke 24.4. The group of women enter the tomb, notice that the body is absent, and have only a moment to feel perplexed when suddenly two men in white are standing near them, actually in the tomb. The impression, just as in John, is that these angels have the ability to appear at will. The fact that the male disciples do not see them in John 20.5–8 certainly does not mean that they do not manage to arrive at the tomb until Mary Magdalene comes for a second visit.

The unforced error is compounded, though partly also explained, when Licona says more about the differences:

> Is John's account closer to what was originally taught, while the resurrection narratives in the Synoptics have conflated and greatly compressed various elements?
> …[I]f the resurrection narratives in the Synoptics have not been conflated and greatly compressed, why is the initial appearance of the angels to the women absent in John? If Matthew (and the Synoptics) conflated and compressed elements in the narrative, of necessity they would have needed to redact other elements in order to improve the flow of the narrative.[16]

This is still quite cryptic. It is difficult to see what Licona's argument is. Taken together with the earlier statement, the reasoning *appears* to be something like

---

[16] Licona, *Why Are There Differences*, p. 176.

this: If John's story is true, this must mean that *none* of the women had an encounter with angels at the first visit and that they *all* saw angels only later, with Mary Magdalene. But if that were true, then the Synoptic narratives would be misleadingly written (conflated and greatly compressed), for they give the strong impression that a group of women saw angels on their *first* visit. So John and the Synoptics cannot both be engaging in normal reportage.

This is the flip side of the confusion over whether Mary Magdalene could have left the group. In the last section we saw Licona rejecting the idea that Mary Magdalene could have left the group according to the version of the story in Matthew, because one would not "get that impression" from reading Matthew alone. The error here is more evident, since John says nothing that gives *any impression at all* about whether the other women stayed with Mary Magdalene. He does not mention where they were when she ran to Simon Peter. In John 20.2, Mary Magdalene does show that multiple women went to the tomb by saying, "We do not know where they have laid him," a nice point of consonance between the Gospels. John does not deny that other women went with her to the tomb. But this certainly doesn't mean that all of the women ran back immediately with her and were standing there with her at that very moment, speaking to Peter and John. Why should it mean any such thing? She could certainly use the word "we" when speaking about what she and the other women were thinking without having them physically with her. Licona's reasoning here (insofar as we can reconstruct it) treats the women as though they are chained together. Mary Magdalene can't leave the others, and they can't let her go back to Peter without them. They must all have all of their experiences at the same time in any one Gospel. This leads to the idea that no women saw any angels during the first morning visit, as portrayed in John. Why think a thing like that?

Without such a strange assumption about the behavior of human beings, Licona's question is easily answered. The initial appearance to the women is absent in John's report because he is describing what happened to *Mary Magdalene alone* during those minutes, and she wasn't with them when they saw the angels. She herself did not see angels on the first occasion, because she and the other women did not enter the tomb together. The other women stayed at the tomb, entered the tomb, and had the encounter with angels as described in the Synoptics, while she ran to Peter and the beloved disciple. Isn't it great that we have both the Synoptics and John, to tell us what happened to different women? This does not require any compression or conflation in the Synoptic accounts of the women's encounter with the angels. It does not even require any hypothesis of achronological narration. The Synoptic accounts just tell us what happened to a group of women who came to the tomb on Easter morning.

4. How many male disciples were present at Jesus' first appearance?

The question addressed in this section does turn on a minor appearance of discrepancy between two of the resurrection accounts, but, as elsewhere, this does not support fictionalizing literary devices in the resurrection stories. The apparent discrepancy is just this: John tells us that Thomas was not present on the first occasion when Jesus appeared to his male disciples and was reluctant to believe that Jesus had risen and appeared to the others (John 20.24–25). Thomas's skepticism is the set-up for the subsequent vivid scene in John 20 in which Jesus confronts him and invites him to touch his hands and side. This would mean that, of the original group of twelve chosen disciples, only ten could have been present on that first occasion, since Judas had betrayed Jesus and hanged himself. Luke, in telling of what appears to be the first appearance by Jesus to his group of male disciples, says that "the eleven and those who were with them" were "gathered together" on this occasion (Luke 24.33, 36). If one takes the term "eleven" in Luke as a counting term, and if this was the same occasion reported in John 20, then there is an apparent discrepancy about how many of this inner ring were present at this time.

Licona sees this discrepancy as irresolvable and makes a startling pair of conjectures as possible explanations:

> Moreover, with Judas now dead, there were eleven main disciples. Thus Luke 24:33 can speak of Jesus's first appearance to a group of his male disciples as including "the eleven and those with them." However, John 20:19–24 tells us Thomas was absent during that event. Thus, only ten of the main disciples would have been present. Accordingly, either Luke conflated the first and second appearances to the male disciples, or John crafted the second appearance in order to rebuke those who, like Thomas, heard about Jesus's resurrection and failed to believe.[17]

Licona repeats this dichotomy in his summary:

> Either Luke conflated two appearances into one or John has crafted an appearance.[18]

This is quite striking. The two "finalist" theories, listed here as our *only* two live options for explaining this minor apparent discrepancy, are either that Luke

[17] Ibid., p. 177.
[18] Ibid., p. 182.

deliberately mashed two appearances of Jesus together to make them look like one, though he knew that this was not the case, or else that John *entirely fabricated* the doubting Thomas sequence. Notice that this idea that John "crafted" an appearance would mean that John first made a blatantly false statement that Thomas was not present on the first occasion (though he really was) and then fabricated out of whole cloth the subsequent appearance (John 20.26–29) in which Jesus confronts Thomas. This is an extremely important piece of testimony, from the disciples, in favor of Jesus' resurrection, since it shows Jesus appearing to someone initially skeptical and offering empirical evidence of his identity. It also includes an important Christological statement by Thomas (vs. 28). John immediately follows his account of the appearance to Thomas with these evidentially emphatic verses:

> Therefore many other signs Jesus also performed in the presence of the disciples, which are not written in this book; but these have been written so that you may believe that Jesus is the Christ, the Son of God; and that believing you may have life in His name. (John 20.29–30)

The casualness with which Licona suggests the complete fabrication of this crucial sequence is notable. He elevates that theory above more than one simpler alternative (discussed below) that would not involve John's making up an evidentially important series of events. When he does narrowly prefer his other fictionalization theory, it is *not* on the grounds that John, deeply concerned with reporting the truth about Jesus' resurrection, would have been antecedently very unlikely to engage in so radical an invention. Such considerations feature nowhere at all in his analysis.

As mentioned repeatedly throughout this book, historians who raise theories and treat them as extremely live options, as one of only a small number of finalist explanations for some conundrum, are signaling something about the probability they give to those theories. The fact that a scholar narrowly rejects a given theory in the end does not mean that it is illegitimate to take notice of the unwarranted high probability he gives to it. Licona's treatment of entire scene fabrication by John here indicates a low estimate of John's factual reliability. It reminds us of Licona's statement that "John often chose to sacrifice accuracy on the ground level of precise reporting, preferring to provide his readers with an accurate, higher-level view of the person of Jesus and his mission"[19] and of Richard Burridge's claim,

---

[19] Ibid., p. 115.

explicitly asserting that John often fabricates information about Jesus, that "the negative connotation of 'fabrication' is modern."[20] Licona does decide in the end to prefer the theory that Luke deliberately made it look like two meetings were one, though it is unclear that any rigorous argument has brought him to the conclusion that Luke, *rather* than John, has altered the facts.[21]

There is, in fact, no reason for such suggestions at all. Consider first an idea that Licona expressly rejects—that Luke was using the term "the eleven" for the group of the main disciples, without intending to indicate that precisely eleven disciples were present on that occasion. The expression "the eleven and" some indefinite other group appears to be an expression that Luke liked. Verse 9 says "the eleven and all the rest," and verse 33 says "the eleven and those who were with them." The difference in the two is just that verse 9 does not say that these were all together at one place and one time, whereas verse 33 says that the men who met Jesus on the way to Emmaus returned to Jerusalem and found this group "gathered together." Of course, in verse 9, there was no reason why, over the course of the day, the women could not eventually have told their stories to all of the eleven in a literal sense, including Thomas. Still, Luke's use of the term in verse 9 in a rather sweeping and imprecise passage is some reason to think that he is not exactly counting noses. Interestingly, when John says that Thomas was not with the disciples, he calls him "one of the twelve" (John 20.24), though "the twelve" no longer strictly speaking existed at the time to which he refers, with Judas dead. Similarly, Paul says in I Cor. 15.5 that Jesus appeared to "the twelve," which is probably a conventional expression by almost any estimation. While Matthias would eventually be inducted into the group of main apostles (Acts 1), he was not counted as one of "the twelve" at the time of Jesus' appearances. So it seems that references to the time of Jesus' resurrection appearances are coupled with group names for his disciples that do not have highly precise numerical value, and it is quite possible that Luke is using such a group name in this case.

---

[20] Richard Burridge, *Four Gospels, One Jesus: A Symbolic Reading* (London: Society for Promoting Christian Knowledge, 2005), pp. 169–170

[21] The only reason Licona gives for saying that it "seems more probable in this instance that Luke has conflated" is his skepticism about the idea that Luke used the term "the eleven" as a group term. But this is confused. The supposition that Luke used "the eleven" to indicate a literal number is what sets up the alleged discrepancy in the first place. In no way does that premise about Luke's use of "the eleven" *distinguish* between Licona's two proposed explanations. If John fabricated the doubting Thomas sequence and if Jesus really met all of the disciples together the first time, then eleven disciples were also present literally at the first appearance.

Licona rejects this suggestion solely on the grounds that "there is no indication that 'the eleven' was ever used in a similar sense."[22] What this must mean is that there is no other, *independent* indication that "the eleven" was ever used in a similar sense. But this is rather a weak argument. After all, the term, whether conventional or specific, would have been relevant only for a brief period of time—between the crucifixion and the selection of Matthias less than forty days later. This is a period of time for which we have relatively few records. The literal eleven were probably often together during this time. Why should we expect to find some independent record of such a usage? And what would such an indication look like *other than* what we have right here, where John is very precise and says that Thomas was not present, while Luke casually refers to the main disciples present as "the eleven"? It is surprising, again, that Licona places this entirely viable theory *lower* in probability than the theory that doubting Thomas is a figment of John's imagination. The latter is a finalist, one of two suggested in Licona's typical "either/or" dichotomy. The idea of "the eleven" as a conventional term for the disciples does not even make it that far.

A somewhat stronger argument against Luke's using "the eleven" in a non-counting sense is just that the period of time during which this term would have been relevant was so short that there would have been little opportunity for its common usage to develop in the Christian community. And Luke was (probably) not part of the Christian body during those specific forty days. So his usage of the term in such a collective sense would seem to be his own idea when writing some years later, which is somewhat improbable. Licona does not give this argument against the non-counting use of "the eleven."

Here I must bring up an option that Licona should certainly consider far more probable than John's inventing doubting Thomas—namely, that Luke just didn't know that Thomas was absent on that first occasion. I have often refrained from mentioning, as I've gone through these alleged discrepancies, that honest, minor error is always an option for consideration by historians and usually a much simpler theory than wholesale invention. Certainly it is simpler in the case of the Gospel authors, when we have plenty of independent evidence of their historical intention and when the trivial differences in question would be quite easy for an honest witness to misremember or for an honest historian not to get precisely correct. In most cases, the literary device theorists ought to consider good-faith error more probable than the more complex idea that the author deliberately wrote

---

[22] Licona, *Why Are There Differences*, p. 178.

falsely. The falsehood is there either way, even though they do not wish to admit that it is a falsehood when they call it a "device." Adding deliberateness to a false statement makes it no less false and merely contradicts much other evidence concerning the literal honesty of these authors.

In this case it would be a serious omission if I did not mention the obvious: Perhaps nobody told Luke about Thomas's absence from Jesus' first appearance or about the subsequent scene recorded in John. Luke was a very careful historian, but he was not told everything. Perhaps he honestly thought that all eleven main disciples were present when Jesus first appeared to them. If this theory makes Luke's reference to "the eleven" count as an error, that does not change the fact that such an error is a far simpler explanation of his using "the eleven" than his *knowing* that Thomas was absent on this first occasion and writing in a deliberately misleading way to make it look like he was present. And it is orders of magnitude simpler than the idea that John made up the entire doubting Thomas sequence.

Saying that Luke is (deliberately) "conflating" two meetings does not explain what we have in any useful way, since Luke does not tell anything else that sounds much like John's description of the second meeting. There is, for example, no confrontation with a specific skeptic nor any invitation to anyone to thrust a hand into Jesus' side. Luke 24 records an invitation to touch Jesus and verify that he is not a spirit, but this is similar to Jesus' showing the disciples his wounds in the *first* meeting in John (Luke 24.39, John 20.20). Conversely, John does not happen to mention in either meeting that Jesus ate at this time. So what does it even mean to say that Luke has conflated two meetings *other than* to say in a less explicit way that he wrote deliberately misleadingly about how many people were present, knowing that Thomas was absent?[23]

Nor does Licona suggest any motive for Luke to falsify the number of disciples present. Given Luke's haste in this last chapter, which I will discuss in a later section, it is certainly plausible that he would not have had space to write about the doubting Thomas sequence had he known about it. But merely leaving it out would not have required deliberately writing falsely about how many people were present. If Luke did think of "the eleven" as a specific counting number, and if he knew that Thomas was not present on the occasion he describes, he could easily have just said "the disciples" instead of "the eleven." And then he could have left out the doubting Thomas sequence. Why should Luke deliberately alter the

---

[23] Remember that, according to Licona's definition, conflation is the deliberate melding of more than one event to make them look like one event. Ibid., p. 20.

number? Once again, the literary device theorist works tacitly on the false premise that falsification is the only way for an author to write briefly. It would make far more sense to hypothesize that Luke didn't know that one detail. Yet the simple explanation that Luke did not know that Thomas was absent the first time Jesus met his disciples after his resurrection does not even make it onto Licona's radar. Instead, he presents his readers with the false dichotomy that either Luke or John changed the facts. This is not carefully considering all reasonable hypotheses.

5. Does Luke put all of the appearances of Jesus on Easter Sunday?

It is often said that Luke compresses the narrative of events in Luke 24 after Jesus' resurrection, and in one sense this claim seems rather obviously true. There is certainly something hurried about Luke's presentation in certain parts of Chapter 24. As I will argue below, the pace picks up notably from verse 44 onward, while the narration of the appearance at Emmaus is by contrast somewhat leisurely. Apparently Luke wanted to give that unique story in some detail. Earlier in the chapter (verses 8–12), I have argued that Luke is "chunking things in," not specifying precisely at what time of the day various women told their story to various disciples.

This is a place where it is absolutely vital to keep clear the distinction between achronological and dyschronological narration. There is nothing very controversial about saying that Luke compresses achronologically in this chapter, not intending to give the impression that all events happened within a shorter period of time than they actually took but just narrating hastily and leaving out details. That is not a fictionalizing literary device, and it seems to be borne out by the details of some parts of the chapter. To say that Luke deliberately *puts* all of the events onto Easter Sunday when he knew that they did not all take place on Easter Sunday is an entirely different matter. It involves Luke's deliberately writing in a manner contrary to fact, and concluding that Luke has done this requires the satisfaction of a much higher burden of proof.

Unfortunately, more than one evangelical scholar is convinced that this is exactly what Luke does do. This theory also sometimes begets another fictionalization theory concerning Luke, which I will discuss in the next section. That second theory is that Luke geographically moves Jesus' first appearance to his disciples to Jerusalem, though it really took place in Galilee. It is only fair to add that the second theory does not follow deductively from the first. One might think that Luke put all of the appearances onto Easter Sunday and believe that he simply left out any appearances in Galilee and a later return to Jerusalem. The further theory that he moved the first appearance geographically requires the further (faulty) premise that Matt. 28.16ff is telling the same event as Luke 24.36–43.

It is important to emphasize that there is no plausible motive for Luke to compress dyschronologically in Luke 24. I noted in the last section that there is no recognizable motive for Luke deliberately to give an incorrect number of male disciples present at Jesus' first group appearance. Similarly here: Why would Luke deliberately try to make it look like events after Easter took less time than they really took? Any motive to write briefly could be satisfied by achronological narration with no intention to make things look contrary to reality. (This is, in fact, what we have in Luke 24.) And since, as the theorists agree, Luke made it quite clear in Acts 1 that Jesus was with his disciples for forty days before his ascension, why would he *want* to make the timeframe look different in Luke 24, especially since he was sending both works to Theophilus? What point would that make? What purpose would it serve? We have again an unstated false premise that it is impossible to compress achronologically, to shorten, without deliberately trying to make things take less time in the world of one's story than they did in reality.

So we have to examine the argument. What is the basis for the claim that Luke dyschronologically compressed events in Luke 24? To begin with, let's look at the passage in question. It will be useful for the analysis to quote a rather large section, though with some ellipses:

> And behold, two of them were going that very day to a village named Emmaus, which was about seven miles from Jerusalem. And they were talking with each other about all these things which had taken place. While they were talking and discussing, Jesus Himself approached and began traveling with them. But their eyes were prevented from recognizing Him. And He said to them, "What are these words that you are exchanging with one another as you are walking?" And they stood still, looking sad. One of them, named Cleopas, answered and said to Him, "Are You the only one visiting Jerusalem and unaware of the things which have happened here in these days?" And He said to them, "What things?" And they said to Him, "The things about Jesus the Nazarene, who was a prophet mighty in deed and word in the sight of God and all the people, and how the chief priests and our rulers delivered Him to the sentence of death, and crucified Him ....Indeed, besides all this, it is the third day since these things happened. But also some women among us amazed us. When they were at the tomb early in the morning, and did not find His body, they came, saying that they had also seen a vision of angels who said that He was alive. Some of those who were

with us went to the tomb and found it just exactly as the women also had said; but Him they did not see." And He said to them, "O foolish men and slow of heart to believe in all that the prophets have spoken! Was it not necessary for the Christ to suffer these things and to enter into His glory?" Then beginning with Moses and with all the prophets, He explained to them the things concerning Himself in all the Scriptures.

And they approached the village where they were going, and He acted as though He were going farther. But they urged Him, saying, "Stay with us, for it is getting toward evening, and the day is now nearly over." So He went in to stay with them. When He had reclined at the table with them, He took the bread and blessed it, and breaking it, He began giving it to them. Then their eyes were opened and they recognized Him; and He vanished from their sight. They said to one another, "Were not our hearts burning within us while He was speaking to us on the road, while He was explaining the Scriptures to us?" And they got up that very hour and returned to Jerusalem, and found gathered together the eleven and those who were with them, saying, "The Lord has really risen and has appeared to Simon." They began to relate their experiences on the road and how He was recognized by them in the breaking of the bread.

While they were telling these things, He Himself stood in their midst and said to them, "Peace be to you." But they were startled and frightened and thought that they were seeing a spirit. And He said to them, "Why are you troubled, and why do doubts arise in your hearts? See My hands and My feet, that it is I Myself; touch Me and see, for a spirit does not have flesh and bones as you see that I have." And when He had said this, He showed them His hands and His feet. While they still could not believe it because of their joy and amazement, He said to them, "Have you anything here to eat?" They gave Him a piece of a broiled fish; and He took it and ate it before them.

Now He said to them, "These are My words which I spoke to you while I was still with you, that all things which are written about Me in the Law of Moses and the Prophets and the Psalms must be fulfilled." Then He opened their minds to understand the Scriptures, and He said to them, "Thus it is written, that the Christ would suffer and rise again from the dead the third day, and that repentance for forgiveness of sins would be proclaimed in His name to all the nations, beginning from Jerusalem. You are witnesses of these things. And behold, I am sending forth the promise of My Father upon you; but you are to stay in the city until you are clothed with power from on high."

And He led them out as far as Bethany, and He lifted up His hands and blessed them. While He was blessing them, He parted from them and was carried up into heaven. And they, after worshiping Him, returned to Jerusalem with great joy, and were continually in the temple praising God. (Luke 24.13–52)

Here are some of Licona's statements that Luke's narration is dyschronological:

> In Luke 24:1–53, Jesus's resurrection, all of his appearances, and his ascension to heaven are narrated as though having occurred on that Sunday. That Luke compressed the events in this manner is clear, since in the sequel to his Gospel, Luke says Jesus appeared to his disciples over a period of forty days before ascending to heaven (Acts 1:3–9).[24]

> As we observed above, Luke compresses all of the appearances and the ascension to have occurred on the same day as Jesus's resurrection. So there is no time to have the disciples go to Galilee.[25]

> Luke employs telescoping. In his Gospel, all of the appearances and the ascension occur on Easter.[26]

The statements of dyschronological narration here are particularly explicit: "All of the appearances and the ascension occur on Easter." "Luke compresses all of the appearances and the ascension to occur on the same day as the resurrection. So there is no time for the disciples to go to Galilee." And so forth. The only argument to be found in these statements, which supposedly is so strong that it makes this conclusion clear, is that in Acts 1 Luke does know that Jesus appeared to the disciples over a period of forty days.

It is rather difficult to see how this premise yields this conclusion. Yes, in Acts 1 Luke knows that Jesus was with his disciples for forty days. How does this make it "clear" that he narrated dyschronologically in Luke 24? There must be some unstated premises here. One unstated premise is apparently that the narration in Luke 24 is so unmistakably "putting" all of the events "on Easter" that the only options are that Luke believed that all of this really happened on Easter when he wrote Luke 24 or that he deliberately made it look that way even though he knew to the contrary. The other unstated premise is apparently that whatever Luke knew when he wrote Acts 1 must be what he knew when he wrote Luke 24; therefore, when he wrote Luke 24, he must have deliberately made events look different from what he knew to be true.

Without these unstated premises, the argument that Licona says is "clear" from the information in Acts 1 will not go through. But both of them are quite false. There is certainly no reason to believe that Acts was written at the same

---

[24] Ibid., p. 177.

[25] Ibid., p. 180.

[26] Licona, *The Resurrection of Jesus*, p. 596, n. 449.

time as Luke. Indeed, it is quite obvious from Luke's own mention to Theophilus of "the former treatise" (Acts 1.1) that they were sent to Theophilus at different times. But if there was a gap of time between Luke's writing Luke 24 and Acts 1, he could have received more information within that time period about how long Jesus was on earth after his resurrection. Indeed, it is quite plausible that he did. For even given that Luke is writing in a rushed, achronological way in Luke 24, and even given that the period in question must be more than one day (as I shall argue), he is certainly *indefinite* in that chapter about how long Jesus was on earth. It is entirely plausible that he left the time period indefinite simply because he didn't know how long it was. Acts 1, then, may well reflect a more detailed knowledge of the facts and perhaps also a fresh scroll with more space to give additional information concerning Jesus' last scenes with his disciples and his ascension. It is astonishing that Licona should so casually assume that Luke's knowledge when writing Acts was identical to his knowledge when writing Luke, since it is virtually beyond question that they were not sent out simultaneously to Theophilus.

What about the premise that Luke 24 appears to place all of the events on a single day? To kick off a discussion of that proposition, here is an argument from William Lane Craig that Luke is narrating dyschronologically. As far as I am aware, this dyschronological change and the alleged moving of the Temple cleansing are the only specific fictionalizing literary devices that Craig has endorsed in the Gospels, though he is quite convinced of these. After expressly stating that John narrates dyschronologically concerning the Temple cleansing, Craig says this about Luke 24:

> Similarly, if you look at Luke's resurrection narrative in Luke 24, it's filled with repeated chronological markers. In 24:1 he says, "But on the first day of the week at early dawn they came to the tomb." Then in verse 13, "Now on that same day two of them were going to a village called Emmaus." And then in the Emmaus story they say to Jesus, "Stay with us because it is almost evening and the day is now nearly over." Then they run back to Jerusalem and find the disciples gathered together saying "The Lord is risen indeed." Then in verse 36, "while they were talking about this Jesus stood among them and said . . ." So the whole thing is narrated in such a way as to look chronologically as though this is all happening on Easter . . .[27]

---

[27] William Lane Craig and Kevin Harris, "An Objection to the Minimal Facts Argument," *Reasonable Faith*, May 6, 2018, https://www.reasonablefaith.org/media/reasonable-faith-podcast/an-objection-to-the-minimal-facts-argument/.

Craig's argument is that Luke 24 cannot contain achronological narration because the chapter is filled with chronological markers. This argument is flawed in two ways. First, Craig gives chronological markers *only before* the point where Luke really starts flying through his material. No one is questioning that all of the events listed by Craig here took place on Easter Sunday evening—Jesus' meeting with the two on the road to Emmaus, their returning to Jerusalem, and Jesus' appearance to the group while they are relating their experience. It's at verse 44 that Luke becomes so hurried, through the end of the book.

Second, the very chronological points that Craig notes help to show that Luke is not really trying to put all of the events on Easter Sunday in his Gospel. For if we note these chronological markers, and if we follow through to the ascension at the end of the chapter, we can see *just from reading Luke alone* that there would not have been time for the ascension reasonably to occur on that same evening. Luke is taking no trouble to try to make it look like everything fits. So the points Craig is raising support the opposite conclusion from the one for which he is arguing.

While the events through verse 43 appear to be placed on Easter Sunday, things change at verse 44, when Jesus begins teaching. Various translations introduce Jesus' teaching in vs. 44 with different English words. The ESV begins, "Then he said to them..." but in fact there is no such temporal indicator. The NASB begins, "Now he said to them..." which is also unfortunate. The King James is more indefinite, with "And he said unto them..." The NIV is perhaps best, with no connective at all, merely, "He said to them..." The Greek connective, in fact, is *de*, which as we have already seen is indefinite as to time. It is sometimes translated "and," sometimes "moreover," as well as in other ways.

Similarly, at verse 50, translated "And he led them out..." in the NASB, the particle is *de*. There are no temporal indicators in these verses, just a summary of Jesus' teaching and a narration of the ascension. Far more than indicating that everything occurred on Easter, the passage from verse 44 to the end of the book reads like an abbreviated summary of events beginning on Easter and for some unspecified time thereafter. As Wenham says,

> These 'thens' [in the RSV at verses 44 and 50] give a much sharper suggestion of chronological continuity than the Greek justifies. The paragraphs are linked by a weak connective non-temporal particle (*de*) which would be better left untranslated.[28]

Looking back in the passage, consider how Luke's earlier time markers show

---

[28] Wenham, *Easter Enigma*, p. 107.

that he is not attempting to compress dyschronologically. In the scene on the road to Emmaus, the two men urge Jesus to stay with them because it is getting on toward evening and the day is far spent (Luke 24.28). They recognize him in the breaking of bread at the evening meal and then, after he disappears, they hurry back to Jerusalem, which is a six or seven mile walk, as Luke notes (vs. 13). This would have taken an hour or two. In Jerusalem they tell their story, and while they are there, Jesus appears in their midst, converses with them, and eats to illustrate that he is not a ghost (vss. 40–43).

After this Jesus opened the disciples' minds to understand the Scriptures about the prophecies concerning himself. Presumably what Luke records here was no-where near the whole of what Jesus had to say on that fascinating topic, making it (if this were on the same day) one of the first very long Sunday evening sermons.[29] And only *after that* did they go to Bethany. Sundown around the first of April in that part of the world occurs about 7 p.m. If this were the same day, it would have been quite dark for a walk back out to Bethany. And how would the disciples have seen Jesus received up to heaven? In other words, the narrative would be unnecessarily implausible if we insisted on taking everything, including the ascension, to occur on one day.

Luke makes no attempt to smooth matters out here to fit everything into one evening. He could have written differently if he really wanted (for some inscrutable reason) to make it all non-factually appear to have happened in one day. This would have been quite easy if, as Licona appears to think, Luke had no scruples about changing facts in his story. In that case, he could have made the meal in Emmaus a noon meal rather than an evening meal. He could easily have left the name and distance of the town unstated, merely saying that they were on a road near Jerusalem and came to a certain village. He could have left out any reference to Jesus' teaching later on. Why make the occurrence of all these events on one day so difficult for himself? But he didn't do any of that. The combination of indefinite, non-temporal connectives in vss. 44 and 50, brief, non-detailed narration, and clues earlier in the same chapter that there was no time for the ascension on that evening provide strong evidence of achronological rather than dyschronological narration.

A careful, fully attentive reader of Chapter 24, rather than thinking that all the events occur on Easter Sunday, might wonder what was the cause of Luke's sudden rush. We may never know whether he was running out of scroll or trying to catch a ship to send his completed work, the Gospel of Luke, to Theophilus. But haste does

---

[29] I owe this point about the long Sunday evening sermon to Timothy McGrew.

not necessitate changing chronology. Indefiniteness and brevity at certain points, such as we *do* have in Luke 24, are quite sufficient for the purpose of abbreviating. We miss something quite important if we conclude that Luke was narrating dyschronologically in Luke 24. That something is the character and purpose of Luke himself. His careful discussion in Acts 1 of Jesus' appearance over forty days, showing himself alive by "many convincing proofs" (Acts 1.3), bespeaks a very different author from one who was trying at the end of the previous book, sent to the *same recipient*, to write as if Jesus did *not* appear on earth over forty days. On the contrary, Luke is being meticulously clear about the time scheme. As already suggested, he may have received more definite information in the meanwhile, since Luke 24 is indefinite. Moreover, he may have realized that the need to narrate achronologically at the end of Luke (whatever the cause) not only left out information but may have inadvertently given the impression that Jesus was with his disciples for only a short time—perhaps a few days. Scrupulously, he clears up any potential misunderstanding, and he does so for transparently evidential reasons. He wants Theophilus to know how much contact the disciples had with the risen Jesus.

Like Luke, a man of the ancient world, we in the 21st century should recall the importance of accuracy in empirical matters in the resurrection narratives.

6. Did Luke move an appearance from Galilee to Jerusalem?

I have not often quoted Bart Ehrman in this book, because my focus is on the way that non-factual interpretations of the Gospels have come into the evangelical scholarly world, and Ehrman is not an evangelical scholar. But the alleged discrepancy I will discuss in this section is a special favorite of Ehrman's, and it is in a debate with Ehrman that evangelical scholar Michael Licona has put forward the theory that Luke geographically moved Jesus' first appearance from Galilee to Jerusalem. Here is Ehrman on the subject:

> One point in particular seems to be irreconcilable. In Mark's account the women are instructed to tell the disciples to go meet Jesus in Galilee...In Matthew's version the disciples are told to go to Galilee to meet Jesus, and they immediately do so. He appears to them there and gives them their final instruction. But in Luke the disciples are not told to go to Galilee. They are told that Jesus had foretold his resurrection while *he* was in Galilee...And they never leave Jerusalem—in the southern part of...Israel, a different region from Galilee, in the north....In Luke's next volume, Acts, we're told that the disciples are in fact explicitly told by Jesus after his resurrection not to leave Jerusalem (Acts 1:4), but to stay there until they receive the Holy Spirit....The disciples do stay in Jerusalem until the

Holy Spirit comes (Acts 2). And so the discrepancy: If Matthew is right, that the disciples immediately go to Galilee and see Jesus ascend from there, how can Luke be right that the disciples stay in Jerusalem the whole time, see Jesus ascend from there, and stay on until the day of Pentecost?[30]

Ehrman's exegesis is wrong or misleading at all the crucial points for producing a discrepancy. Particularly egregious is his attempt to use Acts 1 to support the conclusion that the disciples have never gone to Galilee at all, despite the fact that Acts 1.3 expressly states that Jesus had been with them already for forty days before the ascension. Acts 1.4, which Ehrman cites, says that Jesus commanded them not to leave Jerusalem after "gathering them together" in Jerusalem. Whatever accidental confusion might have been generated by the brevity of the narration at the end of Luke 24, discussed in the previous section, Acts 1 should clear it up. Forty days would be more than enough time for the disciples and Jesus to meet in Galilee and return to Jerusalem. Another candidate for the most misleading statement in this paragraph is the falsehood that in Matthew the disciples see Jesus ascend from Galilee. Matthew does not tell about the ascension at all.

Notice, too, Ehrman's reference to the angel's words about Galilee in different Gospels as if these are somehow in conflict. As Ehrman portrays it, the angel could not have referred to Galilee *both* as the place to which Jesus' followers are to go and also as the place where Jesus predicted his death. It must be one or the other. I dealt with this strange redactive theory, also advocated by Licona, in Chapter XI, section 5. There we saw that the reference to Jesus' prediction in Galilee is *not* part of Luke's redactive fictional artistry but rather part of a coherent picture in all of the Synoptics of this group of women who really did know Jesus in Galilee.

Ehrman's exegesis here also features a blatant argument from silence—a favorite argumentative pattern of his. When he says that in Luke the disciples are *not told* to go to Galilee, he implies that Luke contradicts Matthew and Mark simply because Luke does not *record* an order to go to Galilee.

The entire Lukan side of Ehrman's complaint has already been dealt with in the previous section. Luke neither attempts nor pretends to give an entire account of everything that Jesus did and said to his disciples after his resurrection. He adds some unique information—e.g., the names of some of the women who went to the tomb and the story of the road to Emmaus—and leaves out some

---

[30] Bart D. Ehrman, *Jesus, Interrupted: Revealing the Hidden Contradictions in the Bible* (and Why We Don't Know About Them) (New York, NY: Harper One, 2009), p. 49.

information given in other Gospels, such as the trip to Galilee and the Great Commission. In the last verses of the Gospel his narrative becomes abbreviated and rushed. But nothing in Luke contradicts a trip to Galilee, as Ehrman implies. In fact, as I will discuss below, both the initial appearance of Jesus to his disciples in Jerusalem and the fact that he and his disciples were later in Galilee together are confirmed in independent narratives in John 20–21, so that John ties together Luke and the other Synoptics.

What about the claim that in Matthew the disciples go to Galilee "immediately"? The most that can be said for this is that a) Matthew (like Mark) reports that the women were told to tell the disciples to go to Galilee, b) Matthew doesn't narrate any other activities by the disciples before going to Galilee and c) we don't know why Matthew left out the meetings in Jerusalem. But he certainly does not say that the disciples went immediately to Galilee. That is Ehrman's typical over-reading. Here is Matthew, beginning with the words of the angel to the women:

"Do not be afraid; for I know that you are looking for Jesus who has been crucified. He is not here, for He has risen, just as He said. Come, see the place where He was lying. Go quickly and tell His disciples that He has risen from the dead; and behold, He is going ahead of you into Galilee, there you will see Him; behold, I have told you."

And they left the tomb quickly with fear and great joy and ran to report it to His disciples. And behold, Jesus met them and greeted them. And they came up and took hold of His feet and worshiped Him. Then Jesus said to them, "Do not be afraid; go and take word to My brethren to leave for Galilee, and there they will see Me."

Now while they were on their way, some of the guard came into the city and reported to the chief priests all that had happened. And when they had assembled with the elders and consulted together, they gave a large sum of money to the soldiers, and said, "You are to say, 'His disciples came by night and stole Him away while we were asleep.' And if this should come to the governor's ears, we will win him over and keep you out of trouble." And they took the money and did as they had been instructed; and this story was widely spread among the Jews, and is to this day.

But the eleven disciples proceeded to Galilee, to the mountain which Jesus had designated. When they saw Him, they worshiped Him; but some were doubtful. And Jesus came up and spoke to them, saying, "All authority has been given to Me in heaven and on earth ...." (Matt. 28.9–18)

458 | *The Mirror or the Mask*

The translation of Jesus' message that they should tell his brethren "to leave for Galilee" in the NASB is unfortunate. Better is the ESV's simpler "to go to Galilee." The "brethren" in question need not have been only the eleven main disciples. Jesus' message here to the women (and the angel's similar message to "his disciples and Peter" in Mark 16.7) could have been intended for a much larger group in addition to the eleven. The women could serve as messengers to assist in setting up a meeting in Galilee, which the eleven would be able to help with once they were fully convinced that Jesus had risen. While the women would probably not be heeded on their own, when the eleven also said that they had seen Jesus, the women, with these messages in mind, would help to spread the word.[31]

As Wenham points out, an outdoor location in the hills of Galilee would a better place than Jerusalem for a large meeting of Jesus' followers. The Apostle Paul says (I Cor. 15.6) that Jesus was seen by more than five hundred brethren at once, a number stated nowhere in the Gospels. If this is true, it would have to refer to an appearance in a location where such a meeting would be possible. There would have to be enough space for that many people to gather at once. And they would want to gather without interruption from the authorities and without curiosity from others, since it was apparently Jesus' intention during this period to appear only to a select group of people. As Wenham emphasizes, this would have to be a deliberately convened meeting.[32] Therefore, it is not surprising that Jesus and the angels began early to convey this message via the women. In fact, Galilee was plausibly the next location where these particular women would see Jesus again, along with the larger group of brethren.

Licona does not see it this way and seems to agree with Ehrman's interpretation that the women are told in Matthew to tell the disciples that they are to leave for Galilee instantly:

> In Matthew, the angel instructed the women to "go quickly" to the disciples with the message that Jesus had been raised and was going before them to Galilee, where they would see him (28:7). There was a sense of urgency since Jesus had already left for Galilee.[33]

This cannot be the correct interpretation of the angel's words, since Jesus himself meets the women just a verse or two later right in Matthew. Obviously he has

---

[31] This point answers the claim that Jesus and the angel would not have sent such a message to Peter and the other disciples if Jesus was going to see them again later that day.

[32] Wenham, *Easter Enigma*, pp. 112–115.

[33] Licona, *Why Are There Differences*, p. 178.

not "already left for Galilee" in Matthew, nor does the angel say that he has. The important and exciting nature of the message that Jesus is risen would be quite sufficient grounds for telling the women to go quickly and report it. Perhaps Licona's idea is that the women are to tell the disciples that Jesus "had already left" by the time that the women and the disciples would be speaking. But the passage does not say this, either, and such a hyper-precise understanding of the message is an over-interpretation. It is important not to read the angel's message as telling the *disciples* to "go quickly" to Galilee. That is not at all what the angel says.

Licona also emphasizes that the word for "there" in the angel's message comes first in the sentence, "There you will see him," which is a position of emphasis.[34] For many of the larger group of brethren it was true that they would first see Jesus in Galilee, so in their case, such an emphasis would make especially good sense. On the other hand, it is straining and over-reading the placement of this word to take it to say, "There they will see me first, only there, and *not a single male disciple will see me anywhere else before that time*."[35]

After Matthew says that the women saw Jesus and were going to tell the disciples, he breaks off to give the story of the bribing of the guard at the tomb. I have included it in the above quotation for the following reason: It separates the statement that the women went to the disciples from the further statement that the eleven went to Galilee. And, unsurprisingly, the word translated here as "but" in "But the eleven disciples proceeded to Galilee" is the non-temporal particle *de*, which we have met already in Luke. Matthew's narrative at this point is *consistent* with an immediate departure by the eleven, but it does not at all *require* it. In fact, the story of the bribing of the guards covers a span of time all by itself. Matthew does not say precisely when the Jewish leaders gathered together and bribed the guard, and the statement that the guards did as they were instructed obviously covers an unspecified longer period of time. They presumably went on keeping up the cover story (at least to their superiors) that the disciples stole the body. Matthew even uses the phrase "to this day" when describing how the story continues to be told. It is only after all of that that he jumps back to the disciples and says that they went to Galilee. This interweaving of the stories creates, at a minimum, some degree of temporal distancing and unclarity. Are we jumping back to report a departure the next *hour* after the women ran to the disciples, the next *day*, or a week later?

---

[34] Ibid.

[35] According to I Cor. 15, Peter saw Jesus before the group saw him, so if one were to interpret the angel's message in this extreme way, it would be in some tension with I Cor. 15.

Matthew doesn't say. As Wenham has pointed out, the usual custom of devout Jews would be to remain in Jerusalem for at least six more days, because of the Feast of Unleavened Bread. This point supports the report in John 20 that Jesus appeared to the disciples one week later, apparently before they had gone to Galilee.[36]

One or two more points about Matt. 28 are relevant. Although Matthew does not (as Luke does) include explicit notes of time that make it unlikely that the later events occurred immediately, he does have a few subtle clues. Matthew 28.16 says, "But the eleven disciples proceeded to Galilee, to the mountain which Jesus had designated." When had Jesus designated a particular mountain? It's possible that the message from either Jesus or the angel contained this information and that Matthew and Mark do not record it. It's also possible that Jesus had mentioned this location earlier, perhaps at the point described in Matthew 26.32. But the fact that the disciples repeatedly did not understand or accept Jesus' predictions of his own crucifixion and resurrection makes it somewhat more likely that Jesus would have given them specific directions to a mountain after he rose again. Hence, an interesting possibility is that Jesus designated this mountain when he met with members of the eleven after his resurrection. They were able to direct a gathering of the brethren using this additional information.[37] Directions to a particular place in the Galilean hills would have been easier for the disciples to take in during a series of meetings with Jesus than for the shocked women to take in when first processing the fact of the resurrection.

Matthew's reference to a specific, designated mountain dovetails nicely with the earlier points concerning the desirability of such a location for a meeting with a larger group. But this also implies some need of time to gather those who were to meet there.

Wenham adds a fascinating point based on the Greek of Matthew's account of the meeting in Galilee. Matthew 28.17 reads, "When they saw Him, they worshiped Him; but some were doubtful." Wenham states that this "they did A, but some did B" construction in Greek "normally signifies a change of subject, and the standard grammar translates ['but some' as] ... 'but others'." He scrupulously admits that the language does not "demand that those mentioned in the first part of the sentence and the 'others' mentioned in the second part should be regarded as completely mutually exclusive, but it is natural to take them as referring to different groups."[38]

---

[36] Wenham, *Easter Enigma*, pp. 98–99.

[37] Ibid., p. 113.

[38] Ibid., p. 114.

It is evidently no part of Matthew's plan to write either about the experiences of the men in Jerusalem or about the experiences of the wider company of believers in Galilee. But he chooses a form of words which neatly describes the faith of the eleven and hints at the presence of others with doubts.[39]

If the eleven had already met Jesus on other occasions in various groupings, they would probably not have been doubtful anymore at this point, but others with them, for whom this was the first meeting, might have needed more convincing that they were really meeting the risen Jesus. Hence, though Matthew does not say that anyone other than the eleven was present at this meeting, his language readily allows for that possibility.

A cultural point also applies to Matthew's narrative logic and could easily have occurred to anyone in his first audience: Is it likely that the male disciples would have left for Galilee based upon the word of the women alone? Luke 24.11 mentions the initial skepticism of the male disciples about the women's report. Are we to take this culturally plausible note in Luke to be a bit of cleverness on Luke's part (since they are staying in Jerusalem in Luke), while Matthew's eleven disciples are surprisingly progressive, accept the women's message even though none of them have seen Jesus yet, and immediately depart *en masse* on the long walk to Galilee? And this in the middle of a Jewish festival, while still traumatized by Jesus' arrest and crucifixion? The idea that Jesus had risen from the dead surely took some believing. John's story of Thomas's skepticism even against the testimony of the other male disciples is true to human nature. One might reasonably guess when reading Matthew alone that he has left out some further evidence obtained by the eleven before they went all the way to a specific mountain in Galilee in the hopes of seeing Jesus.[40]

For all these reasons, Matthew's narrative, though incomplete, readily leaves space for further appearances of Jesus in Jerusalem.

Licona, however, further emphasizes his claim of contradiction between Matthew and Luke by insisting that Matthew and Luke record the *same meeting* between Jesus and his disciples:

---

[39] Ibid.

[40] There is a relevant apologetic point here as well. If the disciples first saw Jesus when they were expecting to see him, this might slightly raise the possibility of some sort of hallucination induced by enthusiasm. (Any detailed group hallucination would still be quite improbable, a point that brings us again to the question of whether we can take the Gospels' word for it that the disciples claimed to have had detailed group experiences with an apparently physical Jesus.) Both Luke and John make it clear that the first meeting was *not* expected. The disciples were behind closed doors for fear of the Jewish authorities. They had not made a trek to a designated mountain in the hopes of having a religious experience of the risen Jesus.

> The appearance in Galilee in Matt. 28:16–17 is almost certainly a parallel to the appearance in Jerusalem in Luke 24:36–49, which is narrated as the first appearance to the male disciples as a group.[41]

> If Matt. 28:17 and Luke 24:41 are, as it seems, describing the same event, we have one more reason for understanding Matthew to have located the first appearance of Jesus to a group of his male disciples in Galilee while Luke locates it in Jerusalem.[42]

"Almost certainly" is unusually strong language for Licona, who more often compasses about his suggestions with terms like "perhaps" and "it may be." What is notable about the claim that these are "almost certainly" the same event is that it is so manifestly false. There is nothing remotely certain about the identification of the meeting in Luke 24 in Jerusalem with the meeting in Galilee in Matt. 28. Far from it. They do not appear to be the same event at all. Not only do the meetings occur in different locations and hence at different times (the very points of alleged contradiction), they differ in multiple other ways. The meeting in Luke 24 is unexpected. That in Matt. 28 is by appointment. The meeting in Luke 24 (emphasized even more in John 20) is indoors. The one in Matt. 28 is outdoors on a mountainside. In Luke 24, Jesus suddenly "stood among them" while they were talking. In Matt. 28:18, he "came up and spoke to them." Why think that these are the same event?

Licona's argument to this effect is curious. Over the span of a couple of pages, he discusses at length the fact that in Luke 24.41 they did not believe at first for joy and amazement and that Matt. 28.17 says that some doubted. But the fact that there is some amazement and/or doubt in both meetings, on the part of someone or other, is not a good argument for taking them to be the same meeting. Why would it mean that? Licona has a good deal to say about the Greek words in both passages (describing doubt in Matthew and disbelief from joy in Luke), but it is hard to see how that argument supports his conclusion, since he himself emphasizes that they are entirely different Greek words. Even if they were the same, this would not be a strong argument that the events are the same, but why talk about the Greek words as if they support the argument *at all* when they are completely different words? It becomes evident in Licona's own discussion that a good English translation makes their meanings clear anyway.

In the end, Licona's conclusion appears to be simply that the words have sufficient semantic range that they *could* be used to describe similar emotions, but that

---

[41] Licona, *Why Are There Differences*, p. 179.
[42] Ibid., p. 180.

is not a controversial point nor one that supports the highly dubious conclusion that the two events are the same.

> Thus, Luke uses an even stronger term than Matthew's "doubt" when describing the initial response of the male disciples when Jesus first appeared to them after his resurrection: "unbelieving." Yet it is clear that we are not to imagine those experiencing "unbelief" in Luke 24:41 as though they were standing there looking at Jesus with arms crossed and lips pressed. My mom and dad have both died. If they were to appear before me alive today, I would have a response that could be described in terms similar to what Matthew and Luke employed. I would feel joy and wonder at seeing them. But that would be accompanied by questions in my heart, "How can this be? I held my dad's hand the moment he died and I buried both!" I would exclaim, "Unbelievable!" and have two thoughts—"Wow!" and "How?"[43]

This point is immediately followed by, "If Matt. 28:17 and Luke 24:41 are, as it seems, describing the same event..." but the mere argument that the words in the passages could be describing similar emotions of awe and astonishment hardly supports *that* conclusion.

Perhaps there is an unspoken premise here that no one would have been present in the one scenario who was not present in the other and that the same disciples would have been unlikely to experience similar emotions twice; hence, the eleven must be envisaged as meeting Jesus for the *first* time in *both* descriptions. But that has already been addressed. Though Matthew does not state that anyone else was present besides the eleven, the Greek of Matthew's wording, "They [the eleven] worshiped him, but some doubted" hints that some others may have been present at this outdoor appointment for whom this was a first meeting. We do not have to assume that those who were almost disbelieving for joy as described in Luke were the same people who were doubtful in Matt. 28.

Notice what has happened in this argument: Licona first ignores clear, multiple indicators that the two meetings are different and concludes, against the evidence, that they are the same meeting. Consequently, the fact that one occurs in Galilee and the other in Jerusalem is taken to be a *contradiction* between Matthew and Luke. From this chain of reasoning Licona concludes (as we shall see) that Luke moved one of the appearances not only chronologically but also geographically.

I cannot help noticing the resemblance between this method and that of the 19th-century higher critics, as pointed out in a charming piece of satire by their contemporary German theologian Johannes Ebrard called "Receipt [Recipe] for

---

[43] Ibid., pp. 179–180.

Writing a Life of Jesus like Dr. David F. Strauss." Ebrard recommends as follows in his satiric recipe:

> If the contradictions are really great, and such as to indicate to an unprejudiced person, that the events which two of the sources relate are entirely different from those related in the two others, you are then, either silently to assume the identity of the two accounts, or to seek to render this plausible by urging the points of similarity....You put on now a conscientious mien, and discourse after this wise:—"On account of the differences here, the harmonists have attempted to explain the two accounts as referring to different transactions. But who does not see the violence of this assumption?...That the two narrators wished, therefore, to relate one and the same occurrence, admits of no question. It is quite another matter, whether in the manner in which they relate it, they do not contradict themselves."...Nay, even if the *time* in one authority is *expressly* different from that in the other, still you must assume the identity of the two events; and now your contradictions will become as plentiful as you can wish.[44]

Having concluded that there is a contradiction between Luke and Matthew concerning the location of the first meeting between Jesus and his disciples, Licona must explain this contradiction. In *Why Are There Differences in the Gospels?*, he seems poised between thinking that Matthew and Luke (John here agreeing with Luke) were relying upon different sources that placed the first meeting in different locations and concluding that Luke *knew* that the first meeting occurred in Galilee and deliberately altered it to Jerusalem without any historical warrant.[45] By the time of a later debate with Bart Ehrman, he had evidently concluded that the latter is the correct explanation. When Ehrman pressed his well-loved alleged contradiction concerning the place of the first meeting, Licona replied, "I think that first appearance probably happened in Galilee, but Luke situates it in Jerusalem there. When you compare the two accounts, they're talking about the same one." He further explained, "[Luke's] just compressing the account. I

---

[44] Johannes Ebrard, "Receipt for Writing a Life of Jesus like Dr. David F. Strauss," in *The Journal of Sacred Literature and Biblical Record*, ed. B. Harris Cowper (Edinburgh: Williams and Norgate, 1864), pp. 395–396.

[45] Licona, *Why Are There Differences*, p. 180. "Perhaps Mark and Matthew either preferred or knew only sources that located the appearance in Galilee, whereas the source(s) preferred by Luke and John put the appearance in Jerusalem." There is an oddity here in talking about the "sources" used by John and Matthew for knowledge of the first appearance of Jesus to his disciples. Once again, traditional authorship is left out of account in such a fashion that one must wonder whether Licona thinks it even remotely plausible that the authors of these Gospels were disciples. If John and Matthew were disciples, they would not have relied upon other "sources" to tell them such crucial, memorable information as whether Jesus first met them after his resurrection in Jerusalem or Galilee. Making matters more

see what he's doing. There's no problem there. He's compressing the account for economy of time or space, and then he's wanting to emphasize Jerusalem as the headquarters of the church." When Ehrman pressed by emphasizing that this would be not merely a chronological alteration but also a geographical change, Licona said, "It's both."[46]

While the emphasis throughout Licona's discussion is on Luke, the implications for the resurrection appearances in John are serious. A point not often enough emphasized in discussions about an alleged discrepancy between Luke and Matthew is that John and Luke *agree* that Jesus met a group of his male disciples first in Jerusalem. It would be entirely legitimate to say that a first meeting in Jerusalem is multiply attested. John and Luke really do seem to be recounting the same meeting, but they give complementary information about it, and there is no sign of dependence, either on each other or on some common source, other than reality. It is quite plausible that they have separate access to the event, which would be quite easy for John if he was a disciple.

If, as Licona now says, the first meeting with Jesus took place in Galilee, where does that leave the first meeting recounted in John and the doubting Thomas sequence? As we saw in section 3, Licona raises doubts about the historicity of that incident but decides instead that probably Luke deliberately misstated the number of disciples present at the first meeting. But now the question comes up yet again. Matthew says that it was "the eleven" who went to Galilee and saw Jesus together. On Licona's and Ehrman's interpretation of Matthew, Matthew is saying that this occurred immediately. And as we have seen in the earlier section, Licona is unwilling

tangled, later on that same page Licona suggests (as if this is compatible with the suggestion about preferring or using different sources) that different authors might have "redacted" the message of the angel and of Jesus to fit with their preferred location. But if they were relying on *separate* sources, they would have had no need to "redact" a source that placed a meeting in a different place from their own source. They would either not have known the other source or would simply have ignored it. Licona also suggests that Luke may have "redacted" the message of the angel because he could not fit in a trip to Galilee. This is consonant with the position he has settled on more recently. But it is in tension with the suggestion on the same page that Luke was relying on an historical source that said that the first meeting really *did* take place in Jerusalem. It is almost as though Licona is juggling so many different redactive and fictionalizing theories about these passages that he does not realize that they cannot all be true at the same time.

[46] Debate: Bart Ehrman vs. Mike Licona, "Are the Gospels Historically Reliable," February 21, 2018, minute 1:46:57, https://youtu.be/qP7RrCfDkO4?t=6417. Licona's statement that Luke's motive was merely "economy of time or space" simply confuses achronological and dyschronological narration. It is not necessary for reasons of "time or space" to *put* all of the events *on* Easter Day. Achronological narration, which is in fact what Luke does, makes the account shorter without trying to imply an incorrect timeframe.

to countenance the idea that "the eleven" is anything other than a counting term. Hence, since Licona's theory, stated to Ehrman, is that Jesus really did meet his disciples first in Galilee, per (their interpretation of) Matthew, it looks like doubting Thomas cannot be historical after all. On this theory about who met Jesus first and where, Thomas must have met Jesus right away in Galilee along with the other ten disciples, leaving no room for a doubting sequence. And of course John locates that sequence, beginning with the first meeting on Easter day, firmly in Jerusalem. But according to Licona's most recent theory there was no sequence of meetings between Jesus and his disciples in Jerusalem at first. Jesus first met them in Galilee.

John's series of post-resurrection appearances is the longest recorded in any one extant Gospel resurrection account.[47] So if one thinks that Luke "compresses" and that this is why he moves the first appearance to Jerusalem, one cannot use that same explanation for John's first meeting in Jerusalem. John's statement that Thomas was not present on the first occasion leads to a second, uniquely recorded meeting in Jerusalem eight days later, and there is a unique meeting in Galilee in John 21, though not the same one recorded in Matthew. If Jesus did not first appear to his disciples in Jerusalem and John also moved the first appearance to Jerusalem, John would have had to fabricate scenes for some completely different reason from Luke's, not compression. In that case they would agree with each other that Jesus first appeared to his disciples in Jerusalem by coincidence.

It is entirely possible that Licona does not explicitly intend the implication of ahistoricity for the doubting Thomas sequence by his claim about Luke's moving the location of Jesus' first appearance. He has not addressed the issue and perhaps has not thought of the connection. But the negative connection to John's report is there nonetheless. It would make far better sense to focus on the fact that, on the point at issue in this section—the location of Jesus' first meeting with his disciples—Luke and John are complementary.[48] John 21, on the other side, confirms Matthew by telling us that the disciples did return to Galilee while Jesus was still on earth. There seven disciples could have met Jesus as recounted in John 21 and the eleven (and perhaps many more) could have met him as recorded in Matt. 28. Hence John provides a welcome geographical bridge between Luke and Matthew.

---

[47] I take the long ending of Mark to be non-canonical, so we have no resurrection appearances in our current copies of Mark.

[48] Lest the point go unnoticed, I note that the entire invention of doubting Thomas by John does not correspond to any named compositional device that Licona even claims to have found in Greco-Roman literature.

The idea that Luke moved Jesus' first meeting to Jerusalem and invented the surrounding circumstances, which leads to the conclusion that John must have invented entire scenes, is an unjustified, hyper-complex "solution" to alleged discrepancies that can be far more easily addressed. Both Luke and Matthew left out some of the events after the resurrection and narrated briefly, without contradicting any of the other Gospels. Putting together the four Gospels and Acts gives us a fuller picture of what really happened.

7. Did Jesus breathe and say, "Receive the Holy Spirit"?

In this section we return to utterly unforced errors and to the gratuitous doubt often cast upon the Gospel of John. More than one evangelical New Testament scholar has suggested that Jesus never historically breathed out (presumably upon his disciples) saying, "Receive the Holy Spirit" as recorded in John 20.22–23.[49] This was, allegedly, a place where John crafted in order to "weave mention" of or "allude" to the day of Pentecost.

It is difficult to set up this discussion by acknowledging some apparent discrepancy, because there is no apparent discrepancy among the documents. No other resurrection account in any other Gospel says anything that seems to contradict this incident. Luke doesn't record it in Luke 24 in his account of the same appearance, but mere absence in another Gospel is not a contradiction. Scholars make a suggestion out of the blue that perhaps this incident did not really happen.

Here are the verses in question:

> So Jesus said to them again, "Peace be with you; as the Father has sent Me, I also send you." And when He had said this, He breathed on them and said to them, "Receive the Holy Spirit. If you forgive the sins of any, their sins have been forgiven them; if you retain the sins of any, they have been retained." (John 20.21–23)

To someone not steeped in the subculture of New Testament studies, an historical doubt directed against these specific verses looks quite strange. This is not,

---

[49] D. A. Carson, who unqualifiedly defends the historicity of the event, argues that the idea that Jesus was definitely breathing *upon* the disciples is not clearly expressed by the Greek and that that common translation is somewhat misleading. He argues that the Greek is "absolute" and should not be considered to take an object. *The Gospel According to John* (Grand Rapids, MI: Eerdmans, 1991), pp. 512–513. Carson argues that Jesus, in this action, was not bestowing the Spirit but rather symbolizing the coming of the Spirit. Given this doubt about the Greek word, I have carefully worded my section header accordingly. But since my concern is with the historicity of the literal event and John's truthfulness in reporting it rather than the theological significance—indeed, a major part of my argument is that the former must be fairly considered even if we cannot decide about the latter—I will not always refrain from using some phrase like "breathed on them" in my analysis.

at least in the case of evangelical scholars, a matter of doubting the resurrection. The scholars in question believe in that, and they believe that Jesus appeared to his disciples in a group at some point. So why should they have doubts about the historicity of *this* part of John's narrative? At a minimum, a gratuitous doubt directed against this action and these words of Jesus manifests a low view of John's historical reliability as an individual source.

When one reads further discussion of the passage (see below), one discovers that the alleged problem is not a narrative one but a theological one. If one adopts a specific, strong theological interpretation of the meaning of Jesus' action—that he was giving the disciples the Holy Spirit in the sense that was promised to them elsewhere in John—this creates a theological tension with the book of Acts, in which the promised coming of the Holy Spirit takes place on the day of Pentecost, described in Acts 2, after Jesus has ascended. It is on the basis of this entirely unnecessary theological worry that scholars question the historicity of the event in John, implying that John may have chosen to make up words and deeds of Jesus while on earth to stand in the theological place of Pentecost within his own Gospel.

The arguments for this conclusion are far too flimsy to bear its weight. When Licona presents the theory for serious consideration, he gives nothing that could be called an argument:

> Pertaining to Jesus's breathing on his disciples and saying, "Receive the Holy Spirit" (John 20:22), perhaps John, knowing he would not be writing a sequel as had Luke, desired to allude to the event at Pentecost. So he wove mention of the ascension into his communications with Mary Magdalene (20:17) and of the Holy Spirit at Pentecost into his communications with his male disciples (20:22).[50]

The motive suggested here for John to engage in such a fictionalization makes little sense. No one was stopping John from recording the actual ascension and Pentecost if he wished to. Moreover, it is simply untrue to speak of this as an "allusion" to Pentecost, since the events are obviously completely different. In John 20.22–23, Jesus is visibly on earth, breathing and speaking. In Acts 2 the disciples see what look like tongues of fire and hear a rushing wind. Jesus is not visible, because he has already ascended. If an early Christian reader or hearer

---

[50] Licona, *Why Are There Differences*, p. 180. Again, Licona does not state that this corresponds to any named compositional device that he believes he has discovered in Greco-Roman literature. It is simply a doubt that comes up because of the theological concerns of New Testament scholars, without any reference whatsoever to Greco-Roman tropes.

believed that this somehow "was" Pentecost in John, a substitute for the events in Acts 2, he would simply have been confused and wondered whether John was denying the events on Pentecost.[51]

To be sure, Jesus' actions and words at this point in John 20 are mysterious, but that hardly makes them dubiously historical. One must wonder why John would make up something so cryptic if it did not occur. Indeed, the strangeness and lack of explanation of the event is another reason for taking it to be historical, if any were needed.

If anything in John looks like a foreshadowing of Pentecost, it is Jesus' teaching about the coming of the Paraclete in John 14–16, but that teaching of course is beautifully consonant with the events at Pentecost and looks forward to the benefits that the disciples and other believers will receive after that time. There is no reason whatsoever to think that John found this teaching insufficient and hence would have desired to invent a cryptic act and words of Jesus as an unclear "allusion" to Pentecost.

In the above quotation from Licona, the same scholarly whimsy that calls into question an aspect of the scene in John 20.22–23 also calls into question the historicity of Jesus' words to Mary Magdalene about ascending to the Father in John 20.17. Once again, no reason at all is given for thinking that John invented Jesus' words, "I have not yet ascended to the Father; but go to My brethren and say to them, 'I ascend to My Father and your Father, and My God and your God.'" Licona describes no alleged discrepancy to which this idea is the solution. It is an utterly unforced error.[52]

Craig Keener has more to say about the breathing incident:[53]

[D]o John and Luke refer to distinct events? Or has John invented the setting to include the event before his narrative closes? Because I believe that John takes many more symbolic theological liberties with his story than does Luke, my John commentary addresses this question somewhat more fully than does the treatment here, which rehearses some of my discussion and conclusions there. I

---

[51] Carson makes this point. *The Gospel According to John*, p. 514.

[52] In these two cases, there is not even the claim that John is "paraphrasing" some other teaching of Jesus recorded in the Synoptic Gospels. Apparently not even the inventiveness that seriously put forward "I thirst" as a "dynamic equivalence" for "My God, why have you forsaken me" is sufficient to suggest some entirely different sayings of Jesus that John is "paraphrasing" here. The suggestion is flatly that Jesus did not say these words at all while on earth and that John has made them up out of whole cloth.

[53] I refer to this as an "incident." Someone might quibble that the "incident" is the first resurrection appearance to a group of male disciples, of which this is but one detail. This complaint would be

believe that there may have been historical experiences behind both reports but that Luke is accurate about a subsequent setting for the Spirit's empowering the church for mission ... [T]he Johannine "Pentecost" (John 20:19–23) shares some common features with Luke's Pentecost, but their primary relationship is their mutual affirmation that Jesus imparted or sent the Spirit shortly after his resurrection. John's report is far less dramatic and does not occur in the era of Christ's exaltation, but John completes his account before the promised exaltation ... and hence presses into this event the narrative fulfillment of Christ's promises concerning the Spirit. It is possible that historically the disciples experienced a foretaste in 20:22 that was fulfilled more dramatically on a later occasion.... But for those who must choose one account or the other and regard Luke's as too dramatic: Luke seems more likely to report the events as he has them from his tradition than does John. John takes significant liberties with the way he reports his events, especially in several symbolic adaptations in the passion narrative, whereas Luke follows, where we can test him ..., the procedures of a good Hellenistic historian .... [54]

Here Keener does not *entirely* deny the historicity of the breathing incident in John 20, but it is entirely fair to say that even in this passage (and more so in his commentary on John, quoted below) he calls its historicity seriously into question. The most he will say in favor of it is that "there may have been historical experiences behind both reports" and "it is possible that historically the disciples experienced a foretaste" of Pentecost in 20.22. In the same breath, however, he insists that John takes many "symbolic theological liberties with his story" and "significant liberties with the way he reports his events." This low evaluation of John's literal, historical reliability apparently makes it impossible to draw anything more than the extremely tentative conclusion that maybe *something or other* happened while Jesus was on earth that constituted a "foretaste" of Pentecost and that "lies behind" the report in John 20. What exactly that something was like is left entirely fuzzy, and the reader is left with the strong impression that, given John's penchant for theological invention, there may be no such historical experience "behind" the narrative at all. Given Keener's evaluation, we could not

pedantic and unenlightening. The portion of that appearance in which Jesus breathes and speaks to the disciples about receiving the Holy Spirit is a separable event, an important thing in itself, theologically interesting (especially given his statement about their authority to forgive sins, apparently related to the reference to the Holy Spirit), which either did or did not occur. For John to invent it *ex nihilo* would not be for him to tweak a little "detail," and it is important that we resist the expansive concept of "details" or mere "aspects of incidents" to trivialize such an invention.

[54] Craig Keener, *Acts: An Exegetical Commentary* (Grand Rapids, MI: Baker Academic 2012), vol. 1, pp. 790, 793.

confidently take John's narrative in this passage at face value as reliably reporting something Jesus recognizably did and said, something you could have seen and heard if you had been there.

Keener's discussion in the commentary on John is longer but by the same token less clear:

> Views on the relation between this passage and a later impartation of the Spirit, such as Acts 2 depicts, vary. Some would argue that John retains a distinction between Easter and a later Pentecost, perhaps by John 20:22 symbolically pointing forward to the historical Pentecost. Whatever its historical plausibility, however, the view that Jesus merely symbolically promises the Spirit here does not pull together an adequate narrative climax on the literary-theological level of John's earlier promises of the Spirit. Certainly the verb for Jesus breathing on the disciples means more than mere exhalation. Whether John might use Jesus' breathing symbolically, however, is a different question than whether Jesus is portrayed as acting merely symbolically in the story world.[55]

So did the event happen in the real world, or not? The passage is unclear, though Keener seems to be insisting here that John means to portray Jesus theologically as really giving the disciples the Holy Spirit.

Keener continues,

> Some of [Max] Turner's observations may suggest legitimate complexities or incongruities in John's language. These in turn may suggest that John is aware of a subsequent Pentecost event and lays emphasis on an earlier event that also provided an encounter with the Spirit.[56]

This looks like another cautious and qualified acknowledgement that *maybe* something like the event described in John really happened, though Keener bases this suggestion upon "incongruities" in John's language (whatever those might be) rather than upon the plain facts of John's narrative. But then we have this:

> John completes his Gospel in ch. 21; if he is to narrate any fulfillment of his Paraclete promises that provide continuity between the missions of Jesus and his followers, he must do so here....Even if the giving of the Spirit in the tradition behind 20:22 represents merely a symbolic or partial impartation, it must bear in John's narrative the full theological weight equivalent to Luke's Pentecost.

---

[55] Craig Keener, *The Gospel of John: A Commentary* (Grand Rapids, MI: Baker Academic, 2003), p. 1196.

[56] Ibid., pp. 1198–99.

But if its narrative function (in terms of its full theological weight) is in some sense symbolic of an outpouring of the Spirit, one need not seek a chronological harmonization with Acts 2. As [Gary] Burge emphasizes, Luke-Acts itself provides a similar chronological situation: because Luke must end his Gospel where he does, he describes the ascension as if it occurs on Easter (Luke 24:51) even though he will soon inform or remind his readers that it occurred only forty days afterward (Acts 1:3, 9). Likewise, "knowing his Gospel would have no sequel," the Fourth Evangelist theologically compressed "the appearances, ascension, and Pentecost into Easter. Yet for him, this is not simply a matter of literary convenience.... John weaves these events into 'the hour' with explicit theological intentions."[57]

This piles confusion upon confusion. Once again, it makes no sense to speak as though John was prohibited from narrating Pentecost if he wished to. Who was to stop him? The statement that, if he wanted to narrate the fulfillment of the promises he "must do so here" because his Gospel ends at Chapter 21 gives the curious impression of an author who has no control over where in the story his Gospel ends, as though this were somehow dictated from outside.

The assumption that John must do something or other to narrate the fulfillment of the promises of the Spirit within his own Gospel and the claim that he gives this scene the "full theological weight equivalent to Luke's Pentecost" are likewise quite unjustified. Why think that this scene has to bear any such weight at all? The idea that John made up something fictitious and unclear and gave it the "full theological weight" of Pentecost is a bizarre supposition based upon no compelling reason at all.

Moreover, the claim that the cryptic narration of Jesus' breathing *does* appear to fulfill the promises in John is inconsistent with the content of the promises themselves. It does not even work literarily. To the contrary, Jesus' repeated promises of the Holy Spirit in John indicate that he (and the Father) will *send* the Holy Spirit. Jesus even emphasizes his own on-going *absence* as a prerequisite for the sending of the Holy Spirit. The strong implication of the earlier promises is that Jesus will not be physically present with them when the Spirit comes:

> "I will ask the Father, and He will give you another Helper, that He may be with you forever; that is the Spirit of truth, whom the world cannot receive ..." (John 14.16–17)

> "These things I have spoken to you while abiding with you. But the Helper, the Holy Spirit, whom the Father will send in My name, He will teach you all things, and bring to your remembrance all that I said to you." (John 14.25–26)

---

[57] Ibid., p. 1200.

"When the Helper comes, whom I will send to you from the Father, that is the Spirit of truth who proceeds from the Father, He will testify about Me, and you will testify also, because you have been with Me from the beginning." (John 15.26)

"But I tell you the truth, it is to your advantage that I go away; for if I do not go away, the Helper will not come to you; but if I go, I will send Him to you." (John 16.7)

The emphasis in all of these verses upon the prophesied physical absence of Jesus and his (and the Father's) consequent *sending* the Paraclete certainly does not set up any expectation of a scene such as that described in John. That cryptic scene does not look at all like a "narrative climax" of these promises.

All of this fits very well with what one gathers from the complementary promise in Luke and Acts, coming before the ascension:

"You are witnesses of these things. And behold, I am sending forth the promise of My Father upon you; but you are to stay in the city until you are clothed with power from on high." (Luke 24.48–49)

Gathering them together, He commanded them not to leave Jerusalem, but to wait for what the Father had promised, "Which," He said, "you heard of from Me; for John baptized with water, but you will be baptized with the Holy Spirit not many days from now....but you will receive power when the Holy Spirit has come upon you; and you shall be My witnesses both in Jerusalem, and in all Judea and Samaria, and even to the remotest part of the earth." (Acts 1.4–5, 8)

Far from being in tension, Luke and John speak in the same terms. In both places, Jesus makes an emphatic prediction that he will send the Holy Spirit later, after he returns to the Father and is no longer physically with them, and that, as a result of the Spirit's arrival, the disciples will be his witnesses. Peter's words about electing a new apostle in Acts 1.21 echo the language of "witnesses from the beginning" in John 15.26, and we see the Spirit's role of empowering the disciples as witnesses in Acts 2.

It is easily possible for Jesus to predict something in John that does not occur until after the end of John's Gospel. Once we think of these as real events rather than as parts of a highly literary "story world," we do not have to strain the text to find a "narrative climax" within John itself for Jesus' promises to send the Spirit.

Burge's statement, quoted by Keener, that Luke describes the ascension as though it occurs on Easter has already been dealt with at length earlier in this chapter. But the comparison fails even on its own terms. Luke *does* clearly tell about the ascension in Luke 24, albeit briefly. He doesn't tell about a completely different event as a darkly coded *substitute* for the ascension.

Keener ends his entire discussion of this matter with the quotation from Burge, giving the distinct impression that he is taking Burge's words as his own. Burge, at any rate, seems to take the literal event in John 20.22–23 as little more than John's theologically freighted invention. He says that "many items point" in the direction of concluding that Jesus' breathing in John 20 "fulfills the Paraclete promises and duplicates the Acts event." This would mean that one or the other of them, presumably the breathing in John, must be ahistorical. Burge merely says that the case for this conclusion falls short of "absolute confirmation."[58] He is fairly definite that he sees a contradiction between John and Acts, saying, "What Luke records on Pentecost, John refers to Easter." This is flatly false in historical terms, since the two events do not appear to be the same. Burge appears to give no negative weight to the radical nature of this theory in relation to the historicity of John, and he clouds the issue with theological euphemisms. For example, he says that the disciples were "experiencing in John 20 the eschatological Spirit predicted in 1:33" and that "[I]t comes as no surprise that John has a clear motive for bringing the Spirit into Easter."[59]

What is missing in all of this speculation is the desire and ability to ask a clear question and give a clear answer: Did this happen or did it not? If John's Gospel has any significant degree of historical credibility, and if Jesus did appear to his group of disciples after his resurrection, what concrete reason is there to doubt that this brief event and these sayings of Jesus did recognizably occur?

Also absent is the crucial capacity to separate our ability to know what such an event would have *meant* or would have accomplished on a theological plane from our justification for believing that it occurred in the world of space and time. Jesus often did and said things that were, and remain, hard to understand. It *is not necessary* for us to decide "how much" of the Holy Spirit the disciples received if Jesus actually did this in order to be rational in believing that the event took place historically, that if you spoke the relevant language (whether Aramaic or Greek), you would have heard Jesus saying recognizably what he is recorded as saying and would have seen him breathing if you had been there. Perhaps the disciples themselves were never entirely sure what had happened on that occasion or its precise relationship

---

[58] Gary M. Burge, *The Anointed Community: The Holy Spirit in the Johannine Tradition* (Grand Rapids, MI: Eerdmans, 1987), p. 148.

[59] Ibid.

to the tongues of fire on Pentecost and their subsequent power for spreading Jesus' message. But John did not have to *understand* the event himself in order accurately to *report* it. Theological speculation here darkens historical counsel. The theologizing of the historical question gives a false impression of an *historical* problem with John 20.22–23 when, in fact, there is no special problem at all for these verses. John reports that Jesus did this. His *doing it* does not in any way contradict what Luke narrates in Acts 2 or what any of the other Gospels narrate anywhere. Of course it was an odd thing for Jesus to do, and his words in the context were cryptic as well. (Was he really endorsing a unique ability of the apostles to forgive sins?) We may never know precisely what he meant by doing it or what theologically happened at that moment. But the mere oddity of his action does not in any way, shape, or form undermine the reasonableness of thinking that John, with his desire to report truthfully what Jesus did and said, told us truly about something that observably happened on that day in the upper room. To think otherwise is an unforced error.

8. Harmonization and the vindication of the reportage model

At the end of his own harmony of the resurrection accounts, John Wenham writes,

> Forced harmonizing is worthless. The tendency today, however, is the opposite—to force the New Testament writings into disharmony, in order to emphasize their individuality. The current analytical approach to the gospels often has the effect of making scholars more and more uncertain at more and more points, till eventually their view of Jesus and his teaching is lost in haze.[60]

This chapter has analyzed one example after another of forcing the New Testament writings into disharmony in order to emphasize their individuality. Again and again, scholars either ignore or reject reasonable harmonizations, or (as in the last section) they create a problem out of nowhere, when there is not even any apparent discrepancy.

Wenham continues,

> The harmonistic approach, on the other hand, enables one to ponder long and conscientiously over every detail of the narrative and to see how one account illuminates and modifies another. Gradually (without fudging) people and events take shape and grow in solidity and the scenes come to life in one's mind. Such study is beautifully constructive and helps to vindicate the presuppositions on which it is based.[61]

---

[60] Wenham, *Easter Enigma*, p. 128.

[61] Ibid. I should make it clear that, although I have used several of Wenham's harmonizations in

What does "helps to vindicate the presuppositions on which it is based" mean? I do not think that this phrase needs to refer to any presuppositionalist approach to philosophy or apologetics. Rather, Wenham seems to be talking about what a philosopher would call hypothesis testing. He also seems to be referring to what T. R. Birks calls "reconcilable variation," discussed in Chapter XII, section 3. We say to ourselves, "Suppose that these *were* historically accurate accounts. Then we should find that they can be rationally harmonized when all relevant information is known." We then test that hypothesis by attempting to harmonize them, using real-world imagination and the data before us. When we find that they are harmonizable across a large set of passages, this legitimately strengthens our confidence in their historicity.

The way that, as Wenham says, people and events take shape and grow in solidity is a result of the confirmation of the reportage model. We are getting a picture of reality. Not of "traditions," not of fuzzy "events that may lie behind" the Gospels, not of one evangelist's "story world," which may or may not be the same as someone else's. Of the real world. In this way, harmonization is like putting together a puzzle; the full picture gradually emerges.

Sometimes there are apparent discrepancies that still seem recalcitrant. Luke's reference to "the eleven" as present at Jesus' first meeting may be one such, depending on one's evaluation of the probability that he was using the term collectively. But in that case, the reasonable thing to do from an historical point of view is to consider the simplest remaining hypothesis that accords with our other knowledge of human behavior. In that case, one considers that people aren't always told every detail and that it is not at all improbable that Luke simply didn't know that Thomas was absent on that occasion.

Sometimes there are puzzles about motive that remain, such as the fact that we don't know why Matthew does not make a clearer reference, perhaps in passing, to Jerusalem meetings or to the fact that the eleven themselves had seen Jesus before

this chapter, I do not agree with all of his views. Above I noted his unnecessary insertion of a gap between two verses in Matthew 28. I also do not think that Mary Magdalene was Mary of Bethany, and I think it unnecessary to hypothesize that the rest of the eleven, other than John and Peter, were lodged as far away as Bethany on the night before the resurrection. Wenham also thinks that Mark's family was close to Jesus, whereas patristic evidence indicates that Mark did not personally know Jesus. But none of these points are central to Wenham's harmonization. I also think that, when he uses the term "telescopes" (p. 89) concerning the place in Luke 24 where the women "were telling" the "eleven and all the rest," he means what I mean by "chunking in," not what a literary device theorist would mean by dyschronological telescoping or conflation. Wenham's important accomplishment is to use his learning in a constructive way to show the plausibility of the harmonization of the resurrection accounts, and he is generally on the right lines.

they met him in Galilee. But a lack of knowledge of motive does not eliminate the obligation, in responsible historical practice, to take all evidence into account and to learn about the events from multiple available sources. Matthew's brevity and his focus on a Galilee meeting does not contradict the multiply-attested claim that Jesus did first appear to a group of his disciples in Jerusalem.

What is clear from this survey of alleged contradictions and fictionalizations in the resurrection accounts is that literary device theories do not bring new insight from specialized knowledge of ancient literary practices. The passages on which Licona concentrates tend to be long-standing points of controversy between harmonizers and anti-harmonizers. The grounds of complaint about those passages will already be familiar to those who have studied skeptical claims of contradiction or have read scholarly redactive speculations, without any reference to specialized devices. The factual accuracy of these passages is not called into question in some new way by any uncanny resemblance between the Gospel accounts and some objective, independently verified, fact-changing compositional devices. It is neither helpful nor convincing to assert broadly, on the basis of an alleged tension, that the authors of the Gospels felt free to "vary the tradition" or "craft the story." And it sheds no new light on the subject.

An examination of alleged contradictions in the resurrection accounts also makes clear, once again, the stakes in the debate between the reportage model and the literary device model. The scope of the suggestions surveyed in this chapter, which include the "crafting" of entire scenes and the elimination of entire actions and sayings of Jesus from the realm of history, flatly refutes any claim that the literary changes in question are trivial. And once again, the view of the authors is radically different between the two models. The "Luke" who moves the risen Jesus and his apostles around Palestine like chess pieces and the "John" who may well have made up the doubting Thomas sequence, the initial meeting with Mary Magdalene, or Jesus' cryptic act of breathing and saying, "Receive the Holy Spirit" are not conscientious about historical matters. They are wrapped up in creating theologico-literary artifacts that satisfy them, and this interest repeatedly trumps their desire to tell what happened, even at that most crucial moment of human history—the resurrection of the Son of God.

Most of all, the examination of resurrection difficulties shows that such theories are unnecessary. Again and again the scholar wheels in the elaborate machinery of redactive and other higher critical theories because of an unjustified bias—a bias against harmonization, a bias against a particular Gospel (such as John), a bias in favor of theological or redactive speculation, a bias in favor of complexity over simplicity. That machinery does not become more epistemically legitimate because one dubs its outputs "literary devices." It must stand or fall on its own, on the basis of the arguments. I propose that, in the resurrection accounts as elsewhere, it cannot stand. We should replace it with the reportage model, which repeatedly provides a better explanation of the data and is independently attested by multiple lines of evidence about the Gospels and their authors.

Summary
Fictionalizing Literary Devices and the Resurrection Accounts

- The claim that the Gospel authors felt free to craft scenes and change facts in the resurrection narratives has serious implications for Christianity.

- Scholars make many fictionalization suggestions about the resurrection narratives.

- Literary device theories about the resurrection illustrate the methodological errors discussed in previous chapters: utterly unforced errors, fictions only need apply, and over-reading.

- Two suggested theories of whole scene invention in the resurrection stories, considered as plausible options by Michael Licona, are 1) that John may have invented the scene between Jesus and Mary Magdalene at the tomb and 2) that John may have invented the doubting Thomas sequence.

- Scholars have suggested that John invented Jesus' breathing and saying, "Receive the Holy Spirit" as recorded in John 20. There is no contradiction in the New Testament that suggests such a theory. It is a result of an excessively theological approach to evaluating the historicity of the Gospels.

- Other claims rebutted in this chapter are that Luke put all of Jesus' appearances after his resurrection on Easter Sunday and that John contradicts the Synoptics on whether or not there were angels at the tomb when the women first came.

- Evangelical scholars' fictionalization theories concerning the resurrection stories do not arise from specialized knowledge of Greco-Roman literature but rather from accommodating long-standing critical doubts about these accounts.

- The rational harmonization of the resurrection accounts is a fruitful enterprise that vindicates the reportage model.

Claiming the Forward Position Once Again

The Gospels undeniably *present themselves* as true accounts of the life and teachings of Jesus of Nazareth. Without any need for a highly specific genre identification, one can say that the immediate impression one gets is that the evangelists intend to tell what really happened. In this extremely broad, non-technical sense, the Gospels appear to be biographical.

C. S. Lewis makes this commonsense point eloquently in response to the claim that the Gospels are legends:

> A man who has spent his youth and manhood in the minute study of the New Testament texts and of other people's studies of them, whose literary experiences of those texts lacks any standard of comparison such as can only grow from a wide and deep and genial experience of literature in general is, I should think, very likely to miss the obvious things about them. If he tells me that something in a Gospel is legend or romance, I want to know how many legends and romances he has read, how well his palate is trained in detecting them by the flavour; not how many years he has spent on that Gospel.[1]

Using John as an example of Gospel realism, Lewis continues,

> I have been reading poems, romances, vision-literature, legends, myths all my life. I know what they are like. I know that not one of them is like this. Of this text there are only two possible views. Either this is reportage—though it may no doubt contain errors—pretty close up to the facts; nearly as close as Boswell. Or else, some unknown writer … without known predecessors or successors, sud-

---

[1] C. S. Lewis, "Modern Theology and Biblical Criticism" in Christian Reflections, edited by Walter Hooper (Grand Rapids, MI: Eerdmans, 1967), p. 154.

denly anticipated the whole technique of modern, novelistic, realistic narrative. If it is untrue it must be narrative of that kind. The reader who doesn't see this has simply not learned to read.[2]

This robust approach to the Gospels' genre suggests that the question is not so fraught with difficulty as the oceans of ink spilled on it would suggest. Nor is its answer so esoteric as literary device theorists would lead us to believe. That is to say, it does not require a highly specific answer at all. Lewis did not need the category of Greco-Roman βίοι to refute Rudolf Bultmann's absurd claim that Jesus in the Gospels does not have a personality and to see that the Gospels are realistic biographical reportage.[3]

Against this realistic view of the Gospels, from before Lewis's time to the present, rolls the tide of skepticism. Even if not explicitly using the categories of myth and legend, the skeptic suggests that the Gospels exhibit carelessness about historical truth and that they were written at many removes. A modern scholar like Bart Ehrman will suggest that, even if the Gospel authors believed what they wrote, they did not have good reason to believe it, they were not close up to the facts, and they included not just a few small errors but a great many, including errors on topics central to Christianity, such as the deity of Jesus.[4]

Such skepticism is bolstered in both the public and the scholarly mind by a welter of alleged contradictions, tensions, and improbabilities in the Gospels. Nor (and this is important) do the vast majority of these objections bear any anti-miraculous bias on their face. Often, as we have seen throughout the preceding chapters, the event or saying called into question is not a miracle at all. Or, if the accounts do concern a miracle, as in the case of the resurrection, the allegation is that they are in contradiction or tension with each other or that they bear marks of redaction, not that they are improbable *per se* because they are miracle stories.

This means that those who have no anti-miraculous bias can become just as tangled up in claims of discrepancy or tension between the Gospel accounts as those who do have an anti-miraculous bias. In fact, as we have seen throughout

---

[2] Ibid., p. 155.

[3] In response to Bultmann's absurd claim that Jesus in the Gospels does not have a personality, see Ibid., pp. 155–157.

[4] See, for example, Bart Ehrman, *Jesus, Interrupted: Revealing the Hidden Contradictions in the Bible (and Why We Don't Know About Them)* (New York, NY: Harper One, 2009), pp. 59–60, 147, 245–254. On p. 147 Ehrman uses one of his favorite analogies—the "telephone game," in which a message is distorted by being whispered from one person to another over a long chain.

this book, various evangelical scholars have widespread doubts that the Gospels are harmonizable in any traditional fashion. Other scholars and laymen who hear that an evangelical scholar has decided that two Gospel accounts are in tension often assume that he *must* have come to this conclusion because of an overwhelming argument. After all, they reason, this is an evangelical Christian scholar. He would not say that there is a problem with harmonization unless the argument were strong, because he doesn't have an anti-miraculous bias. And if the specific objection bears no anti-miraculous bias on its face either, this seems to strengthen further the assumption that the scholarly reasoning behind it is both neutral and compelling.

But these assumptions turn out repeatedly to be false. Unfortunately, it is *entirely* possible for a scholar who has no bias against the supernatural to conclude on flimsy grounds that some portion of the Gospels is really non-historical or that two or more of the narratives are in irreconcilable tension. Such claims are legion in mainstream New Testament scholarship, and poor methodology is entrenched. There is intense pressure to agree that there are multiple problems with traditional harmonization, thus supposedly proving oneself to be an objective scholar working with integrity, untrammeled by *a priori* theological commitments.

The issue of inerrancy raises the pressure still higher. Sociologically, scholars may lose credibility in conservative Christian circles if they say that they are not inerrantists. Both jobs and speaking opportunities are sometimes at stake. Speakers and scholars who believe that they have something important to offer to the Christian world, while holding views that might be thought liberal, want to maintain these opportunities from laudable motives; they think that they can help the Body of Christ and don't want to be locked out of doing so.

I am not saying that nothing *should* be at stake if one refuses to affirm inerrancy. That it has been a line in the sand is quite understandable in many ways. I am merely pointing out the social incentive to redefine the term. Redefinition can allow a scholar to agree in certain ways with the consensus of mainstream biblical scholarship while still claiming that he is an inerrantist. This problem may be unavoidable. The possibility that those who affirm a statement of faith will be tempted to fudge is a consequence of any creed with countercultural content. In general, I strongly support robust statements of faith and the often thankless task of keeping up the standards of Christian institutions, churches, and organizations in an increasingly hostile secular world. We must, however, see these efforts as part of a sociological context in which some scholars come to think of themselves as a beleaguered, reasonable, moderate minority, fighting for their scholarly careers against opposition from both the "left" and the "right."

Psychologically, an evangelical immersed in the milieu of New Testament scholarship with its continual derision directed against harmonization may come to feel weary and even guilty. He is trying to be a good scholar, following what he has been taught are the objective norms of his discipline. If he continues to try to harmonize alleged contradictions in the Bible, he may begin to suspect himself of failing to be objective or of acting from motives of fear. The sheer number of alleged problems may seem overwhelming, leading to a worry that he is just one irresolvable problem away from losing a great deal, both theologically and socially.

Into this fraught situation, literary device theories come with a promise of deliverance. After all, all good conservatives who read the Bible want to understand the books in their original cultural context, don't they? The consideration of genre ought to make a difference to our understanding of a biblical book or portion thereof, shouldn't it? Jesus did tell parables. We don't think that the accuracy or reliability of the Bible is called into question if the story of the Good Samaritan didn't literally happen. Maybe these principles can be somehow applied more broadly so that we can continue to say that the Bible is reliable, even *inerrant*, while also thinking that the Gospel authors changed the facts on various occasions. As long as these were literary devices accepted at the time, perhaps recognizing them is just understanding the document in its correct cultural context, as all responsible biblical scholars are supposed to do. And then we don't have to keep trying to harmonize, or at least we can do so much less often. What a relief!

At first it may seem like bad news to point out to someone who reasons thus that the fictionalizing literary device approach is completely wrong. As discussed in Part One, it is theoretically wrong because, if changing facts invisibly were accepted in a culture, that wouldn't mean that a document that does so is historically *reliable*. It would just mean that it was accepted at the time to create documents that are historically shaky, like movies merely based on true events in our own time. The fact that such devices, if they existed, would not have been individually visible in the document in question, even to the original audience, may come as a surprise to those who hear only an outline of the literary device views. Once that fact is understood, it should make a considerable difference to one's understanding of the relationship of such devices to document reliability. For it is not as though one could "tag" specific passages as partially fictional based upon some recognizable indication in the text itself, while treating everything not "tagged" as historical reportage. What was supposedly "accepted at the time" was the unpredictable alteration of fact. *Where* facts have been altered must be a matter of guesswork, and this would have been so for the original audience as well. If these invisible fictionalizations really were accepted at the time and incorporated into the Gospels, if partial fictionalization were part and parcel of their genre, anyone who wants to know what happened with any great degree of historical confidence needs better primary source documents than these. But the canonical Gospels *are* our best shot at primary source documents for the life of Jesus.

The literary device theories are empirically wrong for the many reasons given in Part Two of this book: Several of the Gospel authors plausibly were not exposed to Greco-Roman literature at all, and the theorists have not countered this *prima facie* case with any good evidence that they were knowledgeable about such literature and educated in its conventions. Moreover, the fictionalizing devices labeled and defined, such as dyschronological displacement, compression, and fictionalizing transferral, are not well established even in Greco-Roman works. Both the claims about exercise textbooks and the supposed inductive case from Greco-Roman biographers and historians fail to establish their existence. The fabrication of set-piece speeches in some ancient works does not imply fabrication of short sayings or other events, even in those works. And such speech invention itself was accepted by some historians and rejected by others. Nor do such rhetorically showy, composed speeches resemble what we find in the Gospels. Moreover, Michael Licona, the theorist arguing at the greatest length that specific compositional devices were accepted at the time, repeatedly conjectures fictionalization in the Gospels even when, by his own account, no device more specific than "crafting" or "artistry" is in question. But that sort of vague "device" label could be applied anywhere; it does not permit any objective control upon free-ranging conjecture.

The refutation of the literary device views is not bad news. It is good news. The failure of a false promise of deliverance returns us to the reportage model that was on the table at the beginning. It returns us to asking what the prospects are for that model. And as it turns out, the prospects are excellent, as discussed in Part Three. Multiple lines of evidence, including undesigned coincidences, external confirmations, and the lesser-known arguments from unexplained allusions, unnecessary details, reconcilable variation, and unique personalities show us the historical intention of the authors as well as their success in getting the facts right. External confirmations also support these conclusions. This is the *real* good news. It opens up a wide field for the study and assimilation of a wealth of confirmatory information. There is not only a *prima facie* case that the Gospel authors intended to report what really happened. There is a hefty empirical case that the Gospels are mirrors of Jesus rather than literary masks.

When we examine alleged problems in the Gospels as in Part Four, we should have four things in mind: One is the refutation of the literary device claims concerning genre and the ancient milieu. This erases an artificial expectation that the Gospel authors would have deliberately changed the facts. The second is the positive, evidentially based confidence that the Gospels are historical reportage. The third is a clear understanding of the complexity of literary device claims concerning particular passages and the burden of proof this creates. The fourth is a recognition that harmonization among documents is part of good historical practice. It is not a desperate, religiously motivated activity.

With these tools in hand, it is exciting to see how well harmonization works for passages that are allegedly in conflict. It is simultaneously disturbing (concerning the theories) and reassuring (concerning the Gospels) to see how often scholars conjecture fictionalization on the flimsiest grounds—utterly unforced errors. Sometimes the claims of literary devices in the Gospels are based on the same dubious methodology used for secular literature—discrepancy-hunting followed by the hasty claim of a device, without consideration of more common sources of variation. By contrast, the reportage view fares very well inductively in the Gospels. The documents provide complementary information and are virtually always harmonizable. Their differences are readily attributable to the possession of different evidence and knowledge rather than to an elaborate intention to write what the author knows to be his own invention. This is also good news.

I do not have a crystal ball and can only guess how literary device theories will fare in the future among Christian scholars, laymen, and the apologists who bridge the gap between them. We see already that the labels vary. Sometimes a scholar tells us that the devices come from Greco-Roman literature and gives them names like "displacement" and "transferral." Sometimes the claim is that students were taught *chreia* elaboration; hence, a license to alter facts is traced broadly to the alleged pedagogy of the Greek world.[5] But sometimes, scholars

---

[5] See especially Chapters V, VIII, and IX. The whole of Part Two documents and responds to these claims.

give alleged devices Jewish names such as "midrash"[6] or "wisdom literature."[7] The sheer variety of terms and the breadth and arbitrariness of their application suggest that such labeling is more subjective than not. Two factors that remain constant are the claim that the Gospel authors thought of themselves as licensed to invent and the attempt to place that claim within a cultural context by giving invention a technical-sounding name. The theorist often then takes the claim, using his chosen name, and matches it to a case where mainstream New Testament scholars have *already* questioned a passage's historicity. In other words, he pastes his preferred terminology over existing mainstream rejection of reportage in the Gospels. I predict that this will continue to be the case, even if new terms become popular in the future.

There is simply no good evidence that the evangelists thought of themselves as licensed to invent, and there is a wealth of evidence to the contrary. This evidence, too, will remain to be accounted for, even if some new specific fictionalization theory arises. This is a wonderful conclusion, because it returns us to the fruitful, constructive reportage approach advocated by older scholars and abandoned only because it fell out of fashion, not because it was refuted. We can once more investigate and make known the positive evidence for the factual reliability of the Gospels. We need not and should not qualify and confuse this message by saying that the authors sometimes considered themselves licensed to change the facts. In this way both Christian laymen and scholars can hold a forward position without apology.

We cannot resolve a crisis of confidence in the Gospels by throwing up our hands and deciding that the evangelists were making deliberate factual changes. Such a conclusion only further undermines confidence in the documents' truth, and it is not supported by the evidence. Instead, we should recognize both how normal variations are in truthful witness testimony and how deep is the well of positive evidence that the evangelists were reliable reporters.

---

[6] See Chapter XI, section 6, on the use of "midrash" for both Luke's and Matthew's infancy stories in a speculation made by Michael Licona. As mentioned there, the idea that Matthew is "midrash," meaning that it embodies the "spirit of free adaptation and embellishment," was previously suggested by Robert Gundry. Robert H. Gundry, *Matthew: A Commentary on His Literary and Theological Art* (Grand Rapids, MI: Eerdmans, 1982), 634ff. Gundry, "A Response to Matthew and Midrash," *JETS* 26 (1983), pp. 50, 54–55. Gundry did not extend the idea to Luke's Gospel.

[7] Craig A. Evans says that Jesus sounds like Lady Wisdom in the Gospel of John, that John itself is rightly compared to "wisdom literature," and that this calls into question the literal historicity of various "I am" sayings. Craig A. Evans vs. Bart Ehrman, "Does the New Testament Present a Historically Reliable Portrait of the Historical Jesus?" Saint Mary's University, January 19, 2012, minute 1:34:00, https://youtu.be/ueRIdrlZsvs?t=1h33m58s.

With this knowledge, Christians can look once more into the Gospels and see mirrored there the person and teachings of our Lord and Savior Jesus Christ. Then we can proclaim him to the world.

More Points about Theon

Chapter VIII contains an extensive discussion of the exercises of Theon and the ways in which scholars have misunderstood both the concept of *chreiai* and the exercises. This appendix contains a few brief additional points concerning misapplications of Theon.

1. "Narrative is language descriptive of things … as though they had happened"

In his discussion of Theon's *Progymnasmata*, Michael Licona quotes the following definition of "narrative":

> Narrative (*diegema*) is language descriptive of things that happened or as though they had happened.[1]

He then immediately, rather surprisingly, goes on to talk about the construction of speeches, which is not relevant to narrative, as I pointed out in Chapter VII, sections 1 and 3. Moreover, Theon does not actually endorse the invention of speeches in historical work, though as we have seen, some authors did do this. In discussing speech composition, Theon repeatedly talks about writing that is openly fictional or hypothetical. The idea is simply to practice writing speeches.[2] Whether Theon would or would not have endorsed inventing rhetorical speeches in historical work is simply impossible to know from his exercises. Again, he

---

[1] Aelius Theon, "The Exercises of Aelius Theon," in *Progymnasmata: Greek Textbooks of Prose Composition and Rhetoric*, trans. by George Kennedy (Atlanta: Society of Biblical Literature, 2003), p. 28. Cited in Michael Licona, *Why Are There Differences in the Gospels? What We Can Learn From Ancient Biography* (Oxford: Oxford University Press, 2017), p. 11.

[2] See, for example, Theon, *Progymnasmata*, pp. 84–85. Theon gives as examples of speech writing composing something that Andromache might say to Hector or something that Achilles might say to his beloved when going off to war. These obviously would not be speeches in an historical work.

doesn't address the question. In fact, there were ancient professional speechwriters (as there are now), so speech writing even in professional work need not have been a matter of fictionalizing history. In any event, Theon does not intertwine speech writing with his definition of *narrative*, so Licona's sudden allusion to inventing speeches is out of place.

So how does this definition of "narrative" support altering facts in history? Licona does think (as discussed in Chapter VIII) that Theon advocates altering historical facts in realistic historical writing. How does this definition contribute to that perception? Licona does not gloss Theon's definition of narrative in detail, so he does not say precisely what part of it he thinks supports his conclusions. Perhaps Theon is supposed to be advocating fictionalizing history by the phrase "as though they had happened." This, however, would be a misunderstanding of the definition.

Theon's broad definition of "narrative" merely makes it clear that narrative includes both real and imaginary stories. In the same section Theon uses Homer's *Iliad* and *Odyssey* as good rhetorical examples of narrative insofar as they narrate briefly what will distress the hearer and describe at more length what the hearer will find pleasant.[3] In other words, all that Theon means by "things...as though they had happened" is that narrative is a broad form of writing that includes fiction. Obviously, fiction involves narrating a story. This is, again, not historiographical advice or a statement about whether or not a writer of a biography or apparently historical work is licensed to alter the facts. It is merely a garden-variety definition of "narrative."

2. "Doing something more than making a factual statement"

Licona also cites an exercise in which Theon says that one may vary a narrative by "doing something more than making a factual statement":

> Sometimes as making a straightforward statement and sometimes as doing something more than making a factual statement, and sometimes in the form of questions, and sometimes as things we seek to learn about, and sometimes as things about which we are in doubt, and sometimes as making a command, sometimes expressing a wish, and sometimes swearing to something, sometimes addressing the participants, sometimes advancing suppositions, sometimes using dialogue.[4]

In Chapter VIII, sections 8 and 9, we have already discussed the misunderstanding of exercises that involve making a command and writing dialogue. Here I

---

[3] Ibid., p. 29.

[4] Licona, *Why Are There Differences*, pp. 11–12, citing Theon, *Progymnasmata*, p. 35.

want to discuss briefly the phrase "doing something more than making a factual statement." This might be taken mistakenly to mean that Theon is advocating altering facts in historical writing. But not only does he not address that question, the example he gives does no such thing.

Theon gives as an example of "doing something more than making a factual statement" an exercise where one merely suggests the slightly broader historical *implications* of an event. Theon is discussing an exercise example in which one uses a bit of Thucydides as a narrative prompt. The prompt has to do with an incident in which a force of Thebans entered a town allied with the Athenians and tried to take it. Theon says,

> If we want to suggest something more than a simple statement of facts, we shall speak as follows: "The arrival at Plataea of the Thebans was, it seems, the cause of great troubles for Athenians and Lacedaimonians and the allies on each side; for a force of Thebans a little over three hundred in number made an armed entry during the first watch into Plataea in Boeotia."[5]

Theon does not say that one adds without historical warrant the claim that the arrival of the Thebans was a cause of great trouble. Presumably the attack on Plataea would be enough in itself to justify the claim that the arrival of the Thebans was a cause of trouble. This is in any event only a writing exercise. Any real historical author could certainly have reason for the generalization. Theon suggests adding a generalization to a bare narrative of the attempted takeover of Plataea. He is merely illustrating how one might write in a more interesting way by including statements about the larger causes and effects of the action. That's all.

3. Inserting sayings into narrative

Craig Keener has repeatedly implied that ancient writers felt free, in allegedly historical writing, to insert someone's sayings into narratives even if they did not know when the saying was originally uttered. This would make it look like a saying was uttered at a particular time and in a particular context, even though the author had no historical warrant for thinking that it was. While his statements to this effect are brief and somewhat cryptic, they are worth noting and answering, since his citations in Theon do not support this conclusion.

In his commentary on Matthew, Keener discusses the fact that sayings and narrative were not mutually exclusive in ancient writing. For example, he says

---

[5] Theon, *Progymnasmata*, p. 36.

that Q may have contained some narrative rather than being purely a sayings document. In the course of making this point, he says, "Ancient writers regularly reported sayings and narrative separately or combined them at will: although teachers of rhetoric formally distinguished sayings *chreiai* and action *chreiai*, they also formally recognized mixed *chreiai*, which included both."[6] It is the phrase "at will" that gives an apparent implication that the combination—the placement of a saying in a story—did not have to be historically supported. But the portion of Theon he cites at this point merely says that a *chreia* (short, pithy anecdote) may include either just a saying or also some situation that prompted the saying.[7]

Keener makes this implication somewhat more clearly a few sentences later:

> Outside of sayings collections, sayings were regularly transmitted apart from one another....Ancient readers considered inserting sayings from sayings collections into narratives, or from narratives into sayings, a matter of arrangement, not of fabrication.[8]

Why *would* one think that such an insertion was a fabrication? Presumably a modern person would think this if the insertion lacked historical support and was merely placed "at will" by the author. Keener says something similar and clearer elsewhere:

> Sayings could also circulate independently...however, being combined with narratives simply to provide a literary or rhetorical location.[9]

The relevant phrase is "simply to provide a literary or rhetorical location." The suggestion in these passages is that authors considered themselves licensed to take a mix-and-match approach to sayings and narrative. So presumably the Gospel authors would have felt free, because of the standards of the time, to make it look like Jesus said something in response to a particular situation when they had no reason to think that he did so, merely placing the saying there "to provide a literary or rhetorical location." For both of these last two claims, Keener cites two passages in Theon's *Progymnasmata*.

---

[6] Craig S. Keener, *The Gospel of Matthew: A Socio-Rhetorical Commentary* (Grand Rapids, MI: Eerdmans, 2009), p. 34.

[7] Theon, *Progymnasmata*, p. 16.

[8] Keener, *The Gospel of Matthew*, pp. 35–36.

[9] Craig Keener, "Appendix: Before Biographies: Memory and Oral Tradition," in Craig S. Keener and Edward T. Wright, eds., *Biographies and Jesus: What Does it Mean for the Gospels to be Biographies?* (Lexington, KY: Emeth Press, 2016), p. 350.

The first section cited in Theon is literally titled "On Fable." The prospects are dim for finding insight on historiographical standards from a section on fable. Theon is not talking about historical narrative here at all:

> It is possible to provide a conclusion whenever, after the fable has been stated, we venture to bring in some gnomic statement fitting it. For example, "a dog was carrying a piece of meat beside a river, and having seen his reflection in the water he thought it was another dog carrying a larger piece of meat. When he dropped what he had and jumped into the river to seize it, he disappeared under the water." We shall add the following comment: "You should note that often those hankering for greater things destroy themselves as well as losing what they have."[10]

Theon is merely talking about adding a moral to a fable. That is all. This has nothing to do with whether or not ancient readers thought it merely a matter of arrangement for an author of a biography to place an historical character's saying into a context without historical warrant.

The second section in Theon that Keener cites also does not recommend this. In fact, ironically, Theon begins the section on inserting a saying into narrative by expressly saying "Such a thing is not appropriate in historical writing…"

> To add a maxim to each part of the narration is called *epiphōnein*. Such a thing is not appropriate in historical writing or in a political speech but belongs rather to the theater and the stage ….The unnecessary last sentence [in a poet he has quoted] only seeks applause in the theater. Of course, when it is smoothly mixed in and these gnomic statements escape notice, the narration does somehow become charming, as in the first book of Herodotus. There he is speaking about human life, saying how it is not steadfast but has many changes in its course; then, counting the number of days in human life as those in seventy years, he adds: "Of all these days one never brings anything alike to another." Then (Solon) moralizes in this way… "Thus, Croesus, man is wholly accident." Or as Gyges says to Candaules: "Master, what you have said is not sound. Would you order my mistress to be seen naked? A woman puts off her modesty with her clothes." And admittedly there are examples to be found in the orators, not least in the most "political," Demosthenes, and in the most political of his speeches. In the Second Olynthiac, talking about Philip, he says he has around him "mimickers of laughter and poets of shameful songs," and those whom the city of Athens expelled as being too licentious, and that Philip's real nature escapes the notice of everyone because of his success in war. After that, he adds the moral: "Remarkable successes hide and overshadow such shameful doings."[11]

---

[10] Theon, *Progymnasmata*, p. 26.

[11] Ibid., pp. 38–39.

But here, as always, Theon means that the insertion of a maxim into narrative is not usually *rhetorically* appropriate. Theon's focus is on rhetoric. Even when he mostly condemns such insertion, he does so for rhetorical reasons and is not addressing propriety in terms of historiographical standards, one way or another. That is not his topic. He relates the insertion of sayings to the theater, stating that one does such a thing for applause. He then admits slightly grudgingly that inserting a saying into a narrative can be "charming" as in Herodotus and gives an instance in which Herodotus moralizes his history with a maxim when he is "speaking of human life." But this saying is in the voice of the narrator. In other words, the saying is just Herodotus' own moralizing, not an historical claim by Herodotus about what someone else said. Theon does list two such maxims that Herodotus gives in the voices of other people. But Theon speaks merely of the charm of such a usage. He makes no pronouncement on the historicity of the sayings; he does not discuss whether or not he thinks Herodotus had reason to believe that these people uttered these sayings. He is not recommending anything in particular concerning making historical figures speak in an invented context. That is simply not Theon's point. Making his discussion even more mixed, Theon moves immediately to Demosthenes' use of a maxim in political oratory condemning Philip, which obviously has *nothing* to do with historiographic standards.

In all of these cases, the attempt to use Theon as a source of historiographical standards involves misunderstanding and misapplying his work.

More Examples from Greco-Roman Historians

Chapter IX contains detailed discussion of six places where some scholars claim that Greco-Roman authors used culturally accepted, fact-changing literary devices. I rebut two more claims to that effect briefly in footnote 37 of that chapter. For readers who are interested in more evidence against the alleged inductive case for the existence of accepted literary devices in Greco-Roman historical writing, I include four more detailed analyses of such claims in this appendix. Here, too, we will see the method of discrepancy hunting or even just noting differences, followed by the hasty invocation of a literary device.

Here I suggest that the reader refer back to the flowchart in Chapter IX, section 2. See p. 180. We will see once again how failure to consider simpler options causes scholars to conclude without justification that ancient authors are using special literary devices.

1. Did Tacitus change the date of Piso's trial?

Some background will be necessary for understanding this example, which is one reason why I have placed it in an appendix. Gnaeus Calpurnius Piso was a Roman statesman during the time of the Emperor Tiberius. While he was Governor of Syria (A.D. 17–19), he clashed seriously with Germanicus, Tiberius' adopted son (really his nephew) and designated heir, who was governing the province along with Piso. Germanicus became seriously ill and, before he died, accused Piso of poisoning him, though Piso was not physically present at the time of his death. The public perception that Piso had murdered Germanicus was so strong that Tiberius, though somewhat reluctant, ordered the Roman senate to hold a trial for Piso. Piso's trial covered many other allegations of malfeasance against him, but the belief that he had murdered Germanicus was the obvious catalyst. In the midst of the trial, after it had become obvious that the senate was going to find Piso guilty of serious crimes, Piso apparently cut his own throat. Rumors insinuated that Tiberius had instigated the murder of Germanicus, who was becoming insubordinate, and had ordered Piso to be murdered (making it look like suicide) to prevent him from implicating Tiberius at the trial.

Nearly a hundred years after these events, the Roman historian Tacitus wrote about them at some length in his *Annals*. There he reported, though he did not explicitly endorse, the rumors that Tiberius was behind the death of Germanicus and Piso. While Tacitus gives no explicit date for the trial (such dates nearly always have to be inferred indirectly in these works), the inference that his narrative places it some time in the spring of A.D. 20 is fairly firm. The indirect inference goes like this: In the midst of narrating the death of Germanicus and the trial of Piso, Tacitus reports that Drusus, Tiberius' natural son, had been offered an ovation by the Roman Senate for his service. An ovation was a special kind of honor in which the person would process through the streets of Rome. An ovation was similar to a triumph but less imposing. According to Tacitus, Drusus delayed accepting his ovation after the death of Germanicus, his brother by adoption.[1] The impression one gets from Tacitus (though not explicitly stated) is that it was the trial of Piso that caused Drusus to delay the ovation. He needed to enter Rome to be present at the trial; presumably he wanted to enjoy the ovation after the trial was over. Tacitus then reports, in a way that does seem to suggest chronological order, that Drusus had his ovation shortly after the conclusion of the trial.[2] (I will be quoting some of these passages from Tacitus below.) Drusus' ovation can be independently dated to May 28, A.D. 20, by way of the Roman Fasti, an official record of festivals.[3] Hence, though indirect, the argument that Tacitus appears to place Piso's trial and death no later than May 28 is fairly solid.

The question that has been raised is whether or not Tacitus changed the timing of Piso's trial. The claim is that it really took place in November or early December of A.D. 20 but that Tacitus in his narrative implicitly moves it backward in time to approximately May of that same year. This would be dyschronological displacement, though scholars who believe Tacitus did this assign no clear motive for it.

---

[1] Tacitus, *Annals*, 3.11.

[2] Ibid., 3.19.

[3] C. S. Kraus and A. J. Woodman, *Latin Historians* (Cambridge, UK: Cambridge University Press for the Classical Association, 1997), pp. 100–102.

In the 1990s, an inscription turned up in Spain that some scholars took to mean that the trial of Piso happened in November or early December of A.D. 20. In 1999, Roman historian Ronald Mellor endorsed the idea that Tacitus changed the date of the trial, and he generalized about how Tacitus would have viewed such a change:

> In modern times, writers and politicians often deceive through statistics—"Lies, damn lies, and statistics!"—while the ancient writer used instead his rhetorical training. In some instances it is a case of different priorities. A recently discovered bronze text sheds some light on this. This senatorial decree, set up around the Empire to announce the suicide and condemnation of Piso in 20 CE, shows several things about Tacitus' narrative. One is that the decree was intended to squelch precisely the rumors—that Piso might have been murdered—that Tacitus includes by innuendo. That is fair enough; the publication of official edicts rarely stops rumors. A more serious point is that Tacitus seems to have moved the trial from December to the previous spring. If that reconstruction is correct, he presumably did it for the sake of a better narrative. He would regard the precise date of an event as of no great importance to an historian who seeks to convey moral truth through a persuasive narrative.[4]

Several things are noteworthy about what Mellor says here. The first thing that springs to the eye is his use of the words "deceive" and "lies." He seems to be quite explicitly saying that Roman historians sometimes lied, deliberately using their rhetorical training to give a false impression in much the same way that a politician might deliberately use statistics to give a false impression. This, of course, is quite different from the insistence of literary device theorists that an author who uses a compositional device is *not* lying or deceiving, since his audience knew to take his factual claims lightly.[5] Mellor seems to be indicating that Tacitus thought that it was permissible for him to deceive in the service of some higher end, and hence that perhaps Tacitus and his fellow ancient writers would have considered deception acceptable among members of their own class. In other words, the pic-

---

[4] Ronald Mellor, *The Roman Historians* (London: Routledge, 1999), p. 93.

[5] See, for example, Michael Licona's statements that Plutarch "does not bend to mislead," "does not engage in lying," and "does not engage in deliberate falsehood," even though he "felt free to invent an occasional scene" and to "bend the facts." *Why Are There Differences in the Gospels? What We Can Learn from Ancient Biography* (Oxford: Oxford University Press, 2017), pp. 17–18. See also William Lane Craig's statement that it would not be an error for John to move the Temple cleansing dyschronologically, because it allegedly "would be permitted by ancient standards of historiography." "An Objection to the Minimal Facts Argument," May 6, 2018, https://www.reasonablefaith.org/media/reasonable-faith-podcast/an-objection-to-the-minimal-facts-argument/.

ture may be of an elite class of intellectual authors who believe that they have a right to mislead the public for the public's own good. But that is not the same thing as saying that such behavior was *not deception* because it was a device accepted by the audience, understood as part of the terms of interaction between audience and the author. Christian literary device theorists would object in the strongest possible terms if one insinuated that they are portraying the evangelists as deceiving the public.

Second, one notices that Mellor does not explain what "moral truth through a persuasive narrative" Tacitus hoped to convey by moving the date of the trial. Nor does the rest of the context supply any further information on what Mellor thinks that "moral truth" might be. Mellor merely makes the high-toned comment about moral truth and moves on, giving no clearer idea of Tacitus' alleged motive for changing the trial date.

Third, one should note Mellor's slightly cautious qualifier, "If that reconstruction is correct...," which will prove important later on.

Michael Licona accepts the claim that Tacitus changed the date of Piso's trial, quoting a portion of this section from Mellor (though not the sentences about lying and deception). He then continues:

> Like Sallust, Tacitus is regarded as one of Rome's finest historians. Thus, Plutarch's use of synthetic chronological placement was not sloppy writing. Rather, it seems that synthetic chronological placement was a compositional device in both biographical and historical writing and was employed by those held to be among the finest historians and biographers of that era.[6]

Licona overlooks the difficulty caused by Mellor's statements about lying and deception, since compositional devices are supposed to remove the charge of deception from the author. Licona regards this not as a case of ordinary deception or propaganda but as a "compositional device" which he calls "synthetic chronological placement"—i.e., dyschronological narration. Of course, Licona is in full agreement with Mellor's 1999 claim that Tacitus moved the date of the trial.

How does that claim stack up to the evidence? As it happens, very poorly. To begin with, the temporal location of the trial in Tacitus is so indirect that it is impossible to discern any moral or literary point whatsoever in moving the trial chronologically. Tacitus says nothing significant about the time of year. He makes no point of the time of year at all.

---

[6] Licona, *Why Are There Differences*, p. 189.

Tacitus's description of the trial is very long, and I do not wish to quote much of it here and bore the reader, but I will quote the portions that include references to Drusus' ovation. These allow modern historians to figure out where the trial is dated in the *Annals*. Here is the first mention of the ovation, just before the narrative of the trial:

> The difficulties of the inquiry, and the rumours busy with his own character, were not lost upon Tiberius. Therefore with a few intimate friends for assessor, he heard the threats of the accusers, the prayers of the accused; and remitted the case in its integrity to the senate.
>
> In the interval, Drusus returned from Illyricum. The Fathers had decreed him an ovation at his entry, in return for the submission of Maroboduus and his achievements of the preceding summer; but he postponed the honour and made his way into the capital privately.
>
> As his advocates the defendant now specified Lucius Arruntius, Publius Vinicius, Asinius Gallus, Marcellus Aeserninus and Sextus Pompeius. They declined on various pretexts, and Manius Lepidus, Lucius Piso, and Livineius Regulus came to his support. The whole nation was eagerly speculating upon the loyalty of Germanicus' friends, the criminal's grounds for confidence, the chances that Tiberius would be able to keep his sentiments effectively under lock and key. Never had the populace been more keenly on the alert: never had it shown more freedom of whispered criticism and suspicious silence towards the emperor.[7]

The mention of Drusus' decision to postpone the honor of an ovation, useful for dating, comes up entirely in passing. Here is the mention of the ovation itself after Piso's apparent suicide:

> This closed the punitive measures demanded by Germanicus' death: an affair which, not only to the generation which witnessed it, but in the succeeding years, was a battle-ground of opposing rumours. So true it is that the great event is an obscure event: one school admits all hearsay evidence, whatever its character, as indisputable; another perverts the truth into its contrary; and, in each case, posterity magnifies the error.
>
> Drusus, who had left the capital, in order to regularize his command, entered it shortly afterwards with an ovation. A few days later, his mother Vipsania died—the only one of all Agrippa's children whose end was peace. The rest perished, part, it is known, by the sword, part, it was believed, by poison or starvation.[8]

---

[7] Tacitus, *Annals*, 3.10–11, Trans. John Jackson (1931), http://penelope.uchicago.edu/Thayer/E/Roman/Texts/Tacitus/Annals/3A*.html.

[8] Ibid., 3.19. The editor of the *Annals* notes at this point (footnote 46) that the phrase "in order to

The mention of Drusus' ovation here leads Tacitus into the mention of his mother's death. There is no indication that Tacitus intends to do anything, either rhetorically or thematically, with the *date of Piso's trial itself.* Germanicus' death was plausibly not any great grief to Drusus, especially since Germanicus was ahead of Drusus in the succession for the crown despite being only an adopted son. Tacitus indicates at one point that Piso expected Drusus to welcome Germanicus' death. He strongly implies that Drusus was in fact not grieved by the death of Germanicus, though he made a public statement (which Tacitus says was probably dictated by Tiberius himself) that he would be very angry with Piso if he had indeed poisoned Germanicus.[9] But none of this creates any sort of moral out of the dating of the trial. Tacitus' narration of Drusus' ovation, which indirectly dates the trial, comes up in a natural and apparently chronological manner as Tacitus returns to telling about what happened to Drusus. He does not make any connection between it and his own brief aside on the nature of rumor. Whether or not Drusus was upset by the death of Germanicus or by the trial and death of Piso, he would be expected to accept his ovation eventually, though understandably (either way) not before the trial. His postponing it during the trial of his adopted brother's alleged killer and his accepting it afterwards tell us nothing one way or another about his real feelings.

If Tacitus really believed that Piso's trial occurred six months after Drusus' ovation, he concealed it well. If he invented the postponement of the ovation out of whole cloth, he did so for a literary motive so obscure that even those who claim that he did so are apparently unable to tell us what it was.

This brings us to the question of the inscription and its alleged implication that the trial really happened in November or December. What is the argument there? Why doubt Tacitus at all? Historians previously took Tacitus at face value and dated the trial, by indirect inference from his narrative, to the spring.[10] As it turns out, the argument from the inscription is quite thin, for the simple reason that the inscription in question *does not date the trial at all.* It does not even make indirect statements (as Tacitus does) that can be used to *infer* a month for Piso's trial. Rather, the argument is merely that the inscription records a decree of the Senate concerning the Piso affair, and the *decree* is dated December 10. This is

---

regularize his command" refers to the fact that, since Drusus had entered Rome privately in order to attend the trial, he had to reassume command of his troops in an official manner as a requirement for receiving his ovation.

[9] Ibid., 3.8.

[10] Mellor indicates that historians previously accepted the spring date from Tacitus. *The Roman Historians*, p. 93.

supposed to produce a discrepancy between the inscription and Tacitus. Why? Some historians thought that the senatorial decree about the entire affair must have been made very *shortly* after the events themselves and that therefore the trial and death of Piso must have occurred in the fall or winter, many months later than the time of year at which Tacitus indirectly dates it.[11]

But this is quite a weak argument. Tacitus notes the continuation of rumors concerning Tiberius, and Mellor himself notes that one of the purposes of the decree (which asserts Piso's guilt and Tiberius' honorable behavior) was to squelch such rumors. Six months is not very long. There is nothing incredible about the idea that the senate took some time to realize that the rumors were not dying down and to decide upon the wording of an appropriate political declaration. In our own day, congressional commissions can take much longer than six months to issue their reports.

If we are going to make such judgements at all concerning what should be closer to what, we may as well note that historians date the death of Germanicus to October of A.D. 19.[12] A gap of six months between Piso's trial and a senatorial decree about the whole affair is no more implausible on the face of it than a gap of *more than a year* between an alleged poisoning and the trial of the supposed murderer.

These sorts of considerations appear to have appealed eventually to none other than Ronald Mellor himself. For in 2010 he published an edition of Tacitus' *Annals* in which he accounted for the inscription in a manner quite different from his 1999 statement:

> The inscription makes clear that Tiberius had referred the case of Piso, his wife, and his son to the Senate, and it records the decree the Senate issued on December 10, 20 C.E. Since Germanicus died on October 10, 19 C.E., and the trial of Piso took place in May of 20 C.E., it seems likely that it was the public celebration of the anniversary of Germanicus' death in October of 20 C.E. that once again aroused popular discontent and compelled the government to make a public statement.[13]

Here Mellor directly contradicts his own statement more than ten years earlier that Tacitus moved the trial. Instead, he accepts Tacitus' implicit dating of the

---

[11] C. S. Kraus and A. J. Woodman explain the reasoning concerning the senatorial decree. They call it a "natural inference" from the December date of the decree that the trial occurred shortly before. They give very little additional argument except to say that, if the trial and death of Piso occurred in the spring, there would have had to be some reason for the meeting and decree of the Senate later in the year. *Latin Historians*, pp. 100–102.

[12] Ronald Mellor, *Tacitus' Annals* (Oxford: Oxford University Press, 2010), pp. 35–36.

[13] Ibid.

trial and conjectures that the senate may have decided to issue the decree shortly after the one-year anniversary of Germanicus' death. There is no mention anymore of Tacitus' need to teach a "moral truth" by moving the date of the trial. Nor does Mellor acknowledge that he once took a different view. But it seems that he simply reflected further and changed his mind about whether or not Tacitus deceptively dated the trial.

This instance is instructive in several ways. First, it is yet another example of how thin the case is that an author has deliberately changed the facts *at all*. Even if Tacitus had been wrong, it still would have been possible that he simply had a source that confused him. But in fact, there is no reason to doubt his account of the trial. The historians were jumping to conclusions. The dating of the senate decree in December is not a good reason to think that the trial occurred later than May. The trial could easily have occurred six months before the senate decree about the whole affair. Second, it illustrates the unfortunate sloppiness of historians who declare a moral motive for altering facts without even bothering to explain how this motive is supposed to work. Apparently, it sounded good to Mellor in 1999 to say that an ancient writer would have thought a date of no great importance in comparison to moral truth, despite the fact that he had no moral truth to suggest in this instance. Perhaps these sorts of considerations influenced Mellor to change his evaluation in 2010. Third, it shows that not every historian who makes such unfortunate statements about ancient writers thinks of this behavior as non-deceptive. Mellor, whom Licona quotes as if he supports his literary device views, actually thought of Tacitus' action as deceptive and likened it to the behavior of politicians who lie with statistics. So one cannot conclude even from an historian's statement that an author changed the facts that the historian agrees with the entire literary device model. He may actually be stopping at a different point in the flowchart and categorizing the ancient author's action as propaganda. As noted in the case of Josephus in Chapter IX, section 8, such a claim is hardly helpful to an analysis of the Gospels unless the theorist wishes to say that the Gospel authors were deceivers.

2. Plutarch, Coriolanus, and Luke

In a contribution to an anthology of essays by Christian scholars on ancient biographies and Gospel historicity, Youngju Kwon speculates that the Gospels' infancy stories and Luke's story of the boy Jesus in the Temple may be largely or wholly invented. He supports this startling suggestion by a conjecture that

Plutarch invented an incident in the childhood of the general Coriolanus, who lived more than five hundred years before Plutarch.

Says Kwon,

> [D. A.] Russell investigates Plutarch's adaptation of his main source (Dionysius of Halicarnassus's *Roman Antiquities*) in writing the *Marcius Coriolanus*. Russell argues that the ways Plutarch adapted his main source reveal the author's compositional techniques. One of the recurring compositional techniques, Russell claims, is the expansion or elaboration of the material based on what it "must have been like." To give one example among many, in *Marcius Coriolanus* 2.2, Plutarch narrates an episode of rivals' ill-intentioned claim that Marcius's success is not due to his courage or skill but simply because of his physical excellence. It is interesting to note that there is no trace of this episode in Dionysius. In other words, according to Russell, this episode must be a "speculative embellishment…based on the story of Marcius's untiring exploits at Corioli and against Antium." Such a judgment seems to be correct because the two motifs in this episode ("freedom of fatigue" and "the jealous rivals") come up again in the later episodes of the same work.[14]

Here is Kwon's conclusion, based on Russell's theories about Plutarch:

> This statement invites us to explore the possibility that Matthew and Luke felt the freedom to add extended accounts of Jesus's early life due to the conventions of ancient biography. Given that ancient biographers commonly use the accounts of a hero's birth and youth as a means of revealing his or her character, it is a reasonable inference that Matthew and Luke, the more literary-conscious evangelists, decided to add the accounts of Jesus' early life in their writings.[15]

These speculations about Luke and Matthew, so far from being a "reasonable inference," would be wildly out of proportion to the evidence even if it were true that Plutarch invented an incident about Coriolanus's boyhood. But the evidence that Plutarch invented at that point without an historical source is scanty in itself. Kwon accepts Russell's conclusions about Plutarch uncritically, despite the fact that Russell's argument as he summarizes it looks on its face like the purest argument from silence, a suspicion borne out in spades when one turns to Russell himself. In fact, Russell does not *argue* that Plutarch invented all the material about

---

[14] Youngju Kwon, "Charting the (Un)charted: Gospels as Ancient Biographies and Their (Un)explored Implications," in Craig S. Keener and Edward T. Wright, eds., *Biographies and Jesus: What Does it Mean for the Gospels to be Biographies?* (Lexington, KY: Emeth Press, 2016), pp. 73–74.

[15] Ibid., p. 74.

Coriolanus that he did not find in Dionysius. He *assumes* it as a methodological given in his very first paragraph:

> I start from the hypothesis that the *Life* is, in its essentials, a transposition into biographical form of the historical narrative in Dionysius of Halicarnassus, *Roman Antiquities*...This has long been the common view....A careful reading of the two texts side by side tempts me to call it certain, so exact and frequent are the echoes. It is at any rate probable enough to justify an attempt to follow out its consequences by treating the differences between Dionysius and Plutarch, in default of other evidence, as Plutarch's constructions, to be explained in terms of his literary purposes and methods. This is what I shall do in the main part of this paper.[16]

So Russell moves from what he considers to be striking verbal parallels between Plutarch's *Life of Coriolanus* and Dionysius to the extremely strong assumption that Dionysius was Plutarch's *only* historical source and that *every incident* found in Plutarch but not in Dionysius can be assumed henceforth to be Plutarch's literary invention. This is an argument from silence so extreme as to be almost breathtaking. Making the methodological blunder even worse, Russell admits two sentences later that there is inductive evidence against the assumption:

> It was certainly rare for [Plutarch] to base a whole *Life* on one authority: indeed, we have no certain knowledge that he ever did it again.[17]

In that case, perhaps we should be hesitant to think that he did it here. Certainly verbal parallels to a particular source do not mean that it was Plutarch's *only* source. The very fact that, as Kwon notes with some admiration, Russell thinks that he finds "many" examples of Plutarch's invention in the *Life of Coriolanus* presumably means that there are *many places* where Plutarch does *not* appear to be following Dionysius. This suggests that he may have more than one source.

Here is the relevant single sentence in the *Life of Coriolanus*:

> At any rate, those who from time to time contended with him in feats of courage and valour, laid the blame for their inferiority upon his strength of body, which was inflexible and shrank from no hardship.[18]

This scarcely even amounts to an "episode" or story, but beyond that, the mere fact that it is not found in Dionysius' treatment of Coriolanus certainly doesn't mean

---

[16] D. A. Russell, "Plutarch's Life of Coriolanus," *Journal of Roman Studies* 53 (1963), p. 21.

[17] Ibid.

[18] Plutarch, *Life of Coriolanus* 2.2.

that Plutarch had no source for it and made it up. We simply don't know what his other sources might have been. To say that the absence of this mention of youthful jealousy from Dionysius means that it "must have been" Plutarch's unsupported embellishment is a serious *non sequitur*. This example does not even make it past the first question on the flowchart: Do the differences between the accounts create an apparent discrepancy? There is not even an apparent discrepancy between Dionysius' account of Coriolanus' youth and Plutarch's.

The only other argument that Plutarch made up this boyhood envy is the alleged similarity to things that Plutarch says about Coriolanus's adulthood. But what are those? Only that he had great endurance and that people were sometimes jealous of him. When one looks up the references given, one does not find even any very close parallel to the boyhood complaint. For example, one does not find the adult Coriolanus's enemies saying that he did well in war only because his body was strong, as the jealous boys did. One simply finds a reference to his refusal to yield to fatigue as well as many references to the fact that others were jealous of him for his influence and honors. For example, here is one quotation about fatigue:

> Then a fierce battle raged around Marcius, and many were slain in short space of time; but the Romans pressed hard upon their enemies and put them to rout, and as they set out in pursuit of them, they insisted that Marcius, who was weighed down with fatigue and wounds, should retire to the camp. He answered, however, that weariness was not for victors, and took after the flying foe.[19]

Here Plutarch admits that Marcius *was* fatigued but that he refused to give in to it, so this is somewhat different from the statement that he had great bodily strength, though of course it does not contradict that claim. This incident seems to emphasize stoical, military endurance.

Here is one about jealousy:

> The rest of the citizens therefore...envied their more fortunate fellows, and were filled with hostility to Marcius, not being able to endure the reputation and power of the man...[20]

To say that such vague adult parallels to a youthful gripe against Coriolanus mean that the youthful event "seems to be" invented is entirely unconvincing. Obviously, a person whom people envy in adulthood may also have been envied

---

[19] Ibid., 9.6.
[20] Ibid., 13.4. See also 10.4, 15.2, 39.1.

in his youth. An account mentioning both is not *ipso facto* a literary construct, inventing one or the other out of whole cloth for purposes of a motif. One might rather argue that, if Coriolanus really did have the kind of physique and personality that aroused envy in adulthood, perhaps the same was true when he was younger. And for all we know, perhaps Plutarch had a source that mentioned that this was the case.

One may also note that, if Plutarch *did* make such an invention, it does not follow that this was a compositional device of the genre of Greco-Roman biography, accepted by audiences at the time. There are additional nodes of the flowchart to be considered. One might consider, for example, the possibility that Plutarch simply did not care very much about the truth—that he engaged in garden-variety fabrication. As noted concerning Josephus in Chapter IX, section 8, the mere fact that a person writing *in* a genre engages in some behavior does not mean that that behavior is an accepted compositional device *of* the genre. If that were a legitimate inference, then every time a news outlet twists the truth we could conclude that twisting the truth is an accepted compositional device *of* news reportage.

Kwon adds significant, sweeping speculation when he turns to applying these ill-supported conclusions about Plutarch to the Gospels. He accepts Russell's claim that Plutarch believed he "had to expand" the "scanty hints about Marcius's youth" that were available in Dionysius because of the "demands of *bioi*." Here again is what Kwon then says about Luke and Matthew:

> This statement invites us to explore the possibility that Matthew and Luke felt the freedom to add extended accounts of Jesus's early life due to the conventions of ancient biography. Given that ancient biographers commonly use the accounts of a hero's birth and youth as a means of revealing his or her character, it is a reasonable inference that Matthew and Luke, the more literary-conscious evangelists, decided to add the accounts of Jesus' early life in their writings. The fact that the most literary-conscious among the evangelists (Luke) offered the most elaborated accounts of Jesus's birth and youth might strengthen this possibility.[21]

On the contrary, there is no reasonable inference here at all. First of all, to use accounts of a main character's birth and youth as a means of revealing his character is not, in and of itself, to invent those accounts. The similarities or foreshadowings may really be there in the historical facts, in which case the author who knows of them can simply report them truthfully.

---

[21] Kwon, "Charting the (Un)charted," p. 74.

Second, the evidence is scanty that it was a widely accepted part of Greco-Roman biography among ancient authors to make whole incidents up out of whole cloth (see Chapter VI), much less that it was widely accepted by audiences.

Third, there is no good argument that Matthew was even exposed to Greco-Roman biographies (see Chapter V, section 3), so he was probably not "literary-conscious" in that sense.

Fourth, while Luke may have been conversant with Greco-Roman literature, this does not make him "literary-conscious" in any sense that *supports* fictionalization. Indeed, the strong statements here about Luke, including the implication that he was *especially* likely to invent his infancy stories, are surprising in view of the fact that even some literary device theorists consider Luke to be the most historically conscientious of the evangelists. Craig Keener himself, the editor of this anthology, implies as much, using his own view of John as a foil, "John takes significant liberties with the way he reports his events, especially in several symbolic adaptations in the passion narrative, whereas Luke follows, where we can test him ..., the procedures of a good Hellenistic historian ...."[22] If Luke was conscious of Roman history, this seems to have motivated him to emphasize that he *has been* historically careful (see Chapter V, section 3, Chapter VI, section 3). Luke's preface to his Gospel, in which he claims to have taken historical care in investigation, comes before his infancy and childhood stories about Jesus and presumably includes them in its scope (see Chapter X, section 2).

Moreover, Kwon fails to take any account of other major disanalogies between Matthew and Luke and Plutarch's *Coriolanus*. Luke and Matthew are writing about relatively recent past events. They may therefore have had the opportunity to interview people quite close to the events of Jesus' infancy and childhood.[23] This is obviously not the case for Coriolanus, who lived in the 5th century B.C., hundreds of years before Plutarch. Moreover, the sheer quantity of fictionalization

---

[22] Craig Keener, *Acts: An Exegetical Commentary* (Grand Rapids, MI: Baker Academic 2012), vol. 1, p. 793. Compare Daniel B. Wallace's reference to John as the "most theologically sensitive" evangelist and Luke as the "most historically sensitive," with John being expected to change Jesus' words even more than Luke. Daniel B. Wallace, "An Apologia for a Broad Use of *Ipsissima Vox*," unpublished paper presented at the meeting of the Evangelical Theological Society, Danvers, MA, November 18, 1999, p. 5. Needless to say, I do not accept this evaluation of John. I bring up the point merely to show that Kwon is attributing a large amount of fictionalization to Luke and even speaking of Luke as if he is *especially* likely to fictionalize, even though this is not the way that other literary device theorists typically speak of Luke.

[23] See Richard Bauckham, "Luke's Infancy Narrative as Oral History in Scriptural Form," in *The Gospels: History and Christology: The Search of Joseph Ratzinger-Benedict XVI*, ed. Bernardo Estrada, Ermenegildo Manicardi and Armand Puig i Tàrrech (Vatican City: Libreria Editrice Vaticana, 2013) vol. 1, 399–417.

suggested for Luke and Matthew concerning Jesus' infancy is much vaster than the vague, short incident in Plutarch's *Life of Coriolanus*. Most importantly, Luke and Matthew had a strong motivation to be concerned about the true facts of Jesus' infancy, given the messianic and other theological claims involved. Various prophecies, the virgin birth, and Jesus' ancestry are all connected with the infancy stories. Plutarch had no personal stake in the truth of a story about Coriolanus's childhood. Kwon ignores all of this.

Kwon's argument for viewing the infancy and childhood stories about Jesus in Matthew and Luke as non-factual is poor at every step. The argument that Plutarch invented the incident is incredibly thin to begin with, based on untenable methodology, and the subsequent leap to suggest large-scale invention by Luke and Matthew is entirely unjustified. The whole argument is a striking example of where literary device theories go. Once one has decided that the Gospels "are" or "resemble" Greco-Roman biographies, that the Gospel authors were therefore Greco-Roman biographers, and that all Greco-Roman biographers accepted the invention of material, one can extrapolate the reasoning quite widely (as here), without even alleging evidence *against* the historicity of the Gospel narrative.[24] This use of genre encourages utterly unforced errors. If a critic of literary device theories, unacquainted with this essay, had predicted that a literary device theorist would make such a weak and sweeping argument against Matthew's and Luke's infancy and childhood stories, he would have been accused of committing a slippery slope fallacy. Yet Kwon has, in fact, made a major extrapolation to fictionalization on the basis of alleged genre conventions.

3. Did Plutarch transfer a speech to Antony and Cassius?

Christopher Pelling is a classicist who provides many of the alleged examples of Plutarch's factual alteration used by Michael Licona. The following example,

---

[24] Kwon's statement that Luke offers the "most elaborated" accounts of Jesus' infancy and youth hardly counts as an argument against historicity. Without begging the question against the historicity of the accounts in Luke, we cannot assume that they are ahistorically elaborated *at all*. Nor is there any clear metric by which they appear "more elaborated" than Matthew's. Luke has a somewhat larger quantity of material than Matthew, partly because he includes the story of Jesus in the Temple in Chapter 2. But Luke sticks entirely to a Jewish context and to the regions of Galilee and Jerusalem, whereas Matthew includes the Magi from the East, a dialogue between the Magi and Herod the Great, the slaughter of the innocent by Herod's soldiers, and a trip to and from Egypt. Of course I am not arguing at all against Matthew's historicity. I am merely pointing out that the claim that one account appears "more elaborated" than the other is subjective and can be turned in either direction. And in any event, Kwon apparently thinks Matthew's account may well be invented as well, so the comparison is unmotivated within his argument as a whole.

taken directly from Pelling, is another hasty claim of contradiction between two different works by Plutarch. As is often the case, there is not even an apparent discrepancy between the passages, yet Pelling claims that there is a conflict. Having created an artificial discrepancy, Pelling says that Plutarch was engaging in the compositional device of transferral.

Pelling says that, in Plutarch's *Life of Antony*, "Antony and Cassius are given the speech to Caesar's troops before the crossing of the Rubicon." In contrast, in the *Life of Caesar*, "Plutarch says that Caesar incited the troops himself." Pelling calls this "the *transfer* of an item from one character to another," and he speculates about which of the *Lives* "accurately reproduces the source." He concludes that it is probably the *Life of Caesar*.[25]

When one turns to the works of Plutarch, one finds that Pelling is basing this claim upon a highly dubious interpretation of the *Life of Antony* and an inexplicable refusal to engage in the most elementary combination of information. Here is the relevant section of the *Life of Antony*:

These Cato opposed, and Lentulus, in his capacity of consul, drove Antony from the senate. Antony went forth heaping many imprecations upon them, and putting on the dress of a slave, and hiring a car in company with Quintus Cassius, he set out to join Caesar. As soon as they came into Caesar's presence they cried loudly that everything was now at loose ends in Rome, since even tribunes of the people had no freedom of speech, but everyone who raised his voice in behalf of justice was persecuted and ran risk of his life.

Upon this, Caesar took his army and invaded Italy. Therefore Cicero, in his "Philippics," wrote that as Helen was the cause of the Trojan war, so Antony was the cause of the civil war. But this was manifestly false. For Caius Caesar was not a pliable man, nor easily led by anger to act on impulse. Therefore, had he not long ago determined upon his course, he would not thus, on the spur of the moment, have made war upon his country, just because he saw that Antony, meanly clad, with Cassius, on a hired car, had come in flight to him; nay, this merely afforded a cloak and a specious reason for war to a man who had long wanted a pretext for it.[26]

Here is the account Pelling cites in the *Life of Caesar*:

Cicero also tried to persuade the friends of Caesar to compromise and come to a settlement on the basis of the provinces mentioned and only six thousand soldiers,

[25] C. B. R. Pelling, "Plutarch's Adaptation of His Source Material," *The Journal of Hellenistic Studies* 100 (1980), p. 129. Kwon accepts this example, following Pelling, "Charting the (Un)Charted," p. 75.
[26] Plutarch, *Life of Antony*, 5.4–6.3.

and Pompey was ready to yield and grant so many. Lentulus the consul, however, would not let him, but actually heaped insults upon Antony and Curio and drove them disgracefully from the senate, thus himself contriving for Caesar the most specious of his pretexts, and the one by means of which he most of all incited his soldiers, showing them men of repute and high office who had fled the city on hired carts and in the garb of slaves. For thus they had arrayed themselves in their fear and stolen out of Rome.[27]

These two passages are not only compatible but *easily* compatible. To begin with, to call what Antony and Cassius do in *Antony* giving "the speech to Caesar's troops" before they cross the Rubicon is quite misguided. One cannot even tell from *Antony* whether the troops heard what Antony and Cassius said, or how many heard them, if any. Plutarch says merely that they "came into Caesar's presence" and "cried loudly" their complaints about the state of affairs in Rome. This hardly looks like a speech of any kind, much less a speech *to the troops*. It is possible that we should picture this "crying loudly" to Caesar as occurring outside, with soldiers around who passed on to others what they heard, but that is a far cry from their giving "the speech" to incite the troops before taking military action. On the contrary, it is only after they have told their story that Caesar makes up his mind that now is the time to invade.

Moreover, Plutarch goes to some lengths in *Antony* to stress that Caesar had been looking for a pretext to invade Italy and that he made use of the arrival of Antony and Cassius for that purpose. This fits beautifully with the statement in *Caesar* that Caesar displayed Antony and Cassius to his troops in order to incite them. Obviously, they first had to tell their story to Caesar himself when they arrived. This is what *Antony* says. Caesar then found it convenient to parade them in their slaves' garb and rouse his troops to sympathy, as told in *Caesar*. It is quite strange that anyone who reads these accounts would think them to be at odds. In fact, they are complementary. One is just more explicit that Antony and Cassius made their complaint loudly to Caesar, while the other account is more explicit about Caesar's deliberately showing them to his troops.

This example does not even get past the first question in the flowchart: Do these differences create an apparent discrepancy? It illustrates once again the poor historical methodology that lies behind the attribution of special compositional devices to ancient authors. These are merely normal, non-contradictory variations between historical accounts.

---

[27] Plutarch, *Life of Caesar*, 31.2–3.

4. Caesar's toga

As an example of the alleged literary device of displacement, Licona describes two different stories in Plutarch's *Lives* where Julius Caesar, confronted with an embarrassing or vexing situation, pulls back his toga from his throat and dramatically offers his neck to anyone who wishes to kill him. Licona claims that Plutarch moved the event from one scenario to the other and uses this example as an introduction to the concept of dyschronological displacement, which he then applies to the Gospels.[28] Plutarch's alleged motive was that he liked this element of the story and hence wanted to include it in more than one *Life*, but in the *Life of Antony* he was discussing only events in which Antony played a significant role. So, allegedly, in that *Life* he displaced the neck-offering incident to a story in which Antony was more prominent.

The two events that Plutarch describes are quite different. This will create a discrepancy *if* (but only if) one is convinced that Caesar would not have made such a gesture twice. In one incident, probably the earlier in time, senators who wished to honor Caesar approached him while he was seated. Following, says Plutarch, the ill-conceived advice of a flatterer, Caesar remained seated rather than rising to receive them. This would have been considered a social signal that he thought himself superior to the senators. He then spoke dismissively of the honors they were offering him, and with (insincere) modesty stated that his honors should be curtailed rather than increased. The senators were insulted, and most of them left. The people felt that Caesar had insulted the Roman people by behaving curtly to the senators.

The incident illustrates the delicate and dangerous game that Caesar was playing at the time. He was simultaneously pretending not to want to be a king while behaving (e.g., by not rising) as if he were a king. As Plutarch tells the story, when Caesar realized that the incident had made him look bad, he immediately rose to go home, pulling back his toga from his throat and crying out loudly that he would offer his throat to anyone who wished to kill him.[29] Caesar thus attempted to draw attention away from his own error of judgement and consequent embarrassment by an elaborate, passive-aggressive gesture, implying that those who were now angry with him might wish to kill him.

In the other incident, Caesar was (as Plutarch tells the story) witnessing some races at the festival of the Lupercalia. His friend Antony was one of the runners and

---

[28] Licona, *Why Are There Differences*, pp. 85, 185–186. "Why Are There Differences in the Gospels," *Tactical Faith*, April 14, 2014, beginning at minute 38.18, https://youtu.be/xtemSTrkogE?t=2298.

[29] Plutarch, *Life of Caesar*, 60.4–6.

came running up to Caesar bearing a diadem wreathed with laurel, indicative of kingship. He attempted to put it upon Caesar's head, but Caesar refused it (though it may in fact have touched his head, per *Antony* 12.2), and they went back and forth like this a few times. This, again, was a kind of diplomatic game. Caesar was to appear not to desire the crown, while Antony was to insist on offering it. The crowd was, however, not pleased with the idea of Caesar's being crowned king. The applause was slight whenever Antony offered the crown but was loud whenever Caesar refused it. Instead of being pleased that the crowd appreciated his modesty, Caesar was angered by the fact that they did not really want him to be king. In the *Life of Antony*, Plutarch reflects wryly on the people's displeasure at the mere name of "king," though they were "willing to conduct themselves like the subjects of a king."[30] Both the *Life of Caesar* and the *Life of Antony* tell this story about the Lupercalia incident up to this point, but only the *Life of Antony* adds that Caesar then stood up in displeasure, pulled back his toga from his throat, and cried out that anyone might smite him there.[31] The idea, again, seems to be that Caesar is reacting angrily to the crowd's displeasure and his own embarrassment. His elaborate gesture essentially says that, if they do not want him to be king, they might as well kill him.

The first question that arises is why we should be so sure that Caesar did not do this twice. Licona himself thinks that the two contexts are not extremely close in time—according to Licona's estimate, at least a few months apart.[32] Plutarch does not clearly date the Lupercalia incident at all. So if Caesar did do such a thing twice, it (probably) was not within some extremely short period of time (e.g., twice in a few days). Licona only raises briefly and indirectly the possibility that Caesar might have repeated the gesture.[33] He does not say why he rejects it. Perhaps one might object to a repeat performance on the grounds of the specificity of the behavior. Would Caesar have done something so specific and so melodramatic on two occasions?

But the sort of person who would try to manipulate public feeling once by such a gesture might do so again. Caesar would have had to be what we would call a "drama queen" to do such a thing on even a single occasion. But perhaps Caesar *was* something of a drama queen, or perhaps he found it useful to play that role. If so, his doing so once more is not all that improbable.

---

[30] Plutarch, *Life of Antony*, 12.3.

[31] Ibid., 12.4.

[32] Licona, *Why Are There Differences*, p. 83–84.

[33] Ibid., p. 85.

Another problem with the idea that Plutarch moved the incident ahistorically is the thinness of the motive attributed to Plutarch. This is often the case in such claims. Why, for example, would Plutarch even have wanted to move an insult to Caesar (calling him a bandit) from one senator to another? (See Chapter IX, section 5.) In this case Licona at least tries to provide a motive, stated above. But it does not seem terribly plausible. How probable is it that Plutarch just liked the detail about Caesar's offering his neck *so much* that he was not satisfied with telling it once but had to tell it again, in a story where he knew that it did not happen? And if he did want to tell it again, why not briefly repeat the earlier story about the senators approaching to confer honors on Caesar? Licona's claim is that he could not have done that in the *Life of Antony* because that story does not involve Antony. But this exaggerates somewhat the focus on Antony in the *Life of Antony*. It is not quite as laser-like as Licona implies. The digression quoted in the previous section on Caesar's character and his motives for invading Italy occurs in the *Life of Antony* and is far more about Caesar's psychology than it is about Antony. In *Antony* we also find an incident involving garlands placed upon statues and Caesar's interactions with those who placed them there and with those who removed them.[34] So if Plutarch liked the throat-exposing detail so much that he wanted to repeat it, but it only occurred in the interaction with the senators, he probably could have worked a short version of that historical incident into the *Life of Antony*.

If we *were* to try to dream up a purely literary motive for Plutarch to do something fictional concerning Caesar's drawing back his toga, a more literarily attractive theory would be that he put the incident fictionally into the *Life of Caesar* rather than into the *Life of Antony*. Caesar (of course) eventually dies in the *Life of Caesar*, stabbed in the forum by the conspirators, and Plutarch describes his death in detail. Given the circumstances of his death, there is something a bit eerie about Caesar's rash invitation to anyone to strike him in the throat. Interestingly, his toga features in the account of his assassination in *Caesar*. One of the conspirators, Tullius, even pulls down Caesar's toga *from his neck*, and Casca gives him the first blow *in the neck*.[35] Caesar throws his toga over his face when he sees Brutus among the murderers.[36] We might see the earlier offer to any man to strike him in the neck, combined with a gesture of pulling back his toga, as a literary foreshadowing

---

[34] Plutarch, *Life of Antony*, 12.4.

[35] Plutarch, *Life of Caesar*, 66.6.

[36] Ibid., 66.12.

of his assassination within the *Life of Caesar*. But in the *Life of Antony* no detailed description of Caesar's assassination occurs at all. Plutarch says simply, "Caesar fell in the senate-chamber."[37] Licona, however, treats the throat-exposing gesture in the *Life of Caesar* as more likely historical than the account in the *Life of Antony*, and he consequently suggests a less literarily plausible motive.[38]

I do not bring up this theory about Plutarch's foreshadowing invention of the throat exposure in the *Life of Caesar* to endorse it seriously, but rather to show how arbitrary such theories are. It is sometimes possible to think up a more literarily fitting hypothesis than the one that the theorist seriously puts forward. And of course, even if Plutarch had invented something for purposes of foreshadowing, this would not *ipso facto* make it a "compositional device," accepted and expected by audiences of the time. It could simply be literarily-motivated, misleading fabrication. This is also true of Licona's theory. If Plutarch invented the incident in the *Life of Antony* because he liked it, why should we regard this as an accepted literary device rather than sheer disregard for truth?

One other possibility should be considered, and that is carelessness without a real intention to invent. This is relevant if one is convinced that Caesar would not have made this gesture on two different occasions. While in this case, unlike many others, the incident is striking enough that it is not *especially* easy to forget or get confused about it (in contrast to tiny details concerning numbers of sittings of the senate or minute matters of chronology), it would still be possible. Plutarch could have remembered that Caesar did this to cover his embarrassment on some occasion and then could have become confused and attached it to another incident, without checking his sources. We saw in Chapter IX, section 5, that one should not take Pelling's speculation that Plutarch composed six of the *Lives* during *approximately* a year or two to mean that no accidental discrepancies could arise between them.

Certainly such a degree of carelessness about when Caesar dramatically exposed his throat would mean that Plutarch was not much concerned to check up on the truth of the matter, but confusion coupled with carelessness in checking would be, nonetheless, a less blatant and deliberate disregard for truth than reporting something while *knowing* that it was untrue. And a careless error would be a

---

[37] Plutarch, *Life of Antony*, 14.4.

[38] Michael Licona, "Why Are There Differences in the Gospels?" minute 41.23, https://youtu.be/xtemSTrkogE?t=2483. Licona also considers the possibility that it was a "floating" incident that Plutarch placed ahistorically in two specific contexts. *Why Are There Differences*, p. 259 n. 3. But he seems more convinced that the incident in the *Life of Caesar* is the historical event.

simpler source of historical inaccuracy than deliberate fact-changing for vague literary motives. Neither ordinary fabrication nor carelessness is a literary device.

As usual, there are multiple nodes of the flowchart at which the claim of special literary device can founder, but Licona does not consider any of them. It is especially noteworthy that there is not even a *clear* apparent discrepancy between the two accounts in Plutarch to begin with. In order to claim that there is a discrepancy, one must assume that Caesar definitely did not make this melodramatic gesture on two occasions. The fact that neither this point nor any of the other possibilities (up to and including fabrication that is not a literary device) are considered seriously illustrates once more the methodological weakness of the literary device case, even in Greco-Roman literature.

As I have said repeatedly in this book, if we consistently applied such methods to historical research and to modern witness testimony, we would eliminate many things that our historical picture should retain. We would have no repeated, similar events (even though these happen all the time), no complementary accounts that tell different parts of an event, no ordinary errors, no variations merely because witnesses tell things in different ways, no propaganda, no casual fabrication, and no carefully constructed deception. The minds of scholars would reshape normal sources of differences into literary devices, across century after century. But that is not the way to do history.

Matthean Discourses and Fictionalizing Literary Devices

1. Why address this issue?

Suppose, for a moment, that the authors of the Gospels sometimes put together composite discourses of Jesus. What this means in the broadest sense is that an author brought together sayings that Jesus did really utter at different times, combining them in one place in such a way that it could appear at first sight as though he said all of those things on one occasion. Within that broad concept of composites, there are a variety of different possibilities, as I shall make clearer throughout this appendix. Some relevant questions are these: Just *how* reasonable would it be to think that Jesus said all of these things at once? Given what the document says, how strongly does the material in question *look like* a discourse as opposed to a loose collection? *How much* material do we conclude was probably uttered on that occasion and how much was not? What did the author think if he did this? What would the original audience have thought if they heard or read it?

Within the broad category of composite discourses, we can think of circumstances that would render the concept compatible with the reportage model. Suppose, for example, that audiences of the first century understood that sometimes an author reporting someone's teachings "chunked in" material on the same topic, within a setting that applied only to *some* of the material. In other words, suppose that they understood that, while the setting did mean that the speaker uttered some significant proportion of the material at that time, the speaker might have spoken some part of it at another time. The author might have included the other material in that part of the document for the sake of convenience and thematic arrangement. If this were the case, then such an arrangement would be a kind of achronological narration. The fact that Jesus' words in Matt. 6 (for example) come after Matt. 5.1, saying that Jesus went up onto a mountain and began to teach the people, and before Matt. 7.28, stating that Jesus finished all these sayings, would not (if this theory were true) necessarily mean that Matthew was trying to make it look like Jesus taught all of the material in Matt. 6 on that same occasion, and it would not have been so taken by the original audience. This would be (if this were the case) similar to narrating events without indicating when they happened explicitly, not meaning them to be taken to have occurred in that order. One might conjecture that the length of a discourse itself and its thematic ordering, together with the *absence* of any interspersed dialogue or narration that brings the reader back to a concrete setting, would constitute a kind of "tag" for original audiences that there was probably some degree of collection going on.

If that were true, such a composite discourse would be compatible with the reportage model, since achronological narration generally is compatible with the reportage model. Indeed, I am convinced that a large majority of evangelical scholars who accept composite discourses in the Gospels think of them in something like these terms.

An obvious question then arises: If composite discourses are not *per se* incompatible with the reportage model, because they *could* represent a kind of achronological narration, why am I addressing them at all in this book? In particular, why should I spend time and space in this appendix arguing that scholars have oversold the case that Matthew produced composite discourses of Jesus and that this proposition is open to reasonable doubt?

There are three reasons why this topic is important in this book. First, it is important to apply the distinction, as I have just done, between achronological and dyschronological narration *explicitly* to this question, lest people become confused about it and slide from one to the other without realizing that they are doing so. Second, Michael Licona has explicitly used composite discourses in discussing the alleged literary device of displacement. Licona uses the consensus of evangelical scholars concerning Matthew's composite discourses to defend *dyschronological* displacement, as if scholars who accept Matthean composite discourses all must agree that Matthew displaced in a dyschronological manner.

In the same portion of a lecture in which he alleges that Luke has dyschronologically displaced Jesus' teaching about causing little ones to stumble (see Chapter XV, section 3) and that John has dyschronologically displaced the foot anointing in Passion Week (see Chapter XIV, section 6), Licona uses the allegedly

composite nature of the Sermon on the Mount to recruit most evangelical scholars as witnesses in favor of dyschronological narration:

> This [the "little ones" passage] is a very clear example of Luke displacing the story.
> That's okay. Most even evangelical scholars would say that Matthew has done that
> and the Sermon on the Mount is just taking different elements of some of Jesus'
> sermons and putting them together in a single sermon. Now, they will say that
> Jesus did speak and actually gave a Sermon on the Mount. But Matthew took this
> opportunity to include some other teachings that Jesus may not have preached on
> that occasion. That's just called "displacement."[1]

Licona makes not the slightest attempt to distinguish Matthew's trying to make it
look like all of the Sermon on the Mount was uttered at that time though it really
wasn't (dyschronological narration) from his "chunking in" material while knowing that his audience would expect that this might be a topically organized set of
sayings that were not all taught at that time (achronological narration). Nor does
he provide any evidence that most evangelical scholars are endorsing the former
rather than the latter. The issue of the alleged composite discourses thus becomes
at least *prima facie* relevant to the matter of fictionalizing literary devices, since
Licona uses it to support them.

Third, it is not really at all clear that there *was* such an audience understanding
concerning topically collected material in places where the author has *explicitly* set
and bracketed a discourse. By "bracketed" I mean that the author places a statement at the beginning to the effect that Jesus began to teach at a particular time
and place and then places a phrase at the end such as, "When he had finished all
these sayings …." A bracketed discourse is not the same thing as a loose collection
of teachings. We must confront the fact that the case for achronological narration
of explicitly bracketed discourses may be on shaky ground. It therefore becomes
doubly important to go back and ask whether the case for composite discourses is
as airtight as we have been led to believe.

If one comes to think that the placement of the bracketed discourses in Matthew would have appeared literal to the first audience and that they would probably have assumed that all of that material was taught (though not word-for-word)
on that occasion, is one then required to agree with Licona that Matthew narrated
dyschronologically, deliberately making it look like Jesus taught things at a time
when he did not teach them? Not at all. The overall evidence that the evangelists

---

[1] Michael Licona, "Why Are There Differences in the Gospels," April 19, 2014, minute 1:06:37,
https://youtu.be/xtemSTrkogE?t=3027.

would not have wanted to confuse their audiences makes the dyschronological option improbable on other grounds. Indeed, if our only options were to think that Matthew wrote in a way that he knew might confuse his audience about when Jesus taught certain things or that Matthew did not create composite discourses, this tension would be some evidence in itself *against* composite discourses. Moreover, the argument that Matthew created composite discourses is conjectural and open to reasonable question.

2. Bracketed discourses and audience understanding

Chapter VII has addressed at length the allegation that ancient authors *generally* thought that the invention of speeches was acceptable. We saw there that some ancient authors accepted while others rejected the practice of composing speeches for one's historical figures or treating the reportage of speeches loosely. There is therefore no *general* truth that ancient audiences simply expected speeches to be reported in a loose fashion in allegedly historical documents.

Part Two also showed how seldom we find explicit discussion of the alleged accepted literary devices. While a few authors do discuss speech invention, we do not have explicit ancient discussions of dyschronological displacement, nor any explicit indication that such a literary device existed at all. Theorists infer that it was an accepted device only inductively from various passages in which, they claim, we find ancient authors engaging in it. I argued there that the inductive evidence in question is weak. So it should come as no surprise that there is no explicit evidence that either achronological or dyschronological composition of composite speeches *per se*, placed between clear brackets indicating the occasion of the speech, was expected by audiences.

If Jesus really taught the material in question at some time or other, compiling it into a single speech seems a *relatively* conservative form of loose reportage, especially as compared with making up material out of whole cloth, putting into Jesus' mouth what one thinks Jesus should have said. It would certainly be more conservative than the sort of theological extrapolation and invention of Jesus' discourses that scholars often unfortunately attribute to John. Nonetheless, it is a bit disconcerting to realize that there is no explicit evidence to support composite discourses as a convention of the time. The only evidence brought forward is the content of the very discourses in question and their conjectured relationship to other texts.

That being the case, one begins to wonder just how plausible it is that Matthew or any other evangelist deliberately created a composite bracketed discourse even achronologically. To be absolutely clear: I am *not* questioning whether Gospel authors sometimes reported Jesus' sayings in a heaped, achronological way. In fact, the idea that Luke did so will feature prominently in this very appendix and was an important part of the discussion in Chapter XV, section 3. There I argued that Luke does not provide any setting or context *at all* for Jesus' words about causing little ones to stumble and that therefore it is confused to allege that he has moved these words to a different context from the historical one and has suffered "editorial fatigue" in the process. I argued there that the portion of Luke in which these words appear looks like a conglomerated "sayings" section. But that is just the point: The sayings of Jesus in that chapter in Luke do not constitute a *discourse* in a particular setting. Hence, while the evidence is fairly clear that Gospel authors sometimes narrated sayings of Jesus achronologically, it does not follow that they did so, even in part, while placing a group of such sayings explicitly *between brackets on a particular occasion* as a discourse properly so called.

D. A. Carson, who leans toward the conclusion that Matthew's explicitly bracketed discourses are not composite, explains the issue clearly:

As Matthew's gospel stands, we must weigh two disparate pieces of evidence: (1) that all five of Matthew's discourses are bracketed by introductory and concluding remarks that cannot fail to give the impression that he presents his discourses as not only authentic but delivered by Jesus on the specified occasions and (2) that many individual bits of each discourse find synoptic parallels in other settings. Many think the second point to be so strong that they conclude that Matthew himself composed the discourses. Conservative writers in this camp say that all of Jesus' sayings are authentic but that Matthew brought them together in their present form. Therefore the first piece of evidence has to be reinterpreted—i.e., the introductory and concluding notes framing each of Matthew's discourses are seen as artistic compositional devices.

A more subtle approach is to say that Jesus actually did deliver a discourse on each of the five occasions specified but that not all of the material Matthew records is from that occasion. In other words, the evangelist has added certain "footnotes" of his own, at a time when orthography was much more flexible and there were no convenient ways to indicate what he was doing. While either of these reconstructions is possible, each faces two steep hurdles: (1) the introductory and concluding brackets around the five discourses do not belong to any clear first-century pattern or genre that would show the reader they are merely artistic devices and not the real settings they manifestly claim to be; and (2) it is remarkable that each conclusion sweeps together all the sayings of the preceding discourse under some such rubric as "when Jesus had finished saying these things" (a possible exception is 11:1). That the introductory and concluding formulas were not recognizable as artistic devices is confirmed by the fact that for the first millennium and a half or so of its existence, the church recognized them as concrete settings. (This is not a surreptitious appeal to return to precritical thinking but a note on the recognizability of a literary genre.)[2]

Carson repeats the point later concerning the commissioning discourse in Matthew 10:

> The setting Matthew gives must be accepted. Although he arranges much of his material topically, uses loose time connectives, and condenses his sources and sometimes paraphrases them, there is no convincing evidence that Matthew invents settings. Nor will appeal to some elusive genre suffice. If Matthew is a coherent writer, such nonhistorical material must be reasonably and readily separable from his historical material, if the alleged "genre" was recognizable to the first readers. Verse 5a could scarcely be clearer: "These twelve Jesus sent out with the following instructions."[3]

It is important to realize that Carson thinks that these points concerning setting weigh against even *partially* composite bracketed discourses. As Licona says in the above quotation, many evangelical scholars believe that the Sermon on the Mount (for example) was partially uttered on that occasion and partially composed from collected sayings actually uttered at other times. But Carson presses the point that Matthew explicitly brackets the entire discourse.

Here the literary device theorist faces a dilemma such as I have noted elsewhere. On the one hand, if the theorist agrees with Carson that Matthew seems to have been trying to make it look (to his original audience) like a discourse was all delivered on one occasion, and if the theorist insists that Matthew knew that it was *not* all said on one occasion, it becomes difficult for the theorist to argue that such a literary device was not intentionally misleading. On the other hand, if the theorist insists that the original audience *would* believe that a discourse of that length, with such brackets, *probably* contained collected sayings material somewhere within it, the analogy to the alleged displacement of (say) the anointing of Jesus' feet fails. For in that example there is nothing in either John or Mark to clue in even an original reader that anything has been moved. The narratives are entirely realistic, and the temporal placements appear clear. Hence, if deliberate displacement did occur, it was entirely invisible, dyschronological, and had every possibility of confusing the reader or hearer about when that incident occurred, unless the reader was savvy

---

[2] D. A. Carson, *Matthew (The Expositor's Bible Commentary)* (Grand Rapids, MI: Zondervan, 2010), p. 153.

[3] Ibid., p. 284.

enough to put question marks over the narratives more broadly. Similarly, Licona insists that Luke intended to erase the reference to the "little ones" in displacing the saying about causing them to stumble but neglected to do so through "editorial fatigue." In other words, Luke was (on this theory) *trying to make it look like* the saying occurred in a different setting from its real setting but was not fully successful. But such an activity would not be analogous to making a composite discourse where such a composite could be *expected* by the audience.

However, if the scholarship really were settled that Matthew (or others) created collected discourses, even when an author gives clear brackets on either end, the opponent of literary device theories in his turn could face a dilemma: In that case it seems that he must either accept that the discourse is partly achronological, considerations to the contrary notwithstanding, or accept that the author engaged in fictionalizing narration.

Statements about the consensus on this matter can seem daunting, especially for someone who is not an established New Testament scholar. For example, in a radio debate with me, Craig Evans went so far as to say this concerning the Sermon on the Mount:

> [T]hese discourses [in Matthew] have been constructed out of disparate materials. And...the Sermon on the Mount, that's a great example of it. When you look at Luke, the parallel there, and it's half a chapter, it's Luke 6:20–49, the so-called Sermon on the Plain, and in Matthew it becomes three chapters, five, six and seven. And all critical scholars of the Synoptics, and I mean evangelicals, not just...non-evangelicals, recognize this assembling, this constructing of these discourses out of materials. And if Lydia rejects that and says, "No, that's not what happened; it's a recording of what Jesus said on one particular occasion," she's very much out of step with critical gospel scholarship on this point. Maybe she doesn't understand the views of most of us hold to.[4]

The word "all" is rather noteworthy here. I assume that Evans was unaware of Carson's position on the matter. Evans's emphatic comments were especially surprising given that, earlier in our discussion, I had expressly stated that I was *not* closed to the possibility of composite discourses. I meant partially achronological discourses, though we did not discuss the specifics. Why did Evans think that

---

[4] Craig A. Evans vs. Lydia McGrew, "Is John's Gospel Historically Accurate?" *Unbelievable*, May 18, 2018, minute 44, http://unbelievable.podbean.com/e/is-john%E2%80%99s-gospel-historically-accurate-lydia-mcgrew-craig-evans-debate/; see also the debate transcript https://www.premierchristianradio.com/Shows/Saturday/Unbelievable/Unbelievable-blog/Lydia-McGrew-vs.-Craig-Evans-on-the-Historical-Reliability-of-John-s-Gospel-Full-Transcript.

the possibility that Matthew assembled composite discourses was a locus of our disagreement, when I had said that I was open to it? Perhaps I had seemed insufficiently enthusiastic. In any event, his implication is clear: If you have the slightest doubt that Matthew's discourses *definitely are composites*, then you are ignorant and unaware of critical Gospel scholarship, out of step with what *all critical scholars* of the Synoptics know to be true. That attitude has, as this appendix demonstrates, driven me to do further research and to become more doubtful of the composite thesis than I was at that time. If one finds a proposition defended against outsiders by such a heavy-handed use of the bandwagon fallacy, one may well consider taking a look to see whether the evidence stands up to careful scrutiny.

As it turns out, the evidence is by no means so clear, and it is entirely epistemically respectable to conclude that Matthew believed that his bracketed discourses contained only material that Jesus uttered on that historical occasion.[5]

3. Some tools

In evaluating the evidence in this area, several analytical tools and empirical points will be helpful. Some of these are matters of commonsense reflection, while others are facts that we discover about the Gospels when we examine the evidence.

First, we should bear in mind that there is a difference between an author's making an informed conjecture that Jesus said something in a discourse and an author's collecting sayings while knowing that they were definitely said at other times, outside of the discourse. It will always be difficult if not impossible to argue that Matthew *must have known* that Jesus *did not* give a particular parable or saying as part of a particular discourse and therefore must have collected it into that discourse while realizing that it was really uttered at a different time. How could we be reasonably sure of such a thing? Perhaps Matthew was relying on his own memory or on the memory of a witness who thought that a saying was part of that discourse. Perhaps thematic organization means that the author thought that Jesus addressed that issue at that time and therefore that material on that theme *was* part of that discourse.

Here I must briefly address the use that scholars sometimes make of the Q hypothesis in such discussions. They are not content merely to think that Matthew and Luke may both have obtained material from this (hypothetical) source. They insist in addition on assuming that they knew *nothing else* about any

---

[5] As emphasized in Chapter X, section 1, this is *not* the same thing as saying that Matthew or any other Gospel author gave a verbatim recording of what Jesus said. Indeed, given the length of some of the discourses, in a world without recording equipment this would be close to impossible.

"Q material" besides what they found in Q. This would mean that they knew nothing else about when it was uttered.

If material is in both Luke and Matthew but not in Mark, scholars usually consider it to be "Q material," assuming that both Luke and Matthew got it from a common written source. But as examples in *Hidden in Plain View* have already shown, even when there is reason to believe that Matthew is in some way using a written source (Mark, in those cases), it does not follow that he had no additional independent information about the matter recorded.[6] So we certainly should not assume that, if some saying is regarded as "Q material," Matthew could have had no information about when it was said *beyond* what he found in Q. Nor do we possess Q ourselves, which means that we can only guess at what it contained anyway.

The line of inference from the premises that a) Matthew and Luke are both using Q material, b) Matthew places it in a long discourse, and c) Luke does not place it in a long discourse to the conclusion that d) Matthew was deliberately collecting material is highly fallible. Roughly, to reason thus, one must assume

1) Matthew found this saying or parable in Q.

2) Matthew had no information about when this saying or parable was uttered, on any occasion, other than what he found in Q.

3) Q did not have this saying or parable located in a discourse.

4) Matthew was justified in concluding that this saying or parable never occurred in the course of a discourse.

5) Matthew did draw that inference.

6) Matthew chose to collect the saying or parable into a discourse anyway.

This line of argument could fail at any of several points. To take but one example, Matthew may not have drawn the same inference that the modern critic is so quick to draw and may instead have genuinely thought it plausible that the saying or parable was uttered as part of a discourse along with other material on the same topic, a failure at #5. And he certainly may have had some other information, beyond the mere presence in Q, about when Jesus gave some teaching, a failure at #2.

The next commonsense point is this: Preachers and teachers do repeat similar material often. Anyone who has taught over a period of time knows this. But critical scholars, though they may give lip service to this possibility, treat it in practice as a desperate *ad hoc* move and scarcely ever accept it, even when there is direct

---

[6] Lydia McGrew, *Hidden in Plain View: Undesigned Coincidences in the Gospels and Acts* (Chillicothe, OH: DeWard Publishing, 2017), pp. 87–89, 92–94.

evidence for it. We have seen this in Chapter XIII, section 5, where Michael Lico-na acknowledges in theory that Jesus may have said something similar more than once but in practice thinks it at least equally plausible that Matthew is redacting a saying about an animal in distress on the Sabbath and placing it ahistorically in a different context. One saying concerns an ox in a well; the other concerns a sheep in a pit. But neither these differences nor the different occasions in the Gospels nor the commonsense possibility that these indicate the way Jesus thought and spoke are sufficient for Licona to set aside the fictionalizing redactive hypothesis.

Scholars should be far more willing than they are to think that Jesus did say something similar on more than one occasion. As we will see, a great deal of the argument that Matthew created composite discourses arises from lists of similar sayings in Luke that are not located in a discourse there. Sometimes these are just short sayings, sometimes slightly longer, and occasionally a parable. But if Jesus repeated his material even to the extent that we independently know that teach-ers do, these lists appear much less formidable. Again, repetition by teachers and preachers is *independently confirmed* within our own common experience. Hence, it is not an *ad hoc* or undesirable explanation of the data. Moreover, if the data imply different settings in different Gospels, that is *prima facie* evidence in and of itself that Jesus said something like this on more than one occasion.

As Carson notes,

> We must suppose that Jesus preached the same thing repeatedly…; he was an extremely busy itinerant preacher. The pithier the saying, the more likely it was to be repeated word-perfect. The more common the natural phenomenon behind a metaphor or aphorism, the more likely Jesus repeated it in new situations. Any experienced itinerant preacher will confirm the inescapability of these tendencies.[7]

This consideration all by itself should lessen the epistemological, not to mention the psychological, impact of long lists of "Q material parallels" and Markan par-allels that allegedly show Matthew's tendency to collect sayings into discourses.

The next important tool is this: When we come to the alleged parallels them-selves, we find again and again that Luke's "placements" of many of the sayings are far looser than Matthew's, often with no clear context. When Matthew places a saying or parable in a discourse between brackets while Luke merely says, "And he said" or "He said to the crowds" or some such phrase, or even strings together sayings with no introductory wording, it is Luke who appears to be uncertain

---

[7] Carson, *Matthew*, p. 153.

about when Jesus said these things and Matthew who appears more confident. This is not invariably the case, but it is often the case. Even if one is reluctant to think "too often" that Jesus repeated himself (though that resistance can be a mistake in itself), that may be the explanation of some of the parallels while others are instances of achronological narration in Luke. It is rather striking that scholars should so often take Luke to *have* a setting and Matthew to be compiling either achronologically or dyschronologically, in cases where *Luke* has the greater *prima facie* appearance of achronological narration. After one has seen this pattern come up a number of times one begins to suspect that a predetermined picture of a "compiling Matthew" is blinding scholars to the greater achronological appearance in certain sections of Luke.

These two points alone—that teachers often repeat and that Luke is often more achronological in sayings sections than Matthew—are sufficient all by themselves to undermine substantially the allegedly knock-down case for Matthean discourse compilation. But there are a few more points to bear in mind. Sometimes Luke or Mark alone records twice, in more than one setting, a teaching found in a discourse in Matthew. When Jesus uses the same saying in different ways, mixing it with different morals or points, this constitutes independent evidence in the other Synoptic Gospels that it was a favorite with Jesus and that he taught it repeatedly with variations.[8]

Occasionally, it is Matthew who repeats a teaching twice, as in the case of Jesus' saying that one must take up one's cross (Matt. 10.38–39, Matt. 16.24–25). The second of these corresponds closely to Mark's setting (Mark 8.34–35), while the first occurs in Matthew's Commissioning Discourse. When that happens, it is *entirely illegitimate* to cite the non-discourse setting in Mark as if it were evidence that Matthew compiled this teaching into a discourse, taking it out of a non-discourse setting. It makes no sense to imagine Matthew as wishing to compile material into a discourse while at the same time repeating it in the same non-discourse setting found in Mark. Did he want to compile or did he want to repeat? It would be multiplying hypotheses without necessity to say that this teaching occurred only once, that Matthew recorded it in its real setting (parallel to Mark), but that he *also* needlessly repeated it in a discourse where he knew that it didn't occur. Rather, the appearance twice in Matthew alone is evidence that Matthew believed that Jesus taught something like this more than once.

---

[8] As Carson says, "[I]f one distances oneself from the more radical presuppositions of form and tradition criticism, the NT documents themselves confirm this approach...." Ibid.

On occasion Mark agrees with Matthew in placing a saying in a discourse setting while Luke is the outlier, reporting similar material elsewhere. In that case one should not cite the parallel in Luke, neglect the parallel in Mark, and add the parallel in Luke to an impressive-sounding list of citations meant to show that Matthew compiled his discourses. I will cite two such instances later.

One last point is worth mentioning before going into some specifics on the Sermon on the Mount and the Commissioning Discourse. The fact that Luke often gives Jesus' sayings in somewhat vague settings while Matthew gives the same sayings in discourse settings is *some* evidence that Luke was not working directly with Matthew as we have it. In particular, the vagueness may indicate that Luke was working with a source or sources that did not give a clear indication about when Jesus said some things. This may have been a written source, a human source, or a group of human sources. It may have been the much-vaunted Q or an earlier, shorter version of Matthew with fewer sayings. Or it may be that Q *just was* a different version of Matthew. If Luke found a saying in a discourse in Matthew, one wonders why he would not place it in a discourse himself rather than putting it somewhere unclear. So a plausible hypothesis is that Luke did not have constant access to Matthew in the form in which we presently have it but knew of some similar material in another way. That hypothesis, of course, is entirely consistent with a reportage view of both Matthew and Luke and does not in any way commit one to the many dubious uses that redaction critics make of the Q hypothesis. Plenty of other evidence shows that Luke had his own independent sources of specific information as well. See, for just one example, the discussion of the Transfiguration in Chapter XII, section 4.

Here I will discuss the Sermon on the Mount (Matt. 5–7), the Commissioning Discourse (Matt. 10.5–42), and the Woes to the Pharisees (Matt. 23.1–36) in some detail and will give only a few remarks about other Matthean discourses. The points and methods used here should be sufficient to illustrate that we are not obligated to accept collected discourses where Matthew has brackets. By the same token, we are certainly not obligated to accept dyschronological discourses in those places.

4. The Sermon on the Mount

As Craig Evans's remarks above indicate, the Sermon on the Mount is Exhibit A in the supposedly knock-down case that Matthew created composite discourses. And the case is chiefly based on the existence of parallel sayings and passages in the other two Synoptic Gospels (Mark and Luke, especially Luke). Scholars take these lists of parallels to mean that Matthew encountered these teachings in only a scattered form and then collected them into discourses. Thus, in the quotation above, Evans says that half of a chapter in Luke "becomes" three chapters in Matthew. Without listing specific parallels, Evans states that Matthew chiefly carried out this collecting activity with Q material—material shared with Luke but not with Mark:

> Matthew has drawn much of this material from Q, the source also used by Luke (see Luke 6:20–49), only Matthew assembles more of Jesus' ethical teaching, creating a discourse of three chapters, compared with Luke's half chapter.[9]

It is not difficult to find complete lists of the alleged parallels, and they do appear impressively scattered, especially when they are laid out one saying at a time, rather than by blocks of material.[10]

But, as Carson notes, the claim that Matthew is collecting stands in *prima facie* tension with Matthew's explicit bracketing statements:

> When Jesus saw the crowds, He went up on the mountain; and after He sat down, His disciples came to Him. He opened His mouth and began to teach them, saying…(Matt. 5.1–2)

> When Jesus had finished these words, the crowds were amazed at His teaching. (Matt. 7.28)

The question at issue is whether the settled and undeniable results of Gospels scholarship obligate us to take these brackets not to mean what one would first take them to mean, since the discourse in between these brackets is partly collected. If so, should we take this to be some sort of achronological narration or dyschronological narration?

I will not spend time in a verse-by-verse discussion of the parallel passages in Luke that come from what is sometimes called the Sermon on the Level Place (Luke 6.17–49). It is entirely plausible that this passage in Luke actually refers to the very same occasion as the Sermon on the Mount, especially since level places can be found amongst mountains in the region in question, a point on which even

---

[9] Craig A. Evans, *Matthew* (New Cambridge Bible Commentary) (Cambridge: Cambridge University Press, 2012), p. 97.

[10] See a verse-by-verse list of alleged parallels compiled by Robert I. Kirby, "Parallel Passages, Multiple Witnesses," *The Sermon on the Mount Site*, September 15, 2015, http://www.sermononthemount.org.uk/Background/ParallelPassages.html. This page, based on the work of Geza Vermes, also lists alleged parallels with the Gospel of Thomas, which for obvious reasons I am ignoring.

Evans agrees.[11] There is nothing about the temporal setting of the Sermon on the Level Place that places it in competition with Matthew's Sermon on the Mount, and what is most noteworthy is that Matthew and Luke are in apparent agreement that Jesus taught *at least* this material at one time.[12] There is some further confirmation that the two sections refer to the same occasion from the fact that shortly after each of them Jesus heals the centurion's servant in Capernaum (Matt. 8.5ff, Luke 7.1ff).

Besides the material in Luke 6, we can readily deal with other parallels using the tools discussed in the last section. It is important, once more, to remember that the mere occurrence of a passage in Luke somewhere in his large middle section does not constitute *ipso facto* an implication by Luke that such a teaching occurred *later* in Jesus' ministry, even if other events intervene. (See discussion of Luke's famously difficult central section in Chapter XV, section 3.) As Carson says,

> [E]ven if (as I am willing to assume) Luke's central section is framed by certain historical journeys to Jerusalem, used theologically to point to the final journey, it is only to be expected that topical material is also incorporated, because many of Luke's transitions between pericopes (when he uses them at all) are chronologically imprecise. What this means for a commentator on Matthew is that each apparent parallel between a pericope in Matthew and one in Luke's "central section" must be assessed on its own merits. In some cases, they probably refer to the same event, in others not; and in some instances, the evidence may be such that a convincing decision is impossible.[13]

It would therefore be incorrect to list other events in Luke that come somewhere or other before a given saying and to take this *all by itself* to mean that Luke is presenting a much later setting that competes with Matthew's early setting in Jesus' ministry. It seems that Luke possessed teachings of Jesus that he placed in his large middle section while sometimes being fairly openly achronological about exactly when Jesus taught these things. As already noted, while this may mean that Luke was not working with Matthew as we currently know it, or at least that

---

[11] Evans, *Matthew*, p. 97.

[12] Luke 6.12–16 states that Jesus, after praying on a mountain all night, chose twelve disciples. Luke appears to locate this event shortly before the Sermon on the Level Place. But this location is not in conflict with Matthew's list of the names of the Twelve in Matt. 10.1–5. Luke gives the names at the earlier point in his narrative, but Matthew does not state in Chapter 10 that Jesus *first chose* the Twelve at the time when he sent them on a mission to the surrounding villages. In fact, the statement in Matt. 10.1 that he "summoned his twelve disciples" may well mean that these twelve had been chosen at some earlier time.

[13] Carson, *Matthew*, p. 462.

he did not have it constantly available, that is not the same thing as evidence that Luke places Jesus' teachings in definitely different settings from Matthew's. On the occasions where he *does* have clearly different settings, it is entirely possible that Jesus repeated these teachings.

Several sayings in the Sermon on the Mount that are found elsewhere in Luke are in "floating" settings. For example, Luke 11.33 (about putting a lamp on a lamp stand) is similar to Matt. 5.15. But this is "set" in Luke only "as the crowds were increasing" (Luke 11.29), which tells us very little. Interestingly, the saying that one sets a lamp on a lamp stand is also in Luke 8.16, among Jesus' parables, as it is in Mark 4.21. It is not in Matthew's parable discourse (Matt. 13). When it crops up in the parable discourses in Luke and Mark, Jesus uses it to say that nothing is hidden that will not be revealed. In Matthew's Sermon on the Mount Jesus uses the reference to a lamp on a stand to say that his followers are the light of the world and should let their light shine before men. Both the repetition within Luke itself and Jesus' differing applications support the plausibility that Jesus used this metaphor for different purposes on different occasions. And that is in addition to the fact that the "setting" in Luke 11.33 is extremely loose. Similar considerations of looseness apply to the similarity between Luke 11.34–36 about the eye as the light of the body and Matt. 6.22–23.

Or consider Luke 14.34–35—a saying about salt worded very similarly to Matt. 5.13. There is virtually no setting in Luke. If one looks back far enough one comes to Luke 14.25, which says, "Now great multitudes were going along with Him, and He turned and said to them …" Obviously, a large crowd is also the audience in the Sermon on the Mount. And that is in addition to the importance of salt in the ancient world and the brevity of the saying. As Carson says,

> Salt and light are such common substances (cf. Pliny, *Nat.* 31.102: "Nothing is more useful than salt and sunshine") that they doubtless generated many sayings. Therefore it is improper to attempt a tradition history of all gospel references as if one original stood behind the lot.[14]

The probability is quite high that *either* Luke is achronologically recording something Jesus said in the Sermon on the Mount or that Jesus taught thus more than once.

Sometimes, interestingly, Luke has material that appears to be collected topically, or partially topically, *after* an introductory incident but *without* a concluding

---

[14] Ibid., p. 168.

bracket. Such material may be said to begin with a setting and then to "wander" into a sayings collection. Again, the point here is not that one should be *a priori* committed to thinking that Matthew's setting is literal and Luke's setting is topical. That would be arbitrary. When it comes to the Woes to the Pharisees, discussed below, I am inclined to say that Luke is quite definite in setting, perhaps even more so than Matthew. The point rather is not to come to the text with the assumption that Matthew is collecting and then to impose that assumption upon the text even when, looking at the details, it is Luke who happens to be less clear about chronology. To do so would be evidentially backwards.

One example of Luke's "wandering" into what appears to be a collection, without an ending bracket, occurs in Luke 12.13ff. Luke says that someone in the crowd (what crowd?) asked Jesus to tell his brother to divide the inheritance with him. Jesus replies by warning against greed and giving the parable of the rich man who decides to build more barns, whom God calls a fool. This parable is unique to Luke. Verse 22 then begins, "And he said to his disciples..." This extremely vague phrase is followed by more teachings about riches and possessions. Does this refer to the same occasion on which someone in the crowd asked Jesus to tell his brother to divide the inheritance? If it did, this would not necessarily preclude its occurring during the Sermon on the Mount, since Luke is unclear as to when this pericope as a whole took place. But the vagueness is compounded, for the statement that Jesus said more things about riches to his disciples (perhaps to his disciples among others) could well indicate a shift away from the setting in verse 13. What follows does indeed closely resemble some portions of the Sermon on the Mount. Luke 12.22–34 closely resembles Matt. 6.19–21, 25–32 about not being anxious, seeking the Kingdom of God, and laying up treasure in heaven. But it could hardly be said that Luke sets these things in a place that *competes* with Matthew. Even if one is averse to thinking that Jesus taught these chunks of material more than once, this placement in Luke does not require that hypothesis.

A similar instance of "wandering" may well occur in Luke 11. It begins with Jesus giving the Lord's Prayer, to which I will return in a moment. This is followed (introduced only by "and he said to them") by a parable unique to Luke about a friend who comes at night to ask for bread. Then, without further indication as to when this was said, comes Luke 11.9–13, which is closely similar to Matt. 7.7–11, "Ask and it will be given unto you," etc. But there is *no bracket* in Luke at the end of the sayings about prayer, and it is entirely possible that Luke's narrative has wandered from the scene at the outset, when the disciples find Jesus praying and ask him to teach them to pray, to a collection of Jesus' teachings about prayer. Luke may have been conjecturing when Jesus taught these things, or he may have merely collected them achronologically, with the lack of any closing reference to setting as an indication of uncertainty.

These examples are sufficient to show the difficulties with taking parallels in Luke, referring them to "Q material," and drawing summarily the conclusion that Matthew knowingly collected material into the Sermon on the Mount.

There are some places where Luke *does* seem to have different settings for similar sayings or teachings, but what is interesting is that there are relatively few of these once we have set aside the other types of material. Once their number is whittled down accordingly, we should have very little trouble admitting the possibility that Jesus taught these things twice.

In some cases, the appearance of a different setting arises from what Luke says immediately after. For example, Luke 16.13, teaching that no man can serve two masters and that one cannot serve God and money, is followed immediately by the statement in Luke 16.14 that the Pharisees, who were lovers of money, were listening to all these things and scoffing at Jesus. This is fairly specific and not very consonant with the setting of the Sermon on the Mount, though it is quite similar to Matt. 6.24. But it is hardly implausible that Jesus, who had a great deal to say about the dangers of the love of money, would have taught such a thing more than once.

Similarly, Luke 12.58–59, a warning to agree quickly with your opponent and settle before you reach the judge (similar to Matt. 5.25–26), is followed immediately in Luke 13.1 with a transitional statement that "on the same occasion" someone in the crowd mentioned to Jesus something about the Galileans whose blood Pilate mingled with their sacrifices. (This is one of those unexplained allusions described in Chapter XII, section 1, which lends authenticity to the Gospel narratives.) What follows is some of Jesus' teaching on the need for repentance, unique to Luke. While it is not impossible that this exchange occurred in the midst of the Sermon on the Mount, though not reported by Matthew, this seems rather unlikely, as the teaching does not fit very well there. So if we take Luke's "on the same occasion" in 13.1 to refer to the last two verses of Chapter 12, we should probably take it that this describes a different occasion on which Jesus warned to agree with your adversary quickly. Again, that is hardly much of a stretch.

Now we come to the Lord's Prayer, arguably the longest portion of similar material found in the Sermon on the Mount and found definitely elsewhere in Luke.

I would agree that the setting in Luke (Luke 11.1–4) does not appear to be the Sermon on the Mount (Matt. 6.9–13). In Luke the disciples find Jesus praying, and one of them asks Jesus to teach them to pray as John the Baptist taught his disciples. Jesus then gives them a version of the Lord's Prayer, worded somewhat differently from the wording in the Sermon on the Mount. This is followed in Luke 11, as noted above, by further teachings on prayer.

This is one of those occasions when we are quite uncertain when the opening incident in Luke 11.1 took place. Luke says only that Jesus "was praying in a certain place" and that the disciples spoke to him "after He had finished." The story crops up without other chronological indicators in the middle of Luke's central section. But the specifics of the incident do seem to indicate a different setting.

Here I am strongly inclined to think that the two recordings of the Lord's Prayer represent Jesus' repetition. Carson points out,

> Though the evidence for two traditions is strong, equally significant is the fact that there are two entirely different historical settings of the prayer. Unless one is prepared to say that one or the other is made up, the reasonable explanation is that Jesus taught this sort of prayer often during his itinerant ministry and that Matthew records one occasion and Luke another. Matthew's setting is not as historically specific as that of Luke only if one interprets the introduction and the conclusion of the entire discourse loosely or if one postulates Matthew's freedom to add "footnotes" to the material he provides .... The former is exegetically doubtful, the latter without convincing literary controls, and even in these instances the evidence for two separate traditions for the Lord's Prayer is so strong that the simplest comprehensive explanation is that Jesus himself taught this form of prayer on more than one occasion.[15]

It should go without saying that the disciple's request in Luke 11.1 that Jesus would teach them to pray as John the Baptist taught his disciples does not mean that Jesus had never taught them about prayer before or could have never given the Lord's Prayer in a sermon to the gathered crowds. Even if one were to insist (as one should not anyway) that Luke is firmly placing this incident chronologically late in Jesus' ministry, that would only make it all the more likely that Jesus had already taught his disciples about prayer. Prayer was extremely important to Jesus, and on one occasion he even tacitly chided his disciples for being unable to cast out an evil spirit that could be cast out only by much prayer (Mark 9.29, a healing recounted

---

[15] Ibid., p. 202.

in Luke 9.36ff).[16] We don't know exactly what the disciple was expecting in the way of instruction when he made the request in Luke 11.1. What parallels was he expecting to the instruction that John the Baptist gave to his own disciples? Were all those present in Luke 11 also present at the Sermon on the Mount? It would be over-reading in the extreme to argue that Luke is implying by the disciple's request that Jesus had never taught the Lord's Prayer on any previous occasion. Indeed, it is antecedently probable both that Jesus taught about prayer on many occasions throughout his ministry and that a disciple making such a request was hoping for more detailed private instruction than a reiteration of the Lord's Prayer.

One other supposed parallel between material in the Sermon on the Mount and some other location in Mark and/or Luke is worth mentioning. Jesus' teaching on divorce occurs in the Sermon on the Mount at Matt. 5.31–32. It is found in a different setting in Mark 10.1–12. In Mark, Jesus is in the region beyond Jordan in Judea, and the Pharisees come and ask him about divorce. His disciples then ask him further about it in private. As discussed in Chapter XIII, section 6, the wording in the Sermon on the Mount is not the same as in Mark, since in Matthew Jesus adds an exception to his prohibition on divorce. Nor is it identical to the wording in Luke 16.18. What is most important here, however, is that Matthew shows Jesus teaching about divorce twice *within his own Gospel*. The real parallel passage to the setting in Mark 10 is Jesus' teaching about divorce in Matt. 19.3ff. There can be little doubt that those two passages do describe the same incident. It is therefore completely incorrect to try to parallel the Mark 10 teaching with the Sermon on the Mount (Matt. 5.31–32) and to imply that this differing location is evidence for the composite nature of the Sermon on the Mount. Since Matthew *himself* has the actual incident found in Mark 10 later in his own Gospel, Matthew is *not* collecting this teaching of Jesus from a different setting and moving it to the Sermon on the Mount.

In short, there is no clear case from other Synoptic parallels that the Sermon on the Mount is a composite discourse. Some sayings appear to have been taught twice, sometimes even on the basis of independent evidence within a single Gospel, sometimes as seen by combining two Gospels. Others are not placed in any definite different settings in Luke, so the existence of the parallel does not even require the hypothesis of multiple teachings. And the Sermon on the Level Place in Luke 6 could easily refer to the same occasion and therefore separately confirms Jesus' teaching of a body of this material on a single occasion.

---

[16] I owe this point to Brad Cooper.

5. The Commissioning Discourse

The discourse that Jesus gives to his twelve disciples in Matthew before sending them out, sometimes called the Commissioning Discourse, comes in second place in the allegedly knock-down case for composite discourses. Here Craig Evans proposes his own list of alleged parallel passages, which I will use for analysis:

> Matthew 10:5–15 is prefaced by Matthew's version of the calling of the twelve apostles (cf. Matt 10:1–4). He has developed a discourse on the missionary theme (Matt 10:5–42) by pulling together related materials from Mark (especially Mark 3:13–19; 6:7–13; 13:9–13; 8:34–35) and Q (as seen in Luke 6:40; 12:1–12, 48, 49–53). This discourse is preparation for the much shorter, confessional Great Commission in Matt 28:18–20. The discourse begins with a charge to the newly appointed apostles to go to the "lost sheep of the house of Israel" (vv. 5–15). The apostles are to proclaim the good news of the kingdom of God (or heaven) and are to heal and exorcise. But the discourse goes on to warn the disciples of being dragged before Gentiles while offering assurance that they will know what to say when the time comes (vv. 16–23). The tensions between these two parts of the discourse are obvious, indicating its composite nature. The discourse concludes with words of encouragement (vv. 24–33), warnings of conflict (vv. 34–39), and promises of reward (vv. 40–42). These disparate materials were uttered on different occasions and have been assembled and edited by the evangelist, so that he may clarify important principles of Christian mission.[17]

Evans's confident assertion that "these disparate materials were uttered on different occasions and have been assembled" by Matthew notwithstanding, it is not at all clear that this is true. I note, too, that Evans scarcely gives the impression here that Matthew is recording *any* historical discourse at all at this point in his Gospel. As mentioned in the statement by Licona above, many evangelical scholars believe that the Sermon on the Mount is historical, that Jesus did give a sermon or discourse containing a significant segment of what we find in Matthew, but that it is *partially* compiled. Here Evans gives the distinct impression that we should take most or all of Matthew's Commissioning Discourse to be composed by Matthew ahistorically out of disparate materials that were uttered on other occasions. Of course this requires that the opening and closing brackets in Matt. 10.1, 5 and 11.1 are irrelevant. Matt. 10.1 says,

> Jesus summoned His twelve disciples and gave them authority over unclean spirits, to cast them out, and to heal every kind of disease and every kind of sickness.

---

[17] Evans, *Matthew*, pp. 217–218.

This is followed by the list of the names of the Twelve. Verse 5 says,

> These twelve Jesus sent out after instructing them: "Do not go in the way of the Gentiles, and do not enter any city of the Samaritans;..."

11.1 rounds off the discourse with,

> When Jesus had finished giving instructions to His twelve disciples, He departed from there to teach and preach in their cities.

If what comes in between these brackets merely represents something that Matthew has "developed" out of disparate materials, it is difficult to see why the audience would not have been confused. But if Evans thinks that Jesus taught any significant portion of this to his disciples at that time, he does not make this at all clear in his exposition and, in fact, gives the opposite impression.

Evans's case relies on other Synoptic parallels. Beginning with the Markan parallels that Evans lists, what do these amount to? Mark 3.13–19 is just the names of the disciples, and a similar set of names prefaces the commissioning discourse in Matthew 10. In both cases the narrator gives the names; they are not part of the discourse. Evans's inclusion of this passage in his alleged parallels is the sheerest list-padding.

Mark 6.7–13 is the parallel passage in Mark. That is to say, it is Mark's own account of Jesus' commissioning of the Twelve, at the parallel point in Mark's narrative, agreeing with Matthew. It includes four verses of parallel instructions. Hence it is hardly evidence for the composite nature of Matthew 10.

Mark 8.34–35 should not be paralleled with *anything* in the Commissioning Discourse, because its real parallel occurs elsewhere in Matthew. Although Evans does not say what precise verses he is matching these Markan verses to in the Commissioning Discourse, they resemble Matt. 10.38–39, which is presumably why Evans lists them. In both places Jesus says that it is necessary for anyone who wishes to follow him to take up his cross. But, as in the divorce case, this is the *wrong passage in Matthew* to try to parallel with Mark. As in the divorce teaching in the Sermon on the Mount, Matthew has two sayings about taking up one's cross, and the real, obvious parallel, including setting, chronology, and following verses, is clearly Matt. 16.24–25, at the time of Peter's famous confession that Jesus is the Christ. This does not give the appearance of Matthew's collecting sayings from Mark and moving them to a discourse. Rather, it appears that Matthew believed that Jesus made a remark about taking up one's cross on more than one occasion. And this is of course highly probable and independently supported. The Gospels attribute similar ideas about the need to lose one's life in order to gain it in yet a third setting in John 12.25 and also in Luke 9.24, 14.27, which mentions carrying one's cross, and 17.33.

There is only *one passage* in Mark that occurs in a clearly different setting from Matthew, in very similar wording. This is Mark 13.9–13, which is quite similar to Matt. 10.17–22. This is the "apocalyptic" material in the Commissioning Discourse. Jesus predicts in both Mark and Matthew, in similar wording and in the same order, that the disciples will be turned over to be flogged in the synagogues, that they will stand before kings, that family members will betray each other to death, that they will be hated by everyone, and that those who endure to the end will be saved. Mark's setting is quite different: This passage occurs in Mark's version of the Olivet Discourse. Jesus is speaking to his disciples about the end times during Passion Week, probably on Tuesday evening after teaching in the Temple.

It is sometimes said that Matthew omits this passage, found in Mark, from his own Olivet Discourse.[18] The idea is that he has moved it from the Olivet Discourse in order to fill out his Commissioning Discourse. But matters are not so simple. For, while the verbal similarity is greater between Mark 13.9–13 and Matt. 10.17–22 than between Mark 13.9–13 and any passage in Matthew's Olivet Discourse, there are single verses that are identical in their versions of the Olivet Discourse, and there conceptual parallels as well. Immediately after the reference to the "beginning of birth pangs" in both Matthew's and Mark's Olivet Discourses, Jesus in Matthew 24.9 says, "Then they will deliver you to tribulation," which conceptually repeats the prediction in Matt. 10.17 (and parallels that in Mark 13.9) that they will be delivered over to be flogged and persecuted. Matt. 24.14, "This gospel of the kingdom shall be preached in the whole world as a testimony to all the nations" is virtually identical to Mark 13.10, "The gospel must first be preached to all the nations." Matt. 24.9, put together with 24.13, yields, "You will be hated by all nations because of My name…But the one who endures to the end, he will be saved," which is identical both to Mark 13.13 and Matt. 10.22. Matt. 24.10, "At that time many will fall away and will betray one another and hate one another," is conceptually similar to the prediction in Matt. 10.21 and Mark 13.12 that brother will deliver the brother unto death. In other words, even in a section that is so verbally similar between Matthew's Commissioning Dis-

---

[18] Grant R. Osborne, "Round Four: The Redaction Debate Continues," *JETS* 28 (December, 1985), p. 406.

course and Mark's Olivet Discourse, we find both conceptual and verbal parallels to a section in Matthew's *own* Olivet Discourse, giving us reason to believe Jesus taught material very much like this twice. While this does not tell us *why* the wording is so much closer to Mark's in Matthew's Commissioning Discourse than in his Olivet Discourse, it disconfirms the idea that Matthew was just knowingly shifting material said in the Olivet Discourse in order to compose a Commissioning Discourse. If he were doing that, one would not expect so much repetition in his *own* Olivet Discourse.

One conjecture is that Matthew may have used notes taken from Mark (perhaps to jog his memory) in writing the Commissioning Discourse, perhaps remembering that Jesus did make apocalyptic predictions when he sent out the disciples. When writing his own Olivet Discourse, having reason to believe that Jesus again taught similarly, he may have varied the wording, giving a recognizable paraphrase in some verses, in deference to the fact that he had already used notes from this portion of Mark in writing the earlier discourse. This, of course, is only a conjecture. But again, to say that Matthew simply *omits* this material from his own Olivet Discourse in Chapter 24 and that therefore he appears to have *moved* it to the Commissioning Discourse does not do full justice to the details of the evidence.

One more point is relevant here: Matthew's words in 10.15–19 are very similar to a verse in Luke's Olivet Discourse, Luke 21.14–15, and to Mark 13.11. Jesus tells the disciples not to think ahead of time what they shall say, because it will be given to them. Does this mean that one or the other author has moved the saying? No, and for an interesting reason: An even closer verbal parallel to Matthew occurs elsewhere within Luke itself, in Luke 12.11–12. This passage is unclear as to precise setting but contains some other material also found in Matthew's Commissioning Discourse (see below). Luke *himself* therefore repeats the idea and seems to have had reason to believe that Jesus uttered this instruction (not to think ahead of time what they will say) on more than one occasion. Luke even records it in proximity with other material that is similar to Matthew's Commissioning Discourse.

What about the other alleged Lukan parallels that Evans lists? Luke 6.40 (found in the Sermon on the Level Place but not recorded in the Sermon on the Mount) is merely the short saying that the servant is not above his Master. John's Gospel gives us reason to believe that Jesus uttered this saying more than once and was quite fond of it. Jesus says it *twice* in the Farewell Discourse *alone* (John 13.16, 15.20). Hence its appearance in Luke's Sermon on the Level Place is not good evidence that Matthew took it from "Q material" and wove it into the commission to the Twelve, having no reason to think that it was uttered at that time.

Luke 12.2–9 contains several similar sayings to those found in the Commissioning Discourse, and in the same order, though the wording is somewhat different in a few places. These include, *inter alia*, the statement that nothing is hidden that will not be revealed, that they should not fear those who have power only to kill the body, and the famous saying that God watches over the sparrows and that Jesus' followers are of more value than many sparrows. It seems mildly plausible that Luke was working with a source (perhaps written or perhaps a human witness) who was describing the same occasion that Matthew reports as the Commissioning Discourse.

But here, again, Luke's setting is vague. Luke 12.1 says,

> Under these circumstances, after so many thousands of people had gathered together that they were stepping on one another, He began saying to His disciples first of all, "Beware of the leaven of the Pharisees, which is hypocrisy...." (Luke 12.1)

The parallels with Matthew begin immediately after. The injunction to beware of the leaven of the Pharisees, given in a different setting in Mark 8.15, does not occur in Matthew's Commissioning Discourse at all. Luke gives no chronological indicator as to when this was besides the fact that Jesus was followed by thousands, which of course could describe a time just before the Commissioning Discourse. Moreover, Luke indicates that at least some of the words that immediately follow were taught specifically to the disciples. Although one might weakly guess that, in Matthew 10, the crowds were at more of a distance, whereas in the setting at the beginning of Luke 12 they might seem physically closer, this is by no means clear. For what it is worth, Matt. 9.36–38, narrated immediately before Jesus summons the Twelve in Matt. 10.1, says that Jesus saw the crowds and felt compassion on them because they were as sheep without a shepherd. At that time he spoke about this to the disciples, telling them to pray that the Lord of the harvest would send forth laborers. Insofar as the end of Chapter 9 is relevant to the scene of the Commissioning Discourse at the beginning of Chapter 10, it may indeed mean that there were crowds milling about when Jesus pulled the Twelve aside and gave them instruction to prepare them for their mission, as in Luke 12.2–9.

Similar considerations are relevant to the similarity between Luke 12.51–53 and Matt. 10.34–36, about Jesus bringing a sword rather than peace and dividing families. There is no clear different context in Luke. Indeed, there is even less of a context by Luke 12.51 than at the beginning of Luke 12, given Luke's appearance of "wandering" into collected sayings after kicking off a segment of Jesus' sayings with some sort of question or setting.

Another passage sometimes paralleled between Luke and Matthew (though Evans does not list it) is Luke 14.26.[19] In Luke, Jesus says that anyone who comes to him and does not hate his father, mother, and other members of his family cannot be his disciple. Matt. 10.37, somewhat less harsh, says that anyone who loves father and mother more than Jesus is not worthy of Jesus. Luke says that Jesus said this to the large crowds, while in Matthew it is part of the instructions to the disciples. It is in any event a short saying, quite consonant with Jesus' other teaching about the need for commitment, self-denial, and the priority of commitment to himself over family (cf. Luke 9.60), and it is not at all implausible that Jesus said it on more than one occasion.

All of this messy evidence bespeaks the texture of the real life and teaching of a peripatetic rabbi. It also probably indicates that sometimes one of the authors, usually Luke, was not confident about when something was taught and that he wrote with appropriate vagueness in those cases. It certainly does not present any knock-down case for the picture of Matthew as an author who habitually gathered Jesus' teachings into composed discourses, bracketed them with verses seeming to indicate that Jesus gave those teachings on that occasion, but didn't really mean it.

Evans has one other argument for the composite nature of the Commissioning Discourse. He states it rather cryptically:

> The apostles are to proclaim the good news of the kingdom of God (or heaven) and are to heal and exorcise. But the discourse goes on to warn the disciples of being dragged before Gentiles while offering assurance that they will know what to say when the time comes (vv. 16–23). The tensions between these two parts of the discourse are obvious, indicating its composite nature.[20]

Evans does not expound upon these alleged tensions, so one must conjecture about what he thinks they are. It was typical of Jesus to warn of persecution and to reassure in a single breath. (See, for example, John 16.33.) Perhaps the idea is that some of the teaching in Matthew 10 appears to refer to events that would not happen during the upcoming mission of the Twelve but would happen later on, when the church was launched and under persecution. But we don't know that

---

[19] Ibid.

[20] Evans, *Matthew*, p. 218.

Jesus would not have foretold later conflicts and persecutions as part of an initial charge to the disciples. Good trainers and teachers often do look both to the short-term and to the long-term. As Carson points out,

> We have already found Jesus predicting severe persecution (e.g., 5:10–12), seeing a time of prolonged witness to the "world" (5:13–14; 7:13–14) after his departure (9:15), and many Gentiles participating in the messianic banquet (8:11–12). Therefore it is surely not unnatural for Jesus to treat this commission of the Twelve as both an explicit short-term itinerary and a paradigm of the longer mission stretching into the years ahead. For the latter, the Twelve need further instruction beyond those needed for the immediate tour, which they must see as, in part, an exercise anticipating something more.[21]

This does not constitute any significant argument for the "composite nature of the discourse."

6. The Woes to the Pharisees

A short discussion is in order concerning Jesus' condemnation of the Pharisees found in Matt. 23.1–36, which bears resemblances to similar material in Luke 11.37ff.

One error that we should avoid at the outset is treating the condemnation of the Pharisees in Matt. 23 as part of the same sermon that is Matthew's Olivet Discourse in Chapters 24 and 25. Such an amalgamation can make it look like a "single discourse" in Matthew is even longer than it really is. Then, if one lists alleged parallel passages for all of Matt. 23–25, that list will appear to include more passages found elsewhere for a "single Matthean discourse." But the woes upon the Pharisees in Matt. 23 are quite separate from the Olivet Discourse, as both the setting in Matt. 23.1 and the explicit transition in Matt. 24.1–3 make clear. In the woes to the Pharisees, Jesus is speaking to a group of his disciples and to the crowds (at least at the outset). In the Olivet Discourse, in Matthew just as in Luke and Mark, Jesus and his disciples leave the Temple, Jesus predicts the Fall of Jerusalem, and his disciples ask him to tell them more while sitting on the Mount of Olives. The settings, the audiences, and the topics are clearly distinct. These three chapters do not constitute a single discourse in Matthew.[22]

It is certainly true that in several respects what Jesus says in Matt. 23 about the Pharisees resembles what he says to the Pharisees and the teachers of the law in

---

[21] Carson, *Matthew*, p. 282.

[22] Ibid., p. 528.

Luke 11. Moreover, the setting in Luke at this point is fairly definite in its local respects, though the chronological time at which it occurred is not fully clear. Luke says that a Pharisee invited Jesus to dinner (11.37), that there were other Pharisees and lawyers present, and that on this occasion Jesus condemned them harshly. Luke inserts a bit of dialogue in the middle, where a lawyer speaks up to protest and Jesus turns to condemning the lawyers (11.45–46). This draws attention once more to the context. And Luke brackets the incident on the other end by describing how Jesus was surrounded by hostile, questioning Pharisees when he left the meal (11.53–54). Luke narrates this meal in his central section. Hence, the narration comes prior to the Triumphal Entry. In Matthew, not only does the condemnation of the Pharisees in Chapter 23 seem quite definitely to occur during Passion Week, it begins with Jesus talking to his disciples and the crowds (Matt. 23.1), apparently in the Temple, which looks like a different setting. It does not look like he is in a home where he has been invited to dinner.

The verbal resemblances are less than exact, though they become closer as the passages go on. Without going into great detail, I will mention that the similar material is not all in the same order, that some of the condemnations preceded by "woes" in one place are not preceded by "woes" in another, and that there is material in Matt. 23 that fits well in its own context but does not occur in Luke or anywhere else (Matt. 23.15–20, 24). The resemblances are especially marked at the ends of the sections, especially Jesus' references to killing prophets and building monuments in their honor (Matt. 23.29–36, Luke 11.47–52).

Making the evidence even more interesting, Matthew does not explicitly bracket the condemnation of the Pharisees with an ending phrase like "when he had ended all these sayings." There is, as already noted, a transition when Jesus comes out of the Temple and is leaving (24.1), but this is not quite the same thing as an explicit ending bracket that once more refers to and groups the teachings that Jesus has just given.[23] In this sense, though Matthew certainly has a context for the *beginning* of Jesus' condemnation of the Pharisees, one may wonder whether he has done what I have called "wandering" in Luke—beginning with a setting and then not explicitly stating when this setting ends and when he has begun to include other teachings not definitely uttered on that occasion. However, this is less plausible in Matthew than in the places I have discussed in Luke, since the transition in 24.1 does remain chronologically quite clearly in Passion Week, and probably even on a specific day (cf. 26.2, just after the Olivet Discourse, plausibly

---

[23] Ibid.

after sundown on Tuesday). The only way in which it is less explicit than Matthew's usual ending bracket for a discourse is that it does not say anything about Jesus finishing saying these things.

One more point is relevant: Luke and Mark *agree* with Matthew that Jesus did condemn the Pharisees during Passion Week, though what they record at that point is much shorter. Luke 20.45–47 and Mark 12.38–40 resemble Matt. 23.5–7. And at this point Luke repeats himself concerning the Pharisees' love of places of honor in synagogues (Luke 20.46, 11.43). This is not evidence that the condemnations in Matt. 23 were collected from elsewhere. On the contrary, this is some acknowledgement in the other Synoptics that Jesus condemned the Pharisees strongly during Passion Week and said things similar to what he said in Luke 11 at the dinner.

With this mixed evidence, it is probably impossible to draw any strong conclusion concerning precisely what Jesus said when. Which woes did Jesus call down upon the Pharisees and lawyers at which times? Remember that the reportage model does not require us to have answers to all questions. But some combination of Jesus' repeating similar condemnations (with variations) and authorial conjecture about the chronology of his teaching is plausible. Here we should return to the distinction made at the beginning between an author's knowing that material was *not* uttered on a given occasion and his drawing a reasonable conclusion that it *was*. If Matthew knew of or remembered that Jesus condemned the Pharisees to the crowds during Passion Week, and if he knew of the material that he includes in Chapter 23, he may have reasonably believed that Jesus uttered all of these condemnations at that time.

Luke, having (apparently) an independent witness, seems to have learned of a meal with a Pharisee that Matthew does not record. At this meal, recorded in Luke 11, Jesus condemned the Pharisees and lawyers harshly and at length. It is possible that Luke reasonably conjectured that Jesus said all of the material in his Chapter 11 at that time. Luke apparently also knew of a later condemnation of the Pharisees during Passion Week, represented briefly by himself and Mark.

What we do not have here is a cut-and-dried case in which either author collected material that he *knew* was uttered at another time. While Matthew *may* be writing partially achronologically (given the lack of an extremely explicit ending bracket after Chapter 23), even that is not the most plausible theory. Certainly neither author must be taken to be writing dyschronologically.

7. More discourse considerations

I will not take the space to make a comprehensive analysis of alleged parallels with Matthew's other discourses (the Parables of the Kingdom in Matt. 13, the Discourse on the Church in Matt. 18, and the Olivet Discourse in Matt. 24–25). The sermons I have already discussed provide the best case for Matthew's making composite discourses, and the types of points used here are applicable elsewhere.

Here are just a few considerations frequently overlooked: Matthew and Mark are in agreement in placing the (very short) parable of the mustard seed with the other parables of the kingdom (Matt. 13.31–32, Mark 4.30–32). Therefore, the occurrence of this parable apart from the others in Luke 13.18–19 is not evidence that Matthew 13 is a compiled discourse. On this point, Luke is the outlier in separating this parable from the rest, and his presentation of that parable is relatively context-free. Similarly, Matt. 25.17 and Mark 13.15 agree in placing the injunction to flee from the housetop in the Olivet Discourse. Therefore, the fact that Luke (here the outlier) gives this saying separately in a far less clear chronological location in Luke 17.31 is not good evidence that Matthew has created a partially composite Olivet Discourse. Luke 21.21 makes a conceptually related point—that one in the field should not enter the city. Luke may have had reason to believe that Jesus said something like this more than once. When Matthew appears to be similar to and possibly even following Mark, it makes little sense to take vaguer placements of similar sayings and passages elsewhere in Luke to be evidence of Matthean compilation.

It is also worth pointing out that the Olivet Discourse is quite similar in all three Synoptic Gospels. Matthew has some *extra* material, chiefly parables, but nearly all of these are unique to Matthew; hence, one cannot even try to claim that Matthew collected them from some different contexts that we can identify from the other Gospels.

There are a couple of places where Luke does have material in clearly different settings. Luke places the parable of the ten minas with uncharacteristic chronological firmness in 19.12ff. It is similar, though not identical, to Matthew's parable of the ten talents in his Olivet Discourse (Matt. 25.14–28). Jesus tells the parable of the lost sheep in different contexts—in Matthew's discourse to his disciples on the church (Matt. 18.12–14) and in remarks to the judgemental Pharisees (Luke 14.1–7). Jesus could have repeated both of these parables for different purposes.[24] Once again, especially when the number is whittled down to only a few portions of material in clearly different contexts, repetition is scarcely far-fetched.

---

[24] Ibid., p. 578.

The fact that a discourse is unified or structured is certainly not evidence in itself that it is composite. To think so would be to assume that Jesus himself spoke in a haphazard or unstructured fashion. An author without a verbatim recording, possessing material that he believed was spoken on a given occasion, might decide to organize it topically if he lacked exact information about the speaker's own ordering. But in practice, it would be extremely difficult to argue that the organization is the author's rather than the speaker's. As Carson says,

> Jesus himself was a master teacher. In his sayings, whose authenticity is not greatly disputed, there is evidence of structure, contrast, and assonance. So when some scholars tell us that Matthew's account has more structure...than the other Synoptics, is this a sign of greater nearness to or distance from Jesus?[25]

In "sayings" sections without any bracketing or strong chronological markers, topical organization may serve a useful organizational purpose, but it does not follow that, in a bracketed discourse, topically grouped material has been collected from other contexts. We must distinguish between topical organization that is *taking the place of* any other principle of organization, occurring in openly achronological narration, and topical organization *within* a discourse that to all appearances occurred at a particular time.

What all of this means is that one-sided scholarly insistence upon composite Gospel discourses is out of place and exaggerated. The complexity of the evidence means that more humility is in order rather than declarations that there is only one reasonable interpretation. Commonsense considerations of the sort I have brought up throughout this appendix show that the composite view is not the only reasonable possibility. It is entirely plausible that an author who bracketed a discourse reasonably believed that the material was all taught on a single occasion.

Scholarly dogmatism is even less defensible when a scholar insists that composite discourses support *dyschronological* narration and, on that basis, rejects the reportage model. No doubt many scholars currently believe and will continue to believe that some convention existed permitting the *achronological* narration of partially composite discourses, even between brackets. That is theoretically possible, though we lack independent evidence for it. But if one comes to doubt that such a convention existed, one should continue to view the evangelists as honest historical reporters who did not deliberately make it look like Jesus said things at a time when he did not say them.

---

[25] Ibid., p. 153.

AUTHORS

SCRIPTURES

SUBJECTS

Also by Lydia McGrew

Hidden in Plain View
Undesigned Coincidences in the Gospels and Acts

Hidden in Plain View revives an argument for
the historical reliability of the New Testament
that has been largely neglected for more than
a hundred years. An undesigned coincidence
is an apparently casual, yet puzzle-like "fit"
between two or more texts, and its best explanation is that the authors knew the truth about
the events they describe or allude to.

Connections of this kind among passages
in the Gospels, as well as between Acts and the
Pauline epistles, give us reason to believe that
these documents came from honest eyewitness
sources, people "in the know" about the events
they relate. Supported by careful research yet accessibly written, Hidden in Plain
View provides solid evidence that all Christians can use to defend the Scriptures
and the truth of Christianity. 276 pages. $15.99 (PB).

*For a full listing of DeWard Publishing
Company books, visit our website:*

www.deward.com